MCAT
BIOLOGY AND BIOCHEMISTRY

Content Review for the
Revised MCAT

Printed in the United States of America

Third Printing, 2017

ISBN 978-1-944935-07-8

Next Step Pre-Med, LLC
4256 N Ravenswood Ave
Suite 303
Chicago, IL 60613

www.nextstepmcat.com

ABOUT THE AUTHORS

Bryan Schnedeker is Next Step Test Prep's Vice President for MCAT Tutoring and Content. He manages all of our MCAT and LSAT instructors nationally and counsels hundreds of students when they begin our tutoring process. He has over a decade of MCAT and LSAT teaching and tutoring experience (starting at one of the big prep course companies before joining our team). He has attended medical school and law school himself and has scored a 44 on the old MCAT, a 525 on the new MCAT, and a 180 on the LSAT. Bryan has worked with thousands of MCAT students over the years and specializes in helping students looking to achieve elite scores.

Anthony Lafond is Next Step's MCAT Content Director and an Elite MCAT Tutor. He has been teaching and tutoring MCAT students for nearly 12 years. He earned his MD and PhD degrees from UMDNJ - New Jersey Medical School with a focus on rehabilitative medicine. Dr. Lafond believes that both rehabilitative medicine and MCAT education hinge on the same core principle: crafting an approach that puts the unique needs of the individual foremost.

To find out about MCAT tutoring directly with Anthony or Bryan visit our website:

http://nextsteptestprep.com/mcat

Updates may be found here: http://nextsteptestprep.com/mcat-materials-change-log/

If you have any feedback for us about this book, please contact us at mcat@nextsteptestprep.com

Version: 2017-01-01

TABLE OF CONTENTS

BIOCHEMISTRY

FREE ONLINE MCAT DIAGNOSTIC and

FULL-LENGTH EXAM

Want to see how you would do on the MCAT and understand where you need to focus your prep?

TAKE OUR FREE MCAT DIAGNOSTIC EXAM

Timed simulations of all 4 sections of the MCAT

Comprehensive reporting on your performance

Continue your practice with a free Full Length Exam

These two exams are provided free of charge to students who purchased our book

To access your free exam, visit:

http://nextsteptestprep.com/mcat-diagnostic/

CHAPTER 1
Introduction

A. THE NEXT STEP APPROACH TO MCAT CONTENT

The Next Step Biology and Biochemistry Review is designed to help you understand major concepts in these areas and to use this knowledge to solve problems. Each chapter contains a large number of practice questions to help you review your content in the only format that matters: MCAT-style multiple choice questions.

These questions are written to test your understanding of basic science concepts and your problem solving abilities; they stress the memorization that is a necessary first step in mastering the MCAT. It is important to note that you cannot prepare for the MCAT the way you have successfully prepared for science exams in school. In your college classes, simple rote memorization is typically all it takes to get a good grade. On the MCAT, memorizing science material is only the first step in a very long journey.

After memorizing the content, you will then need to practice this material on full, timed practice sections and then on full practice tests. This timed work is the only way to simulate the real conditions of test day.

It is critical to note that the time pressure combined with the lengthy and often confusing presentation of facts in the MCAT's passages make for a very demanding exam. It is not enough to learn MCAT content at the level of recognition that is required by most college classes. For the MCAT, you *must absolutely master the content*. This means that it is not simply enough to recognize a term when you see it. You must know the content so well that you could give a small 10-minute lecture on a given topic, off the top of your head, with no notes whatsoever. This level of mastery requires repetition, practice, and more repetition. That's the main reason we've included hundreds and hundreds of questions through our content review books.

To develop the level of mastery needed, test yourself after completing each chapter. Flip to the table of contents at the front of the book. Using the table of contents as an outline, can you give a little 5-minute lecture on each bullet point? Test yourself here – make yourself speak out loud to an empty room. If you can, great! It means you've really mastered the content at the level needed. If not, go back and re-read the chapter. Take careful notes. Finally, one of the best ways to memorize MCAT content is to make study sheets. While flashcards and notes are good and can help, a study sheet is far more effective. A study sheet is a single piece of paper summarizing the important ideas, concepts, relationships, or structures involved in a given MCAT topic. For example, you might make a study sheet of all of the hormones tested on the MCAT – where they are secreted from, where they go, what they do when they get there, what causes them to be released, etc. Then take that study sheet and make a copy, but blank out a dozen pieces of information. Then make a second blank with another dozen pieces of information missing. Then make a final study sheet with almost the whole page blanked out.

Start your practice by filling in the blank spaces on your first copy. Do this over and over, checking the original study sheet until you can get it perfect. Then fill in the spaces on the second blank over and over until you've mastered it. Finally, take the third copy (which is nearly just a blank sheet of paper) and re-create the entire study sheet from memory. That is the level of mastery demanded by the MCAT (and med school!).

B. BIOLOGY AND BIOCHEMISTRY

We'll start with a simple definition of biology: *biology is the study of life*. This includes examination of the processes that govern how life is maintained and reproduced, and observation of how living things interact with each other and with the environment. Although this sounds rather simple, it involves studying many different and diverse areas, from the molecular level to the global scale.

There are two distinct perspectives from which one can study biological processes: *in vivo* or *in vitro*. *In vivo* means research is done in the body itself. *In vitro* means literally "in glass," as an experiment that is done in a test tube, or outside of the body. *In vivo* experiments, naturally, include all the factors that can influence a process; therefore, the reactions being studied represent a "real life" situation. However, all these factors and reactions can make for a very complex system that is not easily understood. *In vitro* studies, on the other hand, allow researchers to manipulate the system to study only one or two isolated factors. This helps to determine exactly what these factors do.

Although each approach has its merits and drawbacks, both perspectives are needed and work synergistically. For example, the study of AIDS has benefited from both in *vivo* and *in vitro* studies. The course of the illness, from infection with HIV to full blown AIDS, has been well characterized in humans through the use of *in vivo* studies. But the exact mechanism of how the virus invades a cell is known through *in vitro* studies. Drugs designed to fight the virus are first tested in vitro using HIV infected cells grown in the laboratory. Drugs that prove effective *in vitro* are then tested *in vivo*.

Biochemistry is the study of chemical processes and molecules as they relate to living systems. Biochemistry focuses primarily on studying the exact mechanisms by which cells communicate and the chemical processes by which they make and store energy. The techniques of biochemistry are also used extensively in the study of molecular genetics.

Because biochemistry straddles the line between biology and chemistry, drawing clear lines between biology and biochemistry, and between biochemistry and organic chemistry, is just about impossible. For the purposes of MCAT prep, however, we will be able to primarily focus our work on the areas of biochemistry that the AAMC has included in their Official Guide to the MCAT.

In this book, you will see some chapter topics repeated between the biology and biochemistry sections of the book. That's because such topics are listed twice by the AAMC in the MCAT Official Guide. The topics are treated slightly differently in the two subjects, so don't skip over a chapter just because it sounds familiar.

The typical college courses in biology and biochemistry cover an exceptionally broad variety of topics. Succeeding in these courses often means simply memorizing a huge list of names and theories and being able to regurgitate what the textbook said about them. When it comes to mastering these topics, this basic memorization is only a first step - you want to start with a broad-based review of all the topics that the MCAT may ask about. This book has been designed with that goal in mind. To make working with the material more intuitive, we have arranged the chapters as they are usually presented in a typical college textbook. On the following pages is a list of all of the major science topics on the exam, grouped around the exam's central concepts.

BIOLOGY

Biological and Biochemical Foundations of Living Systems

I: Proteins

    A. Structure
        a) Protein Structure: Primary, Secondary, Tertiary, Quaternary
        b) Protein Stability: Folding, Denaturing, Hydrophobic interactions
        c) Separation Techniques: Isoelectric Point, Electrophoresis
    B. Protein Function: Immune System, Motors
    C. Enzymes
        a) Catalysts: Reduction of Activation Energy, Cofactors, Coenzymes
        b) Classification
        c) Substrate interactions: Active Site, Induced Fit
        d) Vitamins
        e) Effects on Enzyme Activity: pH, temperature, etc.
    D. D. Enzyme Control
        a) Kinetics: Michaelis-Menten, Cooperativity
        b) Feedback
        c) Inhibition: Competitive, Non-competitive
        d) Regulatory Enzymes: Allosteric enzymes, Zymogens, Covalently-modified enzymes

II: Molecular Genetics

    A. Nucleic Acids
        a) Structure, Function
        b) Nucleotides, Nucleosides: Sugar-Phosphate Backbone, Purines, Pyrimidines
        c) Watson-Crick Model: Double-Helix, Base-Pair Specificity
        d) Transmission of genetic information
        e) Denaturation, Reannealing, Hybridization

    B. DNA Replication and Repair
        a) Replication Mechanism: Semi-Conservative, Enzymes, Replication Origin
        b) Replicating the ends of DNA
        c) Repair: During Replication, Mutation Repair
    C. Genetic Code
        a) Triplets: Codon-Anticodon, Degeneracy, Wobble Pairing, Missense, Nonsense, Initiation, Termination
        b) Transcription
             i. tRNA, mRNA, rRNA, snRNPs, snRNAs
             ii. introns, exons
        c) Translation
             i. mRNA, tRNA, rRNA
             ii. ribosomes, initiation, termination co-factors
             iii. post-translational processing
    D. Chromosomes: Proteins, Repetitive DNA, Supercoiling, Heterochromatin, Euchromatin, Telomeres, Centromeres
    E. Gene Expression
        a) Prokaryotes: Operons, Jacob-Monod Model, Repression, Positive Control
        b) Eukaryotes
             i. transcriptional regulation, DNA binding proteins, transcription factors
             ii. gene amplification, duplication
             iii. post-transcriptional control, introns, exons
             iv. cancer
             v. regulation of chromatic structure: methylation
             vi. non-coding RNAs
    F. Biotechnology: Cloning, Restriction Enzymes, cDNA, Hybridization, PCR, Blotting, Electrophoresis, Stem Cells, Applications, Ethics

III: Classical Genetics

    A. Mendelian Genetics: Phenotype, Genotype, Gene, Locus, Allele, Zygosity, Wild-type, Recessive, Dominant, Co-dominant, Incomplete Dominance, Leakage, Penetrance, Expressivity, Hybridization, Gene Pool

    B. B. Meiosis and Variability
        a) Significance, Differences with Mitosis
        b) Gene Segregation: Independent Assortment, Linkage, Recombination
        c) Sex-Linkage, Y Chromosome, Sex Determination
        d) Extranuclear Inheritance
        e) Mutation: Types, Effects, Errors of Metabolism, Mutagens and Carcinogens
        f) Genetic Drift
        g) Crossing-over

    C. Analysis: Hardy-Weinberg, Test Cross, Crossover Frequency, Biometry

    D. D. Evolution
        a) Natural Selection: Fitness, Differential Reproduction, Group Selection
        b) Speciation: Polymorphism, Adaptation, Inbreeding, Outbreeding, Bottlenecks
        c) Time as gradual random changes in genome

IV: Metabolism

    A. A. Glycolysis
        a) Aerobic: Substrates and Products
        b) Anaerobic: Fermentation
        c) Net Results

    B. Regulation of Pathways

    C. Krebs Cycle: Reactions, Substrates, Products, Regulation

    D. Metabolism of Fat and Protein
        a) Fats: Digestion, Transport
        b) Fatty Acids: Oxidation, Saturated Fats, Unsaturated Fats
        c) Proteins: Metabolism
        d) Anabolism: Synthesis of Lipids and Polysaccharides

    E. Oxidative Phosphorylation
        a) Electron Transport Chain: Substrates, Products, Function
        b) NADH, NADPH, Flavoproteins, Cytochromes
        c) ATP Synthase, Chemiosmosis
        d) Net Results
        e) Regulation

V: Cell Biology

    A. Plasma Membrane
        a) Composition: Phospholipids, Steroids, Waxes, Proteins
           i. Receptors
        b) Solute transport: Thermodynamics, Osmosis, Passive, Active, Na/K Pump, Channels
        c) Membrane Potential
        d) Exocytosis, Endocytosis
        e) Gap Junctions, Tight Junctions, Desmosomes

    B. Membrane-Bound Organelles
        a) Nucleus: Genetic Information, Nucleolus, Nuclear Envelope, Pores
        b) Mitochondria: Function, Membranes, Replication
        c) Lysosomes: Function
        d) ER: Rough vs. Smooth, Double Membrane, Biosynthesis
        e) Golgi: Structure and Function
        f) Peroxisomes: Function

    C. Cytoskeleton: Microfilaments, Microtubules, Intermediate Filaments, Cilia, Flagella, Centrioles, Microtubule Organizing Centers

    D. Epithelial and Connective Cells

VI: Microbiology

    A. Cell Theory: History, Development, Impact

    B. Prokaryotes
        a) Archaea, Bacteria, Bacilli, Spirilli, Cocci
        b) Lack of Eukaryotic Features
        c) Cell Wall, Flagella
        d) Fission, Exponential Growth

e) Quick Adaptation, Antibiotic Resistance

f) Types: Aerobic, Anaerobic, Parasitic, Symbiotic

g) Chemotaxis

h) Genetics: Plasmids, Transformation, Conjugation, Transposons

C. Viruses

a) Structure, Size, Lack of Organelles

b) Bacteriophages

c) Genome: DNA, RNA

d) Life Cycle: Intracellular Reproduction, Attachment, Replication, Release

e) Transduction

f) Retroviruses

g) Prions, Viroids

VII: Cell Division, Cell Development, Reproduction, Embryology

A. Mitosis: Phases, Structures, Growth Arrest, Control and Loss of Control

B. Reproduction

a) Gametogenesis, Meiosis

b) Ovum, Sperm: Formation, Morphology, Contribution to Zygote

c) Sequence: Fertilization to Birth

C. Embryogenesis

a) Stages: Fertilization, Cleavage, Blastula, Gastrula, Cell Movements, Neurulation

b) Germ Layers: Endoderm, Mesoderm, Ectoderm

c) Neural Crest

d) Environmental Effects

D. Cell Development

a) Specialization: Determination, Differentiation, Tissue Types, Cell communication

b) Cell Migration

c) Stem Cells

d) Gene Regulation

e) Apoptosis

f) Regeneration, Senescence, Aging

VIII: Nervous and Endocrine Systems

A. Nerve Cell

a) Structures: Soma, Dendrites, Axon, Myelin, Nodes of Ranvier

b) Synapse: Structure, Neurotransmitters

c) Resting Potential, Action Potential

d) Excitatory, Inhibitory Fibers, Summation, Firing Frequency

e) Glia, Neuroglia

B. Nervous System

a) Function, Organization

b) Efferent, Afferent

c) Sympathetic, Parasympathetic

d) Reflexes: Reflex Arc, Spinal Cord, Supraspinal Circuits

e) Endocrine System Integration

C. Endocrine System

a) Function, Major Glands, Major Hormones

b) Mechanism of Hormone Action

c) Transport of Hormones and Second Messengers

IX: Physiology

A. Respiratory System: Structure, Function, Thermoregulation, Henry's Law, pH control, Regulation

B. Circulatory System

a) Structures, Functions, Regulation

b) Heart: Chambers

c) Systolic, Diastolic Pressure

d) Pulmonary, System Circulations

e) Arteries, Veins, Capillaries

f) Blood Composition: Plasma, Cells, Chemicals

g) Clotting

h) Gas Transport: Oxygen, Carbon Dioxide, Hemoglobin, Hematocrit

i) Lymphatic System: Structures, Functions

C. Immune System
   a) Innate: Macrophages, Phagocytes
   b) Adaptive: T-cells, B-cells
   c) Tissues: Marrow, Spleen, Thymus, Lymph Nodes
   d) Antigens, Antibodies: Ag Presentation, Ag-Ab Recognition, Structure of Ab
   e) Autoimmune Diseases
   f) Major Histocompatibility Complex

D. Digestive System
   a) Ingestion, Peristalsis
   b) Organs: Stomach, Liver, Gall Bladder, Pancreas, Small Intestine, Large Intestine
   c) Control: Muscular, Endocrine, Nervous

E. Excretory System
   a) Homeostasis: bp, osmoregulation, acid balance, nitrogenous waste
   b) Kidney: Cortex, Medulla
   c) Nephron: Glomerulus, Bowman's Capsule, Tubules, Loop of Henle, Collecting Duct
      i. filtration, counter-current multiplier, secretion, reabsorption, concentration
   d) Storage: ureter, bladder, urethra

F. Reproductive System: Gonads, Genitals, Sexual Development, Menstrual Cycle, Pregnancy, Lactation

G. Muscle System
   a) Function: Mobility, Circulatory Assistance, Thermoregulation, Shivering
   b) Smooth, Striated, Cardiac
   c) Muscle Structure: T-tubule, Contractile Apparatus, Sarcoplasmic Reticulum, Contractile Velocity
   d) Cardiac Muscle: Regulation
   e) Oxygen Debt
   f) Control: Motor Neurons, Neuromuscular Junction, Motor End Plates, Sympathetic and Parasympathetic, Voluntary, Involuntary
   g) Sarcomeres
   h) Troponin, Tropomyosin

H. Skeletal System
   a) Function: Support, Protection, Calcium Storage
   b) Bone Types, Joint Types
   c) Composition of Bone Matrix and Cells
   d) Cartilage, Ligaments, Tendons
   e) Endocrine Regulation

I. Skin System
   a) Structure: Layers, Cell Types, Impermeability to Water
   b) Function: Homeostasis, Osmoregulation, Thermoregulation, Physical Protection
   c) Hormonal Control

Chemical and Physical Foundations of Biological Systems

X: Fluids

    A.   Circulatory System: Pressure and Flow in Arteries and Veins

XI: Electrochemistry and Circuits

    A.   Nerve Cell Propagation: Myelin, Schwann Cells, Insulation, Nodes of Ranvier

XIV: Biological Molecules

    A.   Nucleotides and Nucleosides: Composition, Purines, Pyrimidines, DNA, Double-Helix

XV: Thermodynamics and Kinetics

    A.   Enzymes
        a)   Reaction Types
        b)   Mechanisms: Active Site, Induced-fit, Cofactors, Coenzymes, Vitamins
        c)   Kinetics: Catalysis, Michaelis-Menten, Cooperativity, Environmental Effects
        d)   Inhibition and Regulation

Psychological, Social, and Biological Foundations of Behavior

XVI: Sensation

    A.   Sensory Processing: Thresholds, Adaptation, Pathways, Receptor Types
    B.   Vision
        a)   The Eye: Structure and Function
        b)   Visual Processing: Brain Pathways
    C.   Hearing
        a)   The Ear: Structure and Function, Hair Cells
        b)   Auditory Processing: Brain Pathways
    D.   D. Other Senses
        a)   Somatosensation, Nociception
        b)   Taste, Smell: Pheromones
        c)   Vestibular Sense

XVII: Cognition, Consciousness, and Memory

    A.   Biological Factors Affecting Cognition
    B.   Alertness
    C.   Sleep and Circadian Rhythms
    D.   Emotional Effect on Memory Retrieval
    E.   Memory: Changes in Synaptic Connections, Neural Plasticity, Long-Term Potentiation
    F.   Language: Brain Areas of Language and Speech

XVIII: Emotion and Stress

    A.   Biological Factors in Perceiving Emotion
    B.   Physiological Response to Stress

XIX: Behavior

    A.   Biological Basis of Behavior
        a)   Nervous System: Neurons, Neurotransmitters
            i.   central and peripheral nervous systems
            ii.   brain: forebrain, midbrain, hindbrain, lateralization, methods of study
            iii.   spinal cord
        b)   Endocrine System: Components, Effects on Behavior
        c)   Genetics: Temperament and Heredity, Adaptive Value of Behaviors
            i.   Regulatory Genes and Behavior
            ii.   Behavior Variation Between Populations
    B.   Disorders: Schizophrenia, Depression, Alzheimer's, Parkinson's, Stem-Cell Therapy
    C.   Motivation: Biological Drives

XX: Learning

    A.   Classical Conditioning: Conditioned and Unconditioned Response, Processes

    B.   Operant Conditioning

        a)   a.   Shaping, Extinction

        b)   b.   Reinforcement Schedules and Types

        c)   c.   Punishment, Escape, Avoidance

    C.   Biological Effects on Associative Learning

XXI: Social Interaction

    A.   Animal Signals and Communication

    B.   Social Behavior in Animals: Foraging, Mating, Game Theory, Altruism, Inclusive Fitness

BIOCHEMISTRY

Biological and Biochemical Foundations of Living Systems

I: Proteins

    A. Amino Acids: configuration, dipolar ions, acidic/basic, hydrophobic/hydrophilic

    B. Structure
        a) Protein Structure: Primary, Secondary, Tertiary, Quaternary
        b) Protein Stability: Folding, Denaturing, Hydrophobic interactions, Solvation and Entropy
        c) Separation Techniques: Isoelectric Point, Electrophoresis

    C. Protein Function: Immune System, Motors

    D. Enzymes
        a) Catalysts: Reduction of Activation Energy, Cofactors, Coenzymes
        b) Classification
        c) Substrate interactions: Active Site, Induced Fit
        d) Vitamins
        e) Effects on Enzyme Activity: pH, temperature, etc.

    E. Enzyme Control
        a) Kinetics: Michaelis-Menten, Cooperativity
        b) Feedback
        c) Inhibition: Competitive, Non-competitive, Mixed, Uncompetitive
        d) Regulatory Enzymes: Allosteric enzymes, Zymogens, Covalently-modified enzymes

II: Molecular Genetics

    A. Nucleic Acids
        a) Structure, Function
        b) Nucleotides, Nucleosides: Sugar-Phosphate Backbone, Purines, Pyrimidines
        c) Watson-Crick Model: Double-Helix, Base-Pair Specificity
        d) Denaturation, Reannealing, Hybridization

IV: Metabolism

    A. Bioenergetics
        a) Thermodynamics/Bioenergetics: ΔG, K_{eq}, Concentrations, Spontaneity
        b) Phosphoryl Groups: ATP Hydrolysis, Group Transfers
        c) Redox: Half-Reactions, Soluble Electron Carriers, Flavoproteins

    B. Carbohydrates: Classification, Configuration, Hydrolysis of Glycosides, Monomers and Polymers

    C. Glycolysis and Gluconeogenesis
        a) Aerobic: Substrates and Products
        b) Anaerobic: Fermentation
        c) Net Results
        d) Gluconeogenesis and Pentose Phosphate Pathway

    D. Regulation of Pathways
        a) Regulation of Glycolysis and Gluconeogenesis
        b) Glycogen Synthesis and Breakdown, Regulation
        c) Analysis of Metabolic Regulation

    E. Krebs Cycle: Acetyl CoA Production, Reactions, Substrates, Products, Regulation

    F. Metabolism of Fat and Protein
        a) Fats: Digestion, Transport
        b) Fatty Acids: Oxidation, Saturated Fats, Unsaturated Fats, Ketone Bodies

    G. Oxidative Phosphorylation
        a) Electron Transport Chain: Substrates, Products, Function
        b) NADH, NADPH, Flavoproteins, Cytochromes
        c) ATP Synthase, Chemiosmosis
        d) Net Results
        e) Regulation
        f) Mitochondria: Apoptosis, Oxidative Stress

    H. Hormonal Regulation: High Level Integration, Tissue Specific Metabolism, Obesity

V: Cell Biology

    A.   Plasma Membrane
        a)   Composition: Phospholipids, Steroids, Waxes, Proteins
            i.   Receptors
        b)   Solute transport: Thermodynamics, Osmosis, Passive, Active, Na^+/K^+ Pump, Channels
        c)   Membrane Potential
        d)   Exocytosis, Endocytosis

VIII: Nervous and Endocrine Systems

    A.   Biosignalling: Gated Ion Channels, Voltage and Ligand Gated, Receptor Enzymes, G protein-coupled receptors
    B.   Lipids: Structure, Steroids, Terpenes, Terpenoids

Chemical and Physical Foundations of Biological Systems

XII: Solution Chemistry and Acid/Base

    A.   Brønsted-Lowry Definitions, Auto-Ionization of Water, Conjugates
    B.   Weak Acids/Bases: Salts, pH Calculations
    C.   Constants: K_a, K_b, K_w
    D.   Buffers: Common Systems, Titration Curves
    E.   Ions: Common Names and Charges, Hydration and Hydronium

XIII: Separation and Purifications

    A.   Extraction
    B.   Distillation
    C.   Chromatography: Column, HPLC, Paper, TLC
    D.   Peptides: Electrophoresis, Quantitative Analysis, Size-Exclusion, Ion-Exchange, Affinity

XIV: Biological Molecules

    A.   Nucleotides and Nucleosides: Composition, Purines, Pyrimidines, DNA, Double-Helix, Chemistry, Other Functions
    B.   Amino Acids and Peptides
        a)   Amino Acids: Configuration, Dipolar, Acid/Base, Hydrophobic/Hydrophilic
        b)   Peptides: Sulfur Linkage, Polypeptides, $1°$ - $4°$ Structure, Isoelectric Point

    C.   3D Protein Structure: Conformational Stability, Hydrophobic Interactions, Solvation and Entropy, $4°$ Structure, Folding and Denaturing
    D.   Non-Enzymatic Protein Function: Binding, Immunoglobulins, Motors
    E.   Lipids: Storage, Triacyl Glycerols, Saponification, Phospholipids, Phosphatides, Sphingolipids, Waxes, Fat-Soluble Vitamins, Steroids, Prostaglandins
    F.   Cyclic Molecules: Phenols, Hydroquinones, Ubiquinones, 2e- Redox Centers, Aromatic Heterocycles

XV: Thermodynamics and Kinetics

    A.   Enzymes
        a)   Reaction Types
        b)   Mechanisms: Active Site, Induced-fit, Cofactors, Coenzymes, Vitamins
        c)   Kinetics: Catalysis, Michaelis-Menten, Cooperativity, Environmental Effects
        d)   Inhibition and Regulation
    B.   Bioenergetics: ΔG, K_{eq}, Phosphorylation, ATP, ATP Group Transfers, Redox, Soluble Electron Carriers, Flavoproteins

C. THE SCIENTIFIC METHOD

As with all sciences, biological research involves methodically searching for information. The procedure associated with this search is called the ***scientific method***. It involves

1. asking questions, which are then followed by one or more ***hypotheses*** (educated guesses or hunches that answer or explain the question).
2. making predictions from the hypothesis, usually in the form of "if....then" statements (*if* the influenza virus causes the flu, *then* those exposed to it will become ill).
3. testing the predictions through experimentation, observation, model building, etc., including appropriate controls with which to compare the results.
4. repeating the investigations and devising new ways to further test the hypothesis (this may include modification of the hypothesis based on the results of the tests).
5. reporting the results and drawing conclusions from them.

A theory is similar to a hypothesis in that it is subjected to the scientific method, but a theory usually explains a broad range of related phenomena, not a single one. Theories are well supported hypotheses, shown to be valid under many different circumstances.

In science, there is no real beginning or end. All hypotheses are based on previous work, and all results and conclusions can be expanded in the future. Often experiments raise more questions than they answer.

Understanding this methodical approach to scientific evidence and conclusions is essential for success on the MCAT. Most of the passages you will see in the science sections are ones that describe an experimental procedure and it is critically important that you understand the procedure so that you can answer the questions. You should read the passage carefully, often taking "flowchart" style notes to make sure you've understood the experiment.

D. CHARACTERISTICS OF LIFE

If biology is the study of life, then it is natural to ask: What is life? There is no one definition of life that can encompass all living things. However, there are certain characteristics that all living things share:

♦ ***order and organization***: The basic unit of life is the cell. It is capable of performing all activities of life. For single-celled organisms, this is the limit of their organization. For multicellular organisms, cells may be arranged in tissues, tissues arranged in organs, and organs arranged in systems. Living things are further organized into populations, communities, ecosystems and, ultimately, the biosphere (the combined regions of the earth in which organisms can live). A corollary to this topic is the organization and structure of the genetic material: all living things have nucleic acids as the storage mechanism for genetic information.

♦ ***growth and development***: All living things grow and develop during their life. This may be as simple as a bacterium that increases in size or as complex as a fertilized egg that develops into an elaborate, multicellular organism.

♦ ***reproduction***: Organisms must reproduce in order for the species to survive. The exact mode of reproduction may be different (for example, asexual verses sexual reproduction), but the outcome is the same: an increase in the number of organisms.

♦ *energy metabolism*: All living things require energy to survive. Various processes are necessary in order to supply this energy. First of all, organisms must gain nutrition: those that can make their own food are called autotrophs, all others are called heterotrophs. The nutrients must be converted into energy, which includes the process of respiration. Finally, waste products must be eliminated.

♦ *stimuli response and homeostasis*: The ability to respond to the environment, whether it be the external or the internal environment, is a vital function in all living things. Organisms must regulate their life processes based on what is happening in the environment.

♦ *evolution*: The ability to change, to mutate, is an important characteristic of life. Were it not for this ability, the vast diversity of life would not exist on this planet. For that matter, no life would exist at all.

E. STRUCTURE AND FUNCTION

Another topic which underlies all aspects of biology is the correlation between structure and function. If the structure is known, often the function can be determined, and vice versa. For example, knowing the amino acid sequence of a protein (the structure) can help predict how that protein functions in a cell. Or, as another example, if an animal has the ability to see (the function), then it must have the structures necessary to support that function (eyes, optic nerves, a region of the brain to interpret nerve impulses, etc.).

Data and Figure Interpretation

While the MCAT has always featured figures and graphs quite prominently, with the addition of the psychology and sociology section, the AAMC is significantly ramping up its focus on the correct interpretation of data and figures. To that end, you must be sure to carefully analyze each figure you encounter on the test. Your first task is the most important: correlate the text with the figures. What does the text of the passage tell you about the diagram? What does the diagram show you about the situation described in the text? Overwhelmingly, the medium and high difficulty questions on the test involve this correlation.

When examining the figures themselves, look for the following:
1. Title and axes – what are the units of the axes? Is it a log plot?
2. Trends – are things increasing? Decreasing? No correlation?
3. Extremes – which category or trend is the biggest? Smallest? Changes the most?
4. Inflection points – when does the slope change from flat to positive? To negative?
5. Intercepts – do any lines cross the x or y axis? If so, what do they represent?
6. Intersections – do any trends cross at some point?

Research Methods

In addition to more questions focused on interpreting figures, the MCAT also includes an increase in questions asking about why experiments were constructed in a certain way. The three major factors to keep in mind here are control groups, independent vs. dependent variables, and confounding factors. The control group is, of course, the group which receives no experimental treatment. Most experiments that show up in MCAT passages will explicitly include a control group that is listed either as "control", "wild type" or "placebo" group. Sometimes, however, the group is not explicitly labeled in that way. To see which group is the control group, start with the aim of the experiment – what are they trying to assess? If they are trying to measure the impact of factor X, then any group that does not include factor X is the control group. If there is no such group, then it is a flawed experiment because it does not include a control. Be sure to notice this! A question will surely ask about it.

Next, the test will often ask about which variables in an experiment are the dependent and independent ones. In the simplest sense, the independent variable is the one the researchers control, and the dependent variable is the one they measure. Typically the independent variable might be time, or age, or dosage level of a drug. When plotting data, the independent variable is on the x-axis and the dependent variable is on the y-axis.

Finally, you should always be on the lookout for confounding factors. These are variables the experimenters did not consider which can affect the outcome. Sometimes these will be obvious – the experimenters will fail to control for age, or income level, or previous experience. Other times they won't be obvious, but will be brought up in the questions. Remember to always ask yourself, "Did they control for this variable? Could this variable affect the results?"

F. USING THIS BOOK

Remember: the MCAT stresses your problem solving skills and your knowledge of basic biological concepts. Therefore, the work you do in understanding these concepts is a necessary first step, but the first step only. Next Step's Content Review books will help you in this foundational work through a thorough treatment of the major topics included in the MCAT. Study to understand these topics, not just to memorize them.

As a part of the purchase price of this book you are also entitled to a free copy of Next Step's online MCAT Diagnostic and Science Content Diagnostic exam. See the insert with details for how to activate your free online test. If you've purchased this book by itself, we strongly recommend that you consider purchasing the rest of the Next Step Science Content Review package. Success on the MCAT will require a good foundation in Chemistry, Organic Chemistry, Psychology, Sociology, and Physics as well.

It's not enough to simply go through this book as you would one of your textbooks in a class. On the MCAT, you must truly master the content. You have to know it so well that you could write this book yourself. To gain that mastery, you should follow a few simple steps:

1. Don't write in the book. You will want to be able to come back and re-do the questions to check your mastery.
2. Begin by taking the Final Exam at the end of the book. This test is a pure content assessment of all the biology and biochemistry content on the MCAT. Taking this test first can help guide you for which chapters merit extra attention.
3. Go through each chapter three times using a "spaced repetition" approach. Spaced repetition has been shown to vastly increase a student's ability to recall information.

Day 1: Start by skimming the chapter quickly. Get a general sense of the content. Then go back and read the chapter slowly and carefully. Take notes in a separate notebook, make flashcards or study sheets as needed.
Day 2: Then wait a day.
Day 3: Come back to the chapter. Re-skim the content and only then do the questions at the end of the chapter. Be sure to analyze all of the questions to make sure you've fully understood them.
Day 4-5: Then wait two days.
Day 6: Come back a third and final time. No need to re-skim – simply re-do the questions at the end of the chapter to solidify your understanding.

4. After completing all of the chapters in a section, complete the Section Content Review Problems at the end of the section. These questions are not in the format of the MCAT – they are simply a very large number of short content questions to check that you've understood and memorized the relevant concepts.

5. Come back to the Section Content Review Problems again two days later and re-do them. At this point you should be getting 100% of the questions correct.

6. After working your way through the whole book, come back to the Final Exam and re-take it. As you wrap up your content review work, you should be scoring nearly 100% on this exam.

G. STUDY PLANS

It's absolutely essential that you develop a clear and rigorous study plan and stick to it. Each student's situation is different so you'll need to develop a plan that fits your unique situation.

The best place to start is with Next Step's online Study Plan. We have posted the plan on our MCAT blog on our website. You can find this plan here:

http://nextsteptestprep.com/category/mcat-blog/

H. OTHER RESOURCES

Good MCAT Prep fundamentally requires three things: content review, practice passages, and full test simulation. The book you're holding in your hands can fulfill the first of those goals. To really prepare for the exam, you will also want to pick up materials to provide you with practice and full test simulation

For practice passages, there's no better resource than Next Step's Strategy and Practice books. We have produced one book for each of the four sections on the exam. Each of our Strategy and Practice books includes a concise, focused discussion on strategies for how to deal with the passages, followed by full timed section practice. The timed sections are in the format of the exam, but made slightly harder than the real thing in order to help build up those MCAT muscles.

To get practice simulating the real exam, you'll want to use Next Step's online Full Length exams. These tests are the best approximation available of what you'll see on the real test. We're the only MCAT prep company in the world to build our exams from the ground up for the new MCAT. While other big companies are simply re-purposing their old exams into the new MCAT format, we started totally fresh. Our practice tests simulate the content, format, and difficulty level of the real test perfectly.

http://nextsteptestprep.com/mcat-practice-tests/

Finally, the single best resource for MCAT practice is the testmaker: the AAMC. Every student preparing for the MCAT should purchase the official guide, the official AAMC practice test, and any other AAMC practice sets available.

Good luck!

CHAPTER 1 PROBLEMS

PASSAGE 1.1 (QUESTIONS 1-4)

Kaposi's sarcoma (KS) is a cancer marked by purple tumors on the skin. Although extremely rare in the population, it is found in approximately 25% of those infected with HIV, the virus that causes AIDS. It has been suggested that KS itself is caused by a virus, the human herpesvirus 8 (HHV8). To help confirm this hypothesis, the following observations were made:

Observation 1:

At regular intervals over a two-year period, samples of blood were taken from those who tested positive for HIV at the beginning of the study. In 38 of the subjects, no KS developed, although 18% had antibodies against HHV8 in their blood samples. However, in 40 subjects who developed KS, 80% had HHV8 antibodies. In 11 of these men, HHV8 antibodies were detected from the beginning of the study, but 21 of the men developed HHV8 antibodies during the study. In these subjects, the antibodies appeared several months before the onset of KS.

Observation 2:

Individuals not known to have been infected with HIV were tested for antibodies against HHV8. Out of 141 blood donors, only 1% were found to test positive for the antibodies. In addition, 300 hemophiliacs who had regular blood transfusions were also examined. Three percent had HHV8 antibodies.

Observation 3:

In 176 patients who had syphilis, a sexually transmitted disease, 36 (or 20%) had antibodies to HHV8.

1. What conclusion can be drawn from these observations?
    A. Although HHV8 is associated with KS, it has yet to be proven that it causes KS.
    B. In observation 1, the fact that some individuals tested positive for HHV8 but did not develop KS proves this virus does not cause the disease.
    C. Individuals with syphilis will also develop KS.
    D. Hemophiliacs are at no risk of developing KS.

2. Which is the best hypothesis for the mode of transmission of HHV8?
    A. blood transfusions
    B. casual contact
    C. sexual transmission
    D. airborne particles

3. In another study, it was found that KS is prevalent in transplant patients taking drugs which suppress their immune system to prevent rejection of the new organ. This, along with the above evidence, indicates:
    A. a virus other than HHV8 causes KS.
    B. a weakened immune system is probably necessary for KS to develop.
    C. both A and B
    D. neither A nor B

4. Many researchers argue that viruses are not alive. Which of the following supports this hypothesis?

    I. Some viruses carry their genetic information in the form of RNA, not DNA.
    II. Viruses cannot reproduce by themselves.
    III. Viruses do not evolve; that is, they do not mutate or change.

    A. I only
    B. II only
    C. I and II only
    D. II and III only

SECTION 1
MOLECULAR BIOLOGY

Molecular biology, as the term is often used today, refers specifically to the study of the molecules involved in the transmission and usage of information, that is, molecular genetics. Modern molecular biology is a relatively new field, and its importance cannot be understated. Understanding the structure and function of DNA, how it enables information to be passed on from parent to offspring, and how it controls the cellular activities of an organism have ushered in the most exciting period in the history of biology. This knowledge has made possible potential advances in medicine and technology that are only now being realized. This section will explore the structure and function of DNA and RNA, their roles in protein synthesis, and the central position these molecules occupy in directing cellular activities.

The molecular biology portion of the MCAT, while including this information, has a broader scope, and thus uses the term in a wider sense. Also included in this section are topics that might traditionally be considered the province of biochemistry. These topics include the structure and function of enzymes and the various processes by which cells transform and utilize energy. This field is sometimes referred to as *bioenergetics*, or the study of cellular metabolism. All living things need energy in order to survive. Animals employ a complex series of interconnected chemical reactions in order to extract usable energy from the food they eat, and the pathways involved have been elucidated rather thoroughly.

What all of these topics have in common explains their inclusion in this "molecular biology" section. Whether we are discussing genetics, metabolism, or related topics, this section is looking at the processes of life viewed from the perspective of the molecules involved. It was recognized by early biochemists that the chemicals they extracted from living things were similar in all organisms, and could be grouped into four major categories. Initially referred to as "organic" molecules because they were associated with life, we now recognize that the proteins, nucleic acids, lipids, and carbohydrates we will explore in Chapter 2 comprise a small portion of all the carbon-based molecules that exist. However, they are all vital to the survival of every organism. In this section, we will thus also survey the structures and functions of the major biomolecules, and examine their roles in essential life processes. Biological molecules are also reviewed in the organic chemistry book, as well as the biochemistry portion of this book. You should nonetheless read each section carefully as the MCAT places a ***very*** large emphasis on these foundational concepts, and each discipline has its own slightly different take on biological molecules.

CHAPTER 2
Biological Molecules

A. INTRODUCTION

All important biomolecules are organic, that is, based on the carbon atom. Such molecules are often called *macromolecules*, because they are relatively large in comparison with the molecules studied by traditional, *inorganic* chemistry. Biological macromolecules are often *polymers* - molecules formed by the stepwise addition of smaller subunits (*monomers)*. Four major classes of biological molecules have been identified, each with unique structural properties and different roles.

B. CARBOHYDRATES

Carbohydrates get their name from the fact that they are composed of only three types of atoms in particular combinations. The term literally means "carbon and water", revealing their atomic composition: $[C(H_2O)]_n$. This means that only carbon, hydrogen, and oxygen are present, and there is usually twice as much hydrogen as oxygen or carbon. In animals, the major function of carbohydrates is to provide energy for the organism. The fundamental carbohydrate subunit is the *monosaccharide* (see Figure 2.1). *Monosaccharides* can exist alone, or can be polymerized into larger *disaccharides* (see Figure 2.2) and *polysaccharides*.

- ◆ *Monosaccharides*: These are the simplest carbohydrate subunits found in nature. Along with disaccharides, they have a sweet taste and have thus been referred to historically and nutritionally as *sugars* or *simple carbohydrates*. Many nutritional monosaccharides are six-carbon compounds, such as *glucose* (the body's favorite fuel molecule), *fructose* ("fruit sugar"), and *galactose*. Other important monosaccharides are the five-carbon sugars *ribose* and *deoxyribose*, part of the nucleotides that compose DNA and RNA.
- ◆ *Disaccharides*: Composed of two monosaccharide units joined by a *glycosidic* bond, these are also recognized as sugars or simple carbohydrates nutritionally. *Sucrose*, or common table sugar, consists of one glucose and one fructose subunit. Lactose ("milk sugar") is made up of one glucose and one galactose subunit. Maltose ("malt sugar") is composed of two glucose subunits. All of these molecules must be broken down into their constituent monosaccharides before they can be utilized by the body.

♦ **Polysaccharides**: Polysaccharides are made up of many, often hundreds, of monosaccharide subunits. In nature, all of the important polysaccharides are glucose polymers, differing only in their physical arrangement and the type of bonds that join the subunits. Because they do not taste sweet, they are referred to nutritionally as complex carbohydrates, and include such compounds as starch and fiber. **Starch** is an energy storage molecule found in plants, and often makes up a large part of the human diet in the form of grains and vegetables. Because it is a polymer of glucose, starch is broken down into glucose subunits to be used as fuel in our bodies. Fiber, or **cellulose**, is a structural polysaccharide, composing the cell walls of plants. Due to the nature of the glycosidic bonds joining the glucose subunits, however, most animals (including humans) are unable to digest it. **Glycogen** is very similar to starch, and is sometimes referred to as "animal starch". Animals often store excess glucose in this form in their livers and muscles as an energy reserve.

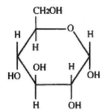

Figure 2.1: Glucose. a monosaccharide

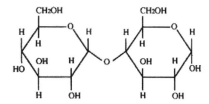

Figure 2.2: Maltose, a Disaccharide

C. LIPIDS

Lipids are macromolecules grouped together for different reasons than are carbohydrates. They do not share any particularly constant chemical structure, but they do share an important physical property brought about by their basic chemical composition: lipids are biological molecules that do not dissolve appreciably in water. This is because they contain nonpolar covalent bonds, and are largely composed of hydrocarbon chains or rings. Since the body is a very watery place, lipids face a challenge, as they are not able to dissolve, and must be handled similarly with regard to their transportation and usage. Several types of lipids exist.

♦ **Triglycerides**: Triglycerides are composed of one molecule of the trialcohol **glycerol** covalently attached to three **fatty acid** molecules, hydrocarbon chains of varying lengths bonded through a terminal carboxylic acid group (see Figure 2.3). Traditionally called **fats** and **oils**, the major role of triglycerides in the body is long-term energy storage. Fats tend to be solid at room temperature because the fatty acid chains are **saturated**, which means they do not contain carbon-carbon double bonds. Chains containing double bonds are called **unsaturated**. The more unsaturated a fatty acid chain, the more liquid the triglyceride. Thus oils are often **polyunsaturated** triglycerides.

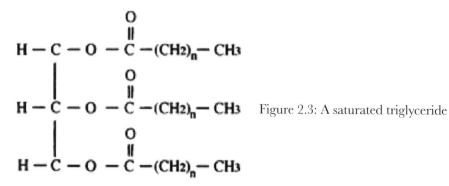

Figure 2.3: A saturated triglyceride

- *Phospholipids*: Phospholipids are a class of related compounds that structurally resemble triglycerides. In place of one of the fatty acids bonded to glycerol, however, is a hydrophilic molecule containing a phosphate group. This gives phospholipids a chemical "split personality". A portion of the molecule is *hydrophobic*, and unable to dissolve in water, while another portion is strongly charged and *hydrophilic*. This interesting combination of properties allows phospholipids to form the structures of plasma membranes and lipoproteins. They also act as emulsifying agents, allowing other lipids to dissolve more easily in the body.

- *Steroids*: Steroids are lipids that do not structurally resemble triglycerides, but are composed of a series of nonpolar rings (see Figure 2.4). *Cholesterol* is the most well known and prevalent steroid compound in the body. Cholesterol plays a role in the structure of cell membranes, as well as serving as the starting compound from which many others are synthesized. Other important steroids include the sex hormones and vitamin D.

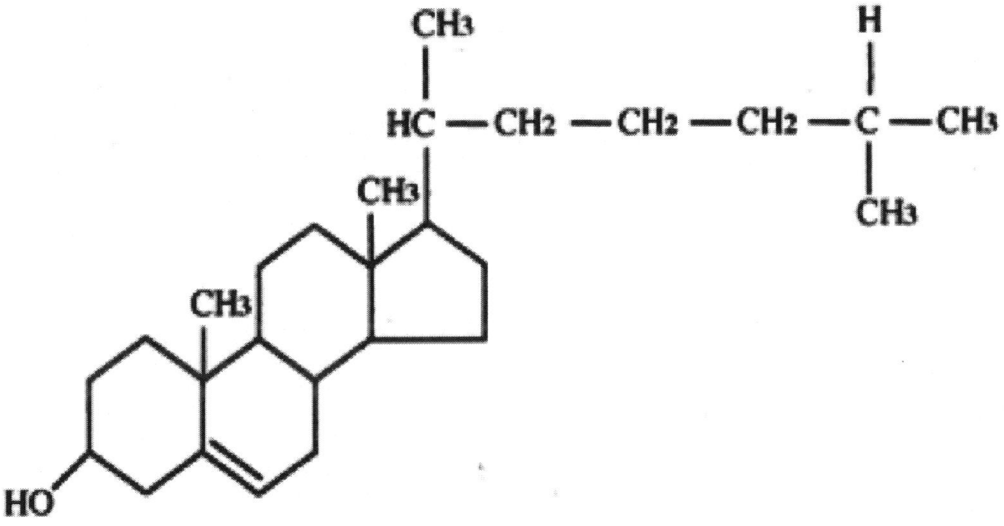

Figure 2.4: Cholesterol, a steroid lipid

D. PROTEINS

Proteins are polymeric macromolecules made up of subunits of *amino acids* (see Figure 2.5). As you might expect, amino acids all contain an amino group and a carboxylic acid group; what differentiates them is a variable portion referred to as the R *group*. In a sense, proteins are structurally simple, since every one consists of a number of amino acids linked by *peptide bonds*. There are twenty different amino acids, however, which can be linked together in any order, and a typical protein contains anywhere from 30 to 1,000 amino acids. Thus, a remarkably vast diversity of different proteins is possible, and this is exactly what we find. There are probably close to 100,000 different proteins in the human body, each with a different function. The remarkable diversity of protein function is made possible by the fact that once a chain of amino acids is linked together (also called a *polypeptide)*, it undergoes additional folding so that the final protein molecule exists in a particular three-dimensional conformation. It is this shape that allows it to function in a unique way. We can identify four levels of protein structure (see Figure 2.6).

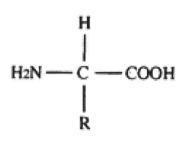

Figure 2.5: An amino acid

- ◆ *Primary structure*: A protein's primary structure simply refers to the linear order of amino acids it contains.
- ◆ *Secondary structure*: The secondary structure of a protein comes about due to local interactions, usually hydrogen bonds between atoms of adjacent amino and acid groups. Common secondary structures include the **alpha-helix** and the **beta-pleated sheet**.
- ◆ *Tertiary structure*: A protein's tertiary structure refers to its ultimate three dimensional shape. It folds uniquely due to long range interactions between the R groups of the amino acids. Such interactions include hydrogen bonding, electrostatic interactions, and hydrophobic interactions. It is the tertiary structure that is responsible for the protein's function.
- ◆ *Quaternary structure*: Not all proteins have a quaternary structure, only those that consist of multiple polypeptide chains. Quaternary folding refers to the interactions between multiple chains of amino acids to achieve a protein that can only function in this complex state.

Proteins perform a vast array of functions, acting as enzymes, antibodies, structural components, hormones, and a wide variety of other functional entities. Well-known proteins include:

- ◆ **Hemoglobin**, which helps carry oxygen in the blood;
- ◆ **Collagen and Keratin**, major components of skin, hair, and connective tissues;
- ◆ **Insulin**, a hormone that regulates blood glucose levels;
- ◆ **Pepsin**, an enzyme that digests other proteins in the stomach;
- ◆ and others too numerous to list!

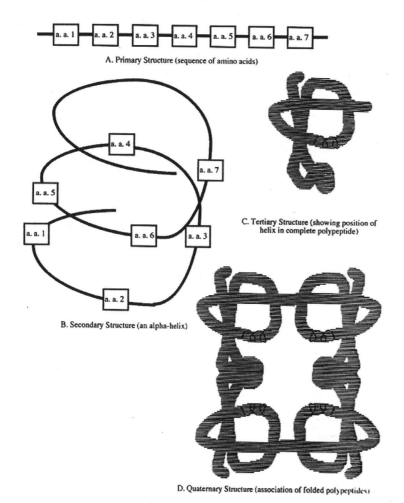

Figure 2.6: Hierarchical folding of a hypothetical protein. aa: amino acid.

E. NUCLEIC ACIDS

Nucleic acids are also macromolecular polymers made up of a particular type of subunit, in this case, the nucleotide (see Figure 2.7). **Nucleotides** are more complex than the other subunits we have considered. Each one is made up of:

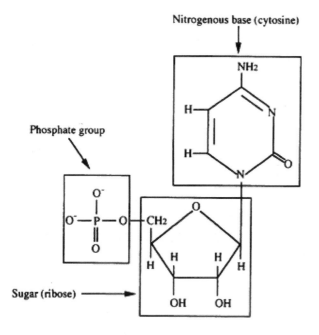

- a five-carbon sugar
- a nitrogenous base
- a phosphate group

Two general types of nucleotides are recognized, depending upon which sugar they contain. Therefore, two major types of nucleic acids can be constructed, depending upon which kind of nucleotide is used.

- **DNA (deoxyribonucleic acid)** is made of nucleotides that contain the sugar deoxyribose.
- **RNA (ribonucleic acid)** is made of nucleotides that contain the sugar ribose.

Figure 2.7: Cytidine monophosphate (CMP),
a ribonucleotide

Deoxyribonucleotides are of four types, depending upon which of four possible nitrogenous bases they contain. The four bases are:

- *Adenine*
- *Guanine*
- *Cytosine*
- *Thymine*

Ribonucleotides are of four types, depending upon which of four possible nitrogenous bases they contain. The four bases are

- *Adenine*
- *Guanine*
- *Cytosine*
- *Uracil*

As you can see, the bases are similar in DNA and RNA, with only one exception: the thymine of DNA is replaced by uracil in RNA. Due to their chemical structures, adenine and guanine are referred to as **purines**, while cytosine, thymine, and uracil are called pyrimidines. You can remember this distinction with the mnemonic "cut the pie" or "CUT the Py" – "Cytosine, Uracil, Thymine are Pyrimidines".

Nucleotides are joined to one another by ***phosphodiester bonds***, creating long chains. As with proteins, what makes one DNA molecule different from another is the sequence of bases that makes up the primary structure. This sequence carries encoded information, and is the basis for the "genetic code". In fact, the major functions of DNA and RNA all deal with the storage, transmission, and usage of genetic information.

It turns out that DNA normally exists in the form of a double helix in nature. Two antiparallel strands of nucleotides are held together by interactions between the bases to form a structure that resembles a twisted ladder (this structure and its consequences are examined in detail in Chapter 5). On the other hand, RNA is usually single-stranded.

CHAPTER 2 PROBLEMS

PASSAGE 2.1 (QUESTIONS 1-5)

Often, bacteria are grown on a medium that contains all of the components they need to survive. This includes an energy source, a carbon source, and sources of all the mineral salts the bacteria require to carry out their metabolic reactions. Sometimes, a mutant bacterium is isolated that needs more than the usual minimum requirements, because it cannot carry out the reactions necessary to produce a needed substance. These mutants are referred to as auxotrophs; if they are to grow, they must be supplemented with the substance they need but cannot manufacture.

Experiment 1

Bacteria were grown on media containing different radioactively labeled atoms to determine which types of biological molecules would be radioactively labeled. Molecules become labeled as they are synthesized by the bacteria using the raw materials provided by the medium. The bacteria were grown for a period of time that was sufficient to label all molecules that could be labeled, and the major types of biomolecules were isolated and tested for the presence of radioactivity. The following table shows the various strains of bacteria and the radioactive element present in the media in which they were grown.

Bacterial strain	Radioactive element
strain 1	carbon
strain 2	phosphorus
strain 3	nitrogen
strain 4	oxygen

Experiment 2

Auxotrophic bacteria were grown on media supplemented with the substance that they need but cannot manufacture. If they were not supplemented in this way, no growth would be observed. The following table shows two auxotrophic strains and the substance with which they were supplemented.

Auxotrophic strain	Supplement
strain A	arginine, an amino acid
strain B	decanoic acid, a fatty acid

Experiment 3

Auxotrophic strain A (from Experiment 2) was grown on a medium that contained supplemental arginine and radioactive phosphorus, and the major types of biomolecules were again isolated and tested for radioactivity.

1. Which of the following biomolecules isolated from Strain 2 would we expect to be radioactively labeled according to the table from experiment 1?
    A. RNA
    B. Proteins
    C. Glucose
    D. Amino acids

2. Which of the following biomolecules isolated from Strain 3 would we expect to be radioactively labeled according to the table from experiment 1?
    A. DNA, but not RNA
    B. DNA and RNA, but not proteins
    C. RNA and proteins
    D. DNA and fatty acids

3. Which of the following biomolecules isolated from Strain 1 would we expect to be radioactively labeled according to the table from experiment 1?
   A. Cholesterol
   B. Phospholipids
   C. Both A and B
   D. Neither A nor B

4. In experiment 2, the arginine-requiring auxotrophic strain A was supplemented with arginine to allow growth. If the cells were not supplemented with arginine, the cells could not grow because arginine is directly required for the synthesis of:
   A. DNA.
   B. proteins.
   C. fatty acids.
   D. RNA.

5. In experiment 3, which of the following biomolecules would we expect to become labeled?
   A. All proteins, DNA, and RNA
   B. Only proteins containing arginine, but not DNA or RNA
   C. DNA, RNA, and only those proteins that contain arginine
   D. RNA and phospholipids

The following questions are NOT based on a descriptive passage.

6. Which of the following sugars does not need to undergo any enzymatic processing before it can be absorbed by the human digestive system?
   A. Lactose
   B. Maltose
   C. Galactose
   D. Sucrose

7. Which of the following is true of the differences between DNA and RNA?
   A. DNA contains a five-carbon sugar, while RNA contains a six-carbon sugar.
   B. DNA contains phosphate groups, while RNA does not.
   C. RNA contains the purine base adenine in place of the purine base guanine contained in DNA.
   D. RNA contains a different five-carbon sugar than DNA.

8. Which of the following statements is true regarding proteins?
   A. All proteins exhibit quaternary folding.
   B. The primary structure of a protein refers simply to the linear order of amino acids it contains.
   C. Not all proteins contain amino acids, only the ones that have extensive three-dimensional folding.
   D. All proteins are composed of one polypeptide chain.

9. Which of the following compounds would one expect to be liquid (with the lowest density) at room temperature?
   A. A saturated triglyceride
   B. A monounsaturated triglyceride
   C. A polyunsaturated triglyceride
   D. None of the above, as all would be solids at room temperature

10. Which of the following carbohydrates is a polymer of the monosaccharide glucose?
    A. Cellulose
    B. Lactose
    C. Ribose
    D. None of the above

CHAPTER 3
Enzymes and Energy

A. INTRODUCTION

The study of energy transformations, or *thermodynamics*, is covered in the chemistry portion of the MCAT. However, it is useful to remind ourselves that the laws of thermodynamics apply as much to living organisms and cells as they do to inanimate objects. Cells therefore had to evolve methods of obtaining and processing energy that are in accordance with the general principles of energy transformations. It is a general chemical principle that in order for a chemical reaction to proceed, a certain amount of energy, the *activation energy*, must be absorbed by the reactants to break the bonds already in place. One way of providing activation energy is simply to add heat to the reactants. This is what we do when we light a match to start a fire, which allows a combustion reaction to proceed. Living systems, however, cannot withstand the high temperatures necessary to overcome the activation energy barriers for biochemical reactions. Another method must exist to allow cells to facilitate and control chemical reactions. *Enzymes* are biological catalysts that facilitate reactions by lowering the necessary activation energy (see Figure 3.1).

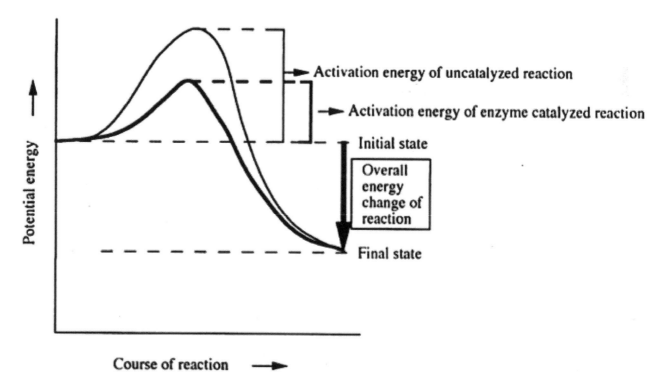

Figure 3.1: Activation energies of catalyzed and uncatalyzed reactions

B. STRUCTURE AND FUNCTION OF ENZYMES

What types of molecules are enzymes and how do they work? Enzymes are almost always large protein molecules, folded into a particular three-dimensional configuration (see Chapter 2). Recently, some RNA molecules have been found to have enzymatic functions, but the vast majority of enzymes are proteins. The protein is folded so that a particular portion of the molecule, the **_active site_**, is accessible and forms a surface that attracts and aligns the reactant(s) in a favorable configuration. The reactant(s) are referred to as the enzyme's **_substrate,_** and when they associate with the enzyme, the intended reaction is able to proceed efficiently at the relatively low temperature of the cell. The amino acids that comprise the active site are close together in space, but may be far apart in the primary structure of the protein. Thus factors that disturb the overall folding of the protein may decrease or totally destroy the enzyme's ability to function.

The way the enzyme interacts with the substrate is only now becoming completely clear. Initially, the association was envisioned as a "lock and key" model, in which the shape of the active site matched the shape of the substrate exactly. This would account for their ability to come together easily. A more modern idea is the "induced fit" model, in which the active site and substrate have an affinity for each other, but the binding of the substrate may change the conformation of the active site, inducing a better fit and perhaps straining the bonds that will be broken in the substrate (see Figure 3.2).

Enzymes have great **_specificity_**, which means that one enzyme can catalyze only one reaction or a set of very closely related reactions. This is of great benefit because it allows the cell to control different reactions independently, by regulating the activity or quantity of the enzyme involved. Furthermore, the enzyme is not permanently altered in any way by participating in the reaction, and so is "recyclable", being used over and over again. Therefore, enzymes typically do not need to be manufactured in large quantities.

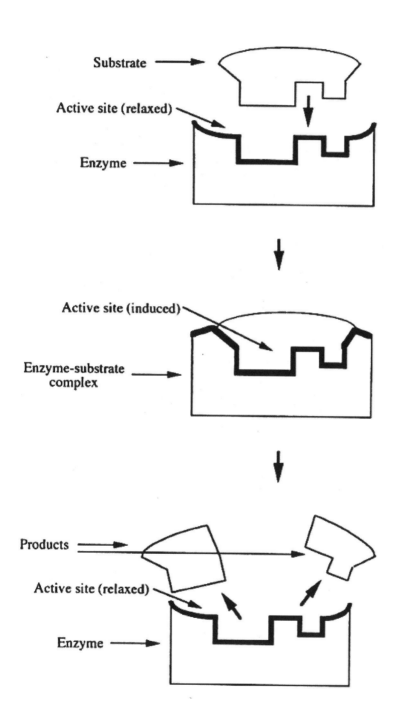

Figure 3.2: A model of enzyme action (induced fit)

C. FACTORS AFFECTING ENZYME ACTIVITY

Sometimes it takes more than just the presence of the substrate and the enzyme to allow a reaction to take place. Many enzymes require the presence of a ***cofactor*** to function. Simple cofactors are usually ionic minerals. For example, many enzymes require magnesium or zinc ions, for which they have binding sites, in order to act as catalysts. If the cofactor is not present, the enzyme will not work or will have reduced activity.

Sometimes the cofactor is a nonprotein organic molecule, called a ***coenzyme***. The coenzyme plays a central role in the catalyzed reaction, often by accepting or providing electrons and becoming ***reduced*** or ***oxidized,*** respectively, in the process. The vitamins of the B-complex group or their derivatives serve as coenzymes in the catabolic reactions that oxidize food molecules to release energy (see Chapter 4).

Environmental conditions also play a major role in determining an enzyme's effectiveness. In particular, temperature and pH influence enzyme activity enormously, and this is the major reason these parameters are so tightly controlled in humans. The temperature and pH of our bodies cannot vary considerably without dire consequences. Why are enzymes affected so profoundly by these environmental conditions?

Enzyme activity, in general, is reduced as the temperature drops and is increased as the temperature rises. If our body temperature becomes colder than normal, enzymes will function, but at slower and slower rates as the temperature falls. Ultimately, these rates will be too slow to sustain life. Raising the temperature will increase enzyme activity, to a certain point. If the temperature is too high, the interactions that maintain the shape of the enzyme will be disrupted, changing the overall shape of the protein and destroying, often irreversibly, the functionality of the active site. When an enzyme loses its activity due to disruption of its three-dimensional configuration, that enzyme has become ***denatured***. Both low and high pH values can also denature enzymes by disrupting the interactions that hold them in their proper orientation, in this case by affecting the charges of various R groups and subsequently changing their affinities for each other. Every enzyme has an optimum pH and temperature at which it functions best; any deviation from these values will reduce its ability to catalyze reactions.

D. CONTROL OF ENZYME ACTIVITY

While ultimately the control of enzymes is accomplished genetically, several other processes affect when and how efficiently an enzyme works, so the cell carries out the desired reactions at the right times and rates. A classic example of an enzyme control mechanism is called ***feedback inhibition***. Many enzymes, in addition to their active sites, contain binding sites for other molecules. These are referred to as ***allosteric sites***, and enzymes that contain them are ***allosteric enzymes***. If the allosteric site has an affinity for the product of the enzyme-catalyzed reaction, a feedback loop will automatically control how much of the product is produced. If product concentrations are low, the cell requires the reaction to proceed; little of the product exists to bind to the allosteric site, and the enzyme functions normally. As the reaction progresses, and enough of the product is made, it binds to the allosteric site. When this happens, the overall shape of the enzyme changes so that the active site is either hidden or disrupted, and the reaction will take place at a reduced rate or not at all. When product levels drop again, the product dissociates from the allosteric site, exposing the active site and allowing the reaction to resume. This process acts like a "thermostat", and is a common cellular strategy for regulating enzyme activity.

Sometimes molecules are present that act to inhibit an enzyme's function, and these are appropriately called ***enzyme inhibitors***. ***Competitive*** inhibitors resemble the substrate, and thus compete with it for binding to the active site. ***Non-competitive*** inhibitors bind to an allosteric site, causing the enzyme's shape to change and affecting its function. Therefore, competitive inhibitors are less effective as the substrate concentration rises, while non-competitive inhibitors work regardless of the substrate concentration.

E. ATP AS THE ENERGY CURRENCY OF THE CELL

Reactions that are **endergonic** require the input of energy. Cells must perform many endergonic reactions in order to remain alive; protein synthesis and DNA replication are just two examples. While enzymes are required to catalyze these reactions, they cannot provide the energy to drive them. Therefore, all endergonic reactions must be coupled to energy-releasing, or **exergonic**, reactions in order to proceed. While cells can ingest energy-containing molecules in many forms (monosaccharides, fatty acids, amino acids, etc.), the energy contained in these molecules must be harvested and stored in a usable form by the cell. In almost all cases, this usable form of energy is the molecule ATP (**adenosine triphosphate**), the triphosphate form of the DNA nucleotide adenosine (see Figure 3.3). When the bond linking the terminal phosphate to the rest of the molecule is **hydrolyzed** (broken), ADP (**adenosine diphosphate**) and free phosphate are the products, and energy is released. Thus, this is an exergonic reaction. Many enzymes that catalyze endergonic reactions associate with ATP, and often contain **ATPase** (ATP hydrolyzing) activity in addition to their other catalytic capabilities. Thus, it is ATP that directly provides the energy required by enzymes to catalyze endergonic reactions. This intimate association of exergonic ATP hydrolysis with endergonic reactions is referred to as **coupling** of reactions. The next chapter addresses the process by which cells transform the chemical energy of food molecules into energy stored as ATP.

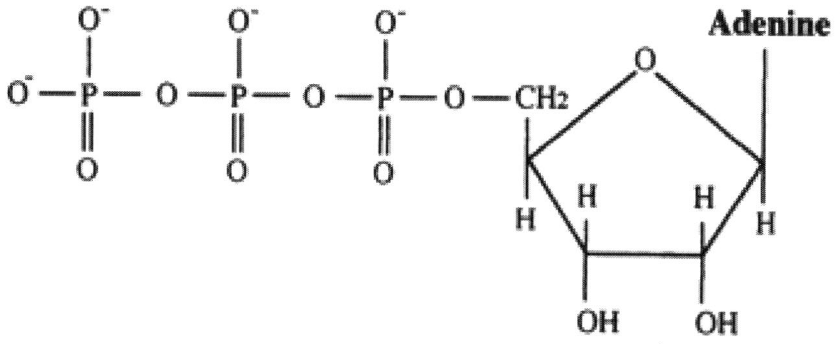

Figure 3.3: Adenosine triphosphate (ATP)

Chapter 3 Problems
Passage 3.1 (Questions 1-5)

In general, enzymes are protein molecules which must be folded in a specific three-dimensional shape in order to function properly. Certain environmental parameters can affect enzyme activity, including pH and temperature. If an enzyme's shape changes significantly and it can no longer function, the enzyme is said to have become denatured.

The enzyme pancreatic amylase is manufactured and secreted by the pancreas into the duodenum (the large, beginning portion of the small intestine). Pancreatic amylase breaks down starch into maltose, a disaccharide. Pepsin is an enzyme that is released by the epithelium of the stomach, and functions in the stomach to break down proteins into smaller polypeptide units.

The following graphs show the activities of enzymes under various environmental conditions.

Graph 1

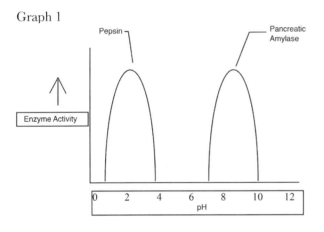

Graph 2

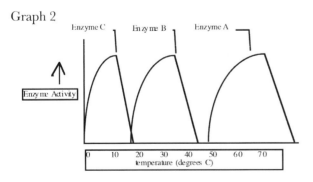

1. Which of the following statements is true with respect to graph 1?
   A. Pepsin and pancreatic amylase could never function together in the same part of the body at the same time.
   B. Pancreatic amylase could function in the stomach, but its activity would be low.
   C. The optimal pH for the functioning of pepsin is approximately 8.5.
   D. Normally, the small intestine must be slightly acidic.

2. Trypsin is a protein digesting enzyme that functions in the small intestine. Which of the following statements should be true about trypsin?
   A. The optimum pH for the functioning of trypsin is approximately 2.
   B. Both trypsin and pepsin would be expected to be found working together in the same part of the body.
   C. The optimum pH for the functioning of trypsin is approximately 8.5.
   D. Trypsin could function well in a solution containing 1 molar hydrochloric acid.

3. Graph 2 depicts the activities of three enzymes. Which curve illustrates the functioning of human DNA polymerase, which functions in the nucleus of cells?
   A. Enzyme A
   B. Enzyme B
   C. Enzyme C
   D. None of the above could represent the activity of human DNA polymerase.

4. Which curve illustrates the functioning of DNA polymerase from a shark?
   A. Enzyme A
   B. Enzyme B
   C. Enzyme C
   D. None of the above, since sharks, like all fish, do not contain DNA polymerase.

5. At what temperature would enzyme B be completely denatured?
   A. 6° C
   B. 15° C
   C. 37° C
   D. 50° C

Passage 3.2 (Questions 6-10)

The reagent iodine potassium iodide (IKI) can be used to detect the presence of starch in a solution. IKI is normally light yellow in color; in the presence of starch it turns a deep blue. IKI can therefore be used to test for the presence and activity of the enzyme amylase, which breaks starch into maltose disaccharide units. (Maltose does not affect the color of IKI). Thus, if starch is initially present and mixed with IKI, the deep blue color created will begin to lighten and disappear if amylase is present as it begins to break down the starch to maltose. Using the same concentration of reagent, the longer it takes for the blue color to disappear, the lower the amylase activity.

Amylase is usually present in vertebrates in two forms that work in different parts of the digestive tract. Salivary amylase, secreted in the saliva by the salivary glands, begins to break down starch in the mouth, which has a slightly acidic pH. Pancreatic amylase is manufactured by the pancreas and released into the small intestine, where it similarly breaks down remaining starch molecules to maltose.

The following tables show the results of an experiment designed to test the activities of one form of amylase at various pH's and temperatures.

pH	Time for blue color to disappear (in minutes)
3	10
6	1
9	5
12	30

Temperature (°C)	Time for blue color to disappear (minutes)
15	10
30	5
37	1
60	blue color never disappears

6. Which of the following is the enzyme being tested?
   A. Human salivary amylase
   B. Shark salivary amylase
   C. Human pancreatic amylase
   D. Shark pancreatic amylase

7. What is the most likely explanation for the observation that the blue color never disappears at 60° C?
   A. The chemical bonds in starch are stabilized by the heat so that it cannot break down even though the enzyme is highly active.
   B. Heat causes the IKI to become unable to stain the starch.
   C. The amylase has become denatured at this temperature.
   D. All of the above are reasonable explanations.

8. What are the enzyme's optimal temperature and pH?
   A. 15°C, pH 12
   B. 37°C, pH 6
   C. 37°C, pH 12
   D. 15°C, pH 6

9. The breakdown of starch is an exergonic reaction, which would occur spontaneously at temperatures of about 200° C. Amylase allows the reaction to proceed at physiological temperatures by:
   A. increasing the activation energy for the reaction.
   B. increasing the potential energy of the reactants.
   C. changing the amount of energy released by the reaction.
   D. lowering the activation energy of the reaction.

10. Which of the following is true of the action of amylase at its optimum pH and temperature?
    A. The enzyme is irreversibly changed, so that one enzyme molecule can only catalyze the reaction once.
    B. It is denatured, and the enzyme's activity is the highest possible.
    C. The active site of amylase consists of every amino acid in the protein.
    D. This pH and temperature represents the physiological conditions under which it functions in nature.

CHAPTER 4
Cellular Metabolism

A. INTRODUCTION

All living organisms, as we have already discussed, require energy in order to survive. Animals obtain this energy by ingesting compounds that contain potential chemical energy (carbohydrates, fats, and proteins), and metabolizing them so that energy is released and stored in the form of ATP. Energy is almost always used directly in the form of ATP. What processes occur at the cellular level to accomplish these energy transformations and create ATP? The net sum of all reactions that take place in a cell or organism is called metabolism, but often the term metabolism is used to refer to the catabolic (breaking down) reactions that make energy available to the cell. These are the reactions on which we will focus in this chapter.

B. TYPES OF METABOLISM

While in theory there are many pathways cells could utilize to metabolize their food, in nature, especially in animals, only a few pathways are used. While rather complex, these pathways vary little from organism to organism. Two major pathways are generally available to heterotrophic animal cells during metabolism: *aerobic respiration* and *fermentation*. Aerobic respiration is an oxygen-requiring series of reactions, and is necessary in all vertebrates. Fermentation does not require oxygen, and while most vertebrates can perform fermentation reactions, it serves them mainly in emergencies when extra energy is needed. Only organisms such as yeast and some bacteria can live entirely by engaging in fermentation.

While many molecules may be metabolized (monosaccharides, amino acids, fatty acids, etc.), most cells prefer glucose as their source of fuel. It is therefore convenient to examine glucose metabolism as a model for the overall process, while keeping in mind that other molecules may also be used. Whichever pathways are ultimately utilized to harvest energy from glucose, they always involve the oxidation of glucose and always begin with a series of reactions called *glycolysis*. If the aerobic pathway is used, glycolysis is followed by two processes: the *Krebs cycle*, a cyclic series of reactions, and the *electron transport chain (ETC)*, where much ATP is synthesized. Let's look at each of these processes in more detail.

C. UNDERSTANDING GLYCOLYSIS

Glycolysis, which literally means "splitting sugar", is a series of nine reactions that partially oxidize glucose and harvest two molecules of ATP. Figure 4.1 shows all nine of the reactions, but it is not necessary to attempt to memorize them all in this context. We are most interested in understanding the major events and the ultimate products of glycolysis.

Glycolysis occurs in the cytoplasm of animal cells, and it is important to remember three major aspects of the process:

- Glucose, a six-carbon compound, is ultimately broken down into 2 molecules of pyruvic acid, a three-carbon compound.
- Two molecules of ATP are produced when glycolysis is complete.
- Two molecules of the coenzyme NAD$^+$ (*nicotinamide adenine dinucleotide*) are reduced to NADH when glycolysis is complete.

A few comments may be helpful at this point.

- Glycolysis is the first step in glucose metabolism in all vertebrates and almost all living cells.
- The ATP made during the process is generated by *substrate level phosphorylation*, which simply means a phosphate group attaches to ADP directly from one of the reactants in the pathway to make ATP.
- NAD$^+$ is a common coenzyme that acts as an electron shuttle. It contains more potential energy when it is reduced to NADH than in its oxidized form, so the generation of NADH represents the temporary storage of energy.

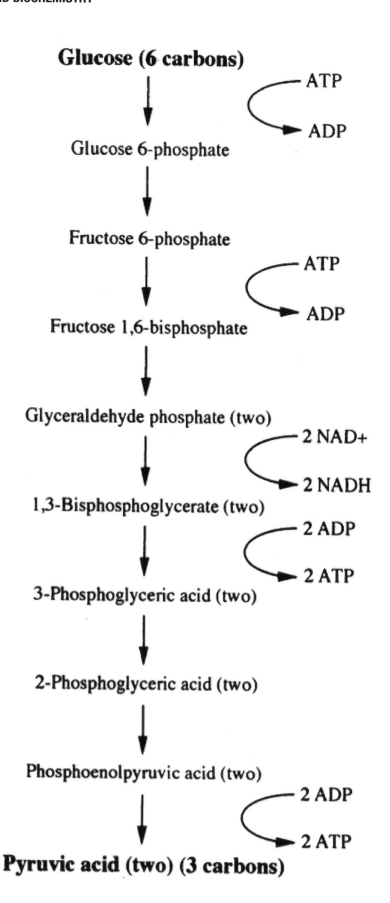

Figure 4.1: A summary of glycolysis

D. THE ANAEROBIC OPTION: FERMENTATION

Glycolysis occurs as the first step in glucose metabolism regardless of whether the cell is performing fermentation or aerobic respiration. It is important to note that glycolysis can never occur alone. It must be coupled to other reactions to be useful. Since fermentation is a comparatively simple process, we will examine it first. If a cell performs fermentation, no oxygen is required, but the pyruvic acid generated in glycolysis must be further processed. While countless variations exist, two major types of fermentation are common (see Figure 4.2):

♦   In *ethanol fermentation*, pyruvic acid is broken down into ethanol (a two-carbon compound) and carbon dioxide (CO_2). This type of fermentation is especially prevalent in yeast, and is utilized in many commercial processes, including the baking of bread and the making of alcoholic beverages.

♦   In *lactic acid fermentation*, the atoms of pyruvic acid are rearranged to form lactic acid (another three-carbon compound). This type of fermentation is carried out by vertebrates, usually in their muscle tissues. During heavy exertion, not enough oxygen may be available to supply ATP needs via the aerobic pathway.

A. Ethanol fermentation

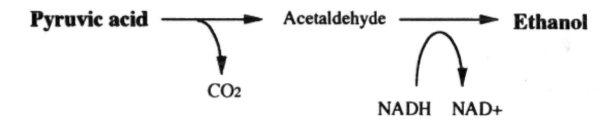

B. Lactic Acid fermentation

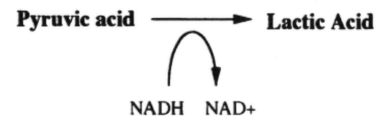

Figure 4.2: A summary of fermentation reactions

It is important to note in examining Figure 4.2 that no additional ATP is produced by either of the fermentation reactions. Why, therefore, must they occur? The answer is simple: the two molecules of NADH formed during glycolysis are oxidized back to NAD^+ during the fermentation reactions. If this did not occur, all of the NAD^+ in a cell would quickly be used up, and glycolysis could no longer continue. This explains why glycolysis can never "stand alone".

E. THE AEROBIC OPTION: CELLULAR RESPIRATION

Vertebrates must perform *aerobic cellular* respiration in order to obtain enough ATP to live. This means that they need a constant supply of oxygen (a major participant in the reactions), and produce carbon dioxide as a waste. This explains the need for breathing, or *physiological* respiration. The reactions of aerobic respiration take place in the mitochondria, so, after glycolysis, the pyruvic acid to be processed must be transported to this organelle. We should note here that the mitochondrion (singular) is surrounded by two membranes; this creates an *intermembrane space*. In addition, the inner membrane is folded to increase its surface area, and the folds are referred to as *cristae*. The inner, liquid portion of the mitochondria is called the *matrix*.

F. THE KREBS CYCLE

Pyruvic acid must now enter a cyclic series of reactions, the *Krebs cycle*, also known as the *citric acid cycle* or the *TCA* (*tricarboxylic acid*) *cycle*. The reactions of the Krebs cycle take place in the mitochondrial matrix, and are summarized in Figure 4.3. Before pyruvic acid can enter the cycle, it must undergo some initial preparatory steps:

- Pyruvic acid is oxidized, releasing one molecule of CO_2 and a two-carbon acetyl group.
- The acetyl group is attached to a molecule called Coenzyme A, to form acetyl CoA.
- In the process, a molecule of NAD^+ is reduced to NADH.

It is important to note that carbon atoms from pyruvic acid can enter the Krebs cycle only in the form of acetyl CoA.

Next, the acetyl group is donated to the four-carbon molecule *oxaloacetic acid* to form citric acid, a six-carbon compound. The citric acid is subsequently broken down, in a series of steps, back to oxaloacetic acid. As with glycolysis, there are three main points to keep in mind regarding the Krebs cycle. Specifically, for each turn of the cycle:

- Two carbons enter the cycle as an acetyl group, and two carbons are released as carbon dioxide.
- One molecule of ATP is harvested.
- Three molecules of NAD^+ are reduced to NADH, and one molecule of another coenzyme, FAD, is reduced to $FADH_2$.

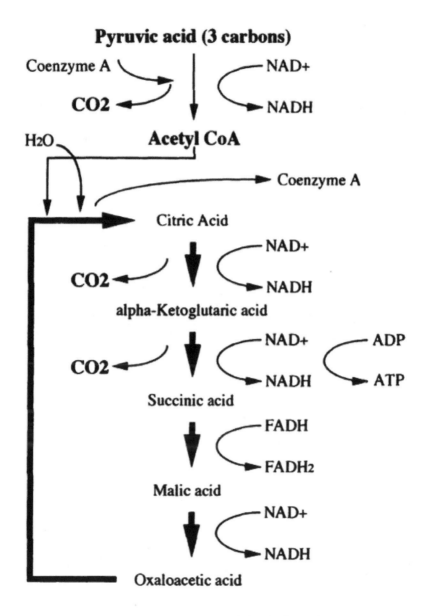

Figure 4.3: Highlights of the Krebs cycle

It is important to remember that for every glucose molecule we started with, two molecules of pyruvic acid were created. Since we have only been keeping track of one pyruvic acid molecule as it travels through the Krebs cycle, we must multiply our totals by two if wish to know the yield per molecule of glucose. If we consider the preparatory events with those of the Krebs cycle itself, we can summarize as follows:

♦ For each three-carbon molecule of pyruvic acid that enter the mitochondria, three molecules of carbon dioxide are released, for a total of six carbon dioxides. This is the source of the CO_2 we exhale.

♦ A total of two molecules of ATP are harvested.

♦ Overall, eight molecules of NAD^+ are reduced to NADH, and two FAD molecules are reduced to $FADH_2$.

G. THE ELECTRON TRANSPORT CHAIN: ATP HARVESTING

After the Krebs cycle, the original glucose molecule has been completely oxidized, which means that its potential energy has been released. One glucose molecule theoretically contains enough potential energy to manufacture close to one hundred molecules of ATP. It is clear that we have not stored a significant amount of the released energy in this form yet. Where is the energy?

The energy is temporarily residing in the reduced coenzyme molecules NADH and FADH$_2$. During the final stages of respiration, the ***electron transport chain***, these coenzymes will donate electrons to a series, or chain, of carriers, and will become oxidized in the process, back to NAD$^+$ and FAD (the coenzymes can then go back and participate in glycolysis and the Krebs cycle). The carriers are physically located in the inner mitochondrial membrane, and include cytochrome proteins, among other molecules. As electrons are passed down the chain, energy is released; the final electron acceptor is molecular oxygen (O$_2$), which is reduced and converted to water as it accepts electrons (this is where the oxygen we inhale is actually used). The energy released is temporarily stored and ultimately used to make ATP by ***oxidative phosphorylation***. The ***chemiosmotic model*** explains how ATP is produced this way (see Figure 4.4). The model highlights three major points:

- The reduced coenzymes NADH and FADH$_2$ ultimately react with oxygen by donating electrons through a series of intermediaries. This reaction causes oxidation of the coenzymes to NAD$^+$ and FAD, and reduction of oxygen to water. A large amount of energy is released in the process. If the intermediate carriers did not exist, all of the energy would be released at once, which would be difficult for the cell to control and manage.
- As energy is slowly released, it is used to ***pump protons*** (H$^+$ ions) from the matrix into the intermembrane space by active transport (see Chapter 11). This establishes an ***electrochemical proton gradient*** which stores the energy that has been released. This gradient can be used to do work.
- The enzyme ***ATP synthase*** is embedded in the inner membrane, and protons diffuse through a channel in this protein back into the matrix. As the protons "fall" through the enzyme, the energy they release is used to do work: the ***phosphorylation*** (addition of a phosphate group) of ADP to make ATP.

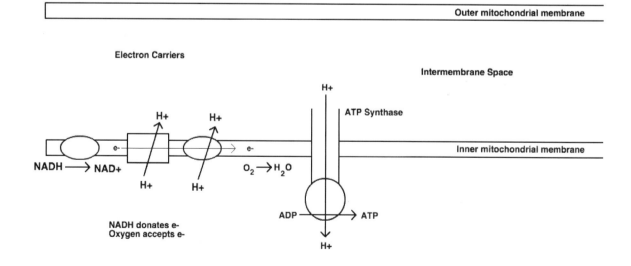

Figure 4.4: The electron transport chain and oxidative phosphorylation

When all is said and done, 32 ATP molecules are harvested by the electron transport chain from all of the reduced cofactors generated through glycolysis and the Krebs cycle. If we add this to the 2 ATP molecules obtained from glycolysis and the 2 produced in the Krebs cycle, we come up with a grand total of 38 molecules of ATP harvested. However, the net amount is 36 ATP molecules because some energy is used to transport pyruvic acid into the mitochondria.

H. OVERALL ENERGY HARVEST

Given that glucose, if burned in a calorimeter, releases 686 kilocalories/mole, and ATP hydrolysis usually yields approximately 7 kilocalories/mole, we can calculate the efficiency of aerobic respiration. If we harvest 36 ATP molecules and multiply by 7 kilocalories/mole, we have obtained 252 kilocalories/mole of glucose burned. This represents an efficiency of 252/686, or approximately 37%. While far from perfect, it is certainly preferable to the efficiency of fermentation, which by the same logic is approximately 2%. Where does the rest of the energy go? The first law of thermodynamics tells us that energy can never be created or destroyed, so it must have been transformed into another type of energy. In fact, it was converted to heat, and is in effect "wasted" energy. Birds and mammals, however, have figured out another use for this energy so that it is not completely wasted: it is the major source of internal heat used to maintain a relatively high body temperature.

I. SUMMARY OF AEROBIC RESPIRATION

After looking at all of the details of respiration, we can formulate a net equation that takes them all into account. That equation is:

$$\text{glucose} + \text{oxygen} + \text{ADP} + \text{P} \longrightarrow \text{carbon dioxide} + \text{water} + \text{ATP}$$

We can make this a proper, balanced chemical equation:

$$C_6H_{12}O_6 + 6O_2 + 36ADP + 36P \longrightarrow 6CO_2 + 6H_2O + 36\,ATP$$

Chapter 4 Problems
Passage 4.1 (Questions 1-5)

Yeast are unicellular fungi that are considered to be facultatively anaerobic. This means that in the presence of oxygen they can and will undergo aerobic respiration, but at the same time they will likely be fermenting glucose. Furthermore, when no oxygen is present they can survive, potentially forever, by fermentation. Yeast use ethanol fermentation, and this produces carbon dioxide as one of its final products.

One way of quantifying the rate of fermentation in yeast is to measure the rate at which the volume of gas changes in a test tube connected to a solution of yeast being fed with glucose. Since carbon dioxide is the only gas involved in fermentation, the rate of gas production should mirror the rate of fermentation.

The following table shows the amount of gas evolved in such an experiment under different environmental conditions.

pH	Gas evolved (in mL)
5	5
6	10
7	20
8	30
9	25
10	10

1. At which pH is the most ethanol produced?
    A. 5
    B. 7
    C. 8
    D. 9

2. It is likely that oxygen is present in this system, such that aerobic respiration is going on at the same time as fermentation. Taking this into account, which of the following statements is true?
    A. Since oxygen will be used up, using the net change in overall gas production as an indicator of the fermentation rate will be inaccurate.

    B. It is irrelevant to our experiment whether or not aerobic respiration is taking place; using the net change in overall gas production as an indicator of the fermentation rate will be accurate.
    C. Under these conditions, no fermentation will occur, since according to the passage yeast only undergo fermentation when no oxygen is available.
    D. The experiment is further complicated by the fact that the yeast will use up some of the carbon dioxide during glycolysis, so using the net change in overall gas production as an indicator of the fermentation rate will be inaccurate.

3. Which of the following statements is true of the yeast in this experiment?
    A. Fermentation reactions will occur in the mitochondria.
    B. Yeast have no mitochondria, and both fermentation and respiration take place in the cytoplasm.
    C. The Krebs cycle, to the extent it occurs, will take place in the mitochondria.
    D. The Krebs cycle clearly does not take place in yeast.

4. Assuming that respiration and fermentation occur at the same time, which of the following statements is true about this experiment?
    A. Since respiration yields more ATP per glucose molecule than fermentation does, the net amount of ATP produced by respiration must be greater than that produced by fermentation.
    B. Even though respiration yields more ATP per glucose molecule than fermentation does, the net amount of ATP produced by fermentation may be greater than that produced by respiration, as long as many more glucose molecules are processed by fermentation than respiration.
    C. Fermentation cannot take place in the presence of oxygen, because it is so inefficient.
    D. The question is impossible to answer, because respiration and fermentation can never take place at the same time.

5. Which of the following statements is true about the electron transport chain in yeast in this experiment?
   A. Yeast do not contain an electron transport chain.
   B. While yeast contain mitochondria and contain an electron transport chain, the energy released during transport is not used to make ATP, it is used to generate carbon dioxide.
   C. The electron transport chain plays no role in ethanol fermentation.
   D. The electron transport chain in yeast functions similarly to that of a human; since yeast do not have mitochondria, however, the chain is located in the yeast cell's plasma membrane.

Passage 4.2 (Questions 6-10)

Many chemicals that are poisons exert their toxic effects by interfering with some aspect of aerobic respiration, usually involving the electron transport chain of the mitochondria. Three such poisons are cyanide, 2,4-dinitrophenol, and the antibiotic oligomycin.

Cyanide is a potent and deadly human poison. It causes its effects by binding to one of the electron carriers and inhibiting the passage of electrons to oxygen, so that electron transport, proton-pumping, and ATP synthesis stop virtually instantaneously.

2,4-dinitrophenol is also a deadly poison to humans. It is an example of the general class of poisons known as "uncouplers", which allow protons to pass back from the intermembrane space to the matrix without passing through the ATP synthase enzyme. Electron transport and proton pumping continue, but ATP is not made. Such uncouplers are also called ionophores.

Oligomycin, an antibiotic, is not deadly to humans, but does interfere with respiration, which is how it kills bacteria, and accounts for its side effects in humans. It is representative of a group of poisons that directly inhibit ATP synthase by blocking the passageway for protons. As with the uncouplers, electron transport and proton pumping continue, but ATP is not made (although for a different reason).

Use the information above, the following observations, and your knowledge of respiration when answering the questions.

Observation 1

When a person breathes a particular deadly poison (compound A), the following effects are observed. Clinically, body temperature quickly increases, causing profuse sweating and ultimately death. At the biochemical level it is noted that normal to greater than normal amounts of oxygen are used, and normal to greater amounts of carbon dioxide are produced. The pH of the mitochondrial intermembrane space does not change appreciably; if it does, it may increase slightly.

Observation 2

When a person ingests a particular toxin (compound B), the following effects are observed. At the biochemical level, it is noted that the Krebs cycle continues to function, producing NADH, and that the NADH is oxidized back to NAD^+ as it donates electrons to the electron transport chain. Strikingly, the pH of the mitochondrial intermembrane space is noted to drop significantly.

6. The toxin ingested that is referred to as compound A in observation 1 is likely to be:
   A. cyanide.
   B. 2,4-dinitrophenol.
   C. oligomycin.
   D. The information presented does not allow differentiation of the three.

7. The toxin ingested that is referred to as compound B in observation 2 is likely to be:
   A. cyanide.
   B. 2,4-dinitrophenol.
   C. oligomycin.
   D. The information presented does not allow differentiation of the three.

8. During cyanide poisoning, which of the following molecules would increase its concentration dramatically?
    A. NAD^+
    B. NADH
    C. Carbon dioxide
    D. FAD

9. In the 1950s, certain weak uncoupling agents were used to promote weight loss. They worked very well; in fact, they worked so well at "burning calories" that many people died from using them and they were pulled from the market. Which of the following statements explains how uncouplers could cause weight loss?
    A. Uncouplers allow ATP to be made but prevent its transport out of the mitochondria, thus uncoupling its manufacture from its use.
    B. Uncouplers increase the metabolic rate, and allow caloric energy temporarily stored in reduced coenzymes to remain "unharvested" as ATP; it is simply released as heat.
    C. Uncouplers prevent oxygen from accepting electrons, so that ATP is not made, and energy is not available to digest and absorb food.
    D. Uncouplers, due to their toxic effects, cause appetite suppression, and lower the overall metabolic rate.

10. Glycolysis could continue to operate indefinitely in all of the following poisoning situations EXCEPT:
    A. cyanide poisoning.
    B. poisoning from a fatal uncoupler.
    C. oligomycin intoxication.
    D. None of the above; glycolysis is not affected by the events of the electron transport chain.

CHAPTER 5

DNA Structure and Function

A. INTRODUCTION

Perhaps the most important molecule in all of biology is ***DNA, deoxyribonucleic acid***. We will devote more than one chapter to this molecule. In addition, the chapters on mitosis, genetics, and evolution rely on a thorough understanding of DNA.

All living things contain DNA as the storage unit of genetic information. The DNA molecule in every organism has the exact same structure and function. How it is copied by the cell (***replication***) and how it is interpreted (***transcription and translation***) may differ in some details; however, the basics are the same in every living entity. We will concentrate on eukaryotic cells in this and the next chapter.

B. THE FUNCTION OF DNA

Earlier, we considered the relationship between structure and function. We will now see how the structure of DNA directly relates to its function. In brief, the functions of DNA are

- ◆ to carry the genetic information of the organism;
- ◆ to control the development of the cell and the organism;
- ◆ to direct the function of the cell, including its reproduction and metabolism.

Since DNA has the same structure in all organisms, and it dictates the function of the cell, it is natural to wonder what makes species different. It is not the basic structure of the DNA, but rather the exact arrangement of the components of DNA that determines this difference. In fact, this arrangement not only accounts for the difference among species, but also for the uniqueness of individuals in the same species.

C. THE CHEMICAL STRUCTURE OF DNA

By the early 1950s, it was well known that DNA was a polymer made up of monomers called ***nucleotides***. Each nucleotide consists of three chemical groups:

- ◆ a 5-carbon sugar, ***deoxyribose***;
- ◆ a nitrogen-rich base attached to the first carbon of the sugar;
- ◆ a ***phosphate group*** attached to the fifth carbon of the sugar.

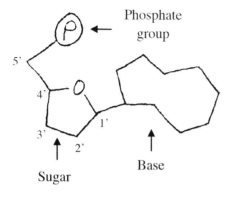

Figure 5.1: General structure
of a nucleotide

Four types of nucleotides exist, and each differ only at the nitrogenous base:

♦ **adenine (A),**
♦ **cytosine (C),**
♦ **guanine (G),** and
♦ **thymine (T).**

In 1953, James Watson and Francis Crick proposed a model for the structure of DNA by considering a wide variety of data from other researchers. In particular, two observations became crucial to their model:

♦ Erwin Chargaff had discovered that, in every molecule of DNA, the amount of **A** was always equal to the amount of **T**, and the amount of **C** was always equal to the amount of **G**.
♦ Rosalind Franklin had obtained X-ray diffraction data that showed DNA exists in a **double helix**, similar in structure to a winding staircase.

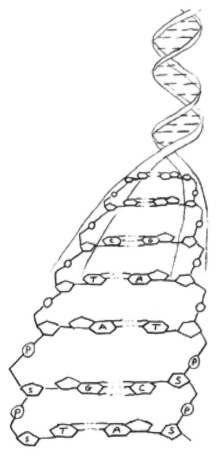

From this information, Watson and Crick were able to correctly determine the structure of the polymer (see Figure 5.2).

The monomers of DNA are linked together via the sugar and the phosphate groups in the nucleotides. This is often called the **sugar-phosphate backbone**, and the bond that forms between the monomeric nucleotides is called a **phosphodiester bond**. Remember how the phosphate group is attached to the fifth carbon on the deoxyribose? The phosphate from one nucleotide attaches to the sugar of another nucleotide at the third carbon. This actually gives DNA a direction, like north and south, except we call it 5' and 3' (pronounced "5 prime" and "3 prime," see Figure 5.2). We'll talk more about this attachment a little later.

One strand (polymer) of DNA is usually found attached to another strand of DNA, forming a double-stranded molecule. The bases on each strand bond to form a pair. This pairing follows a strict rule: **A** always pairs with **T**, and **C** always pairs with **G** (this is what Chargaff saw). We call this **complementary base pairing**. When the strands of DNA come together to form a double strand, the structure twists around itself, creating a double helix (see Figure 5.2). By knowing the **sequence** (arrangements of nucleotides) of one strand, the sequence of the second strand can be determined. It is this sequence that determines the structure and function of the cell and the organism.

The base pairs are held together by **hydrogen bonds**, weak bonds that form between hydrogens and oxygens or hydrogens and nitrogens. The G-C base pairs form 3 hydrogen bonds while the A-T base pairs form only 2. This makes the G-C pairs inherently stronger and more stable.

Figure 5.2: The structure of DNA.
S: sugar; P: phosphate; A, C, G and
T: nitrogenous bases

Another interesting feature of the double helix is that, in order for the bases to pair correctly, the two strands of DNA must run in opposite directions, or in an antiparallel fashion. This means that the 5' end of one strand pairs with the 3' end of the other strand.

D. CHROMOSOME STRUCTURE

Before going any further, let's look at the structure of the DNA as it exists in a cell. If you could remove the DNA from one of your cells and stretch it out, it would be approximately one meter long. How can so much DNA fit into a microscopic cell? The answer is in the packaging. DNA is highly organized into a structure called a ***chromosome***. The chromosome is made up of DNA and proteins. The DNA double helix is wrapped around proteins known as ***histones***, and the histones form complexes called ***nucleosomes*** (see Figure 5.3). The nucleosomes are further packaged into ***supercoiled loops*** sometimes called ***solenoids***. These are packaged into chromosomes.

Human cells contain 23 pairs of chromosomes (46 total). Certain genetic diseases can be diagnosed by examining the chromosome. This is what is done when a pregnant woman has an amniocentesis. The field of biology that studies chromosomes is called cytogenetics.

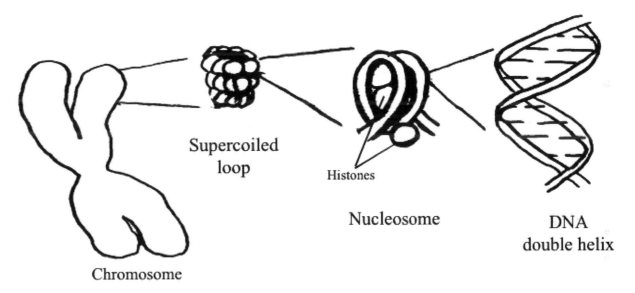

Figure 5.3: Levels of DNA packaging

E. RNA STRUCTURE

Although we will discuss its function later, this is an opportune time to examine the structure of ***RNA (ribonucleic acid)***, a molecule closely related to DNA. RNA is also a polymer of nucleotides, but differs from DNA in three major respects:

- ♦ RNA is usually single-stranded, meaning it is not usually found base paired with another RNA molecule;
- ♦ the sugar in an RNA nucleotide is ***ribose***, not deoxyribose. The difference is found on the 2' carbon of the sugar: ribose has an OH group attached while deoxyribose has only an H;
- ♦ a nitrogenous base called uracil (U) substitutes for thymine (T) in RNA. Uracil is similar in structure to thymine, and will base pair with adenine (this will become important when we discuss transcription and translation).

F. REPLICATION

When a cell divides, the new cell (or **daughter cell**) must receive the same genetic information as the original cell, or the daughter cell will not function correctly. Therefore, before a cell divides, the DNA must be copied, or **replicated**, faithfully. It must also be transferred to the new cell. This entire process is known as **mitosis** and will be addressed in Chapter 12. The details of how DNA is replicated will be discussed here.

The beauty of the structure of DNA is that it simplifies its own replication. Due to the base pairing rules, each strand of the helix serves as a template to make a new strand. The copy is the complement of the template, and is identical to the strand originally bound to the template. This type of replication is referred to as **semiconservative**. Let's consider the details.

G. THE REPLICATION MACHINERY

One of the most important concepts to remember, which will come up again, is that polymers of nucleotides can be built only in one direction, in the 5' to 3' direction. The phosphate from one nucleotide binds to the 3' carbon of the sugar in the preceding nucleotide. The process can never occur in reverse.

Before the DNA can be replicated, the two strands must dissociate (this is sometimes referred to as unzipping, as the DNA double helix resembles a zipper). The physical point at which the DNA is unzipped is referred to as the **replication fork** (see Figure 5.4).

The main enzyme involved in replication is called DNA **polymerase**. It binds to each single-stranded DNA chain and builds a complementary strand by reading the template strand. We will now examine some of the details of this process.

H. LEADING AND LAGGING STRAND SYNTHESIS

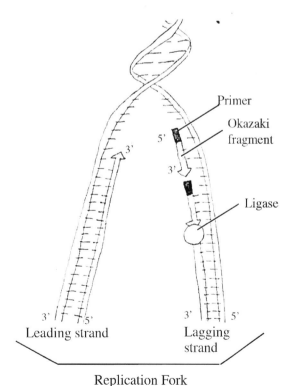

Primer

Okazaki fragment

Ligase

Leading strand

Lagging strand

Replication Fork

Figure 5.4: DNA replication

Since DNA is synthesized from 5' to 3', the template DNA must be read from 3' to 5' (remember the antiparallel structure of the double helix). This causes a problem at the replication fork: one strand can be copied **continuously** as the fork extends, but the other strand must be copied **discontinuously**. This discontinuous replication occurs in the following manner (see Figure 5.4):

1. An RNA **primer** (a short stretch of nucleotides) attaches to one strand via complementary base pairing. The primer is synthesized by a primase enzyme.
2. The DNA polymerase begins synthesizing a new, complementary strand in the 5' to 3' direction. The strands made between RNA primers are known as **Okazaki fragments**.
3. The primers are degraded and the Okazaki fragments are linked together by the enzyme DNA **ligase**.

The strand that is synthesized continuously is called the **leading strand**. The other strand, synthesized discontinuously, is referred to as the **lagging strand**.

I. PROOFREADING AND REPAIR

Everyone makes mistakes, and so does DNA polymerase. When this enzyme puts the wrong nucleotide into the growing chain, the result is a ***mutation*** which changes the genetic makeup of an organism. Therefore, mistakes cannot be tolerated.

Fortunately, DNA polymerase has another ability besides synthesizing DNA strands: it also proofreads its work. If an error is detected, the enzyme cuts out the incorrect nucleotide and replaces it with the correct one.

In addition to random errors during replication, DNA can be mutated by other factors, such as UV light and cancer-causing agents (***carcinogens***). If these mutations are not fixed, the function of the cell will be altered. This may cause the cell to die, or to grow in an unregulated fashion (cancer). Many repair mechanisms exist in the cell to detect and correct mutations, and more often than not they work just fine.

Chapter 5 Problems

Passage 5.1 (Questions 1-4)

Since only four types of nucleotides (adenine, guanine, cytosine and thymine) make up DNA, many scientists were skeptical that this was the hereditary molecule of life. Most believed proteins, with their building blocks of 20 amino acids, provided the complexity necessary to carry the genetic information.

In 1952, Alfred Hershey and Martha Chase designed an experiment to determine whether DNA or protein was the genetic material. They used a bacteriophage (a virus that infects bacteria) called T2. This bacteriophage was only composed of proteins and DNA. A short time after infecting a bacterial cell, the cell would lyse (break open) and release new T2 particles. T2 reprogrammed the cell to make more phage, but did it use DNA or proteins?

Hershey and Chase infected bacteria with T2 phage in growth medium containing radioactive sulfur (which labels proteins) and radioactive phosphate (which labels DNA). The resulting radioactive phages were then incubated with nonradioactive bacteria and allowed to infect these cells. After a short time, the mixture was placed in a blender to shake loose any phage particles remaining outside of or attached to the bacteria. The mixture was then centrifuged: bacterial cells would form a pellet at the bottom of the tube while any phage outside the cell would remain in the liquid portion (the supernatant). The radioactivity in each sample was measured.

1. Radioactive sulfur was found exclusively in the supernatant fraction, while the radioactive phosphate was found in the pellet fraction. This indicated:
   A. phage protein entered the cell, but the DNA did not.
   B. phage DNA entered the cell, but protein did not.
   C. both protein and DNA entered the cell.
   D. the phage did not infect the bacterial cell.

2. If the bacterial pellet were incubated in an appropriate growth medium, what would most likely occur?
   A. No phage would be produced as the protein coat was removed.
   B. Bacteria would survive as there is no proof they were infected with phage.
   C. Phage should be produced and kill the cells.
   D. The radioactive phosphate would kill the cells immediately.

3. A possible alternative to the blender technique used in this experiment would be to:
   A. add a competitive inhibitor to the bacteria before adding phage.
   B. break apart the cell membranes with a strong detergent.
   C. incubate bacteria with a mutant phage that could not bind to the cells.
   D. shake the cell/phage mixture vigorously.

4. A modern experiment that confirms this experiment would be:
   A. injecting DNA into a cell which causes the cell to produce an enzyme it never had before.
   B. fertilizing an egg with a sperm *in vitro*.
   C. prescribing enzyme pills to help cystic fibrosis patients with digestion.
   D. consuming radioactive barium to view internal organs with X-rays.

Passage 5.2 (Questions 5-8)

The Watson and Crick model of the structure of DNA eloquently suggested the method of DNA replication. The double helical nature and the complementary base pairing implied that one strand of DNA provided the information for making the other strand. Once the strands of DNA separated, each would be used as a template to make a new, complementary strand. Therefore, the two resulting strands of DNA would contain both an old strand and a new strand. This is known as the semiconservative theory of replication. The conservative theory stated that one double helix would contain only the newly synthesized DNA while the other would contain only the original strands.

In 1958, Matthew Meselson and Franklin Stahl confirmed the semiconservative model. They grew the bacterium **E. coli** for many generations in a heavy isotope of nitrogen, ^{15}N. The isotope was incorporated into the DNA.

The bacteria were then placed in a medium that contained only the light isotope of nitrogen, ^{14}N. The bacteria were sampled over a period of time. Their DNA was extracted and subjected to centrifugation techniques, which would separate the DNA based on density.

DNA containing solely ^{15}N was "heavy" whereas DNA containing solely ^{14}N was "light". After one round of division in the medium containing ^{14}N, all the DNA was found to be intermediate in size, between the light and heavy types.

This "intermediate" DNA was further analyzed. The hydrogen bonds between the base pairs were broken so the DNA was single stranded. These strands were then centrifuged. Half of the single stranded DNA was in the heavy form, and half was in the light form.

5. If the replication theory suggested by Watson and Crick's model was correct, then the density of the double-stranded DNA after 2 rounds of replication in ^{14}N medium would be:
    A. half heavy, half light.
    B. half heavy, half intermediate.
    C. half intermediate, half light.
    D. all intermediate.

6. Both ^{14}N and ^{15}N were good choices as isotopes because they incorporate into the DNA via:
    I. the deoxyribose sugar
    II. the phosphate group
    III. the bases
    A. I only
    B. II only
    C. III only
    D. I and III

7. If DNA replication was conservative, after 1 round of replication in ^{14}N, the density of the double-stranded DNA would be:
    A. all intermediate.
    B. all heavy.
    C. half intermediate, half heavy.
    D. half heavy, half light.

8. In the Meselson-Stahl experiment, the Okazaki fragments would contain:
    A. only ^{14}N.
    B. only ^{15}N.
    C. neither ^{14}N nor ^{15}N.
    D. both ^{14}N and ^{15}N.

The following questions are NOT based on a descriptive passage.

9. Heat is often used to separate or denature double-stranded DNA into single-stranded DNA by breaking the hydrogen bonds between base pairs. Which of the following statements is true?
    A. G-C base pairs would require higher temperatures to break than A-T base pairs.
    B. A-T base pairs would require higher temperatures to break than G-C base pairs.
    C. All long DNA chains should denature at the same temperature.
    D. DNA-DNA double strands would require higher temperatures to denature than DNA-RNA double strands containing the same sequence.

10. Part of the process of purifying DNA from isolated chromosomes must involve:
    A. adding DNase, an enzyme that breaks apart DNA.
    B. adding proteases, enzymes that break apart proteins.
    C. adding RNase, an enzyme that breaks apart RNA.
    D. adding detergents, chemicals that break apart lipids.

11. An RNA molecule was synthesized to complementarily base pair with a DNA molecule. The sequence of the DNA was: 5' ATCCGCTAAG 3'. The RNA sequence should be:
    A. 5' CUUAGCGGAU 3'
    B. 5' UAGGCGAUUC 3'
    C. 5' CTTAGCGGAT 3'
    D. 5' TAGGCGATTC 3

CHAPTER 6
Transcription and Translation

A. INTRODUCTION

Every cell in an organism contains the same DNA. In multicellular organisms, cells often have different structures and perform different functions. Think about humans: we have heart cells and liver cells, skin cells and bone cells, nerve cells and muscle cells. But how can cells be so different when they contain the same genetic information?

The answer lies in how each cell uses the information. Although they contain the same blueprint, each cell in your body only uses part of the DNA. It's like two people who have access to the Internet. They both have the same information at hand, but they will probably use it differently.

This chapter addresses how genetic information can be transmitted from a stored source (the DNA) into a functional entity (protein). This procedure is traditionally known as the Central Dogma (see Figure 6.1) and details the transmission of the message from DNA into RNA into proteins via the processes of transcription and translation. The process of translation is also known as protein synthesis.

Figure 6.1: The Central Dogma

B. TRANSCRIPTION

Imagine you own a car factory, and there is only one set of blueprints on how to make cars. Many need to see the blueprints-the engineers, the designers, the assembly line foremen. You can't entrust the blueprints, the only set, to everyone who needs them. So what do you do? You make copies of the instructions. This way, everyone has their own set and can complete whatever task they need to.

This is analogous to how a cell works. Instead of directly using its only set of information (the DNA), the cell makes copies of it, in the form of RNA. This is known as *transcription*.

C. THE CLASSES OF RNA

RNA molecules fall into one of three classes: ***ribosomal RNA (rRNA)***, ***transfer RNA (tRNA)*** and ***messenger RNA (mRNA)***. rRNA and tRNA are involved in the process of translation, and we will discuss them in more detail later. In transcription, mRNA is made and carries the instructions for building proteins.

Within the DNA are discrete regions, called ***genes***, which instruct the cell how to make proteins. It is the expression of these regions, which begins with the process of transcription, that determines the functions of cells. When genes are turned on or off they regulate the function of the cell, and, ultimately, the organism.

D. THE SYNTHESIS OF RNA

The synthesis of RNA is similar to DNA replication (see Chapter 5). The template DNA strand is denatured and an RNA copy complementary to the template is synthesized. The same base pairing rules apply (except that U substitutes for T in the RNA molecule). Transcription is similar to replication in that it must proceed (the RNA must be built) in the 5' to 3' direction. Three major differences distinguish transcription from replication:

♦ only one stretch of DNA (the gene) is copied in transcription, unlike the entire DNA molecule in replication. Also, only one strand of the DNA is copied, not both;

♦ the resulting copy of RNA is single-stranded, not double-stranded as in replication;

♦ the enzyme responsible for making RNA is called RNA polymerase.

The transcription of mRNA begins when RNA polymerase binds to a specific sequence of nucleotides just in front of the gene, called the ***promoter***. The enzyme then begins making an RNA copy of the DNA template, and continues until it reaches a stop sequence at the end of the gene. The RNA polymerase then releases the transcript (see Figure 6.2).

At this point, the RNA is technically known as ***pre-mRNA***. All transcripts go through further processing before being translated.

E. PROCESSING THE RNA TRANSCRIPT

Before the pre-mRNA leaves the nucleus to be translated, three additional events occur (see Figure 6.2):

1. A 5' ***cap*** is added. This is a special nucleotide which is added to the 5' end of the message. It contains a methyl group and a phosphate group. The function of the cap is to help regulate translation.
2. A ***poly A tail*** is attached to the 3' end. This long string of 100-200 adenine nucleotides helps to regulate the degradation of the transcript after it leaves the nucleus.
3. The transcript is ***spliced***. In eukaryotic genes, the coding regions of the DNA (***exons***) are interspersed with noncoding regions (***introns***). After the gene is transcribed, the introns are cut, or ***spliced***, from the pre-mRNA so they never are translated. Why does the DNA contain these sequences if they ultimately do not code for the final protein product? It turns out that the presence of introns in the pre-mRNA is necessary for transport of the message out of the nucleus (the splicing machinery appears to be coupled with transport). In addition, ***alternative splicing*** can occur, which results in some exons being removed from the message. Thus, different messages can be made and, ultimately, different proteins can be coded for by the same gene. It is also believed introns play a role in evolution, allowing different regions of genes (i.e. the exons) to be rearranged, leading to new proteins.

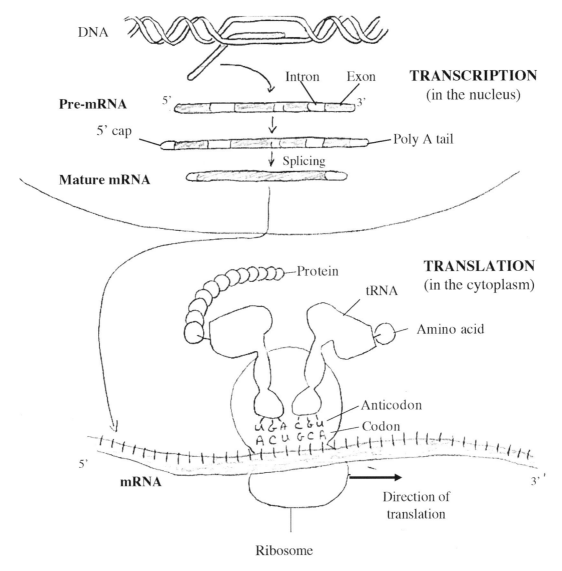

Figure 6.2: Transcription and translation

Once the fully processed mRNA (now called the **_mature mRNA_**) has been transported out of the nucleus and into the cytoplasm, it can be translated into a protein.

F. TRANSLATION

Once the mRNA has been transcribed and processed, the message can now be read and interpreted by the cell. **_Translation_** is the process of making a polypeptide chain based on the instructions in the mRNA. We use the term _polypeptide_ here to denote that not all functional proteins are encoded by a single gene. Many proteins have subunits, each encoded by a different gene.

G. THE GENETIC CODE

To communicate the message, the "words" of the mRNA must be read and understood. These words specify the amino acid that must be placed into the polypeptide chain. If we think of the nucleotides as the "letters" in the alphabet of the genetic code, then groups of those letters make up the words. As it turns out, each word in the mRNA is three letters, or nucleotides, long and is called a ***codon***. Since there are only four letters in the alphabet, and each word contains three letters, there are only 4^3, or 64, possible words. The deciphering of the words is called the ***genetic code*** and is shown in Figure 6.3. By using this chart, an mRNA sequence can be translated. To use this chart, you must begin with the first nucleotide in the codon and find its symbol on the left side of the chart (the first, or 5', position). Then find the second position from the top of the chart, and the third nucleotide from the right side (or 3' end). Now find where all three intersect in the interior of the chart. This is the amino acid the codon specifies. For example, the codon UUG encodes the amino acid leucine.

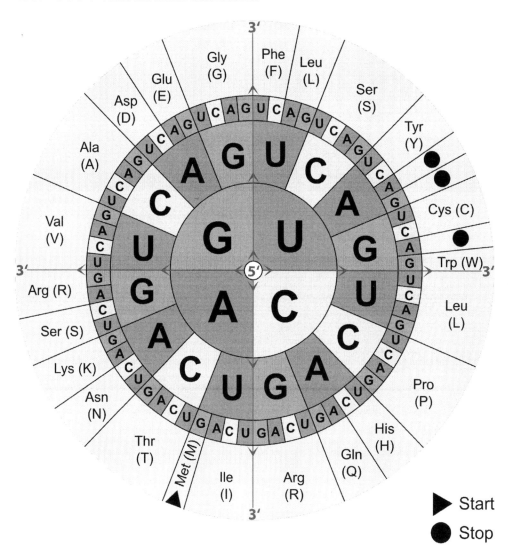

Figure 6.3: The Genetic Code.

Only 20 amino acids are specified by the genetic code, yet 64 different codons are possible. How, exactly, is this code used by the cell? There are three interesting answers to this question:

♦ Three codons, UAA, UAG, and UGA do not specify any amino acids, but rather signal the end of the message. These are often referred to as *stop* or *termination* codons.

♦ Many amino acids are specified by more than one codon. We call this *redundancy*. For example, ACA, ACG, ACU, and ACC all code for the amino acid threonine. You should also note that, in each of these codons, the first two nucleotides are A and C. It doesn't matter what the nucleotide in the third position is. We call this the *wobble* effect.

♦ One codon, AUG, specifies the amino acid methionine. However, it also signals the start of translation for all mRNA molecules. Therefore, all polypeptide chains begin with methionine.

H. TRANSLATING THE MESSAGE

The process of translation involves three distinct steps, all of which occur in the cytoplasm (see Figure 6.2).

1. *initiation*: The mRNA binds to the *ribosome*, a molecular machine made up of rRNA and proteins. The ribosome binds at the beginning of the message.

2. *elongation*: The ribosome helps tRNA molecules bind to the mRNA. Each tRNA has two different regions. One region, called the *anticodon*, contains three nucleotides that bind to the codon in the mRNA transcript via complementary base pairing. The other region has a specific amino acid attached to it. Once the correct tRNA binds with the mRNA, the amino acid on the tRNA is linked to the other amino acids in the growing chain by the ribosome. This results in the formation of a *peptide bond*. Then the tRNA is released and the ribosome moves down the mRNA chain to the next codon. The tRNA is "recharged" with another amino acid by the enzyme *peptidyl transferase*, so it can be used again and again.

3. *termination*: When the ribosome encounters a stop codon, it detaches from the mRNA chain and the polypeptide is released.

Most proteins are further processed before they can function in the cell. This processing may occur in the *endoplasmic reticulum* or in the *Golgi* (see Chapter 10). Proteins are often *phosphorylated* by specific enzymes in the cytoplasm. In addition, most proteins are *cleaved,* or cut, at the beginning of the polypeptide, which removes the initial methionine and other amino acids. So, although every mRNA codes for methionine as the first amino acid, few mature proteins retain this feature.

I. MUTATIONS

Mutations, or changes in the DNA sequence, will often lead to changes in the amino acid sequence of the resulting polypeptide. If the structure of the protein changes, then the function will also change.

Mutations can come from several sources, including environmental mutagens and replication errors. In colloquial terms, mutations are not considered good. However, not all changes are harmful. Some may be neutral, while others may be beneficial. It is these beneficial mutations that can lead to evolution of species (see Chapter 20).

Mutations fall into three main categories (see Figure 6.4):

♦ *base pair substitutions*: When a gene is altered in one nucleotide in the sequence, then only one amino acid in the protein may be altered (but remember the degeneracy of the code and the wobble rules: a nucleotide change may not result in a change in the amino acid). This single amino acid difference may result in a fatal disease, alter the function of the protein (thus creating a new variation or trait: see Chapter 19), or it may not affect the function of the protein at all. However, if a codon specifying an amino acid is changed to a termination codon, the polypeptide will not be translated beyond that point. This truncated transcript will, in all likelihood, not function properly.

NEXT STEP MCAT CONTENT REVIEW: BIOLOGY AND BIOCHEMISTRY

♦ *frameshift mutations*: If one or two nucleotides are either added to or deleted from the DNA sequence, the rest of the transcript will be affected as the codons will be shifted. The resulting polypeptide will have the incorrect amino acid sequence from the point of the mutation, and hence it will have a different function.

♦ *transposable element*: Often referred to as "jumping genes," these pieces of DNA can insert themselves into genes and thereby disrupt the sequence and expression of the gene.

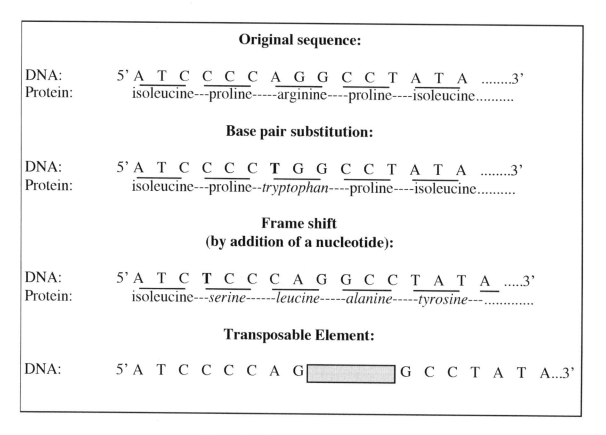

Figure 6.4: Examples of mutations

Chapter 6 Problems

Passage 6.1 (Questions 1-4)

(refer to figure 6.3 throughout this question set)

A newly discovered genetic disease has been observed in several large families. Characteristics of the disease include mental retardation and coronary defects. Researchers studying this disease have isolated the responsible gene. The functional protein encoded by this gene consists of a single polypeptide chain. Experiments were done to determine the exact sequence of the gene with the following results:

Sequencing result 1: In a family with no history of the disease, the gene was found to be 849 nucleotides long, encoding a protein containing 283 amino acids. The mRNA sequence coding for the 22-26th amino acids is shown below:

5' AUUCCUAGUUGCACG 3'

Sequencing result 2: The genetic disease runs in family A. However, in this family, the disease is not severe and most affected individuals lead a fairly normal life. The mRNA transcribed from this gene is shown below (corresponding to the same region of the normal gene in result 1):

5' AUUCCUAGAUGCACG 3'

Sequencing result 3: The disease is also present in family B, but affected individuals are more severely impacted than those in family A. The gene was sequenced, and the corresponding mRNA is shown below (same region as sequence results 1 and 2):

5' AUUCCUAGUUGAACG 3'

1. Using figure 6.3 in the preceding text, what is the predicted amino acid sequence of the normal protein?
    A. isoleucine-proline-serine-cysteine-threonine
    B. phenylalanine-leucine-valine-alanine
    C. serine-stop-leucine-histidine
    D. serine-stop

2. The mutation in family A (sequencing result 2) will cause which of the following results?
    A. A protein will not be made.
    B. There will be a single amino acid change in the protein.
    C. The heart in an individual with the mutation will not develop correctly.
    D. There will be a change in the quaternary structure of the protein.

3. The disease in family B (sequencing result 3) is probably more severe than in family A because:
    A. there is a slight but significant change in the amino acid sequence.
    B. a frameshift mutation caused the amino acid sequence of the protein to be incorrect from the point of mutation on.
    C. a termination codon caused the truncation of the protein, preventing it from functioning.
    D. a point mutation altered a critical amino acid.

4. An ***in vitro*** transcription/translation system was set up to express the isolated genes. Which alteration in the system would allow the gene from family A to be translated into a fully functional protein?
    A. Include a ribosome that would not recognize the codon AGA.
    B. Use a tRNA with the anticodon UCU that carries the amino acid serine.
    C. Replace the normal splicing machinery with one that will remove the incorrect codon.
    D. Substitute the normal RNA polymerase with one that randomly makes mistakes to correct the mutation.

The following questions are NOT based on a descriptive passage.

5. Which of the following mRNA sequences encode the same protein?
    I.   5' UUAAGAUCC 3'
    II. 5' UUGCGUUCU 3'
    III. 5' CUGCGGAGU 3'

    A. I and II
    B. II and III
    C. I and III
    D. I, II and III

6. Due to a problem in the transcriptional machinery of a cell, an mRNA transcript does not have a poly A tail attached. This would probably result in:
    A. faster degradation of the transcript.
    B. unregulated translation of the protein.
    C. translation of a different polypeptide.
    D. deletion of the 5' cap.

7. The mRNA sequence of a particular gene is 5' AUGCCUAUCGUAACA 3'. What is the sequence of the template DNA from which this mRNA was copied?
    A. 5' ATGCCTATCGTAACA 3'
    B. 5' TACGGATAGCATTGT 3'
    C. 5' ACAATGCTATCCGTA 3'
    D. 5' TGTTACGATAGGCAT 3'

SECTION 1

Content Review Problems

1. What is a carbohydrate?
   A. The building block of lipids
   B. The sole building block of RNA
   C. A molecule composed primarily of carbon and hydrogen
   D. The building block of proteins

2. Which of the following is a carbohydrate?
   A. palmitic acid
   B. sucrose
   C. cytosine
   D. glycine

3. Which of the following lists the components of lactose?
   A. one galactose and one glucose
   B. two galactoses
   C. two glucoses
   D. one fructose and one galactose

4. Which of the following lists the components of sucrose?
   A. two fructoses
   B. one fructose and one glucose
   C. two glucoses
   D. one fructose and one galactose

5. Which of the following NOT is a disaccharide?
   A. galactose
   B. lactose
   C. maltose
   D. sucrose

6. Which of the following is a monosaccharide?
   A. lactose
   B. sucrose
   C. fructose
   D. maltose

7. Which of the following is an element in some carbohydrates?
   A. nitrogen
   B. chlorine
   C. helium
   D. oxygen

8. Which of the following are most commonly referred to as sugars?
   A. disaccharides
   B. polypeptide chains
   C. oligosaccharides
   D. polysaccharides

9. What is the main purpose of carbohydrates in the body?
   A. Structure
   B. Genetic Material
   C. Energy storage
   D. Building proteins

10. Which of the following classifications does glucose fall under?
    A. aldohexose
    B. ketohexose
    C. aldopentose
    D. ketopentose

11. Which of the following classifications does fructose fall under?
    A. aldohexose
    B. ketohexose
    C. aldopentose
    D. ketopentose

12. How many stereoisomers are possible for an aldohexose?
    A. 4
    B. 8
    C. 16
    D. 32

13. How many stereoisomers are possible for an aldotriose?
    A. 1
    B. 2
    C. 3
    D. 4

14. Which of the following is true?
    A. Glucose is a D sugar because its OH group furthest from the carbonyl group goes to the right in the Fischer projection.
    B. Glucose is a D sugar because its OH group furthest from the carbonyl group goes to the left in the Fischer projection.
    C. Glucose is an L sugar because its OH group furthest from the carbonyl group goes to the right in the Fischer projection.
    D. Glucose is an L sugar because its OH group furthest from the carbonyl group goes to the left in the Fischer projection.

15. Where does transcription occur?
    A. cytoplasm
    B. nucleus
    C. ribosome
    D. rough ER

16. What are the two possible anomers?
    A. a and b
    B. D and L
    C. R and S
    D. α and β

17. Which of the following classifications does glucose fall under?
    A. pyranose
    B. furanose
    C. pyrulose
    D. ketoacetal

18. Which of the following classifications does ribose fall under?
    A. pyranose
    B. furanose
    C. pyrulose
    D. ketoacetal

19. What is the systemic name for lactose?
    A. β-D-galactopyranosyl-(1, 4)-D-glucopyranose
    B. β-D-fructopyranosyl-(1, 4)-D-glucopyranose
    C. β-D-glucopyranosyl-(1, 4)-D-glucopyranose
    D. β-D-galactopyranosyl-(1, 4)-D-galactopyranose

20. What is a lipid?
    A. a larger fat soluble hydrocarbon
    B. a small hydrophilic hydrocarbon
    C. a large hydrophilic hydrocarbon
    D. a signaling molecule that uses cell-surface receptors

21. Which of the following is not a lipid?
    A. Vitamin K
    B. Cholesterol
    C. Triglycerides
    D. Vitamin B

22. What is a fatty acid?
    A. A ketotic acid with a long aliphatic tail
    B. A carbohydrate with a long amphipathic tail
    C. A carboxylic acid with a long hydrophobic tail
    D. An acidic alcohol with a long hydrophilic tail

23. What are the components of a triglyceride?
    A. A glycerol and 3 phospholipids
    B. A glycerol and 3 fatty acids
    C. A phosphate group and 3 sphingolipids
    D. A phosphate group and 3 fatty acids

24. Where are triglycerides primarily digested?
    A. colon
    B. ileum
    C. duodenum
    D. jejunum

25. What picks up fats from the small intestine?
    A. capillaries
    B. lacteals
    C. micelles
    D. chylomicrons

26. Where are phospholipids found in a cell?
    A. cell membranes
    B. lumen of the duodenum
    C. inside the nucleus
    D. inside lysosomes

27. Which of the following describes a phospholipid?
    A. amphoteric
    B. amphipathic
    C. acidic
    D. hydrophobic

28. Which portion of a phospholipid is on the outside of a bilayer membrane?
    A. The hydrophobic portion
    B. The amphiphilic portion
    C. The lipophilic portion
    D. The hydrophilic portion

29. What is the name of a spherical drop formed by one layer of lipids?
    A. sphingolipid
    B. micelle
    C. liposome
    D. lysosome

30. What is the name of a spherical drop formed by a bilayer of lipids?
    A. sphingolipid
    B. micelle
    C. liposome
    D. lysosome

31. Which of the following is NOT a function of lipids in the body?
    A. Energy storage
    B. Structure
    C. Signaling
    D. Digestion

32. What are the building blocks of proteins?
    A. amino acids
    B. nucleic acids
    C. nucleotides
    D. base pairs

33. Which of the following describes alpha helices and beta pleated sheets?
    A. primary structure
    B. secondary structure
    C. tertiary structure
    D. quaternary structure

34. What is quaternary structure?
    A. The interaction of two or more polypeptides
    B. The folding of the protein
    C. The formation of alpha helices and beta pleated sheets
    D. The order of amino acids

35. In which phase of protein structure would disulfide bonds NOT be involved?
    A. primary
    B. secondary
    C. tertiary
    D. quaternary

36. What is the bond that joins two amino acids?
    A. α linkage
    B. disulfide linkage
    C. peptide bond
    D. β linkage

37. What is a product in the formation of a bond between two amino acids?
    A. COOH
    B. H_2O
    C. CO_2
    D. NH_3

38. Trinucleotide codons directly code for how many α amino acids in the human body?
    A. 19
    B. 20
    C. 21
    D. 22

39. What are the components of nucleic acids?
    I. Ribose
    II. Nitrogenous base
    III. R-COOH
    A. I only
    B. I and II only
    C. II and III only
    D. I, II, and III

40. Which of the following is NOT a nucleic acid, nucleotide, or a nitrogenous base?
    A. ATP
    B. RNA
    C. cysteine
    D. DNA

41. Which of the following is NOT always a component of a nucleotide?
    A. a phosphate
    B. a ribose
    C. a sugar
    D. a nitrogenous base

42. Which of the following is NOT in RNA?
    A. guanine
    B. cytosine
    C. adenine
    D. thymine

43. Which of the following is NOT in DNA?
    A. adenine
    B. cytosine
    C. uracil
    D. thymine

44. What two components are linked together between adjacent nucleotides in DNA?
    A. The sugars
    B. The phosphate groups
    C. The bases
    D. A sugar and a phosphate group

45. Which of the following pairs with uracil?
    A. thymine
    B. adenine
    C. guanine
    D. cytosine

46. Which of the following pairs with guanine?
    A. thymine
    B. adenine
    C. cytosine
    D. uracil

47. Which of the following are purines?
    I. Cytosine
    II. Guanine
    III. Adenine

    A. I and II
    B. I and III
    C. II and III
    D. I, II, and III

48. Which of the following are pyrimidines?
    I. Cytosine
    II. Thymine
    III. Guanine

    A. I and II
    B. I and III
    C. II and III
    D. I, II, and III

49. Which of the following most determines an enzyme's function?
    A. structure
    B. location
    C. pK_a
    D. pI

50. What is the function of an enzyme?
    A. to increase the rate of a reaction
    B. to decrease the free energy change of a reaction
    C. to stabilize the product of a reaction
    D. to increase the free energy change of a reaction

51. Which of the following describes a molecule, other than the substrate, binding the substrate binding site on an enzyme?
    A. competitive inhibition
    B. allosteric inhibition
    C. uncompetitive inhibition
    D. reversible inhibition

52. Which of the following describes a molecule binding an enzyme at a site other than the substrate binding site, resulting in decreased enzyme activity?
    A. competitive inhibition
    B. allosteric inhibition
    C. uncompetitive inhibition
    D. reversible inhibition

53. Which of the following is LEAST likely to affect the rate at which an enzyme is able to function?
    A. temperature
    B. pH
    C. structure
    D. concentration of substrate

54. What is glycolysis?
    A. the process of generating ATP from the addition of hydrogen to oxygen
    B. the process of converting CO_2 to glucose
    C. the process of converting glucose to pyruvate
    D. the process of reducing $FADH_2$

55. What are the products of glycolysis?
    I. Pyruvate
    II. ATP
    III. NADH

    A. I only
    B. I and II only
    C. I and III only
    D. I, II, and III

56. Where does glycolysis occur?
    A. mitochondrial membrane
    B. cytoplasm
    C. mitochondrial matrix
    D. cell membrane

57. What does pyruvate become first in the process of aerobic respiration?
    A. lactate
    B. acetyl CoA
    C. coenzyme A
    D. oxaloacetate

58. What are the products of the Krebs cycle?
    I. ATP
    II. CO_2
    III. Acetyl CoA

    A. I only
    B. II only
    C. I and II only
    D. I, II, and III

59. Where does the Krebs cycle occur?
    A. outer mitochondrial membrane
    B. cytoplasm
    C. mitochondrial matrix
    D. cell membrane

60. Where does oxidative phosphorylation occur?
    A. inner mitochondrial membrane
    B. cytoplasm
    C. mitochondrial matrix
    D. cell membrane

61. What drives the pumping of hydrogen ions across the inner mitochondrial membrane against their gradient?
    A. The transfer of electrons from high energy to low energy states
    B. The hydrolysis of certain compounds
    C. The oxidation of certain compounds
    D. The hydrogens go with their gradient

62. What is an example of anaerobic respiration?
    A. oxidative phosphorylation
    B. reductive phosphorylation
    C. fermentation
    D. lactation

63. During decarboxylation, pyruvic acid combines with what?
    A. lactate
    B. acetyl-CoA
    C. oxaloacetate
    D. coenzyme A

64. Which of the following energetic molecules is used up as a result of the anaerobic reduction of pyruvate?
    A. ATP
    B. NADH
    C. $FADH_2$
    D. Acetyl CoA

65. Which enzyme is responsible for the creation of ATP during oxidative phosphorylation?
    A. Complex IV
    B. Complex III
    C. ATP synthase
    D. ATP reductase

66. What drives H^+ ions to cross the inner mitochondrial membrane into the mitochondrial matrix?
       I. Electrical gradient
       II. Oncotic pressure
       III. Concentration gradient

    A. I only
    B. III only
    C. I and III only
    D. II and III only

67. During anaerobic respiration, where does the ATP come from?
    A. The oxidation of pyruvate
    B. The reduction of pyruvate
    C. Glycolysis
    D. The Krebs cycle

68. What molecule yields the most ATP per molecule when oxidized in the electron transport chain?
    A. pyruvate
    B. NADH
    C. $FADH_2$
    D. Oxygen

69. Where does NADH drop its electrons?
    A. Complex I
    B. Complex II
    C. Complex III
    D. Coenzyme Q

70. Where does $FADH_2$ drop its electrons?
    A. Complex I
    B. Complex II
    C. Complex III
    D. Coenzyme Q

71. How many NADH and $FADH_2$ are produced in the Krebs cycle per glucose molecule?
    A. 3 NADH and 2 $FADH_2$
    B. 6 NADH and 2 $FADH_2$
    C. 6 NADH and 4 $FADH_2$
    D. 4 NADH and 4 $FADH_2$

72. What is the last thing to be reduced in oxidative phosphorylation?
    A. Complex I
    B. Coenzyme Q
    C. O_2
    D. Complex IV

73. What is the last thing to be oxidized in oxidative phosphorylation?
    A. Complex IV
    B. H^+
    C. O_2
    D. ADP

74. In which direction is the lagging strand of DNA replicated?
    A. C terminus to N terminus
    B. N terminus to C terminus
    C. 5' to 3'
    D. 3' to 5'

75. What is the normal *in vivo* structure of DNA?
    A. Helix
    B. Double helix
    C. Alpha helix
    D. Z helix

76. Which of the following is NOT a characteristic of RNA folding?
    A. Hairpin loop
    B. Interior loop
    C. Alpha helix
    D. Bulge

77. Which of the following is NOT part of a replicated chromosome?
   A. Tubulin
   B. Centromere
   C. Sister chromatids
   D. Histones

78. What are the proteins around which chromatin condenses?
   A. Tubulin
   B. Centromeres
   C. Myosin
   D. Histones

79. What is the center of the chromosome where the arms come together?
   A. Chromatid
   B. Centromere
   C. Chromatin
   D. Histone

80. What are the arms of the chromosome called?
   A. Chromatids
   B. Centromeres
   C. Chromatins
   D. Histones

81. What is the structure of an RNA molecule?
   A. Double helix
   B. Hairpin loop
   C. Alpha helix
   D. Not enough information

82. Which of the following is NOT an enzyme involved in DNA replication?
   A. DNA polymerase
   B. Tautomerase
   C. Ligase
   D. Primase

83. What is the function of helicase?
   A. Separating strands of DNA
   B. Joining Okazaki fragments
   C. Adding complementary bases
   D. Initiating replication

84. What is the function of ligase?
   A. Separating strands of DNA
   B. Adding complementary bases
   C. Initiating replication
   D. Joining Okazaki fragments

85. What is the function of DNA polymerase?
   A. Separating strands of DNA
   B. Adding complementary bases
   C. Initiating replication
   D. Joining Okazaki fragments

86. What is the function of primase?
   A. Separating strands of DNA
   B. Adding complementary bases
   C. Initiating replication
   D. Joining Okazaki fragments

87. What is the function of telomerase?
   A. Joining Okazaki fragments
   B. Attaching nucleotides to the ends of chromosomes
   C. Separating strands of DNA
   D. Ensuring that DNA does not wind too tight

88. What is the function of topoisomerase?
   A. Joining Okazaki fragments
   B. Attaching nucleotides to the ends of chromosomes
   C. Separating strands of DNA
   D. Ensuring that DNA does not wind too tight

89. Where does DNA replication occur?
   A. in the nucleus
   B. in the cytoplasm
   C. at ribosomes
   D. in the ER

90. Where do okazaki fragments occur?
   A. The leading strand
   B. The lagging strand
   C. Newly synthesized mRNA
   D. Newly synthesized tRNA

91. Which strand is replicated continuously?
   A. The leading strand, from 5' to 3'
   B. The lagging strand, from 5' to 3'
   C. The leading strand, from 3' to 5'
   D. The lagging strand, from 3' to 5'

92. Which enzyme is the primary DNA proofreader?
    A. DNA polymerase
    B. ligase
    C. primase
    D. helicase

93. Which of the following is NOT a type of DNA damage?
    A. alkylation of nitrogenous base
    B. pyrimidine dimer formation
    C. hydrolysis of nitrogenous base
    D. reduction of nitrogenous base

94. What is transcription?
    A. producing a peptide from an RNA template
    B. copying a DNA segment to a RNA segment
    C. copying the complementary strand of DNA onto itself
    D. replication of an RNA segment

95. Which is the RNA strand transcribed from this DNA strand: 5' AGTCGACAT 3'
    A. 3' UCAGCUGUA 5'
    B. 3' TCAGCTGTA 5'
    C. 3' AGTCGACAT 5'
    D. 3' AGUCGACAU 5'

96. Which of the following is the DNA strand from which the following RNA strand was obtained: 3' AUCGCUUA 5'
    A. 5' AUCGCUUA 3'
    B. 5' ATCGCTTA 3'
    C. 5' TAGCGAAT 3'
    D. 5' UAGCGAAU 3'

97. Which of the following is NOT a class of RNA?
    A. rRNA
    B. tRNA
    C. mRNA
    D. rzRNA

98. What type of RNA codes for proteins?
    A. rRNA
    B. tRNA
    C. mRNA
    D. snRNA

99. What type of RNA bring amino acids to the site of translation of RNA into proteins?
    A. rRNA
    B. tRNA
    C. mRNA
    D. snRNA

100. What type of RNA is a structural component of ribosomes?
    A. rRNA
    B. tRNA
    C. mRNA
    D. snRNA

101. What type of RNA aids in the processing of pre-mRNA in the nucleus?
    A. rRNA
    B. tRNA
    C. mRNA
    D. snRNA

102. Which enzyme transcribes tRNA from DNA?
    A. RNA Polymerase I
    B. RNA Polymerase III
    C. RNA Polymerase II
    D. DNA polymerase

103. Which enzyme transcribes mRNA from DNA?
    A. RNA Polymerase II
    B. RNA Polymerase I
    C. RNA Polymerase III
    D. DNA Polymerase

104. Which enzyme transcribes rRNA from DNA?
    A. RNA Polymerase II
    B. RNA Polymerase III
    C. RNA Polymerase I
    D. DNA Polymerase

105. What is translation?
    A. Copying a DNA strand into a DNA strand
    B. Reading a DNA strand to produce a complementary mRNA strand
    C. Reading an mRNA strand to produce a peptide
    D. Exocytosis of peptides from the cell

106. Where does translation occur?
  A. Smooth endoplasmic reticulum
  B. Ribosomes
  C. In the nucleus
  D. Golgi apparatus

107. Where might ribosomes be found?
  I. Endoplasmic reticulum
  II. Cytoplasm
  III. Cell membrane

  A. I only
  B. II only
  C. I and II only
  D. II and III only

108. How many subunits does a ribosome have?
  A. 1
  B. 2
  C. 3
  D. 4

109. A cell is cultured in a medium with radioactively labeled thymine. After 3 cell divisions and a 4th S phase, how many cells will contain two labeled copies of the cell's DNA?
  A. 1
  B. 4
  C. 6
  D. 7

110. In a double-stranded DNA molecule, if 30% of nitrogenous bases are adenine, what percent are guanine?
  A. 20%
  B. 30%
  C. 40%
  D. 60%

111. In which direction is the leading strand of DNA synthesized?
  A. C terminus to N terminus
  B. N terminus to C terminus
  C. 5' to 3'
  D. 3' to 5'

112. In which direction is DNA read by RNA polymerase?
  A. C terminus to N terminus
  B. N terminus to C terminus
  C. 5' to 3'
  D. 3' to 5'

113. In which direction is RNA synthesized from DNA by RNA polymerase?
  A. C terminus to N terminus
  B. N terminus to C terminus
  C. 5' to 3'
  D. 3' to 5'

114. In which direction are peptides synthesized by ribosomes?
  A. C terminus to N terminus
  B. N terminus to C terminus
  C. 5' to 3'
  D. 3' to 5'

115. Which of the following is NOT a type of mutation?
  A. Insertion
  B. Point deletion
  C. Codon insertion
  D. Substitution

116. Which of the following mutations will MOST drastically change the identity of the peptide coded for?
  A. 1 insertion
  B. 1 substitution
  C. 3 consecutive insertions
  D. 2 consecutive substitutions

117. Which of the following mutations will LEAST likely change the identity of the peptide coded for?
  A. insertion
  B. substitution
  C. deletion
  D. duplication

118. What is a missense mutation?
  A. A mutation that results in a shorter peptide
  B. A mutation that results in a longer peptide
  C. A mutation that results in a substitution of one amino acid for another
  D. A mutation that does not affect the resulting peptide

119. What is a silent mutation?
    A. A mutation that results in a shorter peptide
    B. A mutation that results in a longer peptide
    C. A mutation that results in a substitution of one amino acid for another
    D. A mutation that does not affect the resulting peptide

120. Which of the following is NOT a stop codon?
    A. UAG
    B. UGG
    C. UGA
    D. UAA

SECTION 2
MICROBIOLOGY

Organisms are classified according to the structure and function of their cells and how those cells may be arranged into tissues, organs and systems. Most scientists use the following classification scheme, known as the ***Five-Kingdom system***:

- ***Monera (bacteria)- prokaryotes*** (cells have no nucleus), single-celled;
- ***Protists-*** eukaryotes (cells have a nucleus), usually single-celled;
- ***Fungi-*** eukaryotes, mostly multicellular, ***heterotrophs*** (feed off of other organisms), digest food outside the cell;
- ***Plantae-*** eukaryotes, mostly multicellular, ***autotrophs*** (rely on photosynthesis for food production);
- ***Animalia-*** eukaryotes, multicellular, heterotrophs, ingest food.

Not included in this system are the viruses. Although they are not considered to be alive, viruses have much in common with living cells and depend on them to exist (they exist in a grey area between "alive" and "not alive"). Note that in some modern systems, the monera are divided into eubacteria and archaebacteria, and in even newer systems, life is divided into three domains (eubacteria, archaebacteria, eukaryotes) which are then sub-divided further. For the purposes of the MCAT, you needn't worry about domains, but you should be familiar with the five kingdoms and the six-kingdom variant.

The next three sections of this book will explore the structure and function of different cells in detail. This section focuses on microscopic organisms (viruses, bacteria and fungi), often the cause of devastating diseases.

Humans and microbes have evolved together and now coexist in a variety of ways. This coexistence is known as symbiosis and can be classified based on the exact nature of the relationship:

- ***mutualism***: the relationship is beneficial to both species
- ***commensalism***: one species benefits but the other is unharmed
- ***parasitism***: one species benefits and the other is harmed

Not all relationships are easy to classify into one particular category. In addition, changes in the environment will often alter the relationship. However, these labels help us to think about the nature and consequences of species interactions.

The transmission of microorganisms to humans (infection), and hence the mode of transmission of diseases, is classified into the following categories:

- ◆ *direct contact*: Sexually transmitted diseases, such as gonorrhea and syphilis, can only be transmitted through direct contact.
- ◆ *indirect contact*: Many microorganisms can be deposited on surfaces, including food, which can then be touched or consumed by other individuals. Two examples are typhoid and athlete's foot.
- ◆ *inhalation of airborne organisms*: Some organisms are spread through the air by coughing and sneezing, or can be inhaled from other sources and infect an individual via the respiratory tract. One example of this is the hantavirus.
- ◆ *transmission by biological vectors*: Some microorganisms can be carried by other organisms and, when a human is bitten, the microorganism will be transmitted to the individual. Lyme disease and Rocky Mountain spotted fever are bacterial diseases spread by ticks, and malaria is a parasite carried by mosquitoes.

CHAPTER 7

Viruses

A. INTRODUCTION

As we have already discussed, viruses are not considered to be alive. They cannot, on their own, perform many of the processes that are characteristic of life, including reproduction. Viruses absolutely require a host cell to propagate.

All viruses have the same basic structure. They are comprised of a protein coat surrounding the genetic material (which can be either DNA or RNA). In some viruses, an outer envelope is present, comprised of lipids and proteins derived from the cell membrane of their host.

Viruses come in a wide variety of shapes and sizes and have great capacity to mutate, especially in their protein coat and outer envelope. This often makes it difficult for the host organism to mount an immune response.

B. LIFE CYCLE

Although viruses are not alive, they do have a "life cycle," a series of events that results in their reproduction. In general, viral replication involves four steps:

1. The virus attaches to a specific type of cell.
2. The genetic material enters the host cell.
3. The viral genetic material forces the host cell to produce copies of viral proteins and genetic material.
4. New viruses are released from the cell.

C. BACTERIOPHAGES

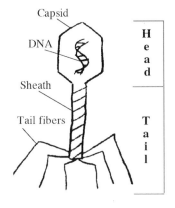

Figure 7.1: Structure of a bacteriophage

Bacteriophages (*phages* for short) are viruses that infect only bacteria. The most widely studied bacteriophages are lambda (λ) and the "T even" phages, T2 and T4. These viruses contain DNA as their genetic material. The basic structure consists of the *head* and *tail* regions (see Figure 7.1). The head contains the protein coat (called a *capsid*) and the DNA. The tail is made up of a tube called a *sheath*, and, in the T even phages, several long *tail fibers* connected to the base of the sheath. The tail region attaches to a bacterial cell, and the DNA is injected into the cell through the sheath.

Once the DNA is inside the cell, two pathways are possible (λ can follow either pathway; the T even phages only follow the lytic cycle):

♦ ***The lytic cycle***: The phage DNA instructs the cell to produce more viral particles. The cell ***lyses***, or breaks, resulting in cell death. New bacteriophages are released and can infect other cells.

♦ ***The lysogenic cycle***: Once infected, the virus enters a latent period, and the host cell is neither damaged nor destroyed. The phage DNA incorporates into the host cell chromosome and is replicated along with the host DNA. At this stage, the virus is technically called a ***prophage***. The viral DNA, therefore, is passed on during cell division. Under appropriate conditions, the phage DNA will excise itself from the chromosome and enter the lytic cycle, thus destroying the host cell.

D. ANIMAL VIRUSES

Animal viruses are very diverse in their size and structure and the exact nature of their genetic material, which can be double- or single-stranded RNA or DNA. We will consider the ***Human Immunodeficiency Virus (HIV)*** as an example of an animal virus (see Figure 7.2).

The first stage of HIV infection involves attachment of the virus to the host cell. HIV has proteins on its outer membrane that recognize a specific protein (the ***receptor***) on the host cell. After docking to the receptor, the virus enters the cell via endocytosis.

Some RNA viruses, such as HIV, must have their RNA copied into DNA for the cell to use it (these viruses are called ***retroviruses***). This is accomplished by the viral enzyme ***reverse transcriptase***. The DNA copy is made in the cytoplasm of the host cell and is then transported into the nucleus, where it can incorporate with the host DNA (the virus is now called a ***provirus***, analogous to a prophage). Newly synthesized viral particles can be released via exocytosis. Therefore, the virus does not always kill the host cell.

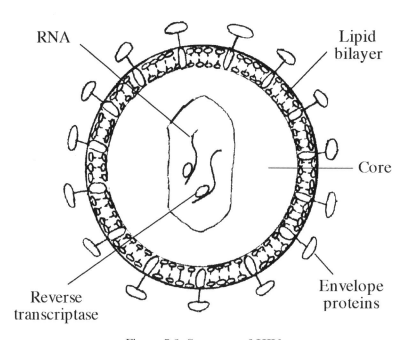

Figure 7.2: Structure of HIV

E. THE EFFECT OF HIV ON HUMANS

HIV is such a deadly virus, and is so difficult to fight off, because it specifically targets cells in the immune system. The receptor for HIV is a protein called CD4, mostly found on helper T cells. In the progression of AIDS, the CD4-bearing cells are killed and the ability of the immune system to fight off other diseases and opportunistic infections is drastically reduced. Individuals do not die from AIDS, but rather from infections that can normally be fought off by a healthy immune system.

Chapter 7 Problems

Passage 7.1 (Questions 1-4)

The activity of bacteriophages is easily assayed. Bacteria are spread on a solid nutrient agar plate. Under appropriate growth conditions, the bacteria will form a cloudy layer completely covering the dish. In microbiology, this is called a *lawn*, as opposed to isolated spots, or *colonies*, of bacteria. If bacteriophages are introduced to the lawn of bacteria, the phages will infect single cells. Once the phages have reproduced, they will lyse the cells and the progeny phages will infect the surrounding bacterial cells. In a relatively short period of time, the phages will have lysed all the bacteria within a radius of the initial infection, causing a clear, circular spot to form in the lawn of bacteria. This is called a *plaque*.

A researcher working with bacteriophages set up the following experiment:

Condition 1:
Bacteria were spread on agar plates and incubated at 37°C for 24 hours. A lawn was clearly visible and no plaques formed.

Condition 2:
The same strain of bacteria was mixed with a preparation of lambda bacteriophage. The mixture was spread on agar plates and incubated for 24 hours at 37°C. An average of twenty plaques formed on the bacterial lawn on each plate.

Condition 3:
The same strain of bacteria was spread on agar plates and then exposed to UV light. After incubation at 37°C for 24 hours, lawns grew and approximately fifty plaques formed on each plate.

1. After incubating the plates from condition 2 for an additional 5 days, the plates became totally clear. What is the most likely explanation for this result?
   A. Newly produced phages infected all bacteria on the dish, thus killing everything.
   B. The bacteria died off due to lack of nutrients.
   C. The bacteria protected themselves from the phages by slowing their growth.
   D. The phage forced all the bacteria to go into the lysogenic cycle and stop growing.

2. What happened in condition 3?
   A. Phage contaminated the dishes causing infection and lysis of the bacteria.
   B. The nutrients in the agar were insufficient to support bacterial growth.
   C. The bacteria were probably a lysogenic strain induced by UV light.
   D. The bacteria were not healthy and died off when exposed to UV light.

3. If a fourth experiment was done, where bacteria were mixed with lambda and exposed to UV light, what result would you predict?
   A. The results would be similar to condition 2, with approximately 20 plaques per plate.
   B. The results would be similar to condition 3, with approximately 50 plaques per plate.
   C. There would be approximately 35 plaques per plate.
   D. There would be approximately 70 plaques per plate.

4. Before the phage life cycle was understood, researchers called the results from condition 3 *autolysis*. They thought an enzyme in the bacteria caused its own destruction and the destruction of surrounding cells. Which of the following would lend support to the viral theory and help to disprove autolysis?
   A. Within a week, all the bacterial cells in condition 3 die.
   B. Viral particles can be purified from the plates in condition 3.
   C. Exposure of bacteria to X rays also causes plaques to form.
   D. With or without exposure to UV light, no bacteria grow at 40°C.

The following questions are NOT based on a descriptive passage.

5. Strategies to fight the AIDS virus include drugs that mimic nucleotides, called ***nucleotide analogs***. Reverse transcriptase incorporates these analogs into the newly formed viral DNA strand. The host cell cannot interpret the DNA correctly, so the virus does not propagate. Unfortunately, this therapy only works for a short time in infected individuals, probably because:

    A. the outer protein coat of the virus mutates so it is no longer recognized by the immune system.

    B. the patient's immune system starts to fight off the analog.

    C. the reverse transcriptase mutates to prevent incorporation of the analog.

    D. the viral DNA no longer incorporates into the host DNA.

6. Immunizations for viruses such as influenza and polio rely on the body's ability to recognize the virus and make antibodies against it. All of the following would allow for antibody production to prevent a virus from entering a cell EXCEPT:

    A. injection of a small amount of "live" virus.

    B. injection of "heat killed" virus.

    C. injection of part of the outer coat of the virus.

    D. injection of viral reverse transcriptase.

CHAPTER 8

Bacteria

A. INTRODUCTION

The kingdom Monera is comprised of an amazingly diverse group of organisms, impossible to characterize using a few simple terms. In general, bacteria have the following features:

♦ all are ***prokaryotes***, meaning they do not contain a nucleus;
♦ all have a single, circular chromosome, and some have ***plasmids*** (small circular pieces of extrachromosomal DNA);
♦ most have a cell wall made of ***peptidoglycan***;
♦ most reproduce by ***binary fission***.

We will highlight the major characteristics of this kingdom, but keep in mind how diverse it is. Remember that for the MCAT, some classification systems actually split Monera into two kingdoms due to this diversity: eubacteria and archaebacteria.

B. ENERGY AND NUTRITION

Bacteria are classified into four groups according to their means of obtaining nutrients:

♦ The ***photoautotrophs*** make food via the process of photosynthesis, using sunlight and carbon dioxide. These include cyanobacteria.
♦ The ***photoheterotrophs*** use photosynthesis but cannot use carbon dioxide. These bacteria need to obtain carbon from another source.
♦ The ***chemoautotrophs*** gain energy from inorganic substances and get their carbon from carbon dioxide.
♦ The ***chemoheterotrophs*** obtain energy from inorganic substances but cannot use carbon dioxide as their carbon source. Most pathogens are chemoheterotrophs. This group is further broken down based on how carbon is obtained:
  • ***parasites*** obtain nutrients from a host.
  • ***saprobes*** obtain nutrients from wastes or the remains of other organisms.

C. SHAPES

Bacteria usually take on one of three shapes (see Figure 8.1):

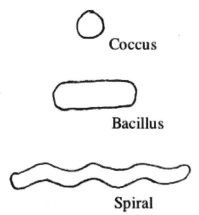

- ◆ **coccus** (plural: **cocci**): spheres.

  - • **diplococci**: pairs of cocci

  - • **streptococci**: chains of cocci

  - • **staphylococci**: sheets or clusters of cocci

- ◆ **bacillus** (plural: **bacilli**): rod shaped

- ◆ **spiral** or **spirochete**: twisted, corkscrew-shape

Figure 8.1: General shapes
of bacteria

D. STRUCTURE

The generalized structure of a bacterial cell is illustrated in Figure 8.2. The main features include:

- ◆ **prokaryotic cell structure**: Although we have stressed that prokaryotes do not contain a nucleus, they also lack other internal structural compartments found in eukaryotic cells
- ◆ **cell wall**: This surrounds the plasma membrane of the cell and helps to retain its shape. The cell wall consists of **peptidoglycan**, a substance composed of polysaccharides linked together via peptides. The exact structure of the cell wall can be determined via the **Gram staining test**. If the bacteria bind the dye used in the staining process, they are said to be **gram positive**, and contain one layer of peptidoglycans (**Staphylococcus** is one example). If cells exclude the dye, they are **gram negative** and the cell wall contains two layers: the inner layer is made up of peptidoglycan, and the outer contains lipoproteins and lipopolysaccharides. **E. coli** is a gram negative bacterium.
- ◆ **glycocalyx**: The glycocalyx, which surrounds the cell wall, consists of a sticky mesh of polysaccharides, polypeptides, or both. If this structure is tightly organized, it forms a protective **capsule**. If it is loosely organized, it forms a slime layer that helps the bacterium attach to surfaces.
- ◆ **flagellum** (plural: **flagella**): Flagella are long, winding protein chains extruding from the bacterial cell. Flagella rotate to move the cell.
- ◆ **pilus** (plural: **pili**): Pili are short, filamentous proteins extending from the cell. They typically are present in large numbers. Pili play an important role in helping bacteria attach to surfaces or to other cells.

E. REPRODUCTION

Most bacteria have the ability to reproduce very rapidly. For example, given the right nutrients and ambient temperature, *E. coli* can reproduce every 20 minutes. The method used to reproduce is called ***binary fission*** and begins with the replication of DNA. Once completed, the two DNA molecules move toward opposite ends of the cell. The cytoplasm then divides to produce two equivalent daughter cells.

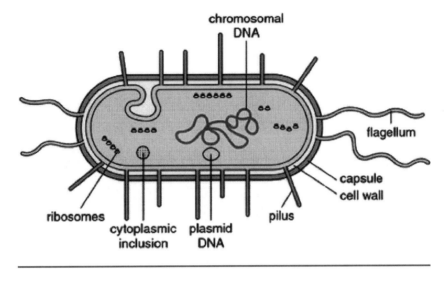

Figure 8.2: General structure of a bacterium

Another process that is often associated with reproduction is ***conjugation***. Although this is not a form of reproduction *per se*, it can change the genetic makeup of the bacterial cell. In conjugation, plasmid DNA is replicated and transferred from one bacterial cell to another via a special pilus, called a ***conjugation tube*** or ***sex pilus,*** which connects the two cells. The plasmid carries bacterial genes that may alter the function of the recipient cell.

When the environmental conditions are not favorable for reproduction, some bacteria have the ability to form ***spores***, which can preserve the cells. Once conditions improve, the bacteria begin to divide and multiply.

F. ANTIBIOTICS

Antibiotics are drugs that kill or prevent the growth of bacteria. These substances are produced naturally in many microorganisms and are used to fight off bacterial infections in humans. Keep in mind, however, that not all bacteria are harmful. Many species are beneficial and, if antibiotics are used to destroy pathogens, beneficial bacteria may also be killed.

The discovery and use of antibiotics has saved millions of lives, and the benefits of these drugs cannot be overstated. However, due to over-prescription and misuse, many bacterial strains have become resistant to antibiotics. One example is the emergence of resistant strains for the bacteria that cause tuberculosis. Once all but purged from the human population, tuberculosis has made a comeback and is stronger and deadlier than ever. It has become increasingly difficult to develop new antibiotics faster than bacteria can adapt to them.

G. ECOLOGY AND BACTERIA

Another important aspect of bacteria is their role in ecology. Bacteria account for a large portion of the *bioremediation* on the planet. They decompose much organic and inorganic matter. Due to recent advances in genetic engineering, some bacteria are being developed that can help clean up toxic substances. Most notably, many companies are designing bacteria that can "eat" oil, which can be used to clean up oil spills.

Chapter 8 Problems

Passage 8.1 (Questions 1-5)

Interestingly, many, if not most, bacterial cells can communicate with other cells in the same species. The bacteria secrete proteins, and, once enough bacteria are present, the concentration of the proteins increases. A high concentration often triggers the bacteria to turn on other proteins so the colony can perform a function. For example, individuals who have impaired immune systems or who have the genetic disease *cystic fibrosis (CF)* are often infected by the respiratory bacterium *Pseudomonas aeruginosa*. Only when enough bacteria have accumulated will *P. aeruginosa* will produce an enzyme that degrades lung tissue, which allows the bacteria to invade the bloodstream.

Although many examples of this intraspecies communication exist, scientists wondered if different species can communicate with each other. To answer this question, researchers examined the relationship between *P. aeruginosa* and *Burkholderia cepacia*. *B. cepacia* causes fatal lung infections in CF patients, but only after these individuals have also been infected by *P. aeruginosa*.

Experiment 1:
P. aeruginosa were grown in an appropriate liquid medium in the laboratory. The culture was centrifuged to remove the bacterial cells. A culture of *B. cepacia* was then grown in the medium. These bacteria increased production of molecules necessary for survival.

Experiment 2:
Mutant *P. aeruginosa* were grown in the laboratory in liquid medium. After centrifugation, the medium was used to incubate cultures of *B. cepacia*. Very few "survival molecules" were produced in the *B. cepacia*.

1. The experiments indicate:
    A. the two bacterial strains can communicate with each other.
    B. the *P. aeruginosa* bacteria help turn on production of survival molecules in *B. cepacia*.
    C. *B. cepacia* bacteria help turn on production of survival molecules in *P. aeruginosa*.
    D. no communication exists between the two bacterial strains.

2. The key to communication between these two bacteria is probably due to:
    A. a soluble protein secreted by *P. aeruginosa*.
    B. direct interaction between the two bacteria, possibly via cells of each species binding to each other.
    C. a soluble protein secreted by *B. cepacia*.
    D. Cannot be determined based on the available data

3. A similar communication system exists between:
    I.   nerve cells
    II. hormones and receptors
    III. photoreceptors in the eye
    A. I only
    B. II only
    C. I and II only
    D. III only

4. One important control that should be included in this experiment is to:
    A. grow *P. aeruginosa* in medium used to grow *B. cepacia* first.
    B. infect mice with both species of bacteria.
    C. grow *B. cepacia* in medium that had not been used to grow *P. aeruginosa*.
    D. no other control is necessary for this experiment.

5. The mutant *P. aeruginosa* used in Experiment 2 were most likely deficient in:
    A. replication.
    B. transcription.
    C. translation.
    D. secretion.

The following questions are NOT based on a descriptive passage.

6. If the doubling time of a strain of bacteria is 30 minutes, approximately how many cells would there be after 5 hours if the original culture had 1×10^5 cells?
    A. 5×10^5
    B. 3.2×10^6
    C. 1×10^8
    D. 1×10^{25}

7. Certain antibiotics work by inhibiting protein synthesis. However, proteins made before exposure to these drugs will continue to function until degraded by the cell. Which of the following would probably be true after adding these antibiotics to a culture of bacteria?

    A. DNA replication would not continue.
    B. Severely damaged flagella could not be repaired.
    C. New pili could be added to the bacteria.
    D. Damage to the glycocalyx would kill the bacterial cell.

SECTION 2

Content Review Problems

1. The protein coat of a virus is called the:
   A. Envelope
   B. Membrane
   C. Capsule
   D. Capsid

2. What is a bacteriophage?
   A. A virus that infects other viruses
   B. A virus that infects bacterial cells
   C. A virus that infects eukaryotic cells
   D. A virus that infects fungal cells

3. Which of the following is NOT true of lytic infection?
   A. Viral DNA integrates into the host genome
   B. The virus hijacks host machinery for reproduction
   C. Virions are made within the cell
   D. The cell eventually lyses

4. Prokaryotes do NOT have which of the following?
   A. Nucleoid
   B. Plasma membrane
   C. Flagella
   D. Mitochondria

5. Which of the following is NOT included in the chemical structure of a phospholipid?
   A. Glycerol
   B. 2 fatty acid chains
   C. Aromatic ring
   D. Phosphate group

6. Which of the following defines a micelle?
   A. A spherical structure made of compounds with a hydrophilic and hydrophobic region
   B. A neurotransmitter carrier in the PNS
   C. A membrane-bound organelle specific to red blood cells
   D. A unique compound found only in prokaryotes

7. The general classification for round-shaped bacteria is:
   A. bacilli.
   B. cocci.
   C. spirilla.
   D. Gram positive.

8. A membrane protein used to help a molecule or compound travel through the membrane is a:
   A. Peripheral protein
   B. G-protein
   C. Carrier protein
   D. Glycoprotein

9. A cell into which water flows can be said to be:
   A. Hypotonic to its surroundings
   B. Isotonic to its surrounding
   C. Hypertonic to its surroundings
   D. Hydrostatic to its surroundings

10. Gram-positive bacteria have all of the following EXCEPT:
    A. thick peptidoglycan cell wall.
    B. capsule.
    C. two exterior membranes.
    D. ribosomes.

11. Bacterial flagella are made from which of the following proteins?
    A. Flagellin
    B. Peptidoglycan
    C. Tubulin
    D. Chitin

12. Which of the following most accurately describes binary fission?
    A. Fungal sexual reproduction
    B. Eukaryotic asexual reproduction
    C. Bacterial sexual reproduction
    D. Bacterial asexual reproduction

13. The use of bacterial plasmids is NOT important in which of the following processes?
    A. Meiosis
    B. Transduction
    C. Transformation
    D. Conjugation

14. A bacterial sex pilus is created during which of the following processes?
    A. Meiosis
    B. Transduction
    C. Transformation
    D. Conjugation

15. Transduction requires which of the following:
    A. A vector
    B. Neutral pH
    C. Low temperature
    D. Limited nutrients

16. The cell walls of fungi are called:
    A. Gram positive
    B. Septa
    C. Chitin
    D. Hyphae

17. Chitin is a:
    A. Polysaccharide
    B. Protein
    C. Nitrogenous base
    D. Glycolipid polymer

18. Fungi are mostly found in which developmental stage?
    A. Haploid
    B. Diploid
    C. Tetraploid
    D. Polyploid

19. Which of the following predominately undergoes budding?
    A. Cardiac cells
    B. Prokaryotes
    C. Yeast
    D. Gram-negative bacteria

20. Bacterial plasma membranes contain all of the following EXCEPT:
    A. Cholesterol
    B. Transmembrane proteins
    C. Phospholipids
    D. Integral proteins

21. Which of the following groups is always an autotroph?
    A. Bacteria
    B. Insect
    C. Plant
    D. Fungi

22. Which of the following defines movement towards or away from certain chemicals?
    A. Chemotaxis
    B. Filibrae–dependent movement
    C. Tumbling
    D. Receptor-specific function

23. The "F" in the F factor that can allow for conjugation stands for which of the following?
    A. Female
    B. Fertility
    C. Franco
    D. Fungal

24. Which of the following houses DNA in prokaryotes?
    A. Ribosomes
    B. Mitochondria
    C. Nucleus
    D. Nucleoid

25. What is the role of most antibiotics?
    A. Destroy viruses
    B. Inhibit viral reproduction
    C. Destroy bacteria
    D. Increase bacterial reproduction

26. A virus that is capable of using reverse transcription to replicate in a host cell is named a:
    A. prion.
    B. active virus.
    C. retrovirus.
    D. viroids.

27. A virus can enter a cell through which of the following methods?
    A. Active transport
    B. Exocytosis
    C. G-protein cascade
    D. Endocytosis

28. When a virus binds to a host cell and before its nucleic acid is injected, which of the following must occur?
    A. Reverse transcriptase must transcribe viral DNA
    B. Viral enzymes must break down a part of the host plasma membrane
    C. The capsid must detach
    D. Viral tail must unravel nucleic acid

29. A temperate virus is one that:
    A. can undergo the lysogenic cycle.
    B. undergoes the lytic cycle.
    C. is temperature sensitive.
    D. is hydrophilic.

30. An injection of a non-pathogenic virus is administered as a:
    A. vaccine.
    B. beta test.
    C. test immune response.
    D. cure.

31. Which of the following are considered prokaryotes?
    A. Archaea
    B. Protists
    C. Fungi
    D. Autotrophs

32. Which of the following are capable of using carbon dioxide as the sole source of carbon?
    A. Chemotrophs
    B. Phototrophs
    C. Autotrophs
    D. Heterotrophs

33. Which of the following use preformed sources of carbon, usually in the form of other organisms, as their carbon source?
    A. Chemotrophs
    B. Phototrophs
    C. Autotrophs
    D. Heterotrophs

34. Phototrophs claim their energy from:
    A. living organisms.
    B. light.
    C. organic matter.
    D. chemicals.

35. Which of the following catabolic processes allow chemotrophs to claim their energy?
    A. Reduction
    B. Oxidation
    C. Phosphorylation
    D. Carboxylation

36. Spirilla are:
    A. spherical.
    B. cylindrical.
    C. helical.
    D. rod-shaped.

37. Bacilli are:
    A. spherical.
    B. cylindrical.
    C. helical.
    D. rod-shaped.

38. The hydrophilic portion of a phospholipid is:
    A. nonpolar.
    B. polar.
    C. neutral.
    D. basic.

39. Phospholipids are examples of:
    A. amphoteric molecules.
    B. amphipathic molecules.
    C. carrier proteins.
    D. degenerative molecules.

40. Phospholipids make up what part of a bacteria's cell structure?
    A. Nuclear membrane
    B. Mitochondrial membrane
    C. Cell wall
    D. Plasma membrane

41. Which of the following forces predominately hold a plasma membrane together?
    A. Intramolecular
    B. Intermolecular
    C. Covalent
    D. Ionic

42. The model that explains how the molecules that make up a membrane can move is the:
    A. symbiotic model.
    B. rigidity model.
    C. fluid mosaic model.
    D. hybridization model.

43. Bacterial transformation is defined as which of the following?
    A. DNA from a vector is incorporated into the genome
    B. DNA from the environment is incorporated into the genome
    C. Bacterial mitosis
    D. The use of a sex pilus to exchange genetic information from one cell to another

44. Binary fission is:
    A. fungal asexual reproduction.
    B. bacterial sexual reproduction.
    C. bacterial asexual reproduction.
    D. eukaryotic asexual reproduction.

45. During which of the following phases does the number of bacteria in the culture double?
    A. G_1
    B. G_2
    C. S
    D. None of the above

46. Which of the following is NOT considered to be a living organism?
    A. Archaea
    B. Protist
    C. Virus
    D. Prokaryote

47. Which of the following accurately describes viruses?
    A. Facultative autotrophs
    B. Obligate anaerobes
    C. Obligate parasites
    D. Facultative chemotrophs

48. Which of the following is NOT possible for a virus to perform without a host?
    A. Translation
    B. DNA replication
    C. Protein synthesis
    D. All of the above

49. Which of the following is the smallest?
    A. Eukaryotic cell
    B. Spermatid
    C. Bacteria
    D. Virus

50. Which part of a bacteriophage first attaches to the host?
    A. Tail fibers
    B. Tail
    C. Capsid
    D. Genetic information

51. What is a requirement for viruses with RNA that enter the lysogenic cycle?
    A. DNA helicase
    B. Reverse transcriptase
    C. Translation
    D. RNA polymerase

52. What is one advantage to the lytic cycle?
    A. Host cell survival
    B. Rapid viral reproduction
    C. Quick viral genomic integration into host genome
    D. Degradation of host machinery

53. A His+ bacterium can survive in medium that does NOT have:
    A. Histidine
    B. Arginine
    C. Tyrosine
    D. Phenylalanine

54. HIV is an example of a:
    A. (+) His virus.
    B. virus that exclusively undergoes the lytic cycle.
    C. retrovirus.
    D. (+) DNA virus.

55. Prokaryotes lack which of the following?
    A. Histones
    B. Nucleic acids
    C. Phospholipids
    D. Inclusion bodies

56. Which of the following can destroy bacterial cell walls?
    A. Amylase
    B. Lysozyme
    C. Trypsin
    D. Acetylcholinesterase

57. A coating of polysaccharides that surrounds a bacterial cell is called the:
    A. capsid.
    B. plasma membrane.
    C. capsule.
    D. cell wall.

58. Motile bacteria must have at least a:
    A. flagellum.
    B. cilium.
    C. frictionless coating.
    D. pulsing mechanism.

59. The ability for flagella to rotate is dictated by the amount of:
    A. genomic replication.
    B. ATP.
    C. action potentials.
    D. internal stimuli.

60. Bacterial pili are used to:
    A. respond to the external environment.
    B. attach to objects.
    C. transport the cell.
    D. act as a signal to the immune response.

61. The commonly used suffix –troph means:
    A. to drink.
    B. to exploit.
    C. to eat.
    D. to make.

62. Photoautotrophs can be identified as:
    A. bacteria that use CO_2 as a carbon source and make their energy from light.
    B. bacteria that build CO_2 from sunlight.
    C. bacteria that oxidize CO_2 as a carbon source and make their energy from glucose.
    D. bacteria that produce CO_2 from glucose.

63. A bacterium that cannot survive in minimal medium is said to be a/an:
    A. chemoheterotroph.
    B. auxotroph.
    C. heterotroph.
    D. autotroph.

64. Bacteria that grow preferentially in high temperatures are said to be:
    A. psychrophiles.
    B. mesophiles.
    C. thermophiles.
    D. hydrophiles.

65. Organisms that can use oxygen, but do not need it are called:
    A. obligate anaerobes.
    B. tolerant anaerobes.
    C. facultative anaerobes.
    D. obligate aerobes.

66. Those organisms for which oxygen is toxic are called:
    A. obligate anaerobes.
    B. tolerant anaerobes.
    C. facultative anaerobes.
    D. obligate aerobes.

67. Organisms that need oxygen to survive are called:
    A. obligate anaerobes.
    B. tolerant anaerobes.
    C. facultative anaerobes.
    D. obligate aerobes.

68. Organisms that can survive in the presence of oxygen, but do not use it are called:
    A. obligate anaerobes.
    B. tolerant anaerobes.
    C. facultative anaerobes.
    D. obligate aerobes.

69. Which of the following is an example of an obligate aerobe?
    A. Virus
    B. Human
    C. Yeast
    D. None of the above

70. An organism that is considered an obligate anaerobe is not capable of which of the following?
    A. Glycolysis
    B. Fermentation
    C. Electron transport chain using O_2
    D. Catabolism

71. Under ideal conditions, bacterial growth can be classified as which of the following?
    A. Sigmoidal
    B. Sinusoidal
    C. Exponential
    D. Linear

72. Yeast is an exception to most fungi in that it is:
    A. multicellular.
    B. unicellular.
    C. a prokaryote.
    D. a eukaryote.

73. Fungi typically digest their nutrients:
    A. outside the cell
    B. inside the cell
    C. with help from a host
    D. without enzymes

74. Which of the following can reproduce both sexually and asexually?
    A. Fungi
    B. Mammals
    C. Birds
    D. Archaea

75. Which of the following processes can most fungi undergo?
    A. Meiosis
    B. Lactic acid fermentation
    C. Conjugation
    D. Binary fission

76. Which of the following cells is able to undergo meiosis, has a nuclear membrane, and is larger than the rest?
    A. Viruses
    B. Eukaryotes
    C. Prokaryotes
    D. Bacteria

SECTION 3
EUKARYOTIC CELL BIOLOGY

Our discussion of cell biology must begin with two principles stated in ***The Cell Theory***:

◆ The cell is the basic unit of life.
◆ New cells can only arise from preexisting cells.

In this section, we will explore the structure and function of eukaryotic cells, specifically animal cells, and how they reproduce. In many instances, cells will develop over time to change their structure and function.

It is important to understand that cells come in many different shapes and sizes. For example, sperm cells are basically DNA with a tail, muscle cells are filled with mitochondria (to supply energy for movement) and neurons have enormously long axons. The typical animal cell is 10-30 micrometers in diameter, whereas an egg cell is 100 micrometers, and the yolk of a chicken egg (which is one single cell!) is 30000 µm. Although all these cells have different shapes, sizes and functions, they all have the same basic structure. In addition, with the exception of sperm and eggs, all cells reproduce in the same manner, via replication of the DNA and cytoplasmic division to produce two equal cells.

The next few chapters will discuss the structure and function of organelles and the cell membrane, and examine the process of mitosis.

CHAPTER 9
Cellular Organelles

A. INTRODUCTION

Organelles form separate compartments within the cell so various enzymatic reactions can occur in suitable environments. The barriers also prevent reactions within the cell from interfering with other cellular activities. Most organelles are membranc-bound sacs. Depending on the function of the cell, various organelles may be more or less prevalent. However, most animal cells contain all the organelles discussed in this chapter. Figure 9.1 is a schematic representation of a typical eukaryotic cell with the various organelles highlighted.

Although not necessarily considered an organelle, it should be noted that the cell is bounded by a lipid bilayer known as the cell or plasma membrane. It maintains an intricate relationship with organelles, and will be referred to in this chapter. It will be discussed in detail later.

B. THE NUCLEUS

The most apparent function of the *nucleus* is to sequester the DNA from the enzymatic reactions occurring in the cytoplasm. However, many activities take place in the nucleus. It contains three separate structures:

♦ *nucleolus:* The nucleolus is a dense mass inside the nucleus. Ribosomal proteins and RNAs are assembled here.

♦ *nuclear envelope:* As stated above, organelles are bounded by membranes. The membrane surrounding the nucleus has been well studied. It consists of two lipid bilayers, each similar to the cell membrane (see Chapter 11). This double membrane creates a barrier to water-soluble substances. *Pores* span both membranes and allow ions and small molecules to pass through. Large molecules are selectively transported across the membrane. The pores are responsible for transport both into and out of the nucleus. Ribosomes, the site of protein synthesis, are often found along the outer membrane, while chromosomes are attached to the inner membrane.

♦ *chromosomes:* Inside the nucleus the DNA is arranged in the structures called chromosomes (see Chapter 5). Chromosomes are made up of the DNA as well as proteins associated with organization, transcription, replication and repair.

C. THE ENDOPLASMIC RETICULUM

The ***endoplasmic reticulum (ER)*** is a network of interconnecting tubes that begins at the nuclear envelope and runs out into the cytoplasm. Two types exist in the cell:

♦ ***rough ER***: Ribosomes are attached to the cytoplasmic side of the ER. The rough ER often looks as though it is "stacked" in the cell. Polypeptides assembling on the ribosomes will be threaded into the ER if they contain a specific sequence of amino acids called a ***signal sequence***. Once inside the ER, proteins become modified through the addition of oligosaccharides. Rough ER is very abundant in cells that secrete large amounts of proteins.

♦ ***smooth ER***: Unlike the rough ER, the smooth ER is not studded with ribosomes. This organelle plays a role in lipid synthesis.

D. PEROXISOMES

Peroxisomes are sacs of enzymes. Fatty acids and amino acids are broken down here. Hydrogen peroxide (H_2O_2), produced as a byproduct from these reactions, is converted into H_2O and O_2 or various alcohols.

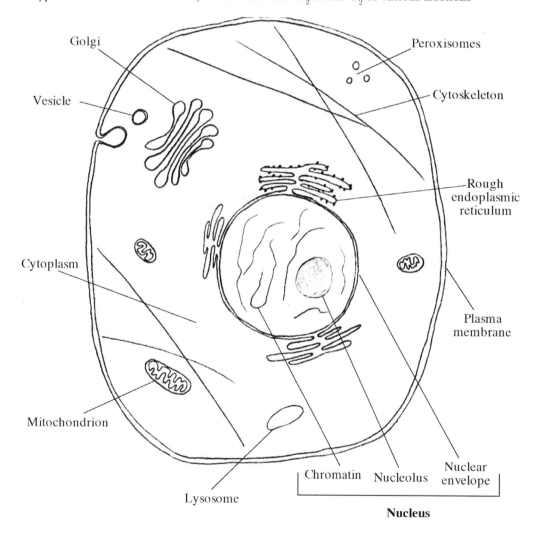

Figure 9.1: Typical eukaryotic animal cell

E. THE GOLGI

The *Golgi* (or *Golgi bodies*, or *Golgi apparatus*) appear as "stacks of pancakes" in the cytoplasm. These organelles function in modifying lipids and proteins that are packaged into membrane-bound *vesicles* for transport to specific locations in the cell. The vesicles form through the budding of the Golgi membrane.

F. LYSOSOMES

One type of vesicle that buds from the Golgi is the *lysosome*. These organelles function in intracellular digestion. They contain enzymes that break down polysaccharides, proteins, nucleic acids and some lipids. Lysosomes can fuse with endocytotic vesicles that have formed from the cell membrane. These vesicles contain molecules, and sometimes cells, obtained from outside the cell. Once the lysosome fuses with an endocytotic vesicle, the digestive enzymes will break down the substances taken into the cell.

Sometimes the lysosomes digest the cell itself. For example, the tail on a tadpole is digested by lysosomes as part of the normal programmed development of a frog.

G. MITOCHONDRIA

As we discussed earlier, ATP is the unit of energy in biological systems. This molecule is generated via the process of *respiration* in the *mitochondria*. Like the nucleus, mitochondria have two membranes (see Figure 9.2). The outer membrane is smooth and faces the cytoplasm. However, unlike the nucleus, the inner membrane is highly convoluted and forms "folds" in the interior of the organelle. These folds are called cristae. Two distinct compartments are bounded by the membranes: an outer compartment is formed between the two membranes, and an inner compartment (called the *matrix*) is bounded by the inner membrane. Most of the processes of respiration critical for the synthesis of ATP occur across the inner membrane, and therefore take place between the matrix and the outer compartment.

The structure of mitochondria is very similar to some bacteria. They contain their own circular DNA and divide on their own. It has been theorized that these organelles evolved from bacteria that were engulfed, but not digested, by other cells. This is known as the *endosymbiotic hypothesis*.

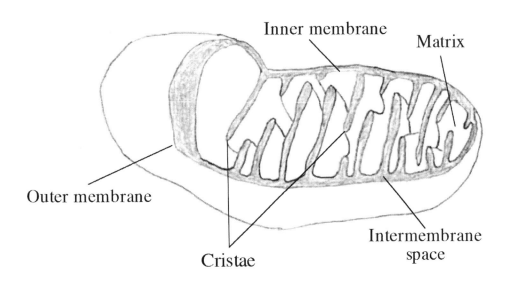

Figure 9.2: A mitochondrion

H. THE CYTOSKELETON

The cytoskeleton is not a membrane-bound organelle, but instead consists of a meshwork of various filaments that extends from the cell membrane and provides the cell with organization, stability, shape and, in some cases, movement. Three main types of filaments make up the cytoskeleton, and each is composed of highly ordered protein subunits:

- ◆ *microtubules:* These structures are made up of ***tubulin*** subunits, arranged in parallel rows that form hollow tubes. Microtubules are critical in vesicle and organelle movement and in cell division.
- ◆ *microfilaments:* These structures differ in their subunits, but always contain the proteins ***actin*** and ***myosin***. They are involved in cell movement.
- ◆ *intermediate filaments:* These cytoskeletal components differ in their protein make up, depending on the type of filament, and most are cell specific. All intermediate filaments form structural meshworks in the cytoplasm or in the nuclear envelope. Researchers can usually determine the type of cell they are working with by identifying which types of intermediate filaments are present.

Chapter 9 Problems

Passage 9.1 (Questions 1-4)

Cells grown in culture are often used to investigate the role of organelles. As culture conditions can be easily manipulated, cells can be subjected to different chemicals and their responses studied and analyzed.

In one such experiment, mouse cells were incubated in the presence of high concentrations of sucrose. The cells were examined under the microscope. Crystals of sucrose were found in the lysosomes of all the cells. When sucrose was depleted from the culture medium, the sucrose crystals in the lysosomes persisted for many days, but did not affect the growth of the cells. Eventually, the sucrose crystals disappeared. The rate of disappearance is shown in the graph below (note: all graphs are the same scale).

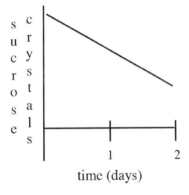

time (days)

Researchers performed two additional experiments:

Experiment 1:

Immediately after sucrose was removed from the culture medium, the enzyme *invertase* was added. Invertase catalyzes the cleavage of sucrose into monosaccharides. The cells were then examined for the presence of sucrose crystals. The results are shown below.

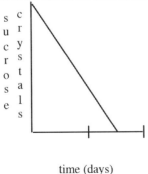

time (days)

Experiment 2:

Mouse cells grown in the presence of invertase (cell type A) were mixed with cells grown in the presence of sucrose (cell type B). A reagent that fuses cells was also added to the culture. After fusion, the cells (cell type AB) were grown in the absence of sucrose. The cells were then examined for the presence of sucrose crystals. The results are shown below.

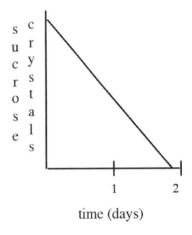

time (days)

1. From the results in Experiment 1, what can you conclude about invertase?
    A. It irreversibly inhibits sucrose production.
    B. It catalyzed the breakdown of sucrose in the medium.
    C. It was internalized by the lysosomes.
    D. It changes the pH of the cytoplasm to catalyze sucrose degradation.

2. Which of the following statements is true for mouse cells grown in culture?
    A. They do not normally have the ability to break down sucrose.
    B. They make invertase but only in low levels.
    C. Fusion with other cells reduces the ability of cells to produce invertase.
    D. High concentrations of sucrose are lethal.

3.   Based on the results in Experiment 2, which of the following could be true?

   I. Invertase diffused from the lysosomes of cell type A into the lysosomes of cell type B.

   II. The lysosomes of cell type A fused with the lysosomes of cell type B.

   III. Invertase destroyed cell type B and only allowed cell type A to survive.

   A. I only
   B. II only
   C. I and II only
   D. III only

4.   Another sugar, mannose, was added to mouse cells, and mannose crystals formed inside lysosomes. Similar to sucrose crystals, the mannose crystals disappeared in a few days after the sugar was removed from the medium. If invertase were added to the culture immediately after mannose was removed, what would you predict would happen?

   A. The mannose crystals would disappear in less than two days.
   B. The mannose crystals would disappear within a few days.
   C. Sucrose crystals would form.
   D. Mannose crystals would appear in the cytoplasm.

The following questions are NOT based on a descriptive passage.

5.   A cell is isolated that does not contain a nucleus. Which of the following organelles might it contain?

   A. Mitochondria
   B. Flagella
   C. Golgi
   D. Endoplasmic reticulum

6.   In eukaryotic cells, DNA replication takes place in

   I. the nucleus
   II. the cytoplasm
   III. the mitochondria

   A. I only
   B. II only
   C. I and II only
   D. I and III only

CHAPTER 10
Plasma Membrane and Transport

A. INTRODUCTION

One of the defining characteristics of life is the need for every living thing to maintain **homeostasis**, the regulation of a specific internal environment regardless of external conditions. One way cells accomplish this is via a **plasma** or **cell membrane**. The membrane functions in two ways:

- ◆ it forms a barrier between the cell and its surroundings.
- ◆ it allows for transport of specific molecules and ions into and out of the cell.

The plasma membrane is the key to the survival of the cell and of the organism. In this chapter, we will investigate the structure of the membrane and consider how it functions to maintain homeostasis.

B. STRUCTURE

The cell membrane is made up of two different types of molecules, **lipids** and **proteins** (you may wish to review the basic structures of these molecules). We will focus on the lipids in this section and discuss proteins later.

The cell membrane is composed mostly of phospholipids. Recall that phospholipids contain two regions; a polar head (comprised of a phosphate group) and a nonpolar tail (made up of two fatty acid chains). The head region is **hydrophilic** (water loving) and the tail is **hydrophobic** (water hating). This poses a problem for the molecule in the aqueous environment of the cell. The lipids solve this problem by forming a **lipid bilayer**: the hydrophobic tails associate to exclude water, while the hydrophilic heads are left exposed to the watery external and internal environments. (see Figure 10.1).

The plasma membrane also contains glycolipids and sterols (such as cholesterol). Proteins that span the membrane (**transmembrane proteins**) are responsible for transport of molecules and ions.

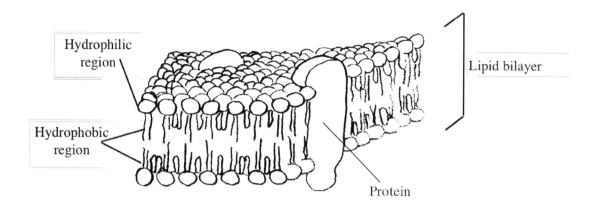

Figure 10.1: Cross section of the plasma membrane

C. THE FLUID MOSAIC MODEL

Our understanding of the structure of the plasma membrane can best be described using the **Fluid Mosaic Model**. The model states that the membrane is not a static network of lipids and proteins, but rather a dynamic matrix that is constantly in motion. In other words, it is fluid. The molecules do not pack together to form a solid layer. Since different types of molecules (i.e., lipids and proteins) make up the membrane, it is said to be a mosaic.

D. DIFFUSION

Before we begin a discussion of transport, we must consider how molecules and ions move in a liquid. This process is called **diffusion**.

Molecules and ions dissolved in a liquid are called **solutes** and are constantly moving in a random fashion. If the solute is more highly concentrated in one area of the liquid, a **concentration gradient** is formed. Due to random movement, the solutes will move, or diffuse, down the concentration gradient: in other words, the molecules and ions will move from an area of high concentration to an area of low concentration. This will occur until the solute is evenly distributed throughout the liquid and equilibrium is achieved. The particles will continue to move, but the concentration will not change. This is called **dynamic equilibrium**.

The rate of diffusion is influenced by many factors, such as:

- ♦ **the "steepness" of the concentration gradient:** Steeper gradients will cause faster diffusion, and, as the gradient decreases, the diffusion slows.
- ♦ **temperature:** The higher the temperature, the faster the diffusion.
- ♦ **size of the solute:** Smaller molecules and ions move faster.
- ♦ **presence of an electrical gradient:** Ions on one side of the membrane will help attract solutes with the opposite charge, thereby increasing the steepness of the concentration gradient of the solute.
- ♦ **presence of a pressure gradient:** Pressure can increase the gradient of a solute.

Transport across membranes can occur by diffusion. Certain solutes that are small, nonpolar and "lipid-y," such as O_2, can diffuses freely across the membrane. All other molecules cannot cross the cell membrane by diffusion, but can cross by the other methods discussed in this chapter. However, the principles of diffusion, especially the notion of concentration gradients, are crucial to most of these other methods of transport.

E. OSMOSIS

Osmosis is closely related to diffusion. It is the diffusion of water across biological membranes. It may be easiest to understand this process if you keep in mind that water is not only a solvent, but also a molecule itself that can have a concentration gradient. As the concentration of solutes increase, the concentration of water decreases. In the cell, the concentration gradient of water is influenced by the total number of molecules of all solutes present on both sides of the membrane. The movement of water in response to this gradient is not referred to as diffusion, but as osmosis.

The direction of water movement is influenced by *tonicity*, the relative concentration of solutes in two liquids. When solutes are in equal concentrations, the liquids are said to be *isotonic*, and there will be no net movement of water molecules. If the concentrations of solutes are not equal, water will move from the *hypotonic* solution (less solutes) to the *hypertonic* solution (more solutes). If the cell cannot adjust to the difference in solute concentrations between the cytoplasm and the external environment, the cell will burst (if placed in a hypotonic solution) or shrivel (if placed in a hypertonic solution).

A phenomenon related to osmosis is *bulk flow*, the movement of water unrelated to a membrane or concentration gradient. It can be due to many factors including pressure gradients, as seen in kidney cells.

F. SELECTIVE TRANSPORT

Transmembrane proteins permit certain molecules to pass through the lipid bilayer. This type of transport is highly specific for molecules and ions. Therefore, the cell needs many different kinds of transport proteins.

In general, all transport proteins function in a similar fashion. The molecule to be transported first binds to the protein. This causes the protein to change its shape. In essence, it "closes" behind the molecule and "opens" to the opposite side of the membrane (remember, molecules can be transported in either direction: from the inside out or from the outside in). This is often referred to as a *gated channel*. Once the protein has allowed the molecule to pass through the lipid bilayer, the molecule is released.

There are two types of selective transport (see Fig. 10.2):

- ◆ *passive transport (or facilitated diffusion):* Transmembrane proteins facilitate the diffusion of a solute down its concentration gradient. Remember our discussion earlier: this process will continue until an equilibrium is reached. However, this rarely happens. For example, once a molecule is transported into a cell, it is usually metabolized right away. Therefore, the concentration gradient does not change and the molecule will continue to diffuse into the cell.

- ◆ *active transport:* Molecules can be pumped across the cell membrane against their concentration gradient, i.e. from an area of low concentration to an area of high concentration. Since this is not the normal behavior for molecules, active transport requires energy, usually in the form of ATP. Once ATP binds, it alters the conformation of the transmembrane protein and the molecule can bind. The molecule is transported across the membrane and is released. The protein returns to its original conformation, preventing the molecule from making the return trip across the membrane.

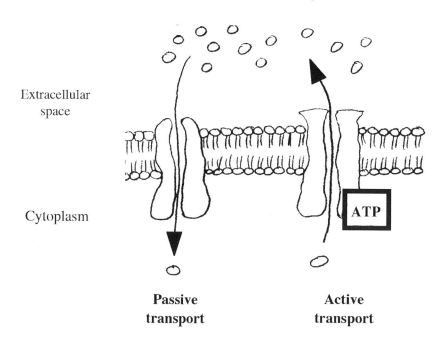

Figure 10.2: Selective transport

G. BULK TRANSPORT

Bulk transport is not used for selective transport of particular molecules but rather, as its name implies, for transporting large amounts of various molecules, and, in some cases, even whole cells. There are two main types of bulk transport (see Figure 10.3):

♦ **exocytosis:** Exocytosis is used to transport molecules out of the cell. In this process, cytoplasmic vesicles move to the plasma membrane and fuse with it. The membrane from the vesicles becomes incorporated in the plasma membrane, and the contents of the vesicles are released to the external surroundings of the cell.

♦ **endocytosis:** The converse of exocytosis is endocytosis. In this process, the plasma membrane "sinks" inward and forms a vesicle around particles and fluids on the extracellular side of the membrane. The newly formed vesicle pinches off from the membrane. The contents are transported to various places into the cytoplasm and may be stored for later use. There are three types of endocytosis:

♦ **pinocytosis:** This type of endocytosis refers to the flow of liquid droplets.

♦ **receptor mediated endocytosis:** This type of transport involves molecules binding to specific receptors clustered at the cell surface. This triggers endocytosis of the molecules. As seen in electron micrographs, the receptors bunch up in the membrane as it sinks into the cytoplasm. Often these structures are called coated pits.

♦ **phagocytosis:** Phagocytosis is usually found in free living cells, such as amoebas. However, it also occurs in multicellular organisms; the best example of this is white blood cells, such as macrophages, in the human immune system (see Chapter 15). In phagocytosis, the cell membrane wraps around an extracellular object, forming a large vesicle that usually fuses with lysosomes in the cytoplasm. The contents of the vesicle are then digested. Phagocytosis is distinguished from other types of endocytosis by the size and amount of material taken in, and the drastic movement and changes that occur in the cell to engulf the object.

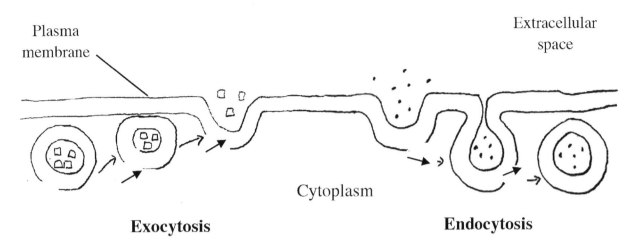

Figure 10.3: Bulk transport

Chapter 10 Problems

Passage 10.1 (Questions 1-5)

The **sodium-potassium (Na⁺/K⁺) pump** is a critical element for many processes of the cell. For example, it is responsible for a neuron's ability to transmit messages. The pump transports sodium out of the cell using energy from ATP (the extracellular matrix has a higher concentration of sodium than the intracellular space). The pump also imports potassium, which is more highly concentrated inside the cell than outside. The pump is an example of a **cotransport system**. Sodium binds to the transport protein and is exported. Once the sodium ion is released, a potassium ion binds and is transported into the cell (actually, for every three sodium ions pumped out of the cell, two potassium ions are pumped in). Thus, sodium and potassium gradients are established and maintained across the membrane. Since the ions are being transported in opposite directions, this type of pump is called an **antiporter**.

The sodium gradient established by the Na⁺/K⁺ pump can be used in many ways. Another cotransport system, the Na⁺/glucose pump, is active in human gut epithelial cells, and results in the uptake of glucose. Due to its concentration gradient, sodium diffuses into the cells through the Na⁺/glucose pump and transports glucose with it (this is called symport). The glucose is processed by the cells and can be used to generate energy.

1. The mechanism used by the Na⁺/K⁺ pump can best be described as
   A. bulk transport
   B. osmosis
   C. facilitated diffusion
   D. active transport

2. The mechanism used by the Na⁺/glucose pump can best be described as
   A. bulk transport
   B. osmosis
   C. facilitated diffusion
   D. active transport

3. If a sodium gradient is formed, whereby there is a vast excess of sodium outside the cell, which is the most likely result?
   A. An electrical gradient is also formed.
   B. A magnetic gradient is also formed.
   C. Other positively charged ions will enter the cell.
   D. Negatively charged ions will enter the cell.

4. A poison was found that prevents binding of sodium to the Na⁺/K⁺ pump. What would be the most likely consequence of this poison?
   I. potassium would not be pumped into the cell
   II. glucose would not be pumped into the cell
   III. nerve impulses would not be transmitted

   A. I only
   B. III only
   C. I and II only
   D. I, II and III

5. In cells where only the Na⁺/K⁺ pump and the Na⁺/glucose pump were functional, and where there were high concentrations of glucose and potassium outside the cell, what would you expect to happen?
   A. There would be a buildup of sodium inside the cell.
   B. There would be a buildup of potassium inside the cell.
   C. There would be an equilibrium of sodium inside and outside of the cell.
   D. There would be an equilibrium of glucose inside and outside of the cell.

The following questions are NOT based on a descriptive passage.

6. A certain transmembrane protein has its amino terminus at the exterior of the cell, carboxy terminus in the cytoplasm and everything in between embedded in the membrane. Which of the following statements is true?
   A. The amino terminus must be hydrophobic.
   B. Much of the protein is hydrophobic.
   C. The protein probably transports sodium.
   D. The protein must have a neutral charge.

7. A single-celled microorganism isolated from the Atlantic ocean was accidentally cultured in a medium formulated for fresh water microorganisms. What probably happened to the organism?

   A. The cell shriveled up and died due to exocytosis of salt.

   B. The cell swelled and burst due to osmosis of water.

   C. The cell died because the membrane transport proteins would not function properly in the new environment.

   D. The cell would try to take up as much sodium as possible via endocytosis from the medium.

CHAPTER 11

Mitosis

A. INTRODUCTION

Reproduction is a crucial, and complex, process. As we have seen, DNA has a method of reproducing itself, called replication. Later we will discuss the process of human reproduction. In this chapter, we will focus on the cellular level of reproduction: how eukaryotic cells divide.

On the cellular level, the parent cell needs to copy the DNA and give enough cytoplasmic components (enzymes, organelles, etc.) to the daughter cells to ensure their survival. There are two types of cellular division, *mitosis* and *meiosis*. Mitosis occurs in the body, or *somatic*, cells, and meiosis occurs in the reproductive, or *germ*, cells. Although the outcomes of these two processes are different, their mechanisms are very similar.

B. THE CELL CYCLE

In the life of a cell, mitosis is only one phase in a cycle. All the phases that describe the activities of the cell are part of *the cell cycle* (see Figure 11.1). This cycle consists of:

◆ *G_1 (gap) phase,* the phase prior to DNA replication in which cellular activities occur.
◆ *S phase (synthesis)*, when the DNA replicates.
◆ *G_2, a second gap*, which occurs after S.
◆ *M phase (mitosis)*, when the cell divides.

G_1, S and G_2 are collectively known as *interphase*. Some cells, such as neurons, function but do not cycle and do not divide. They arrest at a stage in the cell cycle known as G_0.

The time it takes for a cell to go through the cell cycle is characteristic of the cell type. Checkpoints within the cycle ensure that the cell is ready to continue on to the next phase. The cell will not be allowed to continue if certain events are not completed. For example, a checkpoint in G_2 ensures that the cell is physically big enough to divide in M phase. If the cell has not grown to a critical size, the cell will be arrested in G_2 until it is ready to proceed. In many types of cancer, these checkpoints are disabled, and cells divide in an uncontrolled fashion.

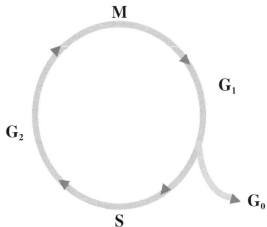

Figure 11.1: The Cell Cycle

C. THE STAGES OF MITOSIS

Four distinct stages have traditionally been observed in the process of mitosis: ***prophase, metaphase, anaphase*** and ***telophase***. An illustration of these stages is depicted in Figure 11.1, and a description of each follows.

D. PROPHASE

Perhaps the most striking event in prophase is the condensation of the chromosomes into threadlike structures that are visible under the microscope. Recall that DNA replication has already taken place by this point in the cell cycle. However, the duplicated strands of DNA are still physically connected. At the chromosomal level, the duplicated strands (called ***sister chromatids***) are attached at the region called the ***centromere***. The ***kinetochore*** is associated with each sister chromatid at the centromere (see Figure 11.2).

During ***spindle formation***, the microtubules in the cell disassemble and reassemble into the spindle, and the nucleus begins to break down. Once the nuclear envelope has disassembled, one end of each microtubule attaches to a kinetochore while the other end connects to one of two areas in the cell called the ***microtubule organizing centers (MTOC)***. The MTOC are located on opposite sides, or ***poles***, of the cell. In some cells, a barrel-shaped structure called a ***centriole*** is associated with each MTOC.

E. METAPHASE

At metaphase, the chromosomes become fully condensed. The main function of metaphase is to ensure each cell gets the correct chromosome complement. After the nuclear membrane has disassembled completely in prophase, and the spindle has assembled, the microtubules pull the chromosomes toward both poles. Since the chromosomes contain two kinetochores, one associated with each chromatid, the chromosomes are pulled toward opposite poles at the same time. The chromatids are still physically connected, so this pulling action results in the chromosomes aligning in the middle of the cell, between the two poles. This also orients the sister chromatids: one to each pole. This region of the cell is often called the ***metaphase plate***.

F. ANAPHASE

During anaphase, the sister chromatids separate and move to opposite poles. At this point in the cell cycle, the sister chromatids are referred to as chromosomes. A complete set of chromosomes now exists at each pole.

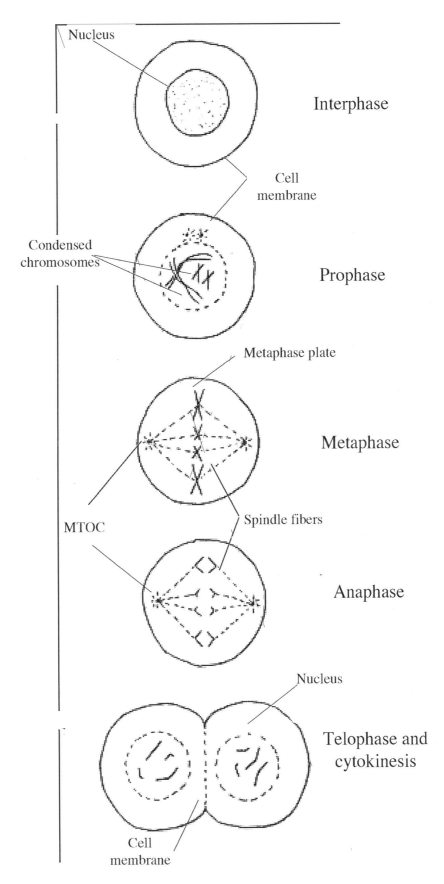

Figure 11.2: Stages of mitosis

G. TELOPHASE

During the final stage of mitosis, the microtubules disassemble and a nucleus forms around each set of chromosomes. The cytoplasm divides by a process called ***cleavage*** or ***cytokinesis*** which is mediated by microtubules. The microtubules "pull" the cell membrane into the cytoplasm. Upon completion of telophase, two new, complete cells exist, and each cell continues on into interphase of the next cell cycle.

Chapter 11 Problems

Passage 11.1 (Questions 1-4)

Cells will often delay entry into mitosis when the DNA has not completed replication, or when the cell is not yet big enough to divide. In yeast, many proteins and enzymes control the cell's ability to detect unreplicated DNA and to determine exactly how big the cell is. This allows for control of the cell cycle.

You wish to study these cell cycle control proteins in detail. You grow yeast cells and then expose them to a chemical mutagen, known to cause mutations in the DNA. You then examine the cells to see if they exhibit any abnormal growth patterns, indicating cell cycle control proteins may have been mutated. Each mutant cell you obtain has only one mutation in one protein.

Experiment 1:
You expose your cells to a drug which speeds up the cell cycle, but you grow the cells in a nutrient-poor medium. This medium normally prevents the cells from growing quickly, although DNA replication still occurs at a normal pace. Most cells take a long time to enter into mitosis. However, you isolate several cells that do not delay entry into mitosis. You call these mutants 1, 2, 3, etc.

Experiment 2:
You add a drug to your yeast cells which does not allow replication to occur. Most of the yeast cells arrest and do not grow. However, several do enter mitosis. You call these mutants A, B, C, etc.

Experiment 3:
Upon careful examination of your mutants, you find a few that allow cells to enter mitosis either when the cell is small or when the DNA has not completed replication. These mutants you call by both previous names (e.g. 5C, 9G, etc.).

Using this data, you try to determine where in the cell cycle these mutations are exerting their influence, and hence, where their normal counterparts act.

1. At what stage in the cell cycle is mutant 8 most likely defective?
    A. G_1
    B. S
    C. G_2
    D. M

2. At what stage in the cell cycle is mutant D most likely defective?
    A. G_1
    B. S
    C. G_2
    D. M

3. At what stage in the cell cycle is mutant 9G most likely defective?
    A. G_1
    B. S
    C. G_2
    D. must be at more than one stage

4. Under your experimental conditions, you find that your mutants quickly die out after a few generations. However, when you culture them without drugs they typically do well. Which of the following mutants would probably die off more quickly than the others under your experimental conditions?
    A. 1
    B. A
    C. 5C
    D. All will die off at the same rate.

The following questions are NOT based on a descriptive passage.

5. A sensitive instrument called a microspectrophotometer can accurately determine the exact mass of DNA in cells. In a culture of diploid cells, the instrument was used to measure DNA in the cells at various stages of the cell cycle. The lowest amount measured was 3.2 picograms (pg) of DNA, while the highest was 6.4 pg. In one cell, 4.8 pg was measured. In what stage of the cell cycle was this particular cell?
    A. G_1
    B. S
    C. G_2
    D. M

6. The drug colchicine prevents microtubules from assembling. If this drug was added to a culture of cells undergoing mitosis, in which phase would the cells be blocked?
    A. Prophase
    B. Metaphase
    C. Anaphase
    D. Telophase

CHAPTER 12
Meiosis

A. INTRODUCTION

While somatic cells undergo mitosis, germ cells, or sex cells, undergo meiosis to create the cells needed for sexual reproduction. The essential difference is that in mitosis, the goal is to produce two identical daughters, whereas in meiosis the goal is to create a cell with only half the normal amount of DNA. When the sperm and egg, each containing half the needed DNA, combine the result is a zygote with the normal DNA complement.

In this brief chapter we will give a short overview of meiosis, how it differs from mitosis, and how spermatogenesis and oogenesis differ. We will then have a fuller discussion in the physiology section.

B. OVERVIEW OF MEIOSIS I AND II

Meiosis consists of two rounds of division, unlike mitosis. The essential differences between mitosis and meiosis occur during the first round of division. Meiosis begins as does mitosis – with an S phase during which the cell doubles its DNA, making sister chromatids. The first major difference occurs during prophase I. Like mitosis, the nuclear envelope begins to break down, the DNA condenses into chromosomes, and microtubules begin the necessary reorganization. However, in prophase I, the cell undergoes ***crossing over***, during which homologous chromosomes may swap genetic material. This serves to increase the variability in the genetic arrangements possible in the sex cells. As with everything in sexual reproduction, the goal is simple – create more variety in the next generation to help increase the overall fitness of the species.

Once prophase I is complete, along with any crossing over that may occur, the second major difference occurs during metaphase I. Instead of chromosomes lining up on the metaphase plate so that sister chromatids may separate, ***homologous pairs*** of chromosomes line up in the middle of the cell and are separated. By pulling apart the homologous pair during anaphase I, the cell converts itself from a diploid cell (two copies of every gene) into a haploid cell (one copy of every gene).

After anaphase I, when the cell has separated homologous pairs of chromosomes, it can then go through meiosis II. This second round of division functions exactly like mitosis – chromosomes line up on the metaphase plate and sister chromatids are pulled apart. See figure 12.1 below for the general outline.

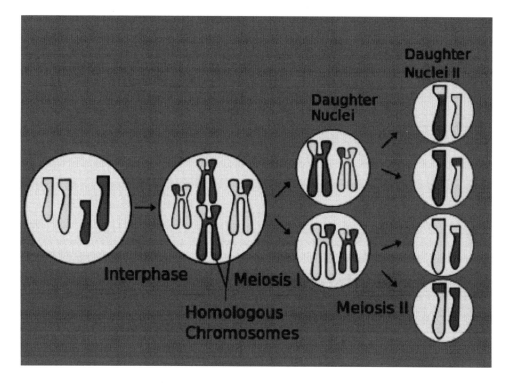

Figure 12.1: Meiosis general outline

C. DIFFERENCES BETWEEN SPERMATOGENESIS AND OOGENESIS

There are several key differences between the two forms of meiosis that occur in the human body. They are summarized in the chart below.

	Spermatogenesis	**Oogenesis**
Number of gametes produced	4 identical sperm	1 ovum, 2 polar bodies
When the process occurs	From puberty to death	Menarche to menopause
Nature of the meiotic process	Continuous – starts at prophase I and doesn't stop	Discontinuous – stops at metaphase II and does not continue until fertilization
"Lifespan" of the gametes	2 weeks then sperm are recycled	Life of the woman – a female baby is born with all of the oogonia she will ever have
Contribution to the zygote	DNA	DNA, mitochondria, organelles, etc.

Chapter 12 Problems

1. During spermatogenesis, how many rounds of division occur and how many sperm cells are produced, respectively?
    A. 1, 4
    B. 2, 4
    C. 4, 2
    D. 2, 2

2. The four sperm cells produced from a single spermatogonium will differ in their:
    A. mitochondrial DNA.
    B. nuclear DNA.
    C. cell structure.
    D. fitness.

3. How many cells are produced by oogenesis?
    A. 2
    B. 3
    C. 4
    D. it can vary between 2 and 6

4. Why does oogenesis NOT produce the same number of gametes as spermatogenesis?
    A. Since a woman can typically only safely carry one fetus at a time, the ovaries don't need to produce as many ova.
    B. Producing ova is physiologically demanding and it would be impossible to meet the energy requirements to produce 4 ova from a single oogonium.
    C. The polar body produced during the first round of division does not divide during the second round.
    D. Spermatogenesis is capable of producing up to eight cells per spermatogonium.

5. The primary function of sexual reproduction is to:
    A. tie the reproductive process to pleasure to motivate individual animals to engage in the reproduction necessary for the continuance of the species.
    B. reduce the metabolic costs of the reproductive process to allow animals to generate more offspring more quickly.
    C. bring together male and female individuals for the reproductive process as a way to cement the social interactions that form the basis of socialization that is necessary for the survival of any vertebrate species.
    D. increase variability in subsequent generations allowing for faster evolution in response to environmental pressure.

6. Each of the following helps to increase genetic variability in the next generation EXCEPT:
    A. crossing over.
    B. genetic recombination.
    C. separation of sister chromatids.
    D. mutations.

SECTION 3

Content Review Problems

1. Which of the following is neither found in nor is a component of the nucleus?
   A. DNA
   B. Double lipid bilayer membrane
   C. Nucleoplasm
   D. tRNA

2. Which of the following is a function of the endoplasmic reticulum?
   A. Synthesize proteins from mRNA
   B. Digest toxic materials in the cytoplasm
   C. Package proteins for leaving the cell
   D. Transport proteins to the Golgi apparatus

3. Where is the endoplasmic reticulum located in a cell?
   A. Connected to the Golgi apparatus
   B. Connected to the nucleus
   C. Connected to the cell membrane
   D. Floating in the cytoplasm

4. Why is rough ER called rough ER?
   A. Because it is the site of toxic waste disposal in the cell
   B. Because it is studded with tRNA
   C. Because it is studded with ribosomes
   D. Because it operates at a low pH

5. What is a function of smooth ER?
   A. Synthesize proteins from mRNA
   B. Synthesize lipids
   C. Provide a site for protein production
   D. Package proteins that will leave the cell

6. Which cells are most likely to have large amounts of smooth ER?
   A. Neurons
   B. Skin oil gland cells
   C. Hepatic acinar cells
   D. Heart cells

7. What is cytokinesis?
   A. The movement of a cell
   B. Signaling between two adjacent cells
   C. Signaling between two cells at a distance
   D. The splitting of a cell

8. Which of the following is a function of the Golgi apparatus?
   A. Synthesize proteins from mRNA
   B. Synthesize lipids
   C. Provide a site for protein production
   D. Package proteins that will leave the cell

9. Which cellular organelle most resembles the Golgi apparatus?
   A. Lysosomes
   B. Mitochondria
   C. Chloroplasts
   D. Endoplasmic reticulum

10. What are the folds called in the Golgi apparatus?
    A. Lumen
    B. Cisternae
    C. Cristae
    D. Cytoplasms

11. Which organelle is capable of replicating itself?
    A. Mitochondria
    B. Ribosome
    C. Golgi apparatus
    D. Endoplasmic reticulum

12. Which organelle is NOT capable of dividing and replicating?
    A. Mitochondrion
    B. Peroxisome
    C. Lysosome
    D. Golgi apparatus

13. What is the function of a lysosome?
    A. Protein synthesis
    B. Waste disposal
    C. RNA synthesis
    D. Digestion of dietary lipids

14. At what pH do a lysosome's enzymes function?
    A. 1
    B. 5
    C. 7
    D. 9

15. Which cell would be expected to contain the most lysosomes?
    A. A red blood cell
    B. A kidney cell
    C. A skin cell
    D. A monocyte

16. Where do lysosomal enzymes originate?
    A. They are packaged at the Golgi apparatus.
    B. They are synthesized at the ER.
    C. They are pinched off from the cell membrane.
    D. They are imported from outside the cell.

17. Which cellular function requires lysosomes?
    A. Apoptosis
    B. Cell division
    C. Translation
    D. Transcription

18. In which of the following processes do mitochondria play the biggest role?
    A. Cellular movement
    B. Cellular respiration
    C. Digestion of lipids
    D. Digestion of proteins

19. Oogenesis differs from spermatogenesis in that it involves:
    A. arresting during meiosis II.
    B. production of only two gametes, not four.
    C. contribution of only nuclear DNA.
    D. a process that ends at death.

20. Which cells have a linearly organized cytoskeleton?
    A. Neurons
    B. Muscle cells
    C. Liver cells
    D. White blood cells

21. Which cell is most likely to do phagocytosis to destroy a foreign antigen?
    A. Neutrophil
    B. Liver cell
    C. Kidney cell
    D. Erythrocyte

22. Which cell is most likely to do phagocytosis to obtain lipids for energy?
    A. Neutrophil
    B. Liver cell
    C. Kidney cell
    D. Erythrocyte

23. How are peroxisomes and lysosomes different?
    A. Peroxisomes are not packaged at the Golgi apparatus.
    B. Peroxisomes are not membrane-bound.
    C. Peroxisomes do not exist in eukaryotes.
    D. Lysosomes do not exist in eukaryotes.

24. Where does spermatogenesis occur?
    A. Somatic line cells
    B. Prostate
    C. Testes
    D. Pancreatic acinar cells

25. Where is rRNA synthesized?
    A. Nucleolus
    B. Cytoplasm
    C. Cell membrane
    D. Mitochondrial membrane

26. Which of the following have flagella?
    A. Spermatagonium
    B. Gametes
    C. Sperm
    D. Neurons

27. The cytoskeleton is composed of which of the following?
    I. Microtubules
    II. Intermediate filaments
    III. Actin

    A. I only
    B. II and III only
    C. I and III only
    D. I, II, and III

28. Which of the following is NOT a purpose of a cell's cytoskeleton?
    A. Give the cell shape
    B. Allow the cell to move
    C. Provide energy to muscle cells
    D. Help with cytokinesis during cellular division

29. What are cellular membranes composed of primarily?
    A. Phospholipids
    B. Sphingolipids
    C. Triglycerides
    D. Microtubules

30. Which of the following is NOT a common component of cellular membranes?
    A. Protein
    B. Cholesterol
    C. Carbohydrates
    D. Peptidoglycan

31. What type of protein is likely to be found in the cell membrane?
    A. Transmembrane immunoglobulins
    B. Ribosomes
    C. Transport proteins
    D. Albumin

32. Which of the following is NOT a purpose of cholesterol in the cell membrane?
    A. Stabilize the membrane
    B. Aid in cell signaling
    C. Allow for greater membrane permeability
    D. Maintain fluidity of membrane

33. Which of the following molecules is likely able to diffuse through a plasma membrane?
    A. CO_2
    B. Cl^-
    C. ATP
    D. Glucose

34. Which of the following molecules is LEAST likely able to diffuse through a plasma membrane?
    A. O_2
    B. CO_2
    C. H_2O
    D. Glucose

35. Which of the following orders the ability of three molecules to diffuse through a plasma membrane?
    A. H_2O, Na^+, glucose
    B. Na^+, H_2O, glucose
    C. Glucose, H_2O, Na^+
    D. H_2O, glucose, Na^+

36. Which amino acid residue is most likely to be found at the center of a transmembrane protein?
    A. Lysine
    B. Arginine
    C. Valine
    D. Aspartate

37. Which amino acid residue is most likely to be found at outer surface of a transmembrane protein?
    A. Isoleucine
    B. Glutamate
    C. Alanine
    D. Leucine

38. Which of the following proteins is most likely to span the cellular membrane?
    A. Potassium channels
    B. Ribosomes
    C. Myosin
    D. Histones

39. What are centrioles?
    A. The center of chromosomes
    B. Proteins around which chromatin is folded
    C. Structures made of tubulin that aid in cell division
    D. Filaments that connect to chromosomes during metaphase

40. Where are spindle fibers synthesized?
    A. Actin filaments
    B. Centrioles
    C. Centromeres
    D. Nucleolus

41. What are histones?
    A. The center of chromosomes
    B. Proteins around which DNA is wrapped
    C. Structures made of tubulin that aid in cell division
    D. Filaments that connect to chromosomes during metaphase

42. What will happen to a cell placed in an isotonic solution?
    A. The cell will lyse.
    B. The cell will shrivel.
    C. The cell will not change in size.
    D. Not enough information

43. What is osmosis?
    A. Net movement of solvent to area of higher solute concentration
    B. Net movement of solvent to area of lower solute concentration
    C. Net movement of solute to area of lower solute concentration
    D. Net movement of solute to area of higher solvent concentration

44. What does hypotonic mean when describing a cell?
    A. Of a higher solute concentration than the surroundings
    B. Of a lower solute concentration than the surroundings
    C. Of equal solute concentration as the surroundings
    D. Of a lower solvent concentration than the surroundings

45. A hypertonic cell has:
    A. A higher solute concentration than the surroundings
    B. A lower solute concentration than the surroundings
    C. An equal solute concentration as the surroundings
    D. A higher solvent concentration than the surroundings

46. What does isotonic mean when describing a cell?
    A. Of a higher solute concentration than the surroundings
    B. Of a lower solute concentration than the surroundings
    C. Of equal solute concentration as the surroundings
    D. Of a lower solvent concentration than the surroundings

Use the following scenario for #47-48: A cell is placed in pure water.

47. Which of the following is true concerning the scenario above?
    A. The cell is hypotonic to its environment.
    B. The cell is isotonic to its environment.
    C. The water is hypertonic to the cell.
    D. The cell is hypertonic to its environment.

48. Which of the following will occur to the cell?
    A. Water will flow into it.
    B. It will shrivel.
    C. There will be no change to the cell.
    D. Not enough information

Use the following scenario for #49-50: A cell is placed in a 1 M solution of NaCl

49. Which of the following is true concerning the scenario above?
    A. The solution is hypertonic to the cell.
    B. The solution is hypotonic to the cell.
    C. The cell is hypertonic to its environment.
    D. The cell is isotonic to its environment.

50. Which of the following will occur to a cell lacking a cell wall?
    A. It will burst.
    B. It will shrivel.
    C. There will be no change to the cell.
    D. Not enough information.

51. If you are lost at sea, why is drinking sea water bad?
    A. Because sea water is hypertonic to your cells and will cause you to lose more water from your cells
    B. Because sea water is hypertonic to your cells and will cause your cells to swell and lyse
    C. Because sea water is hypotonic to your cells and will cause you to lose more water from your cells
    D. Because sea water is hypotonic to your cells and will cause your cells to swell and lyse

52. Which is an example of facilitated diffusion?
    A. Glucose being pumped into a cell
    B. A sodium-potassium pump
    C. H_2O entering a cell through aquaporin channels
    D. K^+ entering a cell against its concentration gradient

53. Which is an example of active transport?
    A. Glucose being digested by an enzyme
    B. A sodium-potassium pump
    C. H_2O entering a cell
    D. K^+ entering a cell through a potassium channel

54. Which is an example of passive diffusion?
    A. Glucose being pumped into a cell
    B. A sodium potassium pump
    C. H_2O entering a cell by pinocytosis
    D. Estrogen entering a cell through the cell membrane

55. Which of the following is true of active transport?
    A. It requires cAMP.
    B. It does not require energy.
    C. It moves particles with their concentration gradient.
    D. It moves particles against their concentration gradient.

56. What is true of facilitated diffusion?
    A. It does not require membrane proteins.
    B. It moves particles from high to low concentration areas.
    C. It moves particles from low to high concentration areas.
    D. It requires ATP.

57. Which of the following is true of osmosis?
    A. Water moves to where solute concentration is greater.
    B. Water moves to where solute concentration is lower.
    C. Water does not move during osmosis; solute particles move from high to low concentration areas.
    D. Water does not move during osmosis; solute particles move from low to high concentration areas.

58. Which of the following is NOT the location of a cell cycle checkpoint?
    A. M phase
    B. G_1 phase
    C. S phase
    D. G_2 phase

59. Which checkpoint checks to see if the cell is large enough to divide?
    A. M phase
    B. G_1 phase
    C. S phase
    D. G_2 phase

60. If a cell has stopped dividing, in which stage of the cell cycle is it likely in?
    A. Prophase
    B. Anaphase
    C. Telophase
    D. Interphase

61. Which checkpoint checks to see if DNA was replicated correctly?
    A. M checkpoint
    B. G_1 checkpoint
    C. S checkpoint
    D. G_2 checkpoint

62. What is the first stage of the cell cycle after mitosis?
   A. G_0
   B. G_2
   C. M
   D. G_1

63. When might G_0 begin?
   A. Between G_1 and S
   B. Before G_1 begins
   C. Between S and G_2
   D. During G_2

64. When does S phase occur?
   A. After M phase
   B. Between G_2 and M phase
   C. Between G_1 and G_2 phase
   D. Before G_1 phase

65. Which phase is not included in M?
   A. Prophase
   B. Metaphase
   C. Telophase
   D. Interphase

66. During which phase of the cell cycle is DNA replicated?
   A. G_0 phase
   B. M phase
   C. S phase
   D. G_1 phase

67. During which phase of mitosis do sister chromatids separate?
   A. Metaphase
   B. Anaphase
   C. Telophase
   D. Prophase

68. During which phase of mitosis do spindle fibers form?
   A. Metaphase
   B. Anaphase
   C. Telophase
   D. Prophase

69. During which phase of mitosis do spindle fibers connect to chromosome centromeres?
   A. Metaphase
   B. Anaphase
   C. Telophase
   D. Prophase

70. During which phase of mitosis do chromosomes line up?
   A. Metaphase
   B. Anaphase
   C. Telophase
   D. Prophase

71. Where do chromosomes line up just before being pulled apart during mitosis?
   A. In the nucleus
   B. Along the cell membrane
   C. Anaphase plate
   D. Metaphase plate

72. During which part of the cell cycle does a cell split into two?
   A. Anaphase
   B. Prophase
   C. Cytokinesis
   D. Metaphase

73. Which of the following gives the correct order of mitosis?
   A. Interphase, metaphase, anaphase, prophase, telophase
   B. Prophase, interphase, anaphase, telophase, metaphase
   C. Interphase, prophase, metaphase, anaphase, telophase
   D. Anaphase, prophase, metaphase, telophase, interphase

74. If a cell has 42 chromosomes to begin with, how many does it have after Meiosis II?
   A. 21
   B. 42
   C. 63
   D. 84

75. If a cell has 42 chromosomes to begin with, how many does it have after Meiosis I?
    A. 21
    B. 42
    C. 63
    D. 84

76. If a cell has 42 chromosomes to begin with, how many does it have after mitosis?
    A. 21
    B. 42
    C. 63
    D. 84

77. Which of the following is most similar to anaphase of mitosis?
    A. Anaphase of meiosis I
    B. Prophase of meiosis I
    C. Prophase of meiosis II
    D. Anaphase of meiosis II

78. Which is a difference between meiosis I and meiosis II?
    A. During metaphase I, chromosomes line up in pairs with their homologous pair.
    B. During metaphase I, spindle fibers attach to centromeres.
    C. After Meiosis I, each cell has 42 chromosomes.
    D. After Meiosis I, each cell has 21 chromosomes.

79. During which cell cycle checkpoint does the cell check that all chromosomes are correctly connected to spindle fibers?
    A. M phase
    B. G_1 phase
    C. S phase
    D. G_2 phase

80. Which of the following human cells undergo meiosis?
    A. Skin cells
    B. Gametes
    C. Germ cells
    D. Somatic cells

81. Which of the following human cells undergo mitosis?
    A. Germ cells
    B. Spermatagonia
    C. Oogonia
    D. Somatic cells

82. How many daughter cells are generated during mitosis?
    A. 1
    B. 2
    C. 3
    D. 4

83. How many daughter cells are generated from spermatogenesis?
    A. 1
    B. 2
    C. 3
    D. 4

84. In which of the following cells is mitosis least likely to occur?
    A. Skin cells
    B. Liver cells
    C. Neurons
    D. Endothelial cells

85. Which of the following cells is most likely to be in M phase?
    A. Skin cells
    B. Liver cells
    C. Neurons
    D. Heart cells

86. What is the process called by which human eggs are developed?
    A. Spermatogenesis
    B. Oogenesis
    C. Gametogenesis
    D. Menstruation

87. Which cell undergoes meiosis I?
    A. Spermatogonium
    B. Spermatid
    C. Primary spermatocyte
    D. Secondary spermatocyte

88. Which cell undergoes Meiosis II?
    A. Spermatogonium
    B. Spermatid
    C. Primary spermatocyte
    D. Secondary spermatocyte

89. What are the products of the second meiotic division in spermatogenesis and how many are produced?
    A. Spermatids, 4
    B. Spermatids, 2
    C. Sperm, 4
    D. Sperm, 2

90. How many secondary oocytes are produced per meiotic division of 1 oogonium?
    A. 1
    B. 2
    C. 3
    D. 4

91. How many primary oocytes are produced per 1 oogonium?
    A. 1
    B. 2
    C. 3
    D. 4

92. How many eggs are produced per meiotic division of 1 oogonium?
    A. 1
    B. 2
    C. 3
    D. 4

93. How many polar bodies are produced during meiosis I from one oogonium?
    A. 1
    B. 2
    C. 3
    D. 4

94. Which of the following cells are haploid?
    I. Sperm
    II. Secondary oocyte
    III. Primary spermatocyte

    A. I only
    B. I and II only
    C. II and III only
    D. I, II, and III

95. During which phase of mitosis does the nuclear envelope disintegrate?
    A. Metaphase
    B. Prophase
    C. Anaphase
    D. Interphase

96. Which of the following do prokaryotes have?
    A. Ribosomes
    B. Nucleus
    C. Mitochondria
    D. Endoplasmic reticulum

97. Which of the following is a characteristic of prokaryotes?
    A. They have lysosomes.
    B. They have circular DNA.
    C. Their DNA is contained in a membrane-bound nucleus.
    D. They do not use oxidative phosphorylation.

98. What is an example of bulk transport?
    A. Transport of electrolytes via facilitated diffusion
    B. Transport of glucose across the cell membrane
    C. Transport of small organelles across the cell membrane
    D. Membrane-bound vesicles transporting materials

99. What is phagocytosis?
    A. The process by which a cell consumes solid particles
    B. The process by which a cell consumes extracellular fluid
    C. The process by which a cell kills itself
    D. The process by which a cell exports particles

100. Which of the following can be referred to as "cellular drinking"?
   A. Phagocytosis
   B. Endocytosis
   C. Pinocytosis
   D. Exocytosis

101. Which of the following is a form of endocytosis?
   I. Phagocytosis
   II. Pinocytosis
   III. Apoptosis

   A. I only
   B. II only
   C. I and II only
   D. I, II, and III

102. After endocytosis, which of the following is the endosome likely to fuse with?
   A. ER
   B. Golgi apparatus
   C. Lysosome
   D. Nucleus

103. What is exocytosis?
   A. The process by which a cell consumes solid particles
   B. The process by which a cell consumes extracellular fluid
   C. The process by which a cell kills itself
   D. The process by which a cell exports particles

104. Which of the following cells uses exocytosis regularly?
   A. Muscle cells
   B. Neurons
   C. Kidney cells
   D. Red blood cells

105. What happens to the volume of the cell directly after endocytosis?
   A. It will grow in volume.
   B. It will shrink in volume.
   C. It will remain the same.
   D. Not enough information

106. What happens to the volume of the cell membrane directly after exocytosis?
   A. A slight decrease
   B. A slight increase
   C. No change
   D. Not enough information

107. What is the primary function of a peroxisome?
   A. Metabolism of fatty acids
   B. Disposal of waste
   C. Synthesis of proteins
   D. Synthesis of amino acids

108. Which of the following cells will contain the most peroxisomes?
   A. Kidney
   B. Skin
   C. Liver
   D. Neuron

109. What do the enzymes in a peroxisome do?
   A. Oxidize energy-rich molecules
   B. Reduce energy-rich molecules
   C. Oxidize toxic material
   D. Reduce toxic material

110. Which of the following is commonly produced as a result of the enzymatic action in peroxisomes?
   A. CO_2
   B. H_2O
   C. H_2O_2
   D. ATP

111. Which of the following is not a membrane-bound organelle?
   A. Lysosome
   B. Mitochondria
   C. Golgi apparatus
   D. Ribosome

112. Which of the following has a double lipid bilayer membrane?
   A. Nucleus
   B. Mitochondria
   C. Peroxisome
   D. Ribosome

113. Which of the following is NOT a component of the fluid mosaic model?
    A. Glycolipids
    B. Cholesterol
    C. Microtubules
    D. Glycoproteins

114. Which cell will likely have the most mitochondria?
    A. Skin cells
    B. Muscle cells
    C. Neurons
    D. Liver cells

115. What is a characteristic of eukaryotes?
    A. They are single celled organisms.
    B. They are multi-cellular organisms.
    C. They have a membrane-bound nucleus.
    D. They have chloroplasts.

116. Which of the following is true?
    A. Mitochondria have circular DNA.
    B. Mitochondria don't have DNA.
    C. Mitochondria have linear DNA.
    D. Mitochondria have ribosomes.

117. Which of the following is the theory that describes how some eukaryotic organelles are derived from prokaryotes?
    A. Pangenesis
    B. Natural selection
    C. Transmutation
    D. Endosymbiosis

118. Which of the following is commonly known as the energy currency of the cell?
    A. ADP
    B. NADH
    C. ATP
    D. cAMP

119. Which of the following is a transmembrane protein?
    A. Coenzyme Q
    B. DNA polymerase
    C. Helicase
    D. T cell receptor

120. Which of the following is not a similarity between mitochondria and bacteria?
    A. they have a double lipid bilayer membrane
    B. they have circular DNA
    C. they generate ATP
    D. they contain enzymes

SECTION 4

VERTEBRATE ANATOMY AND PHYSIOLOGY

Anatomy and physiology are disciplines usually studied together that deal with the structure and function of multicellular organisms. ***Anatomy*** is the science that deals with biological ***structures*** (sometimes called morphology, literally, "the study of form"). How are the parts of an organism arranged, and what are their designs? ***Physiology*** is the science that explores the ***functioning*** of these biological structures. What does each part of an organism do, and how is it accomplished?

Central to the study of anatomy and physiology is a hierarchical way of looking at biological entities. The cell is the fundamental unit of life, even though it has many component parts, so it would not be improper to talk about the anatomy and physiology of the cell itself. Traditionally, however, these terms are more commonly reserved for the study of multicellular organisms, namely animals. We will direct our study at the anatomy and physiology of vertebrate animals (animals with "backbones") because these are the organisms emphasized on the MCAT. Since humans are vertebrates, it is convenient and reasonable to use human anatomy and physiology as an example of vertebrate systems in general.

Returning to the theme of hierarchy, the structure and function of a multicellular animal may be approached on many levels, from the simplest to the most complex. As noted before, the cell is the fundamental living unit, and the general functioning of the cell itself is the subject of previous chapters. In an animal, cells undergo ***differentiation*** and become ***specialized*** - all of the cells in an animal's body are not the same, and the first chapter in this section deals with the major types of cells that exist in vertebrate bodies. Groups of specialized cells working together towards a common function are referred to as ***tissues***. A structure performing a specific function that is made up of more than one tissue type is referred to as an ***organ***, and groups of organs functioning in concert are said to be ***organ systems***. The remaining chapters in this section deal with the various organ systems in the vertebrate body. These are grouped together due to similarities in structure, function, or both. Ultimately, all of the organ systems functioning together will create and sustain the ***organism*** itself, which is the highest level of hierarchy with which we need be concerned here. All of an animal's systems must function harmoniously in order for ***homeostasis*** to be maintained. Homeostasis is the maintenance of the relative constancy of the internal environment of an organism (i.e., temperature, pH, water balance, etc.), and must be preserved if the organism is to remain healthy. A disruption in homeostasis may lead to disease and ultimately death.

NEXT STEP MCAT CONTENT REVIEW: BIOLOGY AND BIOCHEMISTRY

CHAPTER 13
Specialized Eukaryotic Cells and Tissues

A. INTRODUCTION

While all cells share the same fundamental properties, cells in a multicellular animal become specialized to enable them to participate in different functions. Cells that find themselves in a human heart will have to be different structurally than cells found in the brain, due to the different functions these organs perform. Groups of similarly specialized cells working together towards a common function, along with any associated extracellular material, are called tissues. While experts can distinguish almost 200 types of human cells, these are usually grouped into four tissue types, each of which performs a basic function. These tissue types are e*pithelial, connective, muscle,* and ***nervous.***

B. EPITHELIAL TISSUES AND CELLS

Epithelial tissue covers all of the surfaces of the body that come into contact with the environment. This includes the outer surface of the skin, as well as the linings of the respiratory, digestive, and urogenital tracts. Some epithelial cells are specialized to secrete ***mucus*** (which acts as a lubricant and protects inner surfaces from infection), while others often cluster together to form ***glands*** (structures that synthesize and secrete specific substances, often enzymes or hormones). Since epithelial tissue exists wherever the body comes into contact with the environment, it serves a ***protective*** role and also regulates the ***absorption*** of materials (as in the digestive and respiratory systems) and their ***excretion*** (as in the respiratory system and sweat glands). Any particular epithelial tissue is classified according to the shape and arrangement of its cells:

- ♦ ***Squamous*** epithelium consists of cells that are thin and flattened; typically, substances diffuse through these cells rather easily.
- ♦ ***Cuboidal*** epithelium is made up of cube-shaped cells.
- ♦ ***Columnar*** epithelium is composed of elongated, rectangular cells.
- ♦ ***Simple*** epithelium contains cells arranged in a single layer.
- ♦ ***Stratified*** epithelium contains cells arranged in sheets several layers thick.

The epithelial tissue that makes up the outer layer of the skin is ***stratified squamous epithelium***, while the nutrient-absorbing tissue of the small intestine is ***simple columnar epithelium***.

Epithelial tissues of all types are generally attached to underlying connective tissue by a ***basement membrane***, a non-living extracellular conglomeration of proteins and carbohydrates that is secreted by the epithelial cells themselves. Apart from the basement membrane, epithelial tissues generally contain little non-cellular material and are usually continuously turned over. An example of this is the epithelium of the skin, whose cells are constantly shed and replaced by new ones.

C. CONNECTIVE TISSUES AND CELLS

Connective tissues have the most varied structures and functions of any of the four tissue types. In general, they support and connect the other three tissue types, and may play a role in fat storage, the immune response, and the transportation of materials throughout the body. The organization of connective tissue differs from that of epithelial tissue in that connective tissue cells are almost always separated from each other and exist surrounded by an extracellular material known as the *matrix*. The matrix, which is secreted by the cells of the connective tissue, consists of *ground material* that may contain embedded *fibers*. Connective tissues are usually categorized according to the nature of the matrix in which the cells exist.

Many specific cell types may be found in different connective tissues:

♦ *Fibroblasts* are probably the most common type of connective tissue cell. As their name suggests, they secrete proteinaceous fibers into the surrounding matrix. Fibroblasts can produce two basic types of fibers, which will largely determine the character of the matrix surrounding them. *Collagenous* or connecting fibers are composed of the protein collagen arranged in long bundles. They are very strong and resist forces applied to them, and thus are abundant in connective tissues such as bone, cartilage, tendons, ligaments, and the lower layers of skin. *Elastic* fibers are largely made up of the protein *elastin*. As their name implies, they are "elastic" (stretchable without being harmed). These fibers can be found in the walls of arteries and the air passages of the respiratory system.

♦ *Mast cells* are also abundant, but are usually located near blood vessels. They secrete substances into the blood, such as *heparin* (which prevents blood clotting) and *histamine* (often responsible for allergic reactions).

♦ *Macrophages* are important connective tissue cells that are able to actively move around the body, and are specialized for the process of *phagocytosis*. Sometimes called scavenger cells, they can engulf and destroy foreign particles, including pathogens, and thus are important defenses against infection. Since they are mobile, they may be found moving between different connective tissue types, often residing temporarily in the lymphatic system and in tissue fluid.

With the abundance of cells and fibers involved, many types of connective tissues are recognized. Each has a particular role to play in the body. We will list and explore the highlights of each major type.

♦ *Loose connective tissue:* Composed mainly of fibroblasts that secrete both collagenous and elastin fibers, the matrix takes on a gel-like consistency. Loose connective tissue is often found below epithelium; it attaches the skin to underlying organs, binds organs together, and fills the spaces between muscles and bones. *Adipose* tissue is a specialized form of loose connective tissue that stores fat; fat provides energy reserves and insulation, and cushions sensitive body parts.

♦ *Dense connective tissue:* Also consisting mainly of fibroblasts, dense connective tissue has fewer cells and a matrix thickly permeated with collagenous fibers. With its great strength, dense connective tissue largely comprises *tendons* (which attach muscles to bones) and *ligaments* (which bind bones to other bones).

♦ *Cartilage:* Cartilage is a very rigid connective tissue. It is composed of cells called *chondrocytes* surrounded by a matrix abundant in collagenous fibers embedded in a gel-like ground substance. Due to its rigidity, cartilage plays a role in supporting many body structures. It can be found in rings as the major supporting structure of the trachea, and in the ears and nose. It associates with many bones, including the vertebrae and the knees.

♦ ***Bone:*** Bone is even more rigid than cartilage, and provides the major structural framework for the entire body. Bone cells, or ***osteocytes***, exist in cavities separated by a matrix rich in collagen. Bone gains most of its amazing strength, however, from the presence of large amounts of mineral salts, mainly calcium phosphate, in the matrix. In addition to providing major structural support for the body as a whole, bones function to anchor muscles and protect vital organs (as with the sternum and cranium). Bones also contain ***marrow*** that produces blood cells.

♦ ***Blood and Lymph:*** Blood and lymph are connective tissues in which the ground material of the matrix is a liquid called ***plasma***. A variety of specialized cells including ***red blood cells (erythrocytes)*** and ***white blood cells (leukocytes)*** circulate through the body in these tissues by way of the blood and lymphatic vessels. These tissues are involved in the transport of substances throughout the body and in defense against infection.

D. MUSCLE TISSUES AND CELLS

Muscle tissue has one major function and is comprised of only one type of cell. Muscle cells are specialized cells that have the ability to contract; thus muscle tissue is exclusively involved with movement of one kind or another. Muscle tissues are grouped into three major types based on the appearance of the tissue and its interaction with the nervous system.

♦ ***Skeletal muscle:*** Skeletal muscles have a striped or ***striated*** appearance and are controlled voluntarily, or consciously. These muscles are almost always connected to bones, directly or via tendons. Skeletal muscles make up between 20 and 40% of the mass of the entire body, and usually exist in antagonistic pairs. All of the muscles under conscious control, and therefore the ones we usually think about, are skeletal muscles. Examples are the biceps and triceps in the upper arm.

♦ ***Cardiac muscle:*** Cardiac muscle tissue is found only in the heart, and has the distinction of being the only muscle tissue in the body that appears striated but is controlled involuntarily. Also called the myocardium, the importance of this type of muscle tissue cannot be overstated; if it fails to function properly for only a few minutes, death can occur. If a portion of the myocardium does not receive a sufficient supply of oxygen, a myocardial infarction, or "heart attack", may result.

♦ ***Smooth muscle:*** Smooth muscle, as its name implies, does not appear striped, but looks uniformly smooth, and is always controlled involuntarily. Due to this fact, we are often unaware of the actions of smooth muscles within our bodies. Smooth muscle surrounds the walls of hollow internal organs, such as those in the digestive and urogenital systems. Rhythmic contractions of smooth muscles provide the driving force for the unidirectional passage of food through the gastrointestinal tract (called ***peristalsis***), and are largely responsible for blood circulation in veins, where the blood pressure originating from the heart has all but dissipated.

E. NERVOUS TISSUES AND CELLS

Nervous tissue is composed mainly of cells called ***neurons,*** which are highly specialized. They sense certain aspects of their surroundings and respond by transmitting electrical impulses. Nervous tissue also contains ***neuroglial*** (or ***glial***) cells that play several roles, including support, insulation, and transport of nutrients to neurons. The functioning of neurons will be explored in detail in the next chapter, but let us now observe that all neurons follow a generalized structural plan. They typically consist of a centralized ***cell body***, which contains the nucleus; several cytoplasmic extensions called ***dendrites***, which receive information from other cells; and an ***axon*** (also called a nerve fiber), a long extension through which impulses travel away from the cell body, bound for another cell (see Figure 13.1). The axons of many neurons are surrounded by specialized neuroglial cells called ***Schwann cells***, each of which wraps itself around a portion of the axon in such a way that little cytoplasm is present, and multiple layers of cell membrane encircle the axon. Schwann cell membranes are largely composed of a protein called myelin, which is a lipoprotein and thus very hydrophobic. These layers of cell membranes form a ***myelin sheath*** around an axon. Narrow gaps occur in the myelin sheath between each Schwann cell and are referred to as ***nodes of Ranvier***. Axons surrounded by a myelin sheath are referred to as myelinated nerve fibers. The sheath functions to electrically insulate the axon and allow impulses to travel at much greater speeds than would be possible in unmyelinated fibers.

A ***nerve*** is simply a collection or bundle of neurons. Nervous tissue is found in the brain and spinal cord, which together make up the central nervous system, and in the peripheral nerves, which originate from the central nervous system and make up the peripheral nervous system. Nervous pathways, in general, go in two directions. ***Sensory*** nerves bring information (a ***stimulus***) from the sensory organs towards the central nervous system. After the brain processes this information, it usually sends signals through ***motor*** nerves to effector organs (muscles and glands) which can bring about an appropriate response. The multiplicity of connections between neurons, muscles, and glands allows the nervous system to coordinate, regulate, monitor, and integrate many body functions, and makes it possible for us to obtain, process, and react to meaningful information about our environment. More details of the physiology of the nervous system can be found in the next chapter.

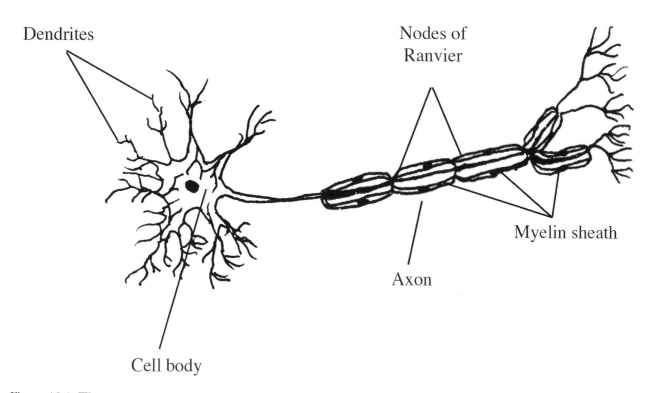

Figure 13.1: The neuron

Chapter 13 Problems

Passage 13.1 (Questions 1-5)

Cancer is a disease in which cells begin to divide when they shouldn't, producing masses of cells called tumors. Cancerous tumors are called "malignant" ones because of their ability to grow aggressively, invade surrounding healthy tissue, and "metastasize", or spread to different locations in the body as tumor cells break off, travel through the blood or lymph, and establish new tumors.

Cancer is generally caused by environmental agents known as "carcinogens", which include chemicals (such as those found in cigarette smoke) and radiation (like the UV rays of sunlight) that mutate cells, causing them to become cancerous.

Tumors that originate from epithelial cells are generally known as carcinomas, and it is estimated that about 90% of all human cancers are carcinomas. Tumors that originate from muscle tissue are called "sarcomas", and tumors can also originate from nervous and connective tissues. Epithelial tissue exists in various locations in the body, including the skin, the mucous membranes lining the lungs and gastrointestinal tract, and the linings surrounding major organs.

1. A person who develops cancer from constantly smoking cigarettes would be most likely to develop
    A. Carcinoma of the skin.
    B. Carcinoma of a mucous membrane.
    C. Sarcoma of the diaphragm.
    D. Carcinoma of the epithelium surrounding the heart.

2. The observation that 90% of human cancers are carcinomas implies that:
    A. Most carcinogens, like UV light, penetrate very deeply into underlying tissues.
    B. Epithelial cells by their very nature are more susceptible to mutation than cells of other tissue types.
    C. Cigarette smoking causes more tumors in humans than does UV light.
    D. Most carcinogens do not penetrate tissues very deeply.

3. A lab worker in Alaska develops a carcinoma of the skin. This particular worker is very dedicated, and almost never leaves the lab. The tumor is most likely the result of:
    A. Excessive cigarette smoking by coworkers.
    B. Excessive ingestion of toxic chemicals.
    C. Exposure to radiation from phosphorus-32, a radioactive isotope the worker routinely uses.
    D. Exposure to ultraviolet rays of sunlight.

4. Which of the following statements is correct?
    A. A tumor located in the liver must be a sarcoma.
    B. A tumor located in a muscle must be a sarcoma.
    C. A tumor composed of epithelial cells must be located in an epithelial tissue.
    D. A tumor in the breast could theoretically consist of cells of any tissue type.

5. Cancer cells can often secrete a substance that has the ability to dissolve basement membranes. This could account for the ability of the cells of a malignant tumor to:
    A. Invade adjacent tissue.
    B. Divide rapidly.
    C. Stop dividing.
    D. Become carcinogenic.

The following questions are NOT based on a descriptive passage.

6. Which of the following tissues is not considered a connective tissue?
    A. Blood
    B. Bone
    C. Lymph
    D. Muscle

7.   A particular muscle is under involuntary control, but appears striated. It is most likely to be:
    A.   The myocardium, the muscular portion of the heart.
    B.   The muscle(s) that surrounds the esophagus and causes peristalsis.
    C.   The biceps, the muscle that moves the forearm.
    D.   The diaphragm, the muscle that allows breathing to occur.

8.   Which of the following tissue types is involved with communication using electrical energy?
    A.   Epithelial
    B.   Connective
    C.   Muscular
    D.   Nervous

9.   The pancreatic cells that manufacture and secrete the hormone insulin are of what tissue type?
    A.   Epithelial
    B.   Connective
    C.   Muscular
    D.   Nervous

10.   Arteries are constantly expanding and contracting due to the force of blood pumped from the heart, the "blood pressure". One would expect the walls of arteries to be composed largely of:
    A.   Cartilage.
    B.   Connective tissue containing mainly collagen fibers.
    C.   Connective tissue containing mainly elastin fibers.
    D.   Muscular tissue.

CHAPTER 14

The Nervous and Endocrine Systems

A. INTRODUCTION

The nervous and endocrine systems are often considered together because they are both involved with communication and send signals from one part of the body to another. Each system sends its messages by different mechanisms, however, and the two systems have correspondingly different, though complementary, structures and functions. The nervous system is designed for very quick communication and uses electrochemical impulses to transmit information through nervous tissue. The endocrine system performs relatively more slowly, and uses chemical *hormones*, which usually circulate in the blood, to convey messages from a point of origin to a group of target cells. Together, the two systems act to coordinate and regulate the activities of the body as a whole, including the major functions of receiving, processing, and reacting to sensory stimuli, as well as the maintenance of homeostasis.

B. PHYSIOLOGY OF THE NERVE IMPULSE

All of the cells in the body have an electric potential difference across their plasma membrane. This means that the inside of each cell is negatively charged with respect to the outside and this difference in voltage, just like a chemical concentration gradient, can be used to do cellular work. The potential difference across a cell membrane (usually about −70 mV) is referred to as the *resting potential*, and exists due to the maintenance of unequal concentrations of positively and negatively charged ions inside and outside of the cell. In addition, a transmembrane protein, the *sodium-potassium pump*, constantly uses active transport to move sodium (Na^+) ions out of the cell and potassium (K^+) ions into the cell, resulting in an electrochemical gradient of sodium and potassium ions across the cell membrane. There is always much more sodium outside of the cell than inside, and potassium is in greater concentration internally. While all cells exist in this state of disequilibrium, it is especially important for the functioning of nervous and muscular tissue cells. The resting potential is maintained due to the impermeability of the cell membrane to any charged atoms or molecules because of its hydrophobic nature (see Chapter 11). Thus, the only way for ions to traverse the membrane is through protein channels which tend to be very specific for a particular type of ion. Since these channels can be open or closed, they are referred to as gated, and we will be most interested in the *gated sodium channels* and *gated potassium channels*.

In a resting neuron (refer to Figure 13.1 for structure), almost all of the gated channels are closed. When a proper *stimulus* is present, the neuron reacts by opening the gated sodium channels in the region being stimulated (usually a dendrite). The result is a sudden influx of positively charged sodium ions, which follow their electrochemical concentration gradient and cause the membrane to become *depolarized*. This is a temporary state during which the polarity of the potential difference is reversed, and the inside of the cell becomes positively charged with respect to the outside. This movement of charges and subsequent depolarization is a form of electrical energy, and causes the gated potassium channels to open. As you would expect, the result is a movement of potassium ions from the inside to the outside of the cell, restoring the resting potential in a process known as *repolarization*. The gated channels of both types then close, and the Na⁺/K⁺ pump restores the concentrations of these ions to their original states. All of these changes taken together are called the ***action potential***, and require only about a thousandth of a second to occur. An important feature of the action potential is its ability to cause similar changes in adjacent regions of the cell; the net result is the unidirectional propagation of a ***nerve impulse*** down the neuron. After the passage of a nerve impulse through any portion of a neuron, there is a brief ***refractory period***, during which the cell is "resetting" itself to be able to receive another stimulus and is unexcitable for a short period of time (about 1/2,500 of a second).

C. SYNAPTIC TRANSMISSION

Signals must travel from one neuron to another, but neurons are separated by a space called the ***synapse,*** or ***synaptic cleft.*** The nerve impulse cannot "jump" across the synapse, so a different mechanism must be used to propagate the signal from the axon of the presynaptic cell to a dendrite of the postsynaptic cell. This is done using ***neurotransmitters***, chemicals that can diffuse across the synapse and stimulate the postsynaptic cells by interacting with specialized receptors located there. Neurotransmitters are synthesized and stored in tiny vesicles near the end of each axon; as the nerve impulse approaches this location, gated channels for calcium (Ca^{2+}) open, allowing calcium ions to diffuse into the cell. This event causes the storage vesicles to fuse with the plasma membrane, and the neurotransmitter molecules are released into the synaptic space. When they couple with their corresponding receptors, an action potential may be triggered in the postsynaptic cell, stimulating a new nerve impulse (see Figure 14.1). After neurotransmitter molecules exert their action, they must be quickly removed as the neuron gets ready to receive another signal. Sometimes they are enzymatically broken down, and in other cases they are reabsorbed by the presynaptic axon to be "recycled" and used again later. To sum up, the propagation of the nerve impulse and subsequent stimulation of adjacent neurons by neurotransmitters explains how electrical signals travel through nerves.

  Acetylcholine is the major neurotransmitter used to stimulate the contraction of skeletal muscles. Others, such as ***serotonin*** and ***dopamine***, function primarily in the brain and are involved with emotional responses and "higher brain functions".

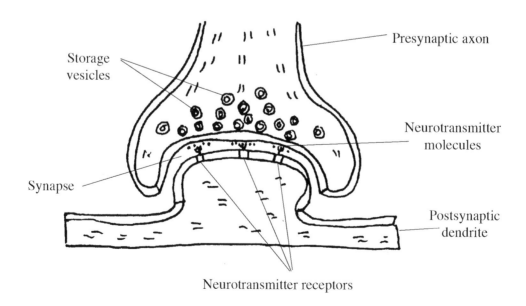

Figure 14.1: Synaptic transmission

D. GENERAL ORGANIZATION OF THE VERTEBRATE NERVOUS SYSTEM

The nervous system is composed almost exclusively of nervous tissue, as you would expect. The system is divided into two major subdivisions:

- ◆ *Central nervous system (CNS)* : consists of the brain and spinal cord.

- ◆ *Peripheral nervous system (PNS)* : consists of all nerves that carry information to and away from the CNS.

Neurons in peripheral nerves can be classified functionally:

- ◆ *sensory neurons* carry signals towards the CNS.
- ◆ *motor neurons* carry signals from the CNS to an effector organ.

Sensory pathways begin with neurons containing specialized ***sensory receptors***, which are able to gather information about both the external and internal environments of the body. This information is sent to the CNS where it is processed and integrated, and a decision is made about an appropriate response. That response is carried out through motor pathways that stimulate an effector, usually a muscle or gland.

As noted previously, a nerve is simply a bundle of neurons held together by connective tissue. If a nerve consists exclusively of sensory neurons, it is referred to as a ***sensory nerve***; likewise, a ***motor nerve*** contains only motor neurons. Many nerves contain both types and are referred to as mixed nerves. Peripheral nerves can also be classified anatomically, depending upon where they are connected to the central nervous system:

- ◆ *spinal nerves* originate from the spinal cord.
- ◆ *cranial nerves* are connected directly to the brain.

Motor pathways in the peripheral nervous system can be further subdivided:

- ◆ *somatic* (voluntary) nerves control the movement of voluntary skeletal muscles.
- ◆ *autonomic* (involuntary) nerves control those functions which occur "automatically", such as the regulation of breathing and heart rate, and the stimulation of glands and smooth muscles.

Furthermore, the autonomic system can be divided again into two subsystems. While the interactions between these two systems (and the endocrine system) are often complex, stimulation usually has the following typical effects:

- ◆ *the parasympathetic* division slows the rate of heartbeat and respiration, as occurs after eating.
- ◆ *the sympathetic* division has the opposite effect, and is often cited for its ability to contribute to the "fight or flight" reaction.

E. STRUCTURE AND FUNCTION OF THE CENTRAL NERVOUS SYSTEM

Both the brain and spinal cord are protected by bones (the skull, or cranium, and the vertebrae, respectively) and membranes called *meninges*. Cerebrospinal fluid exists between layers of the meninges for further cushioning. The spinal cord functions as an intermediary between the brain and the spinal nerves, allowing bi-directional communication along its length. Neurons that exist solely within the spinal cord or brain are referred to as *interneurons*, and can be involved in many functions. The brain is the most important and complex organ of the nervous system, and while we are far from a complete understanding of the way it works, we can list its most important component parts and assign to each particular functions (see Figure 14.2).

◆ *brainstem:* The brainstem connects directly with the spinal cord. It is remarkably similar in all vertebrates, and regulates essential functions such as heart rate and respiration. Often the brainstem is referred to as the medulla oblongata, although technically the *medulla oblongata* is only one part of the brainstem.

◆ *cerebellum:* Located near the base of the brain and dorsal to the brainstem, the cerebellum is responsible for the complex coordination of muscular movements and the maintenance of balance. It is especially large and important in birds, as it plays a crucial role in the coordination of flight.

◆ *diencephalon:* Located just above and ventral to the brainstem, the diencephalon consists of several parts and is associated with various functions. The *thalamus* is involved with the selective sorting and relaying of sensory information to the cerebral cortex. The *hypothalamus* is important in the maintenance of homeostasis, specifically regulating body temperature, water/solute balance, and sensations of hunger and thirst, among other parameters. It is able to produce hormones to aid in its functioning, and therefore is sometimes referred to as a gland. Both the hypothalamus and the thalamus, in association with certain portions of the cerebrum, also comprise what is known as the *limbic system*. The limbic system seems to be associated with the generation of emotions and the control of certain basic behavioral responses. For example, by responding to thoughts or circumstances with a feeling of anger, aggressive behavior might be initiated. Emotions are thought to have evolved precisely for this purpose; for example, fear signals danger, and an organism may have a better chance of survival if it flees a threatening situation. The limbic system also plays a major role in sexual stimulation and behavior, clearly another important function if a species is to remain in existence.

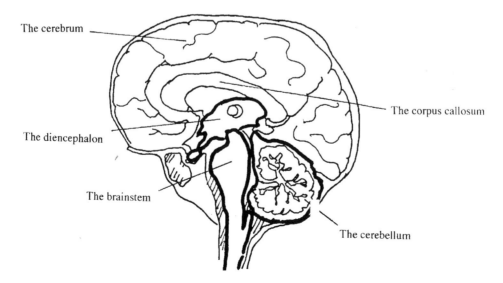

Figure 14.2: The brain

◆ *cerebrum:* The cerebrum is comprised of two **hemispheres** connected by a structure called the **corpus callosum**. The **cerebral cortex** is a relatively thin layer of tissue that forms the outer surface of the cerebrum. In general, the cerebrum is responsible for the most complex nervous functions in an organism. In all vertebrates, this includes the integration of the sensory reception, processing, and motor response functions which we have already mentioned. The cerebral cortex is the most variable portion of the brain in different vertebrates. Fishes and amphibians have no cerebral cortex whatsoever, and even birds and reptiles possess only a rudimentary one. In lower mammals it is more apparent, culminating with the large and folded structure characteristic of primates and humans. The cortex is responsible for all of the so-called "higher brain functions" of humans, including the processes of thought and reasoning and the capacity for complex memory storage, learning, and language.

F. SENSORY PERCEPTION

Since there are potentially many forms in which information can be gathered, several distinct types of receptors have evolved, each specialized to react to a particular stimulus in the environment. Five major types of receptors are recognized in humans.

◆ *chemoreceptors:* Chemoreceptors are sensitive to the quality and concentrations of chemical substances, and are the major receptors for the senses of taste and smell.

◆ *photoreceptors:* Sensitive to the quality and intensity of light, photoreceptors are responsible for our sense of vision.

◆ *mechanoreceptors:* Mechanoreceptors are sensitive to physical pressure, and are involved with several human senses, including hearing, touch, and our ability to determine the relative positions of different parts of our body (**kinesthesis**).

◆ *thermoreceptors:* Sensitive to changes in temperature, these are involved in our sense of touch.

◆ *pain receptors:* These receptors are sensitive to tissue damage, and are also involved in our sense of touch.

Other organisms, for example sharks, have electroreceptors that enable them to sense and react to an electric field. Still other organisms possess magnetoreceptors, which allow them to be aware of the earth's magnetic field. Humans apparently evolved without the need for these other sensory abilities.

In humans, senses can be subdivided into two categories. The **somatic senses** receive information from receptors located on the skin (the sense of touch), as well as from receptors in muscles, joints, and various other internal locations (called **proprioception**). The **special senses** are those whose receptors are collected into large, complex sensory organs located in the head, and include taste, smell, hearing, equilibrium, and vision (sight). We will now list these senses, describing the types of receptors and the major structures and functions involved.

◆ *touch:* The sense of touch is actually mediated through a complex association of different types of receptors located on the skin. A combination of mechanoreceptors, thermoreceptors, and pain receptors collects information that we perceive as a single sensation containing all three types of information.

◆ *proprioception:* While not traditionally classified as a human sense, most of us realize that we obtain sensations giving us information about the interior of our bodies. For example, we can tell if many of our muscles are contracted or relaxed (including the perception of our own heartbeat and breathing), and we can certainly feel internal pain! As with touch, different types of receptors at various internal locations are responsible for this "sense".

♦ *smell (olfaction):* The sense of smell is the product of specialized chemoreceptors, sometimes referred to as olfactory receptors, located in the nasal cavity. It is estimated that these sensitive receptors allow sensations of approximately 10,000 different aromas. Along with the sense of taste, it is thought that the olfactory sense evolved mainly to aid in food selection. Some other vertebrates, for example the bloodhound, have an extremely well developed and powerful sense of smell, approximately 40 times more sensitive than a human's.

♦ *taste:* The sense of taste, like that of smell, is made possible by the presence of specialized chemoreceptors; in the case of taste, however, these receptors are located on so-called taste buds on the tongue. Taste receptors are far less sensitive than olfactory receptors, as there are only five fundamental taste sensations that can be perceived: sweet, sour, salty, savory, and bitter. Various taste sensations result from different combinations of the four basic ones. The overall sensation produced by the consumption of food has a strong olfactory component. You can prove this by eating while holding your nose; whatever you are ingesting suddenly becomes rather "tasteless"!

♦ *hearing:* The sense of hearing is made possible by the existence of the *ear,* a complex organ comprised of an external, middle, and inner section (see Figure 14.3). The stimulus for the sensation of hearing is the physical vibration of the molecules of the medium contacting the ear, usually air, in the form of sound waves. The external ear collects and transmits sound waves from the environment to the ear's interior. The middle ear consists of the *tympanic membrane* (eardrum), which protects the interior of the ear and transmits vibrations of the air to the three ear bones, or *ossicles,* also located in this region. The names of the three ossicles are the *hammer*, the *anvil*, and the *stirrup* (or more technically the *malleus, the incus,* and the *stapes*). The vibrations are transmitted to a structure in the inner ear called the *cochlea* via the ossicles. The cochlea is a fluid-filled compartment that contains the *organ of Corti*, a patch of tissue with many specialized mechanoreceptors. These hearing receptors are stimulated when the cochlear fluid vibrates, sending information to the brain via the *auditory nerves*. The human ear can distinguish frequencies in the range of 20 to 20,000 cycles/second. Other vertebrates can hear higher- or lower-pitched sounds.

♦ *equilibrium:* The sense of equilibrium is again not traditionally looked upon as a human sense, but we should recognize it as one. This sense provides information regarding the movement and orientation of the head in space. As with hearing, specialized mechanoreceptors located in the ear are responsible for the sensations, but the fluid that stimulates these receptors is located in the *semicircular canals* of the inner ear. Like proprioception, equilibrium may be a sense we take for granted!

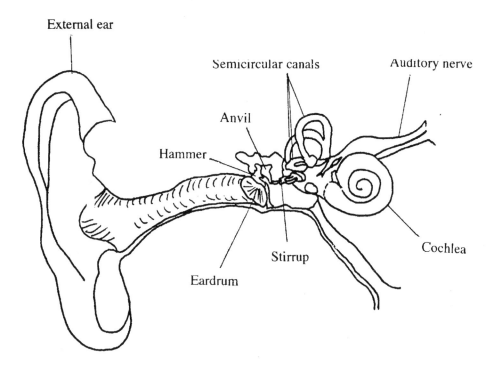

Figure 14.3: The ear

◆ *vision (sight)*: The organ of vision is the **eye**, a complex structure with many component parts that functions in a very similar way to a conventional camera (see Figure 14.4). Light enters the eye through the transparent, protective **cornea**, and then through the **lens**, which focuses the light into an inverted image on the **retina**, located at the back of the eyeball. The amount of light entering the eye is controlled by the **iris** (the colored portion of the eye), a muscular structure that changes the size of the **pupil**, the opening in the iris. The retina contains the photoreceptors, which are classified into two categories based on their shape and function. **Rods**, responsible for "night vision", contain the pigment **rhodopsin**, and are more light-sensitive than the **cones**, which are responsible for color vision. Dim light does not stimulate the cones, but it does affect the rods; that is why we can distinguish shapes but not colors in dim light. Stimulated photoreceptors send information to the brain via the **optic nerves**. Most nocturnal vertebrates have retinas that contain rods only, in large quantities, so that while they can see well at night, they lack color vision almost entirely.

This survey of our senses reveals that instead of the traditional five, humans have at least seven different senses and possibly more (depending upon how they are classified).

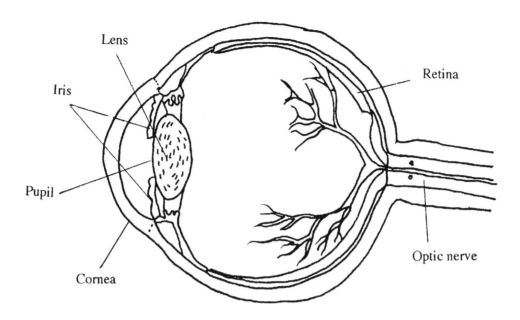

Figure 14.4: The eye

G. THE ENDOCRINE SYSTEM

As we noted at the beginning of the chapter, the endocrine system is related to the nervous system and the two act in concert. The endocrine system sends messages from one part of the body to another using chemical *hormones*. These hormones are manufactured and secreted by *endocrine glands* into the bloodstream, through which they travel and ultimately have certain effects on specific target cells, tissues, or organs.

As we noted in the last chapter, glands are composed of specialized epithelial tissue, and usually function in the production of one or more particular hormones. Hormones themselves can be divided into two classes based upon their chemical nature and corresponding mechanism of action:

- *steroid hormones* are lipids, usually synthesized from cholesterol, that consist of complex ring structures.
- *nonsteroid hormones* include amines, short peptides, and protein hormones; these are related in that they are constructed from amino acids, either by their modification or polymerization.

Hormones are able to act selectively on certain target cells due to the presence or absence of specific protein *receptors*, which exist either inside or on the surface of the target cell. If a cell contains a receptor for a particular hormone, it will respond to the message; if it lacks that receptor, it will be unaffected by the hormone's presence. While both classes of hormones function in a fundamentally similar fashion, steroid hormones have a different mechanism of action than nonsteroid hormones due to the chemical differences that exist between the groups. Since steroid hormones are relatively small lipids, they are soluble in the plasma membrane and can pass relatively easily into all of the body's cells. They will exert their action, however, only when they enter cells that contain the appropriate *intracellular* receptor, with which they then bind. The hormone-receptor complex thus formed is now able to act directly on the DNA in the nucleus, altering gene expression to cause the production of different cellular products (usually enzymes or other proteins). The result is some change in the properties, characteristics, or abilities of the cell. Nonsteroid hormones, in general, cannot diffuse across the plasma membrane and therefore must interact with *membrane* receptors. Receptors of this type are usually transmembrane proteins that contain a hormone-binding domain outside of the cell and another domain inside of the cell that changes its shape when the hormone is bound. It subsequently causes other changes in the cell, usually by activating enzymes through a chemical intermediary. Since the hormone is not causing the changes directly, the intermediary is often referred to as a **second messenger** (the hormone being the "first messenger"). While many such **signal transduction** pathways exist, a common one involves **cyclic AMP (cAMP)** as the second messenger.

H. MAJOR ENDOCRINE GLANDS AND HORMONES

Now that we understand the basic ideas about what hormones are and how they work, we can list the major endocrine glands, the hormones they produce, and the effects they can cause in the body.

♦ *pituitary gland and hypothalamus:* The pituitary gland is located just below the hypothalamus, at the base of the brain. The hypothalamus-pituitary complex is a major point of interface and coordination between the endocrine and nervous systems. As noted before, the hypothalamus, in addition to functioning in the central nervous system, produces many hormones. Most of these are hormones that control the secretions of the anterior and posterior pituitary gland. Two hormones produced by the hypothalamus are stored and ultimately released by the posterior pituitary.

• *antidiuretic hormone (ADH)*, sometimes referred to as *vasopressin*, regulates the ability of the kidneys to reabsorb water, and plays a major role in the body's overall water balance.

• *oxytocin* functions mainly in females to stimulate the release of milk from mammary glands after childbirth.

Six major hormones are generated and secreted by the anterior lobe of the pituitary.

• *growth hormone (GH)*, sometimes called s*omatotropin*, stimulates cells to grow in size and number by causing certain metabolic changes.

• *prolactin (PRL)* causes changes mainly in females, promoting the growth of breast tissue and the secretion of milk after childbirth.

The other four hormones produced by the pituitary gland function in regulating the action of other endocrine glands, and are therefore often called tropic hormones.

• *thyroid-stimulating hormone (TSH)* stimulates the thyroid gland.

• *adrenocorticotropic hormone (ACTH)* controls the production of the hormones of the adrenal cortex.

• *follicle-stimulating hormone (FSH)* and *luteinizing hormone (LH)* influence the regulation and hormone production of the primary reproductive organs in both males and females.

♦ *thyroid gland: Thyroxine (T4)* is the major hormone secreted by the thyroid gland, located in the neck. T4 consists of an amino acid complexed with the mineral iodine, and acts to increase the rate of metabolism (respiration) of all body cells. The thyroid gland also produces *triiodothyronine (T3)*, which functions similarly to T4, and *calcitonin*, which regulates the blood levels of the minerals calcium and phosphorus, which are important for healthy bone formation.

♦ *parathyroid glands:* Located on the surface of the thyroid gland, these tiny structures produce only one hormone, *parathyroid hormone (PTH)*, which is sometimes referred to as *parathormone*. PTH functions in conjunction with calcitonin and vitamin D to precisely regulate the levels of calcium, and less importantly phosphorus, in the blood and various body regions. Since calcium is involved in a wide variety of vital functions (nerve and muscle transmission, bone formation, and blood clotting), its regulation is clearly important for the normal functioning of the body.

♦ *adrenal glands:* The adrenal glands are located on the surface of the kidneys, and are subdivided into two parts, the adrenal *cortex* and the adrenal *medulla*, which are actually distinct glands that secrete different hormones. The adrenal cortex produces two major hormones, *aldosterone* and *cortisol*, both steroids. Aldosterone plays a major role in the regulation of sodium and potassium levels, vital in nerve transmission, via the action of the kidneys. Cortisol raises the level of glucose in the blood by stimulating gluconeogenic pathways (especially the production of glucose from proteins and fats) during periods of stress, and apparently plays an additional role in the regulation of the inflammatory and immune responses. The adrenal medulla secretes two hormones, *epinephrine* (often called *adrenaline*) and *norepinephrine (noradrenaline)*. These hormones are released in conjunction with sympathetic nervous stimulation, and play a role in increasing heart and respiration rates, while additionally raising the blood glucose level, in preparation for potential intense activity.

♦ *pancreas:* The pancreas is the largest gland in the body. In the vicinity of the stomach and attached to the small intestine by connective tissue, it has exocrine as well as endocrine functions. Its exocrine function consists of its ability to produce the major digestive enzymes and release them, through the pancreatic duct, into the duodenum of the small intestine. The endocrine portion of the gland, which is comprised of cell clusters called *islets of Langerhans*, produces and secretes two major hormones, *insulin* and *glucagon*. Both are intimately involved with the maintenance of a relatively constant level of glucose in the blood. Insulin lowers blood glucose concentrations by allowing cells to take up and utilize glucose for fuel, while glucagon has the opposite effect. It reacts to low blood sugar levels by promoting the breakdown of glycogen in the liver and its release as glucose into the blood. Disorders involving these hormones include *diabetes* and *hypoglycemia*.

♦ *ovaries and testes*: These are the primary reproductive organs in females and males, respectively, and in addition to their gamete-producing activities, they also secrete steroid hormones. In females, the ovaries secrete *estrogen* and *progesterone*, which control sexual development, the menstrual cycle, and certain aspects of pregnancy. In males, the testes produce *testosterone*, which stimulates sperm production, controls sexual development, and is responsible for the male secondary sexual characteristics (growth of facial hair, etc.).

♦ *other endocrine activity:* The *pineal gland* secretes *melatonin*, which may play a role in the normal sleep cycle as well as helping to regulate the female reproductive cycle. The *thymus gland* secretes *thymosin*, which helps lymphocytes to mature. Digestive organs, the kidneys, and the heart are all capable of secreting hormones with varying effects.

Chapter 14 Problems

Passage 14.1 (Questions 1-5)

Both the nervous and endocrine systems are involved with communication among body parts, but they exert their actions by different methods. The nervous system uses electrochemical impulses to convey messages through nervous tissue at high speeds, while the endocrine system uses chemical hormones that are released into the blood and directly interact with their target cells. There is some evidence that the nervous and endocrine systems are evolutionarily related.

Hormones can be of two major types chemically: protein (including amines and peptides) or steroid. Each type of hormone normally exerts its effects differently. Protein hormones, such as insulin, epinephrine, ADH, and gonadotropin-releasing hormone (GnRH) interact with a membrane-bound extracellular receptor on their target cells, which causes changes inside of the cell. This usually leads to the activation or inhibition of enzymes through a second-messenger system utilizing cyclic AMP (cAMP) as the second messenger. Steroid hormones such as testosterone, estrogen, and cortisol can diffuse through cell membranes, and usually act by affecting gene expression, but only after interacting with an intracellular receptor.

McCune-Albright syndrome is a genetic disease in which cAMP is synthesized in large quantities even when a signaling hormone is not present; it results in the over-secretion of many hormones, and increased effects of many hormones on their target cells.

1. Target cells of someone who suffers from McCune-Albright syndrome are likely to overreact to the presence of a hormone or respond to a hormone message even when the hormone is not present. Which of the following hormones would not cause overreaction or false message reception in an affected individual?
   A. Insulin
   B. ADH
   C. Testosterone
   D. Adrenaline

2. Some evidence that the nervous and endocrine systems are evolutionarily related comes from the fact that certain molecules function similarly to hormones during transmission of nerve impulses. Which of the following types of molecules fits this description?
   A. The sodium-potassium pump
   B. Gated potassium channels
   C. Neurotransmitters
   D. Neurotransmitter receptors

3. The major connection between the nervous and endocrine systems that allows them to coordinate their activities is represented by:
   A. The cerebral cortex directly stimulating the thyroid gland.
   B. The brainstem controlling heart and breathing rate, which is also controlled by adrenaline.
   C. The ability of the cerebellum to coordinate the actions of several endocrine glands.
   D. The intimate connection between the hypothalamus and pituitary gland.

4. Testosterone is a steroid hormone; its release from the testes in males is controlled by gonadotropin-releasing hormone (GnRH). Which of the following statements is true?
   A. Both of these hormones affect target cells using a second messenger system.
   B. An individual with McCune-Albright syndrome is likely to over-produce testosterone.
   C. An individual with McCune-Albright syndrome is likely to under-produce testosterone.
   D. An individual with McCune-Albright syndrome would produce normal amounts of testosterone, but the target cells responding to testosterone would overreact to the message.

5. Stanozolol is a synthetic steroid that resembles testosterone in its chemistry and action. It is often the drug athletes are ingesting when they are said to be on "steroids". Which of the following statements is true of Stanozolol?

    A. It is likely to exert its effects by binding to an external receptor and triggering a second messenger system.

    B. It is likely to be found in all cells of the body after being ingested.

    C. It will likely only be found in muscle cells after being ingested.

    D. It would affect an individual with McCune-Albright syndrome more drastically than a normal individual.

The following questions are NOT based on a descriptive passage.

6. Often drinking excessive quantities of beer can lead to dehydration later. This can be explained because alcohol inhibits the hormone:

    A. ADH.

    B. Adrenaline.

    C. Norepinephrine.

    D. Glucagon.

7. An action potential is initially triggered by an influx of which of the following that causes depolarization of the membrane?

    A. Potassium

    B. Sodium

    C. Calcium

    D. Neurotransmitter

8. The brainstem is most likely involved in what type of activities?

    A. Coordination of intricate body movements

    B. Thought and memory

    C. Control of breathing and heart rate

    D. Control of emotions and sexual impulses

9. Which of the following statements is true regarding the sense of hearing?

    A. Sound waves cause vibrations of ossicles, which are transmitted to chemoreceptors in the cochlea.

    B. The type of receptors responsible for sensing vibrations that allow hearing are mechanoreceptors.

    C. Since hearing is normally caused by the vibration of air molecules creating sound waves, one could not hear underwater.

    D. The stimulus for hearing is chemical in nature.

10. Some people who have a deficiency of vitamin A exhibit symptoms of night blindness. This condition allows normal sight during the day (in bright light) but virtual blindness when it becomes dark, when people without the condition could at least makes out shapes and outlines. It is likely that this deficiency is causing its effects by:

    A. blocking the passage of information down the optic nerve to the brain.

    B. interfering with the functioning of the cones.

    C. interfering with the functioning of the rods.

    D. interfering with the functioning of all photoreceptors.

CHAPTER 15

The Cardiovascular System and the Immune Response

A. INTRODUCTION

The cardiovascular and lymphatic systems are related in that they both play a role in the movement of substances throughout the body. This transportation system is often referred to as **circulation** (sometimes the term circulatory system is used synonymously with cardiovascular system). The two systems are physically linked, but play different roles in the overall functioning of the body. The major job of the cardiovascular system is to transport nutrients and oxygen from the respiratory and digestive systems to all the cells of the body, and to deliver cellular wastes such as carbon dioxide and urea to their respective points of elimination. Hormones and other important molecules are also transported in the blood. This system functions in the maintenance of homeostasis by helping to stabilize the temperature, pH, and osmotic balance of the body, as well as playing a part in the complex system of defense against disease. The major roles of the lymphatic system include the drainage and return to the cardiovascular system of excess tissue fluid and the absorption of fat from the digestive system. In addition, the immune response, the body's major defense system against specific disease-causing agents, occurs largely in the lymphatic system.

B. GENERAL ORGANIZATION OF THE CARDIOVASCULAR SYSTEM

The cardiovascular system can be thought of as comprised of three major components: **blood**, the fluid connective tissue in which the many substances to be transported are dissolved; blood **vessels**, through which the blood circulates; and a muscular **heart**, which is the pump that provides the driving force for the movement of blood through the vessels. Let us consider each of these "parts" in more detail.

C. THE BLOOD

As noted previously, blood is considered a connective tissue, and like all connective tissues is composed of cells separated by an intercellular matrix, referred to as **plasma**. All blood cells are manufactured in the **bone marrow** from unspecialized **stem cells**, and ultimately differentiate into a variety of cells with different functions and characteristics.

 ◆ **red blood cells (erythrocytes):** Erythrocytes, specialized for the transport of oxygen, are the most plentiful type of blood cell, gaining their red color from large quantities of the protein **hemoglobin**. Hemoglobin contains iron, and binds reversibly to oxygen. Red blood cells are unique among body cells in that they lack a nucleus, which limits their lifetime to a few months. This means that they, like other blood cells, must constantly be produced by the bone marrow. Erythrocytes are also characterized by their unique shape, which resembles a biconcave disk.

- ◆ ***white blood cells (leukocytes):*** White blood cells are involved with some aspect of the body's defense system. There are many types of leukocytes, which can be divided into two major groups based upon their general morphology.
  - • ***granulocytes*** have granular cytoplasm, and include the ***neutrophils, eosinophils,*** and ***basophils.***
  - • ***agranulocytes*** (which lack cytoplasmic granules) are of two major types, ***monocytes*** and ***lymphocytes.***

  Neutrophils, monocytes, and ***macrophages*** (large cells that develop from monocytes) are involved in the process of ***phagocytosis*** (the ingestion and subsequent digestion of foreign agents that enter the body). Eosinophils help to control ***inflammation*** (discussed later), while basophils release heparin (which inhibits blood clotting) and histamine (which is involved in allergic reactions). Lymphocytes are involved in ***specific immunity***, which will be discussed later.

- ◆ ***platelets (thrombocytes):*** Platelets are not truly cells, but fragments of giant cells which break apart and enter the circulation. They play an essential role in blood clotting and repairing breaks in blood vessels. Blood clotting is a complex process requiring a cascade of reactions involving at least fifteen different plasma proteins. When a blood vessel break is detected, the end result is the activation of one of these proteins into fibrin, an insoluble protein which clumps and binds together platelets, forming a clot that covers the wound.

- ◆ ***plasma:*** Plasma is the liquid matrix of the blood, in which all the other components are either suspended or dissolved. Plasma is largely made up of water, with many solutes dissolved in it. The dissolved substances include nutrients (amino acids, monosaccharides, and small lipids); gases (oxygen, carbon dioxide, and nitrogen); wastes (urea, uric acid, ketones, etc.); and a wide variety of simple ions, or electrolytes, which influence the pH and osmotic pressure of the blood and tissue fluids. Also found dissolved in the plasma are a variety of proteins, called plasma proteins, which are involved in several processes including clotting, immune reactions, and the maintenance of osmotic balance.

D. BLOOD TYPES AND TRANSFUSION COMPATIBILITIES

The membranes of red blood cells contain certain markers, or ***antigens***, which may be of different types. Furthermore, there are several major antigenic groups. The most important of these is the so-called ***ABO antigen group***, which is based on the presence or absence of two major antigens, referred to as A and B. Any particular red blood cell can contain only one of four possible combinations of antigens from this group: A only, B only, A and B, or neither. A person whose erythrocytes contain only antigen A has type A blood; likewise, if only antigen B is present, an individual's blood type is B. If both A and B antigens are present, a person is said to have type AB blood, while type O refers to the absence of both antigens. Another blood group is referred to as the ***Rh group***. Individuals whose red blood cells express the Rh factor (antigen) are Rh^+, while those who lack it are Rh^-. This is what is meant when a person's blood type is expressed, for example, as O positive: their red blood cells do not contain antigens A or B (from the ABO group), but do contain the Rh antigen.

E. THE BLOOD VESSELS

The blood vessels are the tubes through which blood passes as it moves from one part of the body to another. They represent a closed system that allows substances to travel to or from any body cell, with the heart as the central pumping organ that allows circulation to occur. Blood vessels are of three major types.

♦ *arteries:* Arteries are major vessels that carry blood away from the heart. Arterioles are smaller branches of arteries that ultimately lead to **capillaries** or **capillary beds.** Since the blood in arteries and arterioles has recently been pumped into them by the heart, it is under considerable pressure, and the walls of arteries are thickened to withstand this blood pressure. They consist of a layer of specialized epithelium called **endothelium**, and are reinforced by smooth muscle and connective tissue rich in elastin.

♦ *capillaries:* Capillaries are the smallest and most permeable of the blood vessels, and it is here that the major function of the cardiovascular system is carried out. Composed of a layer of endothelium only one cell thick, the walls of capillaries allow the diffusion of materials between the blood and the tissue fluid surrounding body cells. This includes the diffusion of nutrients and oxygen into cells and the diffusion of carbon dioxide and other waste molecules out of cells. In addition, plasma fluid is forced through capillary walls due to the pressure of the blood. Most of this fluid is reabsorbed by the venules which are connected to the other end of the capillaries, but some fluid remains in the intercellular spaces. This fluid is normally returned to the cardiovascular system via the lymphatic system.

♦ *veins:* After blood passes through an artery, arteriole, and capillary, the exchange of substances between blood and tissue is complete. The blood must now be returned to the heart, and this is accomplished by its passage through venules (small veins connected to capillaries) and veins. Veins are major vessels that carry blood towards the heart. By this point, most of the initial blood pressure created by the heart has dissipated, so blood flow through veins occurs by contraction of muscles surrounding veins. Valves ensure a unidirectional flow of blood through the veins towards the heart.

F. STRUCTURE AND FUNCTION OF THE HEART, AND THE PATH OF CIRCULATION

The human heart consists of four chambers: the right and left **atria** (located in the upper region), which receive blood from veins, and the right and left **ventricles** (located in the lower region), which are the major pumping portions of the heart and propel blood into arteries (see Figure 15.1). The wall of the heart is largely composed of cardiac muscle, often called the **myocardium**, and the two sides are separated by a thick structure called the **septum**. The entire heart is surrounded by a fluid-filled sac, the **pericardium**, which serves a protective role.

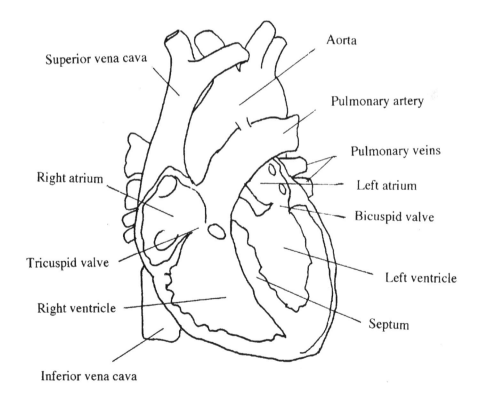

Figure 15.1: Structure of the heart

If we were to follow the path blood takes as it travels throughout the body, we would find that it always flows in one

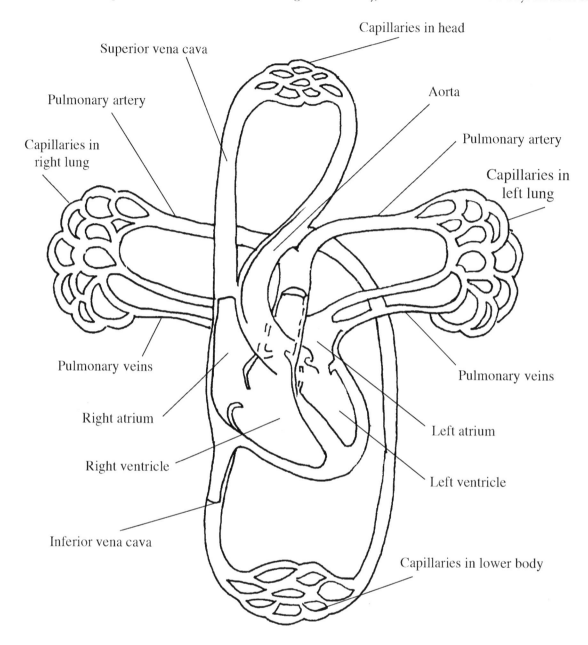

Figure 15.2: Path of circulation

direction, and that we can trace the major vessels through which it flows and their connections with the heart (see Figure 15.2). Arbitrarily starting in the left ventricle, the most powerful pumping region of the heart, oxygen-rich blood is forced into the **aorta**, the largest artery in the body, under considerable pressure. The aorta quickly divides and subdivides, ultimately supplying oxygenated blood to all of the body's tissues via capillaries. As the deoxygenated blood returns towards the heart, venules ultimately merge into two major veins, the superior and inferior **vena cava**, which enter the heart's right atrium. Blood passes into the right ventricle through the **tricuspid** valve, and is pumped out again into the **pulmonary artery**. Notice that the blood present in the pulmonary artery is oxygen-poor, not oxygen-rich as it is in most other arteries. The pulmonary artery branches into two smaller arteries, one leading to each lung, and ultimately terminates in capillary beds surrounding the **alveoli**, or air sacs, of the lungs. It is here that oxygen enters the blood from the lungs, and carbon dioxide leaves, both by the process of diffusion. Venules leading from these capillaries ultimately join to form the ***pulmonary vein***, which deposits oxygenated blood into the left atrium of the heart. Blood then enters the left ventricle through the ***bicuspid*** valve, and the cycle is ready to begin again.

In essence, as we can see from this analysis, the heart actually consists of two separate pumping systems: one which pumps blood from the heart to the tissues and back, referred to as the ***systemic*** circuit; and another, which pumps blood from the heart to the lungs and back, called the ***pulmonary*** circuit. In addition, the cells of the myocardium itself must be supplied with oxygen and nutrients if they are to continue functioning effectively. A small vessel, the ***coronary*** artery, branches off the aorta and supplies the myocardium; ***cardiac*** veins return this blood to the right atrium. If the coronary artery or its branches become blocked, the myocardium may be deprived of oxygen, potentially resulting in a ***myocardial infarction***, or "heart attack".

While the hearts of all mammals and birds are structurally similar, lower vertebrates have different, less efficient heart arrangements. Amphibians, for example, have a three-chambered heart with only one ventricle, but blood destined for the systemic and pulmonary circulation remains relatively unmixed due to ridges in the ventricular wall. In addition, many amphibians respire directly through their moist skin (in addition to their lungs), lessening the need for strict separation. Fish, by contrast, have the most primitive hearts of all, usually consisting of only two chambers, a single atrium and a single ventricle. The ventricle pumps deoxygenated blood directly to the gills, where gas exchange occurs, and then on to the tissues of the body directly. The blood pressure eventually dissipates, and circulation in general is rather sluggish in fish.

G. THE CARDIAC CYCLE AND BLOOD PRESSURE

One complete heartbeat involves the complex coordination of the actions of all four chambers of the heart, during which both of the atria contract simultaneously (while the ventricles are relaxing), followed by the contraction of both ventricles (while the atria are relaxed). These events are called the ***cardiac cycle***, and can be traced electrically using an ***electrocardiogram*** (ECG). The heart is able to "excite itself", i. e., no external nervous stimulus is necessary to initiate the depolarization of the myocardium. Instead, a specialized region of the heart called the ***sinoatrial (SA) node*** initiates impulses at a rate of 70-80 times/minute in an adult. Since it is responsible for the generation of the heartbeat, the SA node, located in the right atrium, is often referred to as the ***pacemaker***. The depolarization spreads across the muscle cells of the atria, causing them to contract, and another critical region, the ***atrioventricular (AV) node***, is stimulated. The AV node is the only electrical connection between the ventricles and the atria; by the time it transmits the "message" to the cells of the ventricles signaling them to contract, the atria have relaxed. An ECG tracing of the cardiac cycle graphically displays these events in detail (see Figure 15.3).

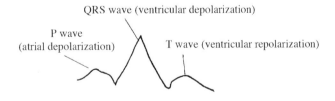

Figure 15.3: An electrocardiogram (ECG)
tracing of a single heartbeat

Although stimulation from the nervous system is not necessary to initiate the heartbeat, it is important in the regulation of the heart rate. This rate must change, for example, during physical exertion. The **cardiac center** of the brain is located in the medulla oblongata of the brainstem; it is able to analyze the levels of carbon dioxide and oxygen in the blood indirectly by sensing blood pH. The heart rate can subsequently be affected through parasympathetic stimulation (decreasing the rate) or sympathetic stimulation (increasing the rate) of the S-A node by motor nerves as is appropriate. (Similar mechanisms usually cause an accompanying change in the rate of respiration.) Additionally, certain hormones have an effect on the heart rate, most notably epinephrine, which causes the rate to increase in response to stressful situations.

As noted earlier, the contraction of the left ventricle forces blood into the aorta, and is responsible for the pressure of blood against the walls of the arteries. This force is what we usually refer to as **blood pressure**, although the pressure of blood can be measured anywhere in the circulatory system. Traditionally, the blood pressure is measured at an artery in the arm by a device that expresses the pressure in terms of its ability to raise a column of mercury (in units of mm Hg). Blood pressure is usually expressed as two numbers: one represents the **systolic** pressure, the highest pressure which occurs as the ventricles contract, with the other representing the **diastolic** pressure, the lowest pressure occurring as the ventricles relax. Normal blood pressure is considered to be 120/80 in an adult male, although many factors can influence an individual's blood pressure at a given time. Chronic high blood pressure, or **hypertension**, can be a significant health threat as it puts undue stress on the cardiovascular system.

H. GENERAL STRUCTURE AND FUNCTION OF THE LYMPHATIC SYSTEM

As noted earlier, the lymphatic system is intimately connected with the cardiovascular system. Its major functions include the drainage and return of tissue fluid to the cardiovascular system and the protection of the body against infection.

As discussed previously, plasma fluid is forced into intercellular spaces near the capillaries by the pressure of blood, and not all of it is reabsorbed into the exiting venule. Lymphatic capillaries, which originate all over the body in tissues, collect this fluid, which is now referred to as **lymph**. (**Lacteals** are specialized lymphatic capillaries that begin in the microvilli of the small intestine and are the primary site of lipid absorption.) The lymph is transported via lymphatic vessels and ducts, which ultimately empty their contents back into the cardiovascular system at the **subclavian veins**, which drain the arms. As with venous circulation, lymph is not under high pressure, and must rely on smooth and skeletal muscular contractions, along with a system of valves, to ensure proper unidirectional flow. In addition to the lymphatic vessels, several lymphatic organs exist that play roles in specific lymphatic functions. The three most important of these are:

- ◆ **lymph nodes:** Located at various positions in the lymphatic system, lymph nodes are masses of tissue through which lymph flows and is cleansed in the process. Two major types of white blood cells collect and function in the nodes: **macrophages**, which ingest foreign particles through phagocytosis, and lymphocytes, which are responsible for the immune response (covered in more detail shortly). Thus the lymph nodes act as filters that remove pathogens and foreign particles before they return to the general circulation.
- ◆ **thymus gland:** Located in the lower neck, the thymus stores certain lymphocytes that were produced in the bone marrow. The thymus produces the hormone **thymosin**, which helps to differentiate these lymphocytes into functional **T lymphocytes** or **T cells**. These T cells then migrate into the lymph nodes and play a role in immunity.
- ◆ **spleen:** Located in the abdominal cavity, the spleen structurally and functionally resembles a giant lymph node. Unlike the nodes, however, it also contains blood. Loaded with macrophages and lymphocytes, the spleen is active in destroying foreign invaders as well as damaged or nonfunctional red blood cells.

I. PROTECTION FROM INFECTION: NON-SPECIFIC DEFENSES

The body is in constant contact with pathogens, microorganisms that can cause disease. These are mainly bacteria and viruses, although some pathogens are protozoa, fungi, or even worms. In any event, the body possesses two major lines of defense to protect itself, the **non-specific** and **specific** defenses. The non-specific defenses protect the body from pathogens in general, while the specific defenses, often called the **immune response**, target and destroy one particular type of pathogen that may be infecting the body at any given time. We will focus on the specific defense shortly.

The non-specific defenses include any physical or chemical barriers able to prevent the colonization of the body by pathogens (**infection**). The skin and mucous membranes provide a continuous surface in direct contact with the environment that should physically prevent the entrance of pathogens. Intact skin is more reliable than the mucous membranes, however, which often must function in the exchange of materials with the environment and tend to be more permeable. Because of this vulnerability, the mucous membranes secrete mucus, a sticky substance designed to trap pathogens before they can breach the membrane. Even so, some microorganisms are able to enter the body through intact mucous membranes, especially in the respiratory tract. Additionally, skin may be punctured or cut so that it is no longer intact, making an inviting target of entry for potential pathogens.

Chemical non-specific defenses include the following:

♦ *enzymes,* such as lysozyme, can kill bacterial cells and are present in tears and saliva.
♦ *perspiration,* secreted from sweat glands, creates osmotically unfavorable conditions for bacterial growth due its high salt concentration.
♦ *acidic conditions* in the stomach kill most of the bacteria ingested in food before they can proliferate.
♦ *interferons* are small proteins effective only against viruses that are released by virally infected cells to signal their neighbors to prepare for invasion.

If a pathogen manages to breach these first lines of defense and enters the body (usually at the skin or mucous membranes), it must deal with the second line of non-specific defenses: **phagocytosis** and **inflammation**. As noted previously, phagocytes are neutrophils and macrophages that can engulf and digest foreign invaders. If pathogens enter through damaged tissue (as with a skin wound), phagocytosis is coupled to a more dramatic inflammatory response. Damaged cells release chemicals that have multiple effects:

♦ *blood supply* to the area is increased and clots often form, isolating the damaged area.
♦ *phagocytic cells* are recruited and enter the region, digesting the invaders they find.
♦ *local temperature* may rise, inhibiting the growth of pathogenic bacteria.

The inflammatory response, while usually painful, is certainly beneficial: it is designed to disable intruders and promote tissue repair before the pathogens can enter the bloodstream. If this defense fails, a systemic infection may result, and the final line of defense is the immune response.

J. THE IMMUNE RESPONSE

The immune response is also called the specific defense system because it is a reaction to a particular type of pathogen and is effective only against that pathogen. The immune response is only activated if a pathogen breaches the non-specific defenses and enters the circulation, creating a *systemic* infection. Two types of lymphocytes are involved in the immune response: **T lymphocytes (**or **T cells)** and **B lymphocytes (or B cells)**. Both are produced by the bone marrow. B cells remain and mature in the marrow, while the T cells migrate to the thymus to continue their maturation. Both cell types eventually move to the lymphatic system and collect in the lymph nodes and spleen (some lymphocytes also circulate in the blood). While both types of lymphocytes are part of the immune response, they approach their respective tasks in different ways.

K. ANTIBODY-MEDIATED IMMUNITY

B-cells are responsible for ***antibody-mediated*** or ***humoral*** immunity. When each individual B cell matures, it begins to express on its surface a single type of ***antibody***, a protein molecule composed of four polypeptide chains (see Figure 15.4). The amazing aspect of this phenomenon is that every B cell displays a different antibody; more than a million (up to 100 million) unique B cells are thus present at any time in an individual. Molecules on the surface of pathogens, known as ***antigens***, bind specifically with existing antibodies. With such a vast diversity of B cells and antibodies in the system, it is overwhelmingly likely that there will be an antibody present to react with any antigen that enters the body. When this antigen/antibody binding takes place, the B cell displaying the antibody is said to be ***stimulated*** or ***activated***, and a series of changes rapidly ensues. The B cell quickly proliferates by mitosis, making more and more B cells, each able to express the same antibody; since each of these cells is a genetic clone of the original, this entire process is often referred to as ***clonal selection and expansion***. Members of the new population of identical B cells soon begin to differentiate into two types of cells with different functions: ***plasma*** B cells and ***memory*** B cells.

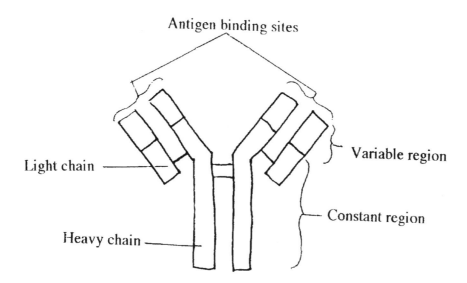

Figure 15.4: Structure of an antibody molecule

Plasma cells are specialized to manufacture and release huge quantities of the antibody that initially responded to the antigen. These antibodies can now bind with virtually all of the stimulating antigen, and, by doing so, they rid the body of the antigen-containing invader in two ways. The binding of the antibody to the antigen may disable the intruder directly. More commonly, the antibody/antigen complex is phagocytized or targeted by a system of plasma proteins known as the ***complement*** system. Complement proteins make holes in the membranes of targeted cells, causing them to lyse and die.

Memory cells, which also have the ability to produce antibodies, persist for long periods of time, sometimes the entire lifetime of an individual. If the same antigen is encountered again in the future, the immediate large scale production of antibodies disables the pathogen before it can cause significant effects. This phenomenon accounts for the ability of the body to acquire active immunity against a specific disease and is the reason why, after an individual contracts a disease once, he or she is often immune to future infection. It is also the explanation behind the effectiveness of *vaccination (immunization)*.

An antibody protein is composed of four polypeptides, each of which has a constant region and a variable region (see Figure 15.4). It is the variable region that differs from antibody to antibody, providing the specificity of the B cell response. Since antibodies are proteins, the amazing diversity of antibodies that exists in any person presents an apparent mystery. Every polypeptide manufactured by a cell must have a corresponding gene to supply the instructions, but there are only about 100,000 genes in the entire human genome. How can over a million different antibodies be produced when it seems there are not enough genes to encode them? It has been established that a unique process called *somatic recombination* provides the answer. The segments of DNA that encode the variable regions of each chain are broken up into several hundred "modules". In any particular B cell, several of the modules are selected and ordered randomly as DNA is cut and rejoined together; this unique combination of modules is then transcribed and translated into a unique antibody. This "shuffling" of DNA segments accounts for the vast diversity of observed antibodies and the paradox of their existence.

L. CELL-MEDIATED IMMUNITY

While B cells and the antibodies they produce play a vital role in the immune response, they do not act alone. As noted above, T lymphocytes, or T cells, constitute another part of the specific defense system. Lymphocytes normally do not react with "self" cells, that is, those that belong in the body. This is due to the presence of a group of proteins present on all "self" cells called the *major histocompatibility complex (MHC)*, which lymphocytes are able to recognize. The MHC proteins also play a role in the functioning of T cells. A T cell cannot interact with an antigen unless that antigen is "presented" by one of the body's own cells that has become infected by the pathogen. For example, if a virus infects a cell, the viral antigens will not be freely circulating in the blood or lymph to be detected by B cells or antibodies. However, the infected cell displays new antigens on its surface. Like B cells, each T cell displays a surface antigen receptor, similar to an antibody, that can bind and recognize only one type of antigen. When a T cell encounters a cell presenting an antigen along with the MHC complex, the T cell becomes stimulated. Thus, T cells are responsible for *cell-mediated immunity*.

There are several classes of T cells, each of which performs a different function in the cell-mediated response. T cells, like B cells, rapidly divide and differentiate after being stimulated, creating cells of the following types:

- ◆ *effector or cytotoxic* T cells (sometimes called T killer cells) act by directly attacking and destroying the infected cell, and also release chemicals called *lymphokines* which attract and stimulate macrophages.
- ◆ *memory* T cells have the same function as do memory B cells.
- ◆ *helper* T cells release chemicals called *interleukins* after being stimulated. These chemicals act to increase the activities of both cytotoxic T cells and B cells, ensuring a speedy and potent response to infection. (It is these helper T cells that are infected by the HIV virus in AIDS, causing a general suppression of the immune response.)
- ◆ *suppressor* T cells seem to play a role in shutting off the immune response after the pathogen has been eliminated, but this process is not yet completely understood.

Chapter 15 Problems

Passage 15.1 (Questions 1-5)

Considering the amazing quantities and diversity of pathogens that exist in the environment, vertebrates had to develop a complex defense system, or they would have perished. In humans, as in most animals, there are multiple lines of defense against potential pathogens. The integumentary membranes (skin and mucous membranes) provide a physical barrier to pathogens. If these are compromised, the inflammatory response is stimulated, during which neutrophils and macrophages phagocytize foreign invaders nonspecifically.

If an infection becomes systemic, the immune response is the last resort. Lymphocytes, specialized white blood cells that mainly reside in the lymph nodes, specifically attack pathogens in the blood and lymph. B lymphocytes are responsible for antibody-mediated immunity, which involves the reaction of protein antibody molecules with antigenic markers on the pathogen. T lymphocytes are responsible for cell-mediated immunity, during which antigens are presented to T cells by antigen-presenting cells of the human body, often macrophages or virally infected cells.

Several diseases can cause the immune system to become weakened or almost completely destroyed. AIDS (Acquired Immune Deficiency Syndrome) is a disease caused by the HIV virus, which attacks helper T cells that normally produce chemicals (interleukins) that stimulate the entire immune system. While functional cytotoxic T cells and plasma B cells can be created, their general activity is low due to lack of interleukin stimulation. Type I diabetes mellitus is an example of an autoimmune disease, in which lymphocytes attack normal body cells, in this case the insulin-producing cells of the pancreas. Perhaps the most devastating immune disease is called severe combined immune deficiency (SCID); individuals with this luckily rare condition have virtually no functioning lymphocytes, and often must live in vinyl bubbles to completely cut them off from any contact with pathogens.

1. What do the diseases AIDS and SCID have in common?
   A. In both cases, functional antibodies cannot be produced.
   B. In both cases, any secondary infection must cause death.
   C. In both cases, T cells are either absent or relatively inactive.
   D. Both diseases are caused by viral infection.

2. During HIV infection:
   A. Bacteria infect helper T cells, leading to compromised immunity.
   B. Functional antibodies to antigens on the HIV virus are produced.
   C. All T cells in the body are destroyed by the virus.
   D. HIV can be found infecting B cells.

3. Which of the following statements is true of the inflammatory response?
   A. B lymphocytes are important during inflammation, as they specifically phagocytize foreign invaders.
   B. Phagocytic white blood cells act nonspecifically to phagocytize invaders.
   C. It does nothing to actually destroy pathogens that enter the body; it only stops them from spreading to other regions of the body.
   D. Red blood cells must be involved in phagocytosis, since swelling and redness are caused by massive amounts of red blood cells entering the inflamed area.

4. Which physical barrier would be most susceptible to infection?
   A. Intact skin
   B. The respiratory mucous membrane
   C. Infection never occurs through skin or mucous membranes.
   D. They both present an equivalent barrier to pathogens.

5. Which of the following statements is true regarding the immune response?
    A. B cells can only be stimulated if an antigen is presented to them by an antigen presenting cell.
    B. T cells can only be stimulated if an antigen is presented to them by an antigen presenting cell.
    C. Macrophages exert their action by producing antibodies.
    D. Macrophages are very specific, and can only phagocytize pathogens of a single type.

The following questions are NOT based on a descriptive passage.

6. By definition, which type of blood vessel must be connected to a ventricle of the heart?
    A. An artery
    B. A vein
    C. A capillary
    D. Any of the above could be connected to a heart ventricle.

7. Which of the following statements is true regarding the blood?
    A. White blood cells contain hemoglobin, and are involved in oxygen transport.
    B. Blood cells are all made in bone marrow.
    C. Red blood cells contain hemoglobin, and are primarily involved with creating blood clots.
    D. Platelets contain hemoglobin, and are responsible for oxygen transport in the blood.

8. Blood located in which major vessel would contain the highest concentration of oxygen?
    A. Superior vena cava
    B. Aorta
    C. Pulmonary vein
    D. Pulmonary artery

9. Which of the following statements is true regarding capillaries?
    A. In a capillary bed, nutrients and oxygen diffuse into cells.
    B. In a capillary bed, plasma is often forced into spaces between cells, and is ultimately picked up by a lymphatic capillary to be returned to the general circulation.
    C. In a capillary bed, urea and carbon dioxide diffuse into the blood.
    D. All of the above are true of capillary beds.

10. Hemoglobin is a _____ that requires the presence of the mineral _____ to function properly.
    A. Protein; iodine
    B. Lipid; iron
    C. Protein; iron
    D. Protein; chromium

CHAPTER 16
Digestive, Respiratory, and Urinary Systems

A. INTRODUCTION

Many of us would not ordinarily consider the digestive, respiratory, and urinary systems to be closely related. There are certainly differences between these systems and the functions they perform. The digestive system is primarily concerned with the breakdown and absorption of nutrients found in the food we eat, which the body uses for energy and as raw material for building macromolecules. The respiratory system is involved with the process of gas exchange, allowing oxygen to enter the body and carbon dioxide to be released to the environment. The urinary system functions primarily in ridding the body of other metabolic wastes (most importantly urea), and is also vital in the maintenance of the water/solute balance of the body. So what is it that these systems have in common? If you think about each of the functions mentioned above, a common theme emerges: each of these systems is involved with the *absorption* (input) or *excretion* (output) of needed substances or metabolic wastes, respectively. While each system deals with various substances in different ways, absorption and excretion represent the fundamental processes by which various substances are exchanged between the cells of our bodies and the external environment.

B. STRUCTURE AND FUNCTION OF THE DIGESTIVE SYSTEM

Since humans and all vertebrates are heterotrophs, we must obtain food from the environment by eating plant or animal tissue. This food contains nutrients, which are needed to supply energy, raw materials for building new molecules, and other substances the body requires but cannot synthesize. Since the material we must consume is often in complex form, it must be chemically broken down into its simpler components before it can enter the body and be used by cells. Thus the digestive system's primary functions are the *ingestion* (taking in), *digestion* (breaking down), and *absorption* (actual entry into the bloodstream) of the nutrients found in food.

While the digestive system consists of many organs, each performing a different function, it in essence is a long tube through which food moves in one direction (see Figure 16.1). The following discussion refers to the human digestive system; while fundamentally similar in all vertebrates, keep in mind that specific differences may exist in different types of organisms.

- ◆ *mouth:* Food initially enters the body through the mouth, the cavity that begins the digestive tract. The actions of the teeth in the process of chewing (mastication) begin the physical breakdown of food, while the salivary glands, located near the base of the tongue, secrete *saliva* into the mouth. This saliva contains *salivary amylase*, an enzyme which breaks down starch into maltose (a disaccharide), and causes the food to become more liquid in consistency. Thus food is both physically and chemically altered while in the mouth.

♦ *pharynx, the esophagus, and swallowing:* When food has been sufficiently chewed and mixed with saliva, it is now referred to as a *bolus* and can be swallowed. Swallowing is a muscular reflex action that causes the rapid movement of the bolus through the pharynx, or throat, and into the esophagus. Since the paths of food and air cross in the pharynx, the *epiglottis*, a flap of tissue, moves during the process of swallowing so that it covers the *glottis*, or entrance to the *trachea* (windpipe), to prevent choking. The esophagus carries food from the pharynx to the stomach. Rhythmic contractions of the smooth muscle that surrounds the esophagus result in the unidirectional movement of food towards the stomach, a process called *peristalsis*.

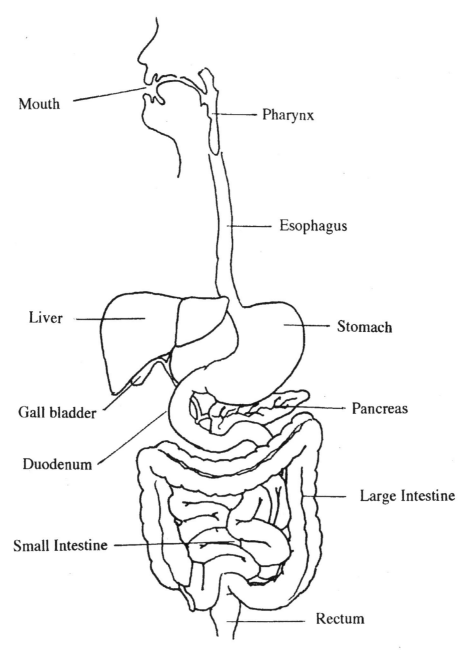

Figure 16.1: The human digestive system

♦ ***stomach:*** The stomach serves several functions. First, it stores food until it can be processed further by the small intestine. Epithelial cells of the stomach wall secrete gastric juice, a combination of hydrochloric acid (HCl), mucus, and ***pepsinogen*** (an enzyme precursor). The epithelium of the stomach also secretes a hormone, ***gastrin***, which controls the secretion of gastric juice. The HCl causes the pH of the stomach to be extremely low, usually with a value of about 2, and these acidic conditions kill many ingested bacterial cells and help to physically dissolve the food further. In addition, the acidic conditions cause pepsinogen to be converted into ***pepsin***, an enzyme that begins to chemically break down proteins. Contractions of the muscular stomach walls cause a churning action which contributes to the continuing physical breakdown of the bolus, until it exists in a homogeneous, semi-liquid state. This partially digested food, referred to as chyme, is now ready for further processing. The ***pyloric sphincter*** is a strong muscle that guards the entrance to the small intestine, and allows chyme to slowly enter. The stomach also has the lower esophageal sphincter (cardiac sphincter) to prevent stomach acid from refluxing back into the esophagus.

♦ ***small intestine - digestion:*** Most of the "action" of digestion occurs in the small intestine. It is here that the chemical breakdown of complex carbohydrates, proteins, and fats is completed. The small intestine is also the site of absorption of the products of digestion into the bloodstream. Chemical digestion is completed in the first portion of the small intestine, the ***duodenum***. Enzymes manufactured by the pancreas attack undigested nutrients, and bile manufactured by the liver aids in the process. Specifically, the pancreas produces pancreatic ***amylase***, which breaks down starch into maltose, ***trypsin*** and other proteolytic enzymes, which break down proteins into amino acids, and ***lipases***, which hydrolyze fats, yielding glycerol and fatty acids. These enzymes are dissolved in pancreatic juice and enter the duodenum via the pancreatic duct. These juices also have the ability to neutralize the acid entering the duodenum from the stomach. The liver produces ***bile***, which is stored in the gall bladder; it travels to the duodenum via the bile duct and participates in digestion by emulsifying fats, which otherwise would not be appreciably soluble and would not be fully exposed to the action of lipases. Finally, the epithelium of the small intestine itself also produces enzymes that break disaccharides into monosaccharides. As you might expect, hormones regulate the production and secretion of digestive enzymes and bile. ***Secretin*** and ***cholecystokinin*** are secreted by the duodenal epithelium in response to acid and the presence of nutrients, and stimulate the pancreas and gall bladder to release their products. When digestion is complete, monosaccharides, amino acids, fatty acids, and glycerol, along with various vitamins and minerals, are ready to be absorbed into the blood.

♦ ***small intestine - absorption:*** Absorption of nutrients occurs in the remainder of the small intestine, which is anatomically broken into two parts, the ***jejunum*** and the ***ileum***. These portions are adapted in several ways to facilitate absorption; many of these adaptations exist to increase the surface area of the intestinal wall, which will allow nutrient absorption to take place at a faster rate and to increase total absorption. Firstly, the length of the small intestine is great, approximately six meters in humans. In order to fit in the abdominal cavity, it must be greatly coiled. Additionally, the walls of the small intestine project fingerlike folds, known as ***villi***, whose surface area is increased even further by the presence of tiny cellular projections known as ***microvilli***. All in all, the total absorptive surface area of the small intestine is over three hundred square meters! Monosaccharides, amino acids, and small fatty acids enter capillaries in the villi by both facilitated diffusion and active transport. Mineral electrolytes also enter the bloodstream directly, usually by active transport, and water follows by osmosis. Larger fatty acids, glycerol, and cholesterol do not enter the capillaries of the villi, but instead are combined and packaged into lipoprotein particles called ***chylomicrons***, which enter a ***lacteal***. The lacteal is a small lymphatic vessel, and the chylomicrons ultimately enter the blood by way of the lymphatic system.

♦ *large intestine:* Following the small intestine is the large intestine, so named because its diameter is greater than that of the small intestine. Its surface area is comparatively small, however, and by the time material reaches the large intestine, most of the nutrients have already been absorbed. The large intestine is anatomically divided into two parts, the pouch-like *cecum*, which represents the beginning of the organ, and the much longer *colon*, which has the shape of an inverted "U". (The *appendix*, a small pouch which apparently plays no role in digestion, is also located near the cecum.) There is a large population of symbiotic mutualistic bacteria, mostly *Escherichia coli*, which reside in the colon of humans and many other vertebrates. They are sustained by particles of food which could not be digested by their host, and find the warm temperature of the colon ideal for their growth. In return, they synthesize certain vitamins and amino acids, most notably vitamin K, which is involved in proper blood clotting. The major digestive role of the large intestine is to reabsorb water that is still in the digestive tract before the remaining waste material is eliminated. To facilitate this, any remaining salts are also absorbed here. The resulting waste, or *feces*, should be relatively solid, and consists of indigestible materials including cellulose fibers, some water, and many bacterial cells. It is stored in the *rectum* until it is eliminated by defecation through the *anus*. (You should note that this elimination is not properly referred to as excretion, as the materials present in the feces have simply passed through, but never entered, the body.)

♦ *pancreas and liver -- accessory organs:* We noted above that the pancreas and liver are important in the overall process of digestion. They are referred to as accessory organs, however, because food never actually passes through them. Instead, they function by producing necessary substances and secreting them into the digestive tract. To reiterate, the pancreas produces digestive enzymes dissolved in an alkaline fluid which is emptied into the duodenum. The liver produces bile, which is stored in the gall bladder and enters the duodenum to help with the digestion of fats. While both organs have other functions, their roles in digestion cannot be overstated.

C. NUTRITION

In this chapter, we alluded to some of the major types of nutrients. The detailed structures of many of these were discussed earlier. We will now consider each in more detail with respect to the needs they fulfill in the body.

♦ *carbohydrates:* Carbohydrates are a group of molecules based on the *monosaccharide*, or simple sugar, subunit. We can consume them in complex form as *polysaccharides* like starch, or in simple forms, as mono- or disaccharide sugars. Carbohydrates are prevalent in plant tissues such as fruits and grains, and function mainly to provide the body with energy.

♦ *proteins:* Proteins are polymers of *amino acids*. They are abundant in animal foods like meat, and are necessary largely to supply amino acid building blocks for the construction of the body's own proteins. Since they can be converted to glucose or fat, they can also provide energy in times of need. Eight amino acids must be ingested and are referred to as *essential*, but the body can synthesize the other needed twelve. A *complete* protein source contains all twenty of the amino acids.

♦ *fats:* Fats are lipids composed of one molecule of *glycerol* attached to three *fatty acid* chains. They are often abundant in animal products, and play several roles in the body, including their primary function in long-term energy storage. Fats are also important in the synthesis of cell membranes and certain hormones. The body needs but cannot manufacture certain polyunsaturated fatty acids, which therefore must be consumed and are referred to as *essential* fatty acids.

♦ *vitamins:* Vitamins are essential organic compounds that the body cannot synthesize but needs for a wide variety of purposes. Many act as *coenzymes* in metabolic pathways, and are usually required in relatively small amounts. Others act as *antioxidants*, protecting important molecules from oxidation and damage by free radicals and thus potentially playing a role in the prevention of cancer. Vitamins are often classified according to their solubility properties; A, D, E, and K are fat soluble, while the many vitamins in the B complex and C dissolve readily in water. The required vitamins can usually be obtained from a variety of plant and animal sources, although supplementation is a common practice, especially if the diet is deficient.

♦ *minerals:* Like vitamins, minerals are essential substances the body must obtain from the environment and are used for a variety of functions. Unlike vitamins, however, minerals are inorganic, usually elemental, substances that are often ingested as ionic salts; thus they dissociate in water and are often referred to as electrolytes. Examples of important minerals are calcium, phosphorus, sodium, potassium, chloride, and iodine. As with vitamins, these can usually be obtained in sufficient quantities from a normal diet, but are sometimes supplemented due to other factors.

♦ *water:* No discussion of nutrition would be complete without a mention of water, probably the most essential nutrient. While we likely take it for granted, water is vital in many ways to the functioning of the body. As the major solvent present in our cells, it accounts for much of the mass of the entire organism, and is especially important as a part of the blood and lymph. Dehydration, if severe enough, will inevitably lead to death. While the body can "manufacture" a certain amount of water as it engages in metabolic reactions, water must be ingested to ensure an adequate supply.

D. GENERAL STRUCTURE AND FUNCTION OF THE RESPIRATORY SYSTEM

We noted in our discussion of digestion that humans, along with other vertebrates, are heterotrophs, and thus must obtain organic molecules from the environment to supply them with energy. That energy is released by a process of oxidation called *cellular respiration*, which requires oxygen and produces carbon dioxide. This means that organisms such as humans have a constant need to obtain oxygen and rid themselves of carbon dioxide. Since both of these substances exist as gases under physiological conditions, a system that allows gas exchange must be present. The process of breathing, or *respiration*, refers to the constant exchange of oxygen and carbon dioxide between the organism and the environment, and is the major function of the respiratory system. The major structures of the respiratory system are, in essence, a series of tubes that ultimately connects with capillaries of the circulatory system (see Figure 16.2). The following discussion refers to the human respiratory system; important differences exist in other vertebrates, especially fish, and will be addressed subsequently.

♦ *nasal passages, the pharynx, and the trachea:* During normal breathing, air enters the body through the nostrils and nasal passages, travels through the pharynx, and enters the trachea, or windpipe. The trachea is a strong tube strengthened by rings of cartilage which maintain its structural integrity. The *larynx*, or upper region of the trachea, contains the vocal cords, which humans use to make sounds.

♦ *bronchi and bronchioles:* The trachea divides into two bronchi (singular, *bronchus*) inside the *lungs*. Each bronchus further subdivides again and again, creating many smaller tubes called bronchioles.

♦ *alveoli:* The smallest bronchioles terminate in tiny air sacs called alveoli (singular, *alveolus*). Each alveolus is thin-walled and surrounded by capillaries from the cardiovascular system. The barrier is so thin that gases can diffuse freely directly across the alveolar wall into or out of the blood. A human's two lungs contain about 300 million alveoli, with an exchange surface area of approximately 75 square meters.

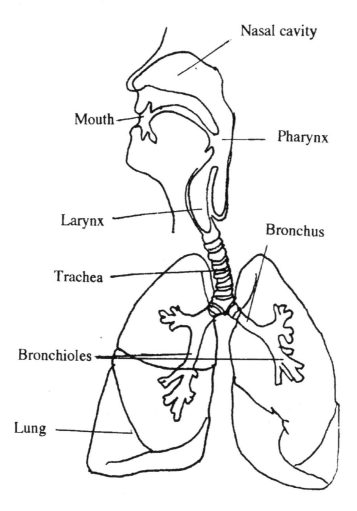

Figure 16.2: The human respiratory system

   The entire inner surface of the respiratory system is composed of epithelial tissue which secretes mucus; it is therefore called a ***mucous membrane***. Since the alveoli have such thin walls, the respiratory system is potentially susceptible to the entry of pathogens, and the mucus secreted by the bronchial tubes and trachea acts to trap any pathogens or foreign particles before they can reach the exchange surfaces. Many of the cells of the mucous membrane also contain ***cilia***, small projections which beat in one direction, causing a current of mucus to move towards the top of the trachea. This flow, known as the ***ciliary escalator***, ensures that material trapped by the mucus is removed from the system, protecting the delicate respiratory surfaces from harm.

E. MECHANICS AND REGULATION OF RESPIRATION

Breathing, or respiration, consists of two complementary processes: *inhalation* or *inspiration*, during which air enters the lungs, and *exhalation* or *expiration*, during which air leaves the lungs. Inspiration occurs when the brain sends a signal to the *diaphragm*, a sheet-like muscle at the base of the thoracic cavity, and the *intercostal* muscles, located between the ribs. When the diaphragm contracts, the overall volume of the thoracic cavity increases, causing the air pressure in the lungs to decrease. Air automatically flows into the lungs due to the external air pressure. When the diaphragm relaxes, the thoracic cavity returns to its initial size, and air is forced out of the lungs. Thus we can see that inspiration is active while expiration is passive.

The respiratory rate is controlled by centers in the brainstem, which normally send out rhythmic impulses to the diaphragm causing a regular cycle of inspiration and expiration to occur involuntarily. (To some extent, breathing can be brought under conscious control.) The respiratory center neurons are also sensitive to information about the chemical composition of the blood, and this allows them to alter the rate of breathing when conditions dictate, as during exercise or physical/emotional stress. The respiratory neurons are mainly sensitive to the pH of the blood (the concentration of H^+ ions, which as we shall soon see, is intimately related to the concentration of carbon dioxide). As metabolic activity increases, the levels of carbon dioxide and hydrogen ions in the blood rise, triggering an increase in the rate of breathing to restore normal levels of these substances. Whenever carbon dioxide concentration increases, oxygen concentration decreases, so there is really no need for the brain to monitor both parameters. There are receptors called the *aortic* and *carotid bodies*, however, which are sensitive to the levels of oxygen in the blood; they transmit this information to the respiratory centers of the brain, enabling "fine-tuning" of the system.

F. TRANSPORT OF GASES IN THE BLOOD

Oxygen diffuses into the blood from the air, but oxygen is not extremely soluble in the plasma of the blood. Therefore, vertebrates have hemoglobin, a protein with a high affinity for oxygen so sufficient oxygen can be transported to meet metabolic demands. Hemoglobin consists of four polypeptide chains combined with an iron-containing heme group. Hemoglobin, which is red in color, is packed into red blood cells, and allows them to play their role in the transport of oxygen around the body. It is also responsible for the red color of blood.

Carbon dioxide is somewhat more soluble in the plasma than oxygen, but much of it reacts with water in the blood to form carbonic acid, H_2CO_3, which subsequently dissociates to form bicarbonate ions and free hydrogen ions. This is why increased levels of carbon dioxide increase the acidity (H^+ concentration) of the blood. Since carbon dioxide can exist in the blood in these different forms, it also plays a major role in buffering the blood against pH changes, a major aspect of homeostasis.

G. GENERAL STRUCTURE AND FUNCTION OF THE URINARY SYSTEM

The urinary system is a special excretory system that plays several roles in maintaining homeostasis. A primary function is the excretion of *urea*, a major nitrogen-containing waste product derived from the catabolism of amino acids. More generally, this system regulates the chemical composition and pH of the blood by analyzing and adjusting the levels of major ions (including H^+), nutrients, and other important substances in the blood. Finally, the urinary system is responsible for maintaining the proper amount of water in the body, a major determining factor in the concentrations of all solutes present in an organism. Anatomically, the urinary system consists of the following (see Figure 16.3):

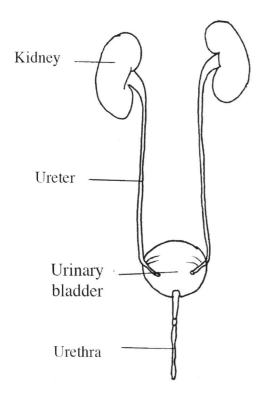

♦ **kidneys:** The kidneys, located dorsally behind the stomach and liver, are the major organs of the urinary system. They filter blood, analyze its composition, and form urine that will ultimately be expelled from the body. Each kidney is divided into an outer **cortex** region and an inner **medulla**.

♦ **ureters:** These tubes transport urine from each kidney to the urinary bladder.

♦ **urinary bladder:** This sac-like structure stores the urine until enough of it has collected to be expelled.

♦ **urethra:** The urethra is the tube through which the urine ultimately exits the body.

Figure 16.3: The human urinary system

H. THE NEPHRON AND URINE FORMATION

The functional unit of the kidney is called the **nephron**, and each kidney contains about a million nephrons (see Figure 16.4). **Renal** arteries supply each kidney with blood; after entering the kidney, they branch and subdivide so that each nephron is supplied with arterial blood through a tiny **afferent** arteriole. The arteriole feeds a capillary bed referred to as the **glomerulus**. Constriction of the arterioles causes the blood pressure to be especially high in this region, and the glomerular capillaries are extremely permeable, causing a significant portion of the plasma, along with its dissolved substances, to be forced out of the arteriole. This **filtrate** collects in **Bowman's capsule**, a cuplike structure which leads to the **renal tubule**. As the filtrate passes through the tubule, its composition will be

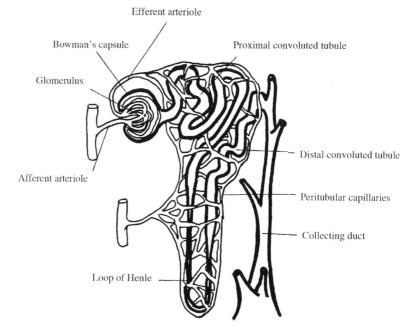

Figure 16.4: The nephron

altered, ultimately forming urine. During the process of filtration, blood cells and large protein molecules cannot pass through the capillary walls, and thus do not leave the blood, but instead leave the capillary bed through an *efferent* (leaving) arteriole. This vessel subdivides again into a set of *peritubular* capillaries, which surround and interact with the renal tubule. This complex arrangement allows the filtrate in the tubule to exchange materials with the blood as urine formation proceeds. The peritubular capillaries merge to form a venule which ultimately joins many others and exits the kidney as a renal vein.

The renal tubule has three main sections: the *proximal convoluted tubule*; a long, "U"-shaped section called the *Loop of Henle*; and the *distal convoluted tubule*, which empties into the *collecting duct*, the tube through which urine ultimately leaves the nephron. As the filtrate moves through the tubule, two important processes occur simultaneously. During *secretion*, some of the molecules that did not enter the filtrate but are still in the blood are actively transported from the peritubular capillaries into the renal tubule. Many drugs and toxic substances are removed from the blood by this method. *Reabsorption* is the other major process that occurs, by which a majority of the materials in the filtrate, including most of the water, glucose, and other nutrients, are returned to the blood. Whatever remains in the renal tubule after these transport processes occur becomes the urine, and leaves via the collecting duct. The urine usually consists of water which contains *urea* (a waste formed by the metabolism of amino acids) as the major solute. Also present in lesser quantities may be *uric acid* (which results from nucleotide metabolism), *creatinine* (from the metabolism of creatine), *ketones* (from the metabolism of fatty acids), and a variety of other substances normally present in trace amounts.

I. REGULATION OF WATER BALANCE

It is important to realize that the amount of water that remains in the urine must be carefully controlled to ensure that we do not become over or underhydrated. As noted earlier, the amount of water present in the body is one of the major factors determining concentrations of all solutes, and its regulation is therefore vital to the maintenance of homeostasis. Additionally, as land creatures, we are in constant danger of losing water to the environment, and mechanisms of excreting urine that is hypertonic to our body fluids have thus evolved for purposes of water conservation. Depending on the circumstances, of course, we also may need to create urine that is hypotonic to body fluids, for example, after we have consumed a large amount of water. How is the nephron able to regulate the amount of water that leaves in the urine?

Firstly, as the filtrate passes through the proximal convoluted tubule, its volume is drastically reduced as sodium ions, glucose, and amino acids are actively transported out, causing water to follow passively by osmosis. In addition, negatively charged ions return to the blood due to the electrical imbalance created by active transport of positive ions. All of these substances are readily picked up by the peritubular capillaries and returned to the blood. As the filtrate begins its passage through the loop of Henle, its composition is altered more dramatically. Both active transport and diffusion of both Na^+ and urea make the area surrounding the loop extremely hypertonic to the filtrate; however, the walls of the ascending branch of the loop and the collecting duct itself are impermeable to water. So as salt is removed from the filtrate and water is not allowed to follow, the urine becomes very dilute (hypotonic). If nothing else was to happen, this would be the end of the process and urine would always be very dilute. Remember, however, that it is the lack of permeability of the collecting duct wall that prevents water from diffusing out of the duct. If the wall could be made permeable to water, it would rapidly move by osmosis out of the urine and back into the surrounding area to be ultimately returned to the blood, causing a concentrated, hypertonic urine to be excreted. As you've probably guessed, there is a way of controlling the permeability of the wall of the collecting duct to water, and thus of regulating the concentration of the urine. This mechanism depends on the action of the hormone ADH (*antidiuretic hormone*), which increases the permeability of the walls of the collecting duct to water, promoting the formation of a concentrated urine.

As we discussed in an earlier chapter, ADH is manufactured by the hypothalamus and stored and secreted by the pituitary gland in the brain. The hypothalamus monitors the osmotic composition of the blood and the blood pressure, and triggers a release of ADH when necessary. If the blood is dilute, as might occur after drinking a lot of fluids, the hypothalamus decreases ADH production, so more water is excreted in the urine. Conversely, if the body is dehydrated, the osmotic pressure of the blood increases, and the hypothalamus steps up ADH production, causing more water to be retained.

The hormone aldosterone, secreted by the adrenal cortex, triggers the nephron to increase reabsorption of sodium ions as well as increase secretion of potassium. Thus, the electrolyte balance of the body is also controlled by the nephron. In addition, the nephron participates in the regulation of pH by secreting hydrogen ions into the urine. All in all, the kidney really is an amazing organ, which performs and controls many processes leading to an incredibly fine-tuned regulation of body fluid composition.

J. OTHER EXCRETORY PROCESSES

While we have explored the major excretory processes carried out by the respiratory and urinary systems, other organs and systems are also involved with excretion. For example, the liver produces pigments called *biliverdin* and *bilirubin* as it breaks down the heme portion of hemoglobin during the process of red blood cell destruction. These pigments are stored in the gall bladder and released with the bile, and are thus referred to as *bile pigments*. They ultimately leave the body in the feces.

Another example would be the sweat produced by *sweat glands* embedded in the skin. While sweat is mostly water and functions in cooling the body, it also contains small amounts of electrolytes, urea, and uric acid. Sweating is thus an excretory function.

Chapter 16 Problems

Passage 16.1 (Questions 1-2)

Some individuals do not produce sufficient amounts of the enzyme lactase to digest the sugar lactose, present in milk and dairy products, and are referred to as "lactose intolerant". Lactose is a disaccharide, which must be broken down by lactase into its constituent monosaccharides, glucose and galactose, before it can be absorbed. If not broken down, it remains in the small intestines and is passed along into the large intestine, a place it does not belong, with waste materials. The results can range from dehydration and diarrhea to intestinal cramps and bloating. The pain and bloating often experienced by the lactose intolerant after lactose ingestion are caused by intestinal bacteria that metabolize the lactose to which they are normally not exposed. Products of this fermentation include organic acids and various gases. Some products are available to allow lactose intolerant individuals to eat lactose-containing products, and are meant to be ingested just before eating milk or dairy products.

1. Which of the following is a reasonable explanation of the observation that lactose intolerant individuals become dehydrated after lactose consumption?
   A. The presence of lactose in the large intestine inhibits the pituitary gland from releasing the hormone ADH.
   B. Large amounts of lactose in the large intestine increase the osmotic pressure, causing water to be retained there and eliminated with wastes, whereas it would normally be reabsorbed into the blood.
   C. Because they cannot drink milk, lactose intolerant individuals are deprived of an important water source.
   D. The presence of lactose in the large intestine causes more frequent urination.

2. What is the likely nature of the products that, if taken before lactose ingestion, will inhibit the symptoms of lactose intolerant individuals?
   A. They are likely antibiotics that kill the bacteria in the intestine so that they cannot metabolize the sugar.
   B. They probably contain the enzyme lactase, which will end up in the small intestine and allow lactose digestion.
   C. They are probably cocktails of various drugs that inhibit urination and help to ease the pain.
   D. They are likely drugs that allow the small intestine to absorb undigested lactose.

Passage 16.2 (Questions 3-5)

After glucose is absorbed by the small intestine, it is transported to the liver, where many "decisions" are made regarding its fate. These decisions are hormonally effected, and include release of some glucose into the blood, storage of some as glycogen, and conversion of some to fat.

The hormones insulin and glucagon are produced by the pancreas; insulin is produced in response to high blood sugar, as after a meal, and tells body cells to take up glucose from the blood, while notifying the liver to store or convert any excess. Glucagon targets the liver when blood sugar is low, telling it to break down some glycogen and release it into the blood as glucose. The interaction of these hormones acts like a thermostat to maintain a relatively constant blood glucose concentration.

In individuals with diabetes mellitus type I, insulin is no longer produced by the pancreas, and must be supplemented by intravenous injection, or the afflicted individual will eventually die.

3. Why must insulin be injected intravenously, while other enzymes such as lactase can be taken orally, by pill?
    A. Insulin is a protein; if it was taken by mouth, it would be broken down into its constituent amino acids, and would never enter the blood.
    B. Since insulin affects glucose concentrations, if it were ingested it would halt the absorption of glucose by the small intestine.
    C. If insulin was taken in pill form, it would interact with glucagon secreted by the pancreas in the small intestine, and the two would "neutralize" each other.
    D. None of the above answers is reasonable.

4. All of the following symptoms might be associated with untreated diabetes mellitus type I EXCEPT:
    A. Extremely high blood glucose.
    B. Extremely low blood glucose.
    C. The excretion of glucose in the urine.
    D. Dehydration due to water loss in the urine.

5. Sometimes if the administration of glucose is not timed properly, insulin is injected but an individual does not eat for a prolonged period of time. This can lead to insulin shock, during which a person loses consciousness and can die. The probable cause of insulin shock is:
    A. The injected insulin causes the blood sugar to become so low that glucose is not available to fuel the body's needs.
    B. The injected insulin causes so much glucose to be released into the blood that the surge of energy can cause heart rhythm irregularities.
    C. The injected insulin suppresses hunger, so that the person does not realize they should eat.
    D. Injected insulin causes the inhibition of glucagon synthesis, so no glycogen can be broken down to glucose by the liver.

The following questions are NOT based on a descriptive passage.

6. Which of the following parameters does the brain monitor most closely in regulating the rate of respiration?
    A. The concentration of oxygen in the blood.
    B. The heart rate.
    C. The concentration of carbon dioxide in the blood and the blood pH.
    D. The concentration of lactic acid in the blood.

7. If release of the hormone ADH was inhibited, the result would be:
    A. Large volumes of concentrated urine
    B. Large volumes of dilute urine
    C. Small volumes of concentrated urine
    D. Small volumes of dilute urine

8. The contraction of the _____ causes active inhalation, and is normally involuntarily controlled by respiratory centers located in the _____.
    A. Diaphragm; brainstem
    B. Diaphragm; cerebellum
    C. Rectus abdominus; brainstem
    D. Rectus abdominus; cerebellum

9. All of the following substances would be found in the glomerular filtrate of the nephron before reabsorption except:
    A. Urea
    B. Glucose
    C. Amino acids
    D. Large plasma proteins

10. Which of the following is an organ that plays a role in digestion, but never has any food actually pass through it?
    A. The large intestine
    B. The stomach
    C. The pancreas
    D. The colon

CHAPTER 17

The Integumentary, Skeletal, and Muscular Systems

A. INTRODUCTION

In this chapter, we will explore three systems that have a close physical connection, and are related in that none of them could function properly without the help of the others. While this is true of all body systems in the widest sense, the integumentary, muscular, and skeletal systems share a particularly intimate connection. The integumentary system, whose major organ is the skin, is responsible for a wide variety of functions, including protection from infection; absorption and excretion (in the sense that organs of the system line all exchange surfaces); temperature regulation; and sensory contact with the environment (in the sense that many sensory receptors, discussed earlier, are located in the skin). Skin is often directly connected to muscles, the major organs of the muscular system. Muscles have but one function: to contract, causing movement. While there are many types of movements, major movements of the body entail the connection of muscles to bones (often via tendons). In fact, it is bones that voluntary muscles cause to move when we raise our arms or lift our legs. In addition, bones, the major organs of the skeletal system, provide the major structural framework of the body. Without bones, there would be no means of supporting the rest of the organism.

B. ORGANIZATION OF THE INTEGUMENTARY SYSTEM

The major organs of the integumentary system are technically referred to as ***membranes***. We tend to think of organs as discrete entities within the body, but remember that, by definition, organs simply consist of at least two tissue types functioning together towards a common purpose. Looked at this way, the skin, perhaps the most important of these membranes, certainly qualifies as an organ. All of the membranes of the integumentary system line body surfaces or internal cavities, and three major types can be identified and described.

♦ ***Serous Membranes:*** Serous membranes are organs that line internal body cavities which lack any connection with the outside environment, and often surround and line other internal organs. They typically have a simple structure, consisting of a single layer of epithelial tissue attached to a thin layer of loose connective tissue. Examples of serous membranes would be the membranes lining the thoracic and abdominal cavities.

♦ ***Mucous Membranes:*** Mucous membranes, to which we have referred previously, are organs which line internal body cavities that are continuous with the external environment. This includes the inner surfaces of all organs of the digestive tract, the respiratory system, and the urinary and reproductive systems. Like serous membranes, mucous membranes are composed of a combination of epithelial and connective tissues. Mucous membranes get their name from the fact that the cells of these organs secrete ***mucus***, a substance that serves to lubricate the surface of the membrane and protect the organism from infection.

♦ ***The Cutaneous Membrane:*** The cutaneous membrane lines the external surfaces of the body and is also the technical term for the skin. Since the skin is the most complex and versatile organ of the integumentary system, we will explore it in more detail.

C. THE CUTANEOUS MEMBRANE: THE SKIN

As noted in the introduction, the skin plays a variety of roles vital to the continuing health of the organism. In previous chapters we examined the excretion of sweat, and the sensory nerve endings located in the skin that help us to gather information about the world around us. Similarly, we noted the role of the skin as a non-specific barrier acting in general defense against infection by pathogens. The skin also plays a major role in thermoregulation, a topic we will consider shortly. Since we have already discussed the many functions associated with the skin, we should now address its structure (see Figure 17.1). The skin can be seen as composed of three layers, each with a unique composition.

♦ ***The Epidermis:*** This outermost layer of the skin is composed exclusively of stratified squamous epithelial tissue. Recall that stratified epithelium is many layers thick, and this has an interesting consequence for the skin. Since only epithelial cells are present, there is no supply of blood to nourish the epidermis. A single layer of cells that lies close to the dermis is nourished by capillaries found in the thicker lower layer. These cells are able to undergo mitosis and continually produce new cells. As

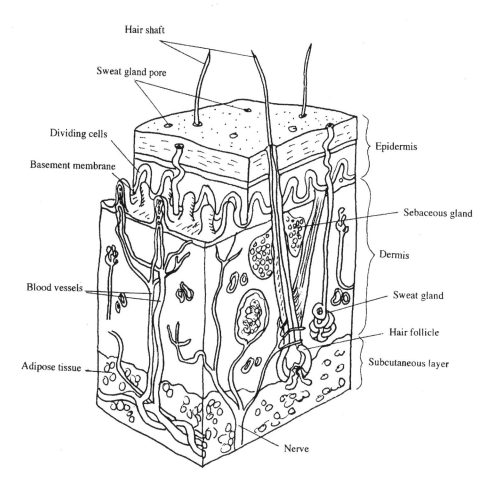

Figure 17.1: The cutaneous membrane (skin)

the new cells are pushed outward, further and further from the blood supply, they become deprived of oxygen and nutrients and die. During this process, the dying cells begin to produce and store large amounts of the fibrous protein *keratin*, which acts as a "sealant". Thus the outer epidermis consists of many layers of tightly packed dead cells containing large amounts of keratin, making the epithelium impermeable to water. Deeper down in the epidermis lie cells which produce the pigment *melanin*, giving skin its color. The presence of melanin and keratin in the epidermis allows it to protect underlying skin layers from water gain/loss, potential damage from ultraviolet radiation, and mechanical damage. The epidermis is connected to the underlying dermis by a *basement membrane*.

♦ *The Dermis:* The dermis is generally three to four times thicker than the epidermis, and is composed of dense connective tissue containing collagen and elastin fibers. This allows the skin to be both strong and pliable. A major function of the dermis is to anchor the epidermis to underlying structures. The dermis also contains blood vessels, some muscular tissue (smooth muscle associated with involuntary movements of the skin and secretions of glands), and nervous tissue (acting in either a sensory or motor capacity). Also located in the dermis are several types of accessory structures:

- *Hair follicles* are composed of epidermal cells protruding into the dermis. As a hair begins to grow, the cells being pushed outward, like other epidermal cells, die and become keratinized. Thus what we perceive as hair is really a shaft of dead, highly proteinaceous cells. Only mammals have true hair, and its function is to act as an insulator. Humans are the only mammalian species in which hair does not cover almost the entire body in large quantities.

- *Sebaceous glands* produce and release sebum, an oily substance that is often secreted into hair follicles. Sebum functions to lubricate the hair and skin; in certain individuals, however, bacterial infection of sebaceous glands can result in acne, a condition in which the skin is covered by inflamed, raised lesions.

- *Sweat glands* produce sweat, usually to cool the body during conditions of high temperature or physical exertion. As we noted in the last chapter, while sweat is mainly water, it may also contain electrolytes and wastes such as urea, so sweating is also considered an excretory process.

♦ *The Subcutaneous Layer:* The subcutaneous layer is a relatively thin basal portion of the skin. It is composed almost exclusively of loose connective tissue which functions in binding the entire skin to the underlying skeletal muscles. Much of this connective tissue is adipose tissue, which as we noted earlier functions in the storage of fat; its location in the subcutaneous layer allows it to contribute to temperature regulation by acting as an insulator against loss of heat. The subcutaneous layer also contains blood vessels that nourish the skin.

D. THERMOREGULATION

All vertebrates create a certain amount of heat as a by-product of their metabolic reactions. In addition, the rate of metabolism is to an extent determined by the temperature of an organism's body, so that temperature cannot vary greatly without metabolic consequences. This is because enzymes are affected by temperature: the colder their environment, the slower the reactions they catalyze will proceed. As temperatures rise, the reactions speed up, but only until a certain point at which the enzyme loses its structural integrity, or *denatures*, and can no longer function properly. So all animals must exist within a temperature range that allows their enzymes to function, and at a reasonable rate.

Vertebrates can be classified based upon the major source of heat that allows their bodies to remain within a reasonable temperature range, and according to whether or not they have the ability to actively regulate their temperature and keep it at an almost constant level. *Ectotherms* absorb most of the heat used to warm their bodies from the environment, while *endotherms* use the heat they generate themselves, during metabolic reactions. *Poikilotherms* have little ability to regulate their body temperatures by internal mechanisms, and are often referred to as "cold-blooded". What this really means is that their body temperature varies with the environmental temperature. **Homeotherms**, often referred to as "warm-blooded", are able to maintain their internal temperatures in a very narrow range that is generally high and advantageous for their metabolic activities. Almost all endotherms are also homeotherms, and almost all ectotherms are poikilotherms. Mammals and birds are the most obvious examples of homeothermic endotherms, while fishes and reptiles are examples of poikilothermic ectotherms. Since fishes live in a watery environment, the external temperature does not vary much, and therefore their body temperatures remain relatively constant, albeit low. Their metabolic processes are similarly slow. Reptiles must absorb heat from the environment, usually by basking on a rock to "get some sun". This raises their body temperature to ensure a reasonable metabolic rate. At night, the temperature of their bodies falls, their metabolism slows, and they become almost completely inactive. Humans, of course, are endotherms and homeotherms, using our relatively high metabolic rates to create heat and to keep our body temperature at a very constant 37°C. Just how do we achieve this thermal constancy?

The hypothalamus, a portion of the brain we encountered in Chapter 14, contains a thermostat set to maintain the body temperature at 37°C. It receives information about the temperature of various parts of the body from internal receptors, and about the external conditions from the temperature sensors located in the skin. If it is very hot outside, and the body temperature begins to rise above the thermostat "set-point", a variety of responses help restore the internal temperature to normal. **Vasodilation** (widening of blood vessels in the skin) increases the blood flow and accelerates the transfer of heat away from the body. In addition, sweat glands are stimulated to excrete sweat; this cools the body because internal heat is used to evaporate the liquid sweat. (Dogs rely more on the evaporation of saliva, which they expose to the environment by "panting".) These mechanisms function in concert to ensure that the body remains at a safe temperature. They are, however, not foolproof. Sweating becomes less effective as the ambient humidity rises; on an extremely hot and humid day, sweat will be produced but will not evaporate, leaving you wet, but still hot! In addition, profuse sweating causes excessive water and electrolyte loss, which must be replaced. Likewise, vasodilation becomes less effective as the temperature rises, and if the external temperature is higher than body temperature, the body may begin to gain heat from the environment! In these cases, it is often advisable for humans to resort to extreme measures -- air conditioners, cool showers, or swimming pools!

The hypothalamus also acts when extreme cold causes the internal temperature to drop below normal. In this case, **vasoconstriction** (narrowing of blood vessels) reduces the blood supply to the skin, thus lowering the rate of heat loss. In addition, the insulating hairs of the skin become erect and trap warm air, and the layer of adipose tissue in the subcutaneous layer serves as an efficient barrier to heat loss. Overall metabolic rate rises as well, so more heat will be produced. This can be accomplished in a number of ways.

- ◆ **Involuntary contraction of muscles** ("shivering") creates heat, as do the voluntary movements we often perform when cold (walking, rubbing hands together, etc.).
- ◆ **Hormones** such as adrenaline may be secreted, signaling the release of glucose into the blood and the increase of heart and respiratory rates.
- ◆ In extreme cases, the thyroid gland may step up its production of thyroxine, which increases overall cellular respiration by directly stimulating mitochondria.

Of course, if it becomes too cold or low temperatures persist for too long, these mechanisms will not be adequate, and death will occur. As a final note, this explains why it is especially dangerous to get wet when cold. This can be thought of as sweating at the wrong time; heat is removed from the body as water evaporates from the skin. **Hypothermia** (a state of reduced body temperature with noticeable negative effects) can occur at temperatures as high as 50°F if an individual is wet.

E. FUNCTIONS AND ORGANIZATION OF THE SKELETAL SYSTEM

The major function of the skeletal system is to provide support for the body. In addition, it plays roles in:

- The storage of calcium.
- The production of blood cells.
- The facilitation of movement.
- The protection of important organs.

Individual **bones**, composed mainly of connective tissue, are the organs of the skeletal system. The skeletal system is divided into the **axial** and **appendicular** portions. The axial skeleton consists of the **skull, hyoid bone, thoracic cage,** and **vertebral column**. The appendicular skeleton consists of the **pectoral girdle** and the **upper limbs** (arms), and the **pelvic girdle** and the **lower limbs** (legs). There are usually a total of 206 bones in the human body, and most of these can be found in the skull, hands, and feet.

F. CLASSIFICATION AND STRUCTURE OF BONES

Bones are classified according to their shape (**long, short, flat,** or **irregular**). A long bone such as the **humerus** is often used to illustrate the major structures of a bone (see Figure 17.2). The shaft, or longest portion of the bone, is referred to as the **diaphysis**, and at each end of the diaphysis lies an enlarged part called an **epiphysis**, which functions in articulating with other bones. The portion of each epiphysis that connects with another bone is covered by **articular cartilage**. The entire bone is covered by the **periosteum**, a fibrous tissue which allows an entrance and exit for blood vessels and nerves, and provides a site for the attachment of **tendons** (which connect muscles to bones) and **ligaments** (which attach bones to other bones). It is also involved in the formation and repair of bone tissue. The hardened part of the diaphysis consists of **compact bone** tissue, while the epiphyses are made up of **spongy bone** tissue. The compact bone of the diaphysis encloses a cylindrical space called the **medullary canal**, which contains blood vessels, nerves, and the **bone marrow**, a soft connective tissue involved in the production of blood cells.

Bone connective tissue, as we noted in Chapter 13, consists of cells called osteocytes which exist in cavities (**lacunae**) separated by a collagenous matrix. The matrix also contains large amounts of inorganic mineral salts, mainly in the form of **hydroxyapatite** (calcium phosphate), which gives bone tissue its great hardness. In the case of compact bone, the cavities are arranged in concentric circles around **Haversian (osteonic) canals**, which contain blood vessels to nourish the osteocytes. Osteocytes concentrically clustered around a Haversian canal form units called **Haversian (osteonic) systems**. Many of these units join together in an orientation that confers resistance to pressure, and make up the substance of the compact bone tissue. In spongy bone, the osteocytes are not clustered around Haversian canals, but instead rest within the spaces formed by the **trabeculae**, bony plates that are irregularly connected and cause spongy bone tissue to be strong but light.

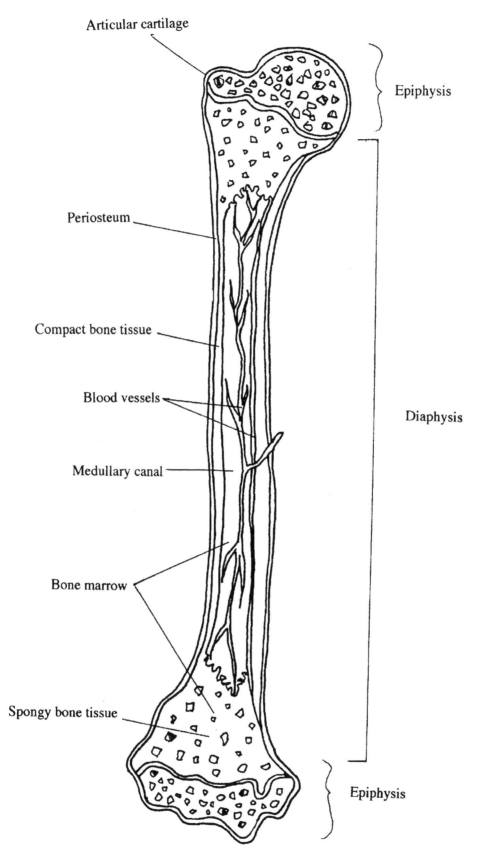

Articular cartilage

Epiphysis

Periosteum

Compact bone tissue

Blood vessels

Diaphysis

Medullary canal

Bone marrow

Spongy bone tissue

Epiphysis

Figure 17.2: Structure of a long bone, the humerus

G. GROWTH AND DEVELOPMENT OF BONES

Most bones are ***endochondral*** bones, which initially develop as cartilage that is gradually replaced by bone tissue in the process of ***endochondral ossification***. (Other bones, mainly in the skull, are termed ***intramembranous*** and develop from layers of non-cartilaginous connective tissue.) An endochondral bone grows in length due to the mitotic activity of cells in an ***epiphyseal disk***, located between an epiphysis and the diaphysis. Ultimately, the disk itself becomes ossified, and no further growth can occur. During an individual's entire life, however, bones are continually "remodeled", as bone tissue is continually ***resorbed*** and new tissue ***deposited***. Many factors are necessary for the proper growth and development of bones, including vitamins A, C and D, the minerals calcium and phosphorus, and growth and thyroid hormones.

H. BONE ARTICULATIONS (JOINTS)

Joints exist wherever bones meet, and are classified according to the means by which the bones are bound together. Most joints where movement occurs are classified as ***synovial joints***. Here, bones are held together by the ***joint capsule*** (which is strengthened by the presence of ligaments). Between the bones involved exists a joint cavity, which is surrounded by the inner surfaces of the capsule. These surfaces are lined with a specialized type of integumentary membrane, the ***synovial membrane***, which secretes ***synovial fluid*** that acts as a lubricant so that the bones do not crunch against each other.

I. FUNCTIONS AND ORGANIZATION OF THE MUSCULAR SYSTEM

The major function of the muscular system is to allow movement. As we noted earlier, muscle tissue can be classified as one of three major types: skeletal, smooth, or cardiac. Individual ***muscles***, composed of a particular type of muscular tissue as well as connective and nervous tissue, are the organs of the muscular system. ***Skeletal muscles*** are responsible for the movements of bones and are under voluntary control. ***Smooth muscles*** facilitate the movement of substances through the body (e. g. food in the digestive tract or blood in a vein), while ***cardiac muscle*** (the myocardium) is found exclusively in the heart and provides the driving force for the movement of blood in the cardiovascular system. Both cardiac and smooth muscles are under involuntary control. By weight, muscle tissue, particularly skeletal muscle, is the most prevalent tissue in the body.

J. STRUCTURE AND ACTIONS OF SKELETAL MUSCLES

An individual skeletal muscle is composed of thousands of ***muscle fibers***, and each muscle fiber is actually a single, specialized muscle cell shaped like a long cylinder, up to several centimeters in length (see Figure 17.3)! Muscle cells contain multiple nuclei and mitochondria, and a specialized plasma membrane called the ***sarcolemma***, which can become depolarized and carry an action potential similar to the action potential of a neuron. Perhaps the most striking feature of the muscle fiber is the presence of thousands of long subunits called ***myofibrils***, surrounded by a tubular membrane system called the ***sarcoplasmic reticulum*** (equivalent to the endoplasmic reticulum of a non-muscle cell). Another membranous network of tubes, the ***transverse tubules***, are invaginations of the sarcolemma that permeate the fiber, allowing an action potential to quickly spread to interior regions of each muscle cell. The functional unit of the myofibril is the ***sarcomere***, each of which is composed of ***thin filaments*** made of the protein ***actin*** associated with ***thick filaments*** made up of the protein ***myosin***. Repeating sarcomeres cause a skeletal muscle to take on its characteristic striated appearance. The sarcomere contains light regions (called I bands), composed exclusively of thin filaments anchored directly to a proteinaceous ***Z line***, and darker regions (called A bands), which consist of thick filaments which overlap thin filaments. The thick filaments are indirectly connected to the Z lines, and the region from one Z line to the next is a complete sarcomere (see Figure 17.4).

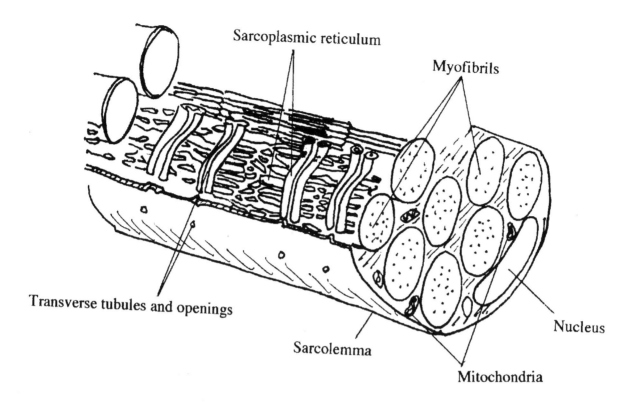

Figure 17.3: A muscle fiber

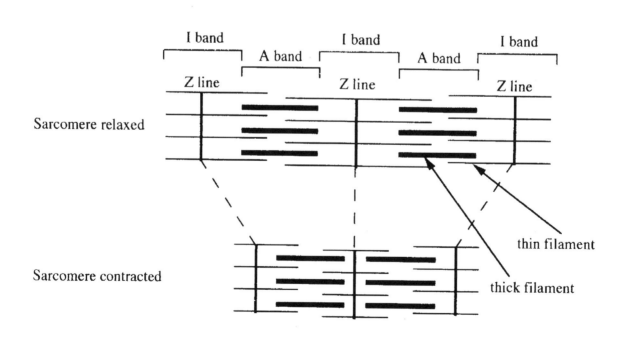

Figure 17.4: The sarcomere

Each muscle is surrounded by layers of fibrous connective tissue referred to as *fascia*. Extensions of the fascia form *tendons*, the structures that connect skeletal muscles to bones. In order to do its job, a skeletal muscle must be attached to at least two bones. Furthermore, if the contraction (shortening) of the muscle is to move a designated bone in a particular direction, one attachment must be immovable and the other movable. The immovable point of attachment is referred to as the origin, and the movable attachment is called the *insertion*. Thus when the muscle contracts, it produces a movement by "pulling on" the bone to which it is inserted. Muscles generally work in opposing pairs referred to as *antagonistic*; this means that since the only action a muscle can perform is contraction, one muscle acts to move a bone in a particular direction, while its antagonistic partner must contract to move it in the opposite direction.

K. THE MECHANISM AND REGULATION OF MUSCLE CONTRACTION

As noted previously, the sarcomere is the functional unit of muscle contraction. The thin filaments are composed of globular actin protein subunits polymerized to form a long chain, two of which are wrapped around each other to form the filament. Thick filaments, on the other hand, are composed of two myosin chains wrapped around each other; each chain is a long, fibrous protein, with an exposed globular "head" at its end and many globular "cross-bridges" protruding along its length. Given the arrangement of thick and thin filaments in the sarcomere, how can we explain and understand the contraction of a muscle fiber?

One of the remarkable aspects of muscle fiber contraction is that although the entire muscle fiber becomes shorter during contraction, nothing actually gets shorter at the molecular level. Instead, the myosin and actin filaments slide past each other, so that they take up less space, in a process explained by the "sliding filament" model. According to this model, when the muscle fiber is stimulated, the head and cross-bridges on the myosin molecule approach and interact with binding sites on the actin molecule. The head hydrolyzes ATP, which provides the energy by which the myosin cross-bridges and head propel the thin filament closer to the center of the sarcomere. Repeated cycles of attachment, movement, and breakage cause the actin filaments to slide past the myosin molecules, so that, at full contraction, the Z lines, which are directly attached to the thin filaments, are almost touching the myosin heads (see Figure 17.4). Thus as the sarcomere gets "smaller", due to changes in the relative positions of the thick and thin filaments, the myofibril as a whole is seen to contract, pulling the bone to which it is attached.

Since skeletal muscles contract in response to voluntary signals from the nervous system, we must explain the mechanism by which the course of events detailed above is set into action and controlled. As we observed in Chapter 14, motor neurons are nervous tissue cells in pathways leading from the brain to an effector organ, usually a muscle. The axon of a motor neuron interacts with the sarcolemma of a muscle cell at the *neuromuscular junction*, which resembles a neuronal synapse in many ways. Often a motor neuron is connected to several muscle fibers, which it stimulates to contract simultaneously. The motor neuron and all its associated muscle fibers are referred to as a *motor unit*. The axon releases the neurotransmitter *acetylcholine* in response to an incoming action potential, which binds to postsynaptic receptors on the muscle cell sarcolemma, triggering a depolarization of the sarcolemma which quickly spreads throughout the muscle fiber by way of the transverse tubules. The acetylcholine is quickly degraded by the enzyme *acetylcholinesterase* in order to "reset" the system for the next signal. How does the depolarization of the membrane lead to contraction?

Two other groups of proteins are involved in the regulatory process. *Tropomyosin* molecules are long and thin, and are associated with globular *troponin* molecules. When the muscle fiber is relaxed, the tropomyosin interacts with the actin filaments so that the binding sites for myosin cross-bridge formation are covered. When the membrane is depolarized, electrical changes occur that cause gated channels for the positively charged ion calcium to open in the membrane of the sarcoplasmic reticulum (SR). Since large amounts of calcium are stored inside the SR, it quickly rushes out into the cytoplasm (often called the *sarcoplasm*) of the muscle cell. Calcium subsequently binds to troponin, causing a conformational change which shifts tropomyosin off the myosin binding sites of the thin filaments, allowing cross-bridge formation, ATP hydrolysis, and the sliding of the filaments. When the sarcolemma is repolarized, calcium is pumped back into the sarcoplasmic reticulum by active transport, the muscle fiber relaxes, and the cycle is ready to begin again.

L. SKELETAL MUSCLES AND ENERGY SUPPLY

As noted above, ATP supplies the energy for a muscle fiber to contract. Since muscular contraction often requires large amounts of energy, especially under extreme exertion, the supply of ATP that can be generated by aerobic cellular respiration is sometimes not enough to fuel the muscle's needs. Under these circumstances, alternate means of generating ATP must be found, or muscle contraction will cease. Firstly, muscles store additional fuel in the form of glycogen, which can be quickly mobilized when energy is needed. Muscles also store another high energy compound called *creatine phosphate*, which reacts with ADP to regenerate ATP by donating a phosphate group. Thus as the ATP supply dwindles, it can be quickly "restocked" by creatine phosphate. If energy demands are still not being met, the body uses its last alternative: the anaerobic process of fermentation begins in the muscle cells. As noted earlier, glucose can be broken down by humans in the process of fermentation to produce two molecules of lactic acid (lactate). While extremely inefficient, the process can provide extra ATP for short periods of time. Since lactic acid is toxic, however, when the "emergency" need for energy is over it must be reconverted to glucose in a process known as *gluconeogenesis*. This process requires energy, which is usually supplied by aerobic respiration. The amount of energy required to dispose of the lactic acid that has been produced corresponds to the so-called "oxygen debt", and explains why heavy breathing often continues even when activity has ceased.

M. SMOOTH AND CARDIAC MUSCLES

In general, the mechanisms of contraction of both smooth and cardiac muscles resemble those of skeletal muscles. Several important differences in both structure and function, however, are apparent. Smooth muscles contain both actin and myosin filaments, but they are more randomly arranged and are not positioned into sarcomeres. Smooth muscle cells also:

- Lack transverse tubules.
- Have only a single nucleus
- Have poorly developed sarcoplasmic reticula.
- Contain the protein *calmodulin* instead of troponin which serves essentially the same function by binding to calcium.
- Are stimulated only by the autonomic division of the nervous system.
- Can recognize the neurotransmitter *norepinephrine (noradrenaline)* as well as acetylcholine. In addition, smooth muscles are often stimulated to contract by hormones.

Cardiac muscle is located exclusively in the heart, and is unique in being the only muscle that is both striated and involuntarily controlled. Its contraction is virtually identical to that of skeletal muscle, as might be expected from the presence of sarcomeres. However, the ends of the muscle cells of the myocardium are connected by *intercalated disks,* which help hold the cells together and allow muscle impulses to travel rapidly from cell to cell. Unlike skeletal muscle, cardiac muscle is self-exciting, and when one portion of the muscle is stimulated, the depolarization quickly travels to other fibers, causing the entire muscle to contract as a unit. The initial stimulation for a single "heartbeat" comes from the *sinoatrial node*, or "pacemaker".

Chapter 17 Problems

Passage 17.1 (Questions 1-2)

Psoriasis is a chronic skin disease in which afflicted individuals develop red patches with a scale-like appearance. The cause of psoriasis is a relatively simple one, but it is difficult to treat. The epidermal cells of an individual with psoriasis are dividing 5-10 times more frequently than they should be! This accounts for the excessive accumulation of cells that leads to the symptoms, as they cannot be sloughed off quickly enough to prevent buildup.

1. Which of the following statements is true of the cells making up the scaly patches of a psoriasis sufferer?
   A. The cells are alive and contain large quantities of melanin.
   B. The cells are dead and highly keratinized.
   C. The dead cells are far from the dermis, but blood vessels from the dermis grow towards the surface of the skin and supply them with nutrients, or else they could not continue to divide.
   D. The cells are dead and contain large quantities of collagen.

2. What type of drugs might be effective in severe cases of psoriasis?
   A. Collagen creams designed to moisturize the skin.
   B. Antibiotics that can kill the bacteria responsible for the problem.
   C. Anticancer drugs that systemically inhibit mitosis.
   D. Drugs that inhibit the formation of sebum, and have also been used to effectively treat acne.

Passage 17.2 (Questions 2-4)

At the neuromuscular junction of a skeletal muscle, neurotransmitters must contact receptors on the muscle fiber sarcolemma to transmit the signal for muscle contraction. That neurotransmitter must subsequently be enzymatically broken down, so that it is removed from the receptor, "resetting it" to receive another message. Many "chemical weapons" are in fact inhibitors of the enzyme necessary to break down the neurotransmitter in question, causing it to remain attached to the receptor indefinitely.

3. The enzyme inhibited by most chemical weapons is probably:
   A. Acetylcholinesterase
   B. Acetylcholine
   C. Seratonase
   D. ATPase

4. Which of the following would probably result after poisoning by one of the agents described in the passage?
   A. The heart would stop, since no messages from the nervous system could signal it to contract.
   B. A person would begin to lose the ability to actively move, and would ultimately die from the failure of the diaphragm to contract, causing suffocation.
   C. The person would suffer from mental confusion, as messages could not be sent within the brain itself.
   D. All muscular functioning in the body would cease.

The following questions are NOT based on a descriptive passage.

5. Under which conditions would normal human body cooling mechanisms work best?
   A. Temperature 80°F, humidity 95%
   B. Temperature 80°F, humidity 35%
   C. Temperature 100°F, humidity 50%
   D. Cooling mechanisms are unaffected by the humidity and/or temperature, and will work just as efficiently under all of the stated conditions.

6. Which of the following connective tissues bind muscles to bones?
   A. Ligaments
   B. Articular cartilage
   C. Tendons
   D. Adipose tissue

7. The release of which ion from the sarcoplasmic reticulum of a muscle fiber directly stimulates muscle contraction?
   A. Sodium
   B. Potassium
   C. Calcium
   D. Phosphorus

8. Which layer of the skin consists mainly of vascularized adipose tissue?
   A. Epidermis
   B. Dermis
   C. Subcutaneous layer
   D. None of the above

9. Hair follicles are located physically in the _____, but hair consists of _____ cells.
   A. Epidermis; dermal
   B. Dermis; epidermal
   C. Subcutaneous layer; epidermal
   D. Subcutaneous layer; dermal

10. Which of the following is not necessary for muscle contraction according to the sliding filament model?
    A. ATP
    B. Calcium ions
    C. Creatine phosphate
    D. Troponin molecules

CHAPTER 18

Reproductive System, Gametogenesis, and Development

A. INTRODUCTION

Almost all vertebrates reproduce sexually, and sexual life cycles always entail two complementary processes: *meiosis* and *fertilization*. Meiosis is a type of cell division which produces genetically *haploid (n)* cells, or *gametes*, from *diploid (2n)* precursor cells. These gametes, the *sperm* and *eggs* (or *ova*) in males and females, respectively, unite in the process of fertilization to produce a new diploid individual, a *zygote*. This zygote then undergoes a series of changes which constitute its *development* into a mature adult form. The reproductive systems of males and females contain the structures and perform the functions that make these events possible.

   Reproductive systems are unique in that they are not necessary to promote and facilitate the life of the individual organism. Their ultimate function is simply to ensure that new individuals can be produced. Specifically, this means that they are involved in the processes of gamete production and delivery and the maintenance of the life of a developing individual. As usual, we will explore sexual reproduction and development in the context of the human process, realizing that while the fundamentals are similar in most vertebrates, differences exist in specific strategies between the vertebrate classes.

   (Please note: some of the terminology used in this chapter, especially with reference to meiosis, presupposes a general knowledge of basic genetic principles and terms. Review the genetics chapters if you are uncomfortable with these concepts.)

B. STRUCTURE AND FUNCTION OF THE MALE REPRODUCTIVE SYSTEM

The male reproductive system is composed of the primary sex organs, the testes, and a variety of accessory organs that function in the transportation and maintenance of sperm cells (see Figure 18.1). The testes play the major role in production of functional sperm cells, and also secrete the major male sex hormone, testosterone. We will first examine the testes, and then consider the contributions of the accessory organs.

◆   *testes:* The testes (singular: testis) are the primary sex organs, or *gonads*, in males (see Figure 18.2). The testes are suspended in a sac called the *scrotum*, which allows them to lie just outside the body. For a variety of reasons, sperm formation is facilitated by the slightly lower temperature of the scrotum, and inhibited by normal body temperature. Sperm are actually produced in coiled *seminiferous tubules*, which fill most of the volume of each testis. Epithelial cells lining the tubules ultimately differentiate into *primary spermatocytes*, each of which undergoes meiosis (refer to the part on meiosis later in this chapter) to produce four haploid *spermatids* (immature sperm cells). Other cells located in the tubules, the *Sertoli cells*, function to nourish the developing sperm

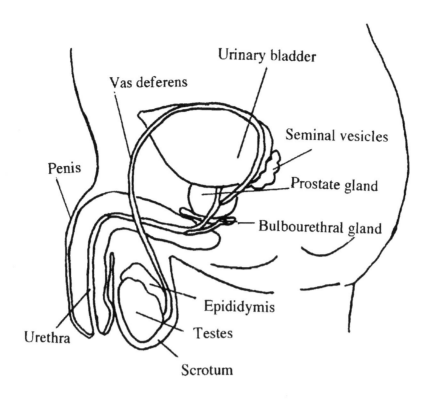

Figure 18.1: The male reproductive system

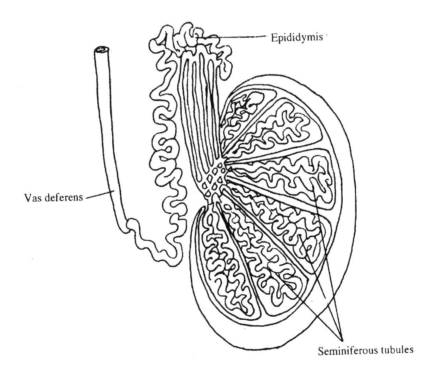

Figure 18.2: A testis (internal view)

cells during this time. It is interesting to note that sperm production begins during adolescence, and continues throughout a male's entire life. Spermatids begin to mature while still in the testis, and the process continues as they move to the *epididymis*.

♦ *epididymis:* The epididymis is a coiled tube that lies just above each testis. Here sperm complete their differentiation, acquiring a distinctive shape and the ability to move. A mature sperm cell consists of a head, which contains the nucleus with the chromosomes; the body, which harbors mitochondria for energy production; and a tail, which allows the sperm to "swim".

♦ *vas deferens:* Each epididymis is connected to a tube called the vas deferens (plural: vasa deferentia), in which many sperm are stored and transported. The vasa deferentia enter the abdominal cavity where they merge and join the duct of the *seminal vesicles*. The seminal vesicles secrete a viscous fluid containing fructose (an energy source for the sperm) and hormones that will stimulate the female system when the sperm are deposited. The sperm then travel through the *prostate gland*, which secretes an alkaline fluid into the *semen* to enhance sperm motility. Ultimately, the sperm enter the *urethra*. The sperm, immersed in semen, exit the body through the urethra, a tube which runs the length of the *penis*, the male organ of sexual intercourse. (Recall that urine also exits the body through the urethra; in males, the reproductive and urinary systems are intimately connected. Special precautions exist that prevent the conduction of both semen and urine at the same time.)

C. STRUCTURE AND FUNCTION OF THE FEMALE REPRODUCTIVE SYSTEM

The female reproductive system is composed of the primary sex organs, the *ovaries*, and a variety of other important organs that function in the transport of egg cells and the maintenance of the life of the developing fetus (see Figures 18.3 and 18.4). The *ovaries* play the major role of producing and releasing functional egg cells, and also secrete the major female sex hormones, *estrogen* and *progesterone*. The *uterus* provides a suitable environment for the development of a new organism.

♦ *ovaries:* The ovaries, located in the abdominal cavity, are the primary sex organs in females. Cells called *primary oocytes* will eventually give rise to mature haploid egg cells through meiosis, similar to sperm production in males. Unlike sperm production, however, all of the primary oocytes a female will ever produce are formed by birth, and all are arrested in prophase of meiosis I. They are surrounded by a structure called the *ovarian follicle*, whose cells provide nutrition for the developing egg. At the onset of puberty, a follicle ruptures and an oocyte is released approximately once every 28 days in a process called *ovulation*; the first meiotic division is completed just before the oocyte is released. Meiosis II will only take place if the egg is fertilized. Females stop releasing eggs at *menopause*, which normally occurs at around age 50.

♦ *oviducts:* After ovulation, the newly released oocyte is swept into a tube called the oviduct or *Fallopian tube*, located near the ovary. The egg travels through the oviduct towards the *uterus* due to smooth muscle contractions. If fertilization occurs, it must happen in the oviduct; whether or not it becomes fertilized, the egg will eventually reach the *uterus*.

♦ *uterus:* A fertilized egg begins dividing during its journey and will implant itself into the uterine wall (called the *endometrium*). Here it will continue to develop and grow, the details of which will be discussed later. If the egg has not been fertilized, it will eventually be expelled from the uterus with most of the uterine lining during *menstruation*.

♦ ***vagina:*** The vagina is a muscular tube which connects the uterus to the external environment. It therefore serves a dual function: it is the female organ of sexual intercourse, which allows the penis to enter and deposit sperm, and it also functions as the birth canal, through which the fetus will emerge when it is born. The ***cervix*** is the muscle surrounding the opening of the uterus into the vagina.

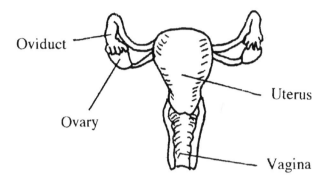

Figure 18.3: The female reproductive system

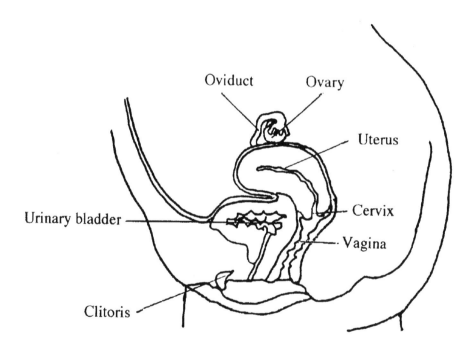

Figure 18.4: The female reproductive system (internal sagittal view)

D. HORMONE PRODUCTION AND REGULATION

As we noted previously, in addition to their roles in creating gametes, the testes and ovaries also produce and secrete the major male and female sex hormones.

Testosterone production begins in males during early embryonic development, and is responsible for the development of an embryo as a male rather than a female. After birth, the production of testosterone is inhibited until about the age of ten, when a surge in its production triggers the onset of puberty. The testosterone produced during this period stimulates the testes to begin producing sperm. It is also responsible for the development of the male secondary sexual characteristics, including the development of facial and body hair, deepening of the voice, and the growth of muscle tissue. The production of testosterone is at all times controlled by various pituitary hormones and the hypothalamus.

In females, the hypothalamus controls the release of various pituitary hormones which interact with estrogen and progesterone to create the ***menstrual cycle***, the period from ovulation to menstruation that occurs on a monthly basis. As in males, the onset of puberty follows increased secretion of sex hormones, and, in addition to initiating the menstrual cycle, causes the development of the female secondary sexual characteristics, which include enlargement of the hips and breasts.

E. SEXUAL RESPONSE AND STIMULATION

In males, sexual excitation causes ***erection*** of the penis due to an influx of blood into the erectile tissue which occupies most of the volume of the penis. Erection is accompanied by the secretion of small amounts of seminal fluid from the ***bulbourethral (Cowper's) glands***, which functions as a lubricant in anticipation of sexual intercourse. If sensory receptors on the penis receive continued stimulation, various muscles involuntarily contract causing the forceful ***ejaculation*** of sperm through the vasa deferentia and urethra, experienced as a series of pleasant sensations referred to as ***orgasm***.

While females may also experience orgasm, it is not necessary in order for conception to take place. The ***clitoris***, which is developmentally homologous to the penis, is the organ of sexual stimulation in females. When arousal occurs, pleasant sensations are accompanied by the secretion into the vagina of a lubricating fluid, and muscular contractions occur similar to those in males.

F. MEIOSIS AND GAMETOGENESIS

Meiosis is the process of cell division that allows haploid cells to be created from diploid parent cells. It occurs only in sexual reproduction, only in the primary sex organs, and only for the purpose of gamete production, or ***gametogenesis***. Meiosis is similar to mitosis (see Chapter 12), but two complete division cycles take place instead of one, and four haploid cells are produced as opposed to two diploid cells.

Meiosis consists of the following stages and events (see Figure 18.5):

- ♦ ***prophase I***: During this phase, chromosomes condense, the nuclear envelope breaks down, and spindle formation begins.
- ♦ ***metaphase I***: At this stage, homologous chromosome pairs line up on the cell's equator; this is the major difference between meiosis and mitosis!
- ♦ ***anaphase I***: The homologous chromosomes separate and begin to move towards the opposite poles of the cell.
- ♦ ***telophase I***: Nuclear membranes may or may not form and cytokinesis may or may not occur; regardless, the haploid sets of chromosomes have been separated, and are now ready to proceed through meiosis II.

- ♦ ***prophase II***: During this phase, chromosomes condense, the nuclear envelope breaks down, and spindle formation begins again.
- ♦ ***metaphase II***: At this stage, chromosomes (which still consist of two chromatids) line up randomly on the cell's equator.
- ♦ ***anaphase II***: The chromatids separate and begin to move towards the opposite poles of the cell.
- ♦ ***telophase II***: As meiosis draws to a close, sets of haploid genomes become enclosed by new nuclear membranes, the chromosomes begin to decondense, and the spindle apparatus is disassembled.

As noted earlier, the result of meiotic cell division is four haploid cells from each parental diploid cell. The process of meiosis itself is virtually identical in the two sexes, except for the timing of the divisions (as mentioned previously). Gametogenesis proceeds differently, however, in males and females. In males, each of the newly created haploid cells, referred to as spermatids, will eventually mature and become a functional sperm cell. In females, on the other hand, only one of the haploid cells produced by meiosis will become a mature egg. The other cells do not grow and are pushed to the side of the follicle. They are visible microscopically as ***dark polar bodies***, and play no further role in the reproductive process. This is probably because the presence of four functional eggs at one time would virtually guarantee multiple births, which might not be desirable depending on the species.

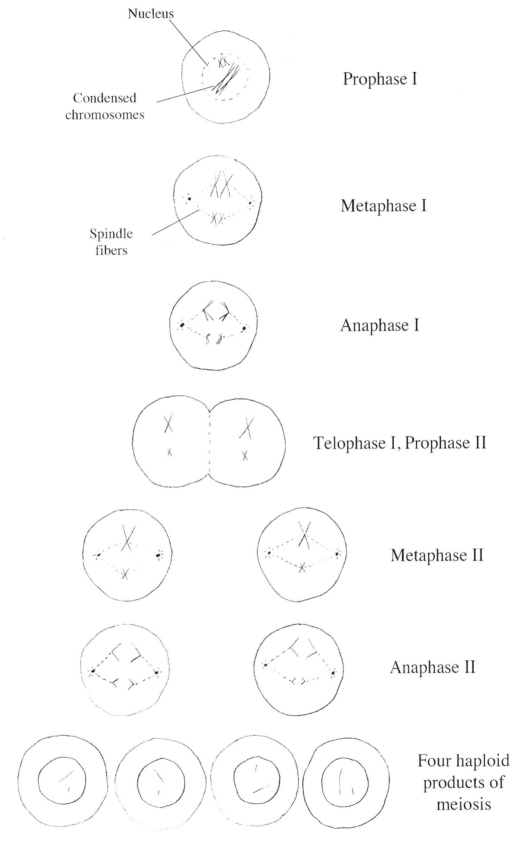

Figure 18.5: The stages of meiosis

G. EARLY DEVELOPMENT

We have already seen how sperm and eggs are produced, and noted the physical processes that allow them to meet. When a sperm contacts an egg (in the oviduct), a chemical reaction takes place between molecules on the surfaces of the sperm and egg. This binding signals the sperm to release enzymes that begin to dissolve the outer layers of the egg's protective coating, and ultimately allows the fusion of the sperm and egg plasma membranes. The sperm nucleus now enters the cytoplasm of the egg, and several changes rapidly ensue:

- ◆ Electrical and physical changes in the egg cause the plasma membrane to become unable to bind with any other sperm; these changes are called blocks to "polyspermy", or the fertilization of an egg by multiple sperm cells. It should be clear why this is necessary, as any cell with more than a diploid set of chromosomes would be inviable.
- ◆ The egg becomes metabolically active, and completes meiosis II. Protein synthesis increases dramatically.
- ◆ When the nuclei of the sperm and egg fuse, a diploid cell is created called a zygote. Now the cell has the potential to continue along its developmental pathway.
- ◆ The zygote begins to prepare for mitotic division.

After fertilization occurs, the egg continues its journey towards the uterus, and more changes take place along the way (see Figure 18.6).

- ◆ *cleavage*, a modified form of mitosis, begins. During cleavage, mitotic cell divisions are not accompanied by cell growth. Thus, the number of cells is increasing, but the overall volume is not increasing. This is because no nutrients are yet available to provide energy for growth processes.
- ◆ *a morula*, or solid ball of cells, has been produced by the time the dividing cells reach the uterus. This usually takes about three days.

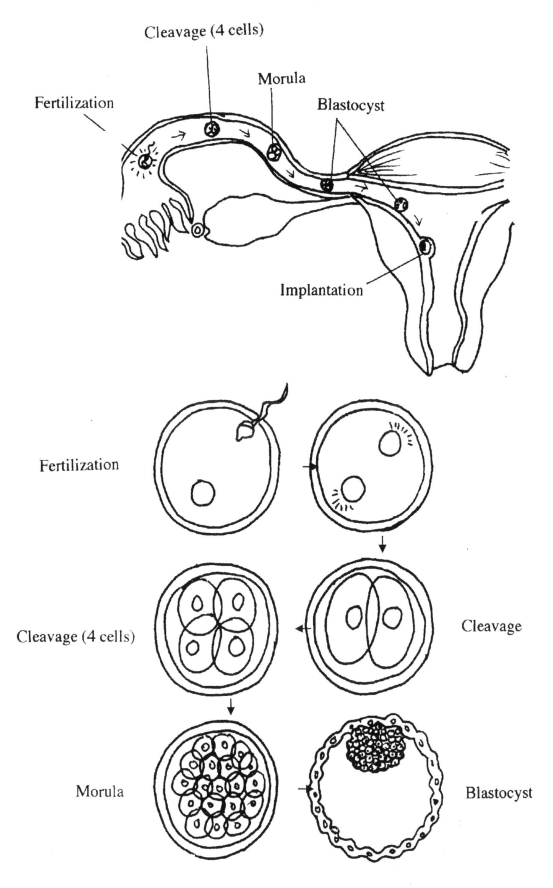

Figure 18.6: Early developmental events

♦ ***a blastocyst*** is formed as the cells of the morula are pushed towards the periphery, and consists of a hollow ball of cells. The blastocyst forms after about six days, and is often called the blastula in other vertebrate species.

♦ ***implantation*** of the blastocyst into the uterine wall (the endometrium) occurs towards the end of the first week.

After implantation, the cell mass that has implanted itself can be properly referred to as the ***embryo***. The embryonic stage lasts until the beginning of the third month of development. This is the most crucial period for proper formation of major structures, and many important changes occur during embryonic development.

♦ The ***placenta*** forms between the embryo and mother, and allows transport of nutrients and oxygen to the embryo for energy production. The placental connection also allows the transport of embryonic wastes from the embryo to the bloodstream of the mother. It is important to note that while small substances such as those mentioned above freely diffuse across the placenta, it is not a direct connection, and the circulation of mother and embryo remain separate.

♦ ***Gastrulation*** changes the overall shape of the embryo so that it resembles a three-layered disc, the gastrula. Three primary germ layers are formed by this process, each of which will eventually give rise to different structures in the adult organism:
  • ***Endoderm***, the inner layer, will give rise to the epithelium lining all inner cavities, including the linings of the digestive, respiratory, and urogenital tracts.
  • ***Mesoderm***, the middle layer, will give rise to internal organs, muscle and connective tissues, and the majority of internal structures.
  • ***Ectoderm***, the outer layer, will give rise to the nervous system and the skin.

♦ The embryo becomes enclosed in a fluid filled sac, the ***amnion***, surrounded by an amniotic membrane and several other membranes.

By the end of the embryonic period, roughly the ***first trimester, organogenesis*** and ***morphogenesis*** (the development of major organs and body shape, respectively) are basically complete. From the third month forward until birth (the second and third trimesters), the developing organism is referred to as the ***fetus***. While the fetal stage lasts the longest, the overall body plan has already been laid out, and most of the time spent as a fetus involves the growth and maturation of existing structures. After a total of approximately nine months, labor begins as the uterus begins to contract and the amniotic membrane ruptures. The baby passes through the dilated cervix and vagina, and enters the world as a new individual.

Chapter 18 Problems

Passage 18.1 (Questions 1-4)

Several genetic disorders are caused by trisomies or monosomies, the presence of one too many or one too few of a particular chromosome, respectively. Some such conditions include Down syndrome, which is caused by the presence of 3 copies of chromosome 21 (trisomy 21); Turner's syndrome, caused by the presence of only one sex chromosome (monosomy X, denoted XO); and Klinefelter's syndrome, caused by the presence of an extra sex chromosome (XXY).

Individuals with Down syndrome are somewhat mentally retarded, exhibit characteristic facial features, and suffer from a wide variety of chronic health problems. Turner's individuals appear female and may suffer slight retardation, while Klinefelter's individuals appear male and likewise may be somewhat retarded. While nondisjunction occurs randomly, no adults with trisomies or monosomies involving any chromosomes other than the sex chromosomes and chromosome 21 are ever observed; if such a condition occurs, it causes miscarriage or early death.

The major cause of trisomies and monosomies is nondisjunction (failure to separate) of homologous chromosomes or chromatids during meiosis, so that gametes are created with 2 copies or no copies of a particular chromosome (when there should be one of each).

1. Which of the following cases of nondisjunction could lead to the development of an individual with Turner's syndrome?
   A. Failure of the X and Y chromosome to separate during meiosis I in the father.
   B. Failure of the two X chromosomes to separate during meiosis I in the mother.
   C. Failure of the two Y chromatids to separate during meiosis II in the father.
   D. All of the above events could lead to Turner's syndrome.

2. The observations that Turner's individuals appear female and Klinefelter's individuals appear male may give us information about sex determination in humans. From this information we can tell that:
   A. Sex is determined by the number of X chromosomes (1=male, 2=female).
   B. Sex is determined by the presence of absence of the Y chromosome.
   C. Sex is determined by the egg, and not the sperm.
   D. Any of the above are consistent with the observations.

3. The fact that trisomies of only chromosome 21 and the sex chromosomes are observed in adults implies that:
   A. Chromosome 21 and the sex chromosomes are more prone to nondisjunction.
   B. Trisomies or monosomies of any other chromosomes have such detrimental effects that they do not allow development and cause death.
   C. There are no genes for fundamental life processes located on chromosome 21.
   D. Both B and C are correct.

4. The older a woman gets, the greater the chances that she will give birth to a Down syndrome child. Which of the following statements is true?
   A. Only the mother (through the egg) can cause Down syndrome in a child; the father (through the sperm) cannot.
   B. Older eggs have a greater chance of undergoing nondisjunction, since all of a female's eggs are present at birth, and meiosis is only completed after fertilization.
   C. The age of a man is completely irrelevant with respect to the chances of his sperm contributing to the formation of a Down syndrome child.
   D. Both B and C are correct.

The following questions are NOT based on a descriptive passage.

5. Which of the following statements is true regarding twin formation?
   A. Identical twins result from the fertilization of one egg by two sperm.
   B. Fraternal twins result when two eggs are mistakenly released at once, and each is fertilized by one sperm.
   C. Fraternal twins result when one egg is fertilized by one sperm, and the developing embryo splits apart, each part being able to grow into a new individual.
   D. Identical twins are not really genetically identical.

6. Fertilization normally takes place in which structure of the female reproductive system?
   A. the vagina
   B. the uterus
   C. the oviduct
   D. the ovary

7. Which of the following statements is true regarding the male and female reproductive and urinary systems?
   A. In both males and females, the urethra carries urine, and also functions in the reproductive system, in males for the delivery of sperm and in females as the orifice that accepts the sperm.
   B. In males, sperm and urine ultimately leave the body through the same tube, the urethra.
   C. In females, the ureters play a role in oogenesis, so the two systems are interconnected, but in a different way than occurs in males.
   D. None of the above statements is true.

8. In the late 1960s, a drug called thalidomide, ironically prescribed for morning sickness, was responsible for the malformation of several babies. In general, at what time during pregnancy would it be most dangerous to take a drug that is toxic or harmful to the developing child?
   A. During the zygote stage
   B. Before implantation
   C. During the embryonic stage
   D. During the fetal stage

9. Which embryonic germ layer ultimately gives rise to the structures of the nervous system?
   A. Endoderm
   B. Mesoderm
   C. Ectoderm
   D. Gastroderm

10. In most marine vertebrates (fish), physical copulation does not occur; instead, eggs and sperm are simply released into the water, where they can meet and fertilization may occur. Humans have various blocks to polyspermy, and fishes have similar mechanisms to prevent fertilization of an egg by more than one sperm. In addition, their method of fertilization probably requires:
    A. the release of far greater amounts of eggs by females.
    B. mechanisms to prevent the fertilization of more than one egg by a single sperm.
    C. mechanisms to avoid potential cross-species fertilization, which would be counterproductive since members of different species are genetically incompatible.
    D. both A and C are correct.

SECTION 4

Content Review Problems

1. A typical neuronal signal travels systemically through which parts of the neuron?
   A. Dendrites, cell body, axon, axon hillock, nerve terminal
   B. Dendrites, axon, cell body, axon hillock, nerve terminal
   C. Dendrites, cell body, axon hillock, axon, nerve terminal
   D. Dendrites, axon, axon hillock, soma, nerve terminal

2. Where are the Nodes of Ranvier?
   A. Soma
   B. Dendrite
   C. Axon
   D. Nerve terminal

3. How is the resting membrane potential in a neuron maintained at a polarized level?
   A. Extracellular signals
   B. Passive diffusion
   C. ATPase pumps
   D. Ca^{2+} infusion

4. As sodium floods into the neuron, the cell is said to be:
   A. hyperpolarizing.
   B. repolarizing.
   C. resting.
   D. depolarizing.

5. Voltage-gated potassium channels are:
   A. peripheral proteins.
   B. transmembrane proteins.
   C. G-protein coupled receptors.
   D. free-floating proteins.

6. Which of the following is made possible when two cells are joined via a gap junction?
   A. Chemical synapse
   B. Neuromuscular junctions
   C. Electrical synapse
   D. Saltatory conduction

7. Which of the following is the next step after an action potential reaches the nerve terminal?
   A. Ca^{2+} enters the nerve terminal.
   B. Ca^{2+} leaves the nerve terminal.
   C. Neurotransmitters are released via endocytosis.
   D. Neurotransmitters are released via diffusion.

8. A neurotransmitter that depolarized the post-synaptic membrane is called:
   A. inhibitory.
   B. excitatory.
   C. temporal.
   D. spatial.

9. Motor neurons that carry an impulse from the CNS to an effector are called:
   A. efferent neurons.
   B. afferent neurons.
   C. sensory neurons.
   D. interneurons.

10. Afferent neurons carry information:
    A. from the CNS.
    B. to the CNS.
    C. to effectors.
    D. to the heart.

11. A reflex:
    A. requires conscious thought.
    B. is a sensory response to a motor input.
    C. is monosynaptic when it requires only 2 neurons.
    D. always uses the brain in some capacity.

12. The voluntary movement of skeletal muscle is considered under which classification of the nervous system?
    A. Somatic
    B. Autonomic
    C. Central
    D. Parasympathetic

13. The parasympathetic nervous system can be informally described as which of the following?
    A. "Fight or flight"
    B. "Rest and strive"
    C. "Rest and digest"
    D. "Fight or plight"

14. Under sympathetic activation, the pupils will do what?
    A. Darkens
    B. Dilates
    C. Constricts
    D. Lightens

15. Stimulation of urination can be due to what?
    A. Parasympathetic NS
    B. Sympathetic NS
    C. Hormonal activity
    D. Circadian rhythms

16. Which part of the brain is directly responsible for controlling blood pressure and rate of respiration?
    A. Cerebellum
    B. Medulla
    C. Posterior pituitary
    D. Frontal cortex

17. Activation of nociceptors typically causes:
    A. pleasure.
    B. pain.
    C. numbness.
    D. sneezing.

18. Olfactory receptors are an example of what?
    A. Electromagnetic receptors
    B. Thermoreceptors
    C. Mechanoreceptors
    D. Chemoreceptors

19. Rod and cone cells of the human eye are an example of:
    A. electromagnetic receptors.
    B. thermoreceptors.
    C. mechanoreceptors.
    D. chemoreceptors.

20. From the auditory canal, sound waves reach:
    A. the auricle.
    B. the tympanic membrane.
    C. the stapes.
    D. the cochlea.

21. A sound's pitch is most directly related to:
    A. amplitude.
    B. polarization.
    C. speed.
    D. frequency.

22. Balance, or lack thereof, is sensed by which of the following?
    A. Eye
    B. Ear drum
    C. Semicircular canals
    D. Cochlea

23. Which part of the eye does light enter first?
    A. Cornea
    B. Pupil
    C. Lens
    D. Retina

24. The optic disk is responsible for:
    A. the most intense vision.
    B. seeing color.
    C. seeing contrast.
    D. the blind spot.

25. Nearsightedness is also called:
    A. myopia.
    B. emmetropia.
    C. hyperopia.
    D. presbyopia.

26. Farsightedness is called which of the following?
    A. Myopia
    B. Emmetropia
    C. Hyperopia
    D. Presbyopia

27. Presbyopia is a result of age in which there is a loss of flexibility in which of the following?
    A. Cornea
    B. Lens
    C. Pupil
    D. Ciliary muscles

28. Our sense of touch can be classified as all of the following receptors EXCEPT:
    A. Thermoreceptor
    B. Nociceptor
    C. Chemoreceptor
    D. Mechanoreceptor

29. What is function of T_3 and T_4?
    A. Increase calcium reabsorption at the level of the bone
    B. Increase basal metabolic rates
    C. Decrease blood pressure
    D. Induce cell growth

30. From where can catecholamines be released?
    A. Thyroid
    B. Pituitary
    C. Adrenal cortex
    D. Adrenal medulla

31. TSH activates which of the following?
    A. Hypothalamus
    B. Kidney
    C. Thyroid
    D. Heart

32. Which of the following is a lipophilic hormone?
    A. Testosterone
    B. Epinephrine
    C. TSH
    D. Vasopressin

33. Which of the following is a peptide hormone?
    A. Calcitonin
    B. Aldosterone
    C. Cortisol
    D. Progesterone

34. Among the following, which is most likely to be hydrophilic?
    A. Tyrosine derivative
    B. Steroid hormone
    C. Peptide hormone
    D. Neurotransmitter

35. Which of the following hormones stimulates the production of testosterone?
    A. Testosterone
    B. Estrogen
    C. FSH
    D. LH

36. Where are steroid hormone receptors?
    A. Outside the target cell
    B. Inside the target cell
    C. Free floating
    D. Within lysosomes

37. Where in the cell are steroids manufactured, and from what are they manufactured?
    A. Smooth ER, cholesterol
    B. Smooth ER, tyrosine
    C. Rough ER, cholesterol
    D. Rough ER, tyrosine

38. ACTH stimulates the release of which of the following?
    A. Angiotensin
    B. Cortisol
    C. Testosterone
    D. ADH

39. Which of the following synthesizes glucagon?
    A. Liver
    B. Gall bladder
    C. Kidney
    D. Pancreas

40. Where can exchange between blood and tissue take place?
    A. Arteries
    B. Veins
    C. Heart
    D. Capillaries

41. The inferior vena cava transports deoxygenated blood into which chamber of the heart?
    A. Left atrium
    B. Right atrium
    C. Left ventricle
    D. Right ventricle

42. Which of the following arteries does not contain oxygenated blood?
    A. Aorta
    B. Carotid artery
    C. Femoral artery
    D. Pulmonary artery

43. Why does backflow of blood in the heart occur without valves?
    A. Higher pressure in atria, lower pressure in ventricles
    B. Higher pressure in ventricles, lower pressure in atria
    C. Higher flow rate in atria, lower flow rate in ventricles
    D. Higher flow rate in ventricles, lower flow rate in atria

44. Blood is able to flow into the ventricles from the atria during:
    A. Diastole
    B. Systole
    C. Inspiration
    D. Exhalation

45. Which of the following initiates systole?
    A. Contraction of atria
    B. Relaxation of ventricles
    C. Contraction of ventricles
    D. Relaxation of atria

46. How can one increase venous return?
    A. Increase blood volume
    B. Increase temperature
    C. Decrease heart rate
    D. Decrease stroke volume

47. The plateau phase during the action potential of a cardiac cell is due to:
    A. Potassium gates
    B. Sodium gates
    C. Sodium-calcium gates
    D. Calcium gates

48. Every heartbeat is initiated with an action potential beginning at the:
    A. AV node.
    B. SA node.
    C. bundle of His.
    D. Purkinje fibers.

49. What allows the action potential to distribute evenly across the heart tissue and allow for a synchronized contraction of the ventricles?
    A. Nodes of Ranvier
    B. Purkinje fibers
    C. Desmosomes
    D. Fast twitch muscle fibers

50. Which of the following is the effect of the vagus nerve on the heart beat?
    A. Increases it
    B. Decreases it
    C. No effect
    D. Causes arrhythmia

51. A person with type B^+ blood can successfully receive which of the following blood types:
    A. AB^+ blood
    B. A^+ blood
    C. O^- blood
    D. A^- blood

52. Which of the following compounds is largely responsible for creating the blood buffer?
    A. Iron
    B. Oxygen
    C. Lactate
    D. Bicarbonate

53. The pH of the blood is normally closest to which of the following?
    A. 4.9
    B. 6.1
    C. 7.4
    D. 8.5

54. Blood's biggest component by volume is what?
    A. Erythrocytes
    B. White blood cells
    C. Plasma
    D. Electrolytes

55. Urea is a product of:
    A. amino acid catabolism.
    B. lipid catabolism.
    C. glucose catabolism.
    D. neuron catabolism.

56. Which of the following proteins has an integral role in blood clotting?
    A. Actin
    B. Myosin
    C. Fibrin
    D. Collagen

57. The ability for hemoglobin to increase its affinity for oxygen once oxygen is bound to one subunit is classified as:
    A. cooperativity.
    B. reactivity.
    C. saturation.
    D. accommodation.

58. In a typical oxygen-dissociation curve of hemoglobin, what type of shift does fetal hemoglobin represent?
    A. Right shift
    B. Left shift
    C. No shift
    D. Down shift

59. As hemoglobin's affinity for oxygen diminishes, a typical oxygen-hemoglobin dissociation curve shifts to the:
    A. right.
    B. left.
    C. up.
    D. down.

60. Within the context of blood-tissue exchange, the hydrostatic pressure is highest where?
    A. Capillaries
    B. Venules
    C. Arterioles
    D. Veins

61. Lymph nodes function to:
    A. filter the lymph.
    B. manufacture white blood cells.
    C. release ADH.
    D. aid in digestion.

62. Which of the following is a part of innate immunity?
    A. Antibodies
    B. Immunoglobulins
    C. Skin
    D. Platelets

63. The generic structure of an antibody is:
    A. T shaped.
    B. B shaped.
    C. C shaped.
    D. Y shaped.

64. Antibodies are produced by:
    A. macrophages.
    B. T cells.
    C. B cells.
    D. platelets.

65. Which of the following is more characteristic of the secondary immune response than the primary immune response?
    A. Slower
    B. Requires memory B cells
    C. Antigens are able to proliferate to a greater extent
    D. No reliance on antibodies

66. HIV kills which of the following?
    A. B cells
    B. Plasma cells
    C. Helper T cells
    D. Epithelial cells

67. Which of the following is not a normal role of Killer T cells?
    A. Destroy healthy host cells
    B. Destroy virus-infected cells
    C. Destroy cancer cells
    D. Destroy foreign cells

68. A phenomenon in which the immune system attacks host cells is:
    A. an exaggerated immune response.
    B. a hyper-reactive immunity.
    C. an autoimmune reaction.
    D. apoptosis.

69. Which of the following cells is able to synthesize all blood cell varieties?
    A. Neuronal stem cells
    B. Nephronal stem cells
    C. Bone marrow stem cells
    D. Thymus cells

70. GI tract muscles are considered to be:
    A. striated.
    B. skeletal.
    C. smooth.
    D. voluntary.

71. What separates an exocrine secretion from an endocrine secretion?
    A. Exocrine secretions pass through ducts.
    B. Endocrine secretions pass through ducts.
    C. Exocrine secretions travel through the blood.
    D. Endocrine secretions always have effectors nearby.

72. The salivary gland produces which of the following enzymes?
    A. Pepsin
    B. Amylase
    C. Trypsin
    D. Lipase

73. The portion of the GI tract that allows a bolus to travel from the epiglottis to the stomach is the:
    A. Trachea
    B. Esophagus
    C. Mouth
    D. Jejunum

74. Mastication is another word for:
    A. swallowing.
    B. spitting.
    C. suckling.
    D. chewing.

75. Which of the following is not true of saliva?
    A. Aids in transport of bolus
    B. Begins carbohydrate absorption
    C. Is produced by the salivary glands
    D. Secreted in the mouth

76. Which of the following is found within saliva?
    A. Lysozyme
    B. Lipase
    C. Trypsin
    D. Proteolysis enzymes

77. Which of the following is the typical pH of the stomach?
    A. -1
    B. 2
    C. 7
    D. 12

78. Chief cells in the stomach secrete which of the following?
    A. Trypsin
    B. Pepsin
    C. HCl
    D. Gastrin

79. The immense surface area of the intestines is a product of all of the following EXCEPT:
    A. villi.
    B. microvilli.
    C. peristalsis.
    D. long length.

80. Where is bile stored?
    A. Liver
    B. Spleen
    C. Gall bladder
    D. Pancreas

81. Which of the following is an important enzyme required for digestion in the small intestine that is also synthesized by the duodenum?
    A. Trypsin
    B. Pepsin
    C. Amylase
    D. Enteropeptidase

82. The role of the colon is to absorb which of the following?
    A. Protein
    B. Water
    C. Bile
    D. Chyme

83. Pancreatic enzymes that are released into the duodenum during digestion are an example of:
    A. exocrine function.
    B. endocrine function.
    C. hormonal function.
    D. neurotransmitter function.

84. Which of the following is not a hormone released from the pancreas?
    A. Glycogen
    B. Insulin
    C. Somatostatin
    D. Glucagon

85. Where is urea synthesized?
    A. Gall bladder
    B. Liver
    C. Intestines
    D. Kidneys

86. The functional unit of the kidney is the:
    A. nephron.
    B. neuron.
    C. cardiac cell.
    D. None of the above

87. As blood flows to the kidney and finally to a nephron it is filtered at the:
    A. proximal convoluted tubule.
    B. distal convoluted tubule.
    C. glomerulus.
    D. collecting duct.

88. Where in the nephron is glucose reabsorbed the most?
    A. Proximal convoluted tubule
    B. Distal convoluted tubule
    C. Glomerulus
    D. Collecting duct

89. Which of the following is true of both ADH and aldosterone?
    A. Act on dilation of blood vessels
    B. Increase blood pressure
    C. Released from anterior pituitary
    D. Exocrine hormones

90. Which of the following attaches muscle to bone?
    A. Tendon
    B. Ligament
    C. Cartilage
    D. Bone

91. Which of the following is NOT a characteristic of skeletal muscle?
    A. Voluntary
    B. Striated
    C. Uses neuromuscular junctions
    D. Has inherent rhythmic contractility independent of innervation

92. During skeletal muscle contraction, myosin is able to bind to the active site on actin because of the role of which of the following ions?
    A. Iron
    B. Magnesium
    C. Potassium
    D. Calcium

93. The sarcoplasmic reticulum:
    A. is a derivative of a ribosome.
    B. sequesters and releases calcium.
    C. sequesters and releases sodium.
    D. is responsible for ion synthesis.

94. Which of the following is true of cardiac muscle cells?
    A. Activated by neuromuscular junctions
    B. Multinucleated
    C. Connected via gap junctions
    D. Does not have sodium-calcium channels

95. Which of the following is true of smooth muscle?
   A. Voluntary
   B. Striated
   C. Mononucleated
   D. Do not have T-tubules

96. The end region of a bone is called the:
   A. end.
   B. diaphysis.
   C. epiphysis.
   D. knob.

97. Inactive bone marrow is called:
   A. yellow marrow.
   B. red marrow.
   C. grey marrow.
   D. blue marrow.

98. Red bone marrow is:
   A. found in every bone.
   B. the site of erythropoiesis.
   C. the site of glucose storage.
   D. a site that releases erythropoietin.

99. Bone is primarily comprised of collagen and what?
   A. Uric acid
   B. Hydroxyapatite
   C. Iron
   D. Keratin

100. Chondrocytes synthesize which of the following?
   A. Bone matrix
   B. Fatty acids
   C. Cartilage
   D. Steroid hormones

101. Bone can be said to undergo constant:
   A. degradation.
   B. dormancy.
   C. construction.
   D. remodeling.

102. Flexible joints are bathed in which of the following?
   A. Synovial fluid
   B. Mucus
   C. Water
   D. Plasma

103. Surfactant coats which of the following?
   A. The intestinal lining
   B. Alveoli
   C. Nephron lumen
   D. Dermis

104. To induce inspiration, the diaphragm:
   A. relaxes, increasing the pressure in the lungs.
   B. relaxes, decreasing the pressure in the lungs.
   C. contracts, increasing the pressure in the lungs.
   D. contracts, decreasing the pressure in the lungs.

105. Where are the intercostal muscles found?
   A. Around the esophagus
   B. Between the ribs
   C. In the neck
   D. Between vertebra

106. The maximum volume of air that can be breathed in is termed:
   A. functional residual capacity.
   B. tidal volume.
   C. total lung capacity.
   D. inspiratory capacity.

107. A decrease in pH can cause respiration to:
   A. increase.
   B. decrease.
   C. stall.
   D. remain unchanged.

108. What is the largest organ of the body?
   A. Heart
   B. Brain
   C. Skin
   D. Legs

109. Keratin is which of the following?
   A. Hydrophilic
   B. Hydrophobic
   C. Lipophobic
   D. None of the above

110. The dermis lies beneath which of the following?
   A. Hypodermis
   B. Epidermis
   C. Muscle
   D. Bone

111. Which of the following is not a thermoregulatory response in humans?
    A. Shivering
    B. Sweating
    C. Dilation of blood vessels
    D. Increase respiratory rate

112. Testosterone is which of the following?
    A. Neurotransmitter
    B. Androgen
    C. Sex cell
    D. Spermatozoan

113. LH stimulates which of the following?
    A. Leydig cells
    B. Sertoli cells
    C. Sperm cells
    D. A fertilized zygote

114. What is the male counterpart to the female ovary?
    A. Penis
    B. Prostate
    C. Testicle
    D. Sperm

115. The process by which spermatids and ovum are created is which of the following?
    A. Gametogenesis
    B. Mitosis
    C. Replication
    D. Binary fission

116. Spermatogenesis begins when?
    A. Before birth
    B. At birth
    C. Before puberty
    D. At puberty

117. Which of the following is true of meiosis I?
    A. It produces primary spermatogonia.
    B. It produces the zygote.
    C. It's the reductive division.
    D. It produces spermatids.

118. The portion of the head of a spermatozoa that contains hydrolytic enzymes to penetrate an egg is called which of the following?
    A. Head
    B. Acrosome
    C. Lysosome
    D. Hydrolase

119. What is responsible for nourishing an implanted and growing embryo?
    A. Ovaries
    B. Fallopian tubes
    C. Endometrium
    D. LH

120. After meiosis in the female, the cell that retains little of the cytoplasm is termed which of the following?
    A. Sickened cell
    B. Primary oocyte
    C. Secondary oocyte
    D. Polar body

121. The primary oocyte is stalled in prophase I until:
    A. birth.
    B. puberty.
    C. menopause.
    D. fertilization.

122. Female meiosis of the oocyte undergoes the second round after which of the following?
    A. Birth
    B. Puberty
    C. Menopause
    D. Fertilization

123. The corpus luteum can produce which of the following?
    A. Estrogen
    B. Progesterone
    C. Both estrogen and progesterone
    D. LH and FSH

124. In the ovulatory phase, an oocyte:
    A. undergoes meiosis I.
    B. undergoes meiosis II.
    C. is ejected from the ovary.
    D. dies.

125. Which is true of hCG? It:
   A. is a steroid hormone.
   B. is produced by the uterus.
   C. is produced by the embryo.
   D. activates uterine contractions.

126. The cleavage stage during embryogenesis leads first to which of the following?
   A. Morula
   B. Blastula
   C. Blastocyst
   D. Zygote

127. The nervous system is derived from which of the following?
   A. Endoderm
   B. Mesoderm
   C. Ectoderm
   D. Epiderm

SECTION 5
GENETICS AND EVOLUTION

The topics of genetics and evolution are closely linked. Not only do they complement each other, but they are central to our current understanding of all aspects of biology. These two topics unite and unify the various fields of biology, including molecular biology, microbiology, and anatomy and physiology. Therefore, the study of genetics and evolution is an absolute necessity for all students of biology.

In addition, the field of genetics is rapidly advancing. This has important consequences in many areas, not the least of which is medicine. Genetics has aided our understanding of cancer, inherited diseases, reproduction, infectious diseases, and much more. In the future, we will rely heavily on genetics to help us diagnose and treat a host of medical conditions.

CHAPTER 19
Genetics

A. INTRODUCTION

During the American Civil War, and at about the time Darwin was proposing his theory of evolution, a monk in what is now the Czech Republic was growing peas in the abbey gardens. Gregor Mendel was using them to unlock the secrets of inheritance.

No one prior to Mendel had undertaken a systematic study to gain insight into how traits are passed from one generation to the next. Breeders of plants and animals were well aware of certain characteristics of inheritance, but there was no theory or explanation of how traits were transmitted from parent to offspring. Mendel advanced our knowledge of the field tremendously, and his principles and theories have been shown to be valid over and over again. We still use his methodologies today.

Mendel was successful for several reasons. First, his choice of the garden pea provided him with an ideal model system. The traits Mendel observed in the peas were easy to score and only had two variations; for example, flowers were either white or purple, plants were either tall or short, and seeds were either wrinkled or round. Plants with different traits could be interbred and huge numbers of progeny could be obtained for analysis. But, perhaps more importantly than his choice of a model system, Mendel kept meticulous records, and he used mathematics to analyze his data.

B. DOMINANT AND RECESSIVE TRAITS

Mendel began his experiments with pure breeding strains. These were strains that had been bred for many generations so their progeny always exhibited the same traits, and these traits were always exactly the same in the parents and offspring. In his experiments, he crossed two pure breeding strains that differed only in one trait. The two original strains in this type of cross are called the ***parental generation***, or P. The resulting progeny are called the ***first filial generation***, or F_1. Mendel noticed that the F_1 plants displayed only one of the traits from the parents. When Mendel allowed the F_1 plants to self-fertilize, they produced the ***second filial generation (F_2)***. In this generation, some of the F_2 plants had the same trait as the F_1 plants (and hence of one of the P plants), but some had the trait not seen in the F_1 generation (but seen in the other P strain).

Mendel proposed that one trait was masking the expression of the other trait in the F_1 generation but the masked trait could reappear in the F_2. He called the trait that was always expressed ***dominant*** and the trait that could be masked ***recessive***.

For example, when Mendel crossed plants that produced yellow seeds with plants that produced green seeds, all the F_1 plants produced only yellow seeds. After self crossing the F_1 plants, some of the F_2 plants produced yellow seeds, and some produced green seeds. Specifically, Mendel found that about three quarters of the F_2 plants displayed the dominant trait (yellow seeds) and one quarter showed the recessive trait (green seeds). Another way to phrase this is to say there was a 3:1 ratio of yellow to green seeds in the F_2. Mendel found that each of the traits he looked at behaved exactly the same way. All had one variation that was dominant in the F_1 generation, and all showed a 3:1 ratio of dominant to recessive expression in the F_2 generation.

C. THE PRINCIPLE OF SEGREGATION

Mendel concluded that each plant contained two "factors" for each trait that could be inherited by the progeny. Each parent contributed one factor to the offspring. If the progeny received at least one factor that was dominant, the offspring would show that trait. Only offspring inheriting two recessive factors would show that characteristic. Since the two factors remain distinct and do not blend, Mendel called this the ***Principle of Segregation***.

Mendel did not know what these factors were, but today we can explain his observations on a molecular level. Mendel's "factors" are ***genes***, and the different varieties of the genes (purple vs. white flowers, for example) are called ***alleles***. Mendel's observations, particularly his Principle of Segregation, are easily explained with our knowledge of meiosis. During meiosis, the pairs of homologous chromosomes (those that carry the same information, or the same genes) line up and one chromosome of the pair moves to one pole of the cell while the other moves to the opposite pole. Therefore, one allele will be distributed to each new cell.

D. PHENOTYPES AND GENOTYPES

If you think about alleles and how they are expressed, you may realize that a dominant trait can be expressed in two ways: if an individual carries two copies of a dominant allele, or if it carries one copy of the dominant allele and one copy of the recessive allele. The only way to display the recessive trait is if two copies of the recessive allele are present. We use two terms in genetics to distinguish between what alleles an individual carries and what trait is expressed. ***Genotype*** refers to the exact alleles present, and ***phenotype*** is the trait that is observed. If the two alleles present are the same (either both dominant or both recessive), the condition is called ***homozygous***. If two different alleles are present in the genotype (the dominant and the recessive), the condition is called ***heterozygous***.

We are now ready to examine the inheritance of traits on a molecular level and to discuss some advanced topics in genetics. Be sure you understand the basics before you move on.

E. MONOHYBRID CROSSES

When only one trait in a cross is examined, the mating is called a ***monohybrid cross***. We can represent the cross in a simple manner and make predictions about the outcome. In crosses, the dominant allele is usually represented by a capital letter and the recessive allele is represented by the lower case. In addition, the dominant allele is used to represent the gene itself. For example, since yellow is dominant to green seeds, the letter Y is chosen to represent the gene for seed color. The dominant allele is Y while the recessive allele is represented as y. Recall that Mendel used only pure breeding strains in his experiments. Therefore, all his parental plants were homozygous.

If we consider the example from above, where Mendel crossed plants having yellow seeds with those having green seeds, we can represent the cross as follows:

$$P: \qquad YY \quad X \quad yy$$

Each parent will contribute one allele (through the gametes) to the offspring. From the homozygous dominant parent, the only allele that can be passed on to the offspring will be Y, while from the homozygous recessive parent, only a y allele can be transmitted. Therefore, all the offspring will be Yy. Remember that Mendel self-crossed the F_1 progeny to obtain the F_2. The results of this cross are shown below:

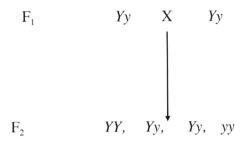

There are three genotypes in the F_2 generation (YY, Yy, and yy) but only two phenotypes (yellow and green seeds). Moreover, there is a 3:1 ratio of yellow to green seeds.

How can you determine the genotypes of the progeny from a cross? Typically, a matrix can be arranged to predict the outcomes of a cross. This matrix is called a ***Punnett square***. On one side of the square, all the possible gametes from one parent are listed, while on the other side, all the gametes from the other parent are listed. The gametes are then combined in the boxes. Consider our example of the parental cross (P) above:

	Y **(P gamete)**	**Y** **(P gamete)**
y **(P gamete)**	Yy (F_1 progeny)	Yy (F_1 progeny)
y **(P gamete)**	Yy (F_1 progeny)	Yy (F_1 progeny)

All the progeny (the F_1 generation) are genotypically heterozygotes, and each has a yellow phenotype. When the F_1 individuals are crossed, the Punnett square looks like this:

	Y **(F_1 gamete)**	**y** **(F_1 gamete)**
Y **(F_1 gamete)**	YY (F_2 progeny)	Yy (F_2 progeny)
y **(F_1 gamete)**	Yy (F_2 progeny)	yy (F_2 progeny)

The F_2 generation shows three genotypes: one quarter homozygous dominant (YY), one quarter homozygous recessive (yy) and one half heterozygous (Yy). The corresponding phenotypes are three quarters yellow and one quarter green, or a 3:1 ratio.

F. TEST CROSSES

Since the homozygous dominant genotype and the heterozygous genotype both express the same phenotype, we cannot be certain of the genotype of a plant that produces yellow seeds. We can determine its genotype by crossing it with a homozygous recessive plant, a true breeding plant that produces green seeds (genotype yy). This is called a **test cross**. The following two Punnett squares illustrate what progeny we would obtain from a test cross involving a homozygous dominant (left) or a heterozygote (right):

	Y	Y
y	Yy	Yy
y	Yy	Yy

	Y	y
y	Yy	yy
y	Yy	yy

If the yellow seed strain is homozygous dominant, all the progeny from the test cross will have the yellow phenotype. However, if the yellow seed strain is heterozygous, half of the progeny from the test cross will have yellow seeds and half will have green seeds. In this manner, test crosses can be very valuable in determining the exact genotype of individuals who express the dominant phenotype.

G. SEX LINKED TRAITS

In humans, sex is determined by the inheritance of two X chromosomes (female) or an X and Y (male). Much information is carried on the X chromosome. This creates a unique situation regarding dominant and recessive genes on this chromosome. In females, the expression of one recessive allele can, of course, be hidden by the expression of a dominant allele on the other X chromosome. But in males, if only one recessive allele is inherited, the trait is expressed. This condition, where only one allele is present and will be expressed, is called the **hemizygous** condition.

When working out crosses with genes carried on the X chromosome, the X and Y chromosomes must both be represented. For example, the trait for color blindness is a recessive X linked trait (we will represent it as X^c). If a heterozygous female ($X X^c$) marries a normal man (XY), the probability that their children will show the trait can be determined using a Punnett square:

	X	X^c
X	XX	XX^c
Y	XY	X^cY

Half of the sons will be colorblind, and half of the daughters will be heterozygotes, or **carriers** of the condition.

We call traits carried on the X chromosome **sex linked** traits. Traits not carried on the X or Y chromosome are called **autosomal** traits. Y linked traits are called **Hollandric** traits. However, due to the lack of genes on the Y chromosome, this type of inheritance is not well characterized and is disputed by many researchers.

H. DIHYBRID CROSSES

We can also examine crosses with two different traits (a ***dihybrid cross***) to see how the traits are inherited by the progeny. Consider a cross between two pure breeding strains, one with yellow seeds and purple flowers, and one with green seeds and white flowers (yellow is dominant to green and purple is dominant to white). We can represent the cross like this:

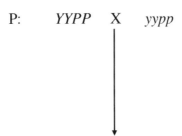

P: *YYPP*   X   *yypp*

F₁   all progeny will have the genotype YyPp
with the phenotype yellow seeds and purple flowers

When the F₁ generation is self-crossed, we can set up a Punnett square of all possible combinations of gametes. Look carefully at the F₁ genotype. Each gamete must contain one allele for the gene for seed color and one allele for the gene for flower color. The analysis would look like this:

	YP	**Yp**	**yP**	**yp**
YP	YYPP	YYPp	YyPP	YyPp
Yp	YYPp	YYpp	YyPp	Yypp
yP	YyPP	YyPp	yyPP	yyPp
yp	YyPy	Yypp	yyPp	yypp

By counting all the squares and combining the phenotypes, you should see that 9/16 of the progeny will have yellow seeds and purple flowers, 3/16 will have yellow seeds and white flowers, 3/16 will have green seeds and purple flowers, and 1/16 will have green seeds and white flowers. Thus, the phenotypic ratio for a dihybrid cross is 9:3:3:1.

I. PRINCIPLE OF INDEPENDENT ASSORTMENT AND LINKAGE

Mendel's second theory, the ***principle of independent assortment***, came from his observations of dihybrid crosses. As you can see in the example above, the distribution of alleles for one trait in the gametes does not influence the distribution of alleles for the second trait. In other words, during meiosis, the alleles segregate, or assort, independently of each other. The traits will be distributed equally in the gametes.

This principle is violated when two genes are physically ***linked***, or joined, on the same chromosome. When this occurs, the alleles for two different traits do not assort independently, but instead are inherited together.

J. EXCEPTIONS TO MENDELIAN INHERITANCE

Most traits are not inherited in a simple dominant/recessive fashion. In fact, most genes have more than two alleles, and most traits are influenced by more than one gene. It can be very confusing. We will not go into an in-depth discussion of all these exceptions, but we will list the most common variations in the dominant/recessive inheritance pattern:

- ◆ *multiple alleles*: more than two alleles exist for a gene. The most common example of this is blood type in humans: the ABO system. Three different alleles exist, designated I^A, I^B and i.

- ◆ *incomplete (or partial) dominance*: the heterozygote displays a phenotype that is intermediate to the phenotypes of the two homozygotes. Flower color in snapdragons is a classic example of this. When two pure breeding plants are crossed, one that has red flowers and one that has white, all the F^1 progeny have pink flowers. When the F^1 plants are crossed, one quarter have red flowers, one half develop pink flowers, and one quarter have white flowers.

- ◆ *codominance:* the heterozygote exhibits both phenotypes of the homozygotes. We can go back to the ABO blood types for an example of codominance. The i allele is always recessive, so individuals who are $I^A i$ are blood type A, $I^B i$ are blood type B, and ii are blood type O. Homozygotes $I^A I^A$ and $I^B I^B$ are A and B, respectively. However, when an individual inherits the alleles $I^A I^B$, that individual expresses both phenotypes, and is said to be blood type AB.

- ◆ *gene interaction*: two genes interact to affect the phenotype of one trait. A novel phenotype will be produced by this interaction. *Polygenic traits* are characteristics that are caused by many genes acting together. For example, skin color is a polygenic trait.

- ◆ *epistasis*: one gene interferes with the phenotypic expression of another gene. This differs from gene interaction in that no new phenotype is produced. A related phenomenon is *pleiotropy*. This refers to one gene affecting many traits. One example of this would be the genetic disorder sickle cell anemia. Individuals with this disease have a mutation in the gene encoding hemoglobin, but have many different organs and systems affected.

K. ENVIRONMENTAL EFFECTS ON GENE EXPRESSION

The development and expression of traits also depends on the external and internal environment. The frequency with which a certain trait is expressed in a population is called *penetrance*, and the extent to which a phenotype is expressed in an individual is called *expressivity*.

The external environment can influence phenotypes. For example, Himalayan rabbits have mostly white fur, while black coat color is found only on the extremities (ears, paws, nose and tail). The gene that produces pigment in the fur is only active at low temperatures, producing the unusual pattern.

Internal factors can influence the expression of genes. Age will often influence the expression of a gene, such as is seen with the development of Huntington's disease in humans. Sex can also determine phenotypes. This is most evident in the preponderance of baldness in human males.

Other factors, such as behavior and intelligence, are also heavily influenced by environment. Although there is currently a debate among scientists (one that may not end for a long time), it is evident that these traits are determined by both "nature" (genetics) and "nurture" (environment).

Chapter 19 Problems

Passage 19.1 (Questions 1-6)

In the fruit fly, ***Drosophila melanogaster***, many different genes influence eye color. Mutations in any one of these genes will change the color of the eyes. Normally, flies have brick red eyes (this is called the ***wild type*** condition). The inheritance patterns of these variations have been extensively studied. The results of some crosses are described below.

Cross 1:
Wild type flies were crossed with brown eyed flies. The F_1 progeny all had red eyes. When the F_1 were crossed with each other, 3/4 of the F_2 had red eyes and 1/4 had brown eyes.

Cross 2:
Wild type females were crossed with white eyed males. All of the F_1's had red eyes. In the F_2 generation, all of the females had red eyes, while half of the males had red eyes and half had white eyes.

Cross 3.
Brown eyed flies were crossed with scarlet eyed flies (scarlet is known to be an autosomal recessive trait). All of the F_1 progeny had red eyes. The F_2 progeny showed a ratio of 9:3:3:1 red to brown to scarlet to white.

Cross 4:
Another mutation affecting the eye, called Bar, does not affect color. Instead, it affects the shape of the eye, changing it from the normal round phenotype to an elongated, oval shape. Wild type flies were crossed with Bar eyed flies. Half of the F_1 progeny had Bar shaped eyes and half had wild type eyes. When the wild type F_1 flies were crossed with the Bar eyed F_1 flies, the F_2 generation showed the same phenotypes as the F_1 generation: half were wild type, half had Bar eyes.

1. The inheritance pattern of brown eyes fits with which of the following mechanisms?
   A. autosomal recessive
   B. autosomal dominant
   C. sex-linked recessive
   D. sex-linked dominant

2. The inheritance pattern of white eyes fits with which of the following mechanisms?
   A. autosomal recessive
   B. autosomal dominant
   C. sex-linked recessive
   D. sex-linked dominant

3. The inheritance pattern of Bar eyes fits with which of the following mechanisms?
   A. autosomal recessive
   B. autosomal dominant
   C. sex-linked recessive
   D. sex-linked dominant

4. What is the best way to describe the genotype of the Bar eyed mutants in the parental generation in cross 4?
   A. homozygous dominant
   B. homozygous recessive
   C. heterozygous
   D. hemizygous

5. To determine the genotype of the red F_2 individuals in cross 1, a test cross could be done. What should be the genotype of the flies used in the test cross? Assume the symbol b+ indicates the wild type allele for the brown gene, while b indicates the mutation.
   A. b^+b^+
   B. bb
   C. b^+b
   D. $X^b X^b$ and/or X^bY

6. The relationship between brown and scarlet eye color is an example of:
   A. codominance.
   B. incomplete dominance.
   C. gene interaction.
   D. epistasis.

The following questions are NOT based on a descriptive passage.

7. A couple has a child with cystic fibrosis, an autosomal recessive disease. Neither parent has the disease. Another child is born, who is unaffected. What is the probability that this unaffected child is a carrier of cystic fibrosis?

   A. 1/4
   B. 1/2
   C. 2/3
   D. 3/4

8. A woman with blood type AB marries a man with blood type B. Which of the following blood types could not be found in their children?

   A. A
   B. B
   C. AB
   D. O

CHAPTER 20
Evolution

A. INTRODUCTION

Evolution is perhaps the most important concept in biology. As discussed before, it is one of the unifying principles of biology. Indeed, most scientists would list it as the unifying topic. It has often been said that nothing in biology makes sense without evolution.

The theory of evolution is not disputed among scientists. Observations and evidence collected and examined over the past 150 years supports this theory as much as, or even more than, other theories such as the atomic theory, the cell theory or the theory of gravity. However, the exact mechanisms of evolution, the details of how it occurred and continues to occur, are, indeed, disputed. This is the challenge and excitement facing researchers today. There are many aspects of and ways to study evolution. We will only discuss some of the basics in this chapter.

B. CHARLES DARWIN

The person usually cited as the key figure in our understanding and development of the theory of evolution is Charles Darwin. He was not the first to propose the idea of evolution, but he was the first to provide extensive support for the process, and he also postulated a mechanism for how evolution occurred.

Darwin's ideas were born on a five-year voyage he took around the world aboard the H.M.S. *Beagle*, beginning in 1831. Darwin was the ship's naturalist, and he made extensive observations and collected specimens, most notably from up and down both coasts of South America and from the Galapagos islands, located off the coast of Ecuador. His book, ***On the Origin of Species by Means of Natural Selection***, was published 22 years after his return to England. Several observations helped Darwin formulate his theory. These include:

♦ *overproduction:* Darwin noted that plants and animals produce many offspring, more than the number necessary for their own replacement. In other words, to replace themselves in a population, a mating pair of sexually reproducing organisms need only have two offspring. The production of large amounts of offspring means that growth will occur in an exponential fashion, creating a huge population in only several generations. In reality, however, this exponential growth is not seen. Many factors limit the population size, some which are discussed below.

♦ *heritable variation:* No two individuals are exactly the same. There is always some variation, something that is different, among individuals. In addition, these variations can be passed on from parent to offspring, as shown through selective breeding of domesticated plants and animals. Darwin did not know the mechanisms behind this process (and Mendel's work was not recognized at the time), but it was obvious that traits were inherited.

♦ *competition:* All species require certain resources in order to survive. Some things, such as soil, food and water, are in limited quantities in the environment. Therefore, different species compete for their use. In addition, a population reproducing geometrically will put individuals of the same species in competition with one another.

♦ *survival and reproduction of the fittest:* Competition results in the survival of some organisms over others. Certain variations will contribute to this survival, and individuals who possess these traits are more likely to reach reproductive maturity. Therefore, the offspring of these individuals will inherit these traits and will have a better chance at survival. In this way, beneficial traits are selected and eventually will increase with frequency in the population.

Thus we can see that overproduction produces a large number of individuals, each having different variations. Competition between species and among individuals of the same species results in survival of the fittest. The best of each generation reproduce and pass on these traits to the next generation. From these observations, Darwin postulated a mechanism that would explain how these factors contribute to evolution. This process is known as *natural selection* and is the cornerstone of the theory of evolution.

C. CAUSES OF EVOLUTION

Darwin's notion of natural selection is not necessarily the only cause of evolution, but it is the key that unifies the theory. Two other important factors are *mutation* and *gene flow*. Before we begin our discussion of these three processes, it is important to note that evolution occurs in populations, not individuals. A *population* is defined as a group of individuals of the same species occupying a given area. Therefore, the remainder of our discussion will focus on populations of individuals, and how changes arise in these populations.

♦ *natural selection:* Natural selection is the result of the interaction of environment and individual variations. When environmental conditions change, selective pressure is placed on a population. Only organisms possessing beneficial variations that allow them to exist in the different environment will survive and reproduce. It is important to understand that natural selection can only work with the variations already present in the population. New variations cannot be produced to help organisms survive. For example, during the evolution of terrestrial vertebrates, the ancestral species was a tetrapod (possessing four legs). Therefore, all terrestrial vertebrates have "four legs." Human evolution involved a transition from walking on "all fours" to walking erect, and an alteration of the forelimbs into arms and hands. Natural selection did not create this situation, but made due with the materials it had to work with. Made due, you say? Aren't humans pretty well off? Well, yes, but ask anyone who's ever had back or knee problems, and they'll tell you these structures are far from perfect. For all intents and purposes, our intellect and logic allowed us to survive, not our physical strength and prowess. Natural selection is responsible for both.

♦ *mutation:* As we discussed above, Darwin was not aware of how variations arose or how traits were inherited, as the field of genetics would not take shape for decades after his death. Today, genetics is central to our understanding of evolution. Earlier, we discussed how mutations alter protein production. This alteration produces new alleles, or variations of genes that may result in a change in the phenotype of an organism. New alleles may change the genetic makeup of the population, and this may lead to evolution.

♦ *gene flow:* Gene flow is described as the movement of alleles from one population to another. This movement could cause changes in the population, either by eliminating variation (as some organisms may leave the population) or by enhancing it (as some organisms enter the population).

Although mutation and gene flow play critical roles, natural selection is cited as the main cause of evolution. As you may have already deduced, the three are not mutually exclusive, and, indeed, natural selection often involves mutation and gene flow. Perhaps the most important thing to remember is that evolution is due to both environment and genetic variation within species. Natural selection is the result of the interaction of these factors and produces changes in the population.

D. ADAPTATION

When selective pressures are placed on populations, natural selection causes certain traits to become more "fit" than others. The variations with the greatest survival value will become more common in each successive generation. Genetic traits that give organisms a better chance at survival will be selected for, and traits that reduce the fitness of individuals will be selected against. This process is known as *adaptation*. Although there are many different definitions of this word, it has a specific meaning in evolutionary theory, and refers to genetics. Adaptation is a change in the genetics of a population with time. An individual cannot change its genetic makeup. Therefore, in evolutionary terms, an individual cannot adapt, only a population can.

Recall that earlier we defined evolution as a change with time, and here we are applying the same definition to adaptation. Evolution is used more often to describe the accumulation of changes or the formation of a new species via the processes of natural selection and adaptation.

E. POPULATION GENETICS

The modern definition of evolution is specific: evolution is defined as the change in allelic frequencies in a population with time. A change in the allelic frequency for one gene does not necessarily result in what we think of evolution, but rather, if changes occur in many genes, the result may be evolution. We usually refer to all of the genes, and all of the alleles, in a population as the *gene pool*. Thus, the diversity and variation of every population can be ascertained by examining the gene pool.

Recall that alleles are different varieties of genes caused by mutations in the DNA. To understand evolution, we must understand the genetics of a population, not just of an individual. In 1908, two researchers, G. H. Hardy and G. Weinberg, set out to understand this via the use of mathematics. They reasoned that, if no genetic changes were taking place over time, then a population would be in equilibrium and would not change. If this were true, the frequency of each allele in a population could be calculated rather easily. Knowing the frequency of each allele would allow for the description of the genotypic frequencies within the population as well.

For example, consider a genetic trait with two alleles, the dominant allele *A* and the recessive allele *a*. Since there are only two alleles of this gene in the population, the sum of the frequency of the two alleles must be one. If we assign symbols to these frequencies (i.e. the frequency of A can be represented by *p*, and the frequency of *a* can be represented by *q*), then we can express this idea as:

$$p + q = 1$$

Furthermore, if we know p and q, we can calculate the frequencies of the various genotypes. If mating is random in a population, then this mating can be expressed as the probability of alleles coming together in any combination. Mathematically we can express this as (p + q) X (p + q). Since p + q = 1, the product of this equation also equals 1. With some algebraic manipulation, this equation becomes

$$p^2 + 2pq + q^2 = 1$$

Each term represents one genotype; specifically, the frequency of the homozygous dominant (*AA*) in the population is expressed by the term p^2, the homozygous recessive *(aa)*, q^2, and the heterozygote *(Aa) 2pq*.

For example, if *p* = 0.85, then we could calculate *q* (1 - 0.85 = 0.15). In addition, we could calculate the frequency in the population of *AA* (0.85 x 0.85 = 0.72), *Aa* (2 x 0.85 x 0.15 = 0.26) and *aa* (0.15 x 0.15 = 0.02). If we consider a population of 1000 individuals, we would predict that 0.72 x 1000, or 720, would be of the genotype *AA*, 0.26 x 1000, or 260, would be *Aa*, and 0.02 x 1000, or 20, would be *aa*.

We can also determine the frequency of the alleles given raw numbers in the population. For example, if, in a population, 800 individuals were found to be of the genotype *AA*, 160 were *Aa*, and 40 were *aa*, then we can calculate allelic frequencies given the formulae:

$$\text{frequency of A} = p = \frac{\text{total number of A alleles}}{\text{total number of alleles}}$$

$$\text{frequency of a} = q = \frac{\text{total number of a alleles}}{\text{total number of alleles}}$$

The total number of *A* alleles in a population is expressed as

$$(2 \text{ x \# of } \textbf{AA}) + (\text{\# of } \textbf{Aa})$$

as homozygous dominant individuals have 2 *A* alleles, and heterozygotes have only 1 *A* allele. Similarly, total number of a alleles in a population is expressed as

$$(2 \text{ x \# of aa}) + (\text{\# of Aa})$$

as homozygous recessive individuals have 2 a alleles, and heterozygotes have only 1 a allele. The total number of alleles in the population is equal to

$$2 \text{ x \# of individuals}$$

as each individual in the population has two alleles for every gene, including the gene of interest. Thus, our equation to find p becomes:

$$p = \frac{(2 \times 800)+(160)}{2 \times 1000} = 0.88$$

We can similarly determine q, or we can remember that *p + q* = 1. Therefore *q* = 0.12.

Also remember that genes can have more than two alleles. Similar equations can be used to describe the frequencies in this case. If all the alleles of a gene occur in the same proportions for many generations, these alleles are called **balanced polymorphisms**. However, if the allelic frequencies are seen to change from one generation to the next, the population is not in equilibrium.

F. HARDY-WEINBERG EQUILIBRIUM

The relationships described above, and the equations that describe them, are known as the ***Hardy-Weinberg equilibrium***. But this brings us to an important point: if a population is in Hardy-Weinberg equilibrium, the allelic frequencies are not changing and therefore evolution could not occur. Hardy and Weinberg identified five tenants that, when violated, would result in the equilibrium being disturbed and, thus, a shift in the allelic frequencies, which may result in evolution. The five principles necessary to maintain Hardy Weinberg equilibrium in a population are:

- ◆ *no mutation:* Mutation would cause the production of new alleles in a population and thus change allelic frequencies.
- ◆ *no migration:* Migration, either immigration or emigration, would result in the exchange of alleles between populations, thus changing allelic frequencies.
- ◆ *no selection:* If particular alleles were selected for, then the frequency of these alleles would increase over time. Similarly, if alleles were selected against, their frequency would be reduced over time.
- ◆ *large population:* With small populations, the allelic frequencies can change by chance due to random fluctuations in the gene pool.
- ◆ *random mating:* If mating is not random, then some alleles would increase in frequency while others would decrease. Usually random mating is violated when sexual selection is in play, which we will discuss shortly.

As you may have guessed, most populations violate at least one of these tenets. However, the principles and equations of Hardy-Weinberg equilibrium are still useful in describing and studying a population. One notable violation of Hardy-Weinberg equilibrium is population size. Several processes have been helpful in understanding genetics of small populations. Some of these include:

- ◆ *genetic drift:* Random chance will cause fluctuations in allelic frequencies. Smaller populations are more susceptible to these chance events, and frequencies can change significantly. For example, natural disasters can decimate small populations. If, by random chance, all the individuals with a certain variation were killed during a hurricane, then the allelic frequency of that trait would be dramatically reduced. Larger populations would not face such drastic changes.
- ◆ *bottlenecks:* When the size of a population is dramatically reduced, usually due to disease or natural disaster, alleles may be lost. The population may be able to recover and increase in number. However, the genetic variation has been reduced and cannot be restored. This is the problem with endangered species today. Although we have protected many species that were on the verge of extinction, diversity has been reduced. If the environment changes, there may not be enough variation within the population to allow the species to survive. Bottlenecks (and genetic drift) can be helped by gene flow. With endangered species, zoos will often exchange animals for mating purposes to increase genetic diversity.
- ◆ *founder effect:* When a few individuals from a population form their own new population, the only genetic variation that exists is what these individuals bring. In essence, they do not bring the whole gene pool to the new population, but rather only a fraction of it. Again, this will reduce diversity and variation.

G. SELECTION

Often, when Hardy-Weinberg equilibrium is violated, natural selection is occurring which will shift allelic frequencies. We can identify four different types of selection which alter these frequencies in different ways.

♦ *directional selection:* Sometimes one allele, or a combination of alleles from different genes, provide an adaptive advantage for an organism. Since these organisms are more likely to survive and reproduce, the frequencies of these advantageous alleles will increase. Directional selection is when the allelic frequency shifts in a steady, constant direction. For example, pesticide resistance in insects is due to alleles which provide protection against these chemicals. Thus, all insects that survive will carry these alleles and will pass them onto their progeny. Soon, all the individuals in a population will have these alleles.

♦ *stabilizing selection:* In this type of selection, an intermediate form of an allele or trait is favored over the extremes. A good example of this is with human birth weight. The average weight of a newborn is 7 pounds. Much lower than this results in medical problems and infant mortality. Much higher and the mother will have difficulty carrying and delivering the child.

♦ *disruptive selection:* Disruptive selection occurs when environmental conditions favor the two extremes of the trait. In this case, the population will, in essence, be split into two. Given enough time, evolution may result in two different species.

♦ *sexual selection:* When competition occurs between individuals of the same sex over mating rights, it is often the bigger, more aggressive animal, or the animal with the more pleasing appearance or courtship display that is allowed to mate. Therefore, these alleles will be passed on to the next generation. Sexual selection has also been implemented in **sexual dimorphism**, the dramatic difference seen between members of the opposite sexes in the same species (for example, the beautifully plumed peacock and his drab counterpart, the peahen.)

H. EVIDENCE FOR EVOLUTION

We have discussed why evolutionary theory arose, the mechanisms that may be responsible for evolution, and a mathematical theory to identify when evolution is occurring. But we still have not investigated one important question: How do we know evolution occurred? Most evidence supporting evolution can be classified in one of the following categories:

♦ *comparative anatomy:* This involves careful comparison of body parts in different organisms. For example, all mammals have hair or fur and have mammary glands used to produce milk to feed their young. Further investigation reveals that mammals also have similar bone structures. These data imply that all mammals had an ancestral relationship. If we further examine the bone structure in mammals, birds, reptiles and amphibians, we can also see amazing similarities, again indicating that even these diverse organisms came from a common ancestral species.

♦ *comparative biochemistry:* Recent advances in biochemical analysis, including protein and DNA sequencing, have allowed for detailed investigations into comparisons of species at the molecular level. This type of comparison reveals differences in sequences that can be used to determine how similar two species are. The rate of change in sequences has also been used as a **molecular clock** to calculate the time of divergence between two species.

♦ *vestigial structures:* Organs or body parts that have no functional value to an organism are called vestigial structures. Since they are present but have no function, they are probably remnants of structures from an ancestral species. For instance, the **appendix** in humans is an example of a vestigial structure. It is the remains of the **cecum**, a structure that acts as a storage chamber in animals that eat a diet high in cellulose. Another example is the pelvic girdle found in whales. This structure has no function and, with time, has been reduced in size and even disconnected from the spine. However, it remains, and gives us evidence that ancestral whales were once land dwelling creatures with hind limbs.

♦ ***embryonic development:*** This is perhaps the most curious and fascinating category we will discuss. When vertebrates are examined, the stages of embryonic development are strikingly similar. Even in organisms as different as turtles and chickens and humans, the form of the developing embryo, and the structures of the embryo, are almost identical. In fact, at one point in human development, ***gill slits*** are apparent. It is argued that these similarities are evidence for a common ancestor for all vertebrates.

♦ ***natural distribution of living things:*** By examining where living things exist in the world, we can compare similarities and differences among the species. This has lead to some interesting findings. For example, species of monkeys in the western hemisphere resemble each other more closely than they resemble species of monkeys in Europe or Africa or Asia. This indicates that, although all monkeys had a common ancestor, geographic separation (different continents) allowed evolution of monkeys in different ways (see the discussion of reproductive isolation below).

♦ ***fossil evidence:*** Probably the most important category of evidence for evolution is the fossil record. Various methods, most notably ***radioactive dating,*** can determine the age of particular rocks. Embedded in these rocks are fossils, preserved specimens of once living organisms. What we know from fossils is that organisms that were alive in the past do not closely resemble organisms alive today, and many species are extinct. What we can see in these fossils are similarities with plants and animals that are alive today, but that these creatures have changed over time. One of the best examples of this is the horse. Fossil evidence over the past 60 million years documents the changes in the horse, including its overall size, hoof structure and jaw and tooth patterns.

♦ ***selective breeding (artificial selection):*** Humans have been cultivating plants and animals for thousands of years. We have selected certain traits and attributes in these organisms and breed organisms to retain and enhance traits that are useful and beneficial to us. This process of selective breeding or artificial selection is quite amazing. For example, the vegetables familiar to us as cabbage, cauliflower, broccoli, Brussels sprouts and kale are all different variations of the same plant. Similarly, dogs, from Chihuahuas to Great Danes, all belong to the same species and were selectively bred from wolves. If humans can exert this type of selective pressure to create so many different varieties from one species, an intuitive leap will tell you it can occur in nature as well.

I. SPECIATION

Natural selection can cause one species to evolve into two or more species. How can this occur? Speciation requires ***reproductive isolation***, the situation whereby one population of a species becomes isolated and can reproduce only with the individuals in that population (remember the premises of Hardy-Weinberg). The different environment of the isolated species will pose different selective pressures on the population, and, given enough time, natural selection may result in evolution of a new species.

Two types of isolation are generally recognized:

♦ ***allopatric:*** When species are divided by a physical barrier, they have undergone allopatric isolation. The most prominent type of allopatric isolation is ***geographic isolation***: Volcanoes, tectonic plate shift, formation of new rivers, species blown by storms to island, etc. can cause geographic isolation. This type of isolation is probably the most common form of reproductive isolation, and, consequently, the most important.

♦ *sympatric:* When no physical barrier divides a population, reproductive isolation can still occur. In this case, daughter species arise within the home range of an existing species. One type of sympatric isolation is ***behavioral isolation***. In this case, a genetic variation may arise within a species that causes behavioral changes. For example, changes may cause some individuals to feed at night. Eventually, these individuals will become nocturnal, essentially isolating themselves from the diurnal individuals. Adaptation may cause changes in eyesight, coloration, and other traits to allow these organism to survive. This may lead to speciation. Another example of sympatric isolation is ***physiological and anatomical isolation***: Variations in physical attributes may prevent breeding among individuals within a population, which may eventually lead to speciation. Consider one example from above: although all dogs are the same species, they can be very different. The Chihuahua will find it difficult, if not impossible, to mate with the Great Dane due to differences in their sizes. Thus, given enough time, the two strains may eventually evolve into two different species.

J. TYPES OF EVOLUTION

When we examine evolution as a process, we see certain patterns. It is helpful to discuss evolution in terms of these patterns to answer questions and make comparisons. These patterns include:

♦ *divergent evolution:* This process refers to what is normally thought of as evolution, and what we have been discussing thus far. Divergent evolution occurs when individuals from one population evolve differently. This, as discussed above, can lead to speciation. For example, the brown bear and the polar bear had a common ancestor. Migration of the bears, leading to geographic isolation, resulted in adaptation to different environments. Divergent evolution often results in individuals having ***homologous structures***, structures that have been adapted differently to perform different functions. For example, the forelimbs in vertebrates evolved into arms (humans), wings (bats) and fins (whales).

♦ *convergent evolution:* When environments are similar or identical, the same selective pressures will be placed on the organisms that live in these environments. Therefore, different species in one environment (or two similar environments) will evolve similar structures to function in the environment. These structures are called ***analogous structures***. One striking example of this is seen in sharks (fish), whales (mammals) and penguins (birds): although very distantly related, all have developed similar structures (fins) that allow them to function in the same environment (the ocean).

♦ *coevolution:* Organisms that share an environment often evolve together due to the selective pressures placed on one or more species in the environment. Thus, one species often changes in response to the change in another species. For example, if rabbits were the main food source for one population of foxes, and the rabbits adapted to become faster runners allowing them to avoid the foxes, then the foxes must adapt and become faster runners in order to continue using the rabbits as a food source.

Chapter 20 Problems

Passage 20.1 (Questions 1-4)

The ability to taste phenylthiocarbamide (PTC) is determined by the **T** gene. Homozygous dominant individuals (**TT**) experience PTC as a very strong and unpleasant taste. Heterozygotes (**Tt**) can taste PTC but experience it as a much weaker taste and do not find it quite as offensive. Homozygous recessive individuals (**tt**) cannot taste PTC at all. As a class assignment, students were tested for their ability to taste PTC, and were asked to test their parents as well. The class data was pooled and the results are shown in the following table:

Ability to taste PTC	Students	Parents
Strong taste	6	11
Weak taste	4	14
No taste	10	15

The class then examined the data and calculated allelic and genotypic frequencies, based on the formulas related to Hardy-Weinberg equilibrium.

1. What is the allelic frequency of **T** in the students?
   A. 0.40
   B. 0.60
   C. 0.16
   D. 0.36

2. In the parents, what proportion have the ability to taste PTC?
   A. 0.28
   B. 0.35
   C. 0.63
   D. 1.00

3. In the parents, what is the value of **q**?
   A. 0.45
   B. 0.55
   C. 0.28
   D. 0.35

4. Is this population in Hardy-Weinberg equilibrium for the ability to taste PTC?
   A. Yes, as the allelic frequencies are relatively the same in each generation.
   B. No, as strong tasters do not occur with the same frequency in each generation.
   C. No, as the values of **p** and **q** in the student generation are not equal.
   D. No, as the values of **p** and **q** are not the same in each generation.

The following questions are NOT based on a descriptive passage.

5. Cystic fibrosis, a recessive genetic disease, occurs in a particular population in approximately 1 of every 2,000 births. What is the frequency of carriers in this population?
   A. 0.0224
   B. 0.9776
   C. 0.0219
   D. 0.0438

6. Many species of marsupials (found mainly in Australia) share similarities to species of placental mammals (found in most other regions of the world) even though they are not very closely related. This is an example of:
   A. divergent evolution.
   B. convergent evolution.
   C. vestigial structures.
   D. sympatric speciation.

SECTION 5

Content Review Problems

1. How many chromosomes does every human cell have, outside of sex cells?
    A. 23
    B. 46
    C. 45
    D. 92

2. The two non-identical copies of a single chromosome are referred to as:
    A. Analogous chromosomes
    B. Different chromosomes
    C. Homologous chromosomes
    D. Genes

3. An individual heterozygote for a certain gene carries:
    A. Both a recessive and dominant allele
    B. Two recessive alleles
    C. Two dominant alleles
    D. Only one allele

4. Which of the following is true of the phenotype?
    A. It is the genetic representation of alleles
    B. It does not represent mutations
    C. It is the physical representation of the genotype
    D. Only one allele codes for the phenotype

5. What is an allele?
    A. An individual's genome
    B. A specific gene
    C. RNA specific to eukaryotes
    D. None of the above

6. Which of the following is an example of an individual with a codominant genotype?
    A. A person with type AB blood
    B. A white flower created from a red and white flower
    C. A person with type O blood
    D. A red flower created from a red and white flower

7. Which of the following is an example of incomplete dominance?
    A. AB blood
    B. A pink flower created from a red and white flower
    C. O blood
    D. A red flower created from a red and white flower

8. What is the probability that a male and a female will have a son?
    A. 0%
    B. 25%
    C. 50%
    D. 100%

9. A female who is a carrier for a sex-linked recessive disease has a son with a male who does not carry the disease. What is the probability that this child has the disease?
    A. 0%
    B. 25%
    C. 50%
    D. 100%

10. A female who is a carrier for a sex-linked recessive disease has a son with a male who has this disease. What is the probability that this child has the disease?
   A. 0%
   B. 25%
   C. 50%
   D. 100%

11. Complete meiosis of a spermatogonium produces how many spermatids?
   A. 1
   B. 2
   C. 3
   D. 4

12. Complete meiosis of an oogonium produces how many ova?
   A. 1
   B. 2
   C. 3
   D. 4

13. Recombination occurring in eukaryotic cells can be referred to as:
   A. Conjugation
   B. Crossing over
   C. Transformation
   D. Transduction

14. What is the probability that a woman will have hemophilia if both of her parents have and show this recessive X-linked disease?
   A. 25%
   B. 50%
   C. 75%
   D. 100%

15. Which of the following about a test cross is true?
   A. An individual with an unknown genotype is crossed with a homozygous dominant individual
   B. An individual with an unknown genotype is crossed with a homozygous recessive individual
   C. An individual with an unknown phenotype is crossed with a heterozygous individual
   D. An individual with an unknown phenotype is crossed with a homozygous recessive individual

16. Chromosomes that don't correctly separate during meiosis create which of the following?
   A. Nondisjunction
   B. Ectopic
   C. Mutation
   D. Linkage

17. Which of the following describes the self-determining separation of alleles of different genes?
   A. Law of independent assortment
   B. Principle of segregation
   C. Inbreeding
   D. Non-Mendelian genetics

18. The phenomenon where a lineage consistently produces identical progeny can be classified as:
   A. Genetic drift
   B. Speciation
   C. Principle of segregation
   D. Pure-breeding

19. A dihybrid cross is used when:
   A. The risk of mutation is high
   B. The probability of a single trait is needed
   C. The probability of two traits is needed
   D. The probability of three traits is needed

20. Genes that do not assort independently can be said to be:
   A. Unlinked
   B. On different chromosomes
   C. Linked
   D. Mutated

21. Because men only have one X chromosome and thus express even recessive X-linked genes, they are said to be:
   A. Degenerative
   B. Hemizygous
   C. Homozygous
   D. Codominant

22. In a typical pedigree, females are represented as:
   A. Squares
   B. Circles
   C. Diamonds
   D. Rectangles

23. Two organisms that cannot produce viable offspring must not be of the same:
    A. Species
    B. Family
    C. Genus
    D. Kingdom

24. The gene pool is:
    A. the same as the population.
    B. the population's sum of all genetic information.
    C. the population's likelihood of survival.
    D. a depiction of a population's mutation history.

25. A tenet of the Hardy-Weinberg principal is:
    A. Non-random mating
    B. Interbreeding
    C. No migration
    D. Small population

26. What is another tenet of the Hardy-Weinberg principal?
    A. Minimal mutation
    B. Absence of natural selection
    C. Divergent evolution must exist
    D. Survival of the fittest

27. If in a population the frequency of the dominant allele for a given gene is 60%, what is the frequency of the recessive allele for the same gene?
    A. 60%
    B. 20%
    C. 40%
    D. 80%

28. If the frequency of the recessive allele for a given gene in a population is 46%, what is p equal to?
    A. 0.46
    B. 0.54
    C. 0.64
    D. 0.04

29. If p is equal to .5, what is the proportion of heterozygotes in the population?
    A. 25%
    B. 50%
    C. 70%
    D. 90%

30. If the frequency of the recessive allele is 40%, then what is the proportion of homozygous dominant individuals in the population?
    A. 40%
    B. 18%
    C. 36%
    D. 64%

31. When 40 out of 100 individuals are heterozygous for a given trait, what is the frequency of the dominant allele?
    A. 28%
    B. 40%
    C. 72%
    D. Not enough info is given

32. The Hardy-Weinberg equilibrium describes:
    A. A possible population dynamic
    B. Impossible circumstances
    C. The likelihood of mutation
    D. Only population of R strategists

33. If part of a flock of geese decides to leave the group, which of the following principles of Hardy-Weinberg have been breached?
    A. Random mating
    B. No natural selection
    C. No migration
    D. No mutation

34. Evolutionary fitness can be described as:
    A. Physical ability
    B. Ability to survive
    C. Ability to produce fertile progeny
    D. Ability to escape predation

35. Speciation is:
    A. The formation of a new species
    B. The formation of a new individual
    C. The result of inbreeding
    D. Impossible for small populations

36. A cat's leg and a human arm can be considered:
    A. Homologous structures
    B. Vestigial structures
    C. Analogous structures
    D. Non-related structures

37. A bird wing and bee wing can be considered (birds and bees do not share a common winged ancestor):
   A. Homologous structures
   B. Vestigial structures
   C. Analogous structures
   D. Non-related structures

38. Similar structures with similar functions that developed in species that do not share a common ancestor are called:
   A. Homologous structures
   B. Vestigial structures
   C. Analogous structures
   D. Non-related structures

39. The generic example of one species becoming two different species can be described by all of the following EXCEPT:
   A. Cladogenesis
   B. Convergent evolution
   C. Speciation
   D. Divergent evolution

40. Which of the following best characterizes parallel evolution?
   A. Part of a shark population that is isolated and eventually becomes a new species
   B. Individuals of two species that are smaller than average and that are both selected for as a result of global warming
   C. Humans' tail bones
   D. Humans' appendices

41. *Homo sapiens* belong to which kingdom?
   A. Animalia
   B. Plantae
   C. Fungi
   D. Protista

42. Which of the following is the phylum for *Homo sapiens*?
   A. Animal
   B. Homo
   C. Chordate
   D. Sapiens

43. Barr bodies are found:
   A. in males.
   B. in females.
   C. in both sexes.
   D. not in mammals.

44. Which classification comes after "Class" in the taxonomy order?
   A. Kingdom
   B. Phylum
   C. Order
   D. Genus

45. Which of the following is the class of *Homo sapiens*?
   A. Sapiens
   B. Animal
   C. Homo
   D. Mammalia

46. Which of the following can be considered an r-strategist?
   A. Humans
   B. Blue whales
   C. Bacteria
   D. Dogs

47. Which of the following describes a crisis so severe that a shift occurs in the allele frequency of a population?
   A. Bottleneck
   B. Carrying capacity
   C. Mutualism
   D. Polymorphism

48. Adaptive radiation is a special case of:
   A. Symbiosis
   B. Speciation
   C. Parasitism
   D. Mutualism

49. A mammal receiving benefits from the bacteria within its gut is an example of:
   A. Parasitism
   B. Mutualism
   C. Commensalism
   D. None of the above

50. A tree using a tree as protection from the environment is an example of:
    A. Parasitism
    B. Mutualism
    C. Commensalism
    D. None of the above

51. All chordates have:
    A. Backbones
    B. Bilateral symmetry
    C. Exoskeletons
    D. Gills

52. What is the probability that a man with hemophilia, a sex linked recessive disease, and a carrier woman will produce a healthy daughter?
    A. 0%
    B. 25%
    C. 50%
    D. 100%

53. What is the probability that a man with hemophilia, a sex linked recessive disease, and a woman who is a carrier for the disease will produce a healthy son?
    A. 0%
    B. 50%
    C. 75%
    D. 100%

54. If a child of a man without hemophilia has a 50% chance of having the sex-linked recessive disease, his mother must:
    A. Have hemophilia
    B. Be a carrier
    C. Be healthy
    D. There is not enough information

55. What is the probability that the second daughter of a man with a sex-linked disease and woman with the same disease expresses this disease?
    A. 0%
    B. 50%
    C. 75%
    D. 100%

56. What comes after "kingdom" in the taxonomy order?
    A. Phylum
    B. Species
    C. Family
    D. Class

57. Which of the following describes the event of becoming lactose intolerant later in life?
    A. Evolution
    B. Genetic drift
    C. Apoptosis
    D. None of the above

58. A typical dihybrid cross showcases the probability of a certain genotype out of how many progeny?
    A. 4
    B. 10
    C. 12
    D. 16

59. What is the standard ratio of genotypes in a dihybrid cross?
    A. 9:3:3:1
    B. 3:3:3:3
    C. 4:8:4:1
    D. 2:2:10:1

60. Among the following genotypes resulting from a dihybrid cross, which is most common?
    A. Heterozygous for both genes
    B. Homozygous recessive for both genes
    C. Homozygous dominant for both genes
    D. Codominant for both genes

61. Which of the following is true of inbreeding?
    A. Changes the allele frequency of the population
    B. Leads to genetic drift
    C. Increases the number of homozygous individuals
    D. Never leads to adverse health outcomes

62. Which of the following is the phenotype ratio in a monohybrid cross?
    A. 2:2
    B. 3:2
    C. 3:1
    D. 4:2

63. Outbreeding increases the number of:
    A. Homozygous dominant individuals
    B. Homozygous recessive individuals
    C. Heterozygous individuals
    D. Codominant individuals

64. What is the probability that a son with hemophilia and Duchenne muscular dystrophy, both X-linked recessive diseases, is produced by a healthy male and a woman who is carrier for both diseases? (consider the genes for these 2 diseases to be unlinked)
    A. 1/2
    B. 1/4
    C. 1/8
    D. 1/10

65. A niche is:
    A. A species' exploitation of their environment
    B. Typically found in dense forested areas
    C. A specialized habitat for birds
    D. A signal of an unsuccessful species

66. What usually occurs after a natural disaster separates a species into two portions that can no longer mate with the each other?
    A. Speciation
    B. Extinction
    C. Increased chance of mutation
    D. Increased chance of homozygous recessive individuals

67. A homozygous dominant individual and homozygous recessive individual for an autosomal gene always produce progeny with what genotype?
    A. Codominant
    B. Homozygous recessive
    C. Heterozygous
    D. Homozygous dominant

68. A homozygous dominant individual and homozygous recessive individual for an autosomal gene always produce progeny with what phenotype (presuming 100% expressivity)?
    A. Codominant
    B. Dominant
    C. Recessive
    D. Incomplete

69. If red hair is dominant and yellow hair is recessive, a son with yellow hair whose mother has yellow hair must have a father with: (consider hair color to be autosomal)
    A. Red hair
    B. Yellow hair
    C. Either red or yellow
    D. None of the above

70. Biometry is another word for:
    A. Niche development
    B. Biostatistics
    C. Epidemiology
    D. Ecological analysis

71. A gene's location on a chromosome is called:
    A. An allele
    B. The locus
    C. Wild type
    D. Phenotype

72. Which is true of the wild-type?
    A. Always homozygous dominant
    B. Always heterozygous
    C. Usually represents the common phenotype
    D. Never homozygous recessive

73. Gene flow between two or more species is termed:
    A. Leakage
    B. Incomplete dominance
    C. Penetrance
    D. Expressivity

74. If someone has the genotype for red hair and has red hair, it can be said without dispute that the red hair gene must have:
    A. 50% Penetrance
    B. 75% Penetrance
    C. 100% Penetrance
    D. There is not enough information

75. 100% penetrance means that:
    A. The phenotype will reflect the genotype
    B. The phenotype may reflect the genotype
    C. The phenotype will not reflect the genotype
    D. It's impossible to say whether the phenotype will reflect the genotype

76. The Y chromosome has:
    A. As many genes as the X chromosome
    B. Very few genes
    C. No genes at all
    D. Not been evolutionarily successful

77. The varying degrees to which a gene is expressed by all individuals whose genotype includes the gene is the gene's:
    A. dominance.
    B. recessiveness.
    C. incompleteness.
    D. expressivity.

SECTION 6
PROTEINS AND AMINO ACIDS

In the biology portion of the book we went through a brief discussion of the basics related to proteins and amino acids. Now that we turn out attention to biochemistry, we must take a much more in-depth look at these molecules. Based on the AAMC guidelines, the foundations of amino acids and proteins will make up a significant portion of both the Biological Foundations section and the Chemical Foundations sections. As such, you should work on building up a strong mastery of this material.

In the following chapters, we will begin our discussion with amino acids and then the proteins that are built from them. We will then go on to discuss the two major functional groupings of proteins: enzymatic protein function and non-enzymatic protein function. Finally, we will wrap up by discussing lab techniques used to analyze these molecules.

NEXT STEP MCAT CONTENT REVIEW: BIOLOGY AND BIOCHEMISTRY

CHAPTER 21
Amino Acids

A. INTRODUCTION

Nearly all human proteins are composed of some combination of the 20 "standard" amino acids (shown in Figure 21.1). Standard amino acids are known as α-amino acids because they contain a primary amino group (—NH$_2$) bound to the central carbon atom (α-carbon atom), which is additionally bound to the carboxylic acid group (—COOH) of the molecule. The α-carbon has two additional substituents, a chemical group referred to as the side chain (—R), which is different for each amino acid, and a hydrogen atom (Figure 21.2).

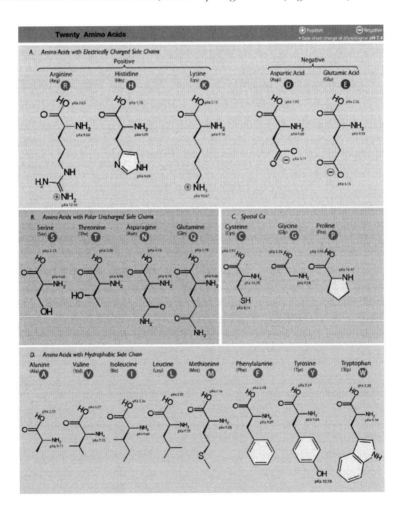

Figure 21.1: The twenty standard amino acids

At physiological pH of approximately 7.4, the amino and carboxylic acid groups of amino acids readily ionize. The α-amino groups of the standard amino acids are protonated and positively charged, while α-carboxylic acid groups are deprotonated and negatively charged. The pK_a of α-carboxylic acid groups for the standard amino acids are ordinarily near 2, while the pK_a of α-amino groups are typically greater than 9. Because of amino acids' capacity to extensively hydrogen bond with water, all standard amino acids are water soluble at physiological pH and are generally more soluble in polar than in nonpolar solvents.

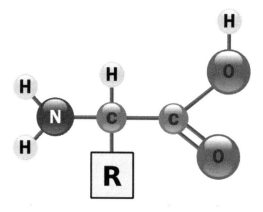

Figure 21.2: α-amino acids

B. CONFIGURATION

In all amino acids other than glycine (where the side chain is hydrogen), the α-carbon is an asymmetrical carbon bound to four unique substituents, displaying point chirality, and existing in one of two optically active, enantiomeric configurations referred to as the D- (dextrorotary) or L- (levorotatory) configuration. Biochemists often use the Fischer convention to describe different forms of chiral molecules. This convention is frequently employed in the nomenclature of amino acids and carbohydrates. Glyceraldehyde contains a single asymmetric center and, in the Fischer convention, the stereochemistry of molecules is assigned depending upon their orientation relative to glyceraldehyde's stereoisomers. Fischer proposed the use of a shorthand notation, known as a Fischer projection, to make this comparison easier. In the Fischer projection, horizontal bonds extend above the plane of the page and vertical bonds extend below it (Figure 21.3).

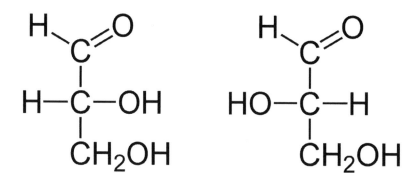

Figure 21.3: D-glyceraldehyde (left) and L-glyceraldehyde (right).

For α-amino acids, the amino, carboxylic acid, R and H groups around the α-carbon correspond to the hydroxyl, aldehyde, CH2OH, and H groups, respectively, of glyceraldehyde. Therefore, L-glyceraldehyde and L-α-amino acids have the same relative configuration. In a Fischer projection of an L-α-amino acid, the amino group will be oriented on the leftmost horizontal bond. In a D-α-amino acid, the amino group will be oriented on the rightmost horizontal bond (Figure 21.4).

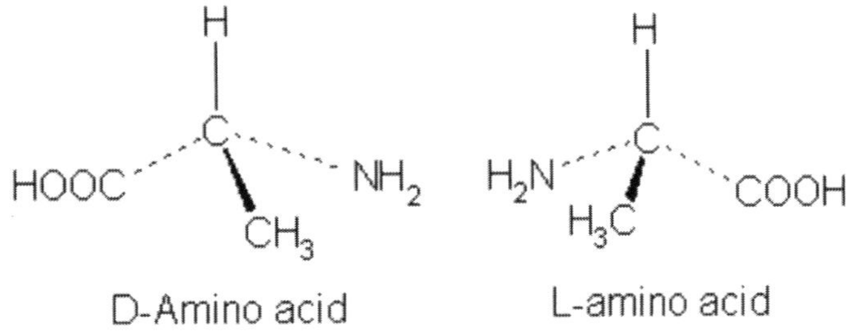

Figure 21.4.: D- and L-stereoisomers of alanine.

The amino acid glycine is neither a D- nor an L-amino acid, because its α-carbon, which is bound to two hydrogens, is non-chiral. L-amino acids are the chiral amino acids found in naturally occurring mammalian proteins. Thus, human metabolic pathways are specific for the synthesis of L-amino acids and nearly always produce enantiomerically pure products, conferring a great deal of stereospecificity on the reactions of many human biological molecules, including enzymes. This is seen in the function of pharmaceuticals, where only a single enantiomer of a drug may be biologically active. While D-amino acids are not synthesized by humans, they can be synthesized by bacterial enzymes, and are found as the components of certain bacterial polypeptides, most often as constituents of bacterial cell walls.

C. HYDROPHOBIC AND HYDROPHILIC AMINO ACIDS

The 20 standard amino acids tested on the MCAT are regularly categorized according to the polarity of their side chains. According to the most common classification scheme, there are three major amino acid types: those with uncharged polar side chains; those with nonpolar side chains; and those with charged polar side chains. These groupings can be useful for describing the typical functional or metabolic roles of the amino acids. But, be forewarned: some acid side chains fit into different categorizations and are therefore grouped differently by different resources. It is, however, extremely unlikely, that correctly answering a question on the MCAT will hinge on a potentially ambiguous amino acid classification.

Alanine and the branched-chain amino acids—valine, leucine, and isoleucine—have large, nonpolar, open hydrocarbon chain side chains. Such aliphatic side chains exhibit significant hydrophobicity. Because of the lack of side chain dipolarity, amino acids with aliphatic side chains are incapable of hydrogen-bonding with water, explaining their inability to interact with it. As part of a protein, hydrophobic amino acids cluster in hydrophobic regions where they are sheltered from the aqueous environment of the cell.

The amino acid proline differs from the other nonpolar amino acids in that it contains a ring involving its α-amino group and its α-carbon. The rigidity caused by this structure disrupts the secondary structure of proline-containing proteins and restricts conformational change in the protein about the location of a proline residue in its polypeptide chain. Glycine is the simplest amino acid. Its side chain contains only a hydrogen atom. Because of the side chain's small size, glycine causes little steric interference in the conformations adopted by the proteins in which it is found. For this reason, glycine is often found in turns and in other sterically restricted regions of proteins.

The aliphatic, polar uncharged amino acids contain a hydroxyl group (serine and threonine) or an amide group (asparagine and glutamine). The hydroxyl and amide groups of these side chains allow these polar amino acids to form hydrogen bonds with water, with the peptide backbone or with other polar compounds (especially in the binding sites of proteins). Due to their relative hydrophilicity, such polar amino acids are frequently found on the surface of globular proteins, where they interact with water in the surroundings.

Both the amino acids cysteine and methionine contain sulfur. The side chain of cysteine contains a sulfhydryl group that is predominately dissociated at physiological pH. The cysteine residues of proteins can spontaneously associate to form covalent disulfide bonds with the thiol groups of other cysteine residues, creating the relatively insoluble amino acid cystine. The formation of disulfide-containing cysteine residues, shown in Figure 21.5, in proteins often link the polypeptide chains of multi-subunit proteins. While methionine also contains a sulfur group, its bulky side chain does not contain a thiol functional group and is therefore not capable of disulfide bonding.

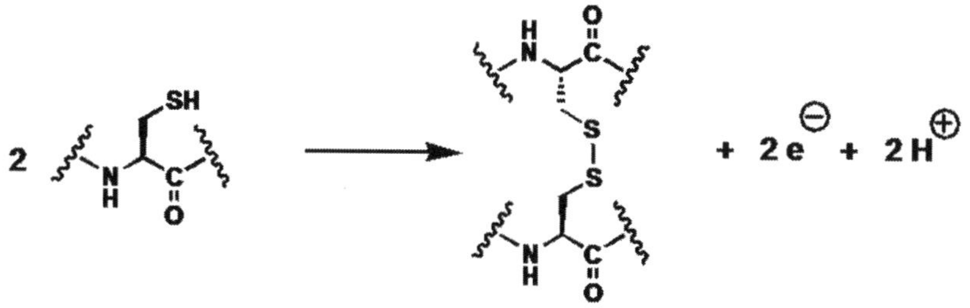

Figure 21.5: Disulfide bond formation

The aromatic amino acids phenylalanine, tyrosine and tryptophan are often grouped together because they contain aromatic ring structures with similar properties. Nonetheless, the polarities of these amino acids differ greatly depending upon the substituents of their aromatic rings. In phenylalanine, the ring is unsubstituted and the amino acid as a whole is quite hydrophobic. In tyrosine, a hydroxyl group bound to the phenyl ring confers additional polarity on the molecule. Tryptophan contains a complex indole ring. The heterocyclic nitrogen of the ring is able to hydrogen bond and, like tyrosine, displays more hydrophilicity than does phenylalanine.

D. ACIDIC AND BASIC AMINO ACIDS

Of the 20 standard amino acids, five are defined as acidic or basic. These amino acids all contain side chains which are charged at physiological pH. The side chains of the basic amino acids (lysine, arginine, and histidine) contain nitrogen and are often found in their protonated and positively charged forms at physiological pH. Lysine contains a butylammonium side chain, and arginine a guanidine group. Histidine, the only amino acid to readily ionize within the physiological pH range, includes an imidazolium moiety. Because of histidine's reversible ionization within the body's predominate pH range, it can be found in both its protonated, cationic form, and its neutral form, in proteins *in vivo*. The reversible protonation of histidine is a common feature of many enzymatically catalyzed reactions.

The side chains of the acidic amino acids (aspartic acid and glutamic acid) are deprotonated and negatively charged at physiological pH values. When ionized, they are often called aspartate and glutamate. The negative charge of the acidic amino acids permits them to form ionic bonds with positively charged groups such as the side chains of basic amino acid residues. For similar reasons, the positive charge of basic amino acids allows them to bind through their side chains to the phosphate groups of co-enzymes. Both basic and acidic amino acid side chains form salt bridges, participate in hydrogen bonding and, when charged, engage in ion-dipole interactions.

E. DIPOLAR IONS

Ultimately, the charge borne by an amino acid at physiological pH is determined by the individual pK_a values for the dissociation of a proton from the α-carboxylic acid group, the α-amino group, and, for acidic and basic amino acids, the side chain. At low pH values, the pH of solution is less than the pK_a of each of an amino acid's acidic protons. As result, all groups remain predominately in their protonated states and the amino acid is positively charged. As the pH of solution increases, protons first dissociate from the most acidic moiety of an amino acid—the α-carboxylic acid group. At a pH equal to the pK_a of the α-carboxylic acid group, approximately half of the α-carboxylic acid groups present in a sample of an amino acid will be protonated, and half will be deprotonated. As the pH increases beyond the pK_a the number of deprotonated α-carboxylic acid groups will continue to increase. The α-amino groups of an amino acid will remain predominately in the protonated form until the pH of solution surpasses their pK_a. In neutral amino acids lacking an acidic or basic side chain, the net charge on the predominate form of the amino acid will have changed from positive to neutral when solution pH is between the pK_a of the α-carboxylic acid and the pK_a of the α-amino groups. In this net neutral charge state, an amino acid is referred to as being in its zwitterion form (Figure 21.6).

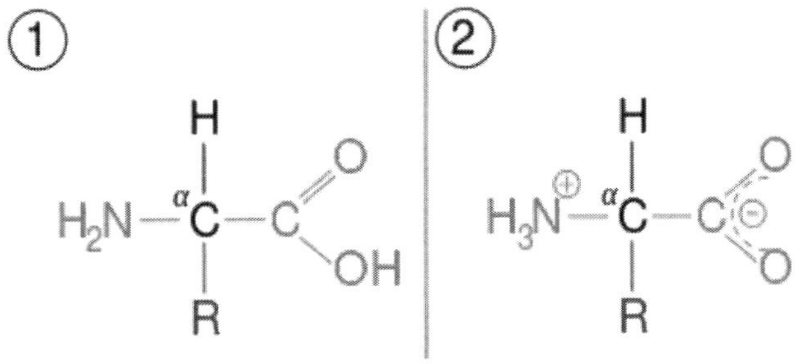

Figure 21.6: The (1) non-ionized and (2) zwitterion
forms of a generic diprotic amino acid

The reversible dissociation of ionizable protons is shown for a generic diprotic amino acid in Figure 21.7

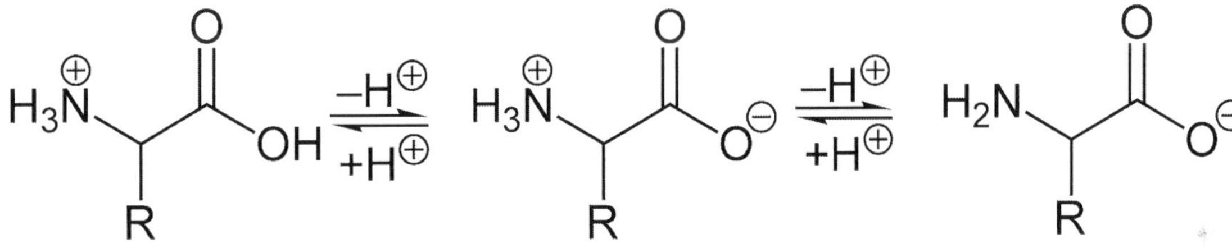

Figure 21.7: Titration of a diprotic amino acid

The pH at which the net charge on a sample of an amino acid in solution is zero, and at which the zwitterion form exists in greatest concentration, is referred to as the isoelectric point (pI). At pH values equal to the pI of a molecule, it will not migrate in an electric field toward a positive pole or a negative pole because of the net neutral charge of the molecules in solution. For the α-amino acids, the pI may be calculated according to the equation

$$pI = (pK_{a1} + pK_{a2}) / 2$$

where K_{a1} and K_{a2} are the dissociation constants of the two ionization states involving the neutral species. For the neutral amino acids, K_{a1} and K_{a2} represent the dissociation constants of the α-carboxylic acid and α-amino groups, respectively. For the dicarboxylic acid amino acids, K_{a1} and K_{a2} represent the dissociation constants of the α-carboxylic acid group and the side chain carboxylic acid, respectively. In the basic amino acids, K_{a1} and K_{a2} represent the dissociation constants of the side chain and of the α-amino group, respectively.

Given that α-amino acids have either two or, for acidic and basic amino acids, three ionizable protons, their titration curves include two or three buffering regions and an equal number of equivalence points. Over the course of a titration with a strong base, protons are lost in a stepwise fashion characteristic of polyprotic acids. The pK_a of each ionizable group is the midpoint of the corresponding leg of the titration curve and is centered around the buffering region for that dissociation. Theoretical titration curves for the 20 standard amino acids using a strongly basic titrant are shown in Figure 21.8.

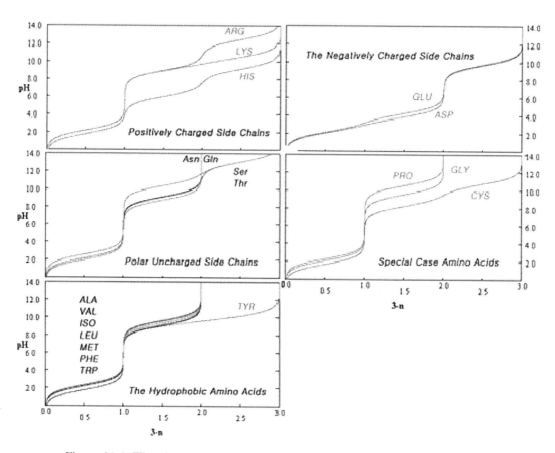

Figure 21.8: Titration curves of 20 standard amino acids grouped by side chain

Chapter 21 Problems

Passage 21.1 (Questions 1-5)

Sickle cell disease (SCD) is an inherited blood disorder characterized by an abnormality in the morphology and function of the oxygen-carrying molecule hemoglobin (Hb). SCD is caused by a point mutation in the β-globin gene of Hb, resulting in the replacement of the amino acid glutamic acid with the amino acid valine.

Association of two wild-type α-globin proteins with two mutant β-globin proteins forms the abnormal hemoglobin referred to as HbS. Under conditions where the partial pressure of oxygen is low, Hb cells non-covalently polymerize, decreasing their elasticity, and leading to blood vessel occlusion and ischemia.

A researcher isolated normal Hb and three abnormal samples of Hb and performed a gel electrophoresis on them at pH 9. The results of the electrophoresis are shown in Figure 1.

Figure 1: Gel electrophoresis of Hb samples

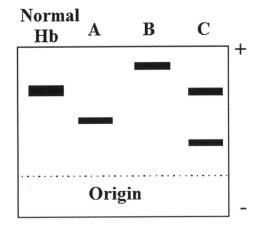

1. Which of the following statements best characterizes the charge at physiological pH of glutamate's side chain and that of the valine for which it is substituted in Hb?
   A. Glutamate carries a negative charge; valine is neutrally charged.
   B. Glutamate carries a positive charge; valine is neutrally charged.
   C. Glutamate is neutrally charged; valine carries a positive charge.
   D. Glutamate is neutrally charged; valine carries a negative charge.

2. At pH = 0, the charge of the predominant form of glutamate is:
   A. one unit greater than valine
   B. equal to that of valine
   C. one unit less than that of valine
   D. two units greater than valine

3. Which of the following sample(s) could NOT be HbS?
   A. Sample A only
   B. Sample B only
   C. Sample A and C
   D. Sample A and B

4. HbS most likely aggregates due to:
   A. hydrogen bonding between the side chains of its residues.
   B. the formation of disulfide bridges.
   C. ionic salt bridging.
   D. hydrophobic interactions.

5. Replacement of a glutamate residue in Hb with which of the following amino acids is LEAST likely to affect the function of Hb?
   A. Cysteine
   B. Isoleucine
   C. Aspartic acid
   D. Alanine

The following questions are NOT based on a descriptive passage.

6. The inclusion of which of the following amino acids in a peptide is most likely to induce the formation of a "kink" in protein secondary structural motifs?
    A. Glycine
    B. Tryptophan
    C. Arginine
    D. Proline

7. Which of the following statements regarding glycine (pI = 6.1) is NOT true?
    A. It will move toward a positive pole at pH 8.
    B. It is optically active.
    C. It will move toward a negative pole at pH 3.
    D. At pH 6.1, its α-carboxylic acid group is most likely negatively charged.

8. Lysine has three pK_a values: 2.18, 8.95, and 10.53. At what pH would its acid residue be deprotonated but its other residues be protonated?
    A. 2.02
    B. 5.48
    C. 9.65
    D. 1.24

9. Which of the following amino acids contains no polar component or functional group in its side chain?
    I. Serine
    II. Valine
    III. Tyrosine

    A. I only
    B. II only
    C. I and III only
    D. II and III only

10. The pI of the amino acid alanine is 6.11 and the pK_a of its α-carboxylic acid group is 2.35. What is the greatest pH value at which a buffering region of the titration of alanine with a strong base is centered?
    A. 2.35
    B. 6.11
    C. 8.45
    D. 9.87

CHAPTER 22
Protein Structure

A. INTRODUCTION

Proteins are composed of amino acids linked linearly as polypeptide chains. The linear sequence of amino acids is genetically encoded and is referred to as the primary sequence of the protein. Polymers composed of two, three, a few, or many polypeptides are referred to as dipeptides, tripeptides, oligopeptides and polypeptides, respectively. In polypeptide biosynthesis, individual amino acid residues are linked enzymatically through the formation of a peptide bond between the carboxylic acid group of one residue and the amino group of the adjacent residue (Figure 22.1).

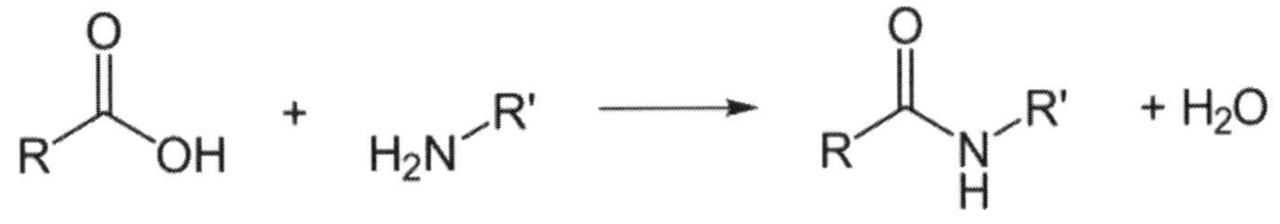

Figure 22.1: Condensation reaction leading to peptide bond formation

The resulting serial linkage between an α-carboxylic acid group, an α-amino group, and an α-carbon form the peptide backbone (Figure 22.2). Peptide bonds ordinarily assume a ***trans*** configuration in which successive α-carbons are located on opposite sides of the peptide backbone. Rotation about the peptide bond is also restricted. The peptide bond is a resonance hybrid of the two principle resonances representing the delocalized electrons of the amide linkage of the peptide bond. Because of this delocalization, the C-N bond of the amide displays partial double bond character, and the carboxyl and amino groups of the peptide bond must remain planar. Other bonds in the peptide backbone are free to rotate.

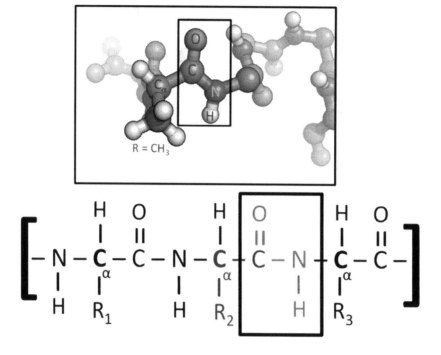

Figure 22.2: Structure of the peptide bond (bottom) and the three-dimensional (tertiary) structure assumed about a peptide bond between alanine and an adjacent amino acid residue (top/inset).

Each chain contains both a carboxy terminal (C-terminus) and an amino terminal (N-terminus). The N-terminus is the amino group of the first amino acid of the chain and the C-terminus is the free carboxylic acid group of the last amino acid of the chain. Extending from the peptide backbone at the α-carbon are the side chains of individual residues. Side chain groups interact with the peptide backbone and the side chains of other residues of the protein, forming hydrogen, disulfide, and ionic bonds, and driving the formation of higher levels of protein structure.

B. PRIMARY TO QUATERNARY STRUCTURE

As mentioned earlier, a protein's primary structure is the amino acid sequence of its polypeptide chain or chains. As the length of a polypeptide chain increases, so too do the number of possible polypeptide sequences. For a protein containing n standard amino acid residues, there are 20^n possible sequences of amino acids. Within the same individual, different isoforms of a protein may exist. Isoforms may differ in terms of their primary sequence, but share the same biological function. The same isoforms of a particular protein may be synthesized over the life of the individual or different isoforms may be expressed at different stages of organismal development.

Polypeptide chains form localized regions of recurring structural patterns known as secondary structure. The two regularly repeating secondary structural patterns, called motifs, that are most likely to appear on the MCAT are the α-helix and the β-pleated sheet. Both are formed by regular backbone hydrogen bonding between the peptide amide hydrogen and peptide carbonyl oxygen of the same or adjacent polypeptides. The α-helix involves intra-peptide hydrogen backbone bonding within a single polypeptide chain that coils in a clockwise manner around a central rotational axis. β-pleated sheets involve backbone hydrogen bonding between adjacent parallel or anti-parallel polypeptides that assume a "pleated" shape, where the side chains of amino residues point in alternation above, and below, the β-strand (Figure 22.3). β-pleated sheets compose fibroin, the most abundant component of silk fibers.

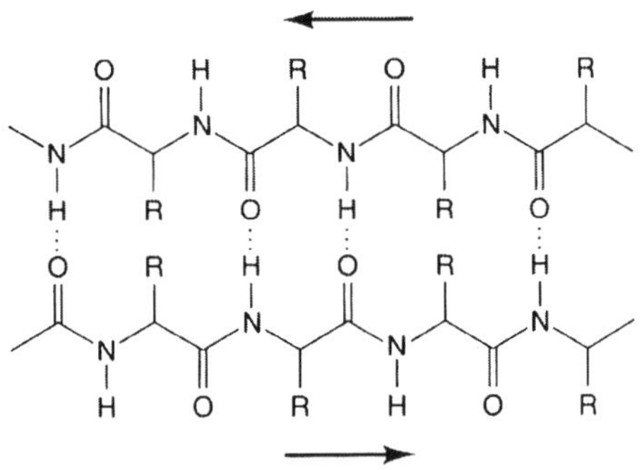

Figure 22.3: Diagram of a β-pleated sheet

Segments with regular secondary structure are often connected by stretches of polypeptides that abruptly reverse direction. These structures are referred to as β-bends when they include β-pleated sheets. These regions are often rich in proline, the presence of which induces formation of bending "kinks" in the polypeptide chain because of its rigid structure. In contrast, proline is rarely found located in α-helices or within long, linear stretches of β-pleated sheets. Other non-regular or non-repeating secondary structures can be formed by polypeptides as well, including coils and loops.

Just as secondary structure follows from the linear amino acid sequence of the protein, so too does the tertiary structure of a protein, which depends upon the three-dimensional conformations adopted by the folded polypeptide chain (Figure 22.4).

Tertiary structure is the pattern of secondary structural elements which fold into flexible, three-dimensional conformations and allow for a protein's emergent functional activity. Unlike secondary structure, which takes into account only the local spatial arrangement of a polypeptide backbone without regard to its side chains, tertiary structure also considers the influence of side chain interactions. Proteins are traditionally classified as fibrous or globular depending upon their shape.

Fibrous proteins tend to serve a protective or structural role and are often characterized by a single recurrent structural element. Fibrous and other structural proteins are extensively linked through covalent bonds. This bonding confers much of the tensile strength and

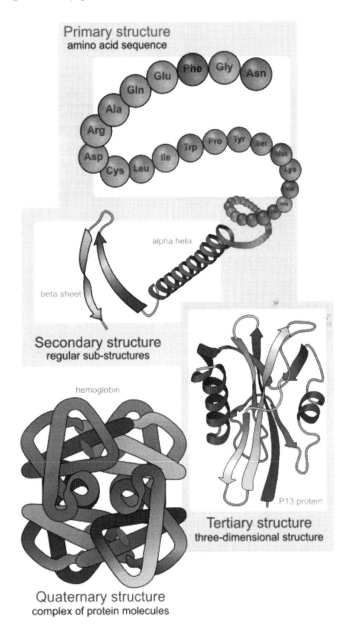

Figure 22.4: Protein structure, from primary to quaternary.

stability possessed by the proteins. Collagens are a family of fibrous proteins secreted principally by fibroblasts (found in connective tissue), muscle cells and epithelial cells. Type I collagen, the most abundant protein found in animals, is an insoluble fibrous protein with significant tensile strength. It is an abundant stress-bearing component of bone, teeth, cartilage, tendon and the fibrous matrix of skin and blood vessels. Type I collage is composed of a triple helix of three inter-wound polypeptide (pro-α) chains (Figure 22.5).

Figure 22.5: Triple helix of tropocollagen
Attribution: en-Wikipedia user;JWSchmidt under CC-BY-SA license

Pro-α chains are rich in glycine, proline and non-standard amino acid residues, including hydroxyproline. The collagen polypeptide amino sequence includes the repeating amino acid triplet sequence Gly-X-Y, where X is often proline and Y is frequently hydroxyproline. Another important structural protein is keratin. It is the principle component of the outer epidermal layer, and is found in hair and nails. The X-ray diffraction pattern of α-keratin, the form of keratin found in mammals, resembles that of two α-helices in a left-handed coiled structure.

Most globular proteins are soluble in the cytosolic environment. Typically, the core of a globular protein contains domains rich in amino acid residues with nonpolar side chains, sequestered from the aqueous medium of the cell, and dominated by attractive hydrophobic interactions. Polar uncharged amino acids are usually found on the exterior of the folded protein. Charged polar amino acid side chains are also typically found on a protein's surface, where they are able to form ionic bonds with each other (salt bridges), the aqueous environment, and with inorganic cations. Such ligand binding serves to decrease repulsion between side chains of like charge.

While tertiary structure in globular proteins is usually driven by van der Waals forces and ionic bonding, covalent disulfide bonds are occasionally involved in the formation of tertiary structures, where they add stability to the folded protein.

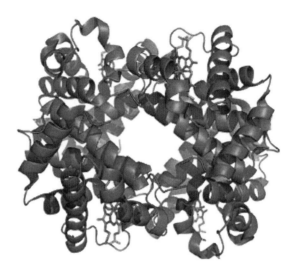

Figure 22.6: Three-dimensional structure of hemoglobin, a globular protein

Many proteins are composed of two or more polypeptide chains, known as subunits, and function in the cell as dimers, tetramers or oligomers, composed of two, four, or more, subunits. A protein's quaternary structure refers to the spatial arrangement and stoichiometric relationship between associated subunits. Subunits ordinarily associate through interactions between closely packed nonpolar side chains, backbone and side chain hydrogen bonding, and salt bridges. They are very rarely bound together by disulfide linkages and never by other forms of covalent bonds.

C. PROTEIN STABILITY: FOLDING, DENATURING, SOLVATION, HYDROPHOBIC INTERACTIONS

As suggested earlier, the structure adopted by proteins is stabilized by hydrophobic effects (the major determinant of a protein's native conformation), electrostatic interactions, chemical cross-linking and hydrogen bonding. Reaching and maintaining the folded state is a fine balance between the forces that stabilize folded proteins, the sum of which may exceed thousands of kilojoules per mole for large proteins, and the thermodynamic disadvantage of remaining in an entropically disfavored state. One example of the chemical thermodynamic considerations associated with the maintenance of protein tertiary structure are the locations at which hydrophobic and hydrophilic amino acid residues are found. As mentioned previously, the core of a globular protein contains domains rich in amino acid residues with nonpolar side chains, located away from the aqueous medium of the cell. The dissolution of solute in solvent— whether polar or non-polar—is exothermic and leads to the formation of a solvation layer around the dissolved solute. However, when hydrophobic residues, including the side chains of hydrophobic amino acids are dissolved in an aqueous solution, their inability to hydrogen bond with water disrupts the existing hydrogen bonding network between molecules of liquid water. This creates a significant entropic disadvantage to the interaction of hydrophobic amino acid residues with an aqueous environment, as water molecules are forced to re-arrange into a more ordered configuration to maximize hydrogen bonding between water molecules in the region around the solvation shell. In net, despite the negative heat of solvation associated with the dissolution of solute, the decreased entropy of dissolving a hydrophobic moiety in water makes the process non-spontaneous. This is in contrast to the spontaneous dissolution associated with the interaction of polar uncharged amino acids and water. Not surprisingly, polar uncharged amino acids are usually found on the exterior of a folded protein *in vivo*.

In order for proteins to remain folded in a particular conformational equilibrium state, solution conditions must remain favorable to that state. Proteins become denatured when their overall shape is disrupted by external factors. However, under certain, normally physiological, conditions they can refold spontaneously into their native state. This is because the tertiary structure adopted by the protein is ultimately determined by its primary amino acid sequence. In certain cases, proteins are aided in folding by heat shock proteins (some of which are referred to as chaperonins) and isomerase enzymes. However, neither chaperonins nor isomerase enzymes change the energy of unwound states of the protein, or of a protein's native conformation.

Protein denaturation can occur due to a variety of processes, environmental conditions and treatments. Heating disrupts a protein's conformation in such a way as to cause a distinct change in the protein's tertiary structure and functional properties. Most proteins reach this so-called "melting" point at relatively low temperatures. Changes in pH due to the addition of acidic or basic salts may alter the ionization states of amino acids, leading to unfolding because of charge redistribution and hydrogen-bonding disruption within the protein. Heavy metal ions such as mercury and lead may bind to anionic side chains, disrupting salt bridges and the secondary and tertiary structures they maintain. Amphipathic detergents associate with nonpolar residues of proteins, interfering with the hydrophobic interactions that maintain the protein's native conformation. Other small molecular or ionic agents, such as urea, disrupt hydrophobic interactions by increasing the water solubility of nonpolar substances.

Chapter 22 Problems

Passage 22 (Questions 1-5)

In 1957, Christian Anfinsen performed a series of experiments on the single chain protein ribonuclease A (RNase A) to evaluate the hypothesis that protein denaturation is reversible under certain conditions.

Step 1

RNase A was completely unfolded and its four disulfide bonds reductively cleaved in a solution containing 8 M urea and the reductant 2-mercaptoethanol. None of the RNase molecules displayed normal enzymatic function.

Step 2

Both urea and the reductant were removed and the remaining solution was exposed to the oxidant O_2 at pH 7.4. Treatment yielded a protein that is structurally and functionally indistinguishable from native RNAse A.

Step 3

RNase A was then reoxided in 8 M urea. After removal of the urea, approximately 1% of the RNase A molecules were able to properly perform their enzymatic function.

1. The level of protein structural organization that was both present and unaffected by the simultaneous treatment of native state RNase A with urea and 2-mercaptoethanol is:
    A. primary structure.
    B. secondary structure.
    C. tertiary structure.
    D. quaternary structure.

2. The shape of an enzyme's native conformation:
    A. does not influence the function of the enzyme's active site.
    B. represents the enzyme's minimum free energy configuration.
    C. is ordinarily temperature insensitive.
    D. is determined exclusively by environmental factors.

3. Which statement is most consistent with the results of Anfinsen's work regarding protein folding?
    A. Protein cannot be denatured under physiological conditions.
    B. Spontaneous refolding of proteins can occur only if denaturation preserves a protein's covalently linked structures.
    C. The renaturation of RNAse A requires enzymatic catalysis.
    D. A protein's primary structure dictates its three-dimensional structure.

4. Based upon the results of the experiments presented in the passage, if non-functional RNase A produced at the end of Step 3 was separated from urea and mixed with a solution containing 2-mercaptoethanol, following removal of the 2-mercaptoethanol and re-exposure to O_2 at pH 7.4:
    A. covalent bonds between cysteine residues would be regenerated.
    B. the protein's peptide linkages would be reductively cleaved.
    C. the majority of enzymes would regain functionality.
    D. its enzymatic function would remain unchanged.

5. In its native state, which intermolecular interaction is most important for the maintenance of the tertiary structure of RNase A?
    A. disulfide bonds
    B. salt bridging
    C. hydrogen bonding
    D. hydrophobic interactions

The following questions are NOT based on a descriptive passage

6. A frameshift mutation resulting in what pair of amino acid substitutions in a polypeptide would most disrupt the salt bridging in which that polypeptide participates?
    A. Val replaced by Phe or Ala
    B. Tyr replaced by Thr or Gln
    C. Asn replaced by Ser or Ile
    D. Asp replaced by Val or Met

7. In laboratory experiments, synthesizing polypeptides by the random polymerization of amino acids under physiological conditions usually leads to the formation of insoluble polypeptide precipitates. Naturally occurring polypeptides of the same length are most often soluble because:
    A. proteins cannot maintain stable tertiary structures without heat shock proteins.
    B. buried salt bridges can only form *in vivo*.
    C. genetically-encoded polypeptide sequences are more likely to be soluble when folded than sequences formed by chance.
    D. the heat of solution of the insoluble polypeptide is less positive than that of the soluble polypeptide.

8. Proteins that perform the same function but have different primary structures:
    A. must arise from different coding regions of a gene.
    B. are known as isozymes if the protein serves a structural role.
    C. may be translated from the products of alternative splicing.
    D. could explain an unexpectedly large number of protein coding regions found in an organism's genome sequence.

9. Pro-α chains found in type I collagen are rich in which amino acid residues?
    A. proline and glycine
    B. glycine and histidine
    C. tryptophan and histidine
    D. proline and tryptophan

10. Which of the following statements is true?
    A. The α-helix domain of a protein can be composed of more than one polypeptide chain.
    B. Domains are a form of secondary structure.
    C. Proline is often found in β-bends.
    D. β-sheets exist only in antiparallel forms.

CHAPTER 23
Enzymes

A. INTRODUCTION

Nearly all of the metabolic events which take place in the body are due to the mediating activity of enzymes. Because of enzymes' ability to act as protein catalysts and increase the rates of the reactions in which they are involved, they are able to direct specific substrates into biologically useful pathways, thus providing a mechanism by which the body can maintain regulatory control over its contents.

B. CATALYSTS

Enzymes speed, specify and regulate biological reactions. Such catalysis is one of the major, and most important, functions of proteins. Enzyme catalysis has three basic steps:

1. Binding of enzyme to substrate
2. Conversion of bound substrate to bound product
3. Release of bound product

Enzymes are extremely specific for reaction substrates, interacting with one or a few substrates and catalyzing only a single reaction. Enzymes function by bringing bound substrates together in the proper orientation for a reaction to occur. Once this orientation of reactants is achieved, enzymes may also participate in the making and breaking of bonds required for product formation. Once formed, the products of the reaction are then released into the cell. Without the efficient catalytic action of an enzyme, many biologically important reactions would occur too slowly to permit complex life to exist.

The catalytic action of an enzyme may be viewed in terms of the energetic pathway provided by the enzyme-catalyzed reaction, which proceeds through a lower energy transition state than the uncatalyzed reaction. An enzyme's catalysis may also be viewed from the perspective of the enzyme's chemical behavior during catalysis. Nearly all chemical reactions proceed through a high-energy transition point, where the energetic difference between the reactants (or products) and the transition point, known as the activation energy, represents an energetic barrier to the reaction proceeding. For substrate molecules to react, they must contain sufficient energy to overcome the energetic barrier of the reaction and achieve the transition state between reactants and products. The overall rate of reaction increases as the number of molecules possessing sufficient energy to overcome the energetic barrier collide with proper orientation per unit time.

The change in the energy of the activated complex for the reversible conversion of carbon dioxide and water to carbonic acid, catalyzed by the metalloenzyme carbonic anhydrase, is shown in Figure 23.1.

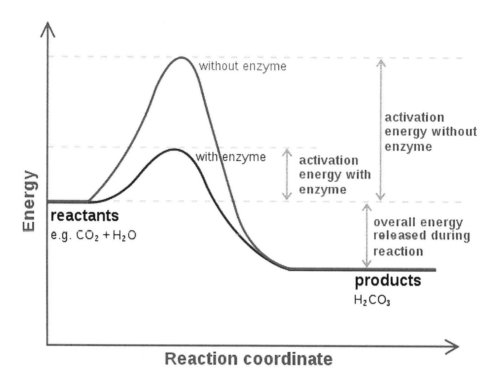

Figure 23.1: Transition state energy changes in reaction catalyzed by the enzyme carbonic anhydrase

Enzymes utilize a number of diverse catalytic strategies to decrease the activation energy of a reaction. By doing so, enzymes increase the overall reaction rate without affecting the free energy of reactants or products, or the position of the reaction equilibrium. Enzymes serve their catalytic role without changing the free energy levels of reactants and products by providing an alternate, lower energy reaction pathway.

C. INDUCED FIT MODEL

In 1894, Emil Fischer proposed that the extreme specificity of enzyme for substrate is because enzymes and their substrates possess perfectly complementary binding site structures. This proposal has come to be known as the "the lock and key" model. However, while this model offers an explanation for enzyme specificity, it fails to address the stabilization of the transition state characteristic of enzyme-catalyzed reactions.

While the shape of enzyme active sites is extremely specific for the substrates to which they bind, this complementarity is not complete. As substrate binds, enzymes undergo a further conformational change, known as induced fit. that repositions the side chains of amino acid residues within the binding pocket. This model reflects the reality that enzyme binding sites are not rigid structures, but flexible three-dimensional spaces created by dynamic surfaces (Figure 23.2).

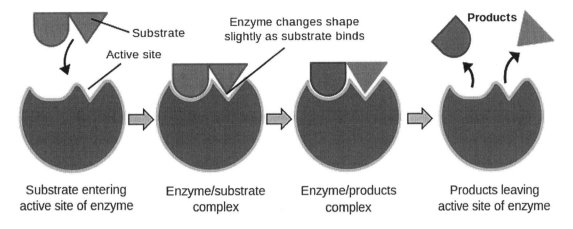

Figure 23.2: Diagram reflecting the induced fit model of enzyme-substrate interaction

Repositioning of functional groups within the active site may increase the strength of substrate binding, enhance substrate recognition, improve binding of a cosubstrate, activate adjacent subunits, or change the relative position of a side chain responsible for a portion of the enzyme's catalytic reaction chemistry.

D. ENZYME CLASSIFICATION

Enzymes may be broadly classified into one of six categories according to the type or types of chemical reactions which they catalyze.

- ◆ The *oxidoreductases* catalyze oxidation/reduction reactions by the transfer of hydrogen atoms, oxygen atoms, or electrons from one substance to another. They include dehydrogenases and oxidases.

- ◆ *Transferases* catalyze reactions involved in the transfer of a functional group from one substance to another. The group transferred may be a methyl-, amino-, acyl- or inorganic phosphate group. Transferases include the transaminases and kinases.

- ◆ *Hydrolases* hydrolyze a single substrate, forming two products. They include the lipases, amylase, and peptidases.

- ◆ *Lyases* non-hydrolytically catalyze the addition or removal of groups from substrates. They cleave a wide variety of bonds, including C-C, C-N, C-O or C-S bonds, depending on the type of lyase. The lyases include decarboxylases.

- ◆ *Isomerases* catalyze intramolecular rearrangement reactions and include both isomerases and mutases.

- ◆ *Ligases* utilize ATP in order to synthesize C-O, C-S, C-N or C-C bonds joining two substrates into a single product. They include synthetases.

E. COFACTORS, COENZYMES, VITAMINS

Cofactors and coenzymes are non-proteins that provide necessary functional groups for an enzyme-catalyzed reaction to proceed. If the non-protein component is an organic molecule, it is referred to as a coenzyme. If it is a metal ion, such as Mg^{2+}, Fe^{2+} or Zn^{2+}, it referred to as a cofactor.

Most coenzymes and cofactors are tightly bound to their associated enzymes and do not dissociate during the course of a reaction. The term holoenzyme refers to the active enzyme bound to its necessary cofactor or coenzyme, whereas the term apoprotein refers to the inactive protein when not bound to the required non-protein moiety. Coenzymes that transiently associate with the enzyme, and then dissociate from the enzyme in a chemically altered state, are referred to as cosubstrates (NAD+ is an example of a cosubstrate). If the coenzyme is permanently associated in the holoenzyme and is returned reversibly to its unmodified form, it is called a prosthetic group (FAD is an example of a prosthetic group).

In humans, coenzymes are often synthesized from vitamins, and individual coenzymes are often specific for the catalysis of reactions involving certain classes of substrates. Vitamins are organic compounds that cannot be synthesized directly from dietary components and must be obtained from the diet. Deficiency in the available pool of metabolically necessary coenzymes may be due to a dietary deficiency of vitamin precursors or from a functional deficiency associated with drug or toxin inhibition of the proteins required for the synthesis of needed coenzymes from dietary vitamins.

Vitamins are often classified as being water-soluble (folate, cobalamin, ascorbic acid, pyridoxine, thiamine, niacin, riboflavin, biotin, pantothenic acid) or fat-soluble (vitamins A, D, E, and K). The majority of water-soluble vitamins just mentioned belong to the B family of vitamins. The names, structures and major metabolic functions of each of the B vitamins is shown in Table 23.1.

Most coenzymes are derivatives of water-soluble vitamins. Only a single fat-soluble vitamin (Vitamin K, along with its derivatives) has a coenzymatic function. Water-soluble vitamins are readily excreted in the urine, but fat-soluble vitamins are absorbed from dietary fats and stored in both the liver and adipose tissues. Because of their poor water solubility, they may potentially accumulate in the body to toxic levels if their excretion is impaired or if they are ingested in sufficient quantity.

Table 26.1: B vitamins and their functions.		
Vitamin	**Name**	**Function**
Vitamin B_1	Thiamin	Thiamin is involved in carbohydrate catabolism, nucleic acid synthesis and nerve function. Its active form is the coenzyme thiamin pyrophosphate (TPP), which is a coenzyme in the conversion of pyruvate to acetyl CoA (CoA).
Vitamin B_2	Riboflavin	Riboflavin is involved in the beta oxidative catabolism of fatty acids, the Krebs cycle and the electron transport chain.
Vitamin B_3	Niacin	Niacin is composed of nicotinic acid and nicotinamide, and exists as two co-enzymes: nicotinamide adenine dinucleotide (NAD) and nicotinamide adenine dinucleotide phosphate (NADP). Both act as carriers of reduced factors in the metabolism of fats, glucose and alcohols. NAD transports reducing equivalents from the citric acid cycle to the electron transport chain, and NADP is a cofactor in lipid and nucleic acid biosynthesis.
Vitamin B_5	Pantothenic Acid	Pantothenic acid is involved in the β-oxidation of fatty acids and carbohydrates. Coenzyme A, which contains pantothenic acid, is involved in fatty acid, amino acid, cholesterol, steroid hormone, phospholipid and neurotransmitter synthesis
Vitamin B_6	Pyridoxine	The active form, pyridoxal 5'-phosphate (PLP), is a cofactor in amino acid and neurotransmitter biosynthesis.
Vitamin B_7	Biotin	Biotin is involved in the metabolism of carbohydrates, lipids, and proteins as a co-enzyme of four important carboxylases.
Vitamin B_9	Folic Acid	Folic acid, as the co-enzyme tetrahydrofolate (THF), is involved in single-carbon transfer reactions during the metabolism of nucleic acids and amino acids. THF is necessary for pyrimidine nucleotide biosynthesis and the production of red blood cells.
Vitamin B_{12}	Cobalamin	Cobalamin is involved in protein, carbohydrate and lipid metabolism and is important for nerve function and blood cell synthesis.

F. EFFECTS ON ENZYME ACTIVITY: TEMPERATURE, PH

The velocity of enzyme-catalyzed reactions is dependent upon a number of external factors, including substrate concentration, temperature and pH. If the activity of most enzymes is measured, the reaction rate is maximized within a specific pH range. The reason for this pH specificity is that most processes require that an enzyme and substrate have moieties that function only in specific, pH-dependent ionization states (Figure 23.3). When pH is significantly below the functional range of a given enzyme, ionized side chains that may be required to catalyze a given reaction become protonated and cannot function in the manner required of the reaction. At increased solution or cellular pH, amino acids may become inappropriately ionized, leading to similarly impaired enzyme function. Extremes of pH can also denature enzymes because the shape, and thus the catalytic activity, of many proteins depends upon the charge character of side chains in the folded state.

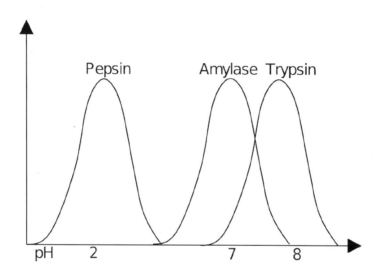

Figure 23.3: Activities of the human digestive enzymes pepsin, salivary amylase and trypsin are plotted as a function of pH.

Most enzymes in the human body function optimally at a temperature near normal body temperature (approximately 37°C). As temperature increases, so too does the kinetic energy of substrate molecules. A greater fraction of relatively higher energy substrate molecules indicates that more molecules possess sufficient energy to overcome the reaction energy barrier and form products. Significant elevation of temperature beyond 37°C often results in temperature-induced denaturation and a dramatic decline in enzyme activity.

Chapter 23 Problems

Passage 23.1 (Questions 1-5)

Chymotrypsin is a proteolytic enzyme which functions in human digestion and has been found to be most active in a small pH range near 7.5. The reaction it catalyzes involves the hydrolytic cleavage of peptide amide bonds where the carboxyl side of the amide bond is a large amino acid containing an aromatic ring side chain that fits into the enzyme's hydrophobic binding (S1) position.

Researchers studying chymotrypsin proposed the mechanism of its action illustrated in Figure 1. Following substrate binding to chymotrypsin, a serine-195 (Ser[195]) and a histidine-57 (His[57]) residue move nearer the active site, entering the proper orientation for serine-195 to nucleophilically attack and briefly become covalently bonded to the substrate, and forming an enzyme-substrate intermediate, the product of (1) in Figure 1. After cleavage of the peptide bond in (2), nucleophilic attack by water on the carbonyl carbon of the serine-bound intermediate during (3) leads to the formation of a second tetrahedral intermediate. Following the collapse of the second tetrahedral intermediate, the hydroxyl group of Ser[195] is regenerated, a proton is created, and the newly cleaved protein fragments are formed.

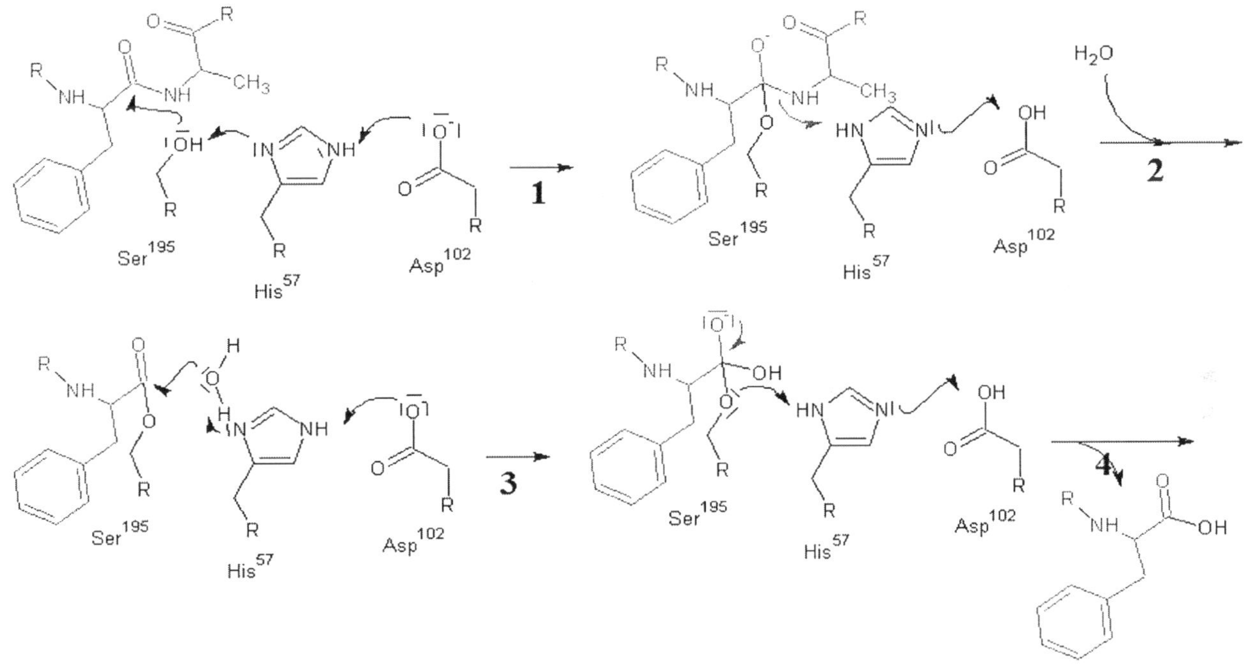

Figure 1. Catalytic mechanism of α-chymotrypsin

1. In the absence of chymotrypsin, the reaction which it catalyzes proceeds slowly for what reason?
   A. The thermodynamics of the reactions are unfavorable.
   B. The free energy of the products exceeds that of the reactants.
   C. Few molecules possess sufficient motional energy for the reaction to proceed more rapidly.
   D. An enzyme is necessary to provide additional energy to the transition state.

2. Step 2 is the rate-limiting step of the reaction shown in Figure 1. One possible explanation for this is:
   A. electrostatic repulsion due to an adjacent carbonyl destabilizes the oxyanion intermediate .
   B. the oxyanion intermediate is stabilized by hydrogen bonding with the adjacent N-H bond of the substrate.
   C. histidine's weakly basic catalysis results in the slow removal of a proton from Asp^{102}.
   D. the strength of the bond between the oxygen of the Ser^{195} residue and the polypeptide substrate makes acyl bond cleavage difficult.

3. Reorientation of chymotrypsin's serine-195 (Ser^{195}) and histidine-57 (His^{57}) residues following substrate binding is best described by what enzyme-substrate binding model?
   A. induced fit; substrate binding creates a conformational change in the active site and increases the number of binding interactions.
   B. lock-and-key; substrate recognizes a complementary three-dimensional surface and binds through multiple interactions.
   C. induced-fit; substrate recognizes a complementary three-dimensional surface and binds through multiple interactions.
   D. lock-and-key; substrate binding creates a conformational change in the active site and increases the number of binding interactions.

4. In an effort to validate the involvement of histidine in the mechanism illustrated in Figure 1, the scientists mentioned in the passage measured chymotrypsin activity under different reaction conditions. Which of the following results most supports the involvement of histidine in chymotrypsin catalysis?
   A. The enzyme was denatured by extreme changes in pH.
   B. The rate of product produced by the enzyme-catalyzed reaction decreased at temperatures below 37°C.
   C. Temperatures substantially greater than 37°C caused inactivation of the protein.
   D. The protein's enzymatic activity was less sensitive to relatively small increases above, than small decreases below, its optimal pH range.

5. In the reaction depicted in Figure 1, which amino acid residue is most likely to be bound to S1 of chymotrypsin?
   A. phenylalanine
   B. glycine
   C. alanine
   D. cysteine

The following questions are NOT based on a descriptive passage.

6. Enzymatic power is defined as the ratio of the rate of an enzyme-catalyzed reaction divided by the rate of the same reaction when uncatalyzed. Which of the following statements regarding enzymatic power is NOT true when comparing enzymes A and B, where each enzyme catalyzes a different reaction and where the enzymatic power of A is greater than B?
   A. Increasing solution temperature beyond the denaturation point of enzymes A and B will reduce both enzymes' enzymatic power.
   B. The rate of the reaction catalyzed by A is greater than the rate of the reaction catalyzed by B.
   C. The rate of product formation is increased more greatly from the uncatalyzed rate for A, than for B.
   D. The percent increase in activation energies between the catalyzed and the uncatalyzed reactions is smaller for the reaction catalyzed by B than for A.

7. Which of the following sequences properly shows the events in an enzyme-catalyzed reaction leading to the formation of product from free substrate? (Note: E represents the enzyme catalyzing the reaction, S the substrate of the reaction, and P the product.)

   A. $S \rightarrow EP \rightarrow E + P$
   B. $E \rightarrow ES \rightarrow EP \rightarrow E + P$
   C. $E + S \rightarrow EP \rightarrow E + P$
   D. $E + S \rightarrow ES \rightarrow EP \rightarrow E + P$

8. An enzyme that is not bound to a non-protein component required for that enzyme's function is referred to as a(n):
   A. holoenzyme.
   B. apoprotein.
   C. cofactor.
   D. coenzyme.

9. All of the following are water-soluble vitamins EXCEPT:
   A. folate
   B. cobalamin
   C. thiamine
   D. vitamin E

10. FAD alone, or bound as part of a holoenzyme, may be accurately categorized as which of the following?
    I. a coenzyme
    II. a cosubstrate
    III. a prosthetic group
    A. I only
    B. III only
    C. I and III only
    D. I, II, and III

NEXT STEP MCAT CONTENT REVIEW: BIOLOGY AND BIOCHEMISTRY

CHAPTER 24
Enzyme Control

A. INTRODUCTION

The structural complexity and functional diversity of enzymes allow them to play a variety of physiological roles, including, notably, the catalysis of the vast majority of biological reactions. In this chapter, we'll examine the structure-function relationship of enzyme catalyzed reactions and the precise regulatory control mechanisms which influence their function.

Myoglobin and hemoglobin are a pair of O_2-binding proteins that illustrate the close linkage between a protein's structure and its enzymatic function. Both myoglobin and hemoglobin share a similar primary structure; however, myoglobin contains a single polypeptide, while hemoglobin is a tetramer composed of two different subunit types. The polypeptide subunits of hemoglobin, like myoglobin's polypeptide, each contain a site for the reversible binding of O_2 to an iron center contained in each heme group.

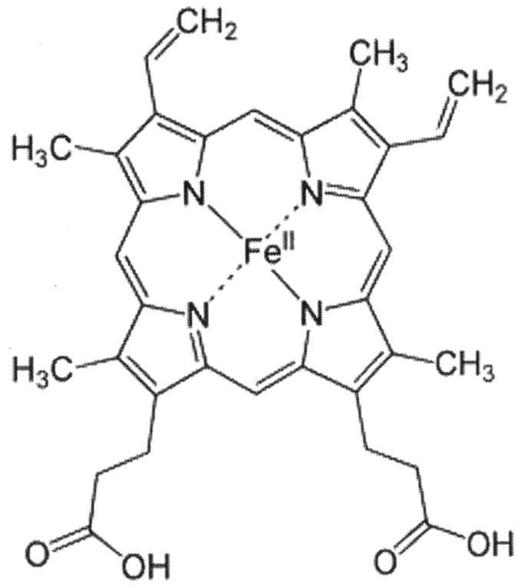

Figure 24.1: Heme prosthetic group consisting of a Fe^{2+} oxygen binding site and the heterocyclic ring structure porphyrin.

The tetrameric structure of hemoglobin permits saturated binding of O_2 in the lungs and release of O_2 in capillary beds. When the amount of O_2-saturated myoglobin or hemoglobin (typically measured as the percentage of total O_2–binding sites in a sample occupied by O_2, referred to as the fractional saturation of O_2, or S) is plotted as a function of the local partial pressure of O_2 (pO_2), the resulting curve is hyperbolic. This curve is identical in form to that relating the total percentage of hormone bound to a cellular receptor as a function of hormone concentration.

It is also identical in form to the curve relating the percentage of small molecular substrate bound to the active site of an enzyme. When an [S] versus pO_2 curve is constructed for hemoglobin and myoglobin, both plots indicate that when the concentration of O_2 is high, the binding sites of myoglobin and hemoglobin are equally saturated. However, at low pO_2 values in aerobic tissues, the percent saturation of hemoglobin is less than that of myoglobin, indicating hemoglobin's binding affinity for oxygen is less than that of myoglobin's at comparably low partial pressures of oxygen.

The relative abilities of hemoglobin and myoglobin to bind oxygen—their relative binding affinities—can be compared quantitatively. The binding ability of a protein for a ligand is given by its association constant, K_a, which is the equilibrium constant for the binding reaction of ligand with protein. K_a is equal to the rate of the forward reaction rate, k_1 (the rate of ligand-protein binding), divided by the reverse reaction rate, k_2 (the rate of ligand-protein complex dissociation). K_d, the dissociation constant for the ligand-protein complex, is the reciprocal of K_a. K_a is directly related to the strength of ligand-protein interaction in the bound complex, and is a useful metric for comparing the affinity of receptors for ligand or the affinity of enzymes for substrate. Good examples are the K_a values of adult and fetal hemoglobin (HbF). Because the subunit composition of fetal hemoglobin differs from that of the predominant form of hemoglobin found in healthy adults (HbA), HbF is able to bind oxygen with greater affinity than HbA. These differential binding parameters provide the developing fetus with improved access to needed oxygen from the maternal circulation.

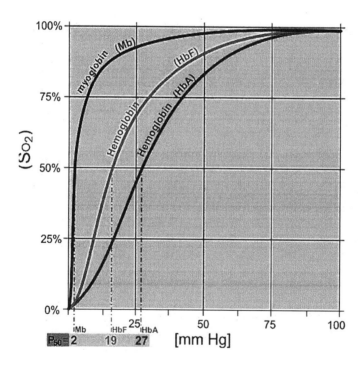

Figure 24.2: Oxygen saturation curves showing the percentage of hemoglobin binding sites saturated by oxygen at different partial pressures of oxygen (measured in millimeters of mercury (mm Hg)) for myoglobin, adult hemoglobin (HbA) and fetal hemoglobin (HbF). Note the sigmoidal shape of the curves for both Hb isoforms versus the hyperbolic shape of the curve for myoglobin.

B. COOPERATIVITY

Upon binding of O_2 to the Fe^{2+} residue in the hydrophobic binding pocket of either myoglobin or hemoglobin, a conformational change occurs. This conformational change has no effect on the function of myoglobin, but leads to a concerted change in the conformation of all four hemoglobin subunits. The conformation of hemoglobin changes from its low O_2 affinity, taut (T) state, to its higher O_2 affinity, relaxed (R) state. Accordingly, the binding rate of the initial O_2 molecule is slow. Subsequent binding of O_2 to hemoglobin subunits in the R state occurs much more rapidly. This increased protein affinity for binding of additional ligand following binding of the initial ligand, known as positive cooperativity, is responsible for the sigmoidal hemoglobin O_2 saturation curve shown in Figure 24.2.

Cooperativity among binding sites is not limited to hemoglobin or other oxygen-binding proteins, but is a common feature of a number of enzymes under regulatory control. The cooperativity of oxygen binding is representative of the behavior of many multi-subunit proteins which display positive cooperativity. For other molecules, ligand binding results in a decrease in affinity at the active site (such as when binding of 2,3-BPG, a glycolytic by-product, decreases the O_2 affinity of hemoglobin). These modulatory effects on protein-ligand binding affinity are collectively referred to as allosteric interactions, and generally require the presence of, and interaction between, at least two protein subunits.

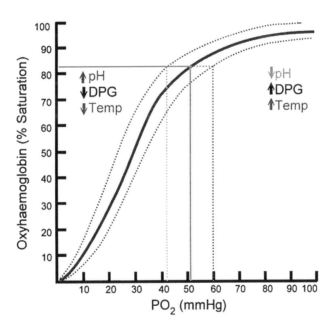

Figure 24.3: The effects on the hemoglobin oxygen saturation curve of changes in pH, 2,3-BPG (DPG) concentration and temperature.

C. ENZYME KINETICS: THE MICHAELIS-MENTEN MODEL

As discussed earlier, enzymes catalyze an enormous variety of reactions using a few basic catalytic mechanisms alone or in combination. Yet despite the diversity of reactions and reaction types in which enzymes are involved, the effects of enzymes can be quantified and the overall efficiency of enzymes studied by a set of common analytical tools. In one model proposed by Leonor Michaelis and Maude Menten, an enzyme reversibly combines with a substrate to form an enzyme substrate (ES) complex that subsequently dissociates, regenerating free enzyme and yielding product. For a single substrate molecule, the two elementary reactions composing the overall reaction may be represented as:

$$E + S \underset{k_r}{\overset{k_f}{\rightleftharpoons}} ES \xrightarrow{k_{cat}} E + P$$

where S is the substrate, E is the enzyme, P is the product, and k_f, k_r and k_{cat} are rate constants. Each of the elementary reactions composing the overall reaction can be described according to characteristic rate constants: k_f and k_r are the forward and reverse rate constants, respectively, for the formation of the enzyme-substrate complex from free enzyme and substrate, and k_{cat} is the rate constant for the irreversible decomposition of the enzyme-substrate complex to free enzyme and product. According to this model, when substrate concentration is sufficiently large to saturate all enzymes present, the second, dissociation step becomes rate-limiting. The overall reaction rate thus becomes independent of substrate concentration.

The Michaelis-Menten equation relates reaction rate (reaction velocity) for an enzymatic reaction rate to initial substrate concentration, where the formation of product from ES displays first-order kinetics. The equation is given by:

$$v = \frac{V_{max}[S]}{K_m + [S]}$$

where v is reaction velocity, V_{max} is the maximal reaction velocity, K_m is the Michaelis constant, and [S] is the substrate concentration. The equation relies on several simplifying assumptions:

1. **Assumption of steady state.** The reaction is assumed to function under a condition in which enzyme is present in substantially smaller concentration versus substrate (a common physiological condition) and where [ES] is assumed to be constant until substrate concentration approaches zero. The resulting rate of ES synthesis must then equal its rate of consumption over the reaction's course—in short, ES maintains a steady, constant-concentration state.

2. **Initial reaction velocity.** In order to consider the effects of complicating factors such as reaction reversibility, feedback inhibition by the reaction product(s) or inactivation of the enzyme, initial reaction velocity, v_o—measured as soon as enzyme is exposed to substrate—is used in place of reaction velocity.

Several important conclusions can be drawn from the Michaelis-Menten equation. First, the rate of the reaction at all substrate concentrations is directly related to the enzyme concentration. If, for instance, the enzyme concentration is doubled, then the initial reaction rate, as well as the maximal reaction velocity, will also double. Secondly, when substrate concentration is much less than K_m, the velocity of the reaction is approximately proportional to substrate concentration. When substrate concentration is much greater than K_m, the rate of the reaction is independent of changes in substrate concentration and the velocity of the reaction is equal to V_{max}.

The Michaelis constant, K_m, for a reaction is the substrate concentration at which the reaction proceeds at half-maximal velocity (V_{max} / 2). Consequently, enzymes with small K_m values achieve a maximal reaction velocity at smaller substrate concentrations than reactions with higher K_m values. K_m is unique for a given enzyme-substrate pair at a particular pH and temperature. K_m is also a measure of an enzyme's affinity for its substrate, provided that k_{cat} / k_r is small compared to K_s, the dissociation constant of ES. (Figure 24.4)

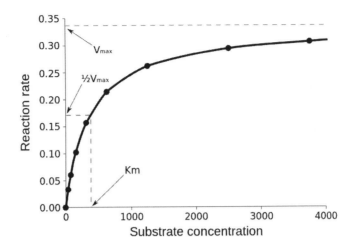

Figure 24.4: Saturation curve for an enzymatic reaction depicting the values of K_m, V_{max}, and $1/2\ V_{max}$. Note the relationship between substrate concentration and initial reaction rate at increasing substrate concentrations.

There are several methods for determining the values of K_m and V_{max}, including through direct measurement of the initial reaction rate and substrate concentration. In practice, however, it is difficult to assess V_{max} directly through plotting v_o versus [S]. A better approach involves plotting the reciprocal of the Michaelis-Menten equation, which is:

$$\frac{1}{V} = \frac{K_m + [S]}{V_{max}[S]} = \frac{K_m}{V_{max}}\frac{1}{[S]} + \frac{1}{V_{max}}$$

A plot of $1 / V$ (where V as measured is actually v_o) versus $1 / [S]$ for this equation, called a Lineweaver-Burk, or double-reciprocal, plot is linear (such a plot is shown in Figure 27.5). In this equation, the x-intercept value is equal to $-1 / K_m$, and the y-intercept value is equal to $1 / V_{max}$.

Figure 24.5: Lineweaver-Burk plot of $1 / V$ versus $1 / [S]$ for an enzyme-catalyzed reaction. Note that the numerical values of the x-intercept, y-intercept and slope are equal to $-1 / K_m$, $1 / V_{max}$ and (K_m / V_{max}), respectively.

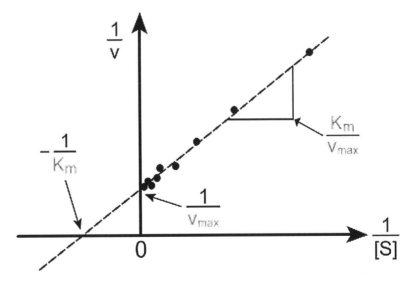

D. INHIBITION

A variety of substances can combine with an enzyme in such a way as to change its interaction with substrate. Substances that reduce an enzyme's activity due to their interaction with an enzyme are known as enzyme inhibitors. Irreversible inhibitors, sometimes referred to as enzyme inactivators, bind in such a way as to permanently decrease an enzyme's activity. This action is in contrast to that of reversible inhibition, whose interaction with enzymes does not lead to a permanent alteration in enzyme function. (Figure 24.6).

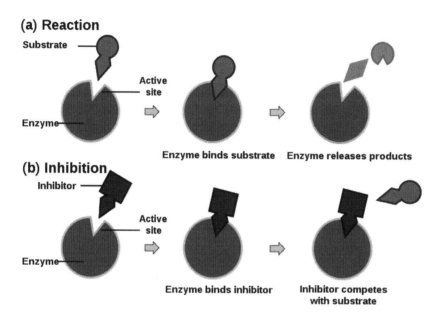

Figure 24.6: Graphic depicting competition between substrate and a competitive inhibitor for the active site of enzyme.

Inhibitors that compete directly with an enzyme's substrate for binding to the enzyme active site are known as competitive inhibitors. This reversible inhibition leads to an increase in the apparent K_m of enzyme for substrate, and an increase in the amount of substrate required to achieve V_{max} / 2. The effects of competitive inhibition can be overcome with increasing substrate concentration. At sufficiently high [S] values, V_{max} for the inhibited reaction equals that of V_{max} for the uninhibited reaction. Changes in the parameters of the reaction due to competitive inhibition are evident by comparing the Lineweaver-Burk plots of the inhibited and uninhibited reactions. The inhibited and uninhibited reaction show different x-axis intercepts, with the competitively inhibited reaction plot intersecting the x-axis at a more positive value than the uninhibited reaction. This indicates that the apparent K_m has increased in the presence of a competitive inhibitor, as the value of x, which equals -1 / K_m, approaches zero from a negative value.

Non-competitive inhibitors characteristically decrease the V_{max} of inhibited reactions. This mode of inhibition occurs when the inhibitor and substrate bind distinct sites on either the enzyme or the enzyme-substrate complex. Binding by non-competitive inhibitors does not interfere with enzyme-substrate binding, and apparent K_m in the presence, or absence, of non-competitive inhibitors is unchanged. On the Lineweaver-Burk plot, the decrease in maximal velocity due to non-competitive inhibition is evidenced by an increase in the value of the y-intercept for the non-competitively inhibited reaction, which equals 1 / V_{max}.

Mixed inhibitors can modify substrate binding or the catalytic activity of an enzyme. They can bind either the enzyme or the E-S complex at an allosteric site, decreasing V_{max} and either increasing or decreasing K_m depending on the binding preference of the inhibitor. If it preferentially binds free enzyme, apparent K_m will increase; if it binds the E-S complex, it will decrease. On a Lineweaver-Burk plot, a mixed inhibition line will intersect the uninhibited line at a point that point lies on neither the x- nor the y-axis (Figure 24.8).

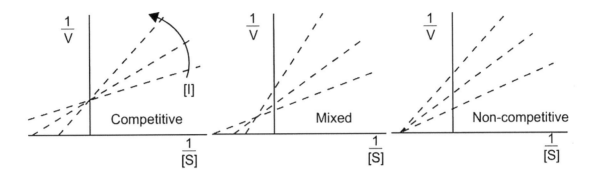

Figure 24.8: Lineweaver-Burk plots of reactions inhibited by competitive, mixed or non-competitive inhibitors.

Uncompetitive inhibitors bind only the enzyme-substrate (ES) complex at a site other than the active site. While non-competitive inhibitors can exert an influence on reaction rate with, or without, substrate binding, uncompetitive inhibitors require the formation of the ES complex. It is the formation of the ES complex that permits a change in the allosteric site to which uncompetitive inhibitors bind.

Upon binding, uncompetitive inhibitors reduce the rate at which substrate leaves the active site and increase the enzyme's apparent affinity for the substrate. This is measured as a decrease in the apparent K_m of the reaction. Stabilization of the ES complex during uncompetitive inhibition also decreases the enzyme's maximum activity (V_{max}), as it takes longer for the substrate or product to dissociate from the active site. Uncompetitive inhibition exerts the greatest influence on reaction kinetics when substrate concentration is high, and the concentration of the ES complex is maximized. The parallel lines of the Lineweaver-Burk plots of uncompetitively inhibited and uninhibited reactions are shown in Figure 24.9, and a general schematic of all four modes of enzyme inhibition is shown in Figure 24.10.

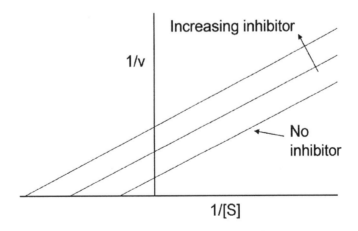

Figure 24.9: Lineweaver-Burk plot of an uncompetitive inhibitor.

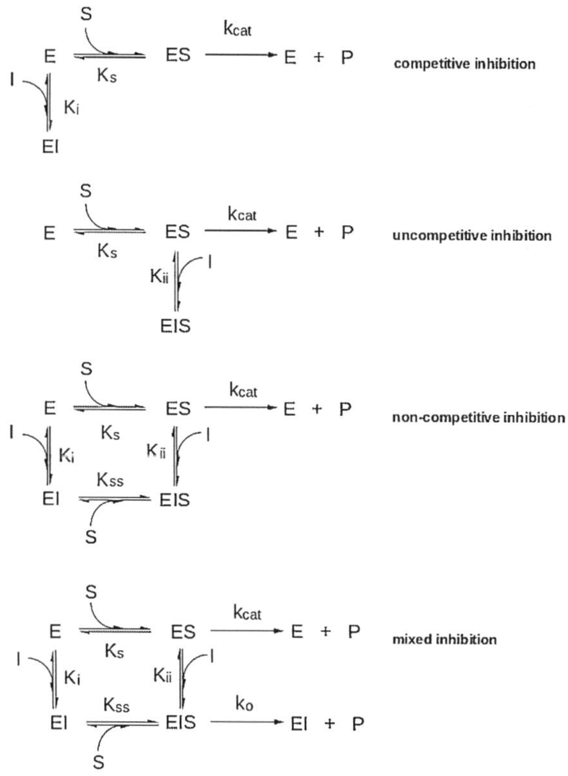

Figure 24.10: Inhibitor types

E. ENZYME CONTROL

Controlling the velocity of enzyme-catalyzed reactions is essential to properly coordinating cellular metabolic activities over time. This is in part accomplished by the inherent sensitivity of enzymes to substrate concentration. As substrate concentration increases in the range of the K_m of a given enzyme, the value of which is ordinarily near that of most intracellular substrate concentrations, the rate of enzyme-catalyzed conversion of substrate to product generally increases, thereby decreasing substrate concentration.

An enzyme's catalytic action can also be regulated directly through structural modification of the enzyme. One such class of changes, known as allosteric modulations, can be brought about by the reversible binding of small molecules, referred to as allosteric effectors. Enzymes which can be regulated by the binding of allosteric effectors are called allosteric enzymes, and are frequently involved in the catalysis of the rate limiting step in reaction pathways. Allosteric enzymes are typically composed of multiple subunits. The presence of an allosteric effector, which binds at a regulatory (allosteric) site which may, or may not, be located on the same subunit as the active site, may alter the enzyme's affinity for substrate, its maximal reaction rate, or both. Allosteric effectors may exert a positive effect on the enzyme, increasing its activity, in which case they are termed positive effectors. In contrast, negative effectors are molecules that decrease enzyme activity. Positive and negative effectors of allosteric enzymes may influence V_{max} or K_m alone, or both V_{max} and K_m.

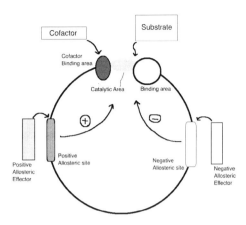

Figure 24.11: Model of positive and negative allosteric regulation

When a substrate acts as an effector on the enzyme to which it binds, most often as a positive effector, it is termed homotropic. In cases of homotropic effector action, substrate binds an allosteric site other than the active site, and through subunit-subunit interactions, cooperatively influences the function of the active site and consequently increases enzyme activity. Such reactions display a characteristic sigmoidal curve when initial reaction velocity is plotted as a function of substrate concentration.

A heterotropic effector is a molecule other than the substrate of the enzyme which it regulates. In feedback inhibition, a heterotropic effector inhibits an earlier step in the pathway of its own biosynthesis. The enzyme involved in the first irreversible step unique to the regulated pathway is most often the enzyme inhibited via feedback inhibition. This mode of inhibition provides the cell a mechanism for control of protein production, by modulating the flow of substrate through the synthetic pathways producing the regulated product. A basic feedback inhibition scheme is shown in Figure 24.12.

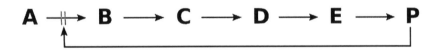

Figure 24.12: Basic mechanism of feedback inhibition, where the product (P) inhibits the committed step of the reaction pathway, in which A is converted to B.

Structural changes to a protein can also occur due to covalent modification. The activity of many enzymes is regulated through phosphorylation by protein kinase enzymes or dephosphorylation by protein phosphatases. Addition of a large, negatively charged phosphate group to a molecule induces a conformational change that may increase the activity of some enzymes or decrease the activity of others. Proteins may also be modified by the addition of ADP-ribose, acetyl or lipid moieties. These modifications may alter the ability of proteins to interact with other proteins or prevent the movement of enzymes within the cell.

Changes in the conformation of the enzyme active site may also be due to direct interactions between enzymes and other proteins. For instance, some protein kinases are tightly bound to a single regulated protein, and regulate that protein only when bound. In another common example, monomeric G proteins, which are small single polypeptide proteins that bind to and hydrolyze the nucleoside GTP, are able to bind to and activate a target enzyme only when bound to GTP. Upon hydrolysis of GTP, they undergo a conformation change, and the complex which they form with the target enzyme becomes unstable and dissociates.

Another method of control is proteolytic activation, which is the activation of an enzyme by proteolytic cleavage. Enzymes controlled in this manner are initially synthesized as inactive precursors known as zymogens, or proenzymes. Proteolytic cleavage of the zymogen reveals a buried active site, irreversibly converting the zymogen into a catalytically active molecule. Because this activation is irreversible, specific inhibitors, known as proteases, are often present intra- and extracellularly to control the active enzyme.

Specific proteolysis is a frequent way of activating enzymes and certain other proteins in biological systems. For instance, digestive enzymes are synthesized by the stomach and pancreas as zymogens and become active only upon specific activation. The activation of another digestive proenzyme, chymotrypsinogen, to its active form, chymotrypsin, is shown in figure 24.13. In another set of instances, coagulation is carried out by a cascade of proteolytically activated enzymes—known as clotting factors—in order to maintain hemostasis in response to specific biological signals.

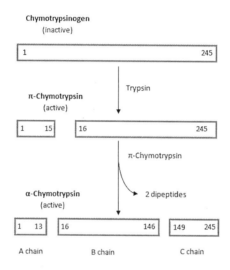

Figure 24.13: Proteolytic activation of chymotrypsinogen in which the subunits of the active form of the enzyme, α-chymotrypsin, are linked by interchain disulfide bonds.

All of the regulatory mechanisms described above modulate the activity of enzymes. However, cells are also able to regulate substrate flux through metabolic pathways by changing the total amount of a particular enzyme present within the cell. By increasing enzyme cellular concentration through induction of enzyme synthesis, or decreasing enzyme cellular concentration by repression of enzyme synthesis, the total number of available substrate active sites may be controlled.

Chapter 24 Problems

Passage 24.1 (Questions 1-5)

Maturity onset diabetes of the young (MODY) is a genetic form of diabetes mellitus in which insulin secretion from the pancreas is impaired, but cellular insulin response is normal. One form of the disease, MODY2, is due to an autosomal dominant mutation in the GCK gene. GCK encodes the enzyme pancreatic glucokinase (PGK), a closely related isozyme of liver glucokinase. Within beta cells, PGK acts as a glucose sensor by catalyzing the rate limiting step of glucose catabolism. In healthy individuals, an increase in the intracellular concentration of the products of glucose catabolism has been shown to directly increase insulin secretion by beta cells.

Researchers studying mutated PGK isolated from individuals affected by MODY first determined that the beta cells of the individuals from which PGK was isolated were are able to normally produce and excrete insulin. However, they found that these cells did so at an altered blood glucose concentration when compared to cells isolated from healthy individuals. X-ray crystallography revealed structural differences between mutant and wild type forms of PGK only at the enzymes' substrate binding site.

Finally, after conducting several initial rate experiments to measure the kinetic parameters of the reaction catalyzed by the mutant PGK enzyme and wild type PGK, they constructed a double reciprocal plot from the data for both enzymes forms, shown below in Figure 1.

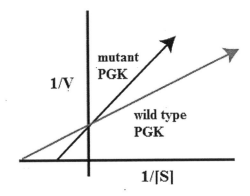

Figure 1: Double reciprocal plots of mutant and wild type PGK. (Note: V is initial reaction velocity and [S] refers to the initial glucose substrate concentration).

1. According to Figure 1, which of the following is true regarding a kinetic parameter of wild type PGK when compared to the same parameter for the mutant form of the enzyme?
   - **A.** V_{max} is greater
   - **B.** V_{max} is smaller
   - **C.** K_m is greater
   - **D.** K_m is smaller

2. The effect of the mutation in the GCK gene discussed in the passage on PGK function is most similar to making which of the following changes to a reaction catalyzed by wild type PGK?
   - **A.** decreasing substrate concentration
   - **B.** reducing the concentration of PGK
   - **C.** introduction of a competitive inhibitor
   - **D.** introduction of a non-competitive inhibitor

3. Based upon information presented in the passage, individuals who carry a single copy of the gene associated with MODY2 are likely to:
   - **A.** respond normally to changes in blood glucose levels.
   - **B.** secrete, at high glucose concentrations, the same amount of insulin as individuals with two wild type genes.
   - **C.** show signs of hypoglycemia under certain physiological conditions.
   - **D.** control MODY2-related symptoms with drugs that increase insulin sensitivity in insulin non-responsive cells.

4. Mutant PGK is most likely to differ from wild type PGK in its:
   - **A.** glucose-binding affinity.
   - **B.** catalytic mechanism.
   - **C.** allosteric binding sites.
   - **D.** site of intracellular function.

5. The substrate concentration of glucose required to reach one-half maximal reaction velocity in wild type PGK is:
   A. greater than that required to reach the same reaction velocity in mutant PGK.
   B. less than that required to reach the same reaction velocity in mutant PGK.
   C. equal to that required to reach the same reaction velocity in mutant PGK.
   D. unable to be approximated directly from measurements of initial reaction velocity and initial glucose concentrations.

The following questions are NOT based on a descriptive passage.

6. Competitive inhibitors bind the:
   A. active site of inhibited enzymes.
   B. substrate of inhibited enzymes.
   C. allosteric sites of inhibited enzymes.
   D. enzyme-substrate complex of inhibited enzymes.

7. Which of the following does NOT cause a decrease in deoxyghemoglobin's affinity for the binding of oxygen?
   A. decreased pH
   B. increased temperature
   C. 2,3-bisphosphoglycerate (2,3-BPG) binding
   D. binding of O_2

8. Which of the following statements is consistent with an assumption of the Michaelis-Menten model of enzyme kinetics?

   I. The percentage of substrate bound by the enzyme at any one time is small.

   II. The rates of formation and dissociation of ES are equal.

   III. The rate of back reaction from product to substrate can be ignored.

   A. I only
   B. II only
   C. I and II only
   D. I, II and III

9. At low concentrations of substrate ($[S] << K_m$), the velocity of an enzyme-catalyzed reaction is, according to the Michaelis-Menten model, nearest what reaction order with respect to substrate and nearest what overall reaction order?
   A. zeroth order with respect to substrate and first order overall
   B. first order with respect to substrate and first order overall
   C. first order with respect to substrate and second order overall
   D. zeroth order with respect to substrate and second order overall

10. The drug allopurinol, used in the treatment of gout, is converted by the enzyme xanthine oxidase to oxypurinol, a compound that binds tightly to the enzyme's active site, inhibiting its further catalytic activity. Given this fact, allopurinol can be most specifically described as a:
    A. negative homotropic effector
    B. reversible inhibitor
    C. suicide inhibitor
    D. negative heterotropic effector

CHAPTER 25
Non-Enzymatic Protein Function

A. INTRODUCTION

With the exception of proteins and certain RNA types, the latter of which serve a handful of specific roles, the vast majority of biological molecules are relatively inert. It is for this reason that, in addition to catalyzing biological reactions, proteins are also responsible for most other functional roles in the body. The set of proteins expressed in a particular cell is known as its proteome, which reflects not only the products of the genetic information contained within the cell, but also the host of functions which it directs.

Proteins may oligomerize to form rigid fibrils, which often play structural roles in the body, where they provide rigidity within the fluid. As discussed in an earlier chapter, most structural proteins are fibrous proteins. Elastin and collagen are two such examples. Some globular proteins can also serve a structural purpose. Actin and tubulin are soluble, globular monomers that polymerize to form insoluble, tough fibers.

Protein–protein interactions control progression through the cell cycle, are involved in the immune response, regulate the activity of enzymes, assemble to form protein complexes, and can bind to or be integrated into cellular membranes. Further, because of the ability of ligand-protein or protein-protein interaction to cause a conformational change in proteins, they serve a vital role in complex signaling networks as receptors and as signaling intermediaries. We will further explore these roles of proteins in this, and in later, chapters.

B. IMMUNE SYSTEM

The adaptive immune system contains protein components known as antibodies. Antibody production is the main function of the humoral subdivision of the immune system. Antibodies principally function to bind foreign material, known as antigens, leading to the immediate neutralization of the antigenic pathogen or toxin, the agglutination (precipitation) and phagocytosis of the antigen-antibody complex, or the opsonization (marking) of the pathogen for destruction by leukocytes.

Antibodies, which are glycoprotein members of the immunoglobin superfamily, irreversibly bind the antigen targets for which they are specific and do so with significantly greater affinity than enzymes bind substrate. Each antibody contains a highly variable region where binding occurs and which is specific for a specific epitope on a specific antigen. This so-called hypervariable region of the antibody allows for millions of antibodies with slightly different antigenic specificity to be produced. The enormous diversity of the hypervariable region is generated by random recombination and mutation of the gene segments encoding antigen binding sites.

Antibodies can be found extracellularly in their soluble form, or anchored to the mature B cells, known as plasma cells, from which they are secreted. In its membrane-bound form attached to the surface of a B cell, an antibody is known as a B cell receptor (BCR). Binding and activation (usually with the assistance of a helper T cell) of a BCR facilitates an antibody's maturation into either an antibody-secreting plasma cell or a memory B cell. While the basic unit of an antibody is an immunoglobulin (Ig) monomer containing a single Ig unit, antibodies may be secreted as dimers, tetramers, or pentamers with two, four or five Ig units respectively.

Antibodies are composed of two primary structural units—one unit containing two identical large heavy chains and another with two identical small light chains. The two polypeptide heavy chains are connected to one another by disulfide bonds, as are the two polypeptide light chains. The structure of a typical human antibody is shown in Figure 25.1.

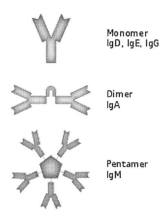

Figure 25.1: Immunoglobin monomer, dimer and pentamer

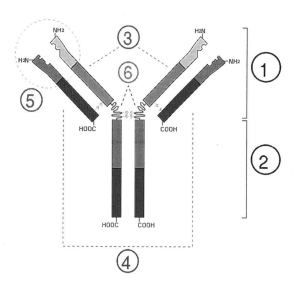

Figure 25.2: Structure of a human immunoglobin. 1. Fab region 2. Fc region 3. Heavy chain with one variable (VH) domain followed by a constant domain, a hinge region, and two additional constant regions. 4. Light chain with one variable (VL) and one constant (CL) domain 5. Antigen binding site (paratope). 6. Hinge regions.

Table 25.1: Antibody Isotypes	
Isotype	**Function**
IgA	Present in mucosal areas, such as the gut, respiratory tract, saliva, tears, breast milk and the urogenital tract, it prevents colonization by pathogens.
IgD	It acts principally as an antigen receptor on B cells that have not been exposed to antigens; it is involved in the activation of mast cells and basophils.
IgE	Involved in allergies and anti-parasitic responses, it binds to allergens causing histamine release from activated mast cells and basophils.
IgG	Four forms of IgG provide for most of the humoral immune response; it is the only antibody which is capable of crossing the placenta and conferring passive immunity on the placenta.
IgM	It is expressed on the surface of B cells as a monomer and secreted by plasma cells as a pentamer; IgM is responsible for mounting an immune response and eliminating pathogens in the early stages of the humoral response before IgG levels increase.

Different antibodies contain different types of heavy chains and can be categorized according to which heavy chains they contain. These different classes of antibodies, known as isotypes, play distinct roles in antigenic recognition and response as part of the immune system (Table 25.1). Each heavy chain has two regions: the constant region, which is identical in all antibodies and contains a flexible hinge region for added flexibility, and a variable region, which differs in antibodies produced by different B cells, but which is the same for all antibodies produced by a single B cell or its clone.

The antibody's binding region is called the Fab region. It is composed of one constant and one variable domain from the heavy and light chain of the antibody. The region of the antibody involved in immune signal transduction is known as the Fc region. The Fc region, which varies between antibody classes, allows the antibody to generate an immune response by binding to a specific class of Fc receptors and complement proteins.

Antibody diversity is further enhanced beyond differences in the hypervariable region by a process called class switching. During class switching, antibody genes rearrange to modify the heavy chain of an antibody, thereby creating a different antibody that still retains the original antigen-specific variable region. Class switching enables a single hypervariable region specific for a particular epitope to rearrange in several different ways during the humoral immune response.

C. MOTOR PROTEINS

Motor proteins, such as myosin, dynein and kinesin, are structural proteins that serve a different role: they generate mechanical force from their conformational change. Motor proteins play an indispensable role in sperm motility, movement of unicellular organisms, intracellular transport mechanisms and the generation of force during muscular contraction.

Kinesins are a class of ATPase motor proteins that are able to travel along the length of microtubule filaments. As the previous description of them as ATPase motor proteins would suggest, the power required for their movement is provided by the hydrolysis of ATP. The movement of kinesins is closely associated with the transport of cellular cargo, such as during axonal transport in neurons, and with mitosis and meiosis. Structurally, kinesins are heterotetramers, wherein their motor domain subunits form a protein-protein dimer that binds two light chains. Each motor subunit contains a head which has separate binding sites for ATP and for a microtubule. The binding and hydrolysis of ATP, as well as the release of ADP, cause a conformational change in the microtubule-binding domains and the orientation of other domains of the kinesin, resulting in unidirectional motion of the protein. Most kinesins transport cargo toward the periphery of the cell by walking towards the plus (+) end of a microtubule. This form of transport is referred to as anterograde transport.

Motility of kinesin

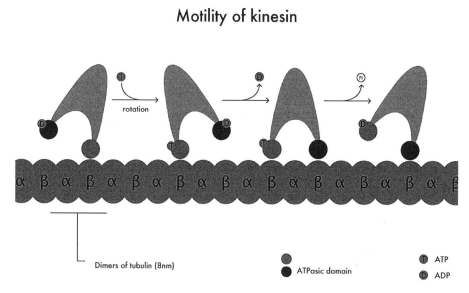

Figure 25.3 Diagram illustrating kinesin motility along a microtubule.

Dyneins are motor proteins that walk toward a microtubule's minus (-) end, which is usually oriented towards the center of a cell, in a form of transport referred to as retrograde transport. Dyneins may be classified into one of two groups: cytoplasmic or axonemal. Axonemal dyneins, sometimes called ciliary or flagellar dyneins, cause some sliding of microtubules found in the structures of cilia and flagella. Cytoplasmic dyneins move processively along a microtubule such that one stalk (a structural element connecting the globular head of a dynein to the microtubule along which it moves) is always attached to a microtubule. In this manner, dyneins may move considerable distances along a microtubule without detaching. Among other functions, dynein is involved in transport of cellular cargo between vesicles, and in the movement of chromosomes and the mitotic spindles during cell division. Dyneins also transport vesicles and organelles along neuronal axons toward the cell body in a process known as retrograde axoplasmic transport.

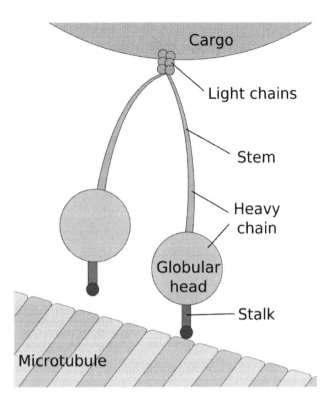

Figure 25.4: Cytoplasmic dynein consists of two heavy chains with globular "heads" that are bound cyclically through "stalks" to the microtubules along which they move.

Another important molecular motor protein family of ATPases are the myosins. Myosins play a central role in actin-based muscular contraction in muscle, as well as in a wide range of other eukaryotic motility processes. Most myosin molecules contain head, neck, and tail domains. Head domains bind the actin of microfilaments and hydrolyze ATP to generate force and induce the movement of the protein along filaments, generally toward the so-called barbed (+) end. During skeletal muscle contraction, multiple myosin II molecules create force by a power stroke mechanism that makes use of the energy released from ATP hydrolysis. The power stroke itself occurs while myosin is tightly bound to actin. When inorganic phosphate is released from myosin following ATP hydrolysis, a conformational change occurs wherein actin is pulled toward myosin. Actin will remain attached until the subsequent binding of an ATP molecule triggers release.

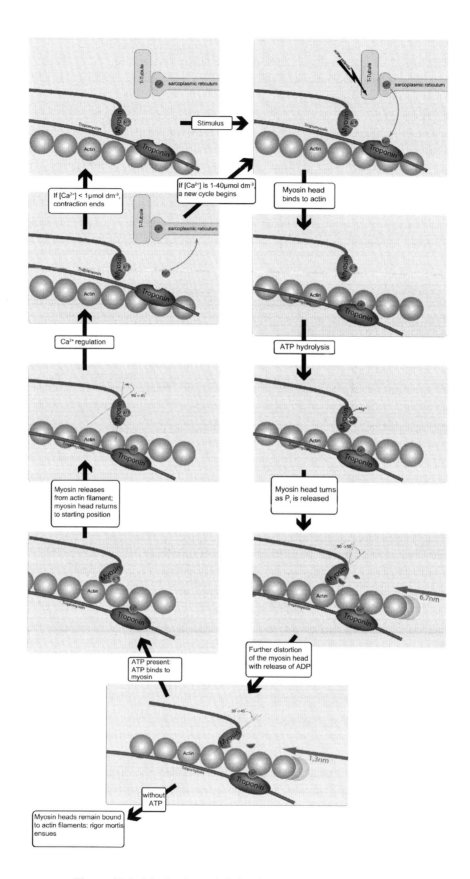

Figure 25.5: Mechanism of skeletal muscle contraction.

D. CYTOSKELETAL PROTEINS

Once formed, actin and tubulin polymers constitute a significant portion of the cytoskeletal system that provides the cell with definitive shape and resistance to deformational force. The three principal types of protein filaments found in the cytoskeleton are microfilaments, microtubules and intermediate filaments. Accessory proteins are able to regulate the function of the cytoskeletal system through their bonding to any of these three filamentous proteins.

Actin microfilaments in the cytoplasm are formed by the polymerization of G (globular) actin monomers into F-actin polymers in an ATP-dependent fashion. Treadmilling is the dynamic process of adding new G-actin monomers to a growing chain at its (+) end, while removing G-actin monomers from the opposite pole, the (-) end, at the same rate. The F-actin polymerization product, the microfilament, helps regulate the physical state of the cytosol and is involved in cell movement and the formation of the contractile ring during cell division.

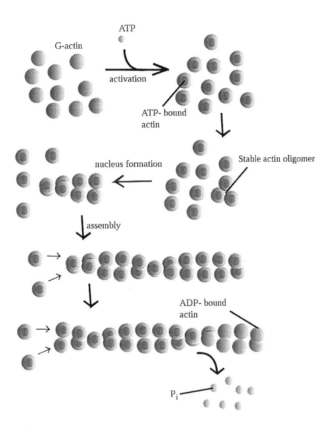

Figure 25.6: Thin filament formation by the ATP-dependent polymerization of G-actin to F-actin.

Intermediate filaments are aptly named, as they are intermediate in diameter between microfilaments and microtubules. Most intermediate filaments are located in the cytosol between the nuclear envelope and plasma membrane and provide structural stability within the fluidic cytoplasm. They are formed by α-helical rod-like protein subunits with globular terminal domains. Two rod-like subunits associate to form a dimer referred to as a coiled coil. Two coiled-coil dimers associate to form a tetramer.

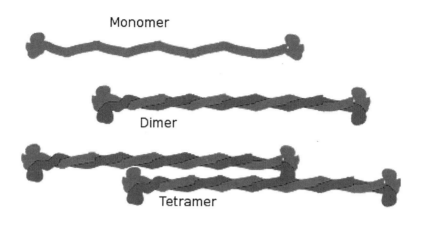

Figure 25.7: Intermediate filament structure

Microtubules are hollow cylinders composed of α- and β-tubulin dimers. Microtubules are involved in the movement of chromosomes during cell division, in intracellular transport, in neutrophil and amoeboid motility and in the formation of cilia and flagella. Microtubule formation is initiated at and organized in microtubule organizing centers (MTOCs). Common MTOCs include the centrosome or the basal bodies found in cilia and flagella. These MTOCs may or may not possess centrioles.

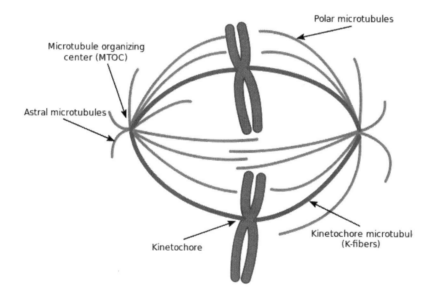

Figure 25.8: The diagram shows the organization of a generic mitotic spindle. Chromosomes are attached to kinetochore microtubules by the kinetochore. Polar microtubules push the spindle poles using motor proteins. Polymerization of both astral and kinetochore (K-fiber) microtubules is nucleated at the microtubule organizing center (MTOC). Astral microtubules anchor the spindle poles to the cell membrane, providing stability during force generation and chromosomal rearrangement.

The building blocks of microtubules are α- and β-tubulin dimers, which polymerize end to end in protofilaments in a GTP-dependent process. Thirteen protofilaments bind laterally forming a single microfilament structure which may be lengthened by the binding of additional protofilaments. In order for polymerization to occur, dimers must be present at a concentration at least equal to a minimum value referred to as the critical concentration.

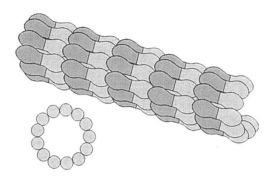

Figure 25.9: Microtubule structure shown axially and in cross-section. Note the organization of protofilaments surrounding a hollow center.

E. CELL ADHESION MOLECULES

Cell adhesion molecules (CAMs) are proteins which are found in association with cytoskeletal elements, as well with cells, where they primarily serve to anchor cells to one another and to the extracellular matrix (ECM). This process is known as cellular adhesion. Adhesion molecules are often categorized into three groups: selectins, cadherins and integrins.

Selectins are a class of CAMs involved in the inflammatory response. Three types of selectins are found in humans: L-selectin, P-selectin and E-selectin. L-selectin is expressed on lymphocytes, monocytes and neutrophils. P-selectin is expressed on platelets and mediates their interaction with the endothelium of blood vessels, which express E-selectin. Cadherins are calcium-dependent CAMs that play a role in the early stages of growth and development and which can bind to the microfilaments of the cell's cytoskeleton. Cadherins are typically expressed in cell-specific forms by different cells. Integrins act not only as adhesion molecules, but also as signaling molecules. They are involved in bi-directional communication across the plasma membrane in a host of cellular processes.

Cell junctions, which are in fact multiprotein complexes at the site of contact between adjacent cells or cells and the ECM, depend upon CAMs. There are three major types of cell junctions: anchoring junctions, tight (occluding) junctions, and gap (communicating) junctions. In anchoring junctions, different classes of CAMs serve as anchoring proteins, wherein they extend through the plasma membrane to link cytoskeletal proteins in one cell to cytoskeletal proteins in neighboring cells or in the extracellular matrix. Desmosomes, hemidesmosomes and adherens junctions, the three anchoring junction types found in cells, can be distinguished from one another by their cytoskeletal protein anchor and the by the transmembrane linker protein found within them. Characteristics of the junctional types are shown in Table 25.2 and their respective structures are shown in Figure 25.10.

Table 25.2: Features of Anchoring Junctions			
Junction	Cytoskeletal Anchoring Fiber	Transmembrane Linker Protein	Binds cells to:
Desmosome	Intermediate filaments	Cadherin	Adjacent cells
Hemidesmosome	Intermediate Filaments	Integrins	ECM
Adherens junction	Actin Filaments	Cadherin/Integrins	Adjacent cells or the EMC

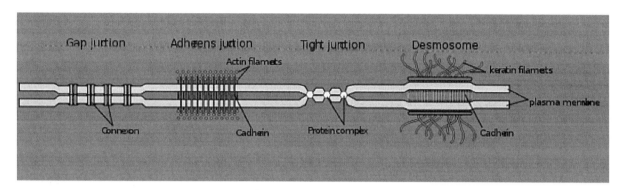

Figure 25.10: Cell junctional complexes

Chapter 25 Problems

Passage 25.1 (Questions 1-5)

The α,β-tubulin heterodimer is the basic structural unit of a microtubule (MT). Microtubules are involved in chromosomal movement, intracellular transport, neutrophil and amoeboid motility and the formation of cilia and flagella. When MTs self-assemble, free tubulin heterodimers join end-to-end to form stable protofilaments if free tubulin dimer concentration is sufficient. These protofilaments then associate laterally to form sheets, and eventually into the hollow cylindrical structure characteristic of MTs.

Heterodimers can add to or dissociate from either end of a MT, referred to as the (+) or (-) end, but do so preferentially at the (+) pole. GTP must be bound to both tubulin heterodimer subunits in order for association to occur between polymerizing heterodimers. GTP on α-tubulin does not hydrolyze, but GTP-bound β-tubulin may, after assembly of a dimer, be hydrolyzed to GDP. It has been shown that MTs are stable and depolymerize slowly if GTP-bound tubulin subunits are present in the heterodimers at a pole, but more rapidly if a GDP-bound tubulin subunit is present.

Within a cell, free tubulin concentrations change locally depending upon free tubulin consumption and the extent of resulting MT polymerization. Researchers hypothesized that below a certain tubulin concentration, rapid shrinkage at the plus end occurs and can be attributed to loss of a "GTP cap", in a process referred to as dynamic instability. A study was conducted to assess the relationship between growth and tubulin concentration during in vitro MT self-assembly. Growth was measured both in the presence and absence of the taxane drug docetaxel. The results of the study are shown in Figure 1.

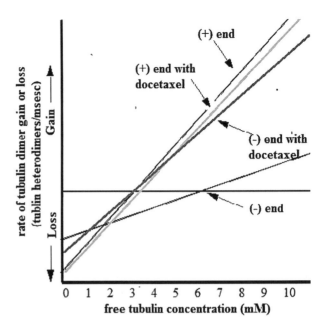

Figure 1: Microtubule polymer state as a function of the concentration of free α- and β-tubulin present.

1. When a new protofilament begins to self-assemble under polymerizing conditions in vitro, the polymer formed is unstable unless:
   A. free tubulin concentration exceeds approximately 2 mM.
   B. free tubulin concentration exceeds approximately 3 mM.
   C. free tubulin concentration exceeds approximately 4 mM.
   D. free tubulin concentration exceeds approximately 7 mM.

2. If additional experiments were conducted, which finding, if true, would most WEAKEN the hypothesis made by researchers in the passage regarding the origins of dynamic instability in microtubules?
   A. GTP-bound dimers are present at both the (+) and (-) ends of stable MTs.
   B. The rate of GTP hydrolysis at the (+) end of MTs is less than that at the (-) end in most cells.
   C. In some cells, MTs appear to grow, while other nearby MTs shorten dramatically.
   D. When the rate of GTP hydrolysis by dimers exceeds the rate of dimer addition, MTs remain stable.

NEXT STEP MCAT CONTENT REVIEW: BIOLOGY AND BIOCHEMISTRY

3. Treatment of an individual with colchicine, a drug which inhibits microtubule polymerization, is most likely to cause which of the following dose-dependent changes in tissues containing actively dividing cells?

   I. Anti-inflammatory effects
   II. Inhibition of mitosis
   III. Disruption of actin binding

   A. I only
   B. III only
   C. I and II only
   D. II and III only

4. Given the research described in the passage, by what mechanism is the drug docetaxel most likely to function?

   A. By stabilizing GDP-bound dimers.
   B. Through increasing the rate of hydrolysis of GTP-bound dimers.
   C. By preventing tubulin heterodimer dissociation into free tubulin.
   D. Through selectively increasing (+) end tubulin binding affinity.

5. At approximately what concentration of free tubulin will the positive rate of growth on the (+) end exceed that of the (-) end in the both the presence and absence of docetaxel?

   A. At any concentration
   B. 1 and 2 mM, respectively
   C. Between 2 and 6 mM and 3 and 6 mM, respectively
   D. At any concentration greater than 5 mM

The following questions are NOT based on a descriptive passage.

6. In attempting to determine the identity of a cytoskeletal component that polymerized only in the presence of ATP, and that, under certain conditions, could be observed to "treadmill", a scientist most likely concluded what about the component?

   A. That it was a microtubule.
   B. That it was a microfilament.
   C. That it was an intermediate filament.
   D. That it was keratin.

7. Which antibody is the first to appear in response to antigen exposure?

   A. IgA
   B. IgD
   C. IgG
   D. IgM

8. The binding of antibody to antigen can best be categorized as:

   A. irreversible.
   B. lower avidity than enzyme-substrate binding.
   C. non-specific.
   D. dependent on the antibody F_c region.

9. Which of the following statements regarding the structure of an individual antibody is NOT true?

   A. Light chains are not connected by disulfide linkages.
   B. Heavy chains are connected by disulfide linkages.
   C. The heavy chain contains a flexible hinge region.
   D. Both light chains are identical.

10. A cellular vesicle is most likely to be transported through a cell toward the (+) end of a microtubule by what transport protein?

    A. kinesin
    B. claveolin
    C. dynein
    D. myosin

CHAPTER 26
Analytic Techniques

A. INTRODUCTION

Studying the properties and interactions of individual proteins requires their purification from complex mixtures including cells and tissues, but accomplishing this task is often not easy. This chapter will outline some of the most commonly tested methods for isolating and characterizing proteins. Many of these techniques can also be used, in somewhat modified form, for the purification of other biologically-relevant macromolecules, including nucleic acids.

The process of protein purification begins with the separation of the protein from the non-protein components of a mixture. This typically begins with removal of biological materials by mechanically lysing a cell, followed by filtration and centrifugation in order to remove large insoluble particles. Centrifugation separates cellular contents according to differences in their masses and densities. When a tube or other vessel containing a mixture of proteins (or cells or cellular components) is rotated rapidly, each particle experiences an inward acting force proportional to its mass. The tendency of a centrifuged particle to move through the liquid because of this force is countered by the resistive force which the liquid exerts upon the particle. The net effect of "spinning" the sample in a centrifuge is that massive, small, and dense particles with greater inertia or less drag tend to move outward faster than less massive particles with less inertia, or with more drag, in the liquid. In most cases, a pellet, enriched in the most massive, or densest, particles will form. Non-compacted particles remain in the supernatant liquid and may be separated from the pellet.

Proteins may then be separated individually until only the protein of interest remains. If the protein target is tightly bound to a membrane, a detergent may be needed to solubilize the lipid membrane components and remove the protein. Proteins are purified through fractionation procedures, where in a series of treatments, differences in the properties of a protein target and other proteins in solution can be taken advantage of to sequentially separate the substances until only the protein of interest remains.

Preparative purifications are intended to produce a significant quantity of purified proteins for subsequent use, while analytical purification produces a relatively smaller amount of a protein intended for analytical purposes, including identification, quantification and functional study.

B. EXTRACTION

A number of strategies can be employed to remove a protein from its surrounding environment, including cycles of freezing and thawing, mechanical agitation, filtration, or treatment with organic solvents. The appropriate choice of how vigorous a method to employ is made in light of the structural stability of the cell, as well that of the protein target. After extraction is complete, the proteins present can be separated from other cellular contents, including DNA and organelles, by ultracentrifugation. Once in solution, proteins become subject to the possibility of irreversible damage by agents and conditions to which they would not be exposed intra-cellularly. For this reason, proteins are ordinarily dissolved in buffers to maintain solution pH and are kept cold to avoid denaturation. During the process of extracting proteins from tissue, proteases are released. To avoid proteolytic degradation of extracted proteins, binding agents which neutralize protease activity can be introduced, and, to the extent that the temperature sensitivity of the protein extract allows, the temperature of the stored protein should be maintained outside the optimal range of the proteases. During long-term storage, additional care must be taken to prevent slow oxidation or microbial contamination. The most common precaution against these possibilities is to store proteins under an atmosphere of inert gas.

C. SOLUBILITY

The solubility of a protein depends on the polarity, pH, temperature, and the dissolved salt concentration of solution. By manipulating these conditions, proteins can be made to selectively precipitate. Protein solubility increases as the ion concentration of a solution is increased by the addition of a salt. This effect is referred to as salting in and is caused by a shielding effect. The ions delivered into solution by the dissolution of the salt protect the charged groups of proteins from protein-protein interaction. This shielding reduces proteins' tendency to aggregate and increases their solubility. However, as salt concentration continues to rise, the dissolved salt ions can begin to compete with the charged groups of proteins for solvent molecules. At very high salt concentrations, there is meaningfully less bulk solvent available to solvate proteins and other solute molecules, decreasing protein solubility. This effect is referred to as salting out. Fractionation by salting out often allows for the purification of a significant quantity of protein. Because different proteins precipitate at differing salt concentrations, adjusting that salt concentration, very often by the addition of ammonium sulfate, to a level just below the concentration at which a target protein precipitates, can separate many unwanted proteins from solution. Ammonium sulfate is the reagent of choice in salting techniques because of its very large solubility, which allows for the preparation of strongly ionic solutions.

D. CHROMATOGRAPHY

Chromatography is an umbrella term that describes a range of laboratory techniques used to separate or identify the components of mixtures. In chromatographic techniques, the mixture is introduced into a mobile phase, which carries it through a separate structure called the stationary phase with which it interacts. Differences in how substances interact with the stationary phase lead to differential retention on the column, and separation of substances contained in the mixture can be analyzed.

One of the earliest chromatographic methods, known as paper chromatography, used filter paper as the stationary phase, and a liquid solvent (also known as a developing solution) as a mobile phase that carries, via capillary action, the tested substance as a dissolved solute along the stationary phase. Thin layer chromatography (TLC) is a similar process, but rather than paper, a different adsorbent is used—very often silica gels are chosen. TLC allows for better separations, faster run times, and a potentially wider variety of stationary phase polarities and properties than does paper chromatography. The development of a TLC plate is shown in Figure 26.1

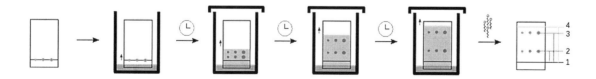

Figure 26.1: Development of a TLC plate, where the initial spotted sample is separated into two products. Their relative distances travelled versus the solvent front (R_f) is indicative of the strength of interaction between the dissolved solutes tested and the stationary phase.

In high performance liquid chromatography (HPLC) or high pressure liquid chromatography (HPLC), solvent is transported under high pressure through a chromatographic matrix of solid absorbent, usually consisting of glass or plastic beads coated uniformly with chromatographic material. High-pressure transport generally increases the speed and resolution of the separation process versus other forms of chromatography. HPLC relies on pumps to pressurize the liquid solvent passing through the solid adsorbent of the column. The pressurized liquid is typically a mixture of solvents of differing polarities, collectively referred to as the mobile phase. Water, alcohols, and acetonitrile are three common components of the solvent preparation. The composition and temperature of the solvent influences the electrostatic interactions which occur between sample components and the granular sorbent, and for this reason are important determinants of the degree of the separation achieved in HPLC.

The most commonly employed method of HPLC is what is called reversed phase HPLC (RP-HPLC). RP-HPLC is so named because it features a reversal of the polarity of the stationary phase and mobile phase found in HPLC. In RP-HPLC, the stationary phase is non-polar and the mobile phase is aqueous. One common stationary phase is silica which has been surface-modified by attaching long-chain alkyl groups. In RP-HPLC, retention times are longer for relatively less polar molecules, while polar molecules elute more rapidly. Retention times can be increased by diluting the solvent through the addition of more water. This acts to increase the attraction of the hydrophobic analyte for the hydrophobic stationary phase when compared to the increased polarity of the mobile phase.

Chromatography can be also be used to separate proteins using porous gels in a technique known as size exclusion chromatography or gel filtration chromatography. In this technique, gel beads containing pores, formed from the cross-linking of the polymer from which the beds are constructed, act as a molecular sieve (Figure 26.2). Proteins that are too large to pass through the pores are excluded from the solvent volume inside the beads. As a result, larger proteins pass through the column more rapidly than do smaller proteins, and demonstrate longer retention times. For the size of proteins typically separated by this method, there is a linear proportionality between the relative elution volume of a protein of a particular shape and the logarithm of its molecular mass.

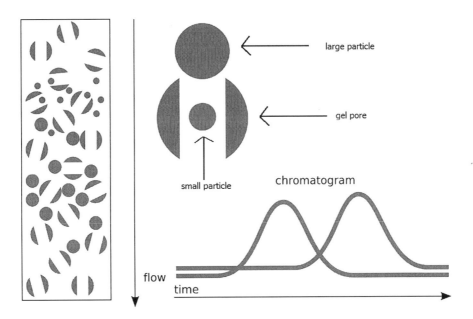

Figure 26.2: Large particles cannot enter the gel, and are thus excluded from the pore and elute sooner with less volume. Small particles are able to enter the gel and elute later with larger volume.

Ion exchange chromatography separates compounds according to the sign and degree of their charge. Anion exchange resins are positively charged and bind negatively charged compounds. Cation exchange resins have a negative charge and bind positively charged molecules. The most frequently used anion exchanger is a matrix with diethylaminoethanol (DEAE) groups attached, while the most frequently seen cation exchanger has a matrix with carboxymethyl (CM) groups bound. Cellulose- and agarose-based resins are frequently used as the matrix material. Proteins, which bear both positive and negative charges at most solution pH values, can bind to cation and anion exchangers (Figure 26.3)

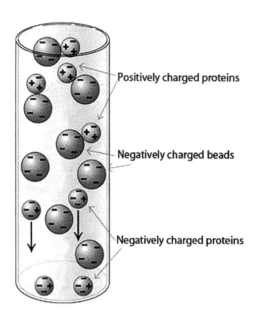

Figure 26.3: Association of ion pairs during ion exchange chromatography.

The binding affinity of proteins for the surface-modified resin of the stationary phase depends on the presence of other ions that compete with protein for binding to the exchanger, and on the pH-dependent net charge of the sample proteins.

After sample is added to the column, the column is washed. The length of retention for each resin-bound solute depends upon the strength of its charge. The most weakly charged compounds will elute first, followed by those with successively stronger charges. Proteins that bind with very high affinity to the column can be eluted (removed) from the ion exchanger by treatment with an eluant (buffered rinse) that modifies the pH of solution to reduce the strength of protein-stationary phase binding.

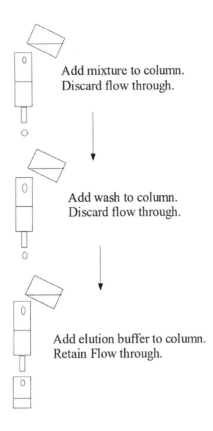

Figure 26.4: Diagram of a simple column chromatography procedure.

Affinity chromatography is a separation technique which frequently uses resin-bound ligands which are specific for the molecules to be separated. Ligand-protein binding takes advantage of the capability that many proteins possess to bind tightly, but non-covalently, to ligands. This "lock and key" fit between the ligand and its target compound means that when an impure protein solution is passed through this chromatographic matrix, the desired protein binds the immobilized ligand, and all other substances are washed through the column with the buffer. The desired protein can then be recovered by changing the elution conditions to release the protein from the matrix. Because separation is achieved due to differences in biochemical, rather than physiochemical properties, the separation power of affinity chromatography often exceeds that of other chromatographic techniques.

Many membrane proteins are glycoproteins and can be purified by lectin affinity chromatography. Lectins are carbohydrate-binding proteins that are highly specific for certain sugar moieties. In this technique, detergent-solubilized proteins bind to a chromatography resin containing lectin. Proteins that do not bind to the immobilized lectin are carried away in the buffered rinse. Those glycoproteins that do bind can be eluted by addition of a highly concentrated solution of competing sugar. In some cases of extremely high-affinity lectin binding, conditions must be modified so as to promote denaturation of the resin-attached lectin.

In immunoaffinity chromatography, an antibody is attached to the matrix in order to purify solutions containing the protein against which the antibody binds. Bound protein is then eluted by washing the column with a solution containing high concentrations of unbound ligand or a solution of differing ionic strength.

In metal chelate affinity chromatography, a divalent metal ion is attached to the matrix material of the column so that proteins containing histidine side chains, which are metal chelators, bind. In a related technique, a so-called "tagged" protein can be engineered to include histidine residues in its sequence. The polyhistidine binds strongly to the divalent ions of metals such as nickel, zinc or cobalt. All untagged proteins pass through the column. The protein can be eluted by decreasing solution pH or by using an imidazole wash, which competes with the polyhistidine tag for binding to the column, as shown in Figure 26.5.

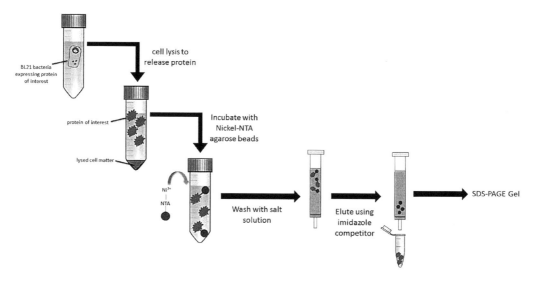

Figure 26.5: Diagram depicting the process of protein purification using nickel immobilized by the chelating agent, nitrilotriacetic acid (NTA).

E. ELECTROPHORESIS

Electrophoresis is a separatory technique that relies on the migration of charged molecules in the presence of an applied electric field. The electrophoresis of proteins typically is conducted in polyacrylamide or agarose gels with characteristic pore sizes. Separation is achieved based on electrophoretic mobility, which is a function of a protein's charge, and gel filtration, which is a function of a protein's size and shape. The pH of the gel chosen is usually at or above 9. As a consequence of the gel pH exceeding the pI of nearly any protein, those proteins contained in the sample will have net negative charges and move toward the positive pole (the anode) of the gel. Molecules possessing similar size and charge will move as a coherent band through the gel.

Following electrophoretic separation, bands may be visualized by exposing the gel to an agent which tightly binds proteins. One of the most popular protein stains is the anionic dye Coomassie Brilliant Blue, which non-specifically binds to proteins. If the proteins separated are radioactive, the gel can be placed over X-ray film and, once developed, an autoradiograph displaying an identifiable banding pattern results. If an antibody to a separated protein target exists, it can be used to detect the presence of that protein specifically in a process known as Western blotting, which is also known as immunoblotting.

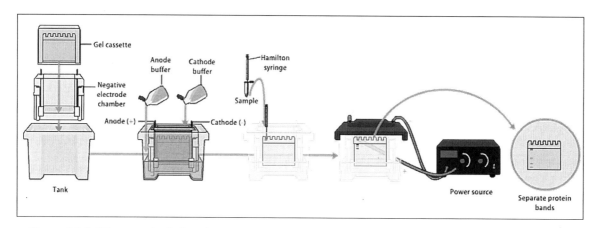

Figure 26.6: Diagram depicting the separation of proteins by a generic gel electrophoresis procedure.

One particular gel electrophoretic technique, known as SDS-PAGE, uses the strong anionic detergent SDS to denature native proteins into their unfolded, unassociated polypeptide states. Proteins are separated according to their electrophoretic mobility—in the unfolded state, this is a function of the charge and the length of a polypeptide. Binding by SDS imparts most proteins with an even distribution of charge per unit mass. More specifically, when highly anionic SDS associates with the polypeptide backbone, the intrinsic charge of polypeptides becomes negligible when compared to the negative charges due to SDS. SDS's anionic character denatures secondary and non-disulfide–linked tertiary structure. Proteins may additionally be heated while being treated with a reducing agent. Dithiothreitol (DTT) and 2-mercaptoethanol (β-mercaptoethanol) are two common examples of reductants added to reduce disulfide linkages left intact by SDS-PAGE treatment. When SDS-PAGE is performed with a reductant, it is known as reducing SDS-PAGE. Because SDS binding controls for variation in the charge per unit length of protein, the electrophoretic mobility of sample proteins becomes solely a function of polypeptide length. Fractionation, then, occurs due to differences in approximate size of the proteins separated during SDS-PAGE. The electrophoretic mobility displayed by these proteins will be a linear function of the logarithms of their molecular weights.

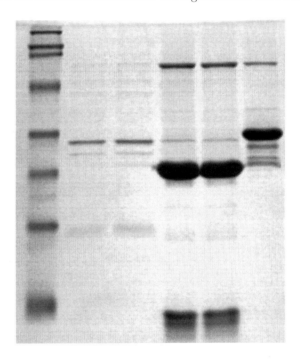

Figure 26.7: Proteins separated by length using SDS-PAGE and visualized using Coomassie Brilliant Blue staining. Molecular markers (protein ladder) are shown in the leftmost lane.

Isoelectric focusing (IEF) is a related electrophoretic technique that separates proteins according to their isoelectric point (pI). In one approach, IEF begins by adding a sample into immobilized pH gradient (IPG) gels—gels which contain a stable gradient of increasing pH. A protein that is in a region of the gel where the pH is below its isoelectric point (pI) will be positively charged and will migrate towards the negatively charged plate—the cathode—of the gel. Migration will cease when, as the protein's overall charge decreases, it reaches the pH region of the gel where pH equals its pI. At this pH, the protein will be neutrally charged. The proteins focused will separate based on the relative number of acidic and basic residues which they contain. In two-dimensional gel electrophoresis, proteins are first isoelectrically focused and separated by their pI. They are then separated in a follow-on step by molecular weight by SDS-PAGE. Because the likelihood of two molecules being similar in two distinct physical properties is small, two-dimensional electrophoresis offers significant advantages over one dimensional electrophoresis in many applications.

F. PROTEIN ASSAYS

The process of protein purification often also requires some means of quantification. This is the purpose of an assay. A common assay technique for the detection of enzymes that catalyze reactions involves the measurement of their products. This is because the rate of product formation in an enzyme catalyzed reaction bears a proportional relationship to the concentration of enzyme present in a sample. Substances that form colored or fluorescent products are often used as the substrates in such reactions. In other cases, if no such substance is available, the product of an enzymatic reaction can be converted into another, more easily detected substance, for use in quantification. This approach is referred to as a coupled enzymatic reaction scheme. The concentration of a substance in solution can be measured by absorbance spectroscopy. For a solution formed from a light-absorbing solute, there is a logarithmic dependence between the transmission of light through a substance and the product of the absorptivity, concentration and path length through the attenuating solution. This is often expressed in the form of the Beer-Lambert law,

$$A = -\ln\left(\frac{I}{I_0}\right) = \varepsilon \ell c \; :$$

where A is the solute's absorbance, also known as its optical density, I is the transmitted intensity of a given wavelength of light, I_0 is the intensity of incident light at the given wavelength, ε is the molar extinction coefficient (alternatively called the molar absorptivity) of the solute at the wavelength of light transmitted, c is the concentration of attenuating solute and l is the path length in cm of the transmitted light. If the molar extinction coefficient for a protein is known, then its concentration can be determined spectroscopically. While polypeptides do not absorb light in the visible region of the spectrum, they do absorb very strongly from 200 nm to 400 nm—the ultraviolet (UV) range—because of the presence of residues containing aromatic side chains (Phe, Tyr and Trp). Absorbance spectroscopy at 280 nm, near a relative maximum for the UV absorbance curve for all three aromatic amino acids, is a convenient means of measuring protein content during a purification. However, this approach isn't without complicating factors when analyzing a sample which is not pure for a single protein. Nucleic acids and other molecules also have significant molar absorptivity in the UV spectral range, and proteins vary in their aromatic amino acid residue content. Colorimetric protein assays, such as the Bradford assay, addresses several of the difficulties described. The Bradford assay is based on the absorbance shift of the previously mentioned dye, Coomassie Blue. At an acidic pH, the dye is converted from a red form into a blue form—in the latter form, it stably and non-covalently binds proteins present in an assay. The bound blue form of the dye-protein complex has an absorption spectrum maximum near 595 nm. The concentration of the resulting blue complex, as measured by the increase in absorption at 595 nm, can be used as an accurate measure of protein concentration.

Immunochemical procedures are an alternative to spectrophotometric analysis. Immunoassays operate on the principle that antibodies cultured from antibody-producing cells recovered from the serum of an immunized source will bind with great specificity to a protein antigen of interest. A protein present in a mixture can be detected, in a technique known as a radioimmunoassay (RIA), when bound to antibody indirectly by measuring the extent to which the protein competes with a radioactively labeled standard for antibody binding sites. A similar, and now more popular technique, is the enzyme-linked immunosorbent assay (ELISA). ELISA encompasses a range of specific protocols, but in general, ELISA uses a solid-phase enzyme immunoassay (EIA) which detects the presence of an antigen. In the procedures, a sample containing an unknown amount of antigen is applied to a solid phase support. After the antigen contained in the sample becomes attached to the solid support, a specific detection antibody is applied to, and binds with, the antigen. The antibody is then covalently linked to an enzyme directly or through a secondary antibody conjugated to an enzyme. Between steps, the plate is often washed with a detergent to rinse unbound proteins or antibodies. Following addition of the enzyme's substrate, a reaction occurs producing a visualizable signal that may be related, based on its intensity, to the quantity of protein antigen present in the original sample. This signal most often involves a measurable color change in solution. Because ELISA can be performed to determine the presence of antigen or the presence of antibody in a sample, it is a useful method for determining serum antibody concentrations and as a rapid screen for certain classes of chemical agents and toxins.

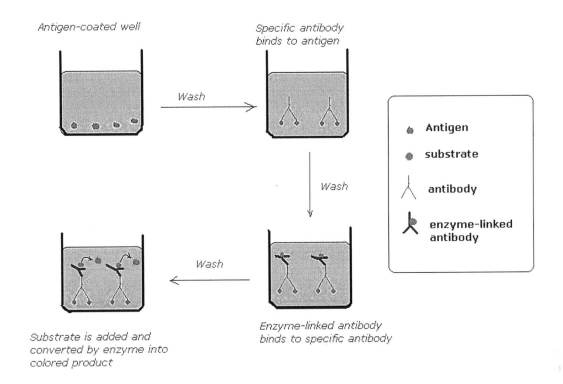

Figure 26.8: Schematic depicting the indirect ELISA procedure.

Chapter 26 Problems

Passage 26.1 (Questions 1-5)

A biochemist sought to purify and isolate a series of antibodies present in a serum sample as part of a six-step protocol.

She prepared three immunoadsorbent columns, labelled Columns 1, 2 and 3. Each consisted of a solid agarose gel matrix coupled to a single antigen which was specific for one of the antibodies that she wished to isolate. Each column contained a different coupled antigen.

She passed the serum over one of the three immunoadsorbents (Column 1) and collected the material that was obtained from the outlet of the column, labelling it as Fraction 1.

She then rinsed the column from Step 2 with an eluting agent containing an acidic salt, and collected the material that was obtained from the column's outlet, labelling it Fraction 2

Fraction 1 was passed through Column 2, and the material obtained from the column's outlet was labelled Fraction 3. Column 2 was then eluted with the same solution used in Column 1, and the solution obtained was labelled Fraction 4.

In the final fractionating step, Fraction 3 was passed over Column 3. Fraction 5 was obtained first and Fraction 6 was collected following treatment with the same eluent used to treat Columns 1 and 2.

Following dialysis of each fraction, UV spectroscopy was performed. Conjugated ring systems absorb UV light strongly at 200 nm. As a result, aromatic amino acid residues are primarily responsible for decreasing the transmittance of UV light by proteins. During UV spectroscopy, the absorbance of UV radiation is inversely related to its transmittance, which decreases with increasing protein concentration. The absorbance data collected was then used to approximate the concentration of protein present in each fraction. The results of the spectroscopic analysis are shown in Figure 1.

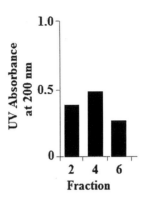

Figure 1: Results of the UV spectroscopy preformed on selected fractions.

1. During the dialysis mentioned in the passage, fractions 2, 4, and 6 were enclosed within a dialysis membrane constructed to prevent the passage of macromolecules, but permit passage of small molecules and ions. Each membrane-enclosed fraction was then placed in a sample of pure water. What was the net effect of this procedure on the dialyzed fraction?
    A. Proteins present in the membrane-contained fractions were concentrated.
    B. The fractions were purified by allowing only small proteins to escape from the membrane.
    C. Solutes originally found in eluent solutions were removed from the fractions.
    D. The charge gradient across the membrane increased.

2. Which purified fraction contained the greatest concentration of Phe, His, Trp and Tyr residues?
    A. Fraction 4, because it transmitted the least UV radiation at 200 nm.
    B. Fraction 4, because it transmitted the most UV radiation at 200 nm.
    C. Fraction 6, because it transmitted the least UV radiation at 200 nm.
    D. Fraction 6, because it transmitted the most UV radiation at 200 nm.

3. The biochemist applied an eluent to all three columns in order to:
    A. rinse non-specifically bound proteins from the column.
    B. bind antibodies for which the eluent's dissolved solutes were specific.
    C. disrupt noncovalent interactions between antibody and antigen.
    D. release the antibody-antigen complex as a unit from the solid support.

4. Which fact, if true, would most *weaken* an assertion that the UV spectroscopy data presented in Figure 1 can be used to accurately approximate the protein content of the fractions analyzed?
    A. The fractions analyzed were contaminated with nucleic acids.
    B. A significant quantity of eluent remained in each fraction.
    C. The UV absorbance of a given protein varies with wavelength within the UV band.
    D. The relative aromatic amino content of most proteins is approximately constant.

5. If immediately following its collection, Fraction 1 had been dialyzed and its UV absorbance measured, then, when compared to the absorbance measurements reflected in Figure 1, what statement is most likely to be true of Fraction 1's absorbance?
    A. It would be smaller than that of Fraction 6.
    B. It would be greater than Fraction 6 but less than that of Fraction 2.
    C. It would be greater than Fraction 2 but less than that of Fraction 4.
    D. It would be greater than that of Fraction 4.

The following questions are NOT based on a descriptive passage.

6. Which peptide absorbs 280 nm UV light most strongly?

    A. Gln-Leu-Phe-Asp
    B. Ala-Ser-His-Leu
    C. Gln-Trp-Tyr-Glu
    D. Glu-Thr-Val-Asp

7. If buffer pH were slowly decreased, in what order would the amino acids lysine, aspartate and leucine be eluted from a diethylaminoethyl (DEAE)-cellulose ion exchange column to which they were bound?
    A. lysine, leucine, aspartate
    B. aspartate, leucine, lysine
    C. leucine, aspartate, lysine
    D. leucine, lysine, aspartate

8. Both a native polyacrylamide gel electrophoresis performed under non-denaturing conditions and SDS-PAGE separate proteins according to what property or properties of the proteins analyzed?
    I.   size
    II. charge
    III. shape

    A. I only
    B. II only
    C. I and II only
    D. I, II and III

9. The mass of a certain protein is determined to be approximately 100 kD when estimated using gel filtration, but only 75 kD when estimated by SDS-PAGE in the presence, or absence, of a reductant. What explanation best accounts for the difference in measured masses?
    A. SDS-PAGE underestimates the protein's true mass because its electrophoretic mobility in the gel depends only upon its size.
    B. Gel electrophoresis is a more accurate estimate because the protein migrates in its native state.
    C. Gel electrophoresis overestimates the protein's true mass because the protein's non-uniform charge distribution retards its migration through the gel.
    D. SDS-PAGE more accurately estimates the protein's true mass because SDS-binding does not cause a change in the protein's conformation.

10. In order to most effectively salt out a protein (pI = 8.1), the pH of solution should be adjusted:
    A. to 7 specifically.
    B. to a value much less than 8.1.
    C. to a value much greater than 8.1.
    D. to 8.1 specifically.

Content Review Problems

1. Enzymes serve which function biologically?
   A. reaction catalysis
   B. structural support
   C. cell recognition
   D. cellular adhesion

2. The residues bound together by a peptide linkage constitute what organic chemical functional group?
   A. amide
   B. ester
   C. lactone
   D. imide

3. Non-protein components of enzymes required for enzyme action are referred to as what?
   A. holoenzymes
   B. prosthetic groups
   C. apoproteins
   D. zwitterions

4. Of the two optical isomers of α-amino acids, what is the form NOT naturally synthesized by humans?
   A. S
   B. R
   C. L
   D. D

5. What substituent of a naturally occurring α-amino acid has the lowest pK_a?
   A. hydrogen atom
   B. –R group
   C. α-carboxylic acid
   D. α-amino group

6. The protonation state of an α-amino acid depends upon:
   A. the pH of the solution in which it is contained.
   B. the pK_a of the α-amino group
   C. the pK_a of the α-carboxylic acid group
   D. all of the above

7. When the pI of an amino acid dissolved in solution is greater than that of the pH in which it is contained, what is the net charge on that amino acid?
   A. positive
   B. negative
   C. zero
   D. the charge cannot be determined from the information given in the question.

8. The pK_a of glycine's α-carboxylic acid residue is 2.35 and the pK_a of its α-amino residue is 9.78. The pI of glycine is nearest to what value?
   A. 1.05
   B. 4.85
   C. 6.05
   D. 10.8

9. The pK_a of aspartate's α-carboxylic acid residue is 2.05, the pK_a of its α-amino residuc is 10.25, and the pK_a of its side chain is 3.86. The pI of aspartate is nearest to what value?
   A. 1.86
   B. 2.95
   C. 9.40
   D. 11.68

10. When pH is plotted against volume of base added for the titration of a triprotic amino acid, the plot indicates the presence of:
    A. two buffering regions and two equivalence points.
    B. three buffering regions and two equivalence points.
    C. three buffering regions and three equivalence points.
    D. three buffering regions and four equivalence points.

11. The presence of an ionizable group in an amino acid buffers the pH of solution at a pH value:
    A. near the pI of the amino acid in which the group is found.
    B. near the pK_a of the ionizable group.
    C. substantially less than that of the pK_a of the ionizable group.
    D. substantially less than the pI of the amino acid in which the group is found.

12. The side chains of which of the following amino acids can form hydrogen bonds?
    A. Asparagine
    B. Aspartic acid
    C. Glutamine
    D. All of these

13. The isoelectric point of an amino acid is defined as the pH where:
    A. the molecule carries no net electric charge.
    B. the α-carboxyl group is uncharged.
    C. the α-amino group is uncharged.
    D. the amino acid experiences maximum electrophoretic mobility.

14. The transamination of aspartic acid results in the production of what molecule containing aspartic acid's former carbon skeleton?
    A. α-ketoglutarate
    B. Fumarate
    C. Oxaloacetate
    D. Succinate

15. Which amino acids would most likely reside in the membrane-anchoring domain of a membrane-embedded protein?
    A. Isoleucine, valine and phenylalanine
    B. Phenylalanine, valine, and aspartate
    C. Leucine, threonine, and lysine
    D. Lysine, arginine and histidine

16. An essential amino acid is:
    A. constitutively synthesized by the body.
    B. required as an energy source for the body
    C. an amino acid which cannot be easily synthesized in sufficient quantities by the body.
    D. an amino acid which can be synthesized in sufficient quantities by the body only under certain conditions.

17. D-alanine and L-alanine are best described as:
    A. anomers.
    B. enantiomers.
    C. epimers.
    D. diastereomers.

18. Which of the following pairs of amino acids would carry a negative side chain charge at pH 8.0?
    A. Asparagine & Glutamine
    B. Leucine & Glycine
    C. Histidine & Lysine
    D. Aspartate & Glutamate

19. Which pair of amino acids displays the greatest UV band absorption at 280 nm?
    A. Threonine and histidine
    B. Tryptophan and tyrosine
    C. Cysteine and asparagine
    D. Phenylalanine and proline

20. Which of the following is a nonstandard amino acid?
    A. Cysteine
    B. Isoleucine
    C. Hydroxyproline
    D. Histidine

21. Which of the following amino acids is involved in the formation of disulfide bonds?
    A. Cysteine
    B. Isoleucine
    C. Valine
    D. Histidine

22. Which of the following amino acids contain an imidazolium moiety?
    A. Alanine
    B. Valine
    C. Cysteine
    D. Histidine

23. Coomassie Blue stains proteins via reaction with:
    A. arginine residues.
    B. free carboxy-termini.
    C. peptide bonds.
    D. aromatic rings.

24. During a successful protein purification scheme, it may be expected that:
    A. measured specific activity increases.
    B. measured specific activity decreases.
    C. protein concentration in the sample decreases.
    D. both A and C are true.

25. What is true regarding the separation of proteins by ion-exchange chromatography?
    A. proteins are separated on the basis of their net charge
    B. proteins are separated on the basis of their size
    C. proteins are separated on the basis of their shape
    D. proteins are separated on the basis of both their shape and size

26. Gel-filtration chromatography separates proteins on the basis of:
    A. both their size and their shape.
    B. their size only.
    C. their shape only.
    D. their net charge only.

27. Purification of proteins on an affinity chromatography column takes advantage of what interactions in order to achieve separation?
    A. specific binding of a protein constituent for another molecule
    B. protein - protein interaction
    C. protein - carbohydrate interaction
    D. none of the above interactions

28. A purified protein sample contains 1.0 μg of protein and has an enzyme activity of 1 mmole of ATP synthesized/sec (1 unit). What is the specific activity of the final purified sample?
    A. 1,000 units/mg
    B. 10,000 units/mg
    C. 100,000 units/mg
    D. 1,000,000 units/mg

29. The conformational change from the T to the R state of hemoglobin is initiated by what event?
    A. The binding of oxygen to the heme of the molecule.
    B. The movement of the proximal histidine residue within heme.
    C. The movement of the F-helix structure, which contains the proximal His residue of heme.
    D. The reorganization of protein-protein contacts between the individual hemoglobin subunits.

30. Binding of an allosteric activator:
    A. decreases oxygen binding affinity of hemoglobin.
    B. increases the binding affinity of hemoglobin.
    C. stabilizes the R state of the hemoglobin protein.
    D. Both B and C

31. The binding affinity of oxygen for hemoglobin is increased by an increase in the measurement of which value?
    A. 2,3-BPG concentration
    B. the partial pressure of CO_2
    C. pH
    D. temperature

32. The specificity of a ligand binding site on a protein is based upon:
    A. the absence of competing ligands.
    B. the amino acid residues lining the protein binding site.
    C. the presence of hydrating water molecules in solution.
    D. the opposite chirality of the binding ligand versus that of the protein.

33. Beta pleated sheets are examples of what level of protein structure?
    A. primary structure
    B. secondary structure
    C. tertiary structure
    D. quaternary structure

34. Signal sequences encoded within a protein's linear amino acid sequence serve what function?
    A. To direct folding of the protein
    B. To cause dissociation of the ribosome during termination of translation
    C. To mark proteins for transport to other sites within cells following translation
    D. To target improperly translated proteins for degradation

35. Marfan's syndrome is a genetic disorder of connective tissue synthesis. The causative mutation of the syndrome is most likely associated with a mutation affecting what process?
    A. hemoglobin synthesis
    B. collagen synthesis
    C. metabolism of homogentisic acid
    D. synthesis of thyroid hormone

36. Cyclins are proteins that directly regulate what cellular process?
    A. endocytosis of extracellular material
    B. cell division
    C. apoptosis of damaged cells
    D. repair of damaged nuclear material

37. Damage to or synthesis of non-functional protein p53 is implicated in the progression of cancer. This protein is most likely categorized as what?
    A. a cyclin
    B. a tumor suppressor
    C. an oncogene
    D. an anti-apoptotic protein

38. Protein folding is:
    A. non-spontaneous.
    B. mediated by chaperone proteins.
    C. mediated by ribosomes.
    D. none of the above

39. The spatial and stoichiometric arrangement of hemoglobin's tetrameric subunits constitutes what level of its protein structure?
    A. primary structure
    B. secondary structure
    C. tertiary structure
    D. quaternary structure

40. Enzyme-driven metabolic pathways can be made more efficient by:
    A. concentrating enzymes within specific cellular compartments.
    B. grouping enzymes into multienzyme complexes.
    C. anchoring related enzymes in adjacent positions within cellular membranes.
    D. All of the above

41. Which of the following statements regarding the structure or function of enzymes is NOT true?
    A. Enzymes do not alter the overall change in free energy for a reaction.
    B. Enzyme function is dependent upon their three-dimensional conformation.
    C. Enzymes modify the rates of the reactions they catalyze by increasing reaction activation energy.
    D. Enzymes are unchanged by the reactions which they catalyze.

42. One means by which enzymes catalyze reactions is through changing the free energy of reactions. This change may be achieved through what means?
    A. Altering the three-dimensional shape of the reactant molecule.
    B. Oxidizing the reactant molecule.
    C. Providing a small amount of activation energy.
    D. Altering the final free energy of product molecules.

43. Hydrogen bonds in α-helices are:
    A. parallel to the principal axis of the helix.
    B. found at regular intervals in the backbone of the polypeptide.
    C. between carbonyl oxygen atoms and free amino residues.
    D. not a type of intermolecular interaction.

44. What statement accurately describes a characteristic of peptide bonds in proteins?
    A. They cannot be formed between proline residues.
    B. They are most often found in the cis configuration.
    C. They are most often found in the trans configuration.
    D. They are planar because of the steric hindrance of adjacent residues.

45. The molecular formula of glycine is $C_2H_5O_2N$. What would be the molecular formula for a linear oligomer synthesized from the condensation of ten glycine molecules?
    A. $C_{20}H_{50}O_{20}N_{10}$
    B. $C_{20}H_{32}O_{11}N_{10}$
    C. $C_{20}H_{40}O_{10}N_{10}$
    D. $C_{20}H_{68}O_{29}N_{10}$

46. Which of the following is an example of tertiary structure in a protein?
    A. A multimeric protein
    B. An α-helix
    C. A β-pleated sheet
    D. A globular domain

47. In deoxyhemoglobin (Hb), the Fe (II) is coordinated to what ligands?
    A. four nitrogens of heme, the proximal His, and a water molecule
    B. four nitrogens of heme and a water molecule
    C. two nitrogens of heme and three His residues in Hb
    D. two nitrogens of heme and three water molecules

48. Disulfide bonds most often stabilize the native structure of what type of proteins?
    A. extracellular proteins
    B. dimeric proteins
    C. hydrophobic proteins
    D. intracellular proteins

49. Cleavage of an IgG molecule by a specific protease can produce:
    A. an antigen-binding site and two constant regions.
    B. two heavy chain-light chain dimers.
    C. an inactive mixture consisting solely of individual amino acids.
    D. two F_{ab} fragments and one F_c fragment.

50. Which of the following is true regarding IgE or its function in humans?
    A. It is involved in the immune response to parasitic infection.
    B. It aids in the complement-mediated killing and phagocytosis of cells.
    C. It is secreted.
    D. all of the above.

NEXT STEP MCAT CONTENT REVIEW: BIOLOGY AND BIOCHEMISTRY

SECTION 7
MOLECULAR GENETICS

We discussed molecular genetics earlier in the biology review. The AAMC have listed molecular genetics as being both a biology and a biochemistry topic, however, so in the next short section we will have one chapter to review DNA from the perspective of biochemistry.

NEXT STEP MCAT CONTENT REVIEW: BIOLOGY AND BIOCHEMISTRY

Nucleic Acids

A. INTRODUCTION

Nucleic acids, which include DNA (deoxyribonucleic acid) and RNA (ribonucleic acid), are macromolecular polymers of nucleotides. Nucleotides are composed of a pentose sugar, a phosphate group, and a nitrogenous base. In DNA, the sugar found in nucleotides is deoxyribose; in RNA, it is ribose. The order in which nucleotides appear in the polymeric sequence of nucleotides is the mechanism by which nucleic acids encode genetic information. That information is then conveyed in the transmission and ultimate expression of that genetic information in living organisms via protein synthesis, and between organisms and their offspring hereditarily.

B. NUCLEOTIDES, NUCLEOSIDES AND THEIR FUNCTION

As mentioned previously, a nucleotide is composed of a nitrogenous base, a five-carbon pentose sugar (either ribose or 2-deoxyribose), and at least one phosphate group.   In ribonucleotides, the pentose is ribose. In deoxyribonucleotides, the sugar, 2'-deoxyribose, lacks a hydroxyl group at the 2'-carbon. A nitrogenous base bound to a pentose sugar which lacks an attached phosphate group is referred to as a nucleoside. When bound to a single phosphate, it becomes a nucleotide—a nucleoside monophosphate. When two or three linked phosphate groups are attached, the nucleotide is a nucleoside diphosphate or nucleoside triphosphate, respectively. The bound phosphate or phosphates are most commonly attached at the 5'-carbon (that is, the number 5 carbon of the pentose sugar), but may be attached at either the 2'- or 3'-carbon as well.

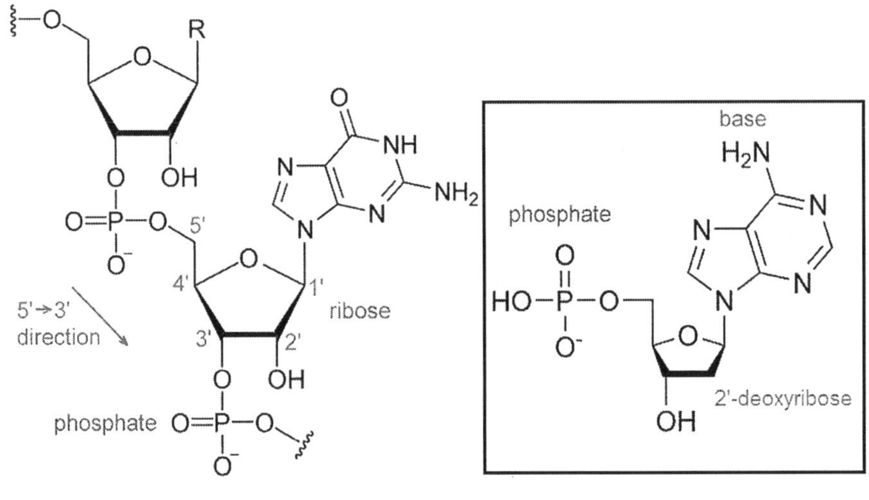

Figure 27.1: A ribonucleotide linked via phosphodiester bonds to adjacent nucleotides; structure of a 2-deoxyribonucleotide (dAMP) (inset).

Cyclic nucleotides, such as cGMP and cAMP, form when the phosphate group is bound to two of the sugar's hydroxyl groups, specifically between the phosphate group and the 3' and 5' hydroxyl groups of the sugar (Figure 30.2).

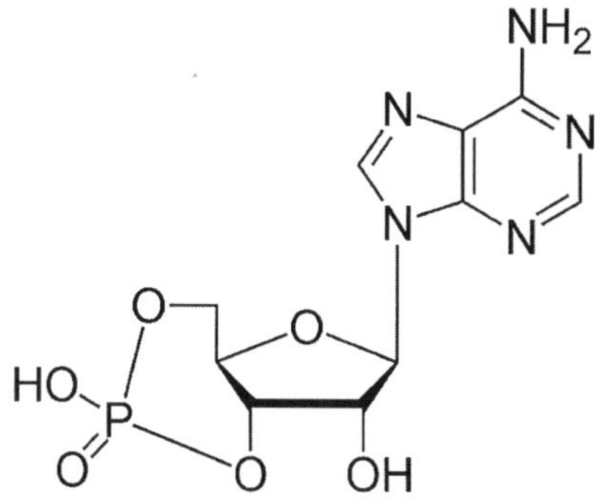

Figure 27.2: Structure of 3'-5'-cyclic adenosine monophosphate (cAMP).

Ribonucleotides are found in ribonucleic acid (RNA), whereas deoxyribonucleotides are found in deoxyribonucleic acid (DNA). RNA and DNA contain one of two classes of nitrogenous base—pyrimidines or purines. Sugars are bound to the nitrogenous base in an N-glyosidic linkage between the ring nitrogen (N-1 for pyrimidines and N-9 for purines) and the 1'-carbon of the pentose sugar. The purine bases adenine and guanine, which consist of a pyrimidine ring fused to an imidazole ring, are found in both DNA and RNA. Pyrimidines are aromatic heterocyclic organic compounds which have nitrogen located at positions 1 and 3 of the ring. The pyrimidines thymine and cytosine are found in DNA, while the pyrimidines uracil and cytosine are found in RNA, which uses uracil in place of thymine. Because of their respective structures, in a nucleic acid adenine bases pairs with thymine by forming two hydrogen bonds, while guanine pairs with cytosine via the formation of three hydrogen bonds.

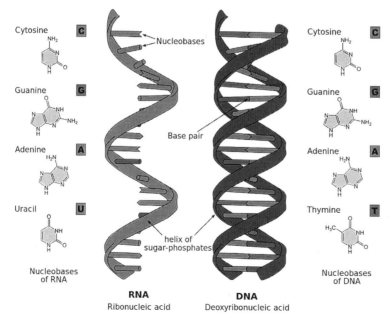

Figure 27.3: Structure of DNA and RNA and the structure of the purine and pyrimidine nucleobases which they contain.

The majority of nucleotides found intracellularly are in the form of either DNA or RNA, where they function in the storage and transfer of genetic information. However, free nucleotides and nucleosides serve other roles as well. Nucleoside triphosphates such as ATP, GTP, UTP and CTP transfer energy during metabolism, participate in cell signaling as second messengers in hormone and ion channel signaling (cGMP and cAMP), and partly compose the cofactors of enzymatic reactions. Such nucleotide-containing cofactors include FAD, FMN, NAD, NADP$^+$, and CoA.

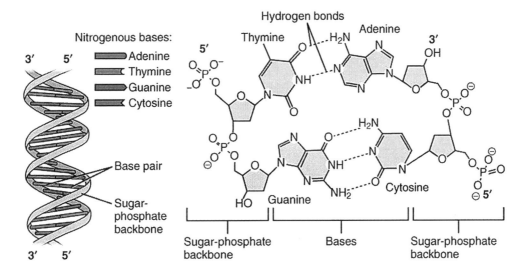

Figure 27.4: Figure depicting the structural association of a nucleic acid via hydrogen bonded nucleobases and the covalently linked backbone sugars.

C. NUCLEIC ACID STRUCTURE AND THE WATSON-CRICK MODEL

Nucleic acids vary widely in terms of their size, but are generally large linear polymers of nucleotides which can range in length into the millions of base pairs. Most DNA molecules are double-stranded, while RNA molecules may be double- or single-stranded. In certain cases, nucleic acid structures with three or more chains have been observed.

The sugars and phosphates in standard nucleic acids are linked in an alternating sugar-phosphate chain, called the sugar-phosphate backbone, by phosphodiester linkages. In the polynucleotide, the terminal residue where the 5'-carbon is not bound to another nucleotide is called the 5'-end and the terminal residue whose 3'-carbon is not linked to another nucleotide residue is called the 3'-end. Because of this convention, nucleotides have directionality.

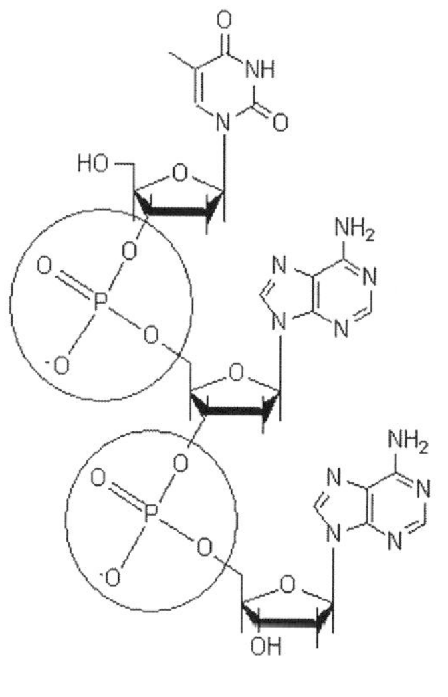

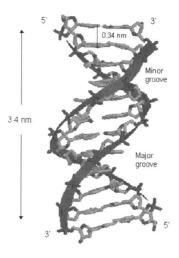

Figure 27.5: Phosphodiester linkage between adjacent nucleotides

Nucleic acids may occur as linear or circular molecules. Linear double-stranded nucleic acids contain complementary sequences. The regularity of base pairing results in a DNA's characteristic double-helical structure. These two strands of the double helix are aligned in opposite directions relative to one another in what is referred to as an anti-parallel alignment. Linear single-stranded RNA and DNA molecules do not exhibit a regular secondary helical structure, but instead adopt highly complex three-dimensional structures. DNA contained in the chromosomes of prokaryotes, plasmids and mitochondrial DNA often adopt a circular, double-stranded conformation. Most RNA molecules are linear and single-stranded, but more complex circular and branched forms can arise from splicing.

When examining the structure of DNA, voids, also known as grooves, can be seen. These grooves are adjacent to the base pairs and differ in size. The wider groove is referred to as the major groove and the narrower groove is referred to as the minor groove. These grooves serve as a binding site for transcription factors, usually at the sides of the bases exposed through the more accessible major groove.

Several different DNA conformations are believed to exist in nature. B-DNA is that which was originally described by James Watson and Francis Crick. It extends approximately 34 Å per 10 base pairs of sequence, making one complete turn about its axis every 10.5 base pairs in solution. This frequency of twist (known as the helical pitch) is driven by hydrophobic interactions between adjacent nitrogenous bases.

Figure 27.6: Structure of the major and minor grooves of B-DNA

A-DNA and Z-DNA are also helical forms, but their geometries differ substantially from those of B-DNA. A-DNA is most probably a dehydrated form of B-DNA that can also be formed by DNA-RNA hybrid helices. It is a right-handed double helix but with a shorter helical structure, resulting in an increase in the number of base pairs per rotation, a deeper major groove, and a shallower minor axis. DNA that has been methylated, usually because of epigenetic modification, can display a left-handed double helical geometry in what is referred to as the Z form of DNA.

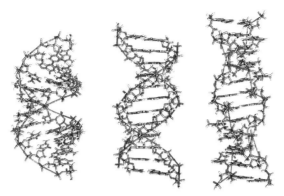

Figure 27.7: From left to right, the structure of the A, B and Z forms of DNA

A DNA segment which is over- or under-wound is referred to as being positively or negatively "supercoiled", respectively. Such supercoiling is a function of torsional strain in the molecule. In a relaxed double-helical segment of B-DNA, the two wound strands complete a cycle of rotation about the helical axis once every 10.5 base pairs. Additional twisting, or unwinding, causes supercoiling, and thus strain. *In vivo*, DNA is usually negatively supercoiled. This conformation makes unwinding of the double-helix—a requirement of transcription—more energetically favorable. Many topoisomerase enzymes are responsive for the supercoiling state of DNA and either create or relieve supercoiling as they catalyze a transformation of DNA's topology.

D. HYBRIDIZATION, DENATURATION, AND REANNEALING

Hybridization is the process by which complementary base pairs contained in two or more strands combine. During hybridization, bonds between A and T and G and C are formed. Binding between G and C is more stable than binding between A and T, because in the hybridization between G and C, three hydrogen bonds are formed; when A and T hybridize, only two hydrogen bonds are formed. In the case of two complementary strands combining, the duplex product forms a double helical structure. Perfectly complementary strands of DNA, RNA, or short stretches of nucleic acids, known as oligonucleotides, will bind one another readily. A single inconsistency between the nucleotides positioned along either of the two strands will decrease the energetic favorability of the strands' annealing. While strands that are not perfectly congruous will still very often anneal, they will do so—to an extent determined by their complementarity—with decreasing avidity. The degree of sequence similarity between two base-paired strands may be quantified by measuring the temperature at which the strands anneal. In the reverse process, heating of annealed strands imparts the energy required in solution to overcome hydrogen bonding between nitrogenous bases of annealed strands. This thermal denaturation, also referred to as melting, can cause the reversible dissociation of the based-paired complex. Once hydrogen bonds are overcome during DNA denaturation, the strands of the double helix unwind as the hydrophobic stacking attractions between the bases are insufficient to maintain the base-paired complex. The temperature at which half of the DNA strands of a sample are present in their single-stranded (ssDNA) state is defined as the melting temperature T_m of the nucleic acid. T_m depends on the length and nucleotide sequence of a molecule. Denaturation can also cause dissociation of complementary strands by chemical means using denaturants such as urea.

DNA denaturation can be a useful analytical tool to determine certain properties of annealed strands. Because C-G base-pairing is generally stronger than A-T base-pairing, during thermal denaturation, the melting point of annealed strands containing increasing amounts of cytosine and guanine, known as the GC content, relative to that of adenine and thymine, known as AT content, will increase. DNA denaturation can also be used to detect the extent of sequence homology between annealed strands. In one procedure, DNA is heated, and the mixture is cooled. As the temperature of solution decreases, the separated strands rehybridize. Hybrid molecules are formed between similar sequences and any differences between those sequences will result in a disruption of the base-pairing.

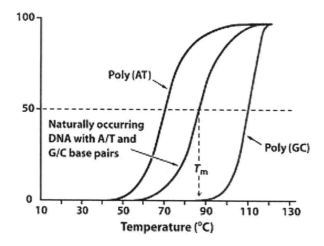

Figure 27.8: Comparison of the melting temperature (T_m) for AT-rich (poly (AT)), naturally occurring and GC-rich (poly (GC)) nucleic acid sequences.

The annealing of complementary base pairs in separate strands can be seen in the binding of a DNA probe or of a primer to a DNA strand during a polymerase chain reaction (PCR). In PCR, DNA is repeatedly heated to a temperature above its melting point, and then allowed to cool, in a process known as thermal cycling. During the cooling process, DNA strands become templates for DNA polymerase enzymes to selectively amplify target DNA within regions flanked by primers specific to the start and end points of the replicated regions. This process is illustrated in Figure 27.9.

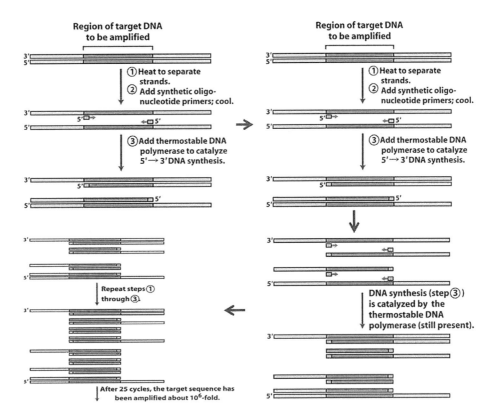

Figure 27.9: Schematic depicting the major steps in polymerase chain reaction (PCR) amplification of a target DNA sequence.

Chapter 27 Problems

Passage 27.1 (Questions 1-5)

On average, homologous chromosomes differ in their nucleotide sequence at every 1250 base pairs. A restriction enzyme is an enzyme that cleaves DNA at or near specific nucleotide recognition sequences known as restriction sites. Homologous chromosomes that produce nucleic acid fragments of different lengths during restriction enzyme digestion are said to exhibit restriction fragment length polymorphisms (RFLPs).

Hemophilia A, which causes deficient synthesis of clotting factor VIII, is a human X-linked disease that causes a known RFLP. Two forms of the alleles exist: the mutant allele and the wild type allele. One form gives a 1.2 kb fragment upon restriction digestion with the enzyme BclI, while another yields a 0.9 kb fragment. DNA samples collected from an affected male and an unaffected female, as well as their three offspring—a son and two daughters—were digested using BclI. The resulting DNA fragments were separated according to their length by agarose gel electrophoresis—wherein larger fragments migrate more slowly—and transferred to a membrane. The membrane was then exposed to a radioactively labelled-DNA hybridization probe with a sequence specific for the region of interest. Prior to hybridization, both the fragments and DNA probe were exposed to strongly basic, denaturing conditions. During visualization of the RFLP analysis, it was observed that the band shown in lane 2 (Figure 1) was approximately twice as intense as the bands present in lanes 1, 3, 4 or 5.

Figure 1: Results of the agarose gel electrophoresis of

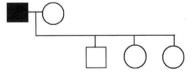

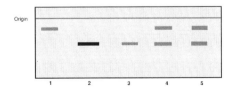

restriction digest fragments from subjects 1-5

1. Which statement regarding the direction and extent of the migration of the restriction fragments shown in Figure 1 is true?
   A. The 1.2 kb fragment migrated the greatest distance and lies nearer the cathode than does the 0.9 kb fragment.
   B. The 1.2 kb fragment migrated the greatest distance and lies nearer the anode than does the 0.9 kb fragment.
   C. The 0.9 kb fragment migrated the greatest distance and lies nearer the cathode than does the 1.2 kb fragment.
   D. The 0.9 kb fragment migrated the greatest distance and lies nearer the anode than does the 1.2 kb fragment.

2. Given the information presented in the passage, the most likely explanation for the increased intensity of band 2 is that:
   A. cells of the female donor contained twice the number of X-chromosomes of any male donor.
   B. it bound the radio-labeled probe more strongly than did other bands.
   C. each sibling received only a single chromosome from subject 2.
   D. it contains more identical genetic information than that found in other bands.

3. The mutant form of the allele mentioned in the passage is most likely to differ from the wild type in what way?
   A. the elimination of a restriction site in the region of DNA for which the probe was specific
   B. its ability to successfully hybridize with a DNA probe specific for the wild type allele
   C. the presence of an additional restriction site in the region of DNA for which the probe was specific
   D. its resistance to cleavage by restriction enzymes

4. The wild type and mutant forms of the allele both possess how many BclI restriction sites in the nucleotide sequence from which the restriction fragments shown in Figure 1 were produced?
   A. 1
   B. 2
   C. 3
   D. It cannot be determined from the information provided in the passage.

5. If a single condition under which the DNA fragments were hybridized to a probe specific for the wild type allele were altered, how would the extent of the hybridization of the probe and the fragment produced from the mutant allele be affected?
   A. it would increase if hybridization temperature were increased
   B. it would be unchanged by an increase in hybridization temperature
   C. it would be unchanged by a denaturant that acts only to strengthen binding of fragments to the membrane
   D. it would increase if the DNA probe had been exposed to a less alkaline environment prior to hybridization

The following questions are NOT based on a descriptive passage.

6. The sequence of a small gene was found to contain 35 adenine, 22 guanine, 30 cytosine and 41 thymine residues in one of its strands. How many pyrimidines and purines are found in the complete double-stranded molecule?
   A. 128 pyrimidines and 128 purines
   B. 110 pyrimidines and 126 purines
   C. 142 pyrimidines and 114 purines
   D. 126 pyrimidines and 110 purines

7. Incorporation of which of the following radiolabeled molecules could be used to measure the extent of RNA synthesis occurring in a cell?
   A. adenine
   B. thymidine
   C. uracil
   D. cytosine

8. Which statement best describes the linear sequence of nucleotides found in both DNA and RNA?
   A. They are linked by phosphodiester bonds between 5' sugars and nitrogenous bases.
   B. They are exclusively found in a double-stranded and antiparallel form.
   C. Cytosine can be found hydrogen bonded to thymine.
   D. Their monomeric units consist of a nitrogenous base, a five-carbon sugar and phosphate.

9. Fluoroquinolones are antibiotics that interfere with prokaryotic enzymes directly responsible for inducing changes in the supercoiling state of bacterial chromosomes. The enzyme targeted by fluoroquinolones most likely belongs to what class?
   A. DNA polymerases
   B. DNA topoisomerases
   C. DNA ligases
   D. DNA nucleases

10. Which of the following DNA sequences has the highest T_m?
    A. CGACGTTAG
    B. GTACAAACT
    C. ATCGACTCA
    D. TTATGACTG

SECTION 7

Content Review Problems

1. The synthesis of DNA from nucleotides is termed:
   A. transcription.
   B. translation.
   C. replication.
   D. gene expression.

2. The primary site of mRNA synthesis in the cell is:
   A. the cytosol.
   B. the nucleus.
   C. the lysosome.
   D. the Golgi apparatus.

3. Eukaryotic DNA differs from that of prokaryotes in what way?
   A. It is contained within a membrane-bound organelle.
   B. It contains thymidine.
   C. It is arranged in circular plasmids.
   D. Prokaryotic histones are smaller than those of eukaryotes.

4. DNA is a polymer of:
   A. nucleotide triphosphates.
   B. nucleosides.
   C. nitrogenous bases.
   D. nucleotide monophosphates.

5. In DNA or RNA, which carbons of ribose or 2-deoxyribose participate in phosphodiester bonds?
   A. 3 and 5.
   B. 4 and 5.
   C. 1 and 3.
   D. 1 and 5.

6. In a molecule of DNA, what functional group is present at the 3' end of the strand?
   A. a nitrogenous base.
   B. a hydroxyl group
   C. a phosphate group.
   D. an epoxide oxygen.

7. How many different trinucleotides can be constructed using any of the four nitrogenous bases found in DNA?
   A. 3
   B. 12
   C. 16
   D. 64

8. Which statement regarding the form of the DNA double helix most commonly found in the human cell is NOT true?
   A. The two strands of the double helix have opposite polarity.
   B. The 2-deoxyribose-phosphate backbone faces the nucleoplasm.
   C. Phosphate groups in opposite strands interact by hydrogen bonding.
   D. The two grooves of the double helix are often of unequal size.

9. The base stacking phenomenon observed in DNA is primarily driven by what intermolecular interaction?
   A. hydrophobic
   B. covalent
   C. ionic
   D. hydrogen bonding

10. When compared to an annealed DNA molecule rich in A-T base pairs, what is true of the melting of a DNA molecule of similar length but rich in G-C base pairs?
    A. Its melting point will be greater.
    B. Its melting point will be lower.
    C. Both molecules' melting points will be equal.
    D. The relative magnitude of the melting point cannot be determined from the information given.

11. Most cellular DNA:
    A. exists in a "right-handed" conformation.
    B. is neither negatively nor positively supercoiled..
    C. requires synthesis from a double-stranded DNA template.
    D. is replicated in the 3' to 5' direction.

12. What statement regarding the heat of denaturation of a DNA double helix is true?
    A. The viscosity of the denatured molecule is greater.
    B. Reannealing of the single-stranded DNA occurs spontaneously under any environmental conditions.
    C. It occurs by the same mechanism as pH denaturation.
    D. The reannealing of DNA with more A/T content is thermodynamically less favored than that of DNA molecules with more C/G.

13. In semiconservative replication:
    A. one strand of each daughter molecule is from the parent molecule, while another strand in each daughter molecule is newly synthesized.
    B. both strands of one daughter molecule are from the parent molecule, while another daughter molecule contains only newly synthesized strands.
    C. the strands of both daughter molecules are newly synthesized.
    D. the strands of both daughter molecules were previously present in a parent molecule.

14. As monomeric precursors are incorporated into a growing DNA molecule, the hydrolysis of what molecule powers the synthetic reaction?
    A. nucleotides.
    B. nucleotide monophosphates.
    C. nucleotide diphosphates.
    D. nucleotide triphosphates.

15. The unwinding of the parental double helix during DNA replication:
    A. is aided by positive DNA supercoiling.
    B. is accomplished by DNA toposiomerases.
    C. requires the hydrolysis of ATP.
    D. requires the activity of a DNA polymerase functional domain.

16. During DNA replication, DNA polymerase moves along the template strand in what direction?
    A. $5' \rightarrow 3'$
    B. $3' \rightarrow 5'$
    C. Both $5' \rightarrow 3'$ and $3' \rightarrow 5'$
    D. Neither $5' \rightarrow 3'$ nor $3' \rightarrow 5'$

17. What class of enzymes is responsible for the cleavage of internal phosphodiester bonds in nucleic acids?
    A. exonucleases
    B. DNA primases
    C. endonucleases
    D. DNA ligases

18. The products of 5'-exonuclease activity are:
    A. nucleoside 5'-monophosphates.
    B. nucleoside 3'-monophosphates.
    C. nucleoside 5'-diphosphates.
    D. nucleoside 3'-monophosphates.

19. What is the major synthetic enzyme of bacterial DNA replication?
    A. DNA polymerase I
    B. DNA polymerase II
    C. DNA polymerase III
    D. RNA polymerase

20. Binding of initiator proteins to bacterial DNA:
    A. leads to unwinding and synthesis bidirectionally from multiple origins of replication.
    B. leads to unwinding and synthesis in one direction, beginning at the origin of replication.
    C. requires initial unwinding of the strand by single-stranded DNA binding proteins.
    D. requires the action of DNA gyrase.

21. What enzyme is responsible for the addition of the initial nucleotide of a new strand during the initiation of DNA replication?
    A. DNA polymerase I
    B. primase
    C. DNA gyrase
    D. DNA polymerase III

22. Okazaki fragments of the lagging strand during DNA synthesis are connected by the enzyme:
    A. DNA polymerase I.
    B. DNA ligase.
    C. primase.
    D. DNA gyrase.

23. In prokaryotes, DNA polymerase:
    A. reads the lagging strand in the 3' → 5' direction.
    B. synthesizes the lagging strand 3' → 5'.
    C. reads the leading strand in the 5' → 3' direction.
    D. synthesizes the leading strand in the 3' → 5' direction.

24. What statement is true regarding the ligation of adjacent Okazaki fragments?
    A. The phosphorylated 3'-terminus of one fragment of one terminus is linked to the free 5'-terminus of another fragment.
    B. The reaction requires the hydrolysis of a phosphoanhydride bond of NADH in humans.
    C. The phosphorylated 5'-terminus of one fragment of one terminus is linked to the free 3'-terminus of another fragment.
    D. Removal of RNA primers at the 3' end of Okazaki fragments is required prior to fragment ligation.

25. Synthesis of DNA beginning at a single origin of replication requires the simultaneous action of how many molecules of the bacterial enzyme, DNA polymerase III?
    A. 1
    B. 2
    C. 3
    D. 4

26. The pentose sugar contained in RNA differs from that contained in DNA in terms of its substitution at what carbon?
    A. carbon 2
    B. carbon 3
    C. carbon 4
    D. carbon 5

27. What statement regarding RNA is true?
    A. RNA is incapable of forming a double helix structure *in vitro*.
    B. Not all cellular RNAs are copied from a DNA template.
    C. The rate of cellular tRNA degradation exceeds that of mRNA degradation under most conditions.
    D. Cellular RNA is typically single-stranded.

28. Transcription requires:
    A. a double-stranded template.
    B. a single-stranded template.
    C. a double- or single-stranded template.
    D. no template.

29. Which of the following incorrectly describes transcription?
    A. A subunit of RNA polymerase recognizes a promoter region in order to initiate transcription.
    B. Strand separation is required prior to RNA synthesis.
    C. RNA polymerase moves processively along the translated DNA template.
    D. The rate of transcriptional initiation of all genes is constant.

30. The promoter regions of transcribed DNA:
    A. are highly conserved at regions located approximately 10 and 35 base pairs upstream of the transcriptional start site.
    B. are specific to the σ subunits of only certain RNA polymerase molecules.
    C. contain identical consensus sequences.
    D. do not contain any base pairs transcribed by RNA polymerase.

31. Which of the following nucleotide triphosphates is not incorporated into RNA by RNA polymerase?
    A. ATP
    B. CTP
    C. TTP
    D. UTP

32. During the action of RNA polymerase, all of the following are true, EXCEPT that:
    A. no RNA primer is required.
    B. the DNA template strand is complementary to the synthesized RNA.
    C. the coding strand has the same sequence as the RNA transcript.
    D. RNA polymerase contains no proofreading nuclease activity.

33. During transcriptional termination:
    A. hairpin loops form by covalent bonding between base pairs.
    B. transcription of palindromic sequences leads to the formation of hairpin loops.
    C. the formation of hairpin loops leads to the binding of transcriptional termination factors.
    D. RNA polymerase recognizes consensus sequences, signaling an end to transcription.

34. Rifampin is a drug which inhibits transcription by tight binding to a subunit of bacterial RNA polymerase. However, a point mutation affecting the rifampin binding site can lead to bacterial resistance. One consequence of rifampin treatment is:
    A. an inhibition of eukaryotic transcription.
    B. the rapid proliferation of a resistant mutant within a population of rifampin-sensitive bacteria.
    C. the induction of rifampin-resistance point mutations due to rifampin treatment.
    D. the inhibition of translation of existing mRNA within bacterial cells.

35. Modification of mRNA after its synthesis by RNA polymerase:
    A. is referred to as post-translational processing.
    B. occurs in both prokaryotes and eukaryotes.
    C. takes place immediately following transcription in prokaryotes.
    D. can involve the addition of 7-methylguanosine to the primary transcript.

36. Processing of pre-mRNA at the 3' end of the molecule involves the addition of what nucleotide residues?
    A. adenine
    B. cytosine
    C. guanine
    D. uracil

37. The process by which RNA is spliced:
    A. involves the addition of introns from other pre-mRNA sequences to the mature mRNA molecule.
    B. is catalyzed by a complex containing only protein.
    C. may produce multiple mature RNA molecules from a single pre-mRNA sequence.
    D. results in the re-formation of a continuous strand of exons.

38. Which of the following statements is true regarding rRNA?
    A. Bacterial and eukaryotic ribosomes contain the same molecules of rRNA.
    B. rRNA is not post-transcriptionally modified.
    C. Ribosomal RNA is transcribed as a single, large precursor molecule.
    D. rRNA serves only a structural role in eukaryotic ribosomes.

39. The ribosome reads codons in what direction?
    A. 5' → 3'
    B. 3' → 5'
    C. Both 5' → 3' and 3' → 5'
    D. Neither 5' → 3' nor 3' → 5'

40. All of the following accurately describe the genetic code EXCEPT that:
    A. the sequence of amino acids in the polypeptide, read from N- to C-terminus, correspond exactly to the sequence of their codons in mRNA read from 5' to 3'.
    B. each codon specifies a single amino acid.
    C. each amino acid is specified by a single codon.
    D. with the exception of the start codon, the genetic code is identical in prokaryotes and the nuclear DNA of multi-cellular eukaryotes.

41. All of the following are stop codons EXCEPT:
    A. UGA
    B. UAG
    C. AUG
    D. UAA

42. An activated ester bond between an amino acid and transfer RNA is formed:
    A. by aminoacyl-tRNA synthetase to the 3' end of the tRNA molecule.
    B. by peptidyl transferase to the 3' end of the tRNA molecule.
    C. by aminoacyl-tRNA synthetase to the 5' end of the tRNA molecule.
    D. by peptidyl transferase to the 5' end of the tRNA molecule.

43. Formation of the activated aminoacyl-tRNA complex produces, in addition to aminoacyl-tRNA, what other products?
    A. ADP and Pi
    B. GDP and Pi
    C. GMP and PPi
    D. AMP and PPi

44. Gene regulation in prokaryotes and eukaryotes most commonly occurs at what level?
    A. At the level of transcription
    B. Post-transcriptionally
    C. By alterations of an organism's gene sequence
    D. Following translation

45. In prokaryotes, the codon AUG codes for which amino acid?
    A. methionine
    B. selenocysteine
    C. lysine
    D. trimethyllysine

46. In order to initiate translation in bacteria, the Shine-Dalgarno sequence of mRNA must be:
    A. recognized by the small ribosomal subunit approximately 10 nucleotides upstream of the start codon.
    B. recognized by the large ribosomal subunit approximately 10 nucleotides upstream of the start codon.
    C. recognized by the small ribosomal subunit approximately 10 nucleotides downstream of the start codon.
    D. recognized by the large ribosomal subunit approximately 10 nucleotides downstream of the start codon.

47. During initiation of translation, binding of initiator tRNA occurs at the:
    A. E site, while the A site remains empty.
    B. P site, while the A site contains an incoming aminoacyl-tRNA molecule.
    C. A site, while the P site contains an incoming aminoacyl-tRNA molecule.
    D. P site, while the A site remains empty.

48. How many high-energy bonds, in the form of either hydrolyzed ATP or GTP, are required for the formation of a single peptide bond during translation?
    A. 1
    B. 2
    C. 3
    D. 4

49. What description of a property of peptidyl transferase is correct?
    A. It is an enzymatic activity of the large ribosomal subunit.
    B. It catalyzes translocation of the ribosomal subunit following peptide bond formation.
    C. Its activity is powered by the hydrolysis of GTP.
    D. It may be described as a ribozyme.

SECTION 8
Metabolism

As with the prior section on DNA, we once again turn our attention to a topic that was already discussed briefly in the biology review material. However, unlike in the genetics section we will now go much more in-depth in our analysis of cellular metabolism. In a typical college biochemistry course, the various molecular pathways involved with metabolism can make up the bulk of the class, and they are equally important for the MCAT. Be sure to review the following chapters thoroughly.

CHAPTER 28
Bioenergetics

A. INTRODUCTION

The bewildering array of biological macromolecules and the diversity of their chemical compositions serves a simple purpose for the organisms in which they are found: to provide the necessary flexibility to assemble them into a dynamic, life-sustaining structure. However, to fully understand the function of these individual molecules and the higher-order structures which they facilitate, we must also understand the chemical reactions in which they participate. These reactions use free energy to both synthesize and break down biological molecules, and harness or produce free energy to facilitate the work of the organism. Metabolism, the overall process by which organisms gain and employ chemical free energy, is often divided into two broad subdivisions: catabolism, the degradation of biological macromolecules or the cell constituents which they compose, and anabolism, the biosynthesis of molecules and structures from less complex components.

Bioenergetics is the study of the energy involved in the formation and the breakage of the chemical bonds found in living organisms, as well as the transformation between forms of the energy involved in these bonds.

The growth, development and ongoing metabolism of the human body constantly involves transfer of energy. During the body's minute-by-minute function, energy is constantly transferred and transformed between forms and functions. This exchange and transformation of energy is critical to any organism's ongoing function, and occurs both within the body and with the surroundings.

During biological processes, the energy stored in chemical bonds can be exchanged during the breaking of bonds. When weak bonds are broken and stronger bonds formed, the energy released can be used for other purposes, including the performance of mechanical work or the chemical synthesis of anabolic or growth-associated processes.

Living organisms obtain energy from organic and inorganic substrates by different strategies. Autotrophs can produce ATP from the energy contained in light by photosynthesis. Heterotrophs, such as humans, use ingested organic materials as their primary energy source. These are mostly carbohydrates, fats, and proteins. Other, more unusual organisms, known collectively as lithotrophs, can obtain energy from the oxidation of sulfur- and nitrogen-containing compounds. Regardless of the materials from which organisms harvest energy, the process is not perfectly efficient: there are variable energetic costs associated with transfer and transformation of energy as it is obtained and used biologically.

B. BIOLOGICAL THERMODYNAMICS

Gibbs free energy describes the maximum amount of non-PV work that can be performed within a closed system in a completely reversible process. It is an indication of the total amount of chemical potential energy available in a system and reflects the overall favorability of the reaction which it describes. ΔG, or the Gibbs free energy change for a chemical reaction, is given by the equation

$$\Delta G = \Delta H - T\Delta S$$

where ΔH is the change in enthalpy (heat) during the reaction, T is the absolute temperature (measured in Kelvins) at which the reaction occurred, and ΔS is the change in entropy during the process. A reaction, or process, will occur spontaneously provided that the Gibbs free energy change for the reaction is negative. These reactions, where $\Delta G < 0$, are referred to as exergonic.

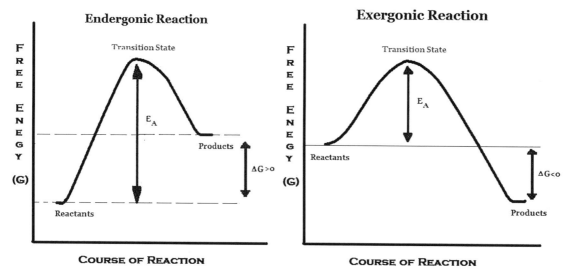

Figure 28.1: Free energy diagrams for an endergonic (left) and an exergonic (right) reaction

The standard free energy change of a reaction, $\Delta G°$, assumes that the concentration of reactants and products is 1 M. This assumption allows for a direct relationship to be drawn between the $\Delta G°$ for a reaction, the equilibrium constant for the reaction, and the thermodynamic stability of reactants and products at these non-physiological conditions, according to the equation

$$\Delta G° = -RT \ln K_{eq}$$

where R is the universal gas constant and K_{eq} is the equilibrium constant for the reaction.

In contrast, the ΔG of a reaction depends not only upon $\Delta G°$, but also upon the concentration of both its products and reactants. By rearranging the previous equation, at constant temperature and pressure, ΔG may be related to $\Delta G°$, T, and the reaction quotient, Q, by the equation

$$\Delta G = \Delta G° + RT \ln Q$$

$\Delta G°$ then is an accurate predictor of reaction spontaneity only under standard conditions. A reaction with a positive $\Delta G°$ can proceed spontaneously in the direction of product production if Q—the ratio of products to reactants—is sufficiently small to make the magnitude of the negative of $RT \ln Q$ greater than $\Delta G°$. One example of this not-infrequent incongruity between $\Delta G°$ and ΔG is the conversion of glucose-6-phosphate to fructose-6-phosphate during glycolysis. Because of the high metabolic flux through the pathway and the comparatively high concentration of glucose-6-phosphate versus fructose-6-phosphate that results, the reaction proceeds spontaneously despite having a positive $\Delta G°$.

Another important property of Gibbs free energy is that the ΔG values for individual reactions that are linked sequentially by common intermediates are additive. Two reactions have a common intermediate when they occur sequentially such that the product produced by one reaction serves as the reactant of a second reaction. For biochemical pathways through which substrates must pass sequentially, the additive property of free energy changes allows for the possibility that the overall free energy of a pathway is negative, even while some of its steps have positive free energy changes. It is for this reason that cells are often able to drive thermodynamically unfavorable reactions by coupling exergonic and endergonic reactions. Due to coupling, the overall free energy change of a chemical process can be made exergonic in order to spontaneously produce a needed metabolic product.

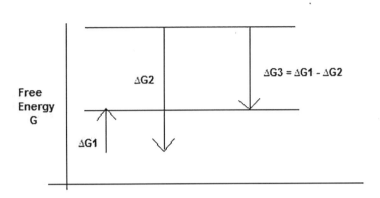

Figure 28.2: Gibbs free energy change of coupled reactions

C. PHOSPHORYL GROUPS

Most reactions employ a coupling strategy to drive anabolism by using the nucleotide adenosine triphosphate (ATP), the structure of which is shown in Figure 28.3, as a coupled intermediate. The hydrolysis of phosphoanhydride bonds between phosphate groups found in ATP, yielding either adenosine diphosphate (ADP) or adenosine monophosphate (AMP) (depending upon whether one or two bonds are hydrolyzed), releases a significant amount of energy. This significant release of energy is due to several features related to the structure of ATP. First, ADP and inorganic phosphate, the products produced during hydrolysis of a single ATP phosophoanhydride bond, have greater resonance stabilization than does ATP. Secondly, at physiological pH, the triphosphate unit of ATP carries four negative charges. Because of the proximity of these charges to one another, their repulsion is significant and can be minimized by hydrolysis. Lastly, ADP and inorganic phosphate are more stabilized by hydration than is ATP, because additional negatively charged groups are made available to interact with and bind water following hydrolysis.

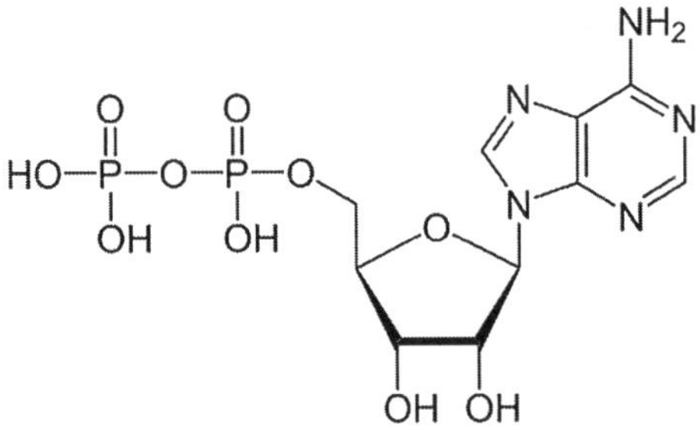

Figure 28.3: Structure of adenosine diphosphate.

One such example of a phosphoryl group transfer reaction is the glycolytic conversion of glucose to glucose-6-phosphate. The direct reaction is thermodynamically unfavorable ($\Delta G° = +13.8$ kJ/mol), but the reaction is coupled to the exergonic cleavage of ATP ($\Delta G° = -30.5$ kJ/mol), so that the overall reaction is favorable, allowing the pathway to operate in the forward direction ($\Delta G° = -16.7$ kJ/mol).

ATP can be similarly regenerated by coupling its synthesis to the even more exergonic cleavage of phosphoenolpyruvate (PEP). The free energy of the so-called "high-energy" phosphoanhydride units contained in ATP and similar molecules can be used to drive reactions even when there is no direct transfer of phosphoryl groups. This was the case in the example of the conversion of glucose to glucose-6-phosphate.

The binding of ATP can induce conformational changes in certain proteins to which it binds. Upon binding, ATP is hydrolyzed and the energy released ensures the change is irreversible, thereby driving the process forward. GTP hydrolysis functions similarly, driving certain reactions that occur during biosignalling and protein synthesis in the forward direction.

Many cellular processes rely on the use of high-energy intermediates, including not only phosphorylated nucleotides such as ATP, but also compounds that contain thioester bonds, including CoA, and reduced coenzymes such as NADH. Each of these serves as a source of energy that, upon exergonic breakdown, can be used to drive endergonic processes.

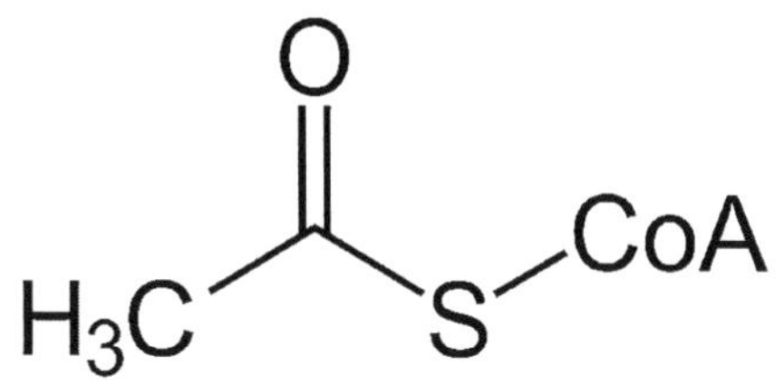

Figure 28.4: Structure of acetyl-coenzyme A

ATP itself is being continually broken and regenerated. Once hydrolyzed, ATP can be regenerated, as mentioned earlier, by coupling its formation to a more exergonic biological process. During substrate-level phosphorylation, ATP is formed from ADP by direct transfer of a phosphoryl group from a higher-energy compound. Other cellular mechanisms generate ATP indirectly, using energy supplied by transmembrane concentration gradients. During oxidative metabolism, discussed later in this text, this is accomplished in a process known as oxidative phosphorylation. The flow of energy from ATP, which occupies a relative middle-point in the energetic spectrum between higher- and lower-energy compounds, to lower-energy phosphate compounds is often accomplished in reactions catalyzed by kinases. These enzymes are responsible for the transfer of phosphoryl groups from ATP to other compounds, or from phosphorylated compounds to ADP.

Cells which have an extremely high ATP usage rate—most often cells found in nervous and skeletal muscle tissue—rely on phosphocreatine (Figure 28.5) as a reserve from which they can quickly regenerate ATP. Phosphocreatine can be synthesized from ADP and creatine by the enzyme creatine kinase. Under physiological conditions, where the concentration of reactants and products is nearly equal, phosphocreatine and ADP can be reversibly converted to creatine and ATP.

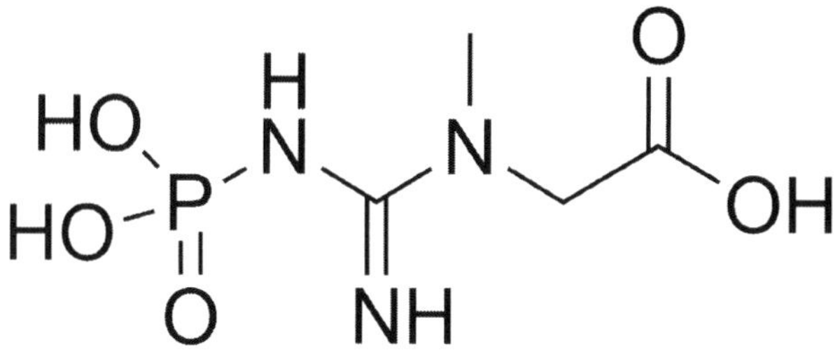

Figure 28.5: Structure of phosphocreatine

Other phosphoryl group transfer reactions take place in the body as well. The biosynthesis of proteins and nucleic acids requires nucleosides other than ATP. Several different kinases reversibly convert specific nucleoside monophosphates to their diphosphate forms—nucleoside diphosphates (NDPs)—using ATP. All nucleoside triphosphates (NTPs) are synthesized from ATP and the NDP in a reaction catalyzed by the nonspecific enzyme nucleoside diphosphate kinase, wherein ATP and an NDP combine reversibly to yield ADP and an NTP.

While human metabolism is replete with examples of phosphorylation reactions, other high-energy compounds exist as well. Thioesters are a prominent case. The thioester bond is found in acetyl-CoA, the common product of fatty acid, carbohydrate and amino acid catabolism. In acetyl-CoA, an acetyl group is part of a thioester bond to the sulfhydryl portion of β-mercaptoethylamine. Coenzyme A (CoA) is a β-mercaptoethylamine group linked to pantothenic acid through an amide linkage. The panthothenic acid is additionally linked via a pyrophosphate bond to a 3'-phosphoadenosine moiety.

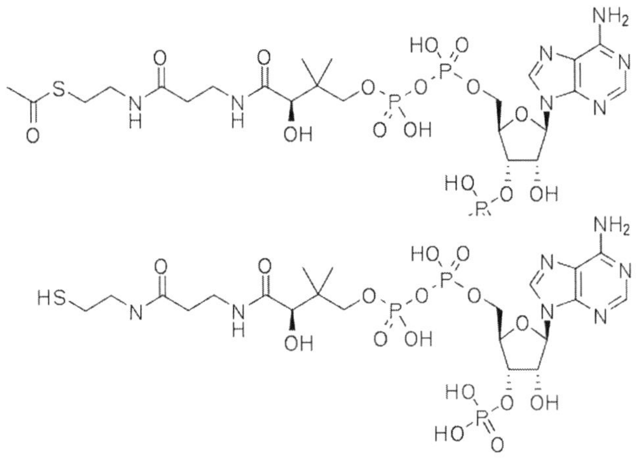

Figure 28.6: Expanded structures of acetyl-CoA (above) and coenzyme A (below). Note that the β-mercaptoethylamine moiety is involved in an amide bond with the vitamin pantothenic acid through an amide linkage, and that the acetyl group of acetyl-CoA is part of a high-energy thioester bond along with the sulfhydryl group of β-mercaptoethylamine.

D. REDOX REACTIONS

Oxidation-reduction reactions are those involving electron transfer. Oxidation is the loss of electrons or an increase in oxidation state of a chemical species, while reduction is the gain of electrons or a decrease in oxidation state of a chemical species. In redox reactions, the reducing agent transfers electrons to the oxidant, wherein the reducing agent is oxidized and loses electrons, and the oxidant is reduced and gains electrons. Collectively they are called a redox pair, and the individual reduction and oxidation processes which they undergo are referred to as half-reactions.

Reduction
Oxidant + e⁻ ⟶ Product
(Electrons **gained**; oxidation number **decreases**)

Oxidation
Reductant ⟶ Product + e⁻
(Electrons **lost**; oxidation number **increases**)

Figure 28.7: Schematic depicting the behavior of redox pair half-reactants.

Each half-reaction has a standard electrode potential (E°_{cell})—also known as a standard reduction potential (E°_{red})—which is equal to the potential difference (E°_{cell}) at equilibrium, under standard conditions, of an electrochemical cell in which the cathode reaction is the half-reaction for the species being measured, and the anode is a standard hydrogen electrode. The reduction potential can be thought of as the tendency for a material to be reduced in a half reaction. The standard reduction potential for $H^+ + e^- \rightarrow \frac{1}{2} H_2$ is taken, by definition, to be zero. For a redox reaction that takes place in a cell, the potential difference is given by the equation:

$$E^\circ_{cell} = E^\circ_{cathode} - E^\circ_{anode}$$

where $E^\circ_{cathode}$ represents the standard reduction potential of the species being reduced, and where E°_{anode} represents the standard reduction potential of the half-reaction involving the species being oxidized. The oxidation potential associated with the reverse reaction for a given half-reaction can be expressed in terms of the oxidation potential of that reaction, where $E^\circ_{ox} = -E^\circ_{red}$. In terms of the oxidation potential of the oxidation half-reaction, the cell voltage equation may be written as

$$E^\circ_{cell} = E^\circ_{cathode} + E^\circ_{(oxidation)\ anode}$$

Oxidation-reduction reactions are the primary energetic source for nearly all organisms, which rely on the oxidation of organic material to drive the synthesis of ATP. When metabolic substrates are oxidized, the liberated electrons are transferred—in aerobic metabolism—to molecular oxygen via intermediate electron carriers.

Two of the most common electron carriers are nicotinamide adenine dinucleotide and flavin adenine dinucleotide (FAD). Nicotinamide adenine dinucleotide exists in an oxidized form (NAD^+) and a reduced form (NADH), allowing it to donate or accept electrons during redox reactions, depending upon the state in which it is found. In reactions involving NAD^+, two electrons are removed from two hydrogen atoms present in a reactant, producing a hydride ion (H^-) and a proton (H^+). The proton is released into solution, the reactant is oxidized, and the electrons from hydride are transferred to the NAD^+, reducing it to NADH (Figure 28.8). During the reduction, one electron from the hydride is transferred to the positively charged nitrogen of the nicotinamide ring of NAD^+, while a second is transferred to a ring carbon. The reduction of NAD^+ can be readily reversed, when NADH reduces another molecule and is returned to its oxidized state, NAD^+, allowing the compound to be recycled without net consumption during electron transfer.

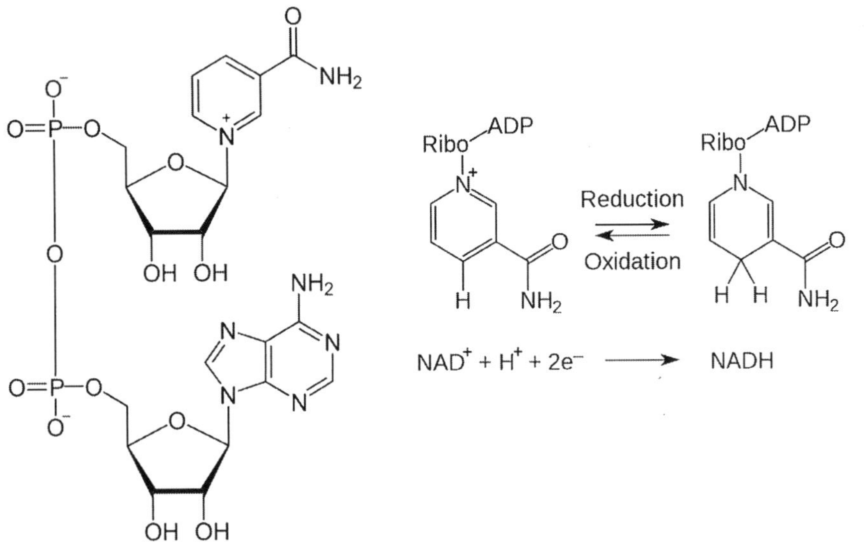

Figure 28.8: Structure of nicotinamide adenine dinucleotide (left) and
the reversible redox reaction in which it participates (right).

Like NAD$^+$, flavin adenine dinucleotide exists in two forms: its fully oxidized, quinone form, FAD, which can accept two electrons and two protons to become FADH$_2$, and its fully reduced, hydroquinone form. FADH$_2$ can then be oxidized to the semireduced form (semiquinone) FADH by donating one electron and one proton. The semiquinone is then oxidized once more by losing an electron and a proton, returning to its original, fully oxidized quinone form (FAD) (Figure 28.10). Since O$_2$, the terminal electron acceptors in aerobic organisms, can accept only unpaired electrons, FAD serves as an important bridge between the electrons carried by NADH, and oxygen. Electrons that are removed from metabolites in pairs can be transferred to FAD, which can undergo both one- and two-electron transfers.

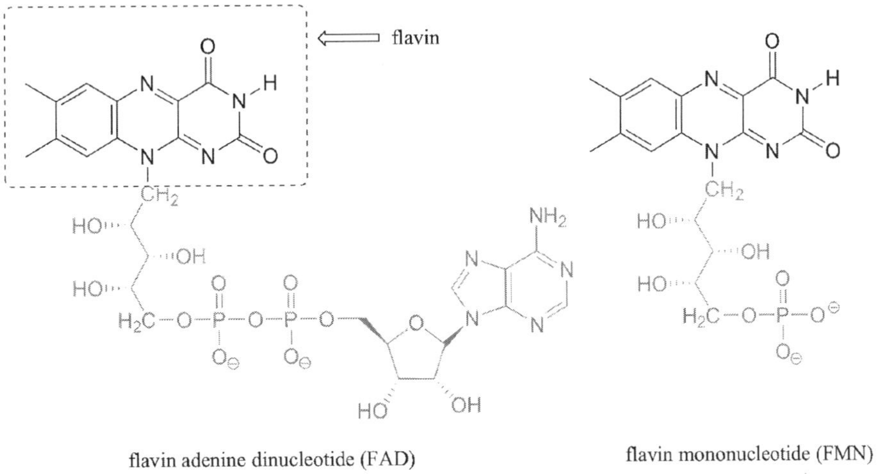

flavin adenine dinucleotide (FAD)   flavin mononucleotide (FMN)

Figure 28.9: Structures of the flavin nucleotides FAD and FMN.

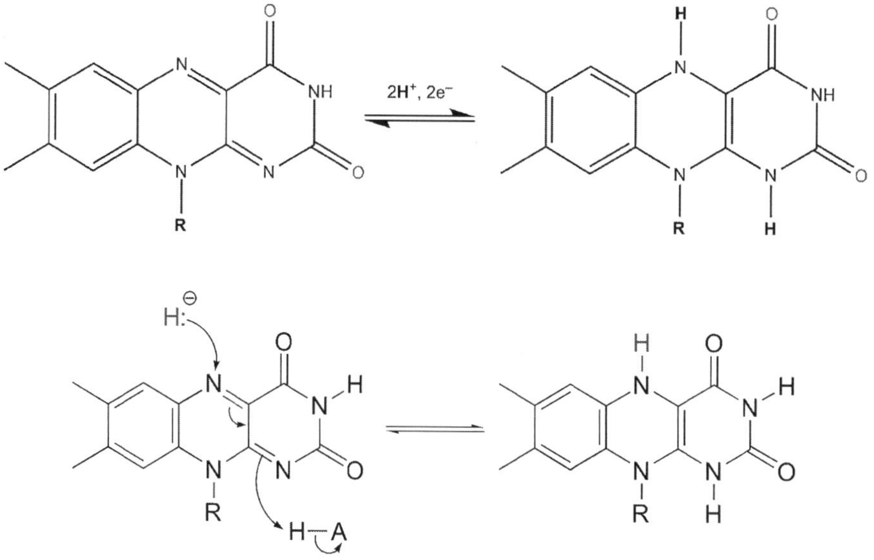

Figure 28.10: Reversible reduction of an oxidized flavin molecule (FAD or FMN) to a reduced flavin molecule (FADH$_2$) (above). FAD and FMN are able to accept a hydride ion and a proton, shown forming FADH$_2$ (below).

Chapter 28 Problems

Passage 28.1 (Questions 1-5)

The standard conditions used in the measurement of $\Delta G°'$ do not readily occur in the human body. The real concentrations of products and reactants, as well as the pH, in metabolic processes often deviate substantially from those in standard conditions.

Researchers examining the free energy changes associated with the conditions found in cultured hepatocytes noted that ATP concentrations within cells at normal body temperature were maintained in a relatively narrow range between 2-10 mM, but that the concentrations of ADP and inorganic phosphate, P_i, were more variable. They further estimated the NAD^+ concentration in cell cytosol to be in a range near 0.3 mM—about ten times the concentration of NADPH found in the same cells.

NAD^+ and NADH represent a redox pair, which can undergo the following reversible reaction: $NAD^+ + H^+ + 2\ e^- \rightarrow NADH$ ($E° = -0.315$ V). NADP and NADPH undergo a similar reaction: $NADP^+ + H^+ + 2\ e^- \rightarrow NADPH$ ($E° = -0.320$ V). Under standard conditions, both reactions operate with a free energy change permitting the reversibility of the redox reactions. The balance between the oxidized and reduced forms of nicotinamide adenine dinucleotide is called the NAD^+/NADH ratio. This ratio is an important component of the redox state of a cell, a measurement that reflects both the metabolic activities and the health of cells. The researchers found the ratio of NAD^+ and NADH in the cytoplasm to be near 700; in contrast, the $NADP^+$/NADPH ratio was maintained at a steady state near 0.005.

1. Considering the values of the NAD^+/NADH and $NADP^+$/NADPH ratios given in the passage, which of the following statements is most likely to be accurate regarding hepatocytes?
   - **A.** The mitochondrial and cytosolic concentration of NAD^+ equilibrate by diffusion across the outer mitochondrial membrane.
   - **B.** Cytoplasmic concentrations of intracellular $NADP^+$ exceed those of NAD^+.
   - **C.** The cytoplasmic NAD^+/NADH ratio is favorable to oxidative reactions.
   - **D.** $NADP^+$ is the dominant form of the nucleotide, nicotinamide adenine dinucleotide phosphate.

2. If $\Delta G°'$ for the hydrolysis of ATP to ADP and P_i is -30.5 kJ/mol and if the ratio [ADP][Pi]/[ATP] < 1 in hepatocytes, then $\Delta G'$ for the hydrolysis of ATP at 37°C in hepatocytes is:
   - **A.** less than -30.5 kJ/mol.
   - **B.** between -30.5 kJ/mol and 0 kJ/mol.
   - **C.** between 0 kJ/mol and 30.5 kJ/mol.
   - **D.** greater than +30.5 kJ/mol.

3. The researchers noted that ATP was hydrolyzed quickly in hepatocytes, but much more slowly when placed in a vessel containing only water. What might account for this observation?
   - **A.** ADP is optimally stabilized at cytosolic pH.
   - **B.** The temperature of the water was greater than the temperature of the hepatocyte cells.
   - **C.** The product of the concentrations of ADP and P_i is greater than the concentration of ATP in hepatocytes.
   - **D.** ATP is kinetically stable in the absence of hydrolytic enzymes.

4. Calculate the electromotive force for the complete oxidation of NADH by FAD, if the standard reduction potential of the half-reaction $FAD + 2\ H^+ + 2\ e^- \rightarrow FADH_2$ is -0.219 V.
   - **A.** -0.534 V
   - **B.** -0.021V
   - **C.** +0.096 V
   - **D.** +0.534 V

5. Cleavage of what bond type in the ATP of hepatocytes resulted in the formation of ADP and inorganic phosphate?
   A. A thioester bond
   B. A phosphoester bond
   C. A peptide bond
   D. A phosphoanhydride bond

The following questions are NOT based on a descriptive passage.

6. Metabolic reactions which operate near equilibrium:
   A. produce product *in vivo* slowly.
   B. often serve as control points of metabolic reactions.
   C. have free energy changes near zero.
   D. always favor reactants at equilibrium.

7. How is the free energy change for the hydrolysis of ATP in the body modified by the binding of Mg^{2+} to ATP?
   A. It is reduced, because Mg^{2+} interferes with the negative charge state of phosphoanhydride.
   B. It is reduced, because Mg^{2+} decreases the electrostatic repulsion of phosphoanhydride.
   C. It is increased, because Mg^{2+} interferes with the negative charge state of phosphoanhydride.
   D. It is increased, because Mg^{2+} decreases the electrostatic repulsion of phosphoanhydride.

8. In the redox reaction shown below, what species acts as the reducing agent?

   $$NADH + FAD + H^+ \rightarrow NAD^+ + FADH_2$$

   A. NADH
   B. FAD
   C. NAD^+
   D. $FADH_2$

9. A certain irreversible metabolic pathway involving compounds A, B and C is depicted below. If the free energy changes associated with the reactions are -17.3 kJ/mol for the irreversible conversion of A to B, -16.2 kJ/mol for the irreversible conversion of B to C, and -0.2 kJ/mol for the conversion of C to D, then which of the following statements is correct?

   $$A \rightarrow B \rightarrow C \rightarrow D$$

   A. The reaction operates predominately in the reverse direction.
   B. The presence of an inhibitor which blocks the conversion of C to D would not lead to conversion of C to B.
   C. The presence of an inhibitor which blocks the conversion of C to D would not change the concentration of D.
   D. B has greater free energy than A.

10. Glycolysis generates ATP, NADH, and protons from glucose, NAD^+, ADP and inorganic phosphate. Given this, what would be the most efficient means by which glycolysis could be regulated according to the metabolic needs of the cell?
    A. Inhibition of the initial irreversible step by glucose
    B. Inhibition of the final irreversible step by ATP
    C. Inhibition of the initial irreversible step by ADP
    D. Inhibition of the initial irreversible step by ATP

CHAPTER 29

Glycolysis and Gluconeogenesis

A. INTRODUCTION

In a previous chapter, metabolism was defined as the sum of the chemical changes—anabolic and catabolic—that take place in the body. In the following chapters, we will discuss many of the catabolic and anabolic pathways relating to the synthesis and degradation of carbohydrates, nucleic acids, proteins and amino acids. This chapter will discuss both pathways that either begin with, or end with, glucose—thus encapsulating the transformations which it encounters during the processes of catabolism and anabolism.

B. GLYCOLYSIS

Glycolysis is an exergonic reaction pathway through which the cells of nearly all organisms, both aerobic and anaerobic, convert glucose into pyruvate. The free energy released in this process is used by to synthesize ATP and NADH—two high-energy molecules. The intermediates of glycolysis—formed during ten enzyme-catalyzed reactions in the cytosol—serve not only their primary purpose of permitting the oxidation of glucose, but also provide entry points for other molecular substrates to enter glycolysis as those intermediates.

The steps of glycolysis can be broadly divided into two phases: the "preparatory phase", during which time ATP is consumed in order to drive the reaction to the "payoff" phase, over the course of which ATP is produced.

The first five steps of glycolysis—the preparatory phase—begin with entry of glucose into the pathway by which it is converted into two triose phosphates at the expense of 2 ATP per glucose molecule. The second half of glycolysis, the payoff phase, leads to the production of 2 ATP and 1 NADH per triose sugar, for a total of 4 ATP and 2 NADH per glucose molecule. Considering the energy investment made in the preparatory phase, glycolysis produces, in net, 2 NADH molecules and 2 ATP molecules per glucose molecule.

1. Glucose to Glucose-6-phosphate

In the first step of glycolysis, glucose is phosphorylated by the enzyme hexokinase, producing glucose 6-phosphate (G6P) at the expense of ATP. This reaction, which requires Mg^{2+} as a cofactor, maintains the intracellular concentration of glucose at a relatively low level, thus promoting glucose's transport into the cell through the plasma membrane by a family of glucose transporters, known as GLUT proteins. Once phosphorylated, glucose is effectively trapped within the cell as G6P—the negative charge of G6P prevents its free diffusion from the cell cytoplasm. In humans, an isozyme of hexokinase—glucokinase—is found in the liver. Glucokinase's affinity for glucose is much lower than that of hexokinase, allowing the liver to continue to metabolize glucose even at high intracellular glucose concentrations.

2.   Glucose-6-phosphate to Fructose-6-phosphate

G6P is then rearranged into fructose 6-phosphate (F6P) by the enzyme glucose-6-phosphate isomerase (also known as phosphoglucose isomerase or phosphohexose isomerase). This reaction is easily reversed under standard conditions. However, it is ordinarily forced forward because of the low intracellular concentration of F6P, which is constantly consumed by the next step of glycolysis.

3.   Fructose-6-phosphate to fructose-1,6-bisphosphate

F6P is phosphorylated again, this time by the enzyme phosphofructokinase-1 (PFK-1) in a reaction which is coupled to the hydrolysis of ATP and which requires Mg^{2+} as a co-factor. This reaction is the rate-limiting step of glycolysis and a key regulatory point in the pathway.

4.   Fructose 1,6-bisphosphate to glyceraldehyde-3-phosphate and dihydroxyacetone phosphate

Fructose 1,6-bisphosphate is destabilized by the electrostatic repulsion between its two negatively charged phosphate groups, allowing aldolase to easily split the hexose ring into two triose sugars, dihydroxyacetone phosphate (DHAP), a ketose, and glyceraldehyde 3-phosphate (GADP), an aldose.

5.   Glyceraldehyde 3-phosphate to dihydroxyacetone phosphate

In the final step of the preparatory phase, the enzyme triosephosphate isomerase converts DHAP into GADP, the only substrate that will continue further through glycolysis.

6.   Glyceraldehyde 3-phosphate to 1,3-bisphosphoglycerate

The enzyme glyceraldehyde phosphate dehydrogenase catalyzes the dehydrogenation and phosphorylation of both molecules of GADP, forming 1,3-bisphosphoglycerate (1,3-BPG). The hydrogen is used to reduce two molecules of NAD^+ to NADH and a proton for each triose.

7.   1,3-bisphosphoglycerate to 3-phosphoglycerate

In this step, phosphoglycerate kinase transfers a phosphate group from the dephosphorylated molecule 1,3-bisphosphoglycerate to ADP to form 3-phosphoglycerate (3PG) and ATP. This process is referred to as substrate-level phosphorylation. Because this reaction requires ADP, it is sensitive to the energy balance of the cell—when ATP levels are high, the reaction is inhibited because of the unavailability of the reaction substrate, ADP. As with previous steps, Mg^{2+} is again a required cofactor. During the reaction, it coordinates with ADP, thus decreasing the electrostatic repulsion between ADP's phosphate groups and stabilizing the molecule.

8.   3-phosphoglycerate to 2-phosphoglycerate

Phosphoglycerate mutase catalyzes the isomerization of 3-phosphoglycerate to 2-phosphoglycerate (2PG).

9.   2-phosphoglycerate to phosphoenolpyruvate

Enolase, a lyase, then catalyzes the conversion of 2-phosphoglycerate to phosphenolpyruvate (PEP) in a reaction requiring 2 Mg^{2+}.

10. Phosphoenolpyruvate to pyruvate

In the final reaction of glycolysis, pyruvate kinase, using Mg^{2+} as a cofactor, converts phosphoenolpyruvate into pyruvate and, in the final substrate level phosphorylation, yields ATP.

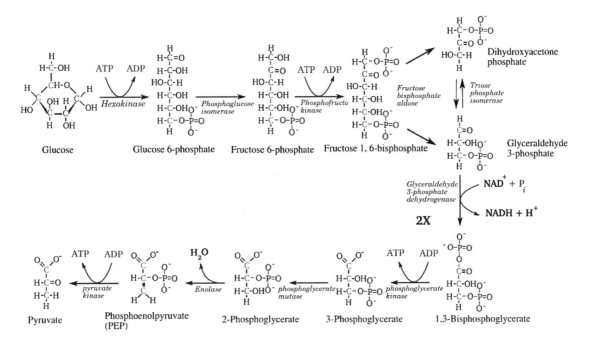

Figure 29.1: The reactions of glycolysis.

The net chemical equation describing glycolysis is:

$$\text{Glucose} + 2\ NAD^+ + 2\ ADP + 2\ P_i \rightarrow 2\ \text{Pyruvate} + 2\ NADH + 2\ H^+ + 2\ ATP + 2\ H_2O$$

If NAD^+ is not regenerated, glycolysis ceases. In order to avoid this, organisms must regenerate NAD^+ from NADH. Organisms accomplish this re-oxidation of NADH by a number of means that differ with respect to the electron acceptor employed.

During lactic acid fermentation, pyruvate is converted to lactate directly. The net chemical equation for the process is:

$$\text{Pyruvate} + NADH + H^+ \rightarrow \text{Lactate} + NAD^+$$

Lactic acid fermentation occurs in bacteria and in the human body for short periods as a cellular energy-producing mechanism of last resort, under the sort of hypoxic conditions that are found in actively exercising skeletal muscle or in infarcted cardiac tissue.

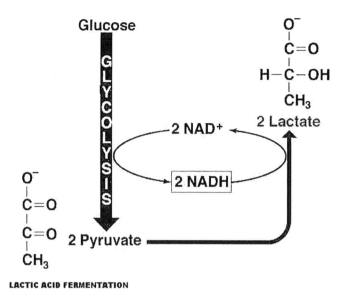

Figure 29.2: Regeneration of NAD$^+$ from NADH during the conversion of pyruvate to lactate.

Alternatively, organisms such as yeast regenerate NAD$^+$ from NADH via ethanol fermentation. During this two-step conversion, pyruvate is first cleaved, producing acetaldehyde and carbon dioxide. Then, the acetaldehyde produced in the first step is reduced by NADH to ethanol, re-forming NAD$^+$.

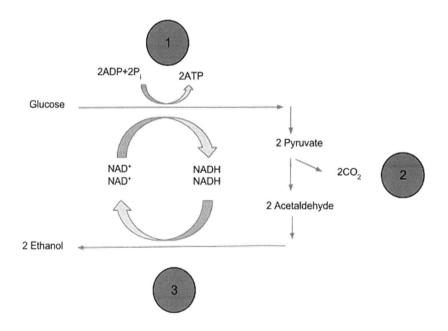

Figure 29.3: During ethanol fermentation, pyruvate produced in glycolysis (1) is cleaved into acetaldehyde and carbon dioxide (2). Acetaldehyde is then reduced to ethanol by transfer of hydride ions from NADH, thereby regenerating NAD$^+$ (3).

Because lactic acid fermentation and ethanol fermentation can occur without oxygen, many anaerobic, unicellular organisms generate energy from the oxidization of substrates entirely by glycolysis.

In general, the anoxic regeneration of NAD^+ is inefficient compared to the much larger ATP yield per molecule of glucose produced by aerobic metabolism of glucose. However, the speed at which ATP can be produced anaerobically in glycolysis is far greater than the speed at which ATP is produced during oxidative phosphorylation. For this reason, it occurs during intense periods of exercise when the metabolic demands of tissues cannot be satisfied by the rate of oxygen delivery to tissue. This process is a self-limiting one. Because of the production of lactic acid during anaerobic metabolism, hydrogen ions accumulate and the pH of tissue declines rapidly, eventually inhibiting glycolytic enzymes.

In other anaerobic organisms, nitrates, nitrites, sulfur-containing compounds and metals are used as the terminal electron acceptor. In aerobic organisms, a complex mechanism has been developed to use molecular oxygen as the final electron acceptor. The enzymes of the pyruvate dehydrogenase complexes irreversibly convert pyruvate to acetyl-CoA and CO_2 within the mitochondria in a process called pyruvate decarboxylation. Acetyl-CoA, the major fuel of the Krebs cycle, is then fully oxidized to carbon dioxide and water during the cycle, producing additional NADH for use in the oxidative phosphorylation of the electron transport chain. These mechanisms will be discussed in detail in a later chapter, but are not the only fate of pyruvate produced during glycolysis.

While glycolysis has thus far been discussed in terms of its use in transferring chemical potential energy from glucose to other molecules, many of the glycolytic metabolites of the pathway are shared with anabolic pathways. Carbon entering the pathway can be extracted prior to the formation of pyruvate, entering pathways directly or via prior conversion, which leads to the synthesis of amino acids, nucleotides, lipids, glucose and other molecules. Pyruvate, the end product of glycolysis, also serves an anabolic role. When oxidatively decarboxylated to acetyl-CoA, it is a building block for the synthesis of fatty acids. If it is carboxylated by the enzyme pyruvate carboxylase, it can replace the intermediates of the citric acid cycle and serve as a gluconeogenic substrate. For these reasons, glycolysis is an important contributor to the pool of carbon skeletons required for the biosynthetic activities of a cell. Glycolysis is also important anabolically because energy stored in the form of NADH can be used to, directly or indirectly, to reduce the pool of $NADP^+$ in the cell to NADPH—the principal reducing agent found in biosynthetic pathways of a cell.

C. GLUCONEOGENESIS

Glycolysis is the process by which glucose is oxidized. This stands in contrast to gluconeogenesis, the metabolic pathway that synthesizes glucose from non-carbohydrate carbon substrates, including pyruvate, glycerol, lactate, odd-chain fatty acids, and the glucogenic amino acids.

Gluconeogenesis is one of the two primary mechanisms by which humans provide glucose to tissue types that consume it constitutively (these tissues include those of the brain, kidney, red blood cells, eye, testes, and exercising muscle) and which prevents glucose levels from dropping substantially during prolonged fasting.

In humans, gluconeogenesis occurs mainly in the liver and, to a much smaller extent, in the cortex of kidneys. During prolonged fasting, however, the contribution of the kidneys to the gluconeogenic synthesis of glucose increases substantially. The process itself is not a simple reversal of glycolysis, which strongly favors the production of pyruvate. Instead, gluconeogenesis features several enzymes, both cytosolic and mitochondrial, not found in glycolysis.

The primary substrates of gluconeogenesis are lactate, glycerol (released during the hydrolysis of triacylglycerols), and the glucogenic amino acids. Transamination and deamination reactions of glucogenic amino acids produce α-keto acids, which may enter the Krebs cycle and be converted into oxaloacetate—a gluconeogenic reactant. Lactate produced during glycolysis can be utilized as well. In the liver, lactate is converted into pyruvate by the enzyme lactate dehydrogenase during the Cori cycle.

Acetyl-CoA, and thus substances that give rise only to acetyl-coA, including the non-glucogenic amino acids lysine and leucine, cannot be converted to glucose in gluconeogenesis because of the irreversibility of the pyruvate dehydrogenase reactions. In humans, an amino acid that can give rise to a ketone body is referred to as being ketogenic. Leucine and lysine are the only exclusively ketogenic amino acids.

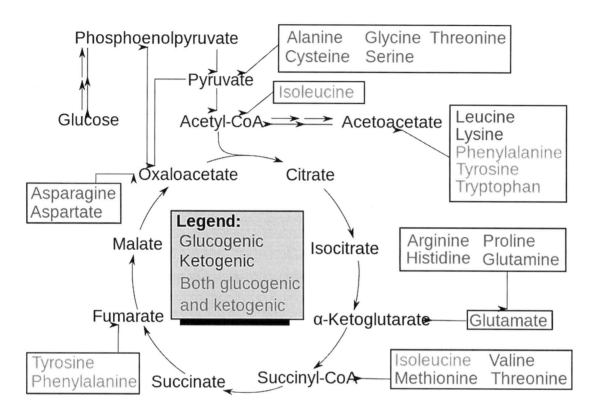

Figure 29.4: Amino acids may be categorized according to their glucogenic potential. Glucogenic amino acids may be anabolized to glucose in gluconeogenesis, while purely ketogenic amino acids may only be used to synthesize lipids or ketone bodies. Some amino acids are both glucogenic and ketogenic, indicating that they can serve either purpose in a cell.

Gluconeogenesis itself is a pathway comprising eleven enzyme-catalyzed reactions. Depending upon the substrate from which glucose is synthesized, gluconeogenesis may begin in either the cytosol or in the mitochondria.

Gluconeogenesis may begin with the carboxylation of pyruvate to oxaloacetate by pyruvate carboxylase in the mitochondria. The reaction requires the hydrolysis of a single molecule of ATP for each oxaloacetate molecule produced. This enzyme is stimulated by high levels of acetyl-CoA, produced by the β-oxidation of fatty acids in the liver, and is inhibited by high intracellular concentrations of ADP and glucose. Oxaloacetate is then temporarily reduced to malate by NADH. This step is required for its export out of the mitochondria. Once in the cytosol, malate is re-oxidized to oxaloacetate using NAD^+ in the cytosol. The remainder of gluconeogenesis occurs in the cytosol, beginning with the decarboxylation and phosphorylation of oxaloacetate, forming phosphoenolpyruvate. The inorganic phosphate used in this reaction is provided by the hydrolysis of GTP to GDP and is catalyzed by the enzyme phosphoenolpyruvate carboxykinase (PEPCK). The reactions that follow are a reversal of the steps of glycolysis, catalyzed by the same enzymes used in glycolysis, until fructose 1,6-bisphosphate is converted by the enzyme fructose 1,6-bisphosphatase—an enzyme not present in glycolysis—to fructose 6-phosphate. The conversion of fructose 1,6-bisphosphate to fructose 6-phosphate consumes one water molecule and releases one phosphate. This conversion is the rate-limiting step of gluconeogenesis. Fructose-6-phosphate is isomerized, forming glucose 6-phosphate, in another reaction common to glycolysis by phosphoglucoisomerase. The glucose-6-phosphate so produced can be dephosphorylated to yield free glucose, or can be shunted into other metabolic pathways.

The dephosphorylation of glucose-6-phosphate takes place in the lumenal space of the endoplasmic reticulum, where glucose-6-phosphate is hydrolyzed by glucose-6-phosphatase to produce glucose and an inorganic phosphate. This reaction again requires the presence of an enzyme not found in glycolysis, as the regulated conversion of glucose to glucose-6-phosphate by hexokinase is irreversible. Once dephosphorylated, glucose may then be transported into the cytoplasm by the glucose transporters found in the endoplasmic reticulum's membrane.

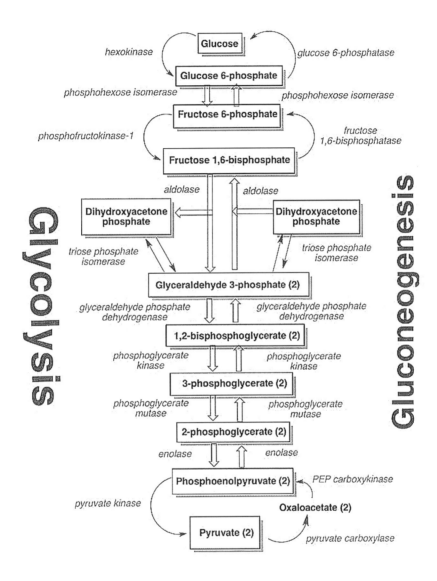

Figure 29.5: Pathways of gluconeogenesis and glycolysis compared

D. REGULATION OF GLYCOLYSIS

Glycolysis is regulated at three points of control: the reactions catalyzed by hexokinase, phosphofructokinase, and pyruvate kinase—the three effectively irreversible enzymes of glycolysis with large negative free energy changes. Regulation of the pathway is accomplished by inhibiting or activating these enzymes, thereby modulating the flux of substrates through glycolysis in response to intra- and extra-cellular conditions.

Glycolysis is regulated in response to the balance of ATP production in the body, the need for glycolytic intermediates in biosynthetic reactions, and blood glucose levels. Blood glucose homeostasis is primarily the responsibility of cells found in the liver and pancreas. In liver cells, glucose-6-phosphate may be converted to glucose-1-phosphate and polymerized to form glycogen, or, in glycolysis, be converted to pyruvate.

Pyruvate can further be converted to acetyl-CoA and then citrate in the Krebs cycle. Excess citrate is exported to the cytosol, where the enzyme ATP citrate lyase will cleave citrate to regenerate acetyl-CoA and oxaloacetate. The acetyl-CoA produced by this means may be used to synthesize fatty acids or cholesterol—an important alternative metabolic fate for glucose when blood glucose concentrations are high and the immediate energy demands of the body are being met. Liver cells contain both hexokinase and its low-affinity isoform, glucokinase. Unlike hexokinase, glucokinase is not inhibited by high glucose-6-phosphate concentrations. This property of glucokinase allows the continued conversion of glucose to fatty acids, glycogen, and cholesterol when blood glucose and intra-hepatic glucose-6-phosphate concentrations are high. When blood glucose levels fall, glucose-6-phosphate can be generated from the stored glycogen and converted to exportable glucose by the enzyme glucose 6-phosphatase (found only in the liver). Because of glucokinase's high K_m for glucose, it will not re-phosphorylate glucose to glucose-6-phosphate at the relatively low glucose concentrations produced by glycogenolysis. In general, when blood glucose concentrations decline, the rate of glycolysis in the liver decreases and the rate of gluconeogenesis increases.

The second control point of glycolysis is the reaction catalyzed by the enzyme phosphofructokinase-1 (PFK-1). The activity of phosphofructokinase is modified by two allosteric effectors: AMP and fructose 2,6-bisphosphate (F2,6BP). Both molecules serve as intracellular signals regarding the abundance of available glucose in cells.

F2,6BP is produced when F6P is phosphorylated by a second bi-functional phosphofructokinase enzyme, phosphofructokinase-2 (PFK2). F2,6BP is the most potent allosteric activator of the glycolytic enzyme phosphofructokinase (PFK-1).

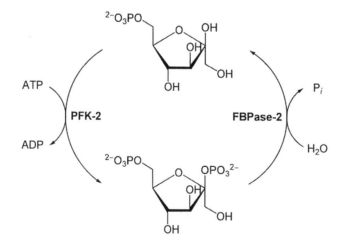

Figure 29.6: Synthesis of fructose-2,6-bisphosphate

In the liver, when blood sugar is low, glucagon levels are elevated. Glucagon causes cAMP concentrations to increase, in turn increasing the activity of protein kinase A, which phosphorylates PFK2. PFK is a bifunctional enzyme which contains both a kinase and a phosphatase activity. Phosphorylation inactivates the PFK2 domain of the enzyme, while the fructose bisphosphatase-2 (FBPase-2) domain of the enzyme is activated. Once activated, fructose bisphosphatase-2 dephosphorylates F2,6BP. This results in the regenerations of F6P and a decline in PFK-1 activity due to lower cellular levels of its positive effector, F2,6BP. In addition to glucagon, the catecholamine hormone epinephrine can also cause cAMP levels in the liver to rise. The result of lower levels of liver fructose-2,6-bisphosphate is a decrease in activity of PFK1 and an increase in activity of fructose 1,6-bisphosphatase, favoring gluconeogenesis. This metabolic preference is in keeping with the role of the liver in maintaining blood glucose levels by generating glucose in response to hormones which indicate glucose is needed. During the well-fed state, glucagon levels decline and insulin levels increase, causing an increase in the amount of F 2,6BP present in the liver and an increase in hepatic glycolysis.

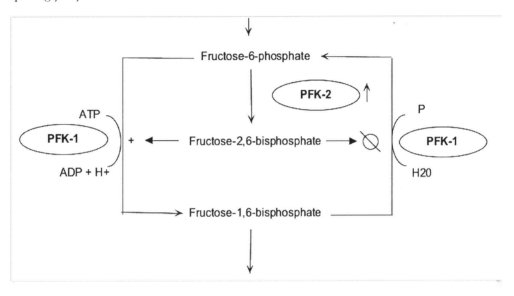

Figure 29.7: Regulation of PFK-1 by fructose-2,6-bisphosphate

PFK-1 is further regulated by ATP, AMP and citrate, the initial compound formed during the Krebs cycle by the condensation of acetyl-CoA and oxaloacetate. High levels of ATP inhibit PFK-1, while AMP and citrate are positive allosteric effectors of the enzyme.

The final step, and the final regulated step, of glycolysis is the conversion of PEP to pyruvate by pyruvate kinase. Pyruvate kinase is activated by its substrate, PEP, and by fructose 1,6-bisphosphate, an earlier intermediate in glycolysis, both of which enhance enzymatic activity when substrate flux through the pathway is high. Pyruvate kinase is negatively allosterically regulated by ATP and the amino acid alanine.

Liver pyruvate kinase is also indirectly regulated by glucagon and epinephrine. Both hormones cause elevation of cAMP and the resulting activation of protein which phosphorylates and inactivates liver pyruvate kinase. Muscle pyruvate kinase is not inhibited by protein kinase A and is thus insensitive to epinephrine. This is consistent with the body's need to inhibit glycolysis in the liver during fasting, but continue glycolysis in muscle.

When blood glucose levels increase, so too do insulin levels. Insulin activates the enzyme phosphoprotein phosphatase I, which dephosphorylates and activates pyruvate kinase. By this regulatory scheme, pyruvate kinase is inactive when the enzymes that catalyze the reverse of this reaction in gluconeogenesis—PEP carboxykinase and pyruvate carboxylase—are active, preventing a futile cycle.

E. REGULATION OF GLUCONEOGENESIS

The glycolytic enzymes hexokinase, phosphofructokinase, and pyruvate kinase are replaced in gluconeogenesis with glucose-6-phosphatase, fructose-1,6-bisphosphatase, and PEP carboxykinase. This system of reciprocal control allows glycolysis and gluconeogenesis to inhibit each other and prevent the formation of a futile cycle of glucose synthesis and immediate degradation.

Control of gluconeogenesis globally is determined mainly by circulating glucagon levels. When blood glucose is low and glucagon is released by the α-cells of pancreas, cAMP levels rise, increasing the activity of protein kinase A. When the targets of protein kinase A become phosphorylated, gluconeogenesis is stimulated and glycolysis is inhibited.

Glucagon exerts its effects through several mechanisms. Glucagon stimulates fructose-1,6-bisphosphatase and inhibits PFK-1 by decreasing fructose 2,6-bisphosphate through its interaction with PFK-2/FBPase-2. Glucagon also converts hepatic pyruvate kinase to its inactive, phosphorylated form, through its cAMP-induced stimulation of protein kinase A, thereby decreasing the rate of production of pyruvate. The PEP which accumulates can be instead shunted into the synthesis of glucose. Finally, glucagon induces increased expression of PEP carboxykinase, increasing the enzyme's availability when the pool of gluconeogenic substrates grows.

FBPase-1 is inhibited by AMP, which is present in increased concentration when the energy balance of the cell is low, and which activates PFK-1, resulting in the reciprocal up-regulation of glycolysis and down-regulation of gluconeogenesis. Conversely, FBPase-1 is activated when ATP levels are high.

For similar reasons, gluconeogenesis is also regulated by acetyl CoA's allosteric activation of pyruvate carboxylase during fasting. During such periods, rapid catabolism of fats in adipose tissue leads to the formation of more acetyl CoA than the liver can oxidize in the Krebs cycle. The acetyl CoA which accumulates activates the enzyme PDH kinase, inhibiting pyruvate dehydrogenase. This inhibition increases the flux of pyruvate through gluconeogenesis and decreases its rate of entry into the Krebs cycle.

F. PENTOSE PHOSPHATE PATHWAY

The pentose phosphate pathway, which is also known as the phosphogluconate pathway and as the hexose monophosphate shunt, is a cytosolic pathway that operates to produce the reducing equivalent NADPH and the pentose sugars necessary for nucleotide biosynthesis. NADPH is the major reductant involved in the biosynthesis of fatty acids, cholesterol and lipids. In addition to its importance in anabolic mechanisms, it also provides the cell a measure of protection against the damaging effects of reactive oxygen species generated from hydrogen peroxide. NADPH provides the reducing equivalents by which reduced glutathione may be regenerated by glutathione reductase, after glutathione peroxidase has converted hydrogen peroxide to water by oxidation of monomeric glutathione to glutathione disulfide.

The pentose phosphate pathway is often described as being divided into two phases: an initial oxidative phase, in which NADPH is synthesized, and a final non-oxidative phase. Pentose synthesis occurs during the non-oxidative phase.

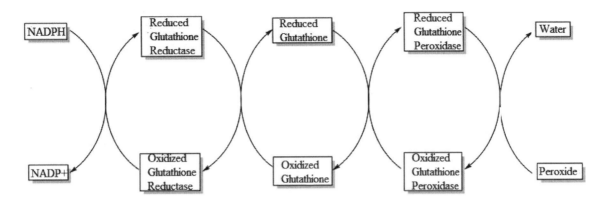

Figure 29.8: Diagram depicting the interaction of glutathione reductase, glutathione peroxidase and glutathione leading to the reduction of hydrogen peroxide to water. Eliminating hydrogen peroxide minimizes its subsequent conversion to oxygen radicals and reduces oxidative stress.

During the three-step oxidative phase, two molecules of $NADP^+$ are reduced to NADPH, while glucose-6-phosphate is oxidized producing ribulose 5-phosphate and carbon dioxide. The first molecule of NADPH is produced during the initial reaction of the process, in which glucose-6-phosphate is oxidized to 6-phosphoglucono-δ-lactone. The reaction is catalyzed by the enzyme glucose-6-phosphate dehydrogenase. The second molecule of NADPH is synthesized during the conversion of 6-phosphogluconate to ribulose 5-phosphate. The reactions of the oxidative phase are shown in Figure 32.9.

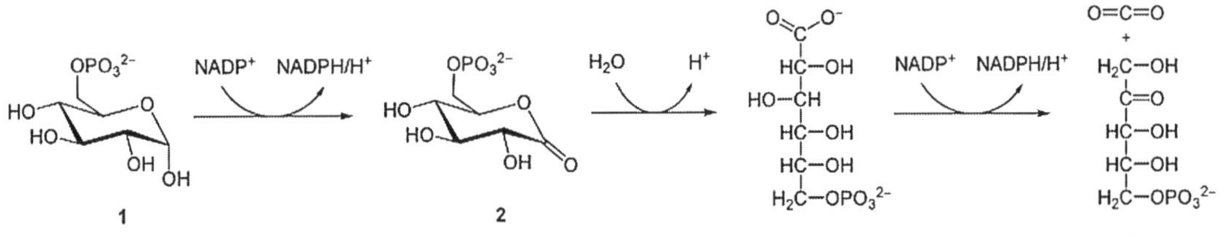

Figure 29.9: Reactions of the oxidative phase of pentose phosphate pathway.
Glucose-6-phosphate (1), 6-phosphoglucono-δ-lactone (2), 6-phosphogluconate (3), ribulose 5-phosphate (4)

All cells synthesizing nucleotides and nucleic acids proceed through the oxidative to the non-oxidative phase of the pentose phosphate pathway, in which 3- to 7-carbon containing sugars are interconverted. During the non-oxidative phase, ribulose-5-phosphate produced during the oxidative phase can be converted to ribose-5-phosphate—required for the synthesis of nucleotides—or to the glycolytic intermediates glyceraldehyde-3-phsophate or fructose-6-phosphate. The reactions of the non-oxidative phase are shown in Figure 29.10. If the cellular need for NADPH exceeds that for ribose-5-phosphate, the thiamine-dependent enzyme transketolase and the aldolase enzyme convert ribulose-5-phosphate to glyceraldehyde-3-phosphate and fructose-6-phosphate via the transfer of two- or three-carbon units. When the need for nucleotide precursors is great when compared to the cell's need for NADPH, ribose 5-phosphate can be synthesized from glyceraldehyde 3-phosphate and fructose-6-phosphate without passing through the oxidative phase of the reaction.

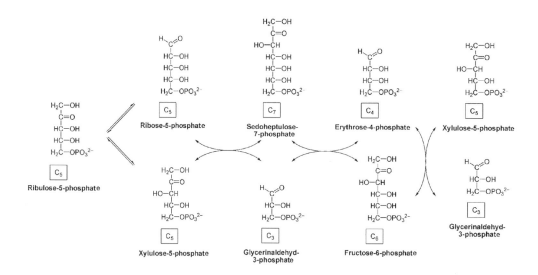

Figure 29.10: Reactions of the non-oxidative phase of the pentose phosphate pathway.

The rate limiting enzyme in the pentose phosphate pathway is glucose-6-phosphate dehydrogenase (G6PD), and the pathway is regulated primarily through this enzyme. G6PD is allosterically inhibited by NADPH and stimulated by $NADP^+$. Under most conditions, the ratio of $NADPH/NADP^+$ is high and the process is inhibited. When demand for NADPH increases, the cellular ratio of $NADPH/NADP^+$ decreases, and flux through the pathway dramatically increases. This makes the cytosol a highly-reducing environment. An NADPH-utilizing pathway forms $NADP^+$, which stimulates glucose-6-phosphate dehydrogenase to produce more NADPH. This step is also inhibited by acetyl CoA.

Chapter 29 Problems

Passage 29.1 (Questions 1-5)

Skeletal muscle consists of slow-twitch (Type I) and fast-twitch (Type II) fibers. Fast-twitch fibers predominate in muscles capable of short bursts of intense activity. Their cells have few if any mitochondria and rely principally on anaerobic metabolism. In contrast, slow-twitch fibers are designed to contract slowly and steadily and are enriched in the mitochondria required by their preferred mode of metabolism.

Fast and slow-twitch fibers were originally referred to as white and red fibers, respectively, because otherwise lightly-colored muscle tissue when enriched with mitochondria assumes a red color. However, in general fiber color is an unreliable indicator of muscle composition.

A physiology student studying skeletal muscle samples, labelled samples A and B, obtained from human sprinters noted that upon microscopic examination, the tissues appeared pale, as did the tissues taken from well-conditioned long-distance runners. In an attempt to reconcile this result by comparing skeletal muscle samples from other species, the student obtained samples of muscle tissue from ducks and geese—migratory birds that need a continuous energy supply to carry out sustained flight—labeled samples C and D. When the student viewed those samples under a microscope, he found that they were rich in slow-twitch fibers, contained abundant intracellular glycogen stores, and appeared red. When he observed samples taken from chickens and turkey—birds that fly only short distances—which he labeled samples E and F, he found that the samples appeared pale and were composed almost entirely of slow-twitch fibers.

When electrical current was applied to cultured goose and duck muscle cells, contraction was stimulated and a small decrease in pH was recorded. When the same procedure was performed on cultured chicken and turkey muscle cells, pH declined rapidly from 7.3 to less than 5.

1. What compound is produced by the reduction of the terminal electron acceptor in the metabolic pathway responsible for the decreased pH found in cultured turkey and chicken muscle cells?
   A. water
   B. lactic acid
   C. ethanol
   D. glucose

2. If the composition-function relationship of muscle cell samples taken from human runners is comparable to that in the birds examined by the student, the skeletal muscle cells of human sprinters are most likely composed of:
   A. predominately Type I fibers.
   B. predominately Type II fibers.
   C. an approximately equal amounts of Type I and Type II fibers.
   D. neither Type I nor Type II fibers.

3. Given passage information, in humans, which of the following enzymes are involved in regulated steps of a major metabolic pathway?
   I.   Hexokinase
   II. Glucose-6-phosphate isomerase
   III. Phosphoglycerate kinase
   IV. Phosphofructokinse-1
   V.   Pyruvate kinase

   A. III and IV only
   B. I, II and V only
   C. II, III and IV only
   D. I, IV and V only

4. When the student visualized samples E and F, they were LEAST likely characterized by:
   A. greater regions of vascularization than in samples C and D.
   B. tissue displaying a striated appearance on micrography.
   C. an inability to undergo anaerobic metabolism.
   D. a slow rate of muscular contraction when electrically stimulated.

5. In humans, the majority of glycogen, by mass, is stored in the cells of skeletal muscle and what other organ?
    A. kidneys
    B. brain
    C. liver
    D. heart

The following questions are NOT based on a descriptive passage.

6. In yeast, NAD^+ is regenerated immediately upon the reduction of what compound?
    A. pyruvate
    B. ethanol
    C. acetaldehyde
    D. lactic acid

7. During gluconeogenesis, the reverse of the reaction catalyzed by hexokinase in glycolysis is carried out by:
    A. fructose 1,6-bisphosphatase.
    B. glucose-6-phosphatase.
    C. PEP carboxykinase.
    D. phosphoglycerate mutase.

8. Which statement correctly describes a cellular response to an increase in blood glucagon concentration?
    A. Protein kinase A activity decreases in the liver.
    B. Phosphofructokinase-2 activity increases in the liver.
    C. Fructose 1,6-bisphosphate is stimulated in the liver.
    D. Pyruvate kinase activity is increased in the liver.

9. Which pair of thermodynamic parameters best describes the regulated reactions of glycolysis?
    A. $\Delta G > 0$ and $K_{eq} < 1$
    B. $\Delta G > 0$ and $K_{eq} = 1$
    C. $\Delta G < 0$ and $K_{eq} > 1$
    D. $\Delta G < 0$ and $K_{eq} = 1$

10. Increased AMP concentrations in the liver:
    A. inhibit gluconeogenesis and stimulate glycolysis.
    B. inhibit glycolysis and stimulate gluconeogenesis.
    C. stimulate gluconeogenesis and glycolysis.
    D. inhibits gluconeogenesis and glycolysis.

CHAPTER 30
Krebs Cycle

A. INTRODUCTION

The Krebs cycle – which is also known as the tricarboxylic acid cycle (TCA cycle) and as the citric acid cycle – generates high-energy compounds through the oxidation of fats, carbohydrates, and proteins in the mitochondrial matrix. During the sequence of Krebs cycle reactions, citrate, a three carbon (tricarboxylic) acid is synthesized from oxaloacetate and acetyl-CoA, reducing NAD^+ to NADH, producing carbon dioxide and regenerating citrate. The NADH generated then enters the oxidative phosphorylation pathway, ultimately to produce usable chemical energy in the form of ATP.

B. ACETYL-CoA PRODUCTION

Acetyl-CoA—the two-carbon substrate of the Krebs cycle—can be generated from a variety of sources. Pyruvate produced during glycolysis is under most circumstances the main source of acetyl CoA used by the Krebs cycle. It is also produced by the β-oxidation of fatty acids in the mitochondrial matrix, yielding acetyl-CoA directly, from the carbon backbone of ketogenic amino acids liberated during protein catabolism, and from ketone bodies and certain alcohols.

As mentioned in a previous chapter, the conversion of ketogenic amino acids (leucine and lysine are exclusively ketogenic, while isoleucine, phenylalanine, tryptophan, tyrosine and threonine are both ketogenic and glucogenic), to acetyl-CoA requires that they first undergo a reaction, referred to as a transamination reaction, in which the amine group of the amino acid is transferred to a keto acid, thus transforming the amino acid into a keto acid. These reactions require the enzyme pyridoxal 5'-phosphate (PLP), the activated form of vitamin B_6, and depend on available α-keto acids. The products of transamination reactions are usually alanine, aspartate and glutamate, since their corresponding α-keto acids are produced during fuel metabolism. The carbon skeleton of α-keto acids can subsequently be converted into acetyl-CoA.

When consumed, alcohols are oxidized by the enzymes alcohol dehydrogenase and acetaldehyde dehydrogenase. Some of the acetyl-CoA that is produced enters the Krebs cycle, but the majority is used in the synthesis of fats.

Ketone bodies, which can serve as an important alternative to glucose as a source of energy for cells of the body—especially in tissues of the brain and heart—during periods of fasting, are ordinarily synthesized from acetyl-CoA in a process referred to as ketogenesis. They can also be broken down to form acetyl-CoA when levels of acetyl-CoA in the cell are low.

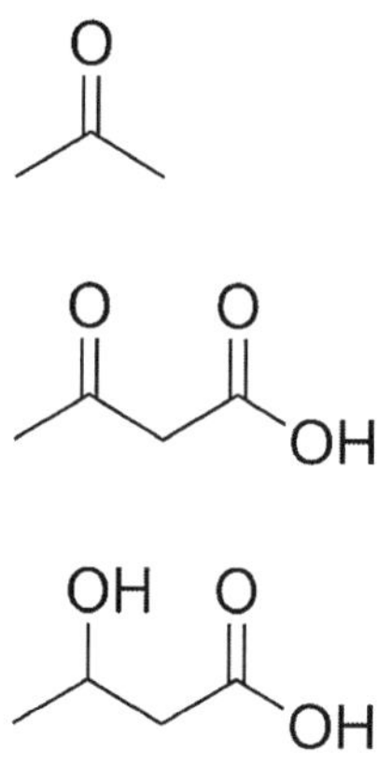

Figure 30.1: Chemical structures of the three endogenous human ketone bodies. β-hydroxybutyric acid (bottom) and acetoacetic acid (middle) are used as a source of energy in the heart and brain, while acetone (top) is a breakdown product of acetoacetic acid.

Before pyruvate—the end product of glycolysis and the major source of acetyl-CoA under most conditions—can enter the Krebs cycle, it must be transported into the mitochondria from the cytosol. The transport of pyruvate into the mitochondria is accomplished by the transport protein pyruvate translocase. After entering the cycle, pyruvate decarboxylation occurs, irreversibly producing acetyl CoA—the two-carbon substrate of the Krebs cycle—NADH and carbon dioxide. This irreversible reaction confines acetyl CoA to the mitochondria unless, under certain circumstances, it is transported from the cell via the citrate shuttle. The pyruvate decarboxylation reaction is catalyzed by the multi-enzyme pyruvate dehydrogenase complex (PDH)—the major cellular producer of acetyl CoA. PDH is a complex of three physically-associated enzymes, each of which catalyzes part of the overall reaction of PDH, shown in Figure 30.2. Intermediates of the process are transferred between the three enzymes—pyruvate dehydrogenase, dihydrolipoyl transacetylase, and dihydrolipoyl dehydrogenase, referred to as E1, E2, and E3 , respectively—without being released.

Collectively, the PDH complex requires five coenzymes. E1 and E2 require coenzymes to act as carriers of reaction intermediates. E1, which oxidizes pyruvate and produces CO_2, requires the coenzyme thiamine pyrophosphate (vitamin B1), as well as the magnesium ion. E2, which oxidizes the remaining two-carbon molecule, requires the oxidant lipoid acid, and CoA, to which the resulting acetyl group is transferred. E3 requires both FAD and NAD^+ to act as oxidants for the intermediates of the reaction. Specifically, FAD is used to re-oxidize lipoid acid. The $FADH_2$ produced in this reaction then transfers electrons to NAD^+. The NADH formed then passes the electrons which it receives from the complex into the oxidative phosphorylation pathway.

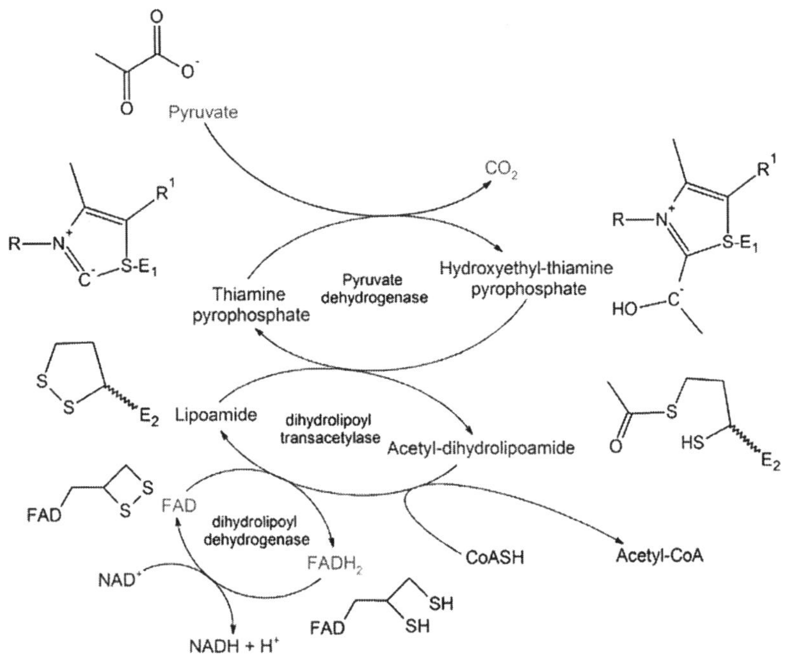

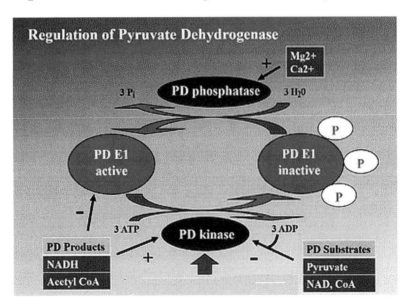

Figure 30.2: Reactions of the pyruvate dehydrogenase (PDH) complex

PDH is regulated by pyruvate dehydrogenase kinase (PDK) and pyruvate dehydrogenase phosphatase (PDP), two regulatory enzymes that are permanently bound within the complex. PDK is activated by an increase in the ratio of the concentrations of ATP/ADP, NADH/NAD$^+$ or of acetyl-CoA/CoA, thereby "turning off" the PDH complex in the presence of increased amounts of high-energy signal. Conversely, when pyruvate—which is a potent inhibitor of PDK—levels are high, E1, the rate limiting enzyme of the complex, is maximally active.

PDK phosphorylates and inactivates E1, halting substrate flow through the PDH complex. E1 can be dephosphorylated, and the complex as a whole re-activated, by PDP. PDP is subject to regulation by its allosteric activators, the Ca^{2+} and Mg^{2+} ions. The scheme or PDH regulation is shown in Figure 30.3.

Figure 30.3: Regulation of E$_1$ (pyruvate dehydrogenase) of the pyruvate dehydrogenase (PDH) complex by pyruvate dehydrogenase kinase (PD kinase; PDK) and pyruvate dehydrogenase phosphatase (PD phosphatase; PDP)

C. REACTIONS AND SUBSTRATES OF THE KREBS CYCLE

Acetyl-CoA, produced by the oxidation of carbohydrates, fats and proteins, entering the Krebs cycle is further oxidized within the mitochondrial matrix during the reactions of the cycle. These reactions drive reduction of three equivalents of NAD^+ to three equivalents of NADH, and one equivalent of FAD to $FADH_2$. It additionally yields one equivalent of GTP, synthesized from an equal number of equivalents of GDP and inorganic phosphate. NADH and $FADH_2$ produced during the Krebs cycle can then enter the oxidative phosphorylation pathway, generating ATP.

The reactions of the citric acid cycle begin with the synthesis of a six-carbon compound, citrate, from an acetyl group donated by acetyl-CoA, and the compound oxaloacetate—a product of the previous turn of the Krebs cycle. In the subsequent reactions of the cycle, two molecules of CO_2 are lost from citrate. The carbons lost as CO_2 originated from carbons which were previously contained in oxaloacetate. Carbons contained in acetyl-CoA are integrated into oxaloacetate and are lost as CO_2 only during subsequent turns of the cycle—provided that the intermediate of the cycle in which they are contained is not shunted from the cycle to serve as a carbon backbone during an anabolic process. At the end of each cycle, the four-carbon oxaloacetate molecule is regenerated and participates in the next turn of the Krebs cycle.

♦ The synthesis of citrate from acetyl-CoA, oxaloacetate and water is carried out irreversibly by the enzyme citrate synthase.

♦ Citrate is then reversibly isomerized to form isocitrate in a reaction catalyzed by the enzyme aconitase.

♦ The isocitrate produced is oxidized and decarboxylated, forming the first of three molecules of NADH produced during the cycle, along with the five-carbon molecule α-ketoglutarate and carbon dioxide. The reaction is catalyzed by one of the rate-limiting enzymes of the Krebs cycle, isocitrate dehydrogenase.

♦ A second molecule of NADH, as well as carbon dioxide and the four-carbon molecule succinyl CoA, is produced from α-ketoglutarate, CoA, and NAD^+. This irreversible conversion is catalyzed by the multi-molecular aggregate of three enzymes, α-ketoglutarate dehydrogenase, the structure of which is very similar to that of the pyruvate dehydrogenase (PDH) complex.

♦ The high-energy thioester bond of succinyl-CoA is then cleaved by the enzyme succinate thiokinase (also known as succinyl-CoA synthetase), producing succinate. The reaction is coupled to the substrate-level phosphorylation of GDP to GTP. GTP can be converted to ATP by the action of nucleoside diphosphate kinase.

♦ Succinate is oxidized to fumarate by the enzyme succinate dehydrogenase, which is embedded in the inner mitochondrial matrix, and functions as Complex II of the electron transport chain. FAD, a prosthetic group which is tightly bound to succinate dehydrogenase, is reduced to $FADH_2$ during the reaction.

♦ Fumarate is hydrated to L-malate in the easily reversible reaction catalyzed by fumarase (also known as fumarate hydratase).

♦ L-Malate is oxidized to oxaloacetate, forming the third molecule of NADH produced during the Krebs cycle. This final reaction of the cycle is catalyzed by malate dehydrogenase. While the standard free energy change of the reaction actually favors malate, the strongly exergonic citrate synthase reaction pushes the malate dehydrogenase reaction in the direction of oxaloacetate by rapidly removing the product of the reaction.

The reactions of the Krebs cycle are summarized in Figure 30.4.

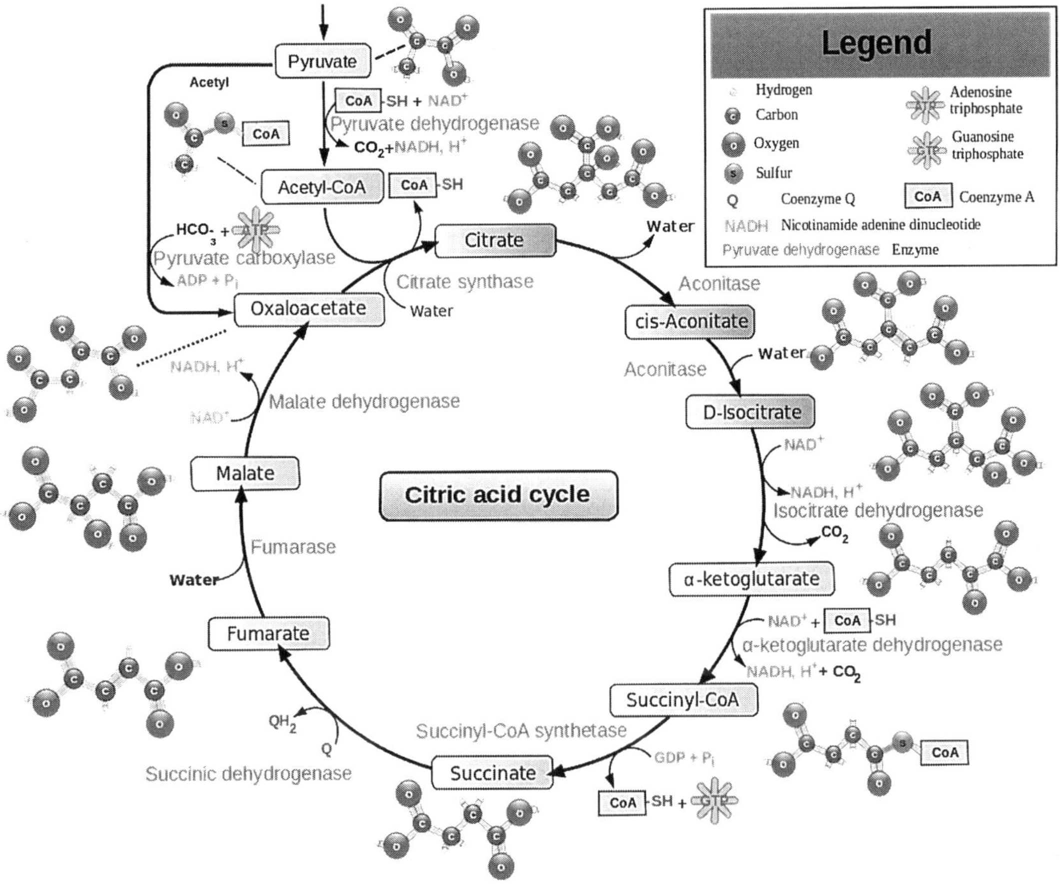

Figure 30.4: Reactions of the Krebs cycle

D. REGULATION OF THE KREBS CYCLE

The Krebs cycle is regulated by product inhibition and the availability of its substrates at four control points: the reactions catalyzed by pyruvate dehydrogenase, citrate synthase, isocitrate dehydrogenase, and α-ketoglutarate dehydrogenase. NADH, a product of the dehydrogenase-catalyzed reactions of the Krebs cycle (other than succinate dehydrogenase) inhibits pyruvate dehydrogenase, isocitrate dehydrogenase, and α-ketoglutarate dehydrogenase, as well as citrate synthase. Additionally, acetyl-CoA inhibits pyruvate dehydrogenase, and succinyl-CoA inhibits α-ketoglutarate dehydrogenase and citrate synthase.

Calcium also regulates metabolic flux through the Krebs cycle. Mitochondrial matrix calcium levels become elevated during active cellular respiration, and, as discussed earlier in the chapter, calcium ions activate PDP which in turn activates the (PDH) complex. In addition to PDP, Ca^{2+} also activates isocitrate dehydrogenase and α-ketoglutarate dehydrogenase, thereby increasing net flux through the Krebs cycle.

Citrate further regulates the cycle, indirectly, through its feedback inhibition of the glycolytic enzyme phosphofructokinase (PFK-1), decreasing glycolytic flux when substrate is present in elevated quantity in the Krebs cycle. The major control points and the effector molecules at those points are shown in Figure 30.5.

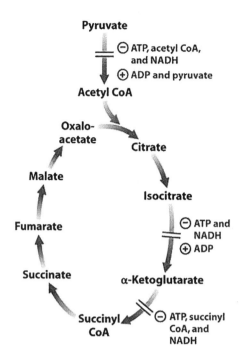

Figure 30.5: Selected control points of the Krebs cycle

Chapter 30 Problems

Passage 30.1 (Questions 1-5)

An early biochemist performing a series of experiments to study cellular respiration noted that, as shown in Table 1, the oxygen consumed by respiring cell samples changed after the addition of certain chemical substances.

Table 1: Results of Experiment 1

Substance Added	Oxygen Consumed (μmol)
None	670
Fumarate	1290
Citrate	1105
Succinate	1520
Malate	1340

He noted that at the conclusion of the reaction, the concentrations of all three reactants were approximately equal to their concentration at the start of the experiment.

The biochemist hypothesized that the substances were intermediates in a biochemical reaction pathway. In order to further clarify the role of the substances, the biochemist added a chemical inhibitor of the reaction which he believed converted succinate into fumarate. At the end of the experiment, he recorded the following results:

Table 2: Results of Experiment 2

Substance Added	Succinate Produced (μL)
None	20.5
Citrate	64.5
Citrate plus inhibitor	387.0

1. The chemical inhibitor chosen by the biochemist interfered with an enzyme embedded in the inner mitochondrial membrane. Which of the following compounds is produced during the reaction catalyzed by the enzyme?
   A. H_2O
   B. NADH
   C. $FADH_2$
   D. CO_2

2. It was later hypothesized that the substances listed in Table 1 formed a biochemical reaction cycle linked metabolically to glycolysis. What additional experimental finding would best support such a hypothesis?
   A. The intracellular concentration of malate decreases when a fumarase inhibitor is added.
   B. Treatment with glucose increases the rate of citrate production.
   C. When pyruvate and oxaloacetate are added, citrate accumulation increases.
   D. When the chemical conversion of succinate is inhibited, oxaloacetate concentrations increase.

3. Assuming that oxygen consumption is directly linked to the rate of production of reduced cofactors during cellular respiration, what might account for the differences in oxygen consumption shown in Table 1?
   A. addition of citrate increases the activity of enzymes involved in its oxidation
   B. conversion of fumarate is a regulated step of the pathway in which it is involved
   C. the reactions of citrate and fumarate are freely reversible under biological conditions
   D. only the reactions of succinate and malate produce electrons passed to the oxidative phosphorylation pathway

4. In evaluating the experimental evidence presented in the passage, which claim, as stated, would NOT be supported?
   A. Table 1 supports the conclusion that the substances added in Experiment 1 may act as catalysts of the reactions of cellular respiration.
   B. The observation that the concentrations of substances added in Experiment 1 did not change supports the conclusion that the substances may act as intermediates of the reactions of cellular respiration.
   C. Table 2 supports the conclusion that the substances added in Experiment 1 may act as catalysts of the reactions of cellular respiration.
   D. Table 2 supports the conclusion that the substances added in Experiment 1 may act as intermediates of the reactions of cellular respiration.

5. If present in the sample, what enzyme could NOT be inhibited by NADH produced by the reactions of Experiment 1?
   A. succinate dehydrogenase
   B. isocitrate dehydrogenase
   C. pyruvate dehydrogenase
   D. α-ketoglutarate dehydrogenase

The following questions are NOT based on a descriptive passage.

6. The Krebs cycle occurs in the:
   A. nucleoplasm.
   B. cytosol.
   C. mitochondrial intermembrane space.
   D. mitochondrial matrix.

7. The metabolism of ingested alcohols produces significant amounts of the coenzyme NADH. Why does very little of the acetyl-CoA produced from the oxidation of alcohol enter the Krebs cycle?
   A. The acetyl-CoA produced by the reaction inhibits the enzymes of the Krebs cycle.
   B. Alcohol dehydrogenase is subject to feedback inhibition by NADH.
   C. NADH inhibits several enzymes of the Krebs cycle.
   D. The cellular demand for the products of the Krebs cycle is low.

8. Which of the following would you most expect to be a symptom of an inborn deficiency of the enzyme pyruvate dehydrogenase?
   A. over-activity of the citric acid cycle
   B. increased triglyceride synthesis
   C. a buildup of lactic acid
   D. an uncoupling of the electron transport chain and ATP synthesis.

9. Fluoroacetate is a potent inhibitor of the enzyme aconitase. A build-up of what Krebs cycle intermediate would you expect as a result of exposure to fluoroacetate?
   A. fumarate
   B. succinyl-CoA
   C. citrate
   D. isocitrate

10. If it were determined that the ATP yield of a molecule of $FADH_2$ in the electron transport chain is 2 ATP/ $FADH_2$, and that the yield of NADH is 3 ATP/NADH, then how many ATP would be produced from the NADH and $FADH_2$ synthesized during a single turn of the Krebs cycle?
    A. 5
    B. 9
    C. 11
    D. 14

CHAPTER 31
Oxidative Phosphorylation

A. INTRODUCTION

As already discussed, the metabolic intermediates of the oxidation of biological substrates donate electrons to the coenzymes NAD^+ and FAD. The reduced coenzymes formed can then donate the electrons which they contain to the specialized set of electron carriers, collectively referred to as the electron transport chain, located in the inner mitochondrial membrane. The electrons from NADH and succinate-bound $FADH_2$ passing through the electron transport chain eventually transfer to oxygen, which is reduced to water. The enzymes of the electron transport chain are a series of electron donors and acceptors. Each electron donor passes electrons to an acceptor with greater reduction potential. That acceptor, in turns, donates those electrons to another acceptor, in a process that continues from species of lesser to greater electron affinity until the transferred electrons are passed to oxygen, the terminal electron acceptor in the chain and the species with the most positive reduction potential. Transfer of electrons between donor and acceptor is an exergonic process, the energy of which is harnessed to pump protons present in the mitochondrial matrix across the intermembrane space, thereby generating an electrochemical gradient across the inner mitochondrial membrane. When protons flow back across the membrane through the ATP synthase complex, the energy stored in the electrochemical gradient is used to perform mechanical work. This work results in the synthesis of ATP from ADP and inorganic phosphate in a process known as oxidative phosphorylation.

A small number of the oxygen molecules reduced during the electron transport chain are not reduced fully, resulting in the formation of the free-radical superoxide, a highly reactive molecule that contributes to cellular oxidative stress. Oxidative stress has been implicated in a number of processes, including specific disease-associated conditions and aging.

That energy not harnessed and stored in the bonds of ATP can be used to perform other functions, including the translocation of Ca^{2+} into mitochondria, or is lost as heat.

As electrons are transferred between carriers down the electron transport chain, much of the energy released is harnessed to drive the production of ATP in a process called oxidative phosphorylation. The energy not captured and transferred to the bonds of ATP is used to drive the translocation of Ca^{2+} into mitochondria or is lost as heat.

B. ELECTRON TRANSPORT CHAIN

The mitochondria contain four inner membrane-bound complexes. Three of these complexes are proton transporters, and the complexes themselves are connected by lipid- and water-soluble electron carriers. The reactions of the electron transport chain are depicted in Figure 31.1.

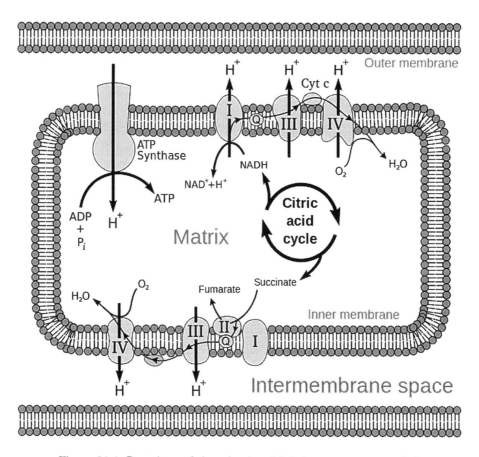

Figure 31.1: Reactions of the mitochondrial electron transport chain

Electrons arriving from the Krebs cycle, or produced in other oxidative pathways, in the form of NADH are first transferred to Complex I of the electron transport chain, NADH dehydrogenase (also known as NADH:ubiquinone oxidoreductase). The two electrons removed from NADH are transferred to ubiquinone (Q) as Complex I translocates four protons (H$^+$) across the inner mitochondrial membrane to the intermembrane space. Once reduced, ubiquinone becomes ubiquinol (QH$_2$). Because ubiquinone is a quinone derivative with a large, hydrophobic isoprenoid tail, it is lipid-soluble and can freely diffuse within the membrane, delivering electrons to Complex III of the electron transport chain.

Complex I is the largest of the respiratory complexes, containing 44 separate polypeptide chains encoded by both the nuclear and mitochondrial genome. Of particular importance is the prosthetic group FMN, and eight iron-sulfur (Fe-S) clusters. Within Complex I, NADH is oxidized to NAD$^+$, and the two electrons removed are transferred in a single step to flavin mononucleotide (FMN), forming FMNH$_2$. The FMNH$_2$ formed in this single-step reduction is then re-oxidized in a two-step process through a semiquinone intermediate. Each electron is transferred individually from FMNH$_2$ to a Fe-S cluster, and from the Fe-S cluster to the coenzyme ubiquinone (Q). Electron flow through Complex I is depicted in Figure 31.3.

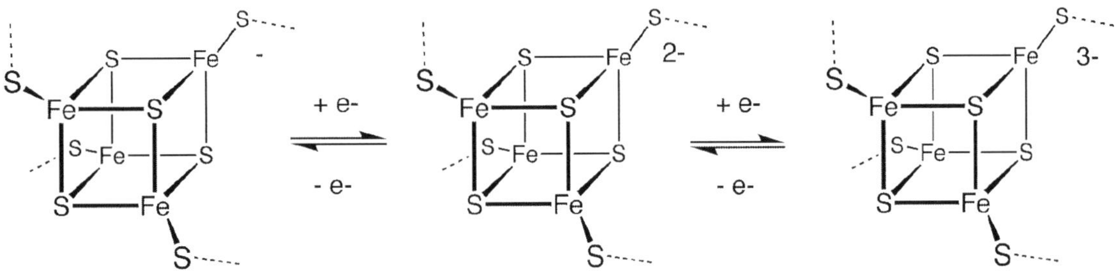

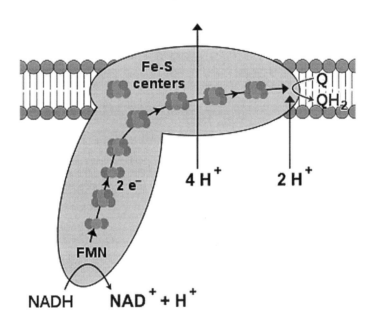

Figure 31.2: Structure and reactivity of the 4 Fe-4 S clusters of the Fe-S centers of Complex I. The Fe centers of each are further coordinated within the protein by cysteinyl ligands. (Note: Complexes II and III also contain Fe-S centers).

Transfer of the first electron results in the free-radical (semiquinone) form of Q, and transfer of the second electron reduces the semiquinone form to the ubiquinol form, QH_2. The reduction of ubiquinone to ubiquinol is shown in Figure 31.4. It is during this electron transfer from Complex I to coenzyme Q that four protons are pumped from the mitochondrial matrix into the intermembrane space.

Figure 31.3: Reactions of Complex I, NADH dehydrogenase.

Coenzyme Q accepts electrons not only from Complex I, but also from Complex II (the Krebs cycle enzyme succinate dehydrogenase), glycerophosphate dehydrogenase (a substrate shuttle for the transport of electrons from reduced coenzymes across the inner mitochondrial matrix), and from acyl-CoA dehydrogenase (an enzyme that produces $FADH_2$ in the initial step of the β-oxidation of fatty acids). Electrons passed directly to ubiquinone, rather than passing first through Complex I, do not cause protons to be pumped into the intermembrane space until their passage through Complex II and thus contribute less energy to the overall process of electron transport.

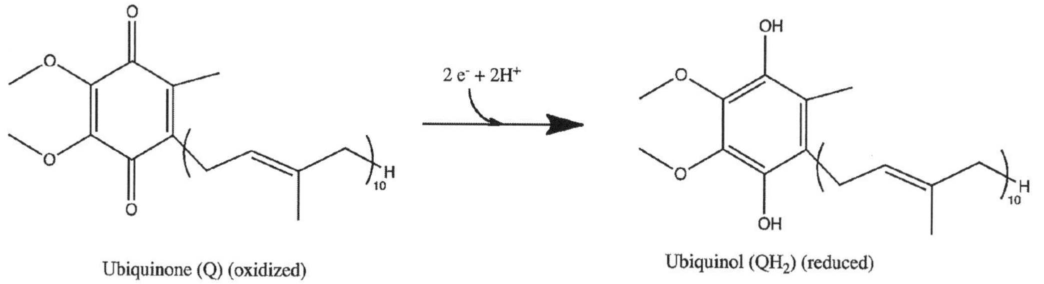

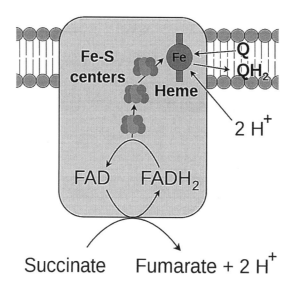

Figure 31.4: The reduction of ubiquinone (Q) to ubiquinol (QH$_2$)

Complex II, succinate dehydrogenase, is the only enzyme that participates directly in both the Krebs cycle and the electron transport chain. The multi-subunit enzyme contains a bound flavin adenine dinucleotide (FAD) cofactor, Fe-S centers, and a heme group. Electron flow through the complex is shown in Figure 34.5.

Figure 31.5: Complex II, succinate dehydrogenase. (Note: the bottom of the diagram represents the mitochondrial matrix; the top of the diagram represents the intermembrane space.)

The remaining members of the electron transport chain are cytochromes. Each cytochrome is composed of a heme group, which is reversibly converted from the ferric (Fe^{3+}) ion to the ferrous ion (Fe^{2+}) when functioning as an electron carrier. In Complex III, also known as the cytochrome bc1 complex , electrons removed from ubiquinol are transferred to heme, forming cytochrome c as part of the Q cycle. In the Q cycle, two molecules of ubiquinol react, transferring four total electrons to the complex. Two electrons pass from the ubiquinols, near the intermembrane space-facing portion of the complex, to a single molecule of ubiquinone near the mitochondrial matrix-facing portion, passing through heme B_L and B_H. The other two electrons removed from the ubiquinol molecules are shuttled through an Fe-S center, and cytochrome c_1, forming reduced cytochrome c. During the transfer of electrons through Complex III, four protons are translocated into the intermembrane space.

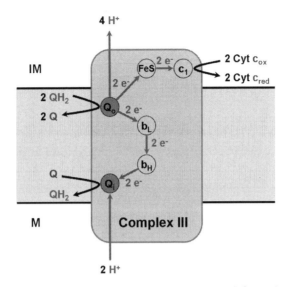

Figure 31.6A: Illustration of the reactions of Complex III

The final protein complex of the electron transport chain is Complex IV—cytochrome oxidase c, sometimes called cytochrome a_3. Four electrons are removed from four molecules of cytochrome c and transferred to a molecule of oxygen, generating two moles of water during the reactions of the complex. As a consequence of the electron transfer, four protons are removed from the mitochondrial matrix, two of which are transported to the intermembrane space.

The complex itself is composed of two heme molecules, cytochrome a and cytochrome a_3, and two copper centers, Cu_A and Cu_B. After cytochrome c is reduced in complex III, it associates with Complex IV near the Cu_A binuclear center. After passing its electron to the binuclear center, cytochrome c is re-oxidized to its Fe^{3+}-containing form, and the reduced Cu_A binuclear center further transfers its electron to cytochrome a. The electron is in turn passed to the cytochrome a_3-Cu_B binuclear center, the site of reduction of molecular oxygen, the terminal electron acceptor of the electron transport chain, to water.

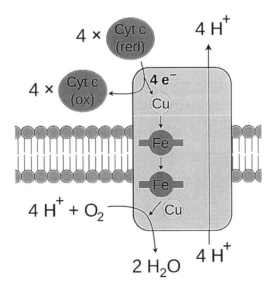

Figure 31.6B: Complex IV, cytochrome c oxidase

Complex V, also known as ATP synthase, harnesses the energy stored in the proton gradient established via electron transport to drive the synthesis of ATP from ADP and phosphate.

ATP synthase is a large, multi-subunit protein. The F_0 domain of the enzyme is embedded within the inner mitochondrial matrix and is surrounded by a ring of c subunits and a proton channel. The head of the protein contains three α and three β subunits, all of which bind nucleotides, while the stalk consists of only a γ subunit. A rod-like subunit anchors the α and β subunits into the enzyme's base. ATP is synthesized at catalytic sites in the β subunits of the F_1 domain, as protons move through ion channel of the F_0 domain. The mechanism of ATP synthesis is currently believed to involve the active site of a β subunit cycling between three states. In the "open" state, ADP and phosphate enter the active site. In the subsequent "loose" state, the protein loosely binds the molecules. The enzyme then undergoes a change of conformation which brings the molecules together in the "tight" state of the enzyme, binding the now-synthesized ATP with great affinity. When the active site returns next to its open state, ATP is released and new ADP and inorganic phosphate are bound, beginning the cycle anew. The mechanism can be described as a form of chemiosmotic coupling, allowing the chemical energy of the electrochemical proton gradient to be used in the synthesis of ATP.

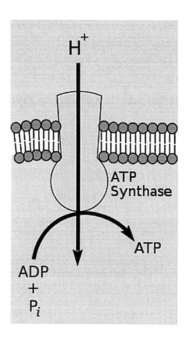

Figure 31.7: Function of the ATP synthase complex during oxidative phosphorylation, illustrating the direction of proton movement from the intermembrane space (top) to the matrix (bottom).

The movement of ions through the synthase complex is driven by two factors: diffusion and electrostatic forces. Protons diffuse down their concentration gradient, flowing from higher concentration in the intermembrane space to lower concentration in the matrix. Protons, being positively charged, also diffuse to regions of lower electrical potential within the matrix, driven from the intermembrane space by its greater concentration of positive charge.

The inner mitochondrial membrane (a lipid bilayer) helps to maintain the electrochemical gradient by acting as an ion barrier. When protons spontaneously flow through the ATP synthase ion channel, it is possible to define a proton-motive force (PMF) created by the electrochemical gradient. It is a measure of the electrical and chemical potential energies stored by the proton concentration and charge gradients across the membrane. The electrical gradient is a consequence of the charge separation across the membrane.

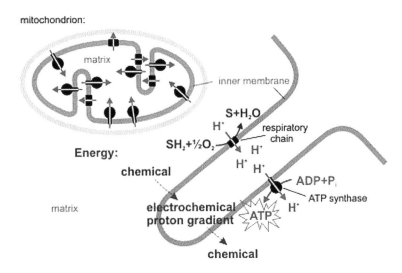

Figure 31.8: Depiction of the manner in which energy is converted in mitochondria. It is accomplished by the chemiosmotic coupling of the chemical energy of redox reactions in the electron transport to the production of ATP in oxidative phosphorylation at the ATP synthase complex.

C. REGULATION

The rates of the electron transport chain and of the Krebs cycle are closely related in a process known as respiratory control. When sufficient oxygen is present, electron transport through the electron transport chain depends upon the availability of ADP. When ADP accumulates, the amount of ATP in the cell increases. An increase in the ADP/ATP ratio activates the Krebs cycle enzyme isocitrate dehydrogenase, accelerating the rate at which NADH and $FADH_2$ are produced and fed into the pathway of electron transport. When the availability of molecular oxygen is limited, the rates at which electrons from NADH and $FADH_2$ can be delivered to it decreases. Accordingly, the concentration of both reduced cofactors increases, feeding back on the Krebs cycle, decreasing its rate.

D. MEMBRANE TRANSPORT SYSTEMS

For the same reason that the inner mitochondrial membrane is impermeable to protons, it is also impermeable to most other charged substances. While the outer mitochondrial membrane is permeable to most species, in order for molecules to pass from the intermembrane space to the mitochondrial matrix, specific transport proteins present in the inner mitochondrial membrane are required.

An adenine nucleotide transporter imports one molecule of ADP into the mitochondria, where it is used, from the cytosol in exchange for the export of one molecule of ATP from the matrix, its site of synthesis during mitochondrial oxidative phosphorylation, into the cytosol. A phosphate transporter is responsible for the transport of inorganic phosphate into the cytosol.

Reducing equivalents produced in the cytosol also require a means of transport across the inner mitochondrial membrane into the matrix. One such means is the glycerol-3-phosphate shuttle. The cytoplasmic enzyme glycerol-3-phosphate dehydrogenase (cGPD) converts dihydroxyacetone phosphate to glycerol 3-phosphate while oxidizing one molecule of NADH to NAD^+ in the reaction shown in Figure 31.9.

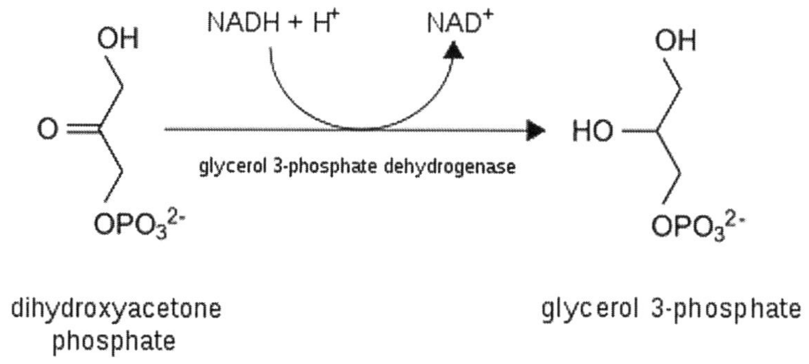

dihydroxyacetone
phosphate

glycerol 3-phosphate

Figure 31.9: Conversion of dihydroxyacetone phosphate (DHAP)
to glycerol 3-phosphate (G3P) by cytoplasmic glycerol 3-phosphate dehydrogenase (cGPD).

Glycerol-3-phosphate is then reconverted to dihydroxyacetone phosphate by membrane-bound mitochondrial glycerol-3-phosphate dehydrogenase 2 (GPDH-M). The re-oxidation of glycerol-3-phosphate is this time tied to the reduction of one enzyme-bound flavin adenine dinucleotide (FAD) molecule to $FADH_2$. $FADH_2$ then reduces ubiquinone to ubiquinol, whereas the shuttle electrons are passed into the electron transport chain. The complete shuttle cycle is shown in Figure 31.10.

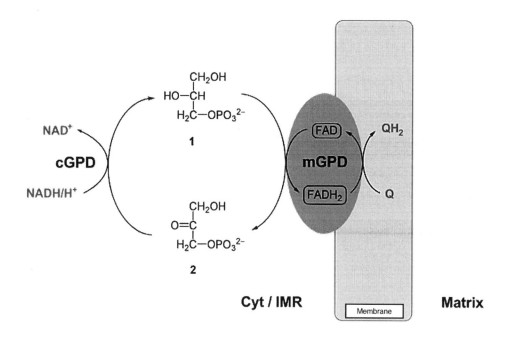

Figure 31.10: Glycerol 3-phosphate shuttle system

Like the glycerol-3-phosphate shuttle, the malate-aspartate shuttle also allows NADH synthesized during glycolysis to contribute to the oxidative phosphorylation of ADP to ATP.

The shuttle integrates the function of four enzymes: malate dehydrogenase, aspartate aminotransferase, the malate-α-ketoglutarate antiporter and the glutamate-aspartate antiporter in the inner membrane. Two forms of malate dehydrogenase—mitochondrial malate dehydrogenase and cytosolic malate dehydrogenase—are used in the shuttle. Cytosolic malate dehydrogenase (present in the intermembrane space) catalyzes the oxidation of NADH to produce malate and NAD$^+$ from oxaloacetate. The malate-α-ketoglutarate antiporter then transfers the malate into the mitochondrial matrix in exchange for alpha-ketoglutarate from the matrix. After malate is imported into the mitochondrial matrix, it is oxidized by mitochondrial malate dehydrogenase into oxaloacetate, while NAD$^+$ is reduced with two electrons, reforming NADH and releasing a proton. The oxaloacetate generated within the matrix cannot be transported back into the cytosol directly. Instead, it is converted to aspartate in a transamination reaction catalyzed by mitochondrial aspartate aminotransferase. The amino group transferred to oxaloacetate is provided by glutamate, which is transformed into α-ketoglutarate during the reaction.

The second antiporter of the shuttle system (the glutamate-aspartate antiporter) transports glutamate from the cytosol to the matrix and aspartate from the matrix to the cytosol. Once exported to the cytosol, aspartate is converted to oxaloacetate by cytosolic aspartate aminotransferase. A depiction of the full shuttle system is shown in Figure 31.11.

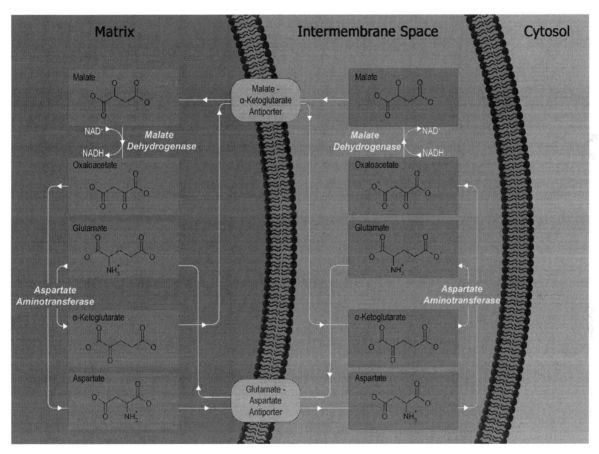

Figure 31.11: Illustration of the malate-aspartate shuttle system

Since the malate-aspartate shuttle regenerates NADH within the mitochondrial matrix, the number of ATPs produced from the NADH generated by glycolysis in the cytosol is maximized—using the shuttle, approximately 3 molecules of ATP are produced per molecule of NADH, ultimately resulting in a net yield of 38 ATP produced from a glucose molecule metabolized aerobically. In contrast, the glycerol 3-phosphate shuttle, which reduces FAD$^+$ to produce FADH$_2$, donates electrons from FADH$_2$ directly to the quinone pool in the electron transport chain, bypassing Complex I, and is therefore able to generate only 2 ATPs per FADH$_2$ molecule generated in glycolysis.

E. APOPTOSIS AND OXIDATIVE STRESS

Molecular oxygen is well suited to serving as the terminal electron acceptor of the electron transport chain because it is a strong oxidant. When it is reduced, the transfer of four electrons and four protons converts a molecule of oxygen into the harmless respiratory by-product, water. However, incomplete reduction—the transfer of one or two electrons – produces reactive oxygen species. These reactive oxygen species, namely superoxide or peroxide anions, as well their reaction products, such as the hydroxyl radical, are highly reactive and potentially quite harmful to the cell because of their ability to act as oxidants of proteins, lipids and nucleic acids. The most deleterious effects of reactive oxygen species are on DNA. DNA damage due to oxidative stress is similar to damage due to ionizing radiation, and has been implicated in the development of cancer and the accumulation of age-related cellular damage.

Oxidative phosphorylation is a major source of reactive oxygen compounds under normal conditions. While the cytochrome c oxidase complex of the electron transport chain is an efficient reductant of water, the extremely large number of electrons passing through the chain still given rise to a small number of incompletely reduced superoxide anions and peroxides. Additionally, during the reduction of coenzyme Q in complex III, a highly reactive ubisemiquinone free radical is formed as an intermediate of the Q cycle. This unstable species can lead to the direct transfer of an electron to oxide, forming the superoxide anion. Cells containing reducing compounds referred to as antioxidant systems, which include vitamins C and E, and the enzymes catalase, superoxide dismutase, and peroxidases, neutralize the reaction products and prevent damage to cells.

While the cell is able to overcome relatively small perturbations due to oxidative stress, more severe oxidation can trigger apoptosis—a process of programmed cell death. The process of apoptosis may be initiated through the so-called intrinsic or mitochondrial-mediated pathway. In this pathway, pores are formed in the mitochondria and cytochrome c is released into the cytoplasm. Once in the cytoplasm, cytochrome c associates with pro-apoptotic factors to form the multi-protein apoptosome complex. Formation of the complexes leads to the cascading activation of a series of cysteine proteases called caspases, beginning with the activation of caspase 9. Activation of key proteins within the cascade leads to the morphological and biochemical changes characteristic of programmed cell death.

Chapter 31 Problems
Passage 31.1 (Questions 1-4)

Investigators researching the relationship between the protein components of mitochondria and the mechanism of ATP synthesis conducted two experiments.

Experiment 1

The investigators immersed isolated mitochondria in a solution at pH 8 with no metabolizable substrate present. After several minutes, the pH of all compartments of the mitochondria, including the matrix and intermembrane space, equalized. The same mitochondria were then moved into an otherwise identical, but acidic, solution of much lower pH. The condition quickly established a proton gradient across the inner mitochondrial membrane. Within several minutes, the investigators detected a sustained increase in ATP concentration within the mitochondria.

Experiment 2

The researchers created artificial vesicles that when immersed in an acidic solution, demonstrated no significant change in the pH of the compartment surrounded by the membrane (Figure 1 (a)). When the vesicles were engineered to include the prokaryotic integral membrane protein bacteriorhodospin (Figure 1 (b)), a light-activated proton pump, and were placed in a solution of neutral pH and exposed to light, the pH within the vesicles decreased. When the investigators further modified the vesicles to include the enzyme ATP synthase from the mitochondria of cow cells (Figure 1 (c)), ATP formed within the vesicles.

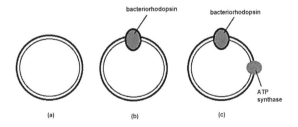

Figure 1: Depiction of the artificial vesicle (a), artificial vesicle containing bacteriorhodopsin (b), and artificial vesicle containing bacteriorhodopsin and ATP synthase (c) used in Experiment 2.

1. Which of the depictions below best represents the reaction condition must likely to exist immediately before the synthesis of ATP by the engineered vesicle?

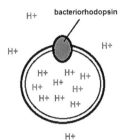

A.

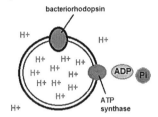

B.

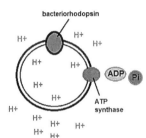

C.

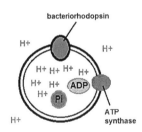

D.

2. To what can the decrease in the pH of the intermembrane space of mitochondria immersed in an acidic solution in Experiment 2 best be attributed?
   A. protons were consumed by the ATP synthase complex
   B. protons were transported from the intermembrane space by bacteriorhodopsin
   C. protons were transported into the mitochondrial matrix by ATP synthase
   D. protons diffused across the inner mitochondrial membrane

3. Which of the following is NOT true of a closed vessel containing normally respiring human mitochondria as they synthesize ATP at physiological pH?
    A. The concentration of O_2 will increase after addition of ADP.
    B. The rate of O_2 consumption will decrease as ADP is consumed.
    C. Inorganic phosphate must be present.
    D. An electron donor is present.

4. The experiments performed in the passage most support what conclusion regarding mitochondrial function?
    A. The establishment of a proton gradient by electron transport is harnessed to drive ATP synthesis.
    B. Substrate metabolism supplies the electron transport chain with energy-rich electron donors.
    C. ATP synthase cannot function without an oxidizable substrate present.
    D. The potential energy of a proton gradient is used by ATP synthase to drive ATP production.

The following questions are NOT based on a descriptive passage.

5. When mitochondria are treated with a decoupling agent that dissipates the proton gradient across their inner membrane, cellular respiration still continues. The energy of ongoing respiration in treated mitochondria is most likely:
    A. used to hydrolyze ATP.
    B. dissipated as heat.
    C. harnessed to synthesize NADPH.
    D. retained for substrate phosphorylation.

6. As the chemiosmotic gradient between the mitochondrial matrix and intermembrane space increases during normal respiration, how does ΔG for the coupled ejection of H^+ by complexes of the electron transport chain if respiration continues and ADP remains available?
    A. ΔG increases
    B. ΔG decreases
    C. ΔG is unchanged
    D. ΔG becomes zero

7. Electrons transferred from $FADH_2$ into the oxidative phosphorylation pathway first enter which respiratory complex?
    A. Complex I
    B. Complex II
    C. Complex III
    D. Complex IV

8. The best candidate for a decoupling agent able to shuttle protons across the inner mitochondrial membrane is a:
    A. lipid-soluble weak acid.
    B. lipid-soluble neutral compound.
    C. water-soluble strong base.
    D. water-soluble neutral compound.

9. Electrons passing from NADH synthesized in the cytosol and from succinate dehydrogenase of the Krebs cycle may enter the electron transport chain via transfer to:
    A. the NADH dehydrogenase complex or coenzyme Q, respectively.
    B. the NADH dehydrogenase complex only.
    C. coenzyme Q or the NADH dehydrogenase complex, respectively.
    D. coenzyme Q only.

10. The transport of two electrons through the electron transport chain, beginning with the enzyme NADH dehydrogenase, will drive the export of how many protons from the matrix?

    A. Two from NADH dehydrogenase, two from the cytochrome bc_1 complex, and two from cytochrome c oxidase.

    B. Four from NADH dehydrogenase, two from the cytochrome bc_1 complex, and two from cytochrome c oxidase.

    C. Four from NADH dehydrogenase, four from the cytochrome bc_1 complex, and two from cytochrome c oxidase.

    D. Four from NADH dehydrogenase, four from the cytochrome bc_1 complex, and four from cytochrome c oxidase.

CHAPTER 32
Macronutrients

A. INTRODUCTION

Humans acquire nutrients from their surroundings and utilize them for fuel, growth and continued metabolic function and regulation of those functions. Macronutrients are the principal oxidizable substrates utilized by the body for fuel and for anabolic processes, and are required in large quantities. Micronutrients are the main source of required metabolic cofactors and are needed on an ongoing basis in relatively small quantities. The human digestive system is specialized for the task of breaking down and absorbing both the macro- and micro-nutrients required for survival. Carbohydrates, fats, and proteins are the principal macronutrients ingested by humans, while vitamins and minerals are the principal micronutrients. A shortage of a required nutrient is referred to as a deficiency.

B. CARBOHYDRATES

Dietary carbohydrates are consumed in order to provide energy, although the ingestion of carbohydrates as a source of energy is not necessary—humans can satisfy their energy needs through the consumption of fats and proteins. However, consuming a diet low in carbohydrates can result in higher level of blood ketone bodies. This condition is known as ketosis.

Dietary carbohydrates are found as monosaccharides, disaccharides, polysaccharides or fibers. Humans metabolize monosaccharides and disaccharides, collectively known as simple sugars, first. Glucose and fructose are the two main monosaccharides found in foods, while sucrose (glucose and fructose), lactose (glucose and galactose), and maltose (glucose and glucose) are the most frequent disaccharide constituents of food products. Sucrose is regularly referred to as table sugar, lactose is the most common sugar found in milk and maltose is a product of the enzymatic breakdown of polysaccharides.

Complex carbohydrates are polysaccharides, most often in the form of glucose polymers that, unlike simple sugars, do not taste sweet. One common example is the starch found in a variety of plants. Other complex carbohydrates, such as cellulose or chitin, cannot be digested by humans.

Dietary fiber is, by definition, a non-digestible, non-starch polysaccharide carbohydrate (and in some cases lignin, another complex polymer). Dietary fiber is divided into two broad categories: soluble and insoluble fiber. Soluble fiber, which dissolves in water, is fermented by colonic flora (commensal bacteria) of the large intestine, producing gas and physiologically active byproducts, and can be prebiotic and viscous. Insoluble fiber, is, as the name suggests, insoluble in water, serves primarily as a bulking agent and is not metabolized. Such fiber absorbs water as it moves through the digestive tract, easing digestion and accelerating the movement of food through the gastrointestinal tract. Sources of dietary fiber are often classified according to whether they are mainly a source of soluble or insoluble fiber.

C. FATS AND FATTY ACID OXIDATION

Fats are esters of long-chain organic acids—fatty acids—and the triol glycerol. Because of their aliphatic nature, fats tend to be predominately hydrophobic and relatively water-insoluble. Fats containing shorter-chain fatty acids are ordinarily liquid at room temperature, whereas fats containing longer-chain fatty acids tend to be solids.

Dietary fats serve both structural and metabolic functions for humans. Fats containing fatty acids that cannot be synthesized by the body are referred to as being as essential. There are two essential fatty acids (EFAs) from which any other fat required by the body can be synthesized: the omega-3 fatty acid α-linolenic acid and the omega-6 fatty acid, linoleic acid. Other lipids needed by the body can be synthesized from these and other fats. Fats and other lipids are broken down in the body by enzymes, called lipases, produced in the pancreas.

Unsaturated fatty acids are often referred to by a naming convention that describes the position of units of unsaturation in the hydrocarbon chain. Omega-3 fatty acids are polyunsaturated fatty acids (PUFAs) with a double bond at the third carbon atom from the end of the carbon chain. The fatty acids have two ends, the carboxylic acid terminus, which is considered the beginning of the chain and the last carbon in the fatty acid tail. The carbon of the carboxylic acid residue of the chain is referred to as being at the "alpha" position, while the methyl end of the chain is referred to as being at the "omega," or tail end. The nomenclature of the fatty acid is taken from the location of the first double bond, beginning from the methyl end. Omega-6 fatty acids possess a double bond at the sixth carbon atom from the end of the carbon chain.

Fats and oils are categorized according to the number and bonding of the carbon atoms in the aliphatic chain. Fats that are saturated fats have no double bonds between the carbons in the chain. Unsaturated fats have one or more double bonded carbons in the chain. Some oils and fats have multiple double bonds and are therefore called polyunsaturated fats. Unsaturated fats can be further divided into cis fats and trans fats. Cis fats occur commonly in nature, while naturally occurring trans fats are very rare. Unsaturated fats can be catalytically reduced to yield a saturated fat when fully hydrogenated. Saturated fats pack more efficiently than do naturally occurring unsaturated fats and tend to remain solid at higher temperatures than unsaturated fats. As an example, animal fats, which contain a significant percentage of saturated fats, tend to be solid at room temperature, while plant-based oils, which contain a greater percentage of unsaturated fat, tend to be liquids at room temperature.

The breakdown of stored fats in the body—a process known as lipolysis—releases glycerol and fatty acids. Those fatty acids can be metabolized in a process referred to as beta-oxidation, while glycerol itself can be converted to glucose by the liver and so become a source of energy.

Beta-oxidation is the process by which fatty acid molecules are catabolized in the mitochondria, generating acetyl-CoA, which enters the citric acid cycle, and NADH and $FADH_2$ for use in the electron transport chain. Before fatty acids released during the lipolysis of stored triglycerides can be beta-oxidized, they are first activated in a two-step, ATP-requiring reaction catalyzed by acyl-CoA synthetase. During activation, the acyl group is irreversibly transferred to coenzyme A (CoA, the same molecule that carries acetyl groups as acetyl-CoA).

Fatty acids are activated in the cytosol, but their subsequent oxidation occurs in the mitochondria. If the fatty acyl-CoA contains a short chain (less than 10 carbons) it is able to diffuse through the inner mitochondrial membrane. Activated long-chain acyl groups (activated fatty acids containing 10 or more carbons) must enter the mitochondria via a shuttle system involving the small molecule carnitine. Acyl CoA is transferred to the hydroxyl group of carnitine by carnitine palmitoyltransferase I (palmitoyltransferase), an enzyme located on the outer mitochondrial membrane. Acyl carnitine is then shuttled inside by a carnitine-acylcarnitine translocase enzyme. Free acyl-CoA is then regenerated by the enzyme carnitine acyltransferase II (palmitoyltransferase), present on the matrix face of the inner mitochondrial membrane. Once liberated, carnitine returns to the cytosol where it continues to function in the shuttle system. The shuttle system is summarized in Figure 32.1.

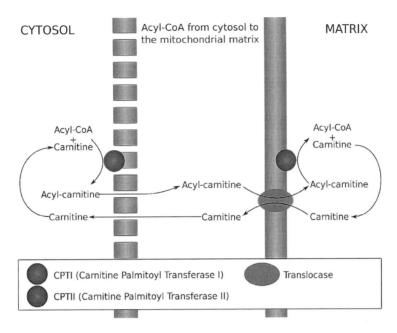

Figure 32.1: Carnitine shuttle system.

Once inside the mitochondrial matrix, beta-oxidation of the long-chain fatty acyl-CoA molecule occurs in four steps. In the first step, the long-chain fatty acid is dehydrogenated to create a trans double bond between carbon two and carbon three. The oxidation is catalyzed by the enzyme fatty acyl-CoA dehydrogenase to produce trans-Δ^2-enoyl CoA while reducing FAD to $FADH_2$.

In the second step, the double bond of trans-Δ^2-enoyl-CoA is hydrated to produce L-β-hydroxyacyl-CoA. This reaction is catalyzed by enoyl-CoA hydratase.

The third step of beta oxidation involves another dehydrogenase reaction. L-β-hydroxyacyl CoA is dehydrogenated by β-hydroxyacyl CoA dehydrogenase to yield β-ketoacyl CoA and NADH.

The final step of the beta-oxidation cycle is the cleavage of the bond between carbon two and carbon three of β-ketoacyl CoA. The reaction, catalyzed by the enzyme thiolase, releases a two carbon units: acetyl CoA, and a fatty acyl-CoA that is two carbons shorter than the parent. The beta-oxidative cycle continues until the original fatty acyl-CoA has been shortened to acetyl-CoA. The reactions of beta-oxidation are shown in Figure 32.2.

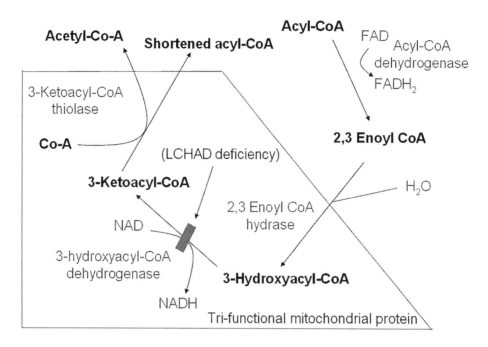

Figure 32.2: Diagram depicting the reaction cycle of mitochondrial
β-oxidation of even-numbered, long-chain fatty acids.

Chains with an odd number of carbons are oxidized by the same pathway as even-chain fatty acids, but the final products of their oxidation are propionyl-CoA and acetyl-CoA. The propionyl-CoA formed in this manner can be converted, in a three-reaction pathway, to form succinyl-CoA. This succinyl-CoA is then able to enter the citric acid cycle as an intermediate.

The position of the cis bond in unsaturated fatty acids can prevent hydration of the trans-Δ^2 bond during beta-oxidation. Accordingly, two additional enzymes are required for the oxidation of unsaturated fatty acids—enoyl CoA isomerase in the case of fatty acids containing an odd number of double bonds or 2,4 dienoyl-CoA reductase in the case of fatty acids containing an even number of double bonds.

The initial oxidation of branched and very long-chain fatty acids (chains longer than 22 carbons) occurs in peroxisomes, followed by mitochondrial oxidation.

One significant difference between peroxisomal and mitochondrial beta-oxidation is that oxidation in peroxisomes is not coupled to ATP synthesis. Electrons are instead transferred to O_2, forming H_2O_2 and producing heat. The hydrogen peroxide produced in the process is converted into water and molecular oxygen by the enzyme catalase—found only in peroxisomes.

Every turn of the beta-oxidation cycle produces one molecule of NADH, $FADH_2$, and acetyl-CoA. For an even-numbered saturated fatty acid containing *n* carbons, *n - 1* cycles of beta-oxidation are necessary to yield the final molecule of acetyl CoA. In addition, two equivalents of ATP are lost during the activation of the fatty acid.

D. PROTEINS

When used as a fuel source, the energy yield of protein oxidation is equal to that of a carbohydrate (approximately 4 kcal/gram) and less than that of lipids (9 kcal/gram). While the consumption of proteins isn't required for fuel, the intake of dietary proteins is required in order to provide the body with certain essential amino acids. There are nine essential amino acids which humans must obtain from the diet: valine, phenylalanine, threonine, tryptophan, methionine, leucine, isoleucine, histidine and lysine. Protein may be obtained from animal products including meats, eggs, fish and dairy products, as well as from grains, nuts, corn, rice and beans. Humans require the essential amino acids in fixed ratios. Protein sources can be rated based upon the relative percentage of amino acids which they contain.

The body is unable to store excess protein. Following the digestion of proteins, amino acids enter the blood and are converted by the liver into other useable molecules, including glucose and ketones, beginning with deamination reactions. Nitrogen liberated during deamination is converted into toxic ammonia, which is further transformed within the liver into urea during the urea cycle. Urea is subsequently excreted by the kidneys. When excess dietary protein is consumed, there is an increase in urea excretion by the kidneys, in order to maintain the nitrogen balance of the body. Most healthy adults are in nitrogen balance, the physiological state in which the mass of nitrogen consumed equals that of the nitrogen excreted by the body. Under starvation conditions the body's own proteins, particularly those of muscle cells, can be catabolized. Protein deficiency and malnutrition in children can lead to mental retardation, growth failure, swelling of the feet and legs, damage to the liver and distention of the abdomen.

E. HORMONAL REGULATION OF METABOLISM

Regulation of fuel metabolism primarily occurs at four locations in the human body: liver, muscle, brain and adipose tissue, as part of a network sensitive to the energy balance of the body. This communication is mediated by both the nervous system and circulating hormones. The regulatory effect of hormones is primarily exerted by the peptide hormones insulin and glucagon, along with the catecholamines epinephrine and norepinephrine. Changes in the levels of these circulating hormones allow the body to up- and down-regulate metabolic processes in response to the need to either create or mobilize the body's energy reserves.

Insulin is synthesized by beta cells in the pancreas. Insulin consists of two polypeptide chains, the A- and B- chains, linked together by disulfide bonds. Preproinsulin contains a 24-residue signal peptide which directs the nascent polypeptide chain to the rough endoplasmic reticulum (RER). The signal peptide is cleaved as the polypeptide is translocated into the lumen of the RER, forming proinsulin. In the RER, proinsulin assumes its correct conformation; the folded product is then stabilized by the formation of three disulfide bonds. After its assembly in the endoplasmic reticulum, proinsulin is transported to the trans-Golgi network (TGN).

Proinsulin matures into its final, active insulin form by proteolytic cleavage. Endopeptidases cleave proinsulin, releasing a fragment known as C-peptide, and two peptide chains, the B- and A- chains, linked together through two disulfide bonds. The sequence of insulin's post-translational modification is shown in Figure 32.3.

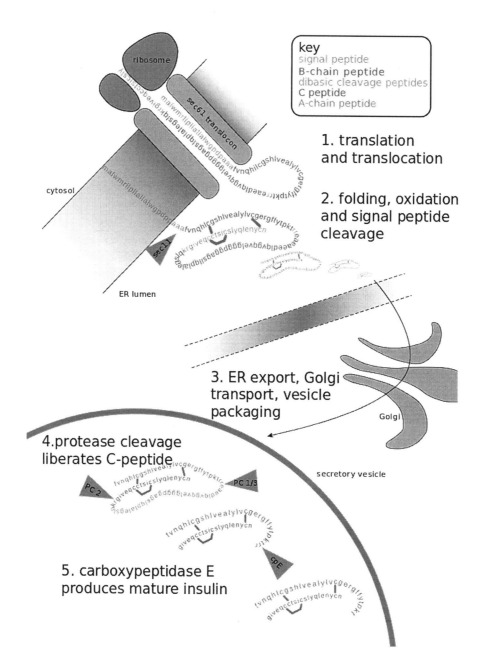

Figure 32.3: Depiction of the posttranslational modification of insulin. Prepared insulin is stored while awaiting secretion. Both c-peptide and mature insulin are physiologically active.

Insulin regulates the metabolism of fats and carbohydrates by favoring the absorption of glucose from the blood into adipose and skeletal muscle tissue. When blood glucose levels fall below a threshold level, the body begins mobilizing stored glucose via glycogenolysis, by breaking down glycogen stored in the liver and muscles for use as an energy source.

Insulin is initially released upon the entry of glucose into the pancreatic β-cells through the glucose transporters, GLUT2. As glucose enters the Krebs cycle within the β-cells of the islets, the ATP:ADP ratio within the cell increases. This increased ATP:ADP ratio leads to the closure of an ATP-sensitive potassium channel and the buildup of intracellular potassium ions. The resultant change in the cell's membrane potential leads to depolarization, and the opening of voltage-gated calcium ion channels within the membrane of β-cells. The entry of calcium ions into the cells triggers the activation of a signaling cascade which results in the release of additional calcium ions from the ER and a substantial increase in the intracellular concentration of calcium ions. Significantly increased amounts of calcium ions in the cells cause the release of previously synthesized insulin, which has been stored in secretory vesicles.

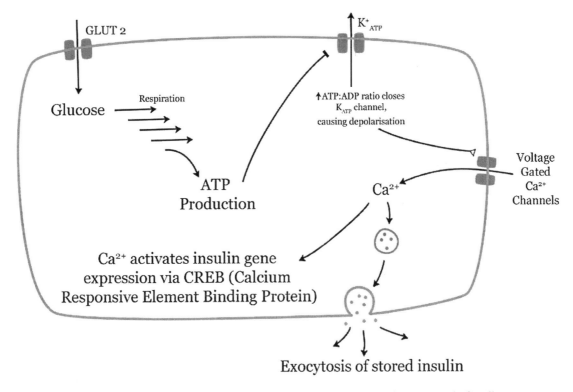

Figure 32.4: Mechanism of glucose-induced insulin release in pancreatic β-cells.

Other substances known to stimulate insulin release include the amino acids arginine and leucine, parasympathetic release of acetylcholine, the digestive enzyme cholecystokinin (CCK) and the gastrointestinally derived hormones glucagon-like peptide-1 (GLP-1) and glucose-dependent insulinotropic peptide (GIP). Release of insulin is strongly inhibited by the stress hormone norepinephrine, leading to increased blood glucose levels during stressful situation as part of the so-called "fight or flight" response.

Insulin release from the pancreas is not continuous, but oscillates over a period of minutes, changing from generating a blood insulin concentration more than about 800 pmol/l to less than 100 pmol/l. This oscillation is thought to avoid down-regulation of insulin receptors at target cells, and to improve the liver's capacity to modulate blood glucose levels.

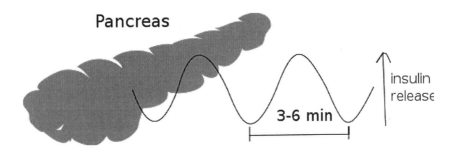

Figure 32.5: Oscillation of insulin release from the pancreas

Insulin in insulin-responsive tissues, including skeletal muscle and fat cells, promotes the recruitment of insulin-sensitive glucose transporters (GLUT-4).

Insulin binds to the extracellular portion of the alpha subunits of the insulin receptor present on the cell surface of insulin-responsive tissue types, such as skeletal and cardiac muscle and adipose tissues. This, in turn, causes a conformational change in the insulin receptor that activates the kinase domain of the insulin receptor's beta subunits. The activated kinase domain autophosphorylates tyrosine residues on the C-terminus of the receptor as well as tyrosine residues in the IRS-1 protein, leading to the phosphorylation and activation of phosphoinositol 3 kinase (PI3) by IRS-1 and, in turn, of protein kinase B (PKB), by PIP3. PKB phosphorylates glycogen synthase kinase (GSK) and thereby inactivates GSK, which is then unable to phosphorylate glycogen synthase (GS) and promote glycogen synthesis. PKB also facilitates vesicle fusion, resulting in an increase in GLUT4 transporters, insulin-sensitive glucose transporters, in the plasma membrane. As the vesicles fuse with the plasma membrane, GLUT4 transporters are inserted and become available for transporting glucose, and glucose absorption increases.

Aside from stimulating absorption of glucose, insulin exerts a range of other effects on human metabolism as well. Insulin forces storage of glucose in the liver and muscle by up-regulating the synthesis of glycogen. In glycogenesis, the process by which glycogen is synthesized, free glucose is first converted into glucose-6-phosphate by the action of glucokinase or hexokinase. Glucose-6-phosphate is then converted into glucose-1-phosphate by the enzyme phosphoglucomutase, through the intermediate glucose-1,6-bisphosphate. Glucose-1-phosphate is then coupled to uridyl diphosphate (UDP), to form UDP-glucose, by the action of uridyl transferase (also called UDP-glucose pyrophosphorylase). During this reaction, pyrophosphate is formed, which is hydrolyzed by pyrophosphatase into two molecules of inorganic phosphate

Glucose molecules are assembled in the polymer glycogen by glycogen synthase, which requires a pre-existing glycogen primer or the small primer protein glycogenin in order to initiate glycogen synthesis. As the polymer grows, additional glucose units are transferred from UDP-glucose to the 4-hydroxyl group of a glucosyl residue, present on the 4 end of the growing glycogen chain.

Glycogen is a branching polymer of large numbers of glucose units linked together. The structure is based on chains of glucose units with linkages between carbon atoms 1 and 4 of each pair of units (α-1, 4 linkages). Every 10 to 14 glucose units, a side branch with an additional chain of glucose units occurs. The side chain attaches at carbon atom 6 of a glucose unit, and the linkage is termed an α-1,6 glycosidic bond. To form this connection a separate enzyme known as a branching enzyme is used. A branching enzyme attaches a string of seven glucose units to the sixth carbon of a glucose unit, usually in an interior location of the glycogen molecule.

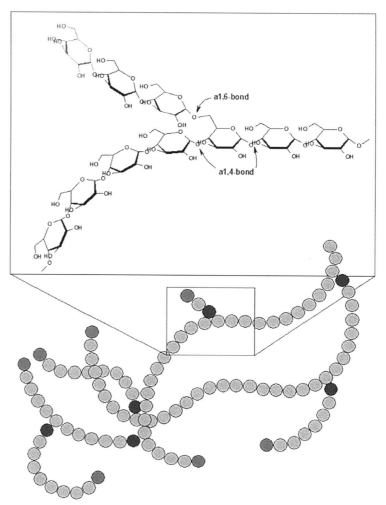

Figure 32.6: Structure of glycogen

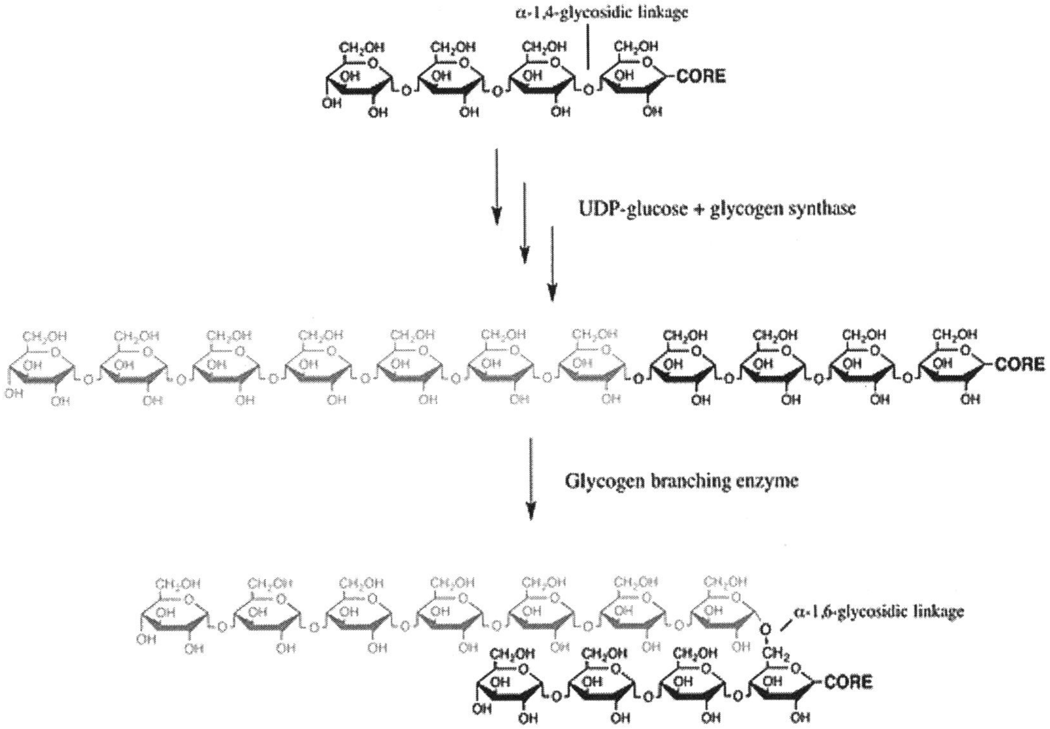

Figure 32.7: Glycogenesis

As discussed in a previous chapter, the enzyme glycogen phosphorylase, the action of which is required for the degradation of stored glycogen, is activated by phosphorylation, whereas glycogen synthase is inhibited by it. Glycogen phosphorylase is converted from its less active "b" form to an active "a" form by the enzyme phosphorylase kinase. Phosphorylase kinase is activated by protein kinase A and deactivated by phosphoprotein phosphatase-1. When insulin binds the insulin receptor, it results in the eventual activation of the enzyme phosphodiesterase (PDE), which degrades cyclic AMP (cAMP) causing the inactivation of protein kinase A. This inactivation indirectly down-regulates the activating of glycogen phosphorylase and up-regulates that of glycogen synthase by preventing both enzymes' phosphorylation.

Protein kinase A is activated by the hormone epinephrine, which binds to a receptor protein (β_2-adrenergic receptors) that activates adenylate cyclase. The latter enzyme causes the formation of cyclic AMP from ATP; two molecules of cyclic AMP bind to the regulatory subunit of protein kinase A. This activates the protein by allowing the catalytic subunit of protein kinase A to dissociate and phosphorylate its protein targets. In this manner, epinephrine, like insulin, can exert reciprocal control on the competing processes of glycogenesis and glycogenolysis, down- and up-regulating the processes, respectively.

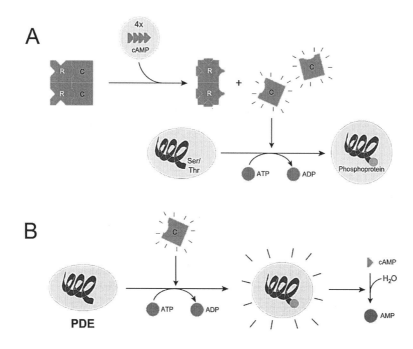

Figure 32.8: Activation of protein kinase A (PKA) (A) and phosphodiesterase (B)

Insulin decreases endogenous synthesis of glucose from non-sugar substrates by suppressing gluconeogenesis, most likely through its negative regulation of the enzyme pyruvate carboxylase.

Insulin also modulates the metabolism of lipids, increasing the rate of triglyceride synthesis. This increased synthesis is due to an insulin-mediated increase in the absorption of fatty acids from circulating lipids, released from lipoproteins in the blood by insulin-sensitive lipoprotein lipase, into fat cells. Those fatty acids are then re-esterified within adipose tissue to form triglycerides. At the same time that insulin promotes the storage of triglycerides, it also opposes their breakdown by inhibiting lipolysis. Lipolysis is stimulated by the hormones glucagon, epinephrine and norepinephrine, growth hormone and the glucocorticoid cortisol, all of which activate adenylate cyclase, and, through its activation of protein kinase A, activate hormone-sensitive lipases found in adipose tissue. Hydrolysis of stored lipids by hormone-sensitive lipase releases free fatty acids and glycerol into the bloodstream. These mobilized free fatty acids may then be taken up by cells and metabolized to produce energy, while glycerol may enter the Krebs cycle after its conversion to glycerol-3-phosphate by glycerol kinase in the liver and kidneys.

Finally, insulin regulates amino acid metabolism. Increasing concentrations of circulating insulin decreases proteolysis—the breakdown of proteins to amino acids and increases their uptake. The global effects of insulin on human metabolism are shown in Figure 32.9.

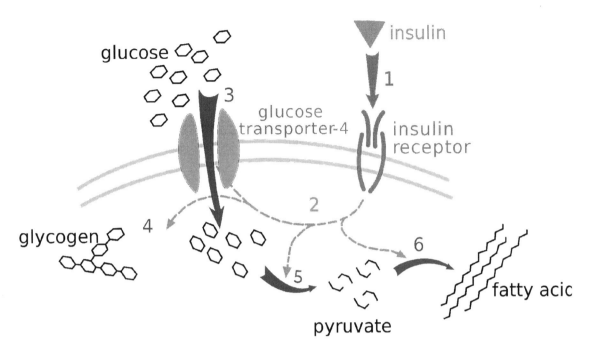

Figure 32.9: Insulin binding to its receptor (1) triggers a protein activation cascade (2). The signaling transduced by this cascade induces the translocation of glucose transporter-4 (GLUT-4) to the plasma membrane, causing an influx of glucose into the cell (3), and an up-regulation of glycogen synthesis (4), glycolysis (5), and triglyceride synthesis (6).

When control of insulin levels fails, diabetes mellitus can result. As a consequence, insulin is used medically to treat some forms of diabetes mellitus. Patients with type 1 diabetes are dependent upon the administration of exogenous insulin, because they no longer produce the hormone in sufficient quantity to properly regulate blood glucose levels. Patients with type 2 diabetes are often insulin resistant—that is, the cells of their body fail to respond to insulin—and, because of such resistance, may suffer from a "relative" insulin deficiency, despite the production of insulin. Some patients with type 2 diabetes may eventually require insulin if dietary modifications or other anti-hyperglycemic medications fail to properly manage their blood glucose levels.

Glucagon is a hormone synthesized by α cells of the pancreas and secreted in response to a low concentration of glucose in the bloodstream. Glucagon induces a compensatory increase in blood sugar levels by causing the liver to convert stored glycogen into glucose, facilitating its release into the bloodstream, and by promoting gluconeogenesis. Glucagon antagonizes insulin's action on blood glucose levels; thus, glucagon and insulin form a feedback system that ensures blood glucose homeostasis in normal individuals.

Upon binding of glucagon to the G-coupled protein glucagon receptors of liver cells, adenylate cyclase becomes activated and produces cAMP. The cAMP produced by adenylate cyclase activates protein kinase A, which in turn phosphorylates and activates glycogen phosphorylase kinase. Activated phosphorylase kinase subsequently phosphorylates glycogen phosphorylase, producing its active "a" form and leading to the release of glucose-1-phosphate. Within liver cells, glucose-1-phosohpate may be subsequently dephosphorylated and released as free glucose into the bloodstream. Glucagon further promotes glycogenolysis by phosphorylating and inactivating phosphoprotein phosphatase-1, preventing its dephosphorylation and deactivation of glycogen phosphorylase.

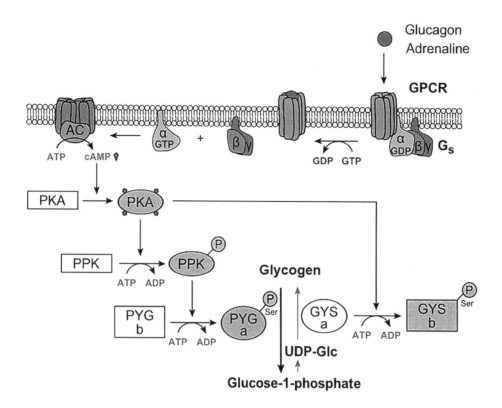

Figure 32.10: Pathway by which glucagon binding in hepatocytes stimulates glycogen phosphorylase, glycogen synthase inactivation and subsequent glycogenolysis. (PKA: protein kinase A; PPK: glycogen phosphorylase kinase; PYG a and PYG b: phosphorylase kinase a and b; GYS a and GYS b (glycogen synthase a and b).

Glucagon further regulates blood glucose levels by influencing the intracellular concentrations of fructose-2,6-bisphosphate, a potent allosteric activator of glycolysis.

Active protein kinase A that was stimulated by the cascade initiated by glucagon will also phosphorylate the bifunctional protein containing the enzymes fructose-2,6-bisphosphatase and phosphofructokinase-2. Phosphorylation stimulates fructsose-2,6-bisphosphatase and inhibits phosphofructokinases-2, thereby decreasing the intracellular concentration of fructose-2,6-bisphosphate (a potent activator of phosphofructokinase-1, the enzyme that is the primary regulatory step of glycolysis), inhibiting flux through the glycolytic pathway and allowing gluconeogenesis to predominate. This process is reversed in the presence of insulin.

Chapter 32 Problems

Passage 32.1 (Questions 1-6)

Insulin, glucagon and epinephrine are the mammalian hormones responsible for the regulation of glucagon metabolism. Mammals store glucose as glycogen after feeding, and degrade it to provide glucose during fasting or upon activation of the sympathetic nervous system. When mobilized, glycogen stores in the liver are largely converted to glucose intended for export into the bloodstream and transport to other tissues. Glycogen degradation is stimulated in the liver by glucagon, as well as by the catecholamine epinephrine in both the liver and skeletal muscle, the latter of which is produced in response to neural signaling. Both epinephrine and glucagon control glycogen metabolism through the enzyme protein kinase A, as shown in Figure 1.

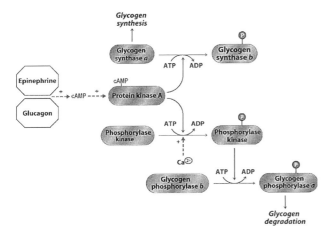

Figure 1: Regulation of glycogen synthesis by glucagon and epinephrine

Insulin, in contrast, exerts its control over glycogenesis, and its control over blood sugar levels, in part through the activation of the enzyme protein phosphatase-1, as shown in Figure 2.

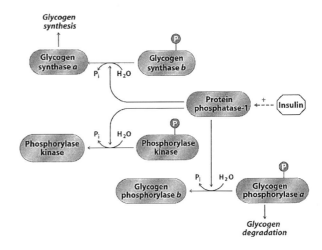

Figure 2: Regulation of glycogen degradation by insulin

Glycogen storage diseases (GSDs) are a group of eleven distinct inborn errors of metabolism involving defects in the pathway of glycogen mobilization including McArdle, Hers' and von Gierke's diseases. McArdle disease is characterized by deficient synthesis of the muscle isoform of glycogen phosphorylase, while Hers' disease is characterized by a deficiency in the liver isoform. Von Gierke's disease results from a deficiency of the liver enzyme glucose-6-phosphatase.

1. In what way do glucagon and epinephrine influence the rate of glycogen degradation in the liver?
    A. They increase it by promoting the dephosphorylation and activation of glycogen phosphorylase.
    B. They increase it by increasing the concentration of a positive allosteric effector of protein kinase A.
    C. They decrease it by promoting the phosphorylation and activation of glycogen synthase.
    D. They increase it by promoting the dephosphorylation and inactivation of phosphorylase kinase.

2. In addition to promoting glycogenolysis in the liver, the signaling cascade initiated by binding of the insulin receptor contributes to an increase in substrate flux through glycolysis by which of the following actions?

   A. Inhibition of phosphofructokinase-2
   B. Inhibition of fructose-2,6-bisphophatase
   C. Stimulation of pyruvate carboxylase
   D. Stimulation of glycogen synthase

3. The hormones mentioned in the passage bind receptors present in or on the:

   A. nucleoplasm.
   B. cytosol.
   C. nuclear membrane.
   D. plasma membrane.

4. The GSD(s) most likely to result in fasting hypoglycemia is:

   A. McArdle disease only.
   B. Von Gierke's disease only.
   C. Hers' and von Gierke's diseases.
   D. McArdle, Hers' and von Gierke's diseases.

5. During fasting, when glycogen stores are depleted, the body attempts to meet its energy demands by all of the following strategies EXCEPT:

   A. the synthesis of ketone bodies.
   B. gluconeogenesis using certain amino acids as substrates.
   C. the mobilization of stored trigylcerides.
   D. gluconeogenesis using free fatty acid as direct substrates.

6. Glycogen phosphorylase's enzymatic action is restricted to cleavage of what type of glycosidic bond?

   A. α-1-4 glycosidic linkage
   B. α-1-6 glycosidic linkage
   C. β-1-4 glycosidic linkage
   D. β-1-6 glycosidic linkage

The following questions are NOT based on a descriptive passage.

7. Into cells of which of the following tissues is glucose transport insulin-sensitive?

   A. Brain
   B. Red blood cells
   C. Adipose tissue
   D. Lens of the eye

8. Which of the following statements regarding glucagon is INCORRECT?

   A. Low blood glucose levels stimulate glucagon release by the pancreas.
   B. It increases intracellular cAMP levels and stimulates glycogenolysis.
   C. Glucagon suppresses the formation of 3-hydroxybutryate within the liver.
   D. Glucagon antagonizes the physiological effects of insulin.

9. Patients deficient in certain enzymes required for the complete mitochondrial beta-oxidation of fatty acids containing an even number of carbon atoms also demonstrate abnormally low fasting blood glucose levels. To what may this be attributed?

   A. Decreased activation of pyruvate carboxylase
   B. Increased production of NADH and ATP inhibit gluconeogenesis
   C. The allosteric effects of increased propionyl-CoA production
   D. Decreased production of acetyl-CoA.

10. A lack of circulating insulin, a physiological condition found in untreated Type 1 diabetics, would NOT cause an increase in what reactions of the liver?

    A. Gluconeogenesis from lactate
    B. Glycogenolysis
    C. Glycogen synthesis
    D. Hormone-sensitive lipase activity

SECTION 8

Content Review Problems

1. If for the unfolding of a protein, $\Delta H° = 210.6$ kJ/mol, then which of the following is true regarding a thermodynamic parameter or property of the reaction?
   A. the enthalpy of unfolding is favored
   B. the enthalpy of folding is favored
   C. the entropy is positive at all temperatures
   D. the entropy is negative at all temperatures

2. Attractive Van der Waals forces occur between:
   A. nonpolar molecules in the liquid state.
   B. any pair of nearby atoms.
   C. polar molecules in the solid state.
   D. molecules only if other forces are less favorable.

3. Which of the following forces or factors is most directly responsible for protein folding?
   A. Conformational entropy
   B. Van der Waals interactions
   C. Hydrophobic interactions
   D. Hydrogen bonds

4. It is NOT correct that at the midpoint of a temperature transition curve representing the folding of a protein that:
   A. half of the protein exists in the denatured state.
   B. $K_{eq} = 1.0$ and $\Delta G = 0$.
   C. the concentration of folded protein equals that of denatured protein.
   D. the energy of transition would not be modified by the addition of a catalyst.

5. Which of the following best describes the position of amino acid residues within the folded structure of globular proteins?
   A. Charged amino acids are never buried in the interior of a protein.
   B. Charged amino acids are seldom buried in the interior of a protein.
   C. All hydrophobic amino acids are buried when a protein folds.
   D. Tyrosine is only found in the interior of proteins.

6. Given that $\Delta G° = -RT\ln K$, what is true regarding the relationship between the magnitudes of ΔG and K for a given reaction?
   A. a 10-fold increase in K decreases $\Delta G°$ by nearly 10-fold
   B. a 10-fold decrease in K decreases $\Delta G°$ by approximately a factor of 2.3*RT
   C. a 10-fold increase in K decreases $\Delta G°$ by approximately a factor of 2.3*RT
   D. a 10-fold decrease in K increases $\Delta G°$ by nearly 10-fold.

7. If the protein found in an egg white, ovalbumin, is denatured when a hard-boiled egg is cooked, then which level of its protein structure is LEAST affected by the heat denaturation?
   A. The primary structure of ovalbumin
   B. The secondary structure of ovalbumin
   C. The tertiary structure of ovalbumin
   D. The quaternary structure of ovalbumin

8. During the unfolding reaction of a helix, breaking a hydrogen bond requires:
    A. less energy than breaking a typical dipole-dipole bond.
    B. not reformed with water.
    C. the same energy as breaking a typical dipole-dipole bond.
    D. more energy than breaking a typical dipole-dipole bond.

9. If the enthalpy change for a reaction is zero, $\Delta G°$ for that reaction must be equal to what?
    A. $T\Delta S°$
    B. $-T\Delta S°$
    C. $-\Delta H°$
    D. $\ln K_{eq}$

10. Reactions that have positive standard free energy changes ($\Delta G° > 0$) can be made to occur in cells by:
    A. coupling them with exergonic reactions via a common intermediate.
    B. manipulating the concentrations of products and reactants such that $\Delta G < 0$.
    C. coupling them to the hydrolysis of ATP.
    D. all of the above

11. How can the standard Gibbs free energy change for a reaction, $\Delta G°$, be described in terms of properties of the reaction reactants and products?
    A. As the residual energy present in the reactants at equilibrium
    B. As the residual energy present in the products at equilibrium
    C. As the difference in the residual energy of reactants and products at equilibrium
    D. As the energy required to convert one mole of reactants to one mole of products

12. If the standard Gibbs free energy for a reversible reaction is positive then:
    A. the reactants of the reaction will be favored.
    B. the products of the reaction will be favored.
    C. the concentration of the reactants and products will be equal when the reaction reaches equilibrium.
    D. all of the reactants will be converted to products.

13. The unfolding of regular protein secondary structure causes what thermodynamic change in a property of the protein?
    A. doubling of the enthalpy of protein
    B. a large decrease in the entropy of the protein
    C. no change in the entropy of the protein
    D. a large increase in the entropy of the protein

14. Glycolytic pathway regulation involves:
    A. allosteric stimulation by ADP.
    B. allosteric inhibition by ATP.
    C. feedback, or product, inhibition by ATP.
    D. all of the above

15. During catabolism, less than half of the energy liberated from the oxidation of glucose is used to synthesize ATP. What is the fate of the energy not stored in the bonds of ATP?
    A. It is lost as heat.
    B. It is used to reduce $NADP^+$.
    C. It remains in the products of metabolism.
    D. It is stored in the form of fat.

16. What is true regarding the direction of operation of the glycolytic pathway?
    A. Three irreversible reactions drive the reaction towards net catabolism.
    B. High levels of ATP induce the pathway to operate exclusively in the forward direction.
    C. The enzymes of glycolysis are exclusively irreversible, favoring glycolysis.
    D. The glycolytic pathway is reversible under sufficiently large product concentrations.

17. Energy released from the oxidation of glucose is stored in what form?
    A. a concentration gradient across a membrane
    B. ADP
    C. ATP
    D. NAD^+

18. A kinase is an enzyme responsible for what modification of the substrates on which it acts?
    A. Removal of phosphate groups
    B. Addition of a phosphate group from ATP
    C. Transfer of electrons from NADH
    D. Dehydration to form a multiple bond

19. For every one molecule of glucose entering glycolysis, how many molecules of pyruvate are produced?
    A. 1
    B. 2
    C. 3
    D. 4

20. In the glycogen synthase reaction, what is the precursor to glycogen?
    A. glucose-6-P
    B. UTP-glucose
    C. UDP-glucose
    D. glucose-1-P

21. Glycogen phosphorylase is in its active form while phosphorylated. What enzyme is activated upon dephosphorylation?
    A. Glycogen synthase
    B. Glycogen semisynthase
    C. Glycogen hydrolase
    D. Glycogen dehydrogenase

22. The enzymes of glycolysis in a eukaryotic cell are located in the:
    A. intermembrane space.
    B. plasma membrane.
    C. cytosol.
    D. mitochondrial matrix.

23. Which of the following is NOT true of glycolysis?
    A. ADP is phosphorylated to ATP via substrate level phosphorylation
    B. The pathway does not require oxygen
    C. The pathway oxidizes two moles of NADH to NAD^+ for each mole of glucose that enters it.
    D. The pathway produces, in net, two moles of ATP per mole of glucose passing the pathway.

24. Which of the following is not a mechanism for altering the flux of metabolites through the rate-determining step of a pathway?
    A. Allosteric control of the enzyme activity
    B. Diffusional coupling between adjacent active sites
    C. Genetic control of the enzyme concentration
    D. Covalent modification of the enzyme

25. Phosphofructokinase, a major rate-controlling enzyme of glycolysis, is allosterically inhibited and activated, respectively, by:
    A. ATP and PEP
    B. AMP and P_i
    C. ATP and ADP
    D. Citrate and ATP

26. Which of the following is true regarding the metabolic regulatory effect of fructose-2,6-bisphosphate?
    A. It is an activator of fructose-1,6-bisphosphatase.
    B. It activates phosphofructokinase-1.
    C. It inhibits fructose-1,6-bisphosphatase.
    D. Both B and C

27. Glucose from the breakdown of glycogen is obtained in:
    A. the liver by phosphorolysis.
    B. the muscles by phosphorolysis.
    C. the muscles by hydrolysis.
    D. both A and B

28. Glucose from the breakdown of glycogen is exported into the blood from:
    A. the liver following phosphorolysis.
    B. the muscles following phosphorolysis.
    C. the muscles following hydrolysis.
    D. both A and B

29. The glyosidic bonds present in glycogen include:
    A. α-1,4 linkages only.
    B. α-1,6 linkages only.
    C. both α-1,4 and α-1,6 linkages only.
    D. both α-1,4 and β-1,6 linkages only.

30. The trans-membrane electrical potential and the proton concentration gradient across the inner mitochondrial membrane:
    A. are both required for oxidative phosphorylation.
    B. are sufficient, separately, to permit synthesis of ATP from ADP and inorganic phosphate.
    C. remain coupled to ATP synthesis in the presence of respiratory inhibitors.
    D. are unchanged upon treatment of mitochondria with a proton ionophore.

31. The irreversibility of the thiokinase reactions (formation of initial acyl-CoA):
    A. makes this activation reaction the committed step in the pathway.
    B. is due to the subsequent hydrolysis of the product.
    C. is true only for the metabolism of even-chain fatty acids.
    D. both A and B

32. The oxidation of methanol (wood alcohol) in human retina tissue leads directly to the formation of:
    A. formaldehyde.
    B. sugars.
    C. CO_2.
    D. lactate.

33. FAD is reduced to $FADH_2$ during what metabolic process?
    A. electron transport phosphorylation
    B. lactate fermentation
    C. Krebs cycle
    D. glycolysis

34. During glycolysis, electrons removed from glucose are passed to what molecule?
    A. FAD
    B. NAD^+
    C. acetyl CoA
    D. pyruvic acid

35. Coenzyme Q is involved in electron transport as:
    A. the immediate reductant of molecular oxygen.
    B. a water-soluble electron donor.
    C. a covalently attached cytochrome cofactor.
    D. a lipid-soluble electron carrier.

36. Carbon dioxide is primarily a product of which of the following aerobic reaction pathways?
    A. Krebs cycle
    B. glycolysis
    C. substrate-level phosphorylation
    D. lactic acid fermentation

37. How many CO_2 molecules are exhaled for each O_2 molecule utilized in cellular respiration?
    A. 1
    B. 3
    C. 6
    D. 12

38. Lactic acid is produced by human muscles during strenuous exercise under conditions which lack what reactive substrate(s)?
    A. oxygen
    B. NAD^+
    C. glucose
    D. ADP and P_i

39. During electron transport, protons are pumped out of the mitochondrion at each of the major protein complexes EXCEPT:
    A. complex I.
    B. complex II.
    C. complex III.
    D. complex IV.

40. In aerobic respiration, which of the following compounds is imported into mitochondria?
    A. acetyl CoA
    B. pyruvate
    C. phosphoglyceraldehyde
    D. oxaloacetate

41. The transport of acyl-CoA for oxidation using a shuttle involves formation of what intermediate?
    A. acetyl-CoA
    B. Acyl-coenzyme A
    C. acyl-carnitine
    D. acyl-malate

42. Each cycle of β-oxidation produces:
    A. 1 $FADH_2$, 1 NAD^+, and 1 acetyl-CoA.
    B. 1 $FADH_2$, 1 NADH and 1 acetyl-CoA.
    C. 1 $FADH_2$, 1 NADH and 2 CO_2 molecules.
    D. 1 FAD, 1 NAD^+ and 2 CO_2 molecules.

43. How many rounds of mitochondrial beta-oxidation are required to completely decompose palmitic acid (C16) to molecules of acetyl-CoA?
    A. 6
    B. 7
    C. 8
    D. 16

44. Ascorbic acid acts as:
    A. a reducing agent.
    B. an oxidizing agent.
    C. a carrier of activated acyl groups.
    D. a phosphorylating agent.

45. The prosthetic group biotin is a carrier of which type of molecule?
    A. Activated carbon dioxide
    B. Ammonia
    C. Methyl groups
    D. Sulfhydryl groups

46. An example of a digestive hormone is:
    A. lipase.
    B. pepsin.
    C. amylase.
    D. gastrin.

47. The enzyme L-folate reductase reduces folic acid to its biological active form:
    A. hydrofolic acid.
    B. dihydrofolic acid.
    C. trihydrofolic acid.
    D. tetrahydrofolic acid.

48. Which of these is a symptom of vitamin A deficiency?
    A. Osteoporosis
    B. Impaired taste perception
    C. Blindness
    D. Impaired blood clotting

49. In terms of its solubility, Vitamin A is similar to all of the following vitamins EXCEPT:
    A. Vitamin E.
    B. Vitamin C.
    C. Vitamin D.
    D. Vitamin K.

50. The vitamin riboflavin is part what molecule?
    A. ferredoxin
    B. FAD
    C. pyridoxal phosphate
    D. pyrophosphate

SECTION 9
Cellular Interaction

We end by returning our focus to the most important topic on the MCAT: the cell. We must consider the biochemical implications of the structure and function of the plasma membrane, and how cells communicate with each other.

CHAPTER 33
The Plasma Membrane

A. INTRODUCTION

The plasma membrane is a biological membrane, consisting of a phospholipid bilayer with embedded proteins, which surrounds all cells and separates them from their extracellular environment. While the plasma membrane is as fragile as a soap bubble, it nonetheless provides an effective diffusion barrier between cell and surroundings, permitting only the entry and exit of those ions and organic molecules for which it is selectively permeable.

Outside of their role as a diffusion barrier, cell membranes are involved in a variety of other cellular processes such as cell adhesion, signaling, the conduction of ions, and as an attachment point for structures, including (when present) the cell wall, glycocalyx, and intracellular cytoskeleton elements of cells. A detailed diagram of the cell membrane and its position relative to the cell and the cell's environment is shown in Figure 33.1

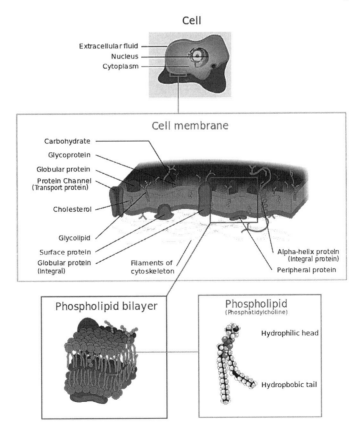

Figure 33.1: Depiction of the cell (top), cell membrane (middle), and the phospholipid bilayer and an individual phospholipid (below).

B. COMPOSITION

According to the so-called fluid mosaic model, biological membranes are two-dimensional, fluid structures in which lipid and protein molecules diffuse readily. The largest structural component of the cell membrane is the lipid bilayer, two layers of amphipathic phospholipids which spontaneously arrange so that the hydrophobic "tail" regions are isolated from the surrounding polar, aqueous environment, causing the more hydrophilic "head" regions to associate with the intracellular (cytosolic) and extracellular faces of the resulting bilayer. A continuous, spherical lipid bilayer is formed by this process. Lipid bilayers are formed primarily in response to hydrophobic forces, but van der Waals forces, electrostatic and non-covalent interactions, and hydrogen bonding contribute to their formation as well.

Three classes of amphipathic lipids are found in cell membranes: phospholipids, glycolipids, and sterols. In most cases, phospholipids are most abundant, but the amount of each depends upon the type of cell. The fatty chains in phospholipids and glycolipids usually contain an even number of carbon atoms, typically between 16 and 20 carbons. Fatty acids may be saturated or unsaturated. Unsaturated double bonds are nearly always found in the cis configuration. The degree of unsaturation and length of fatty acid chains within lipids strongly influences membrane fluidity. Unsaturated lipids create kinks—spatial distortions within chains—that disrupt fatty acid packing, thus decreasing their melting temperature and, for that reason, the fluidity of the membranes. Certain organisms take advantage of this property of membrane lipids in order to regulate the fluidity of their membranes by altering the fatty acid composition of the lipids present within their membrane bilayers.

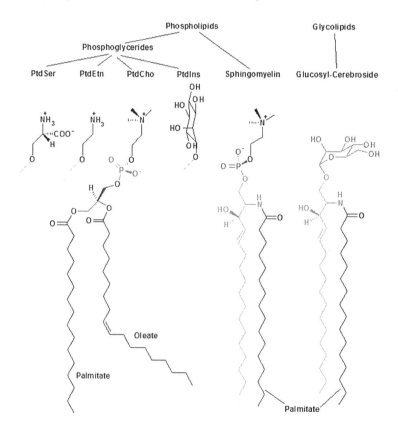

Figure 33.2: Examples of the major membrane phospholipids and glycolipids: phosphatidylcholine (PtdCho), phosphatidylethanolamine (PtdEtn), phosphatidylinositol (PtdIns), phosphatidylserine (PtdSer).

Non-covalent interaction of hydrophobic tails does not strictly restrict the movement of membrane lipids. Under physiological conditions, phospholipid molecules in the cell membrane are able to freely and rapidly laterally diffuse within a membrane. However, the exchange of phospholipid molecules between intracellular and extracellular leaflets of the bilayer is a very slow process that requires enzymatic catalysis.

Proteins are found in significant quantity in cell membranes and serve a variety of biological roles. A number of proteins, found on the extracellular face of the cell membrane, serve as receptors or as identification proteins. Antigens are one such example present on the surface of the plasma membrane. Other membrane proteins can provide for cell–cell contact, surface recognition, cytoskeleton anchoring and communication, signaling, enzymatic activity, or the transport of substances across the membrane. A summary of the three main classes of membrane proteins and their functions is given in Table 33.1.

Table 33.1: Membrane Protein Types		
Protein Type	**Function**	**Examples**
Integral (Transmembrane)	Membrane-spanning proteins with: i) a hydrophilic cytosolic domain that interacts with the interior of the cell; ii) a hydrophobic membrane-spanning domain that anchors it in the cell membrane; iii) a hydrophilic extracellular domain that interacts with extracellular environment. The hydrophobic domain has one or more α-helices and β sheets.	Proton pumps, G protein-coupled receptors, ion channels
Peripheral	Transiently attached to integral membrane proteins or associated with peripheral regions of the lipid bilayer, these proteins tend to interact with the biological membrane only transiently before resuming their function within the cytoplasm.	Hormones, certain enzymes
Lipid-anchored	Covalently bound to single or multiple lipid molecules that anchor the protein within the membrane without the protein contacting the membrane.	G proteins

For proteins destined for insertion or association with the plasma membrane, an N-terminus "signal sequence" directs the newly synthesized proteins to the endoplasmic reticulum, where they are inserted into a lipid bilayer. Once inserted, the proteins are then transported to their final destination in vesicles, where the vesicle fuses with the target membrane.

Plasma membranes also contain carbohydrates, present on the extracellular surface of the plasma membrane. These are most often glycoproteins, but glycolipids (cerebrosides and gangliosides) are present as well. These glycosylated structures contribute to the glycocalyx of the cell, the coat on the external surface of plasma membranes that surround bacteria, epithelia and other cells. The glycocalyx appears "fuzzy" when a cell is visualized. The penultimate sugar is galactose and the terminal sugar is sialic acid, as the sugar backbone is modified in the Golgi apparatus. Sialic acid carries a negative charge, providing an external barrier to charged particles.

Material is incorporated into, or removed from, the cell membrane (notably its protein and lipid content) through one of three means. When intracellular vesicles fuse with the membrane during exocytosis, they not only excrete the contents of the vesicle but they also incorporate the vesicle's membrane components into the cellular membrane. Membrane material may be lost when the membrane forms blebs around extracellular material that pinch off to become vesicles (endocytosis). If a membrane is continuous with a tubular structure made of membrane material, then material from the tube can be drawn into the membrane. Finally, the concentration of membrane components in the aqueous phase is low (stable membrane components have low solubility in water), but an ongoing, slow exchange of molecules between the lipid and aqueous phases does occur.

Lipid vesicles or liposomes are lipid bilayers enclosing a spherical space. These laboratory-derived structures are used by researchers to deliver material to target cells and to test cell membrane permeability with respect to substances of interest by measuring its rate of efflux or influx across the vesicle or liposome. They are formed by first suspending a lipid in an aqueous solution, then agitating the mixture, resulting in a vesicle. Proteins can also be embedded into the membrane through solubilizing the desired proteins in the presence of detergents and attaching them to the phospholipids in which the liposome is formed, thereby allowing a means of simulating the behavior of membrane proteins.

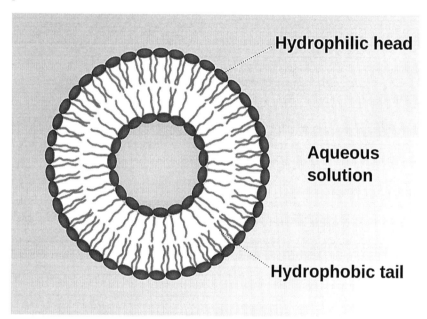

Hydrophilic head

Aqueous solution

Hydrophobic tail

Figure 33.3: Liposome formed from assembly of phospholipids in an aqueous solution

A liposome should not be confused with a micelle, which is an aggregate composed of a single layer of lipids in aqueous solution, where the hydrophilic head region is in contact with the solvent, while the hydrophobic tail region is sequestered within the micelle center. The shape and size of a micelle are a function of the molecular geometry of its surfactant molecules and solution conditions such as surfactant concentration, temperature, pH, and ionic strength. An example of a normal-phase micelle is shown in Figure 33.4.

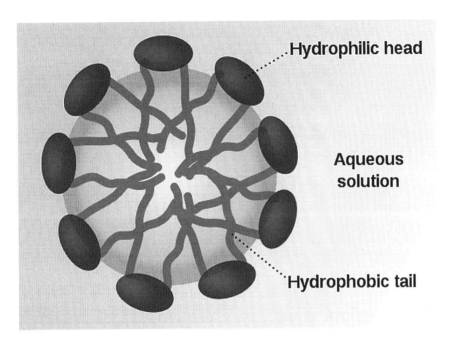

Figure 33.4: Micelle formed from assembly of phospholipids in an aqueous solution

In animal cells, cholesterol is normally found dispersed in varying degrees throughout cell membranes. It is ordinarily present in the irregular spaces between the hydrophobic tails of the membrane lipids, where it confers rigidity upon the membrane and modulates membrane fluidity over a range of temperatures. The hydroxyl group of cholesterol interacts with the polar head groups of the membrane phospholipids and sphingolipids, while the bulky steroid and the hydrocarbon chain are embedded in the membrane, alongside the nonpolar fatty-acid chains of the other lipids. Through the interaction with the phospholipid fatty-acid chains, cholesterol increases membrane packing, which reduces membrane fluidity. The structure of the tetracyclic ring of cholesterol contributes to the decreased fluidity of the cell membrane as the molecule is in a trans conformation, making all but the side chain of cholesterol rigid and planar.

Synthesis within the body starts with one molecule of acetyl CoA and one molecule of acetoacetyl-CoA, which are hydrated to form 3-hydroxy-3-methylglutaryl CoA (HMG-CoA). This molecule is then reduced to mevalonate by the enzyme HMG-CoA reductase. This is the regulated, rate-limiting and irreversible step in cholesterol synthesis and is the site of action for cholesterol-lowering statin drugs. Mevalonate is then converted to 3-isopentenyl pyrophosphate in three reactions that require ATP. Mevalonate is decarboxylated to isopentenyl pyrophosphate, which is a key metabolite for various biological reactions. Three molecules of isopentenyl pyrophosphate condense to form farnesyl pyrophosphate through the action of geranyl transferase. Two molecules of farnesyl pyrophosphate then condense to form squalene by the action of squalene synthase in the endoplasmic reticulum, a precursor of lanosterol. Lanosterol is further converted to cholesterol through a 19-step process.

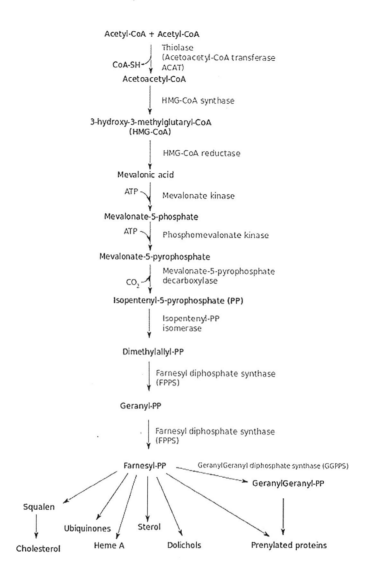

Figure 33.5: Reactions of the mevalonate pathway.

Isopentenyl pyrophosphate (IPP) is an intermediate not only in the synthesis of cholesterol, but is used by organisms in the biosynthesis of terpenes and terpenoids. Terpenes are derived biosynthetically from five carbon-containing isoprene units.

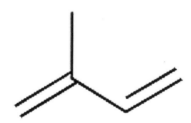

Figure 33.6: Basic structure of an isoprene unit, $(C_5H_8)_n$

The basic molecular formulae of terpenes are multiples of that of isoprene. The activated isoprene unit IPP may be linked with another activated isoprene dimethylallyl pyrophosphate (DMAPP) in a "head to tail" manner in order to form larger terpene chains or rings.

Terpenes may be classified by the number of isoprene units in the molecule. The prefix of the terpene name indicates the number of terpene units needed to assemble the molecule. Monoterpenes consist of two isoprene units and contain 10 carbons. Sesquiterpenes consist of three isoprene units and contain fifteen carbons. Diterpenes are composed of four isoprene unite and contain 20 carbons. They derive from geranyl pyrophosphate and are the basis for biologically important compounds such as retinol and retinal.

Sphingolipids, or glycosylceramides, are a class of lipids containing a backbone of sphingoid bases, a set of aliphatic amino alcohols that includes sphingosine. Sphingolipids are commonly believed to protect the cell surface against harmful environmental factors by forming a mechanically stable and chemically resistant outer leaflet of the plasma membrane lipid bilayer. Certain complex glycosphingolipids are also known to participate in cell recognition and signaling. Disorders of sphingolipid metabolism are involved in a number of diseases which affect neural tissues.

Sphingoid bases are the fundamental building blocks of all sphingolipids. The main mammalian sphingoid bases are dihydrosphingosine and sphingosine. Ceramides, as a general class, are N-acylated sphingoid bases lacking additional head groups.

Complex sphingolipids may be formed by addition of head groups to ceramide. Sphingomyelins have a phosphocholine or phosphoethanolamine molecule with an ester linkage to the 1-hydroxy group of a ceramide.

Glycosphingolipids are ceramides with one or more sugar residues joined in a β-glycosidic linkage at the 1-hydroxyl position.

Cerebrosides have a single glucose or galactose at the 1-hydroxy position. Gangliosides include at least three sugars, one of which must be sialic acid.

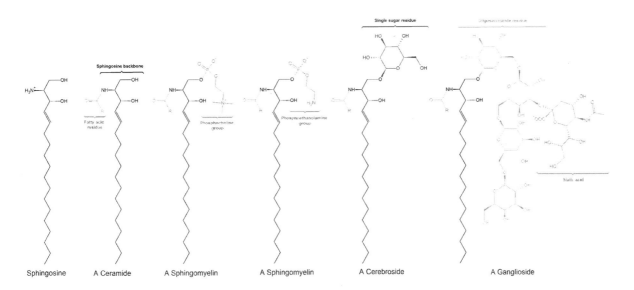

Figure 33.7: General structure of selected sphingolipids

C. SOLUTE TRANSPORT

Lipid bilayers are generally impermeable to ions and polar molecules. The arrangement of hydrophilic heads and hydrophobic tails of the lipid bilayer prevent polar solutes such as nucleic acids, amino acids, carbohydrates, proteins, and ions from diffusing across the membrane, but generally allows for the passive diffusion of hydrophobic molecules, particularly those that are relatively small. Because of this relative impermeability to many substances, the cell is able to selectively allow entry of charged and hydrophilic species through transmembrane protein complexes such as gates, pores and channels. There are four main strategies by which a cell selectively transports materials across its membranes: passive osmosis and diffusion, transmembrane protein channels and transporters, exocytosis and endocytosis.

Table 33.2: Relative Permeability of Substances Across Phospholipid Membranes		
Substance	**Examples**	**Permeability**
Gases	CO_2, N_2, O_2	Permeable
Small uncharged polar molecules	Water, ethanol, urea	Slightly permeable or impermeable
Large uncharged polar molecules	Fructose, glucose	Impermeable
Ions	K^+, Na^-, HCO_3^-, Cl^-	Impermeable
Charge polar molecules	Amino acids, ATP, glucose-6-phosphate	Impermeable

Passive transport is the movement of materials across a cell membrane without the input of chemical energy. Passive transport is a spontaneous process made so by the increase in entropy associated with the transport. The rate of passive transport depends on the permeability of the cell membrane to the transported material, which, in turn, depends on the structure and composition of the lipids and proteins of the membrane. There are four main forms of passive transport: simple diffusion, facilitated diffusion, filtration and osmosis.

Simple diffusion is driven by the net movement of material from an area of high concentration to an area with lower concentration. The difference of concentration between the two areas is often termed the concentration gradient, and diffusion will continue until this gradient has been eliminated. Since diffusion moves materials from an area of higher concentration to lower, it is described as moving solutes down the concentration gradient. Small, generally non-polar molecules such as CO_2 and O_2, may move passively by simple diffusion across the plasma membrane of cells.

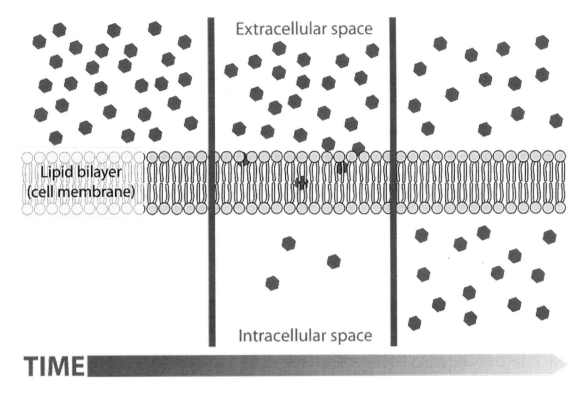

Figure 33.8: Simple diffusion of membrane-soluble solute across the plasma membrane from a region of high concentration (extracellular space) to low concentration (intracellular space).

Osmosis is much like simple diffusion, but it specifically describes the movement of water, rather than solute, across a membrane until there is an equal concentration of water and solute on both sides of the membrane. The net concentration gradient that drives osmosis exists across the membrane because of its relative impermeability to a number of species, thereby creating an osmotic pressure between the extra- and intra-cellular spaces that induces water to flow slowly across the membrane.

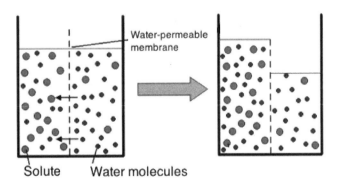

Figure 33.9: A semipermeable membrane separating two compartments of unequal solute concentration. Over time, water flow between the compartments nearly equilibrates the solute concentrations between compartments.

With respect to cells, if the medium in which a cell is placed is of lesser solute concentration than is the cell, we say that the solution is hypotonic relative to the cell cytoplasm, and the cell will gain water through osmosis. If the medium is isotonic, that is, if solute concentration within and outside of a cell is equal, there will be no net movement of water across the cell membrane. Finally, if the medium in which a cell is placed is of greater solute concentration than is the cell, we say that the solution is hypertonic relative to the cell cytoplasm, and the cell will lose water by osmosis. The osmotic effects of placing a red blood cell in hypertonic, isotonic and hypotonic solutions are shown in Figure 33.7.

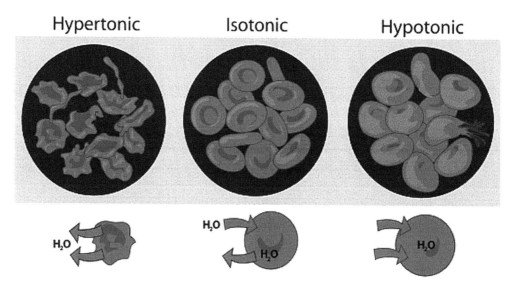

Figure 33.10: A depiction of the osmotic effects on red blood cells placed in solutions of differing tonicities.

Facilitated diffusion is the process of spontaneous passive transport of molecules or ions across a biological membrane via specific transmembrane integral proteins. When dissolved, polar molecules and large ions dissolved in water cannot diffuse freely across the hydrophobic plasma membrane. Hence, the transport of polar molecules requires the use of transmembrane channels. These channels are gated, meaning that they open and close, and thus regulate the flow of ions or small polar molecules across membranes, sometimes against the osmotic gradient. Larger molecules are transported by transmembrane carrier proteins that change their conformation as the molecules are carried across. Transmembrane carrier proteins responsible for the transport of glucose or amino acids function in this manner. Aquaporins, also known as water channels, are transmembrane proteins that selectively conduct water molecules in and out of the cell, while preventing the passage of ions and other solutes. While a small amount of water is able to "leak" across the plasma membranes due to osmosis, rapid changes in the water content of a cell is via the controlled transport of water molecules through aquaporins.

Most ion channels are extremely specific for one ion. For example, most potassium channels are characterized by 1000:1 selectivity ratio for potassium over sodium, though potassium and sodium ions have the same charge and differ only slightly in their radius.

Because transport relies on molecular binding between the cargo and the membrane-embedded channel or carrier protein channels, the rate of facilitated diffusion is not linear, but depends on the enzyme activity of the carrier protein or channel. The rate of transport, then, is saturable, unlike free diffusion in which the rate of diffusion is only dependent on the concentration gradient across a membrane.

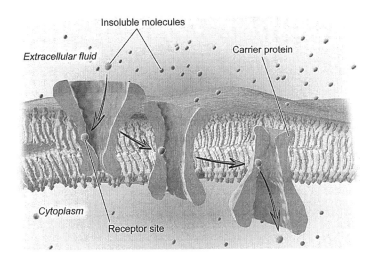

Figure 33.11: Depiction of facilitated diffusion across a cellular membrane

Gated carrier proteins—many of which are classified as uniporters, which bind and facilitate the transport of a single molecule at a time—open in response to a stimulus. There are several ways in which the opening of uniporter channels may be regulated. Voltage-sensitive channels open and close in response to the voltage across the membrane. Voltage-gated sodium channels and calcium channels are made up of a single polypeptide with four homologous domains. Each domain contains 6 membrane-spanning alpha helices. One of these helices is the voltage-sensing helix. It has many positive charges such that a high positive charge outside the cell repels the helix, keeping the channel in its closed state. Depolarization of the cell interior causes the helix to move, inducing a conformational change such that ions may flow through the channel (the open state). Potassium channels function in a similar way, with the exception that they are composed of four separate polypeptide chains, each comprising one domain. During transmission of the neuronal signal from one neuron to the next, dependent upon the opening of sodium ion channels, calcium is transported into the presynaptic neuron by voltage-gated calcium channels. Potassium leak channels, also regulated by voltage, then help to restore the resting membrane potential after impulse transmission.

Ligand-gated channels form another important class; these ion channels open and close in response to the binding of a ligand molecule, such as a neurotransmitter. In the ear, sound waves cause the stress-regulated channels of the cochlea to open, sending an impulse to the vestibulocochlear nerve. Other ion channels open and close with mechanical forces, while yet other ion channels—such as those of some sensory neurons—open and close in response to stimuli, such as light, temperature or pressure.

In active transport, energy is consumed, most typically in the form of ATP, to move a solute against a concentration or electrochemical gradient. In primary active transport, energy is used directly to transport the solute against its gradient, while in secondary active transport, the energy stored in an electrochemical gradient established via primary active transport is used to facilitate movement of a solute.

Most enzymes that perform primary active transport are members of the transmembrane ATPase family. These proteins couple the movement of solutes to the hydrolysis of ATP. One such ATPase is the sodium-potassium pump, which helps to maintain the cell potential across membranes by exchanging Na^+ for K^+ across a membrane, moving both ions against the transmembrane concentration gradients established by the pump.

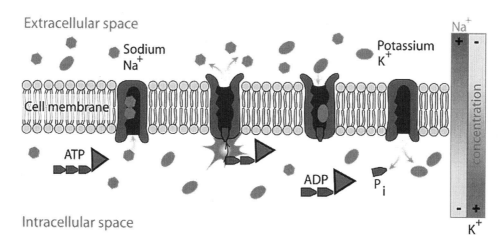

Figure 33.12: Action of the transmembrane sodium-potassium pump

Primary active transporters can also be powered by redox reactions or by energy harnessed from the photons of incident light. An example of the former are the enzymes of the mitochondrial electron transport chain that use the energy released from redox reactions to translocate protons across the inner mitochondrial membrane against their concentration gradient.

In secondary active transport, also known as coupled transport or co-transport, energy is used to transport molecules across a membrane; however, in contrast to primary active transport, there is no direct coupling of the energy-releasing reaction used to drive the translation. Instead, secondary active transport relies upon the electrochemical potential difference created across membranes by active transport.

Co-transporters can be classified as symporters or antiporters. In antiport, two species of ion or other solutes are pumped in opposite directions across a membrane. One of these species is allowed to flow from high to low concentration, which yields the entropic energy to drive the transport of the other solute from a low-concentration region to a region of higher concentration. An example is the sodium-calcium exchanger, an antiporter, which allows three sodium ions to flow down their concentration gradient (established previously by an active transport mechanism) into the cell, while transporting one calcium ion out.

Symport uses the downhill movement of one solute species from high to low concentration to move another molecule in the same direction from low concentration to high concentration, against its electrochemical gradient. An example is the glucose symporter SGLT-1, present in the small intestine, kidneys, heart, and brain of humans, which co-transports one glucose (or galactose) molecule into the cell concomitantly with the transport of two sodium ions it imports into the cell.

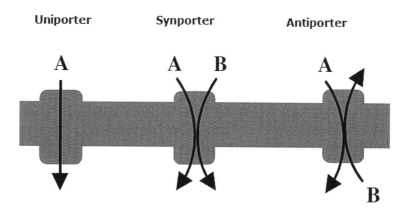

Figure 33.13: Comparison of transmembrane transport proteins

Endocytosis is an energy-using process by which cells absorb molecules by engulfing them. Biologists often categorize endocytosis as pinocytosis and phagocytosis. In pinocytosis, cells engulf liquid particles while in phagocytosis, cells engulf solid particles.

Clathrin-mediated endocytosis involves small vesicles that have a coat composed mainly of the cytosolic protein clathrin. Clathrin-coated vesicles (CCVs) are found in virtually all cells and form domains of the plasma membrane termed clathrin-coated pits. When formed, coated pits can concentrate large extracellular molecules that with receptor-specific for the endocytosis of their ligands, including, in humans, low density lipoprotein (LDL), growth factors, antibodies and other proteins.

Caveolae are the most common non-clathrin-coated endocytotic vesicles. They consist of the cholesterol-binding protein caveolin with a bilayer enriched in cholesterol and glycolipids. Uptake of extracellular molecules is also believed to be specifically mediated via receptors in caveolae.

Phagocytosis is the process by which cells bind and internalize larger materials, such as cellular debris, micro-organisms and, in some specialized cell types, other apoptotic cells. These processes involve the uptake of larger membrane areas than is possible in clathrin-mediated endocytosis or in the caveolae pathway.

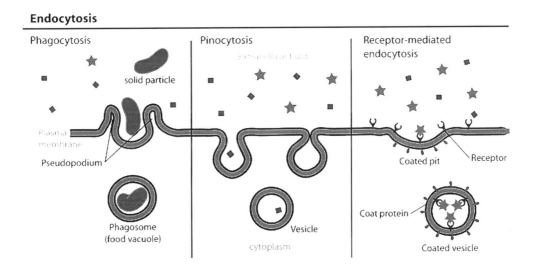

Figure 33.14: Comparison of the mechanisms of endocytosis

The endocytic pathway of mammalian cells consists of distinct membrane compartments, which internalize molecules from the plasma membrane and recycle them back to the surface (in early endosomes), or sort them for degradation (as in late endosomes and lysosomes). The principal components of the endocytic pathway are early endosomes, late endosomes and lysosomes.

Early endosomes are the first cell types of the endocytic pathway. Early endosomes are often located in the periphery of the cell, are mildly acidic, and receive most types of vesicles endocytosed from the cell surface.

Late endosomes receive internalized material en route to lysosomes, usually from early endosomes in the endocytic pathway, from the trans-Golgi network (TGN) in the biosynthetic pathway, and from phagosomes in the phagocytic pathway. Late endosomes often contain many proteins characteristic of lysosomes, including lysosomal membrane glycoproteins and acid hydrolases, and are acidic (pH 5.5). They are thought to mediate a final set of sorting events prior to delivery of material to lysosomes.

Lysosomes are the last compartment of the endocytic pathway. They are more acidic than late endosomes (pH 4.8) and are the principal hydrolytic compartment of the cell, where they function to break down cellular waste products, fats, carbohydrates, proteins, and other macromolecules. These degradation products are then returned to the cytoplasm as new cell-building materials. To accomplish this, lysosomes use some 40 different types of hydrolytic enzymes, all of which are manufactured in the endoplasmic reticulum and modified in the Golgi apparatus.

Just as material can be brought into the cell by invagination and formation of a vesicle, the membrane of a vesicle can be fused with the plasma membrane, extruding its contents to the surrounding medium. This is the process of exocytosis. These membrane-bound vesicles contain soluble proteins to be secreted to the extracellular environment, as well as membrane proteins and lipids that become components of the cell membrane.

There are two main types of exocytosis: Ca^{2+} triggered non-constitutive exocytosis (regulated exocytosis), and non-Ca^{2+} triggered (non-constitutive) exocytosis. Constitutive exocytosis is performed regularly by all cells to release material to the extracellular matrix or to deliver membrane proteins to the plasma membrane. Regulated exocytosis requires an external signal to trigger an intracellular increase in calcium ions, a specific sorting signal on the vesicles, and a clathrin coat. Fusion of secretory vessels with the plasma membrane, in the presence of increased calcium ion concentration, may require the assistance of SNARE proteins, resulting in release of vesicle contents into the extracellular space, or, in case of neurons, into the synaptic cleft, as shown in Figure 33.12.

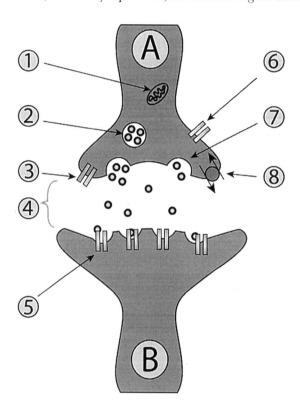

Figure 33.15: Depiction of intraneuronal signaling between neuron A, from which neurotransmitter is released, to neuron B. 1. Mitochondrion 2. Synaptic vesicle with neurotransmitters 3. Autoreceptor 4. Synapse with neurotransmitter released 5. Postsynaptic receptors activated by neurotransmitter (induction of a postsynaptic potential) 6. Calcium channel 7. Exocytosis of a vesicle 8. Reuptake of neurotransmitter

The physical arrangement of cells strongly influences the nature of the transport which occurs across them. The apical membrane of a polarized cell is the surface of the plasma membrane that faces inward to the lumen. This is particularly evident in epithelial and endothelial cells, but also describes other polarized cells, such as neurons. The basolateral membrane of a polarized cell is the surface of the plasma membrane that forms its basal and lateral surfaces. It faces outwards, towards the interstitium, and away from the lumen. Transport proteins such as ion channels and pumps are free to move from the basal to the lateral surface of the cell. Tight junctions join epithelial cells near their apical surface to prevent the migration of proteins from the basolateral membrane to the apical membrane.

D. MEMBRANE POTENTIAL

Membrane potential is the difference in electric potential between the interior and the exterior of a cell. Virtually all eukaryotic cells maintain a non-zero transmembrane potential, usually with a negative voltage in the cell interior as compared to the cell exterior ranging from -40 mV to -80 mV. In non-excitable cells, and in excitable cells in their baseline states, the membrane potential is held at a relatively stable value, called the resting potential. The opening and closing of ion channels can induce a change from the resting potential. This is called a depolarization if the interior voltage becomes more positive, or a hyperpolarization if the interior voltage becomes more negative. In excitable cells, a sufficiently large depolarization can evoke an action potential, in which the membrane potential changes rapidly and significantly for a short period of time, often reversing its polarity. Action potentials are generated by the activation of certain voltage-gated ion channels.

The two types of structures most responsible for creating and maintaining membrane potential are ion channels and ion pumps. Ion pumps influence the action potential by establishing the relative ratio of intracellular and extracellular ion concentration, while the generation of an action potential involves the opening and closing of ion channels. The sodium-potassium pump is the major ion channel contributing to the electrochemical gradient of cell membranes. On each cycle, the pump exchanges three Na^+ ions from the intracellular space for two K^+ ions from the extracellular space. If the numbers of each type of ion exchanged were equal, the pump would be electrically neutral, but, because of the three-for-two exchange ratio, it yields a net movement of one positive charge from intracellular to extracellular space for each cycle, thereby contributing to a positive voltage difference across the membrane, while also establishing a higher sodium concentration in the extracellular space than in the intracellular space and a higher potassium concentration in the intracellular space than in the extracellular space.

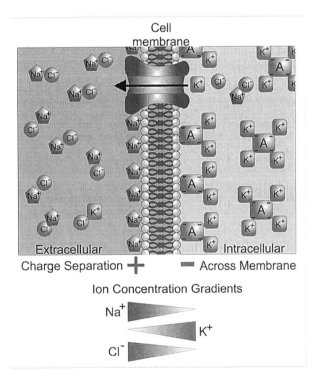

Figure 33.16: Differences in concentration of ions on opposite sides of a cellular membrane are reflected in the membrane potential. Here, potassium (K^+) ions, which are at a high concentration inside and a low concentration outside of the membrane. Sodium (Na^+) and chloride (Cl^-) ions are at high concentrations in the extracellular region, and low concentrations in the intracellular regions.

The reversal potential (or equilibrium potential) of an ion is the value of transmembrane voltage at which diffusive and electrical forces counterbalance, so that there is no net ion flow across the membrane. This means that the transmembrane voltage exactly opposes the force of diffusion of the ion, such that the net current of the ion across the membrane is zero and unchanging. The reversal potential is important because it gives the voltage that acts on channels permeable to that ion—in other words, it gives the voltage that the ion concentration gradient generates when it acts as a battery.

The equilibrium potential of a particular ion is usually designated by the notation E. The equilibrium potential for any ion can be calculated using the Nernst equation:

$$E = \frac{RT}{zF} \ln \frac{[\text{ion outside cell}]}{[\text{ion inside cell}]} = 2.3026 \frac{RT}{zF} \log_{10} \frac{[\text{ion outside cell}]}{[\text{ion inside cell}]}.$$

where R is the ideal gas constant, T is the absolute temperature (Kelvin) and F is Faraday's constant.

E. RECEPTORS

Cell surface receptors, such as membrane and transmembrane receptors, are specialized integral membrane proteins that take part in communication between the cell and the extracellular environment. Extracellular signaling molecules—including hormones, neurotransmitters, cytokines, growth factors or cell recognition molecules—bind to the receptor, initiate a chemical change on the intracellular side of the membrane, and produce a response in the cell as part of a process called signal transduction.

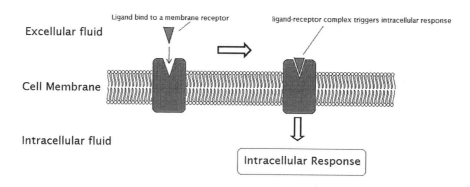

Figure 33.17: Extracellular and intracellular components of signal transduction

Like any integral membrane protein, a transmembrane receptor may be subdivided into three parts or domains: an extracellular, transmembrane and intracellular domain.

The extracellular domain is the portion of a receptor protein that extrudes from the cell or organelle to face the extracellular environment. If the polypeptide chain of the receptor crosses the bilayer several times, the external domain can comprise several loops, each segment of which extends outside of the membrane bilayer. Ligands for which the receptor is specific, for example a neurotransmitter or hormone, bind to the extracellular domain.

In the majority of receptors, alpha helices make up most of the transmembrane domain. In certain receptors, the transmembrane domain forms a protein-lined pore through the membrane, or ion channel. Upon activation of an extracellular domain by binding of the appropriate ligand, the pore becomes accessible to ions, which then pass through. In other receptors, the transmembrane domains are presumed to undergo a conformational change upon binding, which exerts an effect intracellularly.

The intracellular, cytoplasmic, domain of the receptor interacts with the interior of the cell or organelle, relaying the signal. There are two fundamentally different ways for this interaction to occur: the intracellular domain communicates via specific protein-protein-interactions with effector proteins, which in turn send the signal along a signal chain to its destination, through so-called second messengers; alternatively, with enzyme-linked receptors, the intracellular domain has enzymatic activity within the intracellular domain. Often, this is a tyrosine kinase activity.

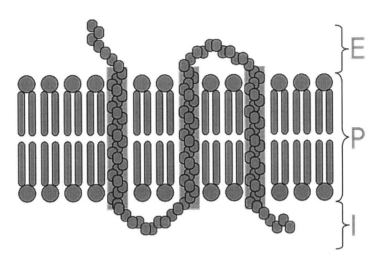

Figure 33.18: Structure of a transmembrane receptor protein. E = extracellular space,
P = plasma membrane, I = intracellular space

Chapter 33 Problems

Passage 33.1 (Questions 1-6)

Sphingomyelin is a type of sphingolipid found in animal cell membranes, especially in the membranous myelin sheath that surrounds certain nerve cell axons. It consists of a phosphocholine head group, sphingosine, and a fatty acid.

 The synthesis of sphingomyelin involves the enzymatic transfer of a phosphocholine group from phosphatidylcholine to a ceramide, as shown in Figure 1.

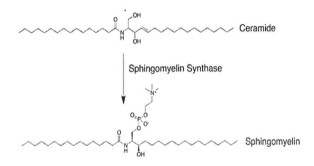

Figure 1: Synthesis of sphingomyelin from ceramide

 The reactions leading to the synthesis of ceramide occur on the cytosolic surface of the endoplasmic reticulum. From there, ceramide is transported to the Golgi apparatus where it can be converted to sphingomyelin.

 Sphingomyelin is degraded within the lysosomes of macrophages, when hydrolyzed by the enzyme sphingomyelinase, which is encoded by the SMPD1 gene of chromosome 7. Mutations in this gene cause Niemann–Pick disease types A and B, diseases characterized by insufficient synthesis of acid sphingomyelinase. In one or both forms of the disease, significant quantities of partially degraded sphingomyelin from the plasma membranes of red blood cells and myelin sheaths accumulate inside the lysosomes of macrophages of certain tissues, causing enlargement and subsequent dysfunction of the spleen and liver, as well as damage to the brain.

1. Sphingomyelin, comprised of sphingosine and fatty acid, can best be described as a:
   A. glucocerebroside.
   B. ganglioside.
   C. phospholipid.
   D. ceramide.

2. Niemann-Pick diseases type A and B can best be described as what?
   A. a non-heritable lysosomal storage disease
   B. a disorder of inappropriate sphingomyelin synthesis
   C. a disease caused by inappropriate macrophage-monocyte lineage activation
   D. a heritable metabolic disorder

3. The immediate developmental precursor from which the lysosomes affected by Niemann-Pick disease develop:
   A. is substantially more acidic than are lysosomes.
   B. contain defective proteins synthesized in the rough endoplasmic reticulum.
   C. fuse directly with autophagosomes to release hydrolytic enzymes.
   D. contain only a single type of hydrolytic enzyme, specific to a cellular target.

4. The enzyme ceramidase is deficient in Farber's disease, a related lysosomal storage disease. If the action of ceramidase results in the removal of only a fatty acid from ceramide, then the product made by the enzyme is best describe as what type of molecule?
   A. sphingosine
   B. choline
   C. cerebroside
   D. sphingomyelin

5. If possible, what strategy would be the least effective treatment for an individual suffering from Niemann Pick diseases type A or B?
   A. Targeting the wild type SMPD1 gene to red blood cells.
   B. Increasing the rate at which the patient's macrophages phagocytize material.
   C. A bone marrow transplant from an unaffected donor.
   D. Replacing degraded red bloods via transfusion from a healthy donor.

The following questions are NOT based on a descriptive passage.

6. Transport of inorganic ions across biological membranes requires a gated channel. The structural elements most likely to be observed in such channels are:
   A. lipid anchors that form covalent bonds while mediating transport.
   B. amphipathic channel-forming α helices.
   C. nonpolar channel-forming α helices.
   D. voltage-sensitive charged proteins.

7. Which of the following statements correctly describes the lipid constituents of plasma membranes?
   A. Most esterified, glycerol-containing lipids of the plasma membrane are glycolipids.
   B. Triglycerides are the most abundant membrane lipid component.
   C. The membranes of nerve cells with relatively low sphingolipid content.
   D. Glycolipids of the plasma membrane are found almost exclusively in the outer leaflet.

8. GLUT1 is a transmembrane protein expressed at high levels in the brain and red blood cells that permits glucose to enter those cells via facilitated diffusion. One characteristic of this transport is that:
   A. the unavailability of ATP will slow movement of glucose through the transporter in brain cells.
   B. the rate of glucose transport in red blood cells depends upon the blood glucose concentration.
   C. no specific inhibitors of GLUT1 exist.
   D. the rate of glucose consumption in brain cells does not influence the rate of glucose flux through the transporter.

9. Within the lipid bilayer of plasma membranes of human cells under physiological conditions:
   A. there is little lateral mobility of membrane lipids.
   B. exchange of phospholipids between the inner and outer leaflet occurs rapidly.
   C. electrical conductivity is too low to permit charge movement across the membrane surface.
   D. cholesterol content does not influence membrane fluidity.

10. Because of tight junctions between the basolateral membranes of stomach epithelial cells, diffusion of glucose, sodium, and other solutes with similar permeability profiles can be accomplished by all of the following means EXCEPT:
    A. facilitated diffusion.
    B. symport.
    C. free trans-membrane diffusion.
    D. antiport.

CHAPTER 34
Biosignalling

A. INTRODUCTION

Cell signaling is part of a complex system of communication that governs basic cellular activities and coordinates the actions of cells. The ability of cells to perceive and respond to their microenvironment is the basis of development, tissue repair, and immunity, as well as of normal tissue homeostasis. Errors in the cells' signaling mechanism are responsible for diseases including cancer, autoimmunity, and diabetes.

Signaling within, between, and among cells is subdivided into intracrine, autocrine, juxtacrine, paracrine, and endocrine signaling. Cells communicate with each other via direct contact (juxtacrine signaling), over short distances (paracrine signaling), or over large distances and/or scales (endocrine signaling). Intracrine signals are produced by the target cell and stay within the target cell. Autocrine signals are produced by the target cell, are secreted, and affect the cell secreting the signal via its own receptors. Juxtacrine signals target cells in contact with the signaling cell. These signals are transmitted along cell membranes and are capable of affecting either the emitting cell or cells immediately adjacent. Paracrine signals target cells in the vicinity of the emitting cell, while endocrine signals target distant cells. Endocrine cells produce hormones that travel through the blood to reach all parts of the body.

Some cell–cell communication requires direct cell–cell contact. Some cells can form gap junctions that connect their cytoplasm to the cytoplasm of adjacent cells. In cardiac muscle, gap junctions between adjacent cells allows for action potential propagation from the cardiac pacemaker region of the heart to spread and coordinately cause contraction of the heart.

Signaling between cells can either be through direct contact—juxtacrine signaling—or through the release of signaling molecules into the extracellular space. When such signaling molecules travel a short distance, the signaling is referred to as paracrine signaling. Autocrine signaling is a special case of paracrine signaling where the secreting cell has the ability to respond to the secreted signaling molecule. Synaptic signaling in neurons is a special case of paracrine signaling (for chemical synapses) or juxtacrine signaling (for electrical synapses) between neurons and target cells. Signaling molecules interact with a target cell as a ligand to the cell surface receptors of the target cells, or by entering into the cell through its membrane. This generally results in the activation of second messengers, and downstream cellular response.

At least three important classes of signaling molecules exist. Hormones are the major signaling molecules of the endocrine system. Neurotransmitters are signaling molecules of the nervous system, and include neuropeptides and neuromodulators. Certain neurotransmitters, such as the catecholamines, are also secreted by the endocrine system into the systemic circulation. Cytokines, including growth factors, are signaling molecules of the immune system. Some signaling molecules can function as both a hormone and a neurotransmitter. For example, norepinephrine, along with epinephrine, can function as a hormone when released from the adrenal gland, or be produced by neurons to function as a neurotransmitter within the brain. Another example is estrogen, which can be released by the ovary and function as a hormone or act locally via paracrine or autocrine signaling.

Signaling molecules can belong to several chemical classes: lipids, phospholipids, amino acids, monoamines, proteins, glycoproteins, or gases. Signaling molecules binding surface receptors are generally large and hydrophilic, while those entering the cell are generally small and hydrophobic. Once inside the cell, a signaling molecule can bind to intracellular receptors or other elements, or stimulate enzyme activity. Two gasses are also known to act as signaling molecules in the human body: nitric oxide and carbon monoxide.

B. GATED ION CHANNELS

Membrane receptors are divided into three general classes: ion channel-linked receptors, enzyme-linked receptors and G protein-coupled receptors.

Ion channel linked receptors, also called ligand-gated channels, are cell membrane-bound receptors that act through synaptic signaling on electrically excitable cells. These membrane-spanning proteins undergo a conformational change when a ligand binds to them so that a transmembrane pore is opened to allow the passage of a specific molecule. The ligands to which the receptor binds can be neurotransmitters or peptide hormones, and the molecules that pass through are often ions, such as sodium or potassium, which can alter the charge across the membrane. The ion channels, or pores, are opened only for a short time, after which the ligand dissociates from the receptor and the receptor is available once again for a new ligand to bind. The opening and closing of ions channels are often controlled by peptide hormones or neurotransmitters, as is shown for the binding of the neurotransmitter acetylcholine to one of its receptors in Figure 34.1.

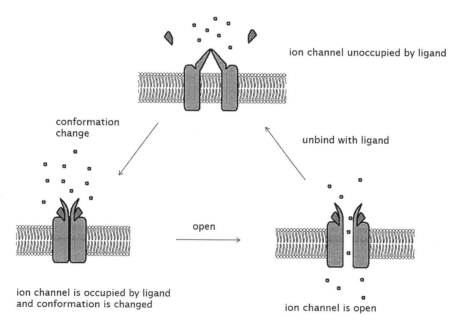

Figure 34.1: Ligand-binding induces conformational changes in the nicotinic acetylcholine receptor.

C. ENZYME LINKED RECEPTORS

Enzyme-linked receptors are either enzymes themselves, or are directly associated with the enzymes that they activate. These are usually single-pass transmembrane receptors, with the enzymatic portion of the receptor being intracellular. The majority of enzyme-linked receptors are protein kinases, or are associated with protein kinases. One prominent class of enzyme-linked receptors are receptor tyrosine kinases (RTK). RTKs are high-affinity cell surface receptors for many polypeptide growth factors and hormones, such as epidermal growth factor (EGF), platelet derived growth factor (PDGF), and fibroblast growth factor (FGF). They have been shown to be key regulators of normal cellular processes, while dysfunctions in these receptors have been implicated in the progression of many types of cancer. Extracellular ligand binding will typically cause or stabilize dimerization of adjacent RTK monomers. This allows a tyrosine in the cytoplasmic portion of each receptor monomer to be trans-phosphorylated by its partner receptor, providing phosphorylated binding sites for adapter proteins.

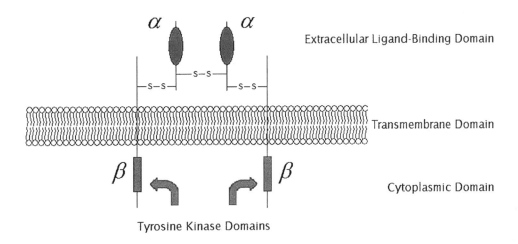

Figure 34.2: Structure of the Insulin-like Growth Factor-1 (IGR-1), a tyrosine kinase receptor.

Binding of adaptor proteins such as GRB2 couple the signal to further downstream signaling processes. For example, one of the signal transduction pathways activated is known as the mitogen-activated protein kinase (MAPK) pathway (also known as the MAPK/ERK pathway). The MAPK protein is a protein kinase that can attach phosphate to target proteins such as the transcription factor MYC and, thus, alter gene transcription and, ultimately, cell cycle progression. Many cellular proteins are activated downstream of the growth factor receptors (such as EGFR) that initiate this signal transduction pathway.

D. G PROTEIN-COUPLED RECEPTORS

G protein-coupled receptors (GPCRs), also known as seven-transmembrane domain receptors because they possess seven transmembrane domains, are a large family of receptors that, upon binding of ligand, experience a conformational change. The ligands that bind and activate these receptors include light-sensitive compounds, odors, hormones, and neurotransmitters, and vary in size from small molecules to peptides to large proteins. The conformational change induced by ligand binding permits the receptor to act as a guanine nucleotide exchange factor (GEF). The GPCR can then associate with and allosterically activate a G-protein. G proteins, which are heterotrimers composed of α, β and γ subunits, are inactive when reversibly bound to GDP but active when bound to GTP. Upon receptor activation, the GEF domain, in turn, allosterically activates the G-protein by facilitating the exchange of a molecule of GDP for GTP at the G-protein's α-subunit. The G-protein's α subunit, together with the bound GTP, can then dissociate from the β and γ subunits to further affect intracellular signaling proteins or target functional proteins directly. The Gα subunit of the G protein has an intrinsic GTP hydrolysis activity, thus the inactive form of the α-subunit (Gα-GDP) is eventually regenerated, leading to its re-association with the Gβγ dimer to re-form the inactive G-protein. The rate of GTP hydrolysis, and thus the rate of G protein inactivation, is often accelerated due to the actions of another family of allosteric modulating proteins, GTPase-activating protein, also known as GAPs.

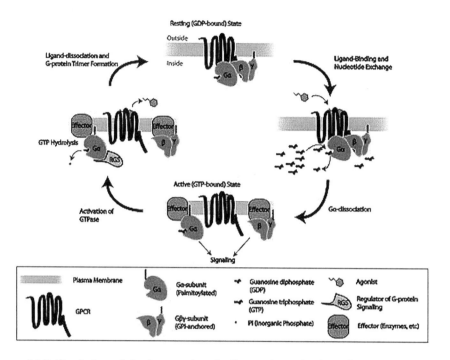

Figure 34.3: Depiction of the heterotrimeric G-protein activation/deactivation cycle

There are two principal downstream signal transduction pathways through which activated G proteins function: the cAMP signaling pathway and the phosphatidylinositol pathway. The pathway affected, and the nature of that effect, depends upon the type of G protein—specifically, the nature of the subunits composing the G protein. While most GPCRs are capable of activating more than one Gα-subtype, they often show a preference for one subtype over another, indicating that the specificity of ligand binding for their respective GPCRs directs the downstream signaling induced by that binding according to the nature of the associated G protein. The effector of both the Gαs and Gαi subunits is adenylate cyclase. Conversion of ATP to cAMP is directly stimulated by G-proteins of the Gαs class, while Gα subunits of the Gαi and Gαo type inhibit adenylate cyclase from generating cAMP. Thus, GPCRs coupled to Gαs and GPCRs coupled to Gαi or Gαo exert reciprocal control upon one another. The level of cytosolic cAMP, a so-called second-messenger, may then determine the activity of various ion channels and downstream proteins through the activity of protein kinase A.

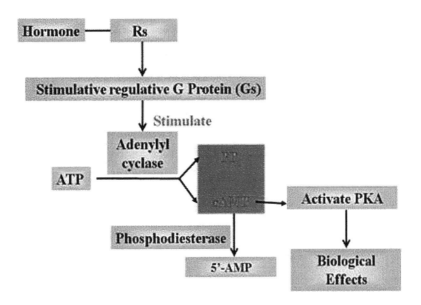

Figure 34.4: Pathway by which hormone activation of the G_s coupled protein receptor stimulates signal transduction through the modulation of cAMP synthesis.

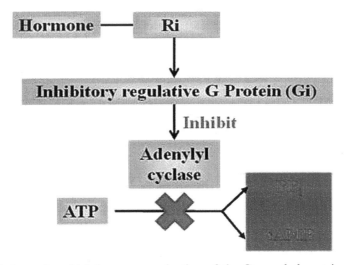

Figure 34.5: Pathway by which hormone activation of the G_i coupled protein receptor inhibits signal transduction through inhibition of cAMP synthesis.

The effector of the Gαq pathway is phospholipase C (PLC), which catalyzes the cleavage of membrane-bound phosphatidylinositol 4,5-biphosphate (PIP_2) into the second messengers inositol (1,4,5) triphosphate (IP_3) and diacylglycerol (DAG).

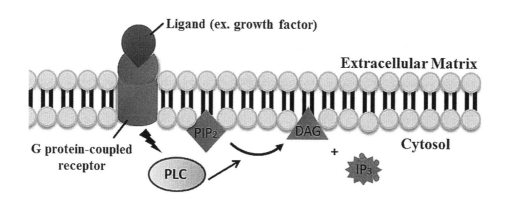

Figure 34.6: PLC-mediated cleavage of PIP_2 to DAG and IP_3

IP$_3$ acts on IP$_3$ receptors found in the membrane of the endoplasmic reticulum (ER) to elicit calcium ion release from the ER, while DAG diffuses along the plasma membrane, where it may activate the membrane-associated kinase, called protein kinase C (PKC). Since many isoforms of PKC are also activated directly by increases in intracellular calcium, these simultaneously-activated pathways can converge a signal through the same secondary effector, PKC. Elevated intracellular calcium also binds and allosterically activates proteins called calmodulins, which in turn go on to bind and allosterically activate enzymes such as calcium/calmodulin-dependent kinases (CAMKs).

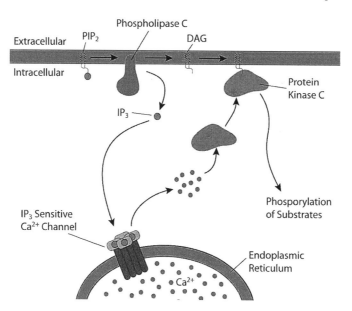

Figure 34.7: PLC cleavage of PIP_2 to IP_3 and DAG initiates intracellular calcium release and PKC activation.

E. STEROIDS

Steroids exert a wide variety of physiological effects by modulating changes in gene expression or by binding membrane-associated steroid receptors, activating intracellular signaling cascades involved in non-genomic actions.

Because most steroids and sterols are lipid-soluble, they can diffuse relatively unhindered from the blood through the cell membrane and into the cytoplasm of target cells. In the cytoplasm, steroid hormones, either in unmodified form or after having undergone enzyme-mediated alterations, bind to their specific metalloprotein receptors, known as nuclear receptors. Upon binding, many steroid receptors dimerize, that is, two receptor subunits join together to form one functional DNA-binding unit that may subsequently enter the nucleus. In the case of some receptors, the receptor is associated with a heat shock protein, which is released at the time of hormone binding. After translocation into the nucleus, the steroid-receptor ligand complex binds to specific DNA sequences and induces up- or down-regulation of the transcription of its target genes.

Nuclear receptors themselves are a class of proteins found within cells that are responsible for sensing steroid and thyroid hormones and certain other molecules. Ligands that bind to and activate nuclear receptors include lipophilic substances such as endogenous steroid hormones, thyroid hormone, vitamins A and D, and certain xenobiotics.

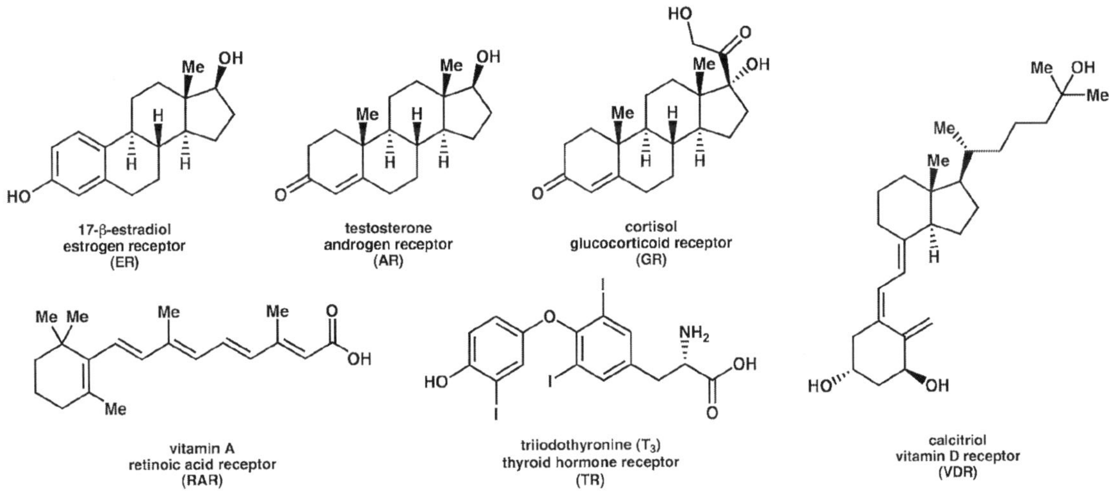

Figure 34.8: Structure of common nuclear receptor ligands and the names of the receptors to which they bind

Nuclear receptors contain a number of functionally distant domains, including a DNA-binding domain, which is a highly conserved domain containing two zinc finger elements that bind to specific sequences of DNA referred to as hormone response elements (HRE), as well as a ligand binding domain (LBD), the structure of which is highly conserved from nuclear receptor to nuclear receptor.

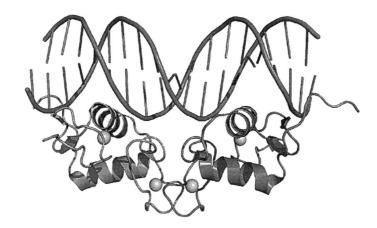

Figure 34.9: Crystallographic structure of the human progesterone receptor DNA-binding domain dimer complexed with double-strained DNA. Zinc atoms are depicted as spheres.

Nuclear receptors (NRs) may be classified into two broad classes according to their mechanism of action and their subcellular distribution in the absence of ligand. Small lipophilic substances such as steroid hormones diffuse through the cell membrane and bind to type I nuclear receptors located in the cytosol (type I NR) or type II nuclear receptors (type II NR) of the cell. Binding causes a conformational change in the receptor which, depending on the class of receptor, triggers a cascade of downstream events that direct the NRs to DNA transcription regulation sites which result in up or down-regulation of gene expression.

Ligand binding to type I nuclear receptors in the cytosol results in the receptor's dissociation from the heat shock proteins to which they are complexed, then receptor dimerization, and finally the receptor translocation from the cytoplasm into the cell nucleus. Once within the nuclear, the receptor-ligand complex binds to specific sequences of DNA known as hormone response elements (HREs). Type I nuclear receptors include the androgen receptor, estrogen receptors, glucocorticoid receptor, and progesterone receptor.

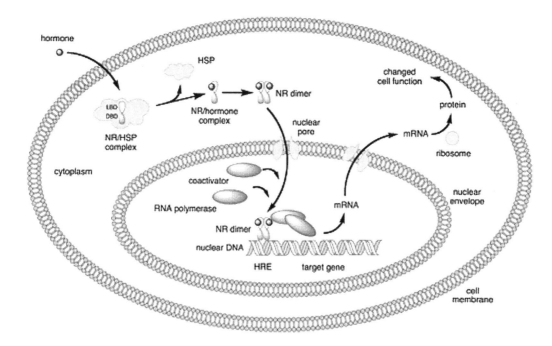

Figure 34.10: Mechanism of type I nuclear receptors (NR)

Type II receptors, in contrast to type I, are retained in the nucleus regardless of the ligand binding status, and exist as hetero-dimers, usually with the protein RXR, when complexed with bound ligand. In the absence of ligand, type II nuclear receptors are often complexed with corepressor proteins. In such cases, ligand binding to the NR causes dissociation of corepressor proteins and recruitment of coactivator proteins. Additional proteins including RNA polymerase are then recruited to the NR-DNA complex, promoting the transcription of target DNA. Type II nuclear receptors include the retinoic acid receptor, retinoid X receptor and thyroid hormone receptor.

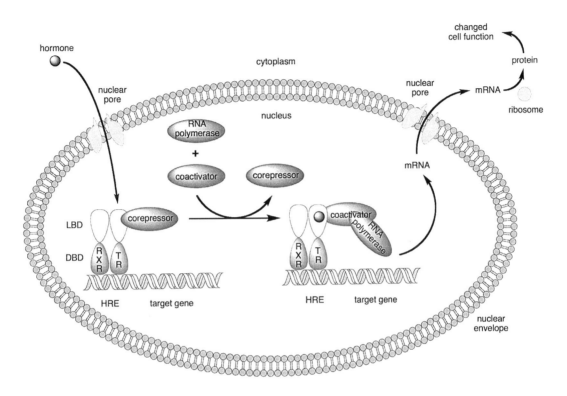

Figure 34.11: Mechanism of type II nuclear receptors (NR)

Nuclear receptors bound to hormone response elements recruit a number of other proteins, referred to as transcription coregulators, which facilitate or inhibit the transcription of the associated target gene into mRNA. The functions of these coregulators are varied and include chromatin remodeling (making the target gene either more or less accessible to transcription) or a bridging function to stabilize the binding of other coregulatory proteins. Binding of agonist ligands to nuclear receptors induces a conformation of the receptor that preferentially binds coactivator proteins. These proteins often have an intrinsic histone acetyltransferase (HAT) activity, which weakens the association of histones to DNA, and therefore promotes gene transcription. Binding of antagonist ligands to nuclear receptors in contrast induces a conformation of the receptor that preferentially binds corepressor proteins. These proteins, in turn, recruit histone deacetylases (HDACs), which strengthens the association of histones to DNA, and therefore represses gene transcription.

F. PROSTAGLANDINS

The prostaglandins are a group of hormone-like lipid compounds that are derived enzymatically from fatty acids, and which contain 20 carbon atoms, including a 5-carbon ring. The prostaglandins, together with the thromboxanes and prostacyclin, form the prostanoid class of fatty acid derivatives, a subclass of eicosanoids.

As signaling mediators, they elicit strong and diverse physiological effects, such as acting upon platelets as well as endothelial, uterine and mast cells. Prostaglandins are not endocrine hormones, but act as local autocrine or paracrine messenger molecules on nearby target tissues. They differ from hormones in that they are not produced at a specific site but at sites throughout the human body.

Their synthesis in the cell begins with the release of arachidonic acid from diacylglycerol or phospholipid via phospholipase-A_2. Once liberated, arachidonic acid enters either the cyclooxygenase pathway or the lipoxygenase pathway. The cyclooxygenase pathway produces thromboxane, prostacyclin and prostaglandin D, E and F. Alternatively, the lipoxygenase enzyme pathway is active in leukocytes and in macrophages and synthesizes leukotrienes.

Prostaglandins synthesis may proceed via the reaction catalysis of either of two cyclooxygenases isoforms, COX-1 or COX-2. Constitutively active COX-1 is thought to be responsible for the baseline levels of prostaglandins, while inducible COX-2 produces prostaglandins through stimulation. While COX-1 and COX-2 are both located in the blood vessels, stomach and the kidneys, prostaglandin levels are increased by COX-2 in scenarios of inflammation and growth.

Through the family of G-protein coupled prostaglandin receptors to which they bind, prostaglandins produce a variety of effects including constriction or dilation of blood vessels, aggregation or disaggregation of platelets, induction of labor, inflammatory regulation, calcium movement, thermoregulation, bronchial smooth muscle tone, and secretion of gastric acid from the parietal cells of the stomach.

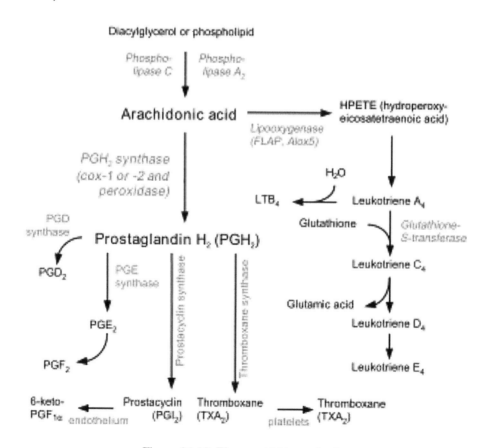

Figure 34.12: Eicosanoid biosynthesis

Chapter 34 Problems
Passage 34.1 (Questions 1-6)

When cells of the liver—hepatocytes— are fractionated by ultracentrifugation, a fraction containing all of the cytosolic components of the cell and a fraction containing all of the membrane components of the cell are obtained.

Glycogen stored in hepatocytes is mobilized in a reaction that requires the activation of the enzyme glycogen phosphorylase in response to binding of the primary messenger, glucagon, in the blood to its receptor on the hepatocyte membrane, a G coupled protein receptor, according to the scheme of cyclic activation and deactivation shown in Figure 1.

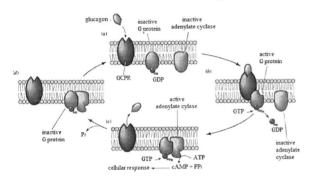

Figure 1: Activation/deactivation-cycle of the glucagon receptor

When the hepatocyte fractions obtained by centrifugation were mixed in various combinations with either glucagon, glycogen, or both, the five results indicated below were observed:

1. cytosolic fraction + glucagon + glycogen + membrane fraction → glucose

2. boiled membrane fraction + glucagon + glycogen + cytosolic fraction → glucose

3. cytosolic fraction + glycogen + glucagon → no glucose

4. membrane fraction + glycogen + glucagon → no glucose

5. boiled cytosolic fraction + glucagon + glycogen + membrane fraction → glucose

1. Which of the following conclusions is LEAST supported by results of the experiments performed in the passage?
   A. Both boiled cytosolic and boiled membrane fractions react to form glucose.
   B. Cytosolic elements are required for the mobilization of the glycogen.
   C. Glucagon is required for the degradation of glucose.
   D. Glucagon induces glycogen breakdown only upon binding of its receptor.

2. In what way is formation of the glucagon receptor-ligand complex linked to an increase in the intracellular cAMP concentration of intact cells through a change in the G protein shown in Figure 1?
   A. complex formation causes the phosphorylation of G-protein bound GDP
   B. exchange of GDP for GTP on the G-protein permits association with the complex
   C. formation of the complex promotes G-protein nucleotide exchange
   D. association of G protein and receptor permit formation of the ligand-receptor complex

3. In addition to cAMP, activation of certain G protein subunits can also transmit intracellular signals through what mechanism?
   A. Increasing intracellular calcium ion concentration
   B. Binding to nuclear receptors in the cytoplasm
   C. Phosphorylation and dimerization of their tyrosine kinase domains
   D. Binding to nuclear receptors in the nucleus

4. Binding of glucagon to a small subset of glucagon receptors causes a decrease in intracellular cAMP levels. Is this observation consistent with the function of G coupled protein receptors?
   A. No, G proteins are activated by binding of the glucagon receptor.
   B. No, activation of Gαs subunits stimulates adenylate cyclase activity.
   C. Yes, binding of the G coupled protein receptor causes exchange of GTP for GTP by Gαi subunits.
   D. Yes, G coupled protein receptors specific for a given ligand may associate with different G protein types.

5. Which of the following can best be described as a second messenger?
   A. Glycogen
   B. cAMP
   C. Glucagon
   D. G coupled protein receptor

The following questions are NOT based on a descriptive passage.

6. A pheochromocytoma is a tumor resulting in the overproduction of catecholamines. In what forms of cell-to-cell signaling can catecholamines participate?
   A. paracrine signaling only
   B. endocrine signaling only
   C. both paracrine and autocrine signaling
   D. neither paracrine nor autocrine signaling

7. Inhibitors of the enzyme lipoxygenase, which are used in the treatment of asthma, inhibit the synthesis of which eiconsanoids?
   I. thromboxanes
   II. leukotrienes
   III. prostaglandins
   A. I only
   B. II only
   C. II and III only
   D. I, II and III

8. 8. All of the following hormones exert their downstream signaling action through binding of an extracellular receptor EXCEPT:
   A. ADH
   B. thyroid hormone
   C. FSH
   D. serotonin

9. Increased intracellular calcium causes the contraction of vascular smooth muscle, however, activation of certain agents that stimulate the production of IP_3 are vasodilators. What fact could explain the action of such agents?
   A. These agents promote the closure of gap junctions between vascular smooth muscle cells.
   B. Calcium ions rapidly equilibrate across the plasma membrane of vascular smooth muscle cells.
   C. The calcium-calmodulin complex stimulates NO synthase in endothelial cells.
   D. Calcium-responsive tropomyosin is not present in vascular smooth muscle cells.

10. All of the following are true of protein kinase A EXCEPT:
    A. its signaling action is enhanced by phosphodiesterases.
    B. it is stimulated by an increase in cAMP.
    C. cAMP binds its two regulatory subunits.
    D. it is capable of inducing a conformational change in target proteins.

SECTION 9

Content Review Problems

1. The amphipathic nature of cholesterol is best reflected in what description of its structure?
   A. It contains a single hydroxyl group and a fused hydrocarbon ring backbone.
   B. Its long branched hydrocarbon chain contains three hydrocarbon rings.
   C. It has five-methyl groups along with its hydrocarbon chain.
   D. It has three six-membered rings fused with a single five-membered ring.

2. During active transport, the molecule that directly facilities solute movement is best described as:
   A. cholesterol.
   B. an integral protein.
   C. a carbohydrate.
   D. a hydrophobic molecule.

3. The model that best describes the structure of biological membranes is the:
   A. fluid mosaic model.
   B. Page model.
   C. lac operon model.
   D. single bilayer model.

4. In terms of their behavior within membranes, phospholipids can best be described as:
   A. hydrophilic molecules.
   B. hydrophobic molecules.
   C. amphiphilic molecules.
   D. amphoteric molecules.

5. Pinocytosis occurs in:
   A. all eukaryotic cells.
   B. all prokaryotic cells.
   C. the mitochondria of eukaryotes.
   D. the nuclei of eukaryotes.

6. Exocytosis of proteins describes their:
   A. secretion across the plasma membrane and into the extracellular space.
   B. secretion across the plasma membrane and into the intracellular space.
   C. uptake from the extracellular space into the cell.
   D. uptake from the cytosol into the mitochondria.

7. The membrane proteins that catalyze active transport reactions differ from soluble enzymes in what respect?
   A. They are permanently changed during the reaction.
   B. The substrates of the reaction are exclusively extracellular.
   C. They do not enhance the rates of reactions.
   D. The products of the reaction move in a specific direction.

8. The movement of molecules across a membrane by passive transport does not in any case require:
   A. an input of metabolic energy.
   B. a concentration gradient.
   C. a protein channel.
   D. A, B or C

9. Peptidoglycan is a complex consisting of what molecules?
   A. oligosaccharides and protein
   B. polysaccharides and protein
   C. monosaccharides and protein
   D. amino acids and carbohydrates

10. The smooth endoplasmic reticulum (SER) is the site of:
    A. phospholipid synthesis.
    B. amino acid synthesis.
    C. carbohydrate synthesis.
    D. protein synthesis.

11. Which of the following is correct concerning biological membranes?
    A. Membranes form boundaries around the cell and distinct subcellular components.
    B. Membranes act as selectively permeable barriers.
    C. Membranes contain varying amount of lipid and protein and some contain small amount of carbohydrates.
    D. All of the above

12. Membrane lipids include:
    A. glycerophospholipids.
    B. sphingolipids.
    C. sterols.
    D. all of the above

13. Arachidonate is a:
    A. unsaturated fatty acid.
    B. saturated fatty acid.
    C. protein.
    D. carbohydrate.

14. Animals cannot convert fatty acids into glucose because:
    A. they lack the enzyme malate synthase.
    B. they lack an appropriate dehydrogenase enzyme.
    C. acetyl CoA cannot be converted directly to pyruvate.
    D. they lack the enzyme alpha-ketoglutarate dehydrogenase.

15. Phospholipids contains:
    A. hydrophilic heads and hydrophobic tails.
    B. long water-soluble carbon chains.
    C. positively charged functional groups.
    D. both B and C.

16. Micelles of fatty acids in water are organized such that the _____ face the solvent and the _____ are directed toward the interior of the cell.
    A. carboxylic acid groups, hydrocarbon chains heads
    B. hydrophilic heads, hydrophobic tails
    C. hydrocarbon chains, carboxylic acid groups
    D. both A and B

17. Chylomicrons are synthesized in the:
    A. blood.
    B. liver.
    C. intestine.
    D. pancreas.

18. Cholesterol is NOT a precursor of which of the following molecules?
    A. steroid hormones
    B. vitamin A
    C. bile salts
    D. both A and C

19. In humans, catecholamine molecules function as:
    A. hormones.
    B. neurotransmitters.
    C. both A and B
    D. neither A nor B.

20. In tyrosine kinase receptors, the SH2 domain of accessory proteins binds to what moiety?
    A. phosphorylated serine residues
    B. phosphorylated tyrosine residues
    C. GDP
    D. Ca^{2+}

21. In paracrine signaling, a secreted signaling molecule affects only:
    A. target cells near the cell from which it was secreted.
    B. target cells distant from its site of synthesis in cells of an endocrine organ.
    C. both A and B
    D. neither A nor B

22. Which of the following molecules does not transduce an intra- or extra-cellular signal through direct binding of an intracellular or cell surface receptor?
    A. Testosterone
    B. Insulin
    C. Thyroxin
    D. Adenylate cyclase

23. Phosphorylation can affect the specific catalytic function of the proteins involved in signal cascades because it:
    A. changes the shape and thus the enzymatic activity of a phosphorylated protein.
    B. increases the affinity of a target protein for a signaling protein.
    C. allows hydrophilic signaling molecules to cross the plasma membrane.
    D. None of the above

24. Which of the following statements regarding G proteins is FALSE?
    A. They are involved in signal cascades
    B. They bind to and are regulated by guanine nucleotides
    C. They become activated when bound to GDP
    D. They must be active before the cell can make needed cAMP

25. When a _____ reaches its _____, there is a specific means of receiving it and transducing the signal received. This task is the responsibility of specialized proteins referred to as_____ .
    A. signaling molecule; receptor; G proteins
    B. signaling molecule; target cell; G proteins
    C. signaling molecule; target cell; receptors
    D. kinase; receptor; proteases

26. If the inhalation of nitric oxide reduces blood pressure only in lung tissue, but not elsewhere in the body, what property of the gas or of the body might explain this observation?
    A. Other body tissues are not responsive to cell signaling molecules.
    B. Nitric oxide cannot penetrate lipophilic cell membranes.
    C. Nitric oxide is degraded rapidly.
    D. None of the above

27. All of the following are cell surface receptors EXCEPT:
    A. enzyme linked receptors.
    B. ion-channel linked receptors.
    C. G protein linked receptors.
    D. type I nuclear receptors.

28. Which of the following is true of a hydrophilic signaling molecule?
    A. Its receptor is located in the cytosol of the target cell.
    B. It might trigger a signal cascade that causes a specific cellular response.
    C. It diffuses across the cell membrane to modulate a specific intracellular process.
    D. It may be categorized as a steroid.

29. cAMP and cGMP are derived from:
    A. ATP and GTP by the actions of adenylate cyclase and guanylate cyclase respectively.
    B. GTP and ATP by the actions of adenylate cyclase and guanylate cyclase respectively.
    C. ATP and GTP by the actions of guanylate cyclase and adenylate cyclase respectively.
    D. none of the above

30. If a disease of the blood vessels caused the endothelial cells of the vessel to die, what effect would this have on the cellular activities associated with vasodilation?
    A. Nitric oxide would no longer be produced within the diseased vessels.
    B. Smooth muscle cells could no longer be made to relax by stimulatory input.
    C. It would be more difficult to increase local blood flow and reduce blood pressure in diseased vessel segments.
    D. All of the above

31. What is the name of the protein signaling molecule that alters glucose uptake by cells globally, and where would its receptors be identified?
    A. Insulin; in fat and skeletal muscle.
    B. Insulin; in the beta cells of the pancreas.
    C. PDGF; in blood vessels.
    D. NGF; in nerve cells.

32. Which of the following molecules only undergoes reduction in the body?
    A. Fatty acids
    B. $FADH_2$
    C. NADH
    D. O_2

33. In the signal transduction mechanism known as protein phosphorylation:
    A. the signaling molecule binds to a surface receptor.
    B. receptor kinases play a key role in triggering the signal cascade.
    C. phosphorylated proteins act with enzymes to trigger the signal cascade.
    D. All of the above

34. The enzyme that catalyzes the splitting of PIP_2 into two molecules of inositol triphosphate (IP_3) and diacylglycerol in cell signaling is:
    A. phosphokinase C.
    B. phospholipase C.
    C. phosphodiesterase C.
    D. lipokinase.

35. The binding of ligands to many G-protein-coupled receptors leads to a(n):
    A. increase in the concentration of certain intracellular signaling molecules called second messengers.
    B. decrease in the concentration of certain intracellular signaling molecules called second messengers.
    C. increase in the concentration of certain extracellular signaling molecules called first messengers.
    D. decrease in the concentration of certain extracellular signaling molecules called first messengers.

36. Which of the following processes involves the combining of a message from one signaling molecule with that of another to either enhance or inhibit a cellular effect?
    A. Signal transduction
    B. Signal reception
    C. Signal integration
    D. Signal amplification

37. A domain of a receptor is particularly rich in leucine residues. This domain:
    A. must be found on the intracellular side of the membrane.
    B. is likely unstable.
    C. must be found on the extracellular side of the membrane.
    D. is more likely to be a membrane-spanning region.

38. Which of the following statements is FALSE?
    A. The principal lipophilic hormones that binds to receptors located in the plasma membranes are prostaglandins.
    B. Prostaglandins are synthesized from arachidonic acid.
    C. Prostaglandins act as paracrine signaling molecules.
    D. None of the above

39. Which of the following is a hormone whose action requires a cell surface receptor?
    A. Nitric oxide
    B. Progesterone
    C. Epinephrine
    D. Growth factors

40. A hormone or ligand can be considered a:
    A. first messenger.
    B. second messenger.
    C. both A and B
    D. neither A nor B

41. Treatment with a drug that interferes with the sodium-potassium ATPase would have what effect on a cell?
    A. High levels of extracellular sodium and potassium.
    B. Increased intracellular sodium concentrations.
    C. Low levels of extracellular sodium and potassium.
    D. Decreased levels of intracellular sodium.

42. Functions of the cell membrane involve all of the following EXCEPT:
    A. direct synthesis of second messengers.
    B. cytoskeletal attachment.
    C. regulation of solute transport.
    D. cellular compartmentalization.

43. A cell junction providing an attachment point between the cell and basement membrane is a:
    A. desmosome.
    B. hemidesmosome.
    C. gap junction.
    D. tight junction.

44. The movement of small amounts of fluid through vesicular infolding is most specifically described as:
    A. phagocytosis
    B. dehydration.
    C. pinocytosis.
    D. endocytosis.

45. Which of the following is most likely to describe the resting membrane potential of a cell?
    A. + 20 mV
    B. + 70 mV
    C. -55 mV
    D. + 55 mV

46. All of the following are sphingolipids EXCEPT:
    A. gangliosides.
    B. cerebrosides.
    C. phosphatidylserine.
    D. sphingomyelin.

47. Of the following forms of transport, the occurrence of which never requires the hydrolysis of ATP?
    A. osmosis
    B. symport
    C. antiport
    D. primary active transport

48. Which of the following is a prominent component of the glycocalyx?
    A. glycolipids
    B. phospholipids
    C. glycoproteins
    D. both A and C

49. The activity of neuromuscular junctions relies on what form of ion channel activation?
    A. ligand-gated channels
    B. ungated channels
    C. enzyme-linked receptors
    D. G protein-coupled receptors

50. Subunits of heterotrimeric G proteins may, upon activation:
    A. increase intracellular cAMP levels.
    B. decrease intracellular cAMP levels.
    C. activate phospholipase C.
    D. all of the above

NEXT STEP MCAT CONTENT REVIEW: BIOLOGY AND BIOCHEMISTRY

Biology and Biochemistry Content Review

1. Which of the following amino acids does NOT have a chiral side chain?
   A. Glycine
   B. Tryptophan
   C. Glutamic acid
   D. Glutamate

2. Which of the following amino acids is NOT basic?
   A. Arginine
   B. Tyrosine
   C. Lysine
   D. Histidine

3. Which of the following amino acids forms disulfide bonds?
   A. Phenylalanine
   B. Serine
   C. Cysteine
   D. Valine

4. All amino acids contain a/an:
   A. Imide functional group
   B. Alkene functional group
   C. Ether functional group
   D. Carboxyl functional group

5. Why does proline have a unique impact on the secondary structure of proteins?
   A. It is achiral
   B. It is extremely reactive
   C. Its R-group is attached to its amino group
   D. It lacks an amino group

6. What is true of leucine?
   A. Leucine has a methyl propyl side chain
   B. Leucine is an acidic amino acid
   C. Leucine is a polar amino acid
   D. Leucine has a nitrogen in its side chain

7. How are tyrosine, phenylalanine, and tryptophan similar amino acids?
   A. They are all acidic
   B. They all lack nitrogen in their side chain
   C. They all have an imide functional group in their side chain
   D. They all have aromatic side chains

8. Glutamic acid can be derived from:
   A. Aspartic acid
   B. Guanine
   C. Glutamate
   D. Lysine

9. Which of the following hormones does the cortex of the adrenal gland produce?
   A. Oxytocin
   B. ADH
   C. Aldosterone
   D. Epinephrine

10. Reducing blood calcium levels is the function of which of the following hormones?
    A. Calcitonin
    B. Parathyroid hormone
    C. Cortisol
    D. Estrogen

11. Reabsorption of just water at the collecting duct of the nephron is the function of which of the following hormones?
    A. Vasopressin
    B. Aldosterone
    C. LH
    D. Erythropoietin

12. Which of the following hormones is a peptide hormone?
    A. T_3
    B. Norepinephrine
    C. Cortisol
    D. TSH

13. Which of the following hormones is a steroid hormone?
    A. LH
    B. hGH
    C. Estrogen
    D. Prolactin

14. Increasing blood glucose levels is the function of which of the following hormones?
    A. Epinephrine
    B. Insulin
    C. Glucagon
    D. hGH

15. Which of the following hormones does the pancreas produce?
    A. Cortisol
    B. Prolactin
    C. Insulin
    D. T_4

16. Which of the following hormones is considered a tyrosine derivative?
    A. FSH
    B. Epinephrine
    C. ACTH
    D. PTH

17. The anterior pituitary produces all of the following hormones except:
    A. Prolactin
    B. Oxytocin
    C. TSH
    D. Human growth hormone

18. What step in mitosis occurs after metaphase?
    A. Interphase
    B. Prophase
    C. Anaphase
    D. Telophase

19. In what phase does the cell exhibit the most growth before division?
    A. Interphase
    B. Prophase
    C. Anaphase
    D. Telophase

20. Where in eukaryotic cells is DNA transcribed?
    A. Nucleoid
    B. Mitochondria
    C. Nuclear membrane
    D. Nucleus

21. Where is translation completed for proteins that are to be transported outside the cell?
    A. Free ribosome
    B. Smooth ER
    C. Rough ER
    D. Golgi apparatus

22. Where in eukaryotic cells is rRNA formed?
    A. Nucleoid
    B. Nucleolus
    C. Ribosomes
    D. Cytosol

23. How does the electron transport chain lead to ATP production?
    A. Hydrolysis of macromolecules
    B. Symport system
    C. Combustion in the presence of oxygen
    D. Establishment of a proton gradient

24. A release of a lysosome's hydrolytic enzymes leads to all of the following except:
    A. Mitosis
    B. Apoptosis
    C. Autolysis
    D. Degradation of cellular components

25. Microfilaments are made up of:
    A. Myosin
    B. Actin
    C. Tubulin
    D. Collagen

26. Which of the following organizes the mitotic spindle during mitosis?
    A. Centrosomes
    B. Centrioles
    C. Plasma membrane
    D. Nucleus

27. Which of the following is NOT an example of connective tissue?
    A. Skin
    B. Adipose tissue
    C. Blood
    D. Neuron

28. Which of the following is an organelle found in eukaryotes and not in prokaryotes?
    A. Flagella
    B. Ribosomes
    C. Plasma membrane
    D. Mitochondria

29. Which of the following organelles is able to synthesize steroids?
    A. Nucleus
    B. Lysosome
    C. Rough ER
    D. Smooth ER

30. The cell wall of bacteria is primarily composed of which of the following polymers:
    A. Peptidoglycan
    B. Chitin
    C. Actin
    D. Tubulin

31. The cell wall of fungi is primarily composed of which of the following polymers:
    A. Peptidoglycan
    B. Chitin
    C. Actin
    D. Tubulin

32. Bacteria are able to manufacture ATP through which of the following processes:
    A. The Krebs cycle
    B. Reduction of glucose
    C. Establishing a proton gradient
    D. Oxidation of pyruvate

33. Bacteria undergo all of the following modes of genetic recombination except:
    A. Conjugation
    B. Transection
    C. Transduction
    D. Transformation

34. Which of the following types of bacterial genetic recombination requires a viral vector?
    A. Conjugation
    B. Transection
    C. Transduction
    D. Transformation

35. Which of the following types of bacterial genetic recombination is considered bacterial sexual reproduction?
    A. Conjugation
    B. Transection
    C. Transduction
    D. Transformation

36. Viruses can contain all of the following except:
    A. Nucleic acid
    B. Capsid
    C. Mitochondria
    D. Enzymes

37. What is the function of reverse transcriptase?
    A. Translates RNA into DNA
    B. Prepares DNA for transcription
    C. Transcribes RNA into DNA
    D. Modifies RNA into mRNA

38. Retroviruses are classified as:
    A. Single-stranded DNA
    B. Single-stranded RNA
    C. Double-stranded DNA
    D. Double-stranded RNA

39. Viral nucleic acid incorporating into the host genome is classified as which of the following viral cycles?
    A. Lytic
    B. Lysogenic
    C. Mitosis
    D. Dormant

40. Which of the following is a characteristic of facultative anaerobes?
    A. Metabolism requires oxygen
    B. Require anaerobic environments for survival
    C. Able to survive in the presence and absence of oxygen
    D. Cannot use oxygen for metabolism, but capable of surviving in oxygen rich environments

41. How many chromosomes are present after the S phase of mitosis?
    A. 23
    B. 46
    C. 92
    D. None of the above

42. How many chromatids are present after the S phase of mitosis?
    A. 23
    B. 46
    C. 92
    D. None of the above

43. How many chromosomes are present in each spermatozoan after Meiosis II?
    A. 23
    B. 46
    C. 92
    D. None of the above

44. Before birth, in what phase of meiosis are primary oocytes arrested?
    A. Prophase I
    B. Telophase I
    C. Prophase II
    D. Anaphase II

45. Where is sperm stored and matured before ejaculation?
    A. Testis
    B. Epididymis
    C. Vas deferens
    D. Seminal vesicle

46. What secretes testosterone?
    A. Sertoli cells
    B. Sperm cells
    C. Leydig cells
    D. Adrenal medulla

47. Which of the following is the final, fully mature product of meiosis in male mammals?
    A. Primary spermatocytes
    B. Secondary spermatocytes
    C. Spermatozoa
    D. Spermatid

48. After ovulation through the peritoneal sac, a woman's egg first enters what part of the woman's reproductive system?
    A. Oviduct
    B. Cervix
    C. Vaginal canal
    D. Uterus

49. How many polar bodies are made from the complete maturation of 1 oogonium?
    A. 0
    B. 1
    C. 2
    D. 3

50. The corpus luteum secretes which of the following hormones?
    A. LH
    B. Testosterone
    C. Progesterone
    D. GnRH

51. Progesterone acts to maintain which of the following?
    A. The vaginal lining
    B. The rigidity of the Fallopian tubes
    C. The endometrial lining
    D. The cervix

52. Where does fertilization normally occur?
    A. Uterus
    B. Fallopian tube
    C. Corpus luteum
    D. Vagina

53. When does cleavage occur?
   A. Pre-fertilization
   B. Post-fertilization
   C. Pre-ovulation
   D. Post-ovulation

54. Fertilization of 2 different eggs results in which of the following?
   A. Conjoined twins
   B. Identical twins
   C. Fraternal twins
   D. Ectopic pregnancy

55. Which of the following cleavage scenarios is placed in the correct order?
   A. Blastula, morula, blastulation
   B. Morula, blastula, blastulation
   C. Blastula, blastulation, morula
   D. Morula, blastulation, blastula

56. Which of the following is true of gastrulation?
   A. It begins pre-implantation
   B. It generates 4 distinct cell layers
   C. It is the process that leads to the creation of the ectoderm, the mesoderm, and the endoderm
   D. It is the process that leads to the creation of a blastula

57. All of the following are at least partially derived from the endoderm EXCEPT:
   A. The pancreas
   B. The thyroid
   C. The gonads
   D. The bladder

58. Cells with the same genes are able to differentiate into cell types with different functions because of a process called:
   A. Conduction
   B. Mitosis
   C. Selective transcription
   D. Neurulation

59. Totipotent cells can differentiate into:
   A. Any type of cell
   B. Certain types of cells only
   C. Sex cells only
   D. Endothelial cells only

60. During normal differentiation, in what sequence does the potency of embryonic stem cells change?
   A. Totipotent, multipotent, pluripotent
   B. Pluripotent, multipotent, totipotent
   C. Totipotent, pluripotent, multipotent
   D. Multipotent, totipotent, pluripotent

61. Which of the following describes signals that act on the same cell that released the signal?
   A. Endocrine
   B. Autocrine
   C. Paracrine
   D. Juxtacrine

62. How is apoptosis defined?
   A. Cell migration
   B. Programmed cell death
   C. Cell development
   D. Programmed cell dormancy

63. Which of the following is used to describe a cell's death due to injury?
   A. Apoptosis
   B. Cell degradation
   C. Necrosis
   D. Programmed cell death

64. If a woman is able to regenerate a liver with identical tissue to the previous liver, this type of regeneration is defined as which of the following?
   A. Complete regeneration
   B. Incomplete regeneration
   C. Detached regeneration
   D. Functional regeneration

65. Umbilical arteries do which of the following?
   A. Carry blood from the fetus's heart to the rest of its body
   B. Carry blood from the fetus's body to its heart
   C. Carry blood from the fetus's heart to the placenta
   D. Carry blood from the fetus's umbilical cord to the fetus's heart

66. During development, when is a human embryo considered to become a fetus?
    A. 9 days after fertilization
    B. 9 weeks after fertilization
    C. 4 months after fertilization
    D. At the end of the second trimester

67. To maintain the resting potential of a neuron, which of the following is true?
    A. Passively, sodium is expelled from the cell and potassium is brought in
    B. Calcium plays an important role
    C. ATP is metabolized
    D. Actively, sodium is collected in the cell and the potassium is expelled

68. After a signal is received by the dendrites of the post-synaptic neuron, the signal travels immediately through which segment of the neuron?
    A. Axon hillock
    B. Soma
    C. Axon
    D. Nerve terminals

69. Axons of neurons in the CNS are myelinated with what type of cell?
    A. Oligodendrocytes
    B. Schwann cells
    C. Alpha cells
    D. Astrocytes

70. Nodes of Ranvier are described as which of the following?
    A. The portion of the axon immediately following the axon hillock
    B. The sections of the axon as they turn into nerve terminals
    C. The unmyelinated sections of the axon
    D. Organelles within the cell body of a neuron in the CNS

71. Sustaining a neuron's resting potential primarily relies on which of the following?
    A. Active transport
    B. Passive transport
    C. Facilitated transport
    D. Symport mechanism

72. Which of the following is true immediately following a signal that reaches threshold and causes an action potential?
    A. Potassium gated channels open
    B. Potassium rushes out of the cell
    C. Sodium rushes out of the cell
    D. Sodium gated channels open

73. The situation in which greater than normal stimulation is required to activate an action potential is called:
    A. Absolute refractory period
    B. Semi-refractory period
    C. Relative refractory period
    D. Neuron inactivation

74. As a signal continues through an axon, its propagation is defined as:
    A. Insulated conduction
    B. Brownian motion
    C. Peristalsis
    D. Saltatory conduction

75. Which of the following is not derived from tyrosine?
    A. T_3
    B. Dopamine
    C. Serotonin
    D. Epinephrine

76. Acetylcholinesterase does which of the following?
    A. Creates acetylcholine
    B. Binds acetylcholine molecules
    C. Degrades acetylcholine
    D. Enhances the signal acetylcholine produces on post-synaptic neurons

77. How does the brain's grey matter differ from white matter?
    A. White matter contains more neurons
    B. Grey matter is less active
    C. Grey matter has unmyelinated axons
    D. White matter has extended axons

78. The sympathetic nervous system is responsible for all of the following EXCEPT:
    A. Heart rate increase
    B. Eye dilation
    C. Penile erection
    D. Blood glucose levels increasing

79. The knee-jerk reflex is an example of which of the following:
    A. Monosynaptic reflex arc
    B. Disynaptic reflex arc
    C. Polysynaptic reflex arc
    D. None of the above

80. Which of the following hormones is classified as a catecholamine?
    A. Norepinephrine
    B. ADH
    C. Cortisol
    D. hCG

81. The hypothalamus directly regulates which of the following glands?
    A. Thalamus
    B. Thymus
    C. Pituitary
    D. Pineal

82. Which of the following hormones undergoes positive feedback during the follicular phase?
    A. Progesterone
    B. hCG
    C. Testosterone
    D. Estrogen

83. What does FSH stand for?
    A. Follicle stabilizing hormone
    B. Fast stimulating hyphae
    C. Follicle stimulating hormone
    D. First stalk hypothalamus

84. How many hormones does the anterior pituitary synthesize?
    A. 5
    B. 6
    C. 7
    D. 8

85. What is the function of prolactin?
    A. Initiates uterine contractions
    B. Stimulates milk production
    C. Induces general growth of cells
    D. Increases water reabsorption at the nephron

86. T_3 and T_4 are released from which of the following glands?
    A. Pineal
    B. Thymus
    C. Thyroid
    D. Pituitary

87. Which of the following cells of the kidney secrete renin?
    A. Cells of the glomerulus
    B. Distal convoluted cells
    C. Proximal convoluted cells
    D. None of the above

88. Renin acts to activate which of the following proteins?
    A. Angiotensin II
    B. Angiotensin I
    C. Angiotensinogen
    D. Aldosterone

89. Glucagon is produced by what cells?
    A. Alpha cells
    B. Beta cells
    C. Delta cells
    D. Gamma cells

90. Somatostatin acts to inhibit the secretion of which of the following?
    A. ADH & aldosterone
    B. Glucagon & calcitonin
    C. Insulin & glucagon
    D. T_3 & T_4

91. What organ releases ANP?
    A. Pancreas
    B. Liver
    C. Heart
    D. Lungs

92. How can Type I diabetes be described?
    A. Receptor-level resistance to insulin
    B. Destruction of beta cells in the pancreas
    C. Autoimmune response to insulin
    D. Destruction of alpha cells in the pancreas

93. Circadian rhythms are regulated somewhat by which of the following hormones?
    A. Melatonin
    B. ADH
    C. Cortisol
    D. Oxytocin

94. Which layer of tissue prevents food from entering the trachea?
    A. Pharynx
    B. Tongue
    C. Tricuspid valve
    D. Epiglottis

95. What normally occurs after the diaphragm contracts?
    A. Expiration
    B. Hiccups
    C. Coughing
    D. Inspiration

96. The diaphragm is considered which of the following types of muscle?
    A. Cardiac
    B. Skeletal
    C. Smooth
    D. It's not a muscle, but endothelial tissue

97. Which of the following best defines residual volume (RV)?
    A. Maximum volume of air in the lungs after complete inhalation
    B. Maximum volume of air in the lungs after complete exhalation
    C. Minimum volume of air in the lungs after complete inhalation
    D. Minimum volume of air in the lungs after complete exhalation

98. Hypoxia is defined as:
    A. Low concentration of hydroxide in the blood
    B. Low concentration of oxygen in the blood
    C. Low concentration of glucose in the blood
    D. Low concentration of potassium in the blood

99. All of the following are true of pulmonary arteries EXCEPT:
    A. They carry blood to the heart
    B. They contain the most de-oxygenated blood
    C. They provide blood to reach the lungs
    D. They originate from the right ventricle

100. How does alkalosis affect the rate of respiration?
    A. It decreases to increase the buildup of carbon dioxide
    B. It decreases to decrease the amount of oxygen the body uses
    C. It increases to increase the rate of gases exhaled
    D. It increases to decrease the amount of carbon dioxide in the body

101. What is the pH considered to be when the individual has acidosis?
    A. Abnormally high
    B. Abnormally low
    C. The blood is basic
    D. The blood does not have sufficient concentration of hydrogen ion

102. What cell type swallows up and digests pathogens?
    A. T cells
    B. B cells
    C. Macrophages
    D. Red blood cells

103. How many chambers does the heart have?
    A. 3
    B. 4
    C. 6
    D. 7

104. Which chamber of the heart is found to be the densest with muscle?
    A. Left atrium
    B. Left ventricle
    C. Right atrium
    D. Right ventricle

105. Blood in the left ventricle is:
    A. Oxygenated and headed for the pulmonary artery
    B. Deoxygenated and headed for the pulmonary artery
    C. Oxygenated and headed for the aorta
    D. Deoxygenated and headed for the aorta

106. Which of the following valves separates the atria of the heart from the ventricles?
    A. Atrioventricular valves
    B. Aortic valves
    C. Pulmonic valves
    D. Pyloric valves

107. The tricuspid valve separates:
    A. Right atrium and left atrium
    B. Left atrium and right ventricle
    C. Right atrium and right ventricle
    D. Left atrium and left ventricle

108. The bicuspid valve separates:
    A. Right atrium and left atrium
    B. Left atrium and right ventricle
    C. Right atrium and right ventricle
    D. Left atrium and left ventricle

109. All of following are functions of the bicuspid and tricuspid valves except:
    A. To create pressure allowing blood to be "pumped"
    B. To prevent oxygenated blood and deoxygenated blood from being mixed together
    C. To prevent backflow of blood once the ventricles contract
    D. To maintain proper heart function

110. What valve separates the left ventricle from the aorta?
    A. Ventricular valve
    B. Aortic valve
    C. Pulmonary valve
    D. Systemic Valve

111. What valve separates the right ventricle from the pulmonary artery?
    A. Ventricular valve
    B. Aortic valve
    C. Pulmonary valve
    D. Systemic valve

112. The heart can contract without a neural input because of impulse initiation from which of the following:
    A. Purkinje fibers
    B. Bundle of His
    C. AV node
    D. SA node

113. How are ventricular muscle cells connected?
    A. Purkinje fibers
    B. Valves
    C. Intercalated discs
    D. Intracalated discs

114. Which of the following about the vagus nerve is true?
    A. It is a nerve of the sympathetic nervous system
    B. It acts to slow down the heart rate
    C. It is a voluntary nerve
    D. It is the longest nerve in the human body

115. Cardiac output in the product of which of the following 2 values?
    A. Heart rate and stroke volume
    B. Heart rate and cardiac output
    C. Stroke volume and vessel resistivity
    D. Stroke volume and systemic blood volume

116. Ventricular contraction occurs during:
    A. Diastole
    B. Systole
    C. Relaxation
    D. Hyperpolarization

117. Where can blood exchange gases and compounds with tissue?
    A. Arterioles and capillaries
    B. Venules and capillaries
    C. Venules and arterioles
    D. Capillaries

118. How is blood transport properly maintained through the veins to the heart?
    A. Veins have valves to prevent backflow
    B. Veins undergo peristalsis to move blood back to the heart
    C. Veins have denser muscle and more rigidity preventing pooling
    D. Veins have the least area and thus limit blood from going anywhere but to the heart

119. Varicose veins result when:
    A. Valves fail
    B. Blood moves too quickly through veins
    C. Blood thins
    D. Veins constrict too tightly leading to impediment of blood flow

120. The superior vena cava does which of the following?
    A. Returns blood to the heart from the portion of the body below the heart
    B. Allows blood to travel to the portion of the body above the heart
    C. Returns blood to the heart from the portion of the body above the heart
    D. Allows blood to travel to the portion of the body below the heart

121. How many portal systems exist in the human body?
    A. 2
    B. 3
    C. 4
    D. 5

122. The cellular portion of the blood consists of 3 major cell types. Which of the following is not a major contributor to the cellular portion of the blood?
    A. Erythrocytes
    B. Leukocytes
    C. Pathogens
    D. Platelets

123. Which of the following organelles does an erythrocyte not have?
    A. Nucleus
    B. Mitochondria
    C. Lysosomes
    D. All of the above

124. Red blood cells obtain their ATP from which of the following processes?
    A. Glycolysis
    B. Krebs cycle
    C. Electron transport chain
    D. All of the above

125. What is hematocrit?
    A. The percentage of white blood cells in a sample of blood
    B. The percentage of platelets in a sample of blood
    C. The percentage of red blood cells in a sample of blood
    D. The percentage of pathogens in a sample of blood

126. Which of the following are not granulocytes?
    A. Neutrophils
    B. Monocytes
    C. Eosinophils
    D. Basophils

127. Which of the following are the 2 cell classes of agranulocytes?
    A. Neutrophils & Basophils
    B. Monocytes & Neutrophils
    C. Lymphocytes & Monocytes
    D. Lymphocytes & Basophils

128. Every individual red blood cell contains roughly 250 million molecules of:
    A. Iron
    B. Oxygen
    C. Hemoglobin
    D. Myoglobin

129. Lymphocytes that mature in the thymus are called:
    A. B cells
    B. T cells
    C. Macrophages
    D. Platelets

130. Which cell is responsible for the production of antibodies?
    A. B cells
    B. T cells
    C. Macrophages
    D. Platelets

131. Platelets are also known as:
    A. Megakaryocytes
    B. Macrophages
    C. Thrombocytes
    D. Erythrocytes

132. What function do platelets serve?
    A. Lubricate compounds in the blood for easier transport
    B. Immune response
    C. Assist in blood clotting
    D. Aid in the replication of red blood cells

133. From what organ is erythropoietin released and what is this hormone's primary function?
    A. Kidney, stimulation of red blood cell development
    B. Liver, stimulation of white blood cell development
    C. Pancreas, stimulation of red blood cell development
    D. Adrenal gland, stimulation of platelet development

134. What organ(s) secrete thrombopoietin and what is this hormone's primary function?
    A. Kidney, stimulation of red blood cell development
    B. Liver & Kidney, stimulation of platelet development
    C. Liver & Pancreas, stimulation of pathogen destruction
    D. Pancreas, stimulation of white blood cell development

135. If a man has type A blood, what type of antigens do his blood cells present?
    A. A antigens
    B. B antigens
    C. B & AB antigens
    D. None of the above

136. If a woman has one type A allele and one type B allele, what is her blood type?
    A. Type A, because A is dominant
    B. Type B, because B is dominant
    C. Type AB, because A and B are codominant
    D. Type O, because one negates the effect of the other

137. What blood type is the universal donor?
    A. Type A
    B. Type B
    C. Type AB
    D. Type O

138. What blood type is the universal recipient?
    A. Type A
    B. Type B
    C. Type AB
    D. Type O

139. On what cells is the Rh factor expressed?
    A. White blood cells
    B. Platelets
    C. Red blood cells
    D. Pathogens

140. The condition in which maternal anti-Rh antibodies cross the placenta and destroy fetal blood cells is called:
    A. Sudden Infant Death Syndrome (SIDS)
    B. Erythroblastosis fetalis
    C. Erythrocyte apoptosis
    D. Erythrocytotic necrosis

141. Where in the body do we find the highest partial pressure of oxygen in the blood?
    A. Lungs
    B. Heart
    C. Capillaries
    D. Superior vena cava

142. Which of the following inhibitors can be overcome by increasing the concentration of substrate?
    A. Noncompetitive inhibitor
    B. Allosteric inhibitor
    C. Competitive inhibitor
    D. None of the above

143. Under what conditions does a right shift NOT occur in the oxyhemoglobin dissociation curve?
    A. Increased partial pressure of carbon dioxide
    B. Decreased pH
    C. Increased acidity
    D. Decreased hydride concentration

144. Fetal hemoglobin:
    A. Is a larger compound than maternal hemoglobin
    B. Has a greater affinity for oxygen than maternal hemoglobin
    C. Has a higher rate of degradation
    D. Has lower oxygen affinity that adult Hb

145. A cell is placed in a hypertonic environment. Which of the following is accurate?
    A. The cell is considered isotonic with regards to its surrounding
    B. The environment has a higher osmotic pressure
    C. There exists no hydrostatic pressure
    D. Water floods into the cell

146. Edema can be defined as:
    A. Demyelination of nerve axons
    B. Abnormal increase in artery rigidity
    C. Excessive fluid accumulation
    D. Insufficient intestinal absorption

147. Coagulation factors are classified as:
    A. Proteins
    B. Carbohydrates
    C. Specialized cells
    D. None of the above

148. Which of the following can convert fibrinogen into fibrin, an important compound in clot formation?
    A. Plasmin
    B. Trypsin
    C. Thrombin
    D. Thromboplastin

149. Innate immunity is also called:
    A. Acquired immunity
    B. Specific immunity
    C. Nonspecific immunity
    D. Adaptive immunity

150. What organ is responsible for blood storage?
    A. Liver
    B. Pancreas
    C. Heart
    D. Spleen

151. Which of the following produces leukocytes?
    A. Bone marrow
    B. Spleen
    C. Thymus
    D. Thyroid

152. As part of adaptive immunity, B-cells can turn into which one of the following cell types?
    A. T-cell
    B. Killer T-cells
    C. Plasma cells
    D. Macrophages

153. Which of the following cells is part of cell-mediated immunity?
    A. T-cells
    B. B-cells
    C. Plasma cells
    D. Mast cells

154. Leukocytes are further classified as either granulocytes or agranulocytes, both of which are derived from:
    A. Erythrocytes
    B. Hematopoietic stem cells
    C. Cardiac stem cells
    D. Gastrulation

155. Which of the following cells can monocytes eventually become?
    A. Leukocytes
    B. Macrophages
    C. B cells
    D. T cells

156. Which of the following drives humoral immunity?
   A. T cells
   B. Killer T cells
   C. Antibodies
   D. Erythrocytes

157. Cells infected with viruses produce which of the following to protect against viral infection?
   A. Interferons
   B. Macrophages
   C. Antibodies
   D. Killer T cells

158. Which of the following is not a type of T-cell?
   A. Helper T-cell
   B. Memory T-cell
   C. Suppressor T-cell
   D. Plasma T-cell

159. Where are lacteals located?
   A. Thymus
   B. Breast tissue
   C. Small intestine
   D. Stomach

160. Where is digestion of carbohydrates initiated?
   A. Stomach
   B. Mouth
   C. Small intestine
   D. Large intestine

161. Peristalsis occurs in which of the following sites?
   A. Small intestine
   B. Mouth
   C. Rectum
   D. Gall bladder

162. After mastication, the bolus is moved from the mouth into which of the following segments of the digestive system?
   A. Larynx
   B. Pharynx
   C. Esophagus
   D. Trachea

163. Chief cells in the stomach secrete:
   A. Pepsinogen
   B. HCl
   C. Gastrin
   D. Bile

164. Protein digestion is started in the:
   A. Mouth
   B. Esophagus
   C. Stomach
   D. Small intestines

165. What is the name of the sphincter that separates the stomach from the duodenum?
   A. Ileocecal sphincter
   B. Pupillary sphincter
   C. Cardiac sphincter
   D. Pyloric sphincter

166. Which of the following cells helps to protect the stomach's inner lining?
   A. Parietal cells
   B. Chief cells
   C. Mucous cells
   D. G cells

167. Which of the following is activated by enterokinase?
   A. Pepsinogen
   B. Secretin
   C. Trypsinogen
   D. CCK

168. What is the primary function of bile salts?
   A. Fat digestion
   B. Fat emulsification
   C. Fat absorption
   D. Fat storage

169. What is the storage form of glucose?
   A. Glycogen
   B. Glucagon
   C. Insulin
   D. Galactose

170. What is the major function of the gallbladder?
    A. Produce bile
    B. Stores bile
    C. Degrades bile
    D. None of the above

171. Which of the following is not a fat-soluble vitamin?
    A. C
    B. A
    C. D
    D. K

172. How can fat-soluble compounds be transported through the body?
    A. They are degraded and rebuilt at their effector site
    B. Chylomicrons act as carriers
    C. Lacteals place hydrophilic antigens on their surface
    D. Red blood cells transport them

173. Filtration from the glomerulus leads to filtrate that first enters:
    A. Proximal convoluted tubule
    B. Collecting duct
    C. Bowman's capsule
    D. Loop of Henle

174. Where is ammonia converted to urea?
    A. Pancreas
    B. Kidney
    C. Liver
    D. Gut

175. In which part of the nephron is glucose primarily reabsorbed?
    A. Distal convoluted tubule
    B. Loop of Henle
    C. Bowman's capsule
    D. Proximal convoluted tubule

176. The descending loop of Henle is only permeable to:
    A. Potassium
    B. Sodium
    C. Glucose
    D. Water

177. The loop of Henle begins in the cortex and moves into what section of the kidney?
    A. Medulla
    B. Glomerulus
    C. Anterior
    D. Superior

178. What compound is the primary regulator of blood acidity?
    A. Oxygen
    B. Bicarbonate
    C. Lactate
    D. Bile

179. Which of the following is created from keratin?
    A. Muscle
    B. Hair
    C. Teeth
    D. Bone

180. Which of the following is produced to protect the skin from harmful UV radiation?
    A. Keratin
    B. Actin
    C. Melanin
    D. Dopamine

181. Thermoregulation is achieved in many ways. Which of the following is not a way for your body to regulate its temperature?
    A. Sweating
    B. Sleeping
    C. Piloerection
    D. Vasodilation

182. The functional unit of skeletal muscle are:
    A. Striated cells
    B. Red fibers
    C. Sarcomeres
    D. White fibers

183. Which of the following muscle groups can be controlled voluntarily?
    A. Smooth
    B. Cardiac
    C. Skeletal
    D. None of the above

184. What is the direct function of the sarcoplasmic reticulum?
    A. To store and release calcium ions
    B. To maintain T-tubules
    C. To regenerate muscle fibers
    D. To maintain a functional pH

185. What role does calcium play in muscle contraction?
    A. Increases the amount of actin
    B. Increases the amount of myosin
    C. Works to expose myosin-binding sites of actin
    D. Works to expose actin-binding sites of myosin

186. Which cell is responsible for breaking down bone matrix?
    A. Osteoblasts
    B. Osteons
    C. Osteoclasts
    D. PTH

187. The bone matrix is made up of all of the following except:
    A. Hydroxyapatite
    B. Calcium
    C. Collagen
    D. Glucose

188. Which of the following can be explained by the concept of incomplete dominance?
    A. A red flower and white flower mate and produce a white flower
    B. A red flower and white flower mate and produce a red flower
    C. A red flower and white flower mate and produce a pink flower
    D. A red flower and white flower mate and produce a red and white flower

189. A mutation that has no ultimate effect on the protein that is synthesized is classified as a:
    A. Missense mutation
    B. Silent mutation
    C. Nonsense mutation
    D. Lethal mutation

190. A mutation that results in a segment of DNA exchanged with another segment of DNA from a separate chromosome is classified as a:
    A. Missense mutation
    B. Insertion mutation
    C. Inversion mutation
    D. Translocation mutation

191. Which of the following increases the prevalence of homozygosity?
    A. Random mating
    B. Inbreeding
    C. Genetic drift
    D. Genetic leakage

192. A test cross is used to:
    A. Find the phenotype of an organism
    B. Find the genotype of an organism
    C. Ensure homozygous recessive organisms mate
    D. Enlarge the gene pool

193. The Hardy-Weinberg principal, if applicable, dictates that a population must:
    A. Be very small
    B. Undergo natural chance of mutations
    C. Undergo random mating
    D. Experience natural selection

194. Many different species arising from a common ancestor can be explained by:
    A. Natural selection
    B. Bottleneck
    C. Adaptive radiation
    D. Convergent evolution

195. Amphoteric species:
    A. Can accept 2 protons readily
    B. Can accept and donate a proton
    C. Can never be amino acids
    D. Can never be zwitterions

196. What is the isoelectric point?
    A. The pH at which a molecule is basic
    B. The pH at which a molecule is relatively acidic
    C. The pH at which a molecule has a net negative charge
    D. The pH at which a molecule is neutrally charged

197. Peptide bond formation can be further classified as a:
  A. Hydration reaction
  B. Dehydration reaction
  C. Hydrolysis reaction
  D. Redox reaction

198. Beta-pleated sheets are an example of a protein's:
  A. Primary structure
  B. Secondary structure
  C. Tertiary structure
  D. Quaternary structure

199. Disulfide bonds do NOT form an essential part of a protein's:
  A. Primary structure
  B. Secondary structure
  C. Tertiary structure
  D. Quaternary structure

200. All of the following are characteristics of catalysts EXCEPT:
  A. They increase the forward rate of reaction
  B. They lower the energy of activation
  C. They do affect the reaction's overall Gibbs free energy
  D. They have specificity

201. The class of enzymes that cleave a functional group from one molecule and incorporate it into another is called:
  A. Oxidoreductases
  B. Hydrolases
  C. Isomerases
  D. Transferases

202. How is an endergonic reaction described?
  A. Energy is produced
  B. Heat is produced
  C. Entropy increases
  D. Energy is required

203. If $\Delta G > 0$, how is the reaction described?
  A. Exothermic
  B. Endothermic
  C. Non-Spontaneous
  D. Exergonic

204. How can V_{max} be increased if an enzyme is saturated in a given reaction?
  A. Increase the concentration of the enzyme
  B. Increase the temperature
  C. Increase the concentration of the substrate
  D. Increase the pH

205. Where do noncompetitive inhibitors bind?
  A. Allosteric site of substrate
  B. Active site of substrate
  C. Allosteric site of enzyme
  D. Active site of enzyme

206. An inhibitor that essentially locks the substrate into the active site of the enzyme is:
  A. A competitive inhibitor
  B. An irreversible inhibitor
  C. A mixed inhibitor
  D. An uncompetitive inhibitor

207. Which of the following is not a cell adhesion molecule (CAM)?
  A. Cadherin
  B. Integrin
  C. Keratin
  D. Selectin

208. Which of the following channels can be opened when it's bound to an activating compound?
  A. Ligand-gated channel
  B. Gated channel
  C. Ungated channel
  D. Voltage-gated channel

209. SDS –PAGE separates proteins on the basis of:
  A. Mass only
  B. Mass and charge
  C. Charge only
  D. Isoelectric point only

210. In electrophoresis, the cathode can attract:
  A. Anions
  B. Positively charged proteins
  C. Neutral species
  D. Negatively charged proteins

211. What can we say if a substance binds tightly to the beads in column chromatography?
    A. It will have a slower elution time for that substance
    B. It will have a faster elution time for that substance
    C. The substance must be very large
    D. The substance must be nonpolar

212. The linear sequence of smaller proteins is best analyzed using:
    A. The Bradford protein assay
    B. Column chromatography
    C. X-ray crystallography
    D. Edman degradation

213. Mannose can best be described as a:
    A. Ketohexose
    B. Aldopentose
    C. Aldotetrose
    D. Aldohexose

214. How does galactose relate to glucose?
    A. Galactose is the C-3 epimer of glucose
    B. Galactose is the C-5 anomer of glucose
    C. Galactose is the C-4 epimer of glucose
    D. They are enantiomers

215. Which of the following accurately describes diastereomers?
    A. They have the same physical properties
    B. They are mirror images of each other
    C. They have different densities
    D. A sample does not rotate plane polarized light

216. Furanose rings are always:
    A. 5-membered carbohydrate rings
    B. 6-membered carbohydrate rings
    C. 6 carbon ketoses
    D. 5 carbon ketose

217. A reducing sugar can be defined as:
    A. Sugars with a hemiacetal
    B. Sugars with a hemiketal
    C. Ketoses
    D. Fructose

218. Tollen's regent is used to detect the presence of a:
    A. Oxidizing sugar
    B. Lactone
    C. Reducing sugar
    D. Aldonic acid

219. Acetals are formed when hemiacetals react with:
    A. Carboxylic acids
    B. Acid halides
    C. Esters
    D. Alcohols

220. Which of the following is not a disaccharide?
    A. Sucrose
    B. Lactose
    C. Ribose
    D. Maltose

221. Homopolysaccharides are:
    A. Composed of a number of different monosaccharides
    B. 20 sugar polysaccharides
    C. Composed of a number of only one monosaccharide
    D. Indigestible to humans

222. What is the difference between saturated and unsaturated compounds?
    A. Saturated compounds have at least 1 double bond
    B. Saturated compounds have at least 1 triple bond
    C. Unsaturated compounds have at least 1 double bond
    D. Unsaturated compounds have at least 1 triple bond

223. Which sphingolipid has a lone hydrogen at its head group?
    A. Sphingosine
    B. Ganglioside
    C. Ceramide
    D. Sphingomyelin

224. Waxes are:
    A. Solid at room temperature
    B. Poisonous
    C. Able to accelerate evaporation
    D. Carboxylic acids

225. Steroids can be derived from:
   A. Wax
   B. Ethers
   C. Cyclic ketones
   D. Terpenes

226. Where is cholesterol normally found?
   A. Phospholipid bilayers
   B. Cell walls
   C. Mitochondria
   D. Ribosomes

227. Rickets, a debilitating condition, is a result of a lack of:
   A. Vitamin A
   B. Vitamin B
   C. Vitamin C
   D. Vitamin D

228. Adipocytes store:
   A. Glycogen
   B. Fat
   C. Water
   D. Potassium

229. The hydrolysis of triacylglycerols is termed:
   A. Transesterification
   B. Saponification
   C. Carboxylation
   D. None of the above

230. How do nucleosides differ from nucleotides?
   A. Nucleosides lack a phosphate group
   B. Nucleotides lack a phosphate group
   C. Nucleotides are only found in DNA
   D. Nucleosides are inactive

231. Guanine binds to:
   A. Adenine
   B. Uracil
   C. Cytosine
   D. Thymine

232. 2 hydrogen bonds are found in the linkage between:
   A. Adenine and thymine
   B. Guanine and cytosine
   C. Guanine and adenine
   D. Thymine and cytosine

233. Which of the following explains Chargaff's rule?
   A. Guanine is the far more reactive purine because it can form more hydrogen bonds
   B. The total number of adenosines must equal the total number of guanines in DNA
   C. The total number of purines must equal to the total number of pyrimidines in DNA
   D. DNA is a double helix by evolutionary error

234. Histones are:
   A. Positively charged
   B. Negatively charged
   C. Found in the cell cytoplasm
   D. Wrapped around chromatin

235. A repeating unit of nucleotides at the end of DNA is called a:
   A. Nucleosome
   B. Poly-A tail
   C. Centromere
   D. Telomere

236. The small amount of chromatin that remains condensed and is late in replicating is called:
   A. Chromatin
   B. Euchromatin
   C. Heterochromatin
   D. Nucleoid

237. What enzyme unzips DNA from its double-stranded helix?
   A. DNA ligase
   B. DNA helicase
   C. DNA nuclease
   D. RNA transcriptase

238. Okazaki fragments are:
   A. Not pieced together and treated as short novel DNA segments
   B. A result of replication of the lagging strand
   C. Seen when the leading strand is replicated
   D. A by-product of transcription

239. Which of the following processes can produce large quantities of DNA copies?
   A. PCR
   B. Southern blotting
   C. Northern blotting
   D. Electrophoresis

240. mRNA is very often polycistronic in:
   A. Fungi
   B. Eukaryotes
   C. Prokaryotes
   D. Vertebrates

241. Every protein translated in eukaryotes begins with:
   A. Alanine
   B. Lysine
   C. Phenylalanine
   D. Methionine

242. The start codon for every eukaryotic mRNA strand during translation is:
   A. AAA
   B. AGA
   C. GUA
   D. AUG

243. Because more than one codon can code for a single amino acid, the genetic code is described as:
   A. Dynamic
   B. Efficient
   C. Degenerate
   D. Collapsible

244. A mutation that results in a premature stop codon is known as a:
   A. Nonsense mutation
   B. Missense mutation
   C. Point mutation
   D. Silent mutation

245. RNA polymerase II, needed for the transcription of DNA into mRNA, binds to:
   A. The TATA box
   B. Free transcriptional factors
   C. DNA polymerase
   D. DNA helicase

246. Post-transcriptional processing in eukaryotes splices out non-coding sequences known as:
   A. Exons
   B. Introns
   C. Poly-A tail
   D. 5' cap

247. How does mRNA, post processing, exit from the nucleus?
   A. Transported inside capsules
   B. Exocytosis
   C. Through nuclear pores
   D. Active transport

248. Phosphorylation can:
   A. Activates proteins
   B. Deactivate proteins
   C. Both activate and deactivate proteins
   D. Signals proteins for degradation

249. What is the main function of chaperone proteins?
   A. Assist in protein translation
   B. Assist in protein folding
   C. Assist in protein transport from the cell
   D. Signal proteins to undergo phosphorylation

250. Prenylation of a protein can be defined by:
   A. Addition of lipid groups
   B. Addition of carbohydrate groups
   C. Addition of phosphate groups
   D. Addition of carboxylic acid groups

251. How can an operon be described?
   A. An on/off switch for transcription
   B. A number of genes that are transcribed into one mRNA strand
   C. Not common in prokaryotic cells
   D. A segment of mRNA that represents one gene

252. Why does acetylation of histones occur?
   A. In order for the cell to undergo apoptosis
   B. To allow for DNA transcription
   C. To fold and condense DNA
   D. In order to combine histone proteins

253. All of the following are characteristics of triglycerides EXCEPT:
   A. Also called triacylglycerols
   B. Made from 2 fatty acids and a glycerol backbone
   C. How lipids are stored in the body
   D. Used in the metabolic process

254. Which of the following forms micelles?
   A. Proteins
   B. Digestive enzymes
   C. Steroids
   D. Phospholipids

255. Proteins that pass completely through the phospholipid bilayer of a cell can be classified as:
   A. Embedded proteins
   B. Transmembrane proteins
   C. Peripheral proteins
   D. Chaperones

256. Which of the following cell-to-cell junctions allows for quick cell communication, like that found in cardiac cells?
   A. Desmosomes
   B. Tight junctions
   C. Gap junctions
   D. None of the above

257. Osmosis is an example of:
   A. Active transport
   B. Facilitated transport
   C. Passive transport
   D. A symport system

258. Osmotic pressure is a colligative property, meaning:
   A. Only the chemical nature of the solute must be known to deduce a solution's osmotic pressure
   B. Only the concentration of dissolved solute particles must be known to deduce a solution's osmotic pressure
   C. The chemical nature and concentration of the solute must be known
   D. The osmotic pressure of a solution is wholly independent of any characteristic of the dissolved solute

259. The phenomenon in which the energy released as one substrate goes down its concentration gradient is used to drive another substrate up its concentration gradient is named:
   A. Active transport
   B. Passive transport
   C. Secondary active transport
   D. Exocytosis

260. Which of the following is not true regarding the Na^+/K^+ ATPase?
   A. It requires ATP to function
   B. It "pumps" 3 Na^+ ions into the cell and 2 K^+ out of the cell
   C. It is responsible for maintaining the negative resting potential for a neuron
   D. It is a transmembrane protein

261. Glycolysis of one molecule of glucose nets:
   A. 3 ATP, 3 NADH, & 3 pyruvate molecules
   B. 3 ATP, 2 NADH, & 2 pyruvate molecules
   C. 2 ATP, 3 NADH, & 3 pyruvate molecules
   D. 2 ATP, 2 NADH, & 2 pyruvate molecules

262. Red blood cells are capable of all of the following except:
   A. Anaerobic respiration
   B. Glycolysis
   C. Aerobic respiration
   D. Oxygen association and dissociation

263. Which of the following can activate PEPCK, an enzyme necessary for gluconeogenesis?
   A. Insulin
   B. Aldosterone
   C. Glucagon
   D. Norepinephrine

264. NADH and $FADH_2$ act as reducing agents needed for the proper function of:
   A. Glycolysis
   B. The Krebs cycle
   C. The electron transport chain
   D. Anaerobic oxidation

265. The formation of ketone bodies is a result of:
   A. Glycolysis
   B. Protein oxidation
   C. Lipid catabolism
   D. Glucogenic amino acid catabolism

266. The ETC functions to produce:
   A. A proton gradient
   B. A neutral pH between the inner membrane space and the intermembrane space
   C. NADH and $FADH_2$
   D. Acetyl CoA

267. The complete combustion of fat gives:
    A. 1 kcal/g
    B. 4 kcal/g
    C. 9 kcal/g
    D. 23 kcal/g

268. During starvation, which of the following hormones would most likely be elevated?
    A. Insulin
    B. Glycogen
    C. Glucagon
    D. Aldosterone

269. When the stomach is empty, which of the following is secreted by the cells of the stomach?
    A. Trypsinogen
    B. Ghrelin
    C. Leptin
    D. Dopamine

SOLUTIONS

CHAPTER 1 SOLUTIONS

1. **A.**
No direct evidence is presented to confirm that HHV8 causes KS, although it appears to be associated with the disease. Answer B is not the best choice as observation 1 was based on a 2-year study: those who tested positive for HHV8 may have developed KS at a later date. A statement about all syphilis patients developing KS is not valid, even if HHV8 is truly the cause of the disease: only a certain percentage would be predicted to develop the disease. And, conversely, it cannot be stated that all hemophiliacs are safe from the disease either.

2. **C.**
KS is prevalent in individuals with HIV and syphilis, two sexually transmitted diseases. Although HIV can also be contracted through blood transfusions, it appears HHV8 cannot due to the hemophiliac data in observation 2. Casual contact and airborne transmission can also be ruled out as HHV8 antibodies are rarely found in HIV negative blood donors.

3. **B.**
No evidence is given that transplant patients had or didn't have HHV8, so the virus as a cause of KS cannot be ruled out based on this statement. However, since these transplant patients have a weakened immune system, as is found in AIDS, it appears KS thrives under this condition.

4. **B.**
Although some may argue that one characteristic of life is the storage of genetic information in the form of DNA, numerous viruses do contain DNA. Also, one outstanding feature of many viruses is their rapid mutation rate. However, all viruses need the host cellular machinery to replicate: they cannot reproduce on their own.

CHAPTER 2 SOLUTIONS

1. **A.**
RNA, a nucleic acid, is the only molecule listed which contains phosphorus (in the phosphate group portion of the nucleotide). Thus radioactive phosphorus will not show up in proteins, glucose (a carbohydrate), or amino acids (protein subunits).

2. **C.**
Both RNA and proteins contain nitrogen, RNA in the nitrogenous base portion of the nucleotide, and proteins in the amino group of every amino acid. A and B are not correct because they exclude RNA or proteins. D is incorrect because fatty acids, constituents of triglycerides, do not contain nitrogen.

3. **C.**
Both cholesterol and phospholipids contain carbon, as do all of the major biomolecules we discussed, as they are organic. Therefore, radioactive carbon would show up in all the biomolecules mentioned.

4. **B.**
We are told that arginine is an amino acid, and amino acids are the building blocks of proteins. DNA and RNA are made up of nucleotides, while fatty acids are long chain hydrocarbons that are not considered polymers, and certainly are not formed from amino acids.

5. **D.**
This question combines aspects of both of the preceding experiments in an attempt to cause confusion. Arginine simply allows the cells to grow, as they could not make proteins without it. However, since neither arginine nor any other amino acids contain phosphorus, no proteins, whether they contain arginine or not, should be labeled. The only remaining choice recognizes that both RNA and phospholipids contain phosphorus, in the phosphate group that each contains as part of its structure.

6. **C.**

The human digestive system can only absorb sugars in the form of monosaccharides. Galactose is the only monosaccharide listed (glucose and fructose are the others). Lactose, maltose, and sucrose are all disaccharides, and must be enzymatically split before absorption.

7. **D.**

One of the major differences between DNA and RNA is that RNA contains the five-carbon sugar ribose, while DNA contains the five-carbon sugar deoxyribose. Both DNA and RNA contain phosphate groups, and both contain adenine and guanine. (RNA contains the pyrimidine base uracil instead of the pyrimidine base thymine.)

8. **B.**

Protein primary structure refers only to the linear order of amino acids. Secondary and tertiary folding are characteristics of all proteins, and involve interactions between various amino acids and ultimately cause specific three-dimensional folding. Both A and D are incorrect for related reasons; some proteins consist of more than one polypeptide chain, and it is only these proteins that exhibit quaternary folding (the association of multiple polypeptides). All proteins contain amino acids, by definition, so C cannot be correct.

9. **C.**

The major factor that determines whether or not a triglyceride will be solid or liquid at room temperature is the level of saturation of the fatty acids it contains. A completely saturated triglyceride is completely "filled" with hydrogen atoms, and is therefore linear in shape. This allows the molecules to pack closely and easily together, which results in a solid phase physical structure. We would call this type of molecule a "fat" or "saturated fat". A point of unsaturation occurs where a carbon-carbon double bond exists, and hydrogen atoms could potentially be added by hydrogenation. The more points of unsaturation, the more "kinks", or bends, the fatty acid will have. This makes packing together difficult, and we obtain a liquid, usually called an "oil".

10. **A.**

Cellulose is the only polysaccharide, or complex carbohydrate, listed. Lactose is a disaccharide, and ribose is a monosaccharide.

CHAPTER 3 SOLUTIONS

1. **A.**

We can tell that this is true because the ranges of activity depicted by the graph do not overlap. Therefore, no pH value exists at which both enzymes will be even slightly active. It is assumed that the general pH values are known for the stomach and small intestine, approximately 2 and 8 respectively. Therefore, the graph confirms that pancreatic amylase will have no activity at pH 2 (choice B), but that this is the optimum for pepsin (not 8.5, as is suggested in choice C.) The graph additionally shows that pancreatic amylase loses all activity at pH 7, so that it could not function in an acidic environment. Since the passage tells us that pancreatic amylase functions in the small intestine, choice D must be incorrect.

2. **C.**

The key here is to understand that trypsin, like pancreatic amylase, functions in the small intestine, and therefore must have a similar optimal pH as does pancreatic amylase. The graph shows that optimum as 8.5. For the same reasons stated above for pepsin and pancreatic amylase, pepsin and trypsin could never work under similar conditions (choice B). Additionally, both choices A and D must be incorrect because they demand that trypsin could function at pH 2 and 0 (the pH of 1M HCl, which you should at least know is acidic).

3. **B.**

Since humans are endotherms and maintain a constant body temperature of approximately 37°C (98.6°F), all human enzymes should share this optimal temperature. Curves A and C depict very different optimal temperatures.

4. **C.**

Since sharks are fish, they are ectothermic and will assume the temperature of their environment. While there is no way for you to know exactly what this value is, it is certainly colder than 37°C, and the optimal temperature of the enzyme shown in the graph, about 12°C (about 50°F), is reasonable for cool water, since you have to pick one choice. D cannot be true; everything that is alive must contain a DNA polymerase!

5. **D.**

Denaturation implies that the enzyme has lost all function because its shape has significantly changed. According to the graph, enzyme B has no activity below 17°C or above 43°C. Therefore, choice A is incorrect because this is the optimal temperature. Both choices B and C are out of the activity range, but cold temperatures do not cause denaturation, they simply cause a slowing of the reaction rate based on general kinetic principles until it is ultimately zero. Only high temperatures will cause denaturation, so choice D (50°C) must be correct.

6. **A.**

From the information given, we can tell that the optimal temperature and pH for the enzyme in question is 37°C, pH 6 (the values at which the reaction proceeds to completion most quickly). As with the previous passage, the high temperature rules out any shark enzymes (choices B and D), and the mildly acidic pH could only exist in the mouth, not the small intestine (which is mildly alkaline).

7. **C.**

A human enzyme would likely become denatured at 60°C, as we saw in the last passage, and this would account for the lack of activity (the failure of the blue color to disappear implies that the starch remains present forever, since the enzyme cannot break it down). Choice A does not make sense, since heat will always tend to destabilize chemical bonds. Choice B could not be correct, because the IKI is still active; it is responsible for the blue color. Logically, this leaves out choice D, too.

8. **B.**

The explanation is the same as in question 6.

9. **D.**

This question is simply testing your general knowledge of how an enzyme functions in the context of this passage. Namely, an enzyme always functions by lowering the activation energy of a reaction (usually by providing a surface at the active site that puts the reactant(s) in a proper orientation and proximity). A is incorrect since it states the opposite of this idea. Choice B reflects what would happen if we were to facilitate a reaction by adding heat; the whole point of enzymes is to facilitate the reaction at a temperature that would not

be harmful to life. With regard to choice C, an enzyme or any catalyst can never alter the change in free energy during a reaction, it can only affect the rate of that reaction! (This is a basic principle of thermodynamics and enzyme function).

10. **D.**

Again, this question is simply testing your general knowledge of how an enzyme functions in the context of this passage. The optimal pH and temperature for any enzyme will reflect the environment in which it normally functions; that is, in fact, why the optimal values are optimal! Choice B must be incorrect, because when an enzyme is denatured, it has no activity, the exact opposite of optimal functioning. Two other ideas you are expected to know regarding the general mechanism of enzyme action are the following: the active site of an enzyme is typically composed of only a few amino acids, and the enzyme is "recyclable", or not irreversibly changed by participating in the reaction. These ideas invalidate choices A and C.

CHAPTER 4 SOLUTIONS

1. **C.**

Ethanol fermentation produces two products from the pyruvic acid made during glycolysis: ethanol and carbon dioxide. Logically, then, the pH at which the most carbon dioxide is produced will be the same pH at which the most ethanol is produced.

2. **B.**

If aerobic respiration is occurring, it should not affect the net amount of gas present because for every molecule of oxygen that is used up, a molecule of carbon dioxide will be produced. Thus the net production of gas will accurately reflect the carbon dioxide produced by fermentation. The passage clearly states that fermentation and aerobic respiration can occur simultaneously, so choice C must be incorrect. Choice D must be wrong because carbon dioxide is never used up or created by glycolysis.

3. **C.**

The passage tells us that yeast are fungi, which are eukaryotic and in addition to a nucleus must possess mitochondria. In general, in all eukaryotic organisms, glycolysis and fermentation reactions occur in the cytoplasm, while the Krebs cycle and electron transport occur in the mitochondria. Choice D must be incorrect; if aerobic respiration occurs, the Krebs cycle must be a part of it.

4. **B.**

It is true that aerobic respiration is much more efficient (36 molecules of ATP harvested per glucose molecule) than fermentation (2 ATP molecules harvested per glucose molecule). The net amount of ATP produced by either process, however, will depend on the number of glucose molecules used by each pathway. If 50 glucose molecules are fermented, for example, the net yield of ATP will be 100 molecules. If, at the same time, 2 molecules of glucose were broken down by respiration, the net yield of ATP would be 72 molecules. Both choices C and D must be incorrect, since the passage clearly states that the two processes can take place simultaneously and that fermentation can take place in the presence of oxygen.

5. **C.**

We have already established that yeast have mitochondria and can carry out aerobic respiration, so they must contain an electron transport chain in the inner mitochondrial membrane (these ideas leave out choices A and D). However, we know that fermentation involves only glycolysis plus the fermentation reactions, which do not take place in the mitochondria and do not involve electron transport. Choice B is impossible since carbon dioxide is a waste product of the Krebs cycle or fermentation, and will not require energy to be made; it would certainly never be produced by electron transport.

6. **B**.

The important information to remember when answering both questions 6 and 7 is the following. First, with cyanide poisoning, electron transport stops completely; this causes a buildup of NADH, and the ultimate shutdown of all previous processes, including the Krebs cycle and glycolysis, due to the unavailability of NAD^+. Cyanide poisoning would therefore not allow any oxygen to be used up or carbon dioxide to

be manufactured. In addition, no energy is released, as all processes are stopped. Since ATP synthase is still functioning, the proton gradient will eventually disappear, causing the pH in the intermembrane space to rise dramatically, as equilibrium with the matrix is reached. With 2,4-dinitrophenol, or any uncoupler, electron transport continues, and so do oxygen consumption and carbon dioxide evolution. Since the membrane is leaky to protons, they will flow back to the matrix without making ATP; the energy released will be dissipated as heat, which accounts for the increased body temperature. To the extent the proton gradient is relieved, the pH will rise in the intermembrane space. With an ATP synthase inhibitor like oligomycin, again, oxygen will continue to be used and carbon dioxide produced, as electron transport will continue. Since protons cannot re-enter the matrix, however, the gradient will become steeper and steeper, and the pH in the intermembrane space will drop dramatically as it becomes very acidic.

So, the high body temperature of the person from observation 1, coupled with continued oxygen consumption and the relatively unchanged or alkaline pH of the intermembrane space, identifies the poisoning agent as an uncoupler.

7. **C.**

Refer to the information from question 6. The dropping pH in the intermembrane space alone allows identification of this toxin as an ATP synthase inhibitor.

8. **B.**

Again, refer to the information from question 6. NADH will build up as electron transport is discontinued, as it has no place to give up electrons. NAD^+ and FAD, the oxidized forms of coenzymes, will eventually decrease in amount until there are none left. Carbon dioxide will ultimately stop being produced, so its concentration will not change very much.

9. **B.**

As we have seen from the solution to question 6, uncouplers function by allowing the inner mitochondrial membrane to become permeable to protons, and we know from question six that energy is released but not used (harvested as ATP); it is simply dissipated as heat. Choice A is incorrect because uncouplers decrease the formation of ATP; choice C is incorrect because it describes a cyanide-like poison that shuts down electron transport. Choice D makes little sense; if anything, an uncoupler would cause the metabolic rate to rise.

10. **A.**

Again referring to the information from question 6, cyanide poisoning is the only situation we mentioned where glycolysis (and the Krebs cycle) will ultimately cease to function, due to the unavailability of oxidized coenzymes.

CHAPTER 5 SOLUTIONS

1. **B.**

Detection of radioactive phosphate in the pellet indicates the bacteria now contain the DNA of the bacteriophage. Radioactive sulfur in the supernatant suggests the protein of the phage did not enter the cell. Since the bacteria took up something from the phage, answer D is unlikely, as it does appear the phage infected the cell.

2. **C.**

The experiment verified that the DNA of the phage entered the cell. Therefore, the bacteria were indeed infected. It is not likely the protein coats are necessary for further functioning of the phage as they never entered the cell. It is also unlikely the radioactive phosphate would immediately kill the cells (after all, phage were propagated in bacteria grown in medium containing the isotope). The most likely answer is that the phage would reproduce as normal.

3. **D.**

Answer D is the only choice that makes any sense. All the other answers defeat the purpose of the experiment: a competitive inhibitor would prevent the phage from entering the cells at all; breaking apart the cell membrane would cause the contents of the cell to be released, where they would be found in the supernatant, along with the components of the phage that did not infect the cell; a mutant phage that could not bind to the cell would probably not infect the cell.

4. **A.**

Bacteriophages work by making the target cell do something it could not do before. Fertilization results in a new type of cell and is the beginning of a developmental cycle, not the best analogy to the phage experiment. Consuming enzymes would not fundamentally change an organism. Although the T2 experiment used radioactivity, not all experiments involving radioactive isotopes examine the same phenomenon.

5. **C.**

After one round of replication, all the DNA was found to be intermediate in density, with one strand containing the light isotope and one containing the heavy isotope. A second round of replication would mean that these intermediate DNA double strands would now serve as the template strands. The resulting copies would contain the light isotope. Therefore, from the template strand containing the heavy isotope, the resulting double strand would be intermediate, and from the template containing the light isotope, the double strand would contain only the light isotope. This would result in half the DNA being intermediate and half being light.

6. **C.**

Only the bases in a nucleotide contain nitrogen.

7. **D.**

Conservative replication implies that the template strands remain together and the copied strands form the new double-stranded DNA molecule. If this were true, then the template strands would contain only ^{15}N, the heavy isotope, and the copy strands would contain only ^{14}N, the light isotope.

8. **A.**

Okazaki fragments are generated during replication of the lagging strand. Therefore, they would contain only ^{14}N.

9. **A.**

Since G-C base pairs contain three hydrogen bonds, whereas A-T base pairs contain only two, the G-C pairing would require more energy, and hence a higher temperature, to disrupt. Extending this idea, long chains of DNA require different temperatures to denature depending on how many G-C pairs they have relative to A-T base pairs. Since there is no difference in the number of hydrogen bonds between a DNA-DNA double strand and a DNA-RNA double strand with the same sequence (A-U base pairs only contain two, just like A-T), there would be no difference in the temperature necessary to denature them.

10. **B.**

Chromosomes contain DNA and proteins. It is necessary to keep the DNA intact during isolation for further experiments, so adding DNase would not be wise. Since chromosomes do not contain RNA or lipids, reagents used to degrade these components are not necessary. However, to purify the DNA, proteins must be removed. Proteases are often used to accomplish this.

11. **A.**

Since RNA contains U instead of T, the answers using T can be eliminated automatically. This question stresses the property of base pairing that requires the strands to be in the opposite orientation (antiparallel). Therefore, although the sequence UAGGCGAUUC (response B) matches the DNA sequence as written, the 5' and 3' ends are not in the correct orientation. If the sequence was reversed, as in answer A, the two strands would complementary base pair.

CHAPTER 6 SOLUTIONS

1. **A.**

Starting at the first nucleotide and reading every three nucleotides as a codon, the predicted amino acid sequence can be deduced. The translation of this sequence requires the use of the genetic code (see Figure 6.3).

2. **B.**

A single nucleotide substitution in the sequence will result in a single amino acid change in the resulting protein (refer to the genetic code). The protein will still be translated, so response A is not true. We cannot infer from the sequencing information or from the family history that the mutation will not allow the heart to develop properly, so response C is incorrect. In addition, we are told the protein functions as a single polypeptide chain, so response D is also incorrect.

3. **C.**

The mutation in the sequence of the gene causes a termination codon to be inserted. This stops the translation of the protein. Since it occurs early in the sequence (the 25th amino acid out of 283 total), the protein will almost certainly not function.

4. **B.**

If the corresponding tRNA was mutated to now allow incorporation of the normal amino acid into the sequence, the protein would function correctly. Responses A and C would not allow for insertion of the correct amino acid at the critical position in the protein, and response D would not guarantee correction of the mutation. As a matter of fact, it would cause more mutations.

5. **D.**

Using the genetic code in Figure 6.3, all of the mRNA sequences can be found to code for the same amino acid sequence.

6. **A.**

Poly A tails regulate the degradation of the transcripts. They are not required for any of the other functions listed in answers B, C and D.

7. **D.**

Recall that the mRNA transcript is manufactured in the 5' to 3' direction, meaning the DNA is copied in the 3' to 5' direction. Also, the mRNA is the complement of the DNA template, not an exact copy of it.

CHAPTER 7 SOLUTIONS

1. **A.**

All the bacteria were infected by the phage and lysed. The other conditions, whether true or not, deal with growth or death of bacteria and would not cause lysis of the bacteria. Therefore, the plate would remain cloudy. Only lysis causes the plates to appear clear.

2. **C.**

The control in this experiment (condition 1) rules out answers A and B. If UV light killed the bacteria, as suggested in D (and as can happen, depending on conditions), then all the bacteria would die. (Although it is possible that only a small percentage would die, it would be highly unlikely that this lethality would show a plaque pattern.) C is the only plausible answer, and we know that UV light can induce lysogenic strains to become lytic.

3. **D.**
Under both conditions, infection and induction, lysis would occur. Therefore, on average for these experimental conditions, infection would produce 20 plaques per plate and induction would produce 50 plaques per plate, for a total of 70 plaques per plate.

4. **B.**
Once induction occurs, viral particles are produced that can go on to infect other bacterial cells. Therefore, the isolation of bacteriophage from cultures would not support the theory of autolysis. Answer A is possible in the realm of either theory, C would not distinguish between the two, and D has nothing to do with either theory, as bacteria that grow well at 37ºC will not grow at 40C.

5. **C.**
The action of the analogs is at the level of reverse transcription. If the reverse transcriptase mutates to no longer allow incorporation of the analogs, then the virus can continue on its normal path. It is unlikely the body would mount an immune response to these analogs (choice B) as these analogs are so similar to normal nucleotides. Although the outer protein coat can and does mutate (choice A), this has nothing to do with the analogs. And the virus must incorporate into the host chromosome, so choice D is also incorrect.

6. **D.**
Antibody production against reverse transcriptase would not prevent the virus from entering the cell. All other conditions would allow the immune system to make antibodies against the intact virus, as it exists outside the cells where the immune system can detect it.

CHAPTER 8 SOLUTIONS

1. **B.**
The experiment shows that a soluble factor released by *P. aeruginosa* is probably present in the supernatant (the medium which was then used to grow *B. cepacia*). This factor induced the production of survival molecules in *B. cepacia*. Therefore, we know that *P. aeruginosa* can communicate with *B. cepacia*. We are given no experimental evidence to indicate if *B. cepacia* is able to communicate with *P. aeruginosa* .

2. **A.**
Since *B. cepacia* were grown in the liquid medium after the *P. aeruginosa* had been removed by centrifugation, a soluble factor, probably a protein, must have been present. No direct cell-to-cell contact could have taken place. In addition, we have no direct evidence that *B. cepacia* secreted any proteins.

3. **C.**
Nerve cells communicate chemically by releasing factors into the synapse between each other. Hormones are released from one gland and travel to a target tissue or organ where they are detected by receptors. Both systems use communication systems similar to the release of protein from one bacterial cell and detection by another.

4. **C.**
It is important to control this experiment. This can be accomplished by incubating *B. cepacia* in medium that had not been used to grow another strain of bacteria. In this manner, we could directly see the effects of *P. aeruginosa* on *B. cepacia*.

5. **D.**
The most likely answer to this question is that the *P. aeruginosa* were defective in secretion. If they had mutations in any other system, they would be unlikely to survive and reproduce.

6. **C.**

After five hours, there would be ten doublings since the doubling time is 30 minutes. Initially, there are 10^5 cells. So, after 30 minutes, there are 2×10^5 cells. After 1 hour, there are $2 \times 2 \times 105$ cells. After 10 iterations, we get:

$$2 \times 2 \times ... \times 2 \times 10^5 = 2^{10} \times 10^5 =$$
$$1024 \times 10^5 \approx 10^3 \times 10^5 = 10^8$$

7. **B.**

DNA replication (response A) would probably continue to occur by utilizing preexisting enzymes. Damage to the glycocalyx (response D) would not necessarily mean the cell would die. However, production of new pili or repair of flagella (B and C) would almost certainly require protein synthesis and therefore could not occur in the presence of this type of antibiotic.

CHAPTER 9 SOLUTIONS

1. **C.**

Since the sucrose crystals appeared in the lysosomes of the cell, the invertase had to have been internalized in order to catalyze the reaction of the crystals into monosaccharides. Given the circumstances, none of the other answers are appropriate.

2. **B.**

Since we are told that the sucrose crystals are broken down within several days of sucrose being eliminated from the medium, it appears that the cells have the ability to produce invertase, but probably in low levels.

3. **C.**

Either conditions I or II would explain the results seen in Experiment 2. There is no indication that invertase would destroy one cell type, so III is not a possibility.

4. **B.**

Recall that enzymes are specific for their substrates. Invertase would probably not catalyze the breakdown of mannose. Therefore, even in the presence of invertase, the mannose crystals would take several days to be eliminated from the cells.

5. **B.**

Cells that do not contain nuclei are prokaryotes, such as bacteria, and do not contain most other organelles. However, bacteria may contain flagella, which aids in locomotion.

6. **D.**

Recall that both the nucleus and mitochondria contain DNA. Therefore, replication can take place in both organelles.

CHAPTER 10 SOLUTIONS

1. **D.**

Since the pump is transporting ions against their concentration gradients, and as it requires ATP to do so, this process is considered active transport. Recall that bulk transport is not specific for molecules or ions, osmosis is the diffusion of water, and facilitated diffusion is possible due to concentration gradients and is a passive process.

2. **C.**

The Na^+/glucose pump uses the concentration gradient established by the Na^+/K^+ pump. It is therefore considered facilitated diffusion.

3. **A.**

The only logical answer is that an electrical gradient will form. In general other ions, be they positive or negative, will not be transported based on sodium concentration. A magnetic gradient will not exist.

4. **D.**

All of the choices would be possible results of preventing transport of sodium.

5. **B.**

Under these conditions, sodium transport out of the cell (by the Na^+/K^+ pump) and its import (via the Na^+/glucose pump) would not be affected, so both of these pumps would be functional, and there would be no buildup of sodium inside the cell (choice A). Equilibrium of sodium and/or glucose (choices C and D, respectively) may occur, but this is unlikely as the pumps will continue to work. However, if no other pump is active, there would be a build up of potassium inside the cell.

6. **B**.

This is the best answer of the choices given. The amino terminus is probably not hydrophobic (choice A) as it is located extracellularly, where there is a great abundance of water. We are given no good reason to assume the protein transports sodium, so choice C is not the best. Transmembrane proteins do not necessarily carry any particular charge, and do not have to be neutral, so answer D is not correct. Answer B relies on your knowledge of the composition of the cell membrane, specifically the lipid component. For a protein to span the membrane, it must be compatible with the environment of the membrane, which is hydrophobic.

7. **B**.

The microorganism is adapted to life in a high salt environment. Remember that water can freely diffuse across cell membranes. Therefore, the tonicity of the organism was probably well suited to its environment. Placing the cell in the fresh water medium, which was hypotonic to the cell, would have caused water to rush into the cell, thereby lysing it.

CHAPTER 11 SOLUTIONS

1. **C.**

Inability to detect whether the cell was large enough to divide would occur at G_2.

2. **B.**

The cell should not be allowed into G_2 if all the DNA has not yet been replicated. Therefore, the mutation probably occurred in S phase.

3. **D.**

It appears that these mutants exert their controls at two different stages in the cell cycle, perhaps at both S and G_2.

4. **C.**

Each mutant would eventually die out under the experimental conditions. However, the mutants that are defective at both checkpoints would probably die out most quickly.

5. **B.**

The amount of DNA in the cell was intermediate to the amount in a cell before DNA replication (3.2 pg, in G_1) and a cell after DNA replication (6.4 pg, in G_2). Therefore, the cell had to be undergoing replication of the DNA and therefore had to be in S phase. Cells in mitosis (M) would contain either 6.4 pg (prior to telophase) or 3.2 pg (just after telophase) of DNA, but never any amount in-between.

6. **B.**

If microtubules cannot assemble, then the chromosomes cannot move via the spindle fibers. Mitosis would proceed up until that point. Therefore, the cells would enter metaphase but never reach anaphase.

CHAPTER 12 SOLUTIONS

1. **B.**

Meiosis always consists of two rounds of division and spermatogenesis produces four physiologically identical sperm cells.

2. **B.**

Sperm cells are physiologically identical – they all have the same basic cell structure. Sperm do not contribute any organelles, including mitochondria, to the zygote, so the only difference between them is the nuclear DNA they contain.

3. **B.**

Oogenesis produces one ovum and two polar bodies.

4. **C.**

During meiosis I, the primary oocyte divides into a secondary oocyte and a polar body. The polar body does not then divide. During meiosis II, the secondary oocyte divides into an ovum and a second polar body, making for a total of three cells.

5. **D.**

The goal of sexual reproduction is not to improve the fitness of any one organism, but rather the fitness of the whole species. By increasing variability, it ensures that each new generation will have a wide variety of individuals with different traits. This means that if there are any shifts in the environment, the species as a whole will be more likely to be able to adjust (even if some individuals cannot).

6. **C.**

Separation of sister chromatids is simply the mechanism by which sexually-reproducing species ensure that their offspring get the normal diploid set of genetic material.

CHAPTER 13 SOLUTIONS

1. **B.**

Since cigarette smoke is inhaled, it is most likely to contact the mucous membrane of the lungs, whose outer layer is composed of epithelium.

2. **D.**

Since carcinogens, whether chemicals or radiation, are contacting the body from the environment, and we know that epithelium is always the tissue that separates the body from the environment, we would expect the carcinogens to initially contact epithelium. If they penetrated tissue deeply, all types of cancers would be equally prevalent; the fact that carcinomas make up 90% of all cancers implies that after the carcinogen contacts the epithelium, it generally does not penetrate much deeper. There is no reason to believe that choice B is correct, and choice C is irrelevant to the question.

3. **C.**

The cause of a carcinoma of the skin would most likely be radiation exposure from the environment, or contact with the skin by carcinogenic chemicals. Since the worker lives in Alaska and rarely goes outside, it is unlikely that excessive exposure to sunlight is the culprit, and radiation from the isotope is a more likely causative agent. Cigarette smoke or ingestion of chemicals would likely affect mucous membranes or internal body parts.

4. **D.**

Due to the possibility of metastasis, a tumor that originated in one part of the body from a particular type of cell may "spread" to virtually any body location, producing a new tumor there. The tumor, however, will still be made up of the type of cells from which it originally grew.

5. **A.**

Since the basement membrane holds epithelium to underlying tissue, it would have to be penetrated by any cells wishing to invade another tissue. It has nothing to do with cell division (leaving out choices B and C) and choice D doesn't make sense -- the cells themselves cannot be carcinogens. The carcinogen is the environmental agent that caused the mutation in the first place.

6. **D.**

Choices A, B, and C all refer to tissues composed of cells and ground material, and all are listed as connective tissues. Muscle tissue is made up of muscle cells, with little intercellular material, and muscle tissue is one of the four fundamental tissue types.

7. **A.**

The only muscle in the body that is involuntary and striated is cardiac muscle, and its only location is in the heart. Smooth muscle is involuntary and unstriated, as is described by choice B. Skeletal muscle is under voluntary control and appears striated, as is described by choice C. The diaphragm is under both involuntary and voluntary control, and is considered a skeletal muscle.

8. **D.**

Nervous tissue is the only tissue type involved with communication using electricity. Muscle tissues use electricity, but for movement; connective and epithelial tissues are not involved with communication, and certainly not by using electricity.

9. **A.**

All glands are composed of glandular epithelium, and all hormone-producing structures are classified as glands.

10. **C.**

Elastin fibers allow stretching, which clearly must take place in the walls of the arteries. Collagen confers strength and is not stretchable; cartilage is even harder and more unyielding. While a small amount of muscle tissue may exist in the walls of arteries, it is not significant with regard to the question.

CHAPTER 14 SOLUTIONS

1. **C.**

Since testosterone is identified in the passage as a steroid hormone, it does not stimulate cells by using cAMP or a second messenger system, and thus should not affect cells abnormally in an individual with the disease. The other three hormones are all identified as proteins, which would use cAMP and thus affect cells abnormally in an individual with McCune-Albright syndrome.

2. **C.**

Hormones are chemical messengers that are produced by a gland, travel to their target cells, and send a message to those cells by interacting with a receptor. While neurotransmitters travel only a short distance, they are secreted by presynaptic dendrites, diffuse across the synaptic cleft, and interact with receptors on the postsynaptic axon, signaling that cell to initiate an action potential. The parallel with hormones is striking. Choices A and B refer to intermembrane proteins that allow transport through a plasma membrane. Choice D refers to proteins that would be more analogous to hormone receptors.

3. **D.**

The hypothalamus, which is composed mainly of nervous tissue and is considered a part of the brain, can also produce hormones, and controls the actions of the pituitary gland almost directly. The pituitary then controls the actions of all other glands in the body. Choices A and C are simply false statements, that may confuse you due to the presence of familiar sounding terminology. While choice B is a true statement, it does not demonstrate any general connection between the two systems, and certainly not one as important as the hypothalamus-pituitary connection.

4. **B.**

Since the release of testosterone is controlled by GnRH, which is identified in the passage as a protein hormone, the cells that secrete testosterone will overreact to the message and secrete excess quantities of testosterone. Choice D describes the opposite of the truth; we know from question one that once produced, testosterone will not have any abnormal effects on target cells. Its presence in large quantities, however, may cause abnormal effects. Choice A is not true because testosterone, being a steroid, does not function using a second-messenger system.

5. **B.**

Steroid hormones diffuse freely through plasma membranes and thus should be found in all cells. They only cause effects, however, in the cells that contain the appropriate intracellular receptor. A is incorrect because it implies a mode of action that would be employed by a protein hormone. D is also incorrect; for the same reason that testosterone will not affect the cells of an individual with McCune-Albright syndrome abnormally, no steroid hormone will, including Stanozolol.

6. **A.**

ADH (antidiuretic hormone) tells the walls of the collecting duct and distal convoluted tubules of the nephron to become permeable to water, allowing it to avoid being excreted in the urine. If it is inhibited, the urine will contain excessive water, causing dehydration. The other hormones listed do not directly affect water balance.

7. **B.**

As positively charged sodium ions quickly diffuse into a neuron through a gated channel, the interior of the cell becomes electrically positive with respect to the outside (depolarization). Potassium is involved in repolarization as it flows out of cells (choice A) and calcium is involved with neurotransmitter release (choice C). Neurotransmitters themselves never actually enter cells, and they are certainly not ions (choice D).

8. **C.**

The brainstem controls autonomic activities such as breathing and heart rate. Choice A is describing the actions of the cerebellum; choice B is describing actions of the cerebral cortex; and choice D is describing actions of the diencephalon.

9. **B.**

Mechanoreceptors react to physical stimulation, and are in fact the receptors for the sense of hearing. Choice A would be correct if "chemoreceptors" was replaced by "mechanoreceptors"; likewise, choice D is incorrect as it implies a chemical stimulus that would be picked up by chemoreceptors. Choice C is incorrect, because sound waves, which are simply vibrations of molecules, can occur in any medium. (Sound would be impossible in a vacuum.)

10. **C.**

The rods are responsible for night vision, or the ability to discern shapes and outlines without color in dim light. If they are inhibited, "night blindness" will occur. If the cones were inhibited, color vision would be affected (choice B). Choices A and D would result in the blocking of all visual information, causing total blindness.

CHAPTER 15 SOLUTIONS

1. **C**

Individuals afflicted by SCID have no T cells, while those with AIDS have T cells whose function has been compromised. Choice A is incorrect because the passage tells us that individuals with AIDS can in fact make antibodies (this is the basis for many common HIV tests). No information from the passage supports choice B or choice D.

2. **B**

As noted in question 1, individuals with AIDS can and do make antibodies to the HIV virus; they simply cannot do it efficiently enough to ward off the disease. A is incorrect because it is a viral infection that occurs, not a bacterial one. Choices C and D are incorrect because the passage does not support them; it implies that T cells are left alive, and it does not say that HIV infects any cell type except helper T cells.

3. **B**

The passage tells us that the inflammatory response acts only in a nonspecific fashion, which leaves out choice A as a possibility. The major blood cells involved in inflammation are the neutrophils and macrophages, which phagocytize foreign invaders. Choices C and

D are not supported by the passage: it says that phagocytes do destroy invaders, and never mentions red blood cells. Red blood cells would never be involved in phagocytosis!

4. **B**

Intact skin, which contains an epithelial layer that is quite thick, is a much better barrier to infection than the respiratory mucous membrane, where most infections are acquired. While the passage does not state this directly, you are expected to be able to reason it through. Since gas exchange occurs across the surface of the respiratory membrane, it must be extremely thin, and could never be as good a barrier as intact skin. Choice C is not true and is not supported by the passage.

5. **B**

The passage states this specifically. B cells can react to circulating antigens, so choice A is incorrect. Choices C and D are incorrect, because the passage tells us that macrophages act by phagocytosis, and also that they are nonspecific.

6. **A**

Since we know that the proper definition of an artery is a vessel that takes blood away from the heart, and that the ventricle pumps blood away from the heart, vessels attached to ventricles must be arteries.

7. **B.**

All blood cells are initially produced in the bone marrow! White blood cells do not contain hemoglobin (choice A); red blood cells are not involved with blood clotting (choice C); and platelets do not contain hemoglobin or transport oxygen.

8. **C.**

Since the pulmonary vein is returning blood to the heart that has just been oxygenated by the lungs, it must contain the highest concentration of oxygen. All of the other vessels mentioned contain varying amounts of oxygen. This question attempts to confuse you because of the general misperception that arteries always contain higher oxygen levels than do veins.

9. **D.**

All of the statements are true.

10. **C.**

Hemoglobin is a protein that must complex with iron in order to perform its function, which is to carry oxygen in red blood cells. Iodine is complexed with the thyroid hormone thyroxin (choice A); hemoglobin is certainly not a lipid (choice B); and chromium is a mineral that interacts with insulin as part of the glucose tolerance factor.

CHAPTER 16 SOLUTIONS

1. **B.**

The normal function of the large intestine is to reabsorb water from the digestive system into the blood; the presence of large amounts of any chemical not usually present will inhibit this function, and allow more water than normal to be eliminated with the feces. This also contributes to diarrhea. None of the other choices make sense, and none are supported by the passage.

2. **B.**

These supplements actually do contain the enzyme lactase; since it is a normal digestive enzyme, it will not be broken down by the proteases present in the digestive system as most other proteins would. Choice A would have far-reaching consequences, as the bacteria of the colon are mutualistic and play an important role in homeostasis. Choice C is unlikely and unsupported by the passage. While choice D is tempting, only monosaccharides may ever be absorbed by the small intestines - this has to do with their size and the lack of any machinery to transport them across the small intestinal wall.

3. **A.**

Since insulin is a protein and should never normally be found in the digestive tract, it would in fact be digested and useless if taken orally. Both choices B and C are unreasonable and unsupported by the passage; you should be aware that glucagon should never be present in the digestive tract. Thus choice D is also ruled out.

4. **B.**

If diabetes type I is untreated, no insulin exists to reduce the blood sugar, causing it to build up to extremely high levels, so much so that it upsets the osmotic balance between the cells and blood, causing water to leave the cells, enter the blood, and be excreted. The tremendous amounts of glucose also tax the kidneys' mechanism for reabsorbing it, so some is excreted in the urine.

5. **A.**

Since the job of insulin is to reduce the blood sugar, excess insulin will do just that, by any means it can. Choice B describes the opposite effect, and therefore must be discarded. Both choices C and D are unreasonable and unsupported by the passage.

6. **C.**

Since the carbon dioxide concentration is so closely linked with the pH of the blood, the brain uses these parameters to gather information about the actions to take to control the respiratory rate. While the concentration of oxygen could be monitored logically (and is, by the carotid and aortic bodies), this is a fine tuning measure, and is not a major source of regulation (choice A). Choice B is incorrect, because the heart rate is regulated by similar mechanisms as the respiration rate; one does not directly affect the other. Choice D is unsupported by the passage, and untrue.

7. **B.**

Since ADH controls the permeability of the walls of the collecting duct of the nephron to water, its absence would cause water to be excreted in large quantities in the urine. This would eventually lead to dehydration.

8. **A.**

The diaphragm is the sheet-like muscle that separates the thoracic and abdominal cavities; its contraction, regulated by the brainstem, is largely responsible for inhalation. The rectus abdominus is an abdominal muscle that moves the body; the cerebellum is involved with the coordination of movement.

9. **D.**

All relatively small molecules initially enter the filtrate, even if they are nutrients; plasma proteins are too large to diffuse across the capillary wall. Glucose and amino acids will normally be completely reabsorbed, leaving urea to be excreted in the urine.

10. C.

The pancreas, known as an accessory digestive organ, is vital to digestion because it manufactures and secretes most of the major digestive enzymes that function in the small intestine. Food never enters it, however, as it is not a part of the gastrointestinal tract. Food does pass through all of the other organs.

CHAPTER 17 SOLUTIONS

1. B.

Like all outer epithelial cells, the cells of a psoriasis blemish are dead and highly keratinized, which is what gives them the scaly appearance. All of the other choices do not make sense, and are not supported by the passage.

2. C.

Since the problem here is excess cell division (which must be by mitosis), anti-cancer drugs that inhibit cell division should be effective (although there are side effects). While collagen is an important component of the dermis, it has nothing to do with psoriasis or the epidermis (choice A). Choice B would only be valid in the case of a bacterial infection, and none exists in this case. Sebum-inhibiting drugs do work against acne, but again, this is due to bacterial infection and is not applicable to psoriasis (choice D).

3. A.

It is expected that you are aware that the neurotransmitter acetylcholine is virtually the only important one that acts at the neuromuscular junctions of skeletal muscles. Acetylcholinesterase is the enzyme that normally degrades it, and if this is inhibited, paralysis will occur. Choice B is incorrect as it refers to the neurotransmitter itself (but might trick you if you weren't careful). Choices C and D are unsupported by the passage.

4. B.

Since only muscles stimulated by acetylcholine will be affected, choice D cannot be true. The heart requires no nervous stimulation to keep beating, and the brain uses different neurotransmitters than acetylcholine (choices A and C).

5. B.

The major cooling mechanisms are sweating and vasodilation. The efficiency of sweating decreases as the humidity increases, and vasodilation becomes less effective as the temperature rises, and counterproductive if it rises above body temperature. So, the conditions with the lowest humidity and temperature would allow the most efficient functioning.

6. C.

All of the tissues listed are connective tissues. Ligaments, however, are involved in the connection of bones to other bones (choice A); articular cartilage occurs also at bone/bone connections (choice B); and adipose tissue is not involved in truly "connecting" things together, although it may be present in a wide variety of locations.

7. C.

Calcium is stored in the sarcoplasmic reticulum of muscle cells, and as the muscle cell becomes depolarized, it is released into the sarcoplasm, where it directly stimulates troponin to initiate contraction. Sodium and potassium are involved only in the nervous signal that depolarizes the sarcolemma (choices A and B), and phosphorus is not relevant in this context.

8. C.

The subcutaneous layer is mainly composed of connective adipose tissue, which requires a steady blood supply. The epidermis is composed solely of epithelial cells (choice A), and the dermis contains all tissue types, but little fat (choice B).

9. B.

Hairs are composed of epithelial cells being pushed outward by a dividing lower layer, and as they get further from the nutrient supply, they die and are keratinized. The follicle itself, however, is located physically in the dermis, where it is protected from bacterial infection, etc.

10. C.

ATP is directly necessary to provide energy, calcium is necessary to activate the complex, and troponin is necessary to bind to calcium and participate in activation. Creatine phosphate is often present, and functions to "recharge" ADP to ATP, but it is not required for contraction.

CHAPTER 18 SOLUTIONS

1. **D.**
All of these events could lead to the production of a Turner's individual in the following ways. If the X and Y chromosomes fail to separate in the father at meiosis I, some of the resulting gametes will contain both X and Y, and some will contain no sex chromosomes. If the latter type joins with a normal egg, an XO individual will result. Likewise, failure of the X's to separate during meiosis I in the mother would lead to some eggs containing two X chromosomes, and some containing none; if the latter combined with a normal male sperm carrying an X chromosome, Turner's would result. Finally, if the two chromatids of the replicated Y chromosome failed to separate during meiosis II, some gametes would end up with two Y chromosomes, and some with no sex chromosomes; if the latter combined with a normal female egg, an XO individual would be produced.

2. **B.**
Since we know that normal human males are chromosomally XY and females are XX, it would not be unreasonable to put forth either of the following hypotheses: 1.) Sex is determined by the number of X chromosomes present; or 2.) Sex is determined by the presence or the absence of the Y chromosome. Consider that Turner's individuals appear female, and yet only possess one X, while those with Klinefelter's syndrome appear male, and yet contain two X's. However, they do contain a Y, while the Turner's individuals do not. Thus, we can postulate that sex is in fact normally determined by the presence or absence of the Y chromosome (which is known to be the case). Choice C is incorrect; since the Y chromosome determines sex, it is the sperm, and thus the father, that contributes the information about the sex of the offspring.

3. **D.**
The passage clearly states that nondisjunction is random, so choice A is ruled out. It also states that if other trisomies or monosomies exist, they are either miscarried or die early; this implies that the effects of such events are extremely detrimental (choice B is true). C also must be true, because if there were genes for fundamental life processes on chromosome 21, Down syndrome individuals could not live to adulthood.

4. **D.**
Question one has established that nondisjunction in either parent can in fact lead to Down syndrome, and there is no reason to believe that it cannot, so choice A must be incorrect. It is true that a female is born with all the eggs she will ever release already formed, but arrested in the early stages of meiosis; the longer they remain in her body, the greater the chances that mutations will occur which might result in nondisjunction (choice B is correct). In addition, males would have the same probability of creating an aberrant sperm at any time in their lives, since sperm are made and turned over continuously until death (C is correct).

5. **B.**
Identical twins result when one egg is fertilized by one sperm, as normal, but for some reason the two cells that result after the zygote divides become separated; at this early stage, each of the cells can go on to produce a complete individual. Fraternal twins are created when two eggs are mistakenly released, and are fertilized by separate sperm. Thus identical twins are in fact genetically identical, while fraternal twins are no more genetically related than any siblings. Of course, identical twins are not identical in all of their characteristics, due to the influence of the environment on development. Choice B is the only answer consistent with this information.

6. **C.**
Fertilization normally takes place in the oviduct (choice C is correct), and cleavage begins as the zygote begins to travel towards the uterus, where implantation occurs (choice B is not). The ovary functions solely in the release of eggs and production of hormones, and the vagina functions as the receptacle for the penis and the birth canal, excluding both choices A and D.

7. **B.**
In males, the sperm and urine do in fact share the urethra as a common pathway out of the body. In females, the urinary and reproductive systems are completely separate anatomically and physiologically; superficially they seem connected due to their external openings in the same general vicinity (choices A, C and D are incorrect).

8. **C.**

The worst effects of any teratogenic (birth-defect causing) drug would occur during the embryonic stage (week two to the end of month two). This is because all of the major events of organogenesis, germ tissue formation, and differentiation occur during this stage. If the drugs were ingested earlier than implantation (choices A and B), the negative effects would likely terminate the zygote or morula before it could implant, or might not harm them at all, depending on the drug. While drugs can certainly harm a fetus, it is usually less severe because all of the major organs have been formed and the general body layout is complete by this stage (choice D).

9. **C.**

The ectoderm gives rise to the skin and the nervous system. The endoderm gives rise to the internal mucous membranes and the gut (choice A). The mesoderm gives rise to most major organs (not in the nervous system), muscles, etc. (choice B). There is no such thing as the gastroderm (choice D).

10. **D.**

Since the eggs and sperm released into the water by fish must find each other virtually "by chance", eggs (and sperm) must be released in very large quantities to ensure that some fertilization occurs (choice A is correct). In addition, since so many species of fish release their eggs and sperm in this fashion (not to mention hundreds of marine invertebrates), species-specific identification methods must exist that allow only sperm and eggs from the same species to attempt to join. While it is theoretically possible for the sperm of one species to fertilize the egg of another, this would be counterproductive so mechanisms have evolved to prevent it (Choice C is correct). Choice B is incorrect as it is impossible for a sperm to fertilize more than one egg in any environment.

CHAPTER 19 SOLUTIONS

1. **A.**

Since the F_1 progeny all are phenotypically similar to one parent (they have red eyes), and the F_2 generation displays a phenotypic ratio of 3:1 red: brown, the brown trait must be recessive. Furthermore, since the pattern does not indicate a difference in heritability in males and females, it must also be an autosomal trait.

2. **C.**

The pattern seen is consistent with a sex-linked recessive trait. Genotypically, the F_1 generation consists of all females heterozygous for the trait (as they inherit one X from the male parent and one from the female parent) and all males will be hemizygous for the normal (wild type) allele (as they can only inherit the X from the female parent). In the F_2 generation, the F_1 females will contribute the wild type allele to half the male progeny and the white allele to the other half, resulting in the phenotypes reflecting the genotypes. However, the male F_1's only have a wild type allele, which will be passed on to the females in the F_2 generation, so all these flies will have red eyes, regardless of what allele they inherit maternally. To extend your knowledge and understanding, determine what would happen if the reciprocal cross was done (white eyed females crossed with red eyed males in the parental generation).

3. **B.**

Since half of the progeny in a cross between affected and unaffected individuals display the mutant phenotype, this condition is autosomal dominant.

4. **C.**

As stated before, the mutation is dominant, but if one parent was homozygous for the allele, all the progeny would show the mutant phenotype. Only a heterozygote could produce unaffected progeny.

5. **B.**

Recall that a test cross is used to confirm the genotype of an individual. The test cross is done with individuals that are homozygous recessive for the allele. When the individual with the unknown genotype is mated to the homozygous recessive individual, only two outcomes are possible: all the progeny are phenotypically dominant (indicated the unknown genotype is homozygous dominant) or half the progeny are phenotypically dominant and half are recessive (indicating the unknown individual was a heterozygote).

6. **C.**

Codominance and incomplete dominance (choices A and B) refer to interactions among alleles for one gene. In this situation, we are looking at the relationship between two genes, and how the alleles for one trait affect the expression of the other trait. Gene interaction and epistasis (choices C and D) describe relationships between genes; however, gene interactions result in new phenotypes (e.g. the white phenotype) whereas epistasis results in one phenotype expressed over another. If epistasis were taking place, the ratio of 9:3:3:1, the typical ratio expected in a dihybrid cross, would change to 9:4:3, if brown was epistatic to scarlet. The genotype representing the 1 in the above ratio is bb/scsc (both alleles at both genes recessive). If brown masks scarlet, as in epistasis, this genotype would phenotypically be brown. If a gene interaction occurs, a new phenotype would result (white).

7. **C.**

The parents must be heterozygotes. They have a 1/4 chance of having a child with the disease, and a 3/4 chance of having an unaffected child. Since we know one child is unaffected, we can eliminate the homozygous recessive genotype, and we are left with only two possibilities: the child is homozygous dominant or heterozygous. If a Punnett square of the cross is examined, there is a 2/3 chance the unaffected child will be a carrier.

8. **D.**

The woman will have the genotype $I^A I^B$, while the man could have either genotype $I^B I^B$ or $I^B i$. Therefore, the only phenotype that could not be produced in the offspring would be blood type O, which, genotypically, is *ii*, which would require the mother to contribute an *i* allele, which she does not have.

CHAPTER 20 SOLUTIONS

1. **A.**
According to the equations given in the chapter, the allelic frequency (p) of the dominant allele is:

[2 x 6 + 4] / 2 x 20 = 16/40 = 4/10 = 0.4

2. **C.**
The question does not specify whether the parents have a weak or strong taste of PTC, only that they can taste it. Therefore, the proportion that can taste it is

$$\frac{11+14}{40} = 0.625 \approx 0.63$$

3. **B.**
Recall that q is the frequency of the recessive allele, in this case t. Using the formulas in the chapter (similar to Question 1), we find that q = 0.55.

4. **D.**
Remember that a population is said to be in Hardy-Weinberg equilibrium if allelic frequencies do not change. Here we see that the values of p and q are different from one generation to the next. It does not require that the genotypic frequencies be the same in each generation (response B).

5. **D.**
You are given the frequency of affected individuals, 1 in 2,000, or 0.0005. This is the frequency of the genotype aa, which is equal to q^2. Therefore, q is equal to 0.0224. Since we know q, we also know p (1 − q = 0.9776). In a population, carriers are heterozygotes, individuals who carry the allele but are not affected by it. The formula to calculate the frequency of heterozygotes is 2pq. Therefore, the frequency of carriers in this population is 0.0438.

6. **B.**
Convergent evolution is the notion that different species evolved similar attributes in similar environments, even though they are not closely related.

CHAPTER 21 SOLUTIONS

1. **A**

Glutamate contains an acidic sidechain residue, which is deprotonated and negatively charged at physiological pH. Valine's side chain is uncharged under the same condition.

2. **B**

At very low pH, glutamate's two carboxylic acid residues are protonated and neutrally charged while its amino group is protonated and positively charged. Glutamate's net charge is therefore +1. Valine contains a neutrally charged, protonated carboxylic acid residue and a positively charged, protonated amino group at the same pH. Its net charge is therefore also +1.

3. **B**

Both samples A and C show at least one band that displays greater electrophoretic mobility toward the negatively charged pole. This is consistent with substitution of a glutamate residue in Hb for a higher pI valine residue able to remain positively charged under less acidic conditions versus normal Hb. Sample B, though, shows enhanced mobility toward the positive electrode. This is inconsistent with substitution with a non-polar uncharged residue for an acidic sidechain residue.

4. **D**

Hb S aggregation must be due to some intermolecular interaction enhanced by the substitution of a non-polar amino acid, valine, for an acidic glutamate residue. This is most likely then due to increased hydrophobic interactions. Choice A requires a polar amino acid residue, choice B requires cysteine and choice C requires acidic or basic residues for such interactions.

5. **C**

Aspartic acid, like glutamic acid, is an acidic amino acid, and would therefore cause the least disruption in the interactions in which glutamic acid had previously participated. Choices A, B and D are nonpolar amino acids.

6. **D**

The distinctive cyclic structure of proline's side chain gives proline an exceptional conformational rigidity compared to other amino acids that tends to introduce "kinks" into the regions of polypeptide secondary structure in which it is found.

7. **B**

Glycine is a non-chiral, optically inactive amino acid because of its hydrogen side chain. At pH 6.1, glycine is most likely to be found in its net neutrally charged zwitterion form, with its carboxylic acid residue deprotonated (choice D). At pH 8, it will be negatively charged and migrate toward the positive pole (choice A). At pH 3, it will be net positively charged and migrate toward a negative pole (choice C).

8. **B**

Lysine will exist as described when pH is greater than that of the carboxylic acid residue, but is less than that of both amino residues. This is true, of the choices listed, only at pH 5.48.

9. **B**

Valine contains only an alkyl group in its side chain. Both serine and tyrosine include polar side chain hydroxyl groups.

10. **D**

The pH range of the second buffering region of alanine will be centered around the pK_a of its α-amino group. This value can be found by using the following equation: $pI = (pK_{a1} + pK_{a2})/2$, where pK_{a2} represents the value of interest. Solving for this value we have = $pK_{a2} = 2*pI - pK_{a1} = 2*6.11 - 2.35 = 9.87$.

CHAPTER 22 SOLUTIONS

1. **A**

Denaturants such as urea, referred to as chaotropic agents, can disrupt hydrogen bonding between water molecules, thereby weakening hydrophobic effects and solvation shells within proteins and between proteins and water. This disruption interferes with the non-covalent forces which stabilize a protein's secondary, tertiary and, if present, quaternary structure: hydrogen bonds, van der Waals forces and hydrophobic interactions. 2-mercaptoethanol will reductively cleave backbone disulfide bonds that the passage described as stabilizing RNase A's tertiary structure. Only RNase's amide-linked peptide bonds will be unaffected by denaturants (choice A).

2. **B**
The native state of a protein is the folded shape that possesses a minimum of free energy (choice B). A protein's native conformation and the tertiary structure which represents it is closely related to and dependent on the shape of an enzyme's active site (choice A) and can be denatured by increased temperature (choice C). While a protein's folded shape is influenced by external patterns, it is also strongly driven by its primary structure (choice D).

3. **D**
The experiment presented in the passage strongly indicates that, under certain circumstances, protein renaturation may occur spontaneously. After completely unfolding RNase A protein in step 1, only the protein's linear amino acid sequence remained unchanged. However, the refolded RNase A obtained as the final product of step 2 was functional and, as described by the passage, undistinguishable from native state RNase A. This suggest that all of the information required to direct adoption of the native state tertiary structure is present in the molecule's linear amino acid sequence (choice D).
The passage does not specifically address whether a protein may be denatured at physiological pH (choice A). Choice B is also false, as treatment with the reductant applied in Step 1 cleaved the covalent disulfide bridges of RNase A, yet the protein was still able to reform its native state spontaneously following removal of the denaturants and reoxidation in Step 2, without the assistance of a catalyst (choice C is also false).

4. **C**
Given the results of the passage, if the protein product of step 3, in which disulfide bonds were randomly reformed, were re-exposed to a reductant in the absence of urea and "unlocked" from its misfolded state, it should be possible for the protein to refold into its native state, as was demonstrated by the results of step 2. Once refolded, the enzyme should regain its catalytic activity (choice C is true and the correct answer; choice D is false). Exposure to a reductant would not lead to oxidation of cysteine and reformation of cystine (choice A), nor would it cause hydrolysis of the peptide backbone (choice B).

5. **D**
Hydrophobic interactions are the most important electrostatic force driving protein tertiary structure folding and subsequent maintenance of the folded state.

6. **D**
Salt bridging occurs between charged polar side groups. Substituting an amino acid with a charged polar side group for an amino with an uncharged polar or nonpolar side group would most disrupt the formation of salt bridges. Only the mutation causing the replacement indicated by choice D is consistent with such a change.

7. **C**
Genetically-encoded proteins with a function that depends on being soluble in the aqueous environments contain an evolutionarily-determined amino acid sequence that allows for their water solubility. The polypeptides synthesized by such random polymerization are not subjected to such functionally selective constraints and less frequently contain a primary sequence permitting the formation of soluble higher-order structures (choice C). Formation of buried salt bridges, or any salt bridge, is possible provided that an amino acid's primary structure allows, and if the conditions to which a protein is exposed don't deviate too greatly from cellular conditions (choice B). The heat of solvation of an insoluble protein is likely more, not less, soluble than that of a soluble protein (choice D). Contrary to choice A, many proteins are able to remain soluble without the assistance of heat shock proteins.

8. **C**
Protein isoforms are proteins which share a similar functional role, but which contain different amino acid sequences. They may be encoded by separate genes, or they may be the product of alternative gene splicing (choice A is false and choice C is true). If the protein isoforms are enzymes, they are referred to as isozymes (choice B). Protein isoforms which serve a similar functional role that are the products of alternative transcription may prove to explain why a smaller

than expected number of protein coding regions are sequenced in an organism's genome, but would not explain why a greater than expected number of coding regions would be found.

9. **A**

Pro-α chains are rich in glycine, proline and non-standard amino acid residues, including hydroxyproline. The collagen polypeptide amino sequence includes the repeating amino acid triplet sequence Gly-X-Y, where X is often proline and Y is frequently hydroxyproline (choice A).

10. **C**

Proline is often found in β-bends, where it introduces the structural "kink" of the bend (choice C). The α-helix involves intra-peptide hydrogen backbone bonding within a single polypeptide chain (choice A). Domains are elements of tertiary structure. The β-pleated sheets involve backbone hydrogen bonding between adjacent parallel or anti-parallel polypeptides (choice D).

CHAPTER 23 SOLUTIONS

1. **C**

Enzymes reduce the activation energy of a reaction, thereby increasing the proportion of substrate molecules with kinetic energies greater than the activation energy. In the absence of enzymatic catalysis, a reaction will precede more slowly because a smaller proportion of substrate pool molecules have the necessary kinetic energy to overcome the energetic barrier of the reaction (choice C). Catalysis do not change the thermodynamic properties of a reaction (choice C), as they do not modify the energy of the reactants (choice A) or products. Enzymes function by providing an alternate reaction pathway with a lower transition state energy, not by transferring energy to a transition state (choice C)

2. **B**

One possible explanation for why Step 2 is the rate-limiting step in the reaction sequence shown in Figure 1 involves stabilization of the reactants in Step 2, thus decreasing the free energy, and increasing the activation energy of Step 2. Choice B, which states that the oxyanion of the tetrahedral intermediate

in Step 2 is stabilized by hydrogen bonding with an adjacent N-H bond, is consistent with this explanation. Destabilization of the oxyanion intermediate would not slow the rate of reaction in Step 2 (choice A). Further, histidine's reversible deprotonation of the aspartate residue of chymotrypsin is dependent upon the rate of deprotonation of histidine by the attacking carbonyl carbon-nitrogen bond in the tetrahedral intermediate of Step 2 (choice C). Cleavage of the Ser^{195} oxygen-tetrahedral carbon bond does not occur until Step 4 (choice D).

3. **A**

The induced fit model posits that the initial interaction between enzyme and substrate is relatively weak, but that these weak interactions quickly induce conformational changes in the enzyme that strengthen binding and enhance enzyme-substrate functional interaction. This model is most consistent with the conformational changes described in the question stem, and the explanation for the model provided in choice A. The lock-and-key model (choices B and D) offers a competing explanation for substrate-enzyme interaction. According to this model, the enzyme and the substrate possess specific complementary geometric shapes that fit perfectly without further modification upon binding. While this model explains enzyme specificity, it fails to explain the stabilization of the transition state that enzymes achieve.

4. **D**

Histidine's imidazole side chain is reversibly protonatable near physiological pH. Of the answer choices listed, only Choice D, which indicates that the protein's enzymatic activity (which requires His^{57} to act as a basic catalyst and abstract a proton from Ser^{195}) is dependent on the protonation state of His^{57}, and thus small changes in pH, provides possible support for histidine's specific involvement in the catalytic mechanism. Increasing pH by a small degree is unlikely to lead to a significant change in histidine's protonation state, and thus its function. However, decreasing pH by a small degree near physiological pH increases the likelihood of histidine's side chain becoming protonated. Of the charged polar amino acids, only histidine is reversibly protonated near physiological pH. Choices A, B, and C all describe functional changes in response to environmental disturbances that are common to most human enzymes.

5. **A**

The passage states that a side chain aromatic ring fits into chymotrypsin's hydrophobic binding position (S1). Of the answer choices given, only phenylalanine (one of the two amino acid residues shown in the polypeptide in Figure 1) contains a hydrophobic side chain.

6. **B**

The question defines enzymatic power as the ratio of the rate of an enzyme-catalyzed reaction divided by the rate of the same reaction when uncatalyzed. Without knowing the rates of the uncatalyzed reactions catalyzed by enzymes A and B, it is impossible to determine, given only the enzymatic power of each enzyme, which enzyme catalyzed reaction proceeds more rapidly (choice B). Choice A, C and D are all true statements. Increasing solution temperature beyond the denaturation point of both enzymes will result in a dramatic decline in the activity of both enzymes, and thus the enzymatic power measured for both (choice A). Because the activation energy is decreased by a smaller factor versus the uncatalyzed reaction in the reaction catalyzed by enzyme B than in the reaction catalyzed by enzyme A (choice D), the rate of production of product is more greatly increased from the uncatalyzed rate for the reaction catalyzed by enzyme A than for enzyme B (choice C).

7. **D**

General enzyme catalysis involves three steps: 1) binding of free enzyme to free substrate forming an enzyme-substrate complex; 2) conversion of enzyme-bound substrate to enzyme bound product; 3) release of bound product from enzyme. Only choice D correctly identifies each of these steps and the moieties involved in each step. Choice A lacks free enzyme in step 1 and does not show formation of an enzyme-substrate complex in step 2. Choice B does not show free substrate in step 1. Choice C also fails to show formation of an enzyme-substrate complex.

8. **B**

An enzyme that is not bound by a non-protein component required for that enzyme's function is referred to as an apoprotein (choice B). A functional enzyme bound to all of its necessary non-protein components is a holoenzyme (choice A). When an enzyme requires binding by an inorganic compound, usually a metal ion, in order to function, that non-protein component is referred to as a cofactor (choice C). If the non-protein component is an organic or a metallo-organic molecule, it is referred to as a coenzyme.

9. **D**

Of the vitamins listed, only vitamin E, a biological antioxidant, is lipid-soluble. Choices A, B, and C are all water-soluble vitamins.

10. **C**

Coenzymes which are permanently bound to an associated enzyme are referred to as prosthetic groups. As such, prosthetic groups are coenzymes that can be more specifically defined as prosthetic groups. Flavin adenine dinucleotide (FAD) is a redox cofactor involved in several important metabolic reactions. FAD is a prosthetic group in the enzyme complex succinate dehydrogenase (complex II) that oxidizes succinate to fumarate during the TCA cycle and, when unbound, FAD serves as a coenzyme to acyl CoA dehydrogenase. Roman numerals I and III are thus both correct. Cosubstrates (Roman numeral II) dissociate from an enzyme in a chemically altered state.

CHAPTER 24 SOLUTIONS

1. **D**

The x-intercept value of mutant PGK is nearer zero, and is therefore a less negative value, than that of wild type PGK. The value of the x-intercept in a double reciprocal plot is equal to $-1/K_m$. Therefore the negative of the value of the x-intercept is inversely proportional to K_m. As the x-intercept more closely approaches zero, thus becoming less negative, K_m must increase. Accordingly, the K_m of wild-type PGK, relative to mutant PGK, must be smaller (choice D). This is the opposite of choice C. The inverse of the y-intercept value in a double reciprocal plot is equal to the value of $1/V_{max}$. Since the y-intercept values for both mutant and wild-type PGK are equal, so too then is V_{max} for each (choices A and B are incorrect).

2. **C**

An increase in K_m with no change in V_{max}, as is true of mutant PGK when compared to wild-type PGK, is the same kinetic change associated with competitive inhibition of an enzyme (choice C). Decreasing substrate concentration would decrease initial reaction velocity, but would not change any kinetic parameter intrinsic to the enzyme (choice A). Reducing concentration of the enzyme PGK would decrease net substrate flux, and thus the total amount of reaction product produced per unit time, but would not modify any parameter of the enzyme (choice B). A decrease in V_{max} with no change in K_m is the same kinetic change associated with non-competitive inhibition of an enzyme (choice D).

3. **B**

Figure 1 indicates that the V_{max} for mutant and wild type PGK are equal. When substrate concentration is saturatingly high for both enzymes, the mutant PGKs lower glucose affinity will be overcome, and its rate of conversion of glucose to glucose-6-phosphate will be equal to that of the wild type enzyme. The passage describes the mutation of the GCK gene which causes MODY2 to be autosomal dominant. Thus, individuals possessing a single mutated allele will be affected by the disease and will show abnormal insulin responses under certain physiological conditions, and, below a threshold level (related to the decreased substrate affinity of mutant PGK), will be mildly hyperglycemic because of decreased insulin secretion compared to unaffected individuals (choices A and C). The passage states that the insulin sensitivity of the cells of those affected by MODY2 is normal (choice D).

4. **A**

Mutant PGK's increased K_m versus that of wild type PGK means that the concentration of substrate at which half-maximal reaction velocity is achieved in a reaction involving mutant PGK is greater than that in wild type PGK because of mutant PGK's decreased affinity for its substrate, glucose, when compared to wild type PGK (choice A). Its active site, and thus catalytic mechanism, is unlikely to be substantially different, if V_{max} for the two enzymes is the same (choice B). There is no indication in the passage that there are differences in the abilities of the two enzymes to interact at their allosteric sites—in fact, the passage indicates that the only structural differences between the two proteins

exists at their substrate binding site. Allosteric sites are by their definition sites other than the enzyme binding site (choice C). The passage also gives no indication that the enzymes' site of intracellular function differ (choice D).

5. **B**

K_m is numerically equal to the substrate concentration at which the reaction achieves half-maximal velocity. Since the K_m of wild type PGK is less than that of mutant PGK, it achieves half-maximal reaction velocity at a lower substrate concentration (choice B is correct; choices A, C and D are incorrect).

6. **A**

Competitive inhibitors bind the active site of the enzymes which they inhibit, competing with substrate for access to the active site (choice A). They do not bind substrate or the enzyme-substrate complex directly (choices B and D). Non-competitive inhibitors most often bind at enzyme allosteric sites (choice C).

7. **D**

Deoxyhemoglobin's oxygen affinity decreases due to decreased pH (choice A), increased temperature (choice B), and the binding of the glycolytic side-product, 2,3-BPG (choice C). However, binding of molecular oxygen to deoxyhemoglobin causes a cooperative change in the binding affinity of the remaining hemoglobin subunits, as the molecule shifts from its T to R conformational state (choice D).

8. **D**

The Michaelis-Menten model assumes that the concentration of substrate is much greater than the concentration of enzyme, so that the statement made in (I) is true. It also assumes that the concentration of enzyme-substrate complex is approximately constant over time, requiring that the statement made in (II) is also true. Finally, initial velocity measurements are often used in in the analysis of enzyme kinetics, since at the time of initial measurement, the concentration of product is very small and the rate of back reaction from product to substrate may be ignored (III).

9. **B**

At low concentrations of substrate ($[S] << K_m$), the velocity of an enzyme-catalyzed reaction is first order with respect to the concentration of substrate only, and therefore also first order overall (choice B).

10. **C**

Oxypurinol, the product of the reaction of allopurinol (a substrate analog of xanthine oxidase's normal substrates, xanthine and hypoxanthine) remains bound to xanthine oxdiase's molybdenum-sulfide (Mo-S) coordination complex, preventing xanthine oxidase's further action. This is an example of a suicide inhibitor, most of which bind covalently and irreversibly to the enzyme active site. A homotropic effector is a substrate molecule which serves as an allosteric effector of the enzyme which catalyzes its conversion, most typically as a positive effector, by binding at a site other than the molecule's active site (choice D). A heterotropic effector is another example of an allosteric effector that binds an allosteric enzyme at some site other than the active site (choice D). Allopurinol's action is, in contrast to reversible inhibition, irreversible (choice B).

CHAPTER 25 SOLUTIONS

1. **C**

During self-assembly, a protein will be unstable unless the rate of heterodimer addition at the (+) end is equal to or greater than the rate of heterodimer loss at the (-) end. Using Figure 1, the rate of (+) addition exceeds that of (-) loss at free tubulin values greater than approximately 4 mM (choice C).

2. **D**

The researchers in the passage hypothesize that MTs are stable when protected by a "GTP cap" at the (+) end. If the rate of GTP-hydrolysis of β-tubulin in associated heterodimers exceeds the rate of GTP-bound dimer addition (association can occur only when both tubulin subunits of a heterodimer are GTP-bound), then the GDP-bound dimers will be exposed at the (+) end and net depolymerization should result. This is the opposite effect indicated by Choice D. Choices A and B are both consistent with maintaining a MT in the polymerized state, and, in the case of choice B, consistent with the rate of tubulin heterodimer

addition versus loss for the (+) and (-) ends shown in Figure 1. The dynamic instability described in the researcher's hypothesis allows for the possibility that changes in free tubulin concentration in regions of the cell, which can vary based upon the number of tubulin heterodimers incorporated, in MTs, can influence the stability of individual MTs at different stages of growth within a single cell.

3. **C**

Colchicine inhibits microtubule polymerization by binding tubulin, the availability of which is crucial to mitosis, thus effectively acting as a mitotic poison. The addition of colchicine near metaphase when chromosomes are aligned along the metaphase plate is part of the standard protocol in karyotyping, effectively halting any further progress through mitosis (Roman numeral II). In addition to inhibiting mitosis, colchicine also inhibits the function of certain leukocytes, including neutrophils, which exhibit amoeboid-like motion. Their movement involves the formation of pseudopodia via the re-arrangement of microtubule and filament structures. The cell surface of a neutrophil projects a membrane process called the lamellipodium, supported by extensions of the cytoskeletal elements mentioned. Cytoplasm flows into the lamellipodium, forming the pseudopodia. Thus, inhibition of neutrophil motility can downregulate the immune and inflammatory responses in which they are involved (roman numeral I). It is for this reason that colchicine is often employed in the management of patient's suffering from gout, a form of acute inflammatory arthritis. There is no indication in the passage or question stem that colchicine influences actin function (roman numeral III).

4. **A**

Figure 1 shows that the rate of dimer loss from the (-) end of MTs decreases due to docetaxel treatment, but little, if any, change occurs in the rate of addition or loss of tubulin heterodimers from the (+). One possible explanation is that GDP-bound dimers are stabilized, and that this effect is more pronounced at the (-) end where the rate of GTP addition is smaller. Both choices B and C would decrease, rather than increase, the rate of tubulin heterodimer addition to the polymer. Choice D does not explain the specific effects shown in Figure 1 at the (-) end of the MT.

5. **D**

According to Figure 1, net growth occurs at the (+) end only at concentrations exceeding approximately 5 mM in both the presence, and absence, of docetaxel (choice D).

6. **B**

Actin filaments require ATP to undergo polymerization, and may demonstrate the phenomena known as treadmilling when added to the (+) pole. Microtubules are composed of tubulin heterodimers that require GPT in order to polymerize (choice A). Intermediate filaments possess stable, rather than dynamic, structures, and are consequently incapable of effects such as treadmilling. Keratin is a type of intermediate filament.

7. **D**

IgM is responsible for mounting the body's initial humoral response and eliminating pathogens before IgG levels increase (choice D). IgA is present in mucosal areas, such as the gut, respiratory tract, saliva, tears, breast milk and the urogenital tract, where it prevents colonization by pathogens (choice A). IgD functions mainly as an antigen receptor on immature B cells that have not been exposed to antigens. It is involved in the activation of mast cells and basophils (choice B). Four forms of IgG provide for most of the humoral immune response. It is the only antibody which is capable of crossing the placenta and conferring passive immunity on the placenta (choice C).

8. **A**

Because of the extremely high specificity (choice C is wrong) and affinity of antibody for antigen (much greater than that of enzyme-substrate affinity, choice B), the binding process is essentially irreversible (choice A). The Fc region is located opposite the antigen binding region of an antibody, and is not involved with the action of antibody binding (choice D). However, the Fc region is important in antibody function. It permits the antibody to interact with cell surface Fc receptors and some proteins of the complement system, allowing for the activation of the immune system.

9. **A**

All of the statements listed in the choices given are correct, except for choice A. Both light chain subunits are disulfide bridged.

10. **A**

Kinesin is the vesicular transport protein most often associated with anterograde transport, trafficking vesicles as it moves toward the (+) end of microtubules that, most often, are oriented toward the periphery of cells (choice A). Dynein, a member of the same microtubule motor protein family as kinesin, walks toward the (-) pole of microtubules and is associated most closely with retrograde transport (choice C). Myosin binds actin, but not microtubules (choice D) and vimentin is a type of intermediate filament (choice B).

CHAPTER 26 SOLUTIONS

1. **C**

If the dialysis membrane described in the passage was constructed of a differentially permeable material which prevents the passage of macromolecules, but permits passage of small molecules and ions, then protein macromolecules would be trapped in the membrane while water and ions would be free to exchange across the membrane, equilibrating the charge and concentration gradient across the membrane. This would lead to a net passage of water into the initially hypotonic membrane interior and, most likely, a net outflow of the salts that remained in the fraction from the elution used to remove antigen-bound antibodies from the column (choice C). Proteins in the passage were diluted due to the fact that at high initial salt concentration, the net inflow of water during dialysis will likely exceed the outflow rate of charge and concentration, equilibrating ions and small molecules. (choices A and D). The question stem states that the membrane is impermeable to macromolecules, a category which includes all proteins. Thus, all proteins will remain trapped within the dialysis membrane (choice B)

2. **A**

The passage states that UV absorbance is principally due to aromatic ring structures. The amino acids phenylalanine (Phe), histidine (His) tryptophan (Trp) and tyrosine (Tyr) are the aromatic amino acids. A fraction purified for the protein with the largest concentration of aromatic amino acid residues should have the greatest absorbance shown in Figure 1, and thus the lowest transmittance at 200 nm. This corresponds to Fraction 4 and the explanation in choice A.

3. **C**

The eluent with a high acidic salt concentration was used to change the ionic strength and decrease the pH on the column to weaken the non-covalent interactions that cause the antibody to be retained on the column through its interaction with immobilized antigen (choice C). Non-specifically bound antigen that did not pass through the column as flow-through was removed by the first buffered wash applied to each column, not, as described the experimental procedure in the passage, the eluent (choice A). While treatment with a competing antigen is a potential method of eluting antibody from antigen immobilized on the affinity column (choice B), the passage states that the eluting agent contained an acidic salt. This suggests that a pH-altering strategies was employed in the elution to separate antibody from immobilized antigen—not the antibody-antigen unit from the column (choice D).

4. **A**

The passage states that UV absorbance is principally due to aromatic ring structures. If nucleic acids, which contain aromatic nitrogenous bases, were present in the fractions tested, the results of the UV spectroscopy upon which estimates of protein concentration were based could be inaccurate (choice A). It's unlikely that the strongly ionic eluent solution would significantly interfere with UV absorption in the wavelength band indicated (choice B). Also, provided that all fractions are tested at the same 200 nm absorbance (the wavelength at which most aromatic amino acid residues in a protein display maximum absorptivity and thus absorb UV light most strongly), the results of the concentration estimates would not be affected (choice C). Further, if the relative content of aromatic amino acids is approximately constant in all proteins—including those proteins found in the fractions—then this eliminates a strong potential objection to using such measures, as all proteins should absorb on a relative basis a similar amount of radiation at a given wavelength in the UV band (choice D).

5. **D**

Fraction 1 contained the antibody which would subsequently become column-bound and eluted into Fractions 4 and 6. The UV absorbance at 200 nm for Fraction 1 should thus exceed that of Fraction 4, or the less absorbent Fractions 2 and 6 (choice D).

6. **C**

Proteins absorb light in the UV region of the electromagnetic spectrum (200-400 nm) due to the presence of aromatic amino acid residues. Of the polypeptides listed, choice C, Gln-Trp-Tyr-Glu, is composed of the greatest percentage of aromatic amino acid residues and will have the greatest absorptivity.

7. **A**

Anion exchange resins are positively charged and bind negatively charged compounds. The most frequently used anion exchanger contains diethylaminoethyl (DEA) groups bound to the stationary phase of the column. At a given pH, basic amino acids which have pI values that are greater than those of polar uncharged, non-polar and acidic amino acids, are least likely to exist in their net negatively charged state and be retained on the anion exchange column. Lysine, leucine and aspartate amino acids, if bound to the anion-exchange resin, must be negatively charged. As buffer pH is decreased, the amino acid with the greater pI (lysine) would reach its pI and be eluted from the column first, followed by, in order of decreasing pI, leucine and aspartate (choice A).

8. **A**

A gel electrophoresis may analyze proteins in their native state, preserving the molecules' secondary, tertiary and quaternary structure. Mobility is a function of the size (Roman numeral I), the charge (roman numeral II) and the shape (Roman numeral III) of the protein. If a chemical denaturant is used in a non-native gel protocol, higher-order structure is lost, and the electrophoretic mobility of proteins will depend only upon their mass-to-charge ratio and their length. Sodium dodecyl sulfate (SDS) is an anionic detergent that denatures proteins and imparts a uniform negative charge to the unfolded, roughly cylindrical polypeptide, resulting in separation by approximate size during electrophoresis (Roman numeral I). When performed using a polyacrylamide gel, this procedure is called SDS-PAGE. SDS-PAGE and native state PAGE, then, share only size (Roman numeral I) as a common basis on which they fractionate proteins (choice A).

9. **C**

SDS-PAGE fractionates proteins only according to differences in their masses, and likely provides a more accurate estimate of protein mass when compared to a gel electrophoresis that overestimates the mass of a protein. This is because gel electrophoresis introduces other potentially confounding variables in an estimate of protein mass, including charge and shape. In a native gel, a protein's conformation can introduce a greater surface area for interaction with the gel then in the unfolded polypeptide, thus retarding the unfolded molecule's migration toward an electrode, leading to an underestimate of the true mass. This is consistent with the reasoning expressed in choice C.

10. **D**

Salting out is most effective when the pH of the solution is set to equal the isoelectric point of the target protein. The procedure results in the precipitation of proteins; precipitation occurs most readily when a protein is bathed in solution at a pH equal to that of the protein's isoelectric point. At the isoelectronic point, the protein exists predominately in its zwitterion form, minimizing its interaction with the surroundings (choice D). This effect complements the effect of high concentrations of certain salts, such as ammonium sulfate, which influence solvent structure in such a way as to decrease the solubility of proteins in a solution of increasing ionic strength. When the concentration of ammonium sulfate increases, proteins begin to aggregate, as the energetics of protein-protein interactions become more favorable than protein-solvent interaction. Proteins have characteristic salting out points (that is to say, salt concentrations at which they actively precipitate)—a fact which can be used in protein fractionation in crude extracts.

CHAPTER 27 SOLUTIONS

1. **D**

Under most conditions, DNA is negatively charged because of the presence of negatively charged phosphate groups. During a gel electrophoresis, DNA will thus migrate toward the positive plate—the anode. The passage indicates that the distance a fragment migrates is inversely related to its size. Therefore, at the completion of the electrophoresis, the larger 1.2 kb fragments will have migrated a shorter distance toward the anode than did the smaller 0.9 kb fragment (choice D).

2. **D**

Subject 2 is homozygous for the wild type allele, as indicated by the presence of only 0.9 kb fragments. While subjects 4 and 5 also possess two X-chromosomes and thus two alleles associated with the RFLP, both subjects are heterozygotes. Subjects 1—an affected male—only has a single mutant allele. The observation that allele 2 is twice as intense as the other alleles is most likely due to the fact that it is composed of chromosomal content from two 0.9 kb fragments (choice D). While the statements in choices A and B are both true, neither explains the increased intensity of band 2 when compared to the intensity of all of the other electrophoretic bands. Additionally, there is no evidence to support the statement that the fragment in lane 2 bound the radiolabeled DNA probe more strongly than did other probes (choice B).

3. **A**

The fragments produced by the digestion of the mutant and wild-type alleles are 1.2 kb and 0.9 kb, respectively. This can be confirmed by inspecting the banding pattern in lane 1 for the hemophiliac father, which shows only a single, lower-mobility banding pattern. The fact that the mutant digestion product is longer than the wild type digestion product suggests that the RFLP eliminates a restriction site, causing the terminal restriction cut to occur at a greater distance from the initial cut in the mutant allele (choice A). Because both 0.9 kb and 1.2 kb fragments were visualized via the Southern blotting procedure described in the passage, the radiolabeled probe's sequence must have been sufficiently similar to that of both fragments to permit its hybridization (choice B). There is nothing in the passage to suggest that one allele is more resistant than another allele is to restriction digestion (choice D).

4. **B**

Both digests were produced by cleavage at two restriction sites. Had either possessed an additional restriction site, more than two sizes of fragments would be produced in the restriction digest (choice B).

5. **C**

Changing reaction conditions to favor binding of the restriction fragments to nitrocellulose would not impact the extent of their complementary base pairing with a DNA probe (choice C). Increasing solution temperature makes hybridization of nucleotide sequences which are not perfectly complementary more difficult (choices A and B are false), as does pre-treatment of the DNA probe with a weaker or less concentrated base. Increased solution alkalinity promotes maintenance of the DNA probe in its single-stranded state, the only state of the probe capable of hybridization. As a result of increasing the amount of probe available as ssDNA, the likelihood of probe hybridization should increase.

6. **A**

Given the content of a single strand of the gene, which contains 57 purines and 71 pyrimidines, the double-stranded molecule should contain 128 each of purines and pyrimidines, since in the double-stranded molecule each purine pairs with a pyrimidine and vice versa.

7. **C**

Uracil is incorporated only into a growing RNA strand. Thus, measurement of uracil utilization by a cell should reflect the rate of synthesis of RNA—uracil's primary synthetic use (choice C). Adenine and cytosine (choices A and D) are incorporated into both DNA and RNA, while choice B, thymidine, is not used by the cell to synthesize RNA.

8. **D**

The monomeric units of RNA and DNA, ribonucleotides and 2'-deoxyribonucleotides, both consist of a nitrogenous base, a five carbon sugar (ribose or 2'deoxyribose, respectively) and phosphate (choice D). They are linked by a phosphodiester bond between the 5' and 3' positions of their sugar moieties (choice A). While DNA is nearly always found as an antiparallel duplex, RNA exists in both a single- and double-stranded form (choice B). Thymine is found only in DNA, but not the nucleotides of RNA (choice C).

9. **B**

First and second generation fluoroquinolones inhibit a domain of prokaryotic DNA topoisomerase II, while third and fourth generation fluoroquinolones selectively inhibit the ligase domain of prokaryotic DNA topoisomerase IV. The action of fluoroquinolones against bacterial topoisomerases can be inferred from the question stem given the function of members of the enzyme class. Topoisomerases regulate the winding state of DNA. During DNA replication or transcription, the double-helical structure may become over- or under-wound. The tension which arises from these topological states can interfere with the ongoing process of DNA replication or transcription. Topoisomerases relieve winding tension by binding ssDNA or dsDNA and cutting the nucleic acid phosphate backbone, allowing the DNA to unwind. Topoisomerases' ligase domains permit reannealing of the strand following re-winding (choice B). DNA polymerases (choice A) are enzymes involved in the replication of DNA. While topoisomerases do include an inherent ligase activity, as a class of independent enzymes, DNA ligases are not directly responsible for changing the winding state of DNA. Nucleases are enzymes capable of cleaving phosphodiester bonds between nucleotides (choice D).

10. **A**

The melting temperature (T_m) of DNA is the temperature at which half of the duplex strands are in the random coil or in the single-stranded state. T_m increases as the length of the DNA polymer increases, and as the GC content of the nucleotide sequence increases. Each of the sequences shown in choices A-D are of equal length; however, in choice A, five of the nine nucleotides are either guanine or cytosine, which form more intermolecular hydrogen bonds than adenine and thymine when base paired. Thus, the T_m of the sequence shown in choice A should be greatest.

CHAPTER 28 SOLUTIONS

1. **C**

According to the passage, the high NAD^+/NADH ratio in hepatocytes indicates that the cellular concentration of NAD^+ greatly exceeds that of NADH. This is consistent with choice C, which indicates that cytosolic conditions favor oxidation of substrates and conversion of NAD^+ to NADH, if the free energy change for the reaction is relatively near zero, and thus permits reversibility, under standard conditions. There is nothing in the passage to indicate the relative concentrations of NAD^+ on either side of the outer mitochondrial membrane. Further, because NAD^+ is positively charged, its ability to freely diffuse across the inner mitochondrial membrane is extremely limited (choice A). The passage states that NAD^+ concentration in cell cytosol is near 0.3 mM, which is ten times the concentration of NADPH found in hepatocytes. The NADPH concentration is thus near 0.03 mM. If the $NADP^+/NADPH$ ratio is approximately 0.005, this can be used to calculate the $NADP^+$ concentration for comparison to that of NAD^+. Accordingly, if $NADP^+/NADPH = 0.005$, then $NADP^+ = 0.005*NADPH = 0.005*0.03 = .00015$. This is less than the cytoplasmic concentration of NAD^+ (choice B). Additionally, given the previous calculations, it can be seen that the concentration of $NADP^+$ is much less than that of NADPH, contradicting choice D.

2. **A**

ΔG can be related to $\Delta G°$ if the concentration of reactants, products and reaction temperature are known according to the equation, $\Delta G' = \Delta G°' + RT \ln Q$. If Q, which equals $[ADP][P_i]/[ATP]$, is less than 1 in hepatocytes, then $RT \ln Q$ must return a negative number. Therefore, $\Delta G°' = -30.5$ kJ/mol $> \Delta G'$ (choice A).

3. **D**

While the hydrolysis of ATP is under most conditions highly exergonic, this thermodynamic property is independent of the rate at which the reaction will proceed. One explanation for the differing rates of hydrolysis of ATP *in vivo* versus *in vitro* could be the lack of enzymes which catalyze the hydrolysis of ATP (choice D). Choices A describe the thermodynamic stability of reactant and does not reflect the rate of the reaction. Nor does Choice C, which again describes the equilibrium position of the reaction, not its rate. While choice B, which mentions temperature, does describe a factor involved in describing reaction rate, if water were at a high temperature, that would tend to increase, rather than decrease, the reaction rate in water relative to the rate in hepatocytes.

4. **C**

The voltage for the reaction can be found by adding the voltage for the oxidation of NADH and the reduction of FAD. The reduction of FAD generates -0.219 V and the oxidation of NADH generates +0.315 V.

5. **D**

Cleavage of one of the terminal phosphoanhydride bond in ATP (shown below) results in the formation of the nucleotide diphosphate, ADP, and inorganic phosphate (choice D). Cleavage of the phosphodiester linkage would result in the free nucleoside, adenosine

(choice B). There are no peptide or thioester bonds present in ATP (choices C and A, respectively).

6. **C**

Metabolic reactions which operate near equilibrium are often reversed by small changes in reactant or product concentration and have free energy changes near zero, since neither the formation of products nor the formation of reactants is favored strongly at equilibrium (choice C is true and choice D is false). The position of a reaction's equilibrium has no bearing on its reaction rate (choice A). The control points in most metabolic pathways are irreversible, rather than reversible, reactions (choice B).

7. **B**

Repulsion of negatively charged oxygen atoms in the phosphoanhydride groups of ATP contribute to its highly exergonic hydrolysis. The coordinate binding of Mg^{2+} to ATP, which is required for its hydrolysis by ATPase enzymes, reduces the thermodynamically destabilizing electric repulsion between oxygen atoms, thereby decreasing the free energy released upon the hydrolysis of ATP—choice B.

8. **A**

During a redox reaction, the reducing agent is the reactant which is oxidized. Of the NADH/FAD pair, NADH is oxidized to NAD^+, making it the reducing agent (choice A). FAD is the oxidizing agent of the reactant. NAD^+ is the oxidized product of the reaction (choice C) and $FADH_2$ is the reduced product (choice D).

9. **B**

The presence of an inhibitor which blocks the conversion of C to D would not lead to a conversion of C to B, as the question stem indicated that the conversion of B to C is irreversible (choice B). The presence of an inhibitor which blocks the conversion of C to D would decrease the concentration of D (choice C is false). The free energy change for the pathway shown is equal to the individual free energy changes associated with each step of the reaction because of the pathway's common intermediates. As a result, the net Gibbs free energy change of the process is negative and will operate in the forward direction (choice A is false).

10. **D**
Glycolysis would be most efficiently regulated in a manner reflective of the energetic state of the cell by feedback inhibition of one of glycolysis' products on glycolysis' initial committed (most likely its first irreversible) step—regulation at a later irreversible step by a product of glycolysis would needlessly shunt substrates into a pathway through which they will not proceed further. Only choice D is an example of a glycolytic product—ATP—feeding back on the committed step of glycolysis.

CHAPTER 29 SOLUTIONS

1. **B**
The rapid decline in pH that occurred following application of electrical current to the cultured chicken and turkey muscle was due to the effects of short-term anaerobic metabolism. In mammalian anaerobic metabolism, the terminal electron acceptor is pyruvate, which is reduced to lactic acid, in order to regenerate the NAD^+ required for continued glycolysis.

2. **A**
The student found that samples taken from chickens and turkeys—birds that fly only short distances—appeared pale and were composed almost entirely of slow-twitch fibers, in contrast to the appearance of migratory birds which required a continual supply of energy to carry out sustained flight. If a human sprinter could be expected to show a similar structure-function relationship between muscle types as found in birds, then it could be expected that they would consist almost entirely of slow-twitch (Type I) fibers.

3. **D**
In glycolysis, the reactions catalyzed by hexokinase, phosphofructokinase, and pyruvate kinase are effectively irreversible in most organisms. The reactions catalyzed by such enzymes are potential sites of control in metabolic pathways, and all three enzymes serve are involved in regulation of glycolytic flux.

4. **C**
The rapid decline in pH that occurred following application of electrical current to the cultured chicken and turkey muscle was due to the effects of short-term anaerobic metabolism. This indicates the tissue contained in the sample was composed of cells capable of anaerobic metabolism.

5. **C**
Most glycogen in humans—a ready store of polymerized glucose—is present in skeletal muscle and in the liver.

6. **C**
Organisms such as yeast regenerate NAD^+ from NADH in ethanol fermentation. During this two-step conversion, pyruvate is first cleaved, producing acetaldehyde and carbon dioxide. Then, the acetaldehyde produced in the first step is reduced by NADH to ethanol, re-forming NAD^+.

7. **B**
During gluconeogenesis, the conversion of glucose-6-phosphate to glucose is catalyzed by the enzyme glucose-6-phosphatase.

8. **C**
Fructose 2,6-bisphosphate (F2,6BP) is a potent activator of phosphofructokinase (PFK-1), which is synthesized when F6P is phosphorylated by a second phosphofructokinase (PFK2). In the liver, when blood sugar is low and glucagon elevates cAMP, PFK2 is phosphorylated by protein kinase A. The phosphorylation inactivates PFK2, and another domain on this protein becomes active as fructose bisphosphatase-2, which converts F2,6BP back to F6P. The result of lower levels of liver fructose-2,6-bisphosphate is a decrease in activity of PFK-1 and an increase in activity of fructose 1,6-bisphosphatase, favoring gluconeogenesis. This is consistent with the role of the liver in such situations, as it acts to increase blood glucose concentrations in response to glucagon (or epinephrine).

9. **C**
In glycolysis, the forward reactions catalyzed by hexokinase, phosphofructokinase, and pyruvate kinase are effectively irreversible in most organisms. Such reactions have large negative Gibbs free energy changes and equilibrium constants much greater than 1.

10. **A**

The reciprocal regulation of glycolysis and gluconeogenesis in the liver is sensitive to changes in the energy state of cells. Increased AMP concentrations stimulate glycolysis, while inhibiting gluconeogenesis. FBPase-1 is inhibited by AMP, which is present in increased concentration when the energy balance of the cell is low, and which activates PFK-1, resulting in the reciprocal up-regulation of glycolysis and down-regulation of gluconeogenesis. Conversely, FBPase-1 is activated when ATP levels are high.

CHAPTER 30 SOLUTIONS

1. **C**

Succinate dehydrogenase is an enzyme complex bound to the inner mitochondrial membrane of mammalian mitochondria. It is the only enzyme that participates in both the Krebs cycle and the electron transport chain. During the Krebs cycle, it catalyzes the oxidation of succinate to fumarate with the reduction of ubiquinone to ubiquinol, producing $FADH_2$.

2. **B**

The most direct evidence that the linked reactants shown in Experiment 1 are connected metabolically to glycolysis would be a demonstration that glucose stimulates production of a reactant of the cycle—in this case, citrate.

3. **D**

Experiment 1 is intended to show the relationship between the cellular consumption of oxygen and metabolism of the substances added. If succinate and malate, the two substances that evoke the greatest increase in oxygen consumption, are the only substances tested that also directly generate electrons which are transferred to the electron transport chain to drive oxidative phosphorylation, then this could explain the elevated oxygen consumption due to their addition.

4. **C**

Table 2 supports the conclusion that citrate is a precursor of succinate in some metabolic pathway. It does not, however, provide any evidence of a connection between the consumption of any given

substance and the reactions of cellular respiration—this finding is evidenced by, among other things, the results shown in Table 1.

5. **A**

NADH inhibits the enzyme citrate synthase, as well as enzymes from which it is produced during the Krebs cycle—pyruvate dehydrogenase, isocitrate dehydrogenase and α-ketoglutarate dehydrogenase. It does not inhibit succinate dehydrogenase.

6. **D**

The Krebs cycle occurs within the mitochondrial matrix.

7. **C**

NADH, produced during the oxidative metabolism of alcohols, inhibits enzymes of the Krebs cycle: citrate synthase, pyruvate dehydrogenase, isocitrate dehydrogenase and α-ketoglutarate dehydrogenase.

8. **C**

A buildup of lactic acid can result in those suffering from a deficiency of pyruvate dehydrogenase. Without the enzyme present in sufficient quantity, the Krebs cycle will slow and pyruvate produced in glycolysis will be converted into lactic acid in order to regenerate the NAD+ consumed during glycolysis.

9. **C**

Aconitase catalyzes the conversion of citrate to isocitrate in the Krebs cycle. An inhibitor of aconitase would cause the substrate of the enzyme, citrate, to accumulate.

10. **C**

A single turn of the Krebs cycle produces 3 molecules of NADH and 1 molecule of $FADH_2$, producing 3*3 + 2*1, or 11, molecules of ATP.

CHAPTER 31 SOLUTIONS

1. **B**

The establishment of a proton gradient across the membrane, as shown in choices A and D, is needed to drive ATP synthesis. Movement of ATP across the vesicular membrane, down its electrochemical gradient, fuels the synthesis of ATP from ADP and inorganic phosphate on the opposite side of the membrane, as depicted only in choice B.

2. **B**

The decline in intermembrane space hydrogen ion concentration mentioned in the question is caused by transport of those ions into the matrix through the channel of ATP synthase's F_o subunit , driving the coupled production of ATP by ATP synthase.

3. **A**

The consumption of O_2 should increase, rather than decrease, upon addition of one of the substrates of its synthesis—ADP.

4. **D**

The two experiments performed in the passage clearly demonstrate only that ATP synthase does not act to synthesize ATP in the absence of a proton gradient, but does synthesize ATP in its presence. This most directly supports the conclusion that ATP synthase harnesses the potential energy of a proton electrochemical gradient in order to synthesize ATP.

5. **B**

When treated with a chemical decoupling agent that dissipates the established H^+ gradient, the energy lost will be dissipated as heat.

6. **A**

As protons are ejected from the matrix by respiratory complexes, they do against the increasingly large electrochemical gradient which they establish, and, accordingly the free energy change of that transport increases. As H^+ is transported from the matrix by the complexes of the electron transport chain, they do so against an increasingly large concentration and charge gradient, increasing the free energy change associated with the process.

7. **B**

Succinate dehydrogenase (Complex II), bound to the inner mitochondrial membrane, contains a covalently attached FAD cofactor which is reduced to $FADH_2$ when succinate is oxidized during the Krebs cycle.

8. **A**

A decoupling agent suitable to shuttle protons across the inner mitochondrial membrane should contain a weakly acidic residue able to be protonated in the strongly acidic environment of the intermembrane space, but able also to be reversibly deprotonated in the higher-pH environment of the matrix. Further, such a molecule should be sufficiently lipophilic—particularly in its protonated state—to permit its diffusion across the inner membrane.

9. **A**

Electrons arriving from the Krebs cycle, or produced in other oxidative pathways of the matrix, in the form of NADH are first transferred to Complex I of the electron transport chain, NADH dehydrogenase. The two electrons removed from NADH are transferred to, ubiquinone (Q) as Complex I translocates four protons (H^+) across the inner mitochondrial membrane to the inter membrane space. Reducing equivalents produced in the cytosol may be transported across the matrix by the malate-aspartate or glycerol-3-phosphate shuttle system. The cytoplasmic enzyme glycerol-3-phosphate dehydrogenase (cGPD) converts dihydroxyacetone phosphate to glycerol-3-phosphate while oxidizing one molecule of NADH to NAD+. Glycerol-3-phosphate is then reconverted to dihydroxyacetone phosphate by a membrane-bound mitochondrial glycerol-3-phosphate dehydrogenase 2 enzyme. The re-oxidation of glycerol-3-phosphate is this tied to the reduction of one enzyme-bound FAD molecule to $FADH_2$. $FADH_2$ then reduces ubiquinone (coenzyme Q) to ubiquinol.

10. **C**

The reactions of the electron transport chain result in the translocation of four protons from NADH dehydrogenase, four protons from the cytochrome bc_1 complex, and two protons from cytochrome c oxidase.

CHAPTER 32 SOLUTIONS

1. **B**

Glucagon or epinephrine binding stimulates adenylate cyclase activity and the production of cAMP. The cAMP is a positive allosteric effort of protein kinase A, which in turn phosphorylates and activates glycogen phosphorylase kinase. Activated phosphorylase kinase subsequently phosphorylates glycogen phosphorylase, producing its active "a" form, stimulating glycogenolysis. Glucagon and epinephrine further promotes glycogenolysis by phosphorylating and inactivating phosphoprotein phosphatase-1, preventing its dephosphorylation and deactivation of glycogen phosphorylase.

2. **B**

Insulin promotes the dephosphorylation of the bifunctional protein containing the enzymes fructose-2,6-bisphosphatase and phosphofructokinase-2. Dephosphorylation inhibits fructsose-2,6-bisphosphatase and stimulates phosphofructokinases-2, thereby increasing the intracellular concentration fructose-2,6-bisphosphate (a potent activator of phosphofructokinase-1, the enzyme that is the primary regulatory step of glycolysis), increasing substrate flux through glycolysis.

3. **D**

Insulin and glucagon are both peptide hormones. Because neither hormone is substantially soluble in the cellular membrane, both bind to receptors located on the cell surface.

4. **C**

Of the GSDs mentioned, Hers' disease and Von Gierke's disease is most likely to result in fasting hypoglycemia. This is because the enzyme deficient in the condition—glucose-6-phosphatase—is present only in liver cells and is responsible for the conversion of glucose-6-phosphate to glucose. In its absence, glucose-1-phosphate, which is further converted to glucose-6-phosphate within liver cells, would remained phosphorylated and trapped within liver cells and would be unable to enter the bloodstream in response to hormonal signaling caused by a decrease in blood sugar. For a similar reason, Hers disease, in which the liver isoform of glycogen phosphorylase is absent, would also handicap the liver's response to low blood glucose levels by preventing its mobilization of stored glycogen as free glucose. Muscle glycogen stores, mobilized by the muscle isoform of glycogen phosphorylase and deficient in McArdle disease, are not used to produce glucose for export from muscle.

5. **D**

During fasting states the body employs the strategies mentioned in choices A, B and C to meet its energetic demands. However, gluconeogenesis cannot make use of fatty acids as substrates directly, although odd-chain fatty acids can be oxidized to yield propionyl-CoA, a precursor for succinyl-CoA, which may be converted into pyruvate and enter into the gluconeogenic pathway. The main gluconeogenic precursors are lactate, glycerol (which is a part of the triacylglycerol molecule) and the glucogenic amino acids alanine and glutamine. Other glucogenic amino acids as well as all citric acid cycle intermediates, the latter through conversion to oxaloacetate, can also function as substrates for gluconeogenesis.

6. **A**

Glycogen phosphorylase cleaves the α-1-4 glycosidic linkage between glucose residues in glycogen.

7. **C**

Muscle cells (myocytes) and fat cells (adipocytes) are the two cell types most strongly influenced by insulin to increase uptake of extracellular glucose. Cells of the tissues in choices A, B and D lack insulin receptors.

8. **C.**

Ketogenesis is the process by which ketone bodies are produced in the mitochondria of liver cells as a result of fatty acid breakdown in response to the unavailability of blood glucose. 3-hydroxybutryate (β-hydroxybutyrate) is one such ketone body. While ketogenesis is principally stimulated by an accumulation of acetyl-CoA, it occurs under condition in which glucagon secretion is high. Accordingly, glucagon has no negative regulatory effective on ketogenesis.

9. **B**

NADH and ATP, both products of mitochondrial beta-oxidation, inhibit gluconeogenesis.

10. **C**

Insulin promotes glycogen synthesis and inhibits gluconeogenesis, glycogenolysis and lipolysis of stored fats. Suppression of insulin would thus promote gluconeogenesis, glycogenolysis and lipolysis but would not result in an increase in the rate of glycogen synthesis.

CHAPTER 33 SOLUTIONS

1. **D**

A ceramide is composed of sphingosine and a fatty acid. The structure of a ceramide is shown below, where R represents the alkyl portion of the fatty acid.

2. **B**

Niemann-Pick Diseases Type A and B both involve an inborn error in the metabolism of sphingomyelin. Further, the passage indicates that this disease is inherited, as it involves a genetic mutation of the SMPD1 gene of chromosome 7.

3. **D**

Late endosomes, the immediate developmental precursors of lysosomes, must contain the defective lysosomal enzyme—sphingomyelinase—transferred to and present in the lysosomes of those suffering from Niemann-Pick Disease. Lysosomal proteins, as well as proteins destined for export from the cell and retention in the cell's plasma membrane are all synthesized on ribosomes of the rough ER.

4. **A**

A ceramide is composed of sphingosine and a fatty acid. The removal of a fatty acid would leave only the unsaturated amino alcohol, sphingosine.

5. **B**

Choices A, C and D all represent potentially beneficial approaches to treating Niemann-Pick disease, as all would either replace diseased red blood cells with healthy cells, or convert existing diseased cells into healthy cells— at least for some period of time. Enhancing the rate of phagocytosis of the patient's own macrophages, however, would only increase the rate of accumulation of partially degraded membranous material.

6. **B**

Ion channels are often α helices with often amphipathic elements capable of interacting both with the hydrophobic membrane lipids and the much more hydrophilic ions passing through the channel.

7. **D**

Three classes of amphipathic lipids are found in cell membranes: phospholipids, glycolipids, and sterols. In most cases, phospholipids, while glycolipids, which contain a highly polar carbohydrate component, are found almost exclusively on the outer leaflet of cells.

8. **B**

Facilitated diffusion is the process of spontaneous passive transport of molecules or ions across a biological membrane via specific transmembrane integral proteins. The process does not require the input of energy, but does dependent on movement of particles down their concentration gradient.

9. **B**

The exchange of phospholipids between the inner and outer leaflet of plasma membranes occurs rapidly in an enzyme-catalyzed process.

10. **C.**

Because of the diffusion barrier established by tight junctions, the solutes mentioned in the question cannot diffuse freely across plasma membranes.

CHAPTER 34 SOLUTIONS

1. **C**

Glucagon is present in each of the five tests performed and thus its requirement for glycogen mobilization could not have been established by the experiments.

2. **C**

Formation of the receptor-ligand complex promotes G-protein nucleotide exchange and activation, thus initiating the downstream signaling cascade tied to G-protein activation.

3. **A**

In addition to activating the adenylate cycle, G proteins can separately increase intracellular calcium ion concentration through the opening of ligand-gated calcium ion channels on the cell surface, and through stimulating the release of intracellular calcium stores via the IP_3/DAG pathway.

4. **A**

G coupled protein receptors specific for a given ligand may associate with different G protein types, thus exerting different downstream targeting effects in different cell and tissue types.

5. **B**

Second messengers are intracellular signaling molecules released by the cell in response to extracellular signals to trigger different physiological changes such as proliferation, differentiation, migration, survival, and apoptosis. Some examples of second messenger molecules include cAMP, cGMP, inositol IP_3, DAG, and calcium.

6. **C**

Certain catecholamines, such as epinephrine and norepinephrine, can act as neurotransmitters and hormones. Hormones are endocrine signalers, while the synaptic signaling in neurons (at chemical synapses) is a special case of paracrine signaling.

7. **B**

Leukotrienes are the only eicosanoids synthesized in the lipooxygenase pathway.

8. **B**

The thyroid hormone T_3 and its prohormone T_4 are modified amino-acid hormones that behave much like steroid hormones in their global regulation of metabolism, transport-protein binding in the blood, and in their binding of the thyroid hormone receptor—a nuclear receptor.

9. **B**

If the calcium-calmodulin complex , which is stimulated by the increased intracellular calcium levels induced by IP_3, increases the activity of NO synthase in endothelial cells, this consequent increase in NO—a potent local vasodilator—could explain the effect mentioned in the question.

10. **A**

The cyclic nucleotide phosphodiesterases comprise a group of enzymes that degrade the phosphodiester bond in the second messenger molecules cAMP and cGMP, thereby antagonizing the normal function of PKA to increase intracellular cAMP concentrations.

SECTION 1 CONTENT REVIEW PROBLEMS

1. C. Carbohydrates are biological molecules involved in energy production and are comprised of carbon, hydrogen and oxygen. These compounds include monosaccharides, disaccharides, and polysaccharides such as glycogen, starch or cellulose. Carbohydrates usually have empirical formulas of CH_2O. Glycogen is a branched polymer of the monosaccharide glucose.

2. B. Sucrose is a disaccharide comprise of glucose and fructose. Palmitic acid is a fatty acid; cytosine is a nucleobase found in DNA and RNA; glycine is an amino acid.

3. A. Lactose is a disaccharide formed from galactose and glucose. Sucrose is a disaccharide formed from fructose and glucose molecule; maltose is a disaccharide formed from two glucose molecules; lactulose is a disaccharide formed from fructose and galactose.

4. B. See the explanation for question 3.

5. A. See the explanation for question 3. Galactose in a monomer, not a dimer.

6. C. See the explanation for question 3.

7. D. See the explanation for question 1.

8. A. "Sugars" commonly refers to disaccharides such as sucrose or lactose.

9. C. See the explanation for question 1.

10. A. The formula for glucose is $C_6H_{12}O_6$ and since there are six carbons it is a hexose, eliminating choices C and D. The structure of the open chain form of D-glucose has the carbonyl functional group in a terminal position, hence it is an aldehyde, with the prefix aldo- in the name.

$$
\begin{array}{c}
H\!\!-\!\!{}^1C\!\!=\!\!O \\
H\!\!-\!\!{}^2C\!\!-\!\!OH \\
HO\!\!-\!\!{}^3C\!\!-\!\!H \\
H\!\!-\!\!{}^4C\!\!-\!\!OH \\
H\!\!-\!\!{}^5C\!\!-\!\!OH \\
{}^6CH_2OH
\end{array}
$$

11. B. Like glucose, fructose has the formula $C_6H_{12}O_6$ with six carbon atoms and is therefore a hexose. The structure of the open chain form has the carbonyl in the second position making it a ketone, with the keto- prefix.

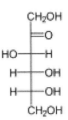

12. C. See the structure for glucose in the explanation for question 10. There are four chiral carbon atoms and hence 2^n possible stereoisomers, where n is the number of chiral centers. $2^4 = 16$

13. B. The formula for an aldotriose is $C_3H_6O_3$ and there is only one chiral carbon. See the explanation for question 12.

14. A. See the structure for D-glucose shown in the explanation for question 10.

15. B. In Eukaryotes, transcription is the process in which DNA is read and produces RNA, which then is transported to the rough endoplasmic reticulum (ER) where it is translated by the ribosomes into a protein.

16. D. Anomers are epimers, diastereomers that have more than one chiral center, but are different from one another by the configuration at a single chiral center. The α and β anomers result from the ring closure reaction between a hydroxyl group and a carbonyl of a straight chain form of a saccharide that forms the hemiacetal or acetal center.

α-D-glucopyranose 36%   < 0.01%   β-D-glucopyranose 64%

17. A. A pyranose is a six membered ring in which one of the atoms is an oxygen and the other atoms are carbon. Furanose is a five membered ring formed by one oxygen and four carbon atoms. A ketoacetal is a molecule that would contain both ketone $[R_2C=O]$ and acetal $[RCH(OR")_2]$ functional groups. In the open form glucose has an aldehyde functional group, and when it closes the ring it forms an acetal functional group.

18. B. See the explanation for question 17.

19. A. See the explanation for question 3.

20. A. Lipids are hydrophobic biomolecules with large alkyl groups, examples of which include triglycerides, phospholipids and cholesterol. Adipocytes are fat cells with high concentrations of triglycerides, which are efficient ways to store energy in the form of high energy carbon-hydrogen bonds.

21. D. K vitamins are a group of hydrophobic vitamins required for the synthesis of certain proteins. For choices B and C, see the explanation for question 20. B Vitamins are a group of water soluble vitamins involved in metabolism and energy production.

22. C. A fatty acid is an organic acid ($R-CO_2H$) with a long hydrocarbon chain, R. When deprotonated, fatty acids can be amphipathic (simultaneously hydrophobic and hydrophilic), but the hydrocarbon tail is always hydrophobic.

23. B. Triglycerides are fatty acid esters of glycerol, an example of which is shown below.

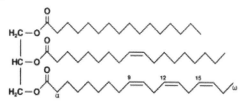

24. C. The duodenum is the beginning of the small intestine, where it connects to the stomach. This is where the stomach acid is neutralized and bile is added to act as a surfactant to help emulsify the fat. The jejunum is the second part of the small intestine where nutrients are absorbed. The ileum is the third portion of the small intestine which then connects to the large intestine or colon.

25. B. Lacteals are similar to capillaries but are part of the lymphatic system, not the blood circulatory system. Micelles are spherical structures formed by lipids and fatty acids in aqueous solution with hydrophobic interiors and hydrophilic exteriors. Chylomicrons are cell-like lipoprotein structures that help transport fats in the blood stream.

26. A. The cell membrane is comprised primarily of amphipathic phospholipids and cholesterol, along with some proteins.

27. B. Phospholipids have two long hydrophobic alkyl groups attached to a negatively charged phosphate group. See the explanation for question 26. Amphoteric means that it can act as both an acid and a base.

28. D. The outside of a phospholipid bilayer is in contact with an aqueous environment and is hydrophilic (water loving).

29. B. See the explanation for question 25.

30. C. The lipid bilayer of a liposome is very similar to the structure of a cell, in that it has interactions with an aqueous phase on both the inside and outside of the sphere. Liposomes tend to be bigger than micelles.

31. D. Lipids are a critical component in fats that are used for energy storage, are a major component of cell membranes and play a significant role in hormone signaling. Bile is not a lipid, but it is comprised of a small percentage (0.5 %) of lipids, with the majority of bile being water (97%). The key word in the question is "function." Fats that are ingested are nutrients that are functioned upon and digested.

32. A. Proteins are polymers of amino acids, connected by peptide (amide) bonds.

33. B. The primary structure of a protein is determined by the sequence of amino acids; the secondary structure is due to the intermolecular forces of the various amino acids which often form alpha helices and beta sheets; the tertiary structure then is the result of how the various secondary structures combine to form the appropriate overall geometric shape; quaternary protein structures result when more than one protein subunit combines to form even larger combinations of shapes.

34. A. See the explanation for question 33.

35. A. Post-translational modifications associated with disulfide bond formation between two cysteine residues is NOT considered part of the primary structure.

36. C. See the explanation for question 32.

37. B. Peptide bonds are formed by dehydration.

38. B. There are twenty naturally occurring amino acid and you need to memorize their names and structures for the MCAT.

39. B. Nucleic acids are polymers such as DNA and RNA, which are comprised of nitrogenous bases, such as adenine (A), cytosine (C), guanine (G), thymine (T) and uracil (U), bonded to ribose and a phosphate group, the so-called nucleotides. Nucleic acids do not contain organic acid ($-CO_2H$) functional groups.

40. C. Cysteine is an amino acid with a thiol side chain. ATP is the triphosphate of a nucleotide in which adenosine, a nitrogenous base, is bonded to ribose, which is bonded to the phosphate groups. See also the explanation for question 39.

41. B. The "D" in DNA stands for deoxyribose, not ribose. RNA contains ribose. See also the explanation for question 39.

42. D. Thymine is one of the four bases (A, C, G and T) found in DNA, but thymine is replaced by uracil in RNA.

43. C. See the explanation for question 42.

44. D. The backbone of nucleic acids are phosphate esters formed between the sugar hydroxyl groups and the phosphate groups.

45. B. In DNA the base pairs are A-T and C-G. Since U replaces T in RNA, the base pair combination of A-T would become A-U during the transcription process.

46. C. See the explanation for question 45.

47. C. The purine bases (A and G) have two fused nitrogenous aromatic rings, whereas pyrimidine bases (C, T and U) only have one ring.

48. A. See the explanation for question 47.

49. A. The shape of an enzyme (catalyst) is critical for helping the activated complex minimize its activation energy.

50. A. By lowering the activation energy an enzyme (catalyst) speeds up a reaction.

51. A. Competitive inhibition is when some other molecule besides the substrate binds to the active site of an enzyme and prevents the desired reaction from being catalyzed. Allosteric inhibition occurs when a molecule binds to some other site on the enzyme besides the active site, causing the shape of the enzyme to change, changing how the substrate binds to the active site. Uncompetitive inhibition occurs when an inhibitor binds to the complex formed between a substrate and the enzyme and prevents further reaction. Most inhibition reactions involving enzymes are reversible (equilibria).

52. B. See the explanation for question 51.

53. D. In most cases, the formation of the substrate/enzyme complex is not the rate determining step in the mechanism for the reaction.

54. C. You should memorize the overall glycolysis reaction, which is the anaerobic oxidation of glucose, in which glucose reacts with two NAD^+, two ADP and two phosphates, to produce two pyruvates, two NADH, two hydrogen ions, two ATPs and two waters.

55. D. See the explanation for question 54.

56. B. The anaerobic process of glycolysis occurs in the cytoplasm of a cell, whereas aerobic respiration occurs in mitochondria (eliminating choices A and C).

57. B. You need to memorize the Krebs cycle. Pyruvate is decarboxylated and combined with coenzyme A to enzymatically produce acetyl CoA, which then reacts with oxaloacetate to produce citric acid, starting the cycle.

58. C. The Krebs cycle produces the high energy molecule ATP and anaerobically converts carbon into carbon dioxide. See also the explanation for question 57.

59. C. See the explanation for question 56.

60. A. This question is really the same as question 59; "Where does aerobic respiration occur?" See the explanation for question 56.

61. A. Since moving the hydrogen ions against a gradient is thermodynamically nonspontaneous, it must be coupled with a more thermodynamically favorable process to supply the energy necessary to drive the reaction. Moving electrons from a high energy molecule to a lower energy molecule produces energy, i.e. in the electron transport chain converting NADH to its oxidized form NAD^+.

62. C. Anaerobic means without oxygen. Oxidative phosphorylation occurs in the mitochondria and uses the oxidation (O_2) processes in the Krebs cycle to produce ATP from ADP. Reductive phosphorylation is essentially the opposite of oxidative phosphorylation and occurs during photosynthesis, where oxygen and carbon dioxide are converted into carbohydrates. Lactation is the physiological process in which a female mammal produces milk.

63. D. See the explanation for question 57.

64. B. Under anaerobic conditions pyruvate can not be used in the Krebs cycle to produce energy. Alternatively, pyruvate is reduced by NADH to produce lactic acid and regenerate NAD^+, which can be used for further energy production by glycolysis. The lactic acid is what makes your muscles hurt when you exercise strenuously, because your respiratory and circulatory systems can't get enough oxygen to your muscles for aerobic respiration to use the Krebs cycle.

65. C. The name of an enzyme is usually related to its function, with the suffix -ase being added to indicate that it is an enzyme. In this case we want to synthesize ATP. Complexes I - IV are transmembrane proteins found in the inner membrane of mitochondria and are part of the electron transport chain.

66. C. The electron transport chain also transfers protons across the inner membrane and out of the inner matrix of the mitochondria, creating both a concentration gradient

and a charge (electrical) gradient across the inner membrane. The movement of protons back across the inner membrane drives the production of ATP.

67. C. See the explanations for questions 54 and 64.

68. B. In the electron transport chain process, NADH is involved in pumping more protons across the membrane because it feeds its electrons into the system at Complex I, whereas $FADH_2$ feeds its electrons into the system at Complex II, as a result NADH essentially produces three ATP per molecule whereas $FADH_2$ produces two ATP per molecule. Elemental oxygen is the final electron acceptor in the electron transport chain and is associated with Complex IV. Pyruvate is not directly associated with the electron transport chain.

69. A. See the explanation for question 68.

70. B. See the explanation for question 68.

71. B. Glycolysis produces two pyruvates per glucose, with each pyruvate going on to produce a single Acetyl-CoA, see the explanation for question 54. The overall reaction "in the Krebs cycle" only, is
Acetyl-CoA + 3 NAD^+ + Q + GDP + P_i + 2 H_2O →
CoA-SH + 3 NADH + 3 H^+ + QH_2 + GTP + 2 CO_2
Doubling the stoichiometric coefficients of this reaction provides the correct answer.

72. C. See the explanation for question 68.

73. D. See the explanation for question 62.

74. C. DNA is always synthesized 5' to 3', regardless of which strand is involved.

75. B. DNA forms a spiral helical structure in which there are two sets of base-pairs in the polymeric chains, hence the double helix. Proteins form alpha helical structures and beta sheets in their secondary structure, see the explanation for question 33.

76. C. See the explanation for question 33 concerning protein structures.

77. A. Tubulin is a fibrous protein that enables a cell to undergo mitosis. A centromere is the linkage that connects sister chromatids after duplication. Histones are proteins that bind to, order and package the DNA into units of chromatin in the nuclei of the daughter cells.

78. D. See the explanation of question 77.

79. B. See the explanation of question 77.

80. A. Chromatids are the arms of the replicated DNA that radiate from the centromere. See also the explanation for question 77.

81. D. There are a number of different kinds of RNA, i.e. messenger (mRNA) codes for a protein, transfer (tRNA) carries an amino acid to the ribosome where it is polymerized into a protein, and ribosomal (rRNA) are structural components of ribosomes, each with significantly different structures and functions.

82. B. DNA polymerase functions as the catalyst that joins nucleotides in the appropriate base pair combinations to extend the length of the DNA polymer. Ligase connects and repairs fragments of DNA strands, such as the Okazaki fragments formed by the lagging strand of DNA during replication. Primase helps initiate the replication of DNA. Tautomerase is an enzyme involved in tautomerization, which is not part of DNA replication.

83. A. Helicase helps break the hydrogen bonding base pair interactions of the two strands of nucleotides in DNA in order to allow replication. See also the explanation for question 82.

84. D. See the explanation for question 82.

85. B. See the explanation for question 82.

86. C. See the explanation for question 82.

87. B. Telomerase adds the polynucleotide unit "TTAGGG" to the 3' end of telomeres, which are the caps on the end of a chromosome. The caps are important in order to help prevent degradation of the chromosome and are implicated in aging processes. See also the explanation for question 82 and 88.

88. D. Topoisomerase regulates the winding of DNA. See also the explanations for questions 82 and 87.

89. A. DNA is located in the nucleus of cells.

90. B. See the explanation for question 82.

91. A. The leading strand is replicated continuously whereas the lagging strand produces fragments. See the explanations for question 74 and 82.

92. A. DNA polymerase serves to both synthesize the growing strand as well as proofread it for mistakes.

93. D. Choices A-C are commonly observed. Alkylation of the nitrogenous bases of nucleotides to form alkyl ammonium ions can disrupt the hydrogen bonding necessary for base pair formation. Ultraviolet light can be absorbed by a double bond in pyrimidine bases (T and C), opening the bond and allowing it to react with neighboring molecules to form covalently bonded dimers. Like alkylation, hydrolysis of a base can lead to the formation of positively charge ammonium ions that would disrupt the structure of DNA.

94. B. Transcription is the first step in the process of gene expression in which DNA is read and converted into mRNA in the nucleus, which is then transported to the ribosomes where translation of mRNA produces a polypeptide or protein.

95. A. The base pair combinations in DNA are A-T and C-G, but since U replaces T in RNA, the complementary base pair combinations during transcription will be A-U and C-G. Choices B and C can be eliminated because RNA will not have T in the sequence.

96. C. See the explanation for question 95. Choices A and D can be eliminated because DNA will not have U in the sequence.

97. D. See the explanation for question 81.

98. C. See the explanation for question 81. Small nuclear (snRNA) ribonucleic acids remain in the nucleus and are involved in splicing together Okazaki fragments during DNA replication.

99. B. See the explanation for question 81 and 98.

100. A. See the explanation for question 81 and 98.

101. B. See the explanation for question 81 and 98.

102. B. RNA Polymerase I transcribes DNA to synthesize rRNA; RNA Polymerase II transcribes DNA to synthesize precursors of mRNA and snRNA; RNA Polymerase III transcribes DNA to synthesize tRNA. DNA polymerase replicates DNA.

103. A. See the explanation for question 102.

104. C. See the explanation for question 102.

105. C. Translation is the conversion of RNA into protein, which occurs at ribosomes.

106. B. Translation is the process in which mRNA is read to produce a specific polypeptide or protein, which occurs in ribosomes.

107. C. Ribosomes are attached to the endoplasmic reticulum, forming the rough ER, of eukaryotic cells. In addition there are free ribosomes that are located anywhere in the cytosol of the cell and produce proteins used by the cell.

108. B. Ribosomes consist of two major subunits: the small ribosomal subunit, which reads the RNA; and the large subunit, which joins amino acids to form a polypeptide chain.

109. C. The first cell will have an unlabeled double stranded DNA (| |), and after it undergoes cell division it will produce two new daughter cells, both with one unlabeled and one labeled DNA strand (| |*). After the second cell division, there will be four cells, two (| |*) and two (|*|*). After the third cell division there will be two (| |*) and six (|*|*). After these cells have undergone the synthesis phase, the DNA has been replicated, but the cell has not yet divided. At this point there will be six cells containing two sets of labeled DNA, (|*|*:|*|*) and two cells containing one labeled and one half labeled set of DNA, (| |*:|*|*).

110. A. Due to the base pair combinations (see the explanation for question 95), if the DNA is 30 % A, then it must also be 30 % T, with the remaining bases being 20% each of C and G.

111. C. See the explanation for question 74.

112. D. DNA is read in the opposite direction from which it is synthesized. See also the explanation for question 74.

113. C. Nucleic acids are all synthesized in the same way. See also the explanation for question 74.

114. B. The 5' and 3' refer to positions on the sugar ribose for nucleic acids. Proteins do not contain sugar residues, hence we can eliminate choices C and D. Proteins are always synthesized from the amino end (N) of the polypeptide to the carboxylate end (C).

115. C. A codon represents a set of three continuous nucleotides. It is highly improbable for this replication error to occur.

116. A. An insertion mutation is when one or more nucleotides are added to DNA. Adding one nucleotide would change all of the codons that follow in a gene and would drastically change the identity of the polypeptide or protein for which the gene codes. Inserting three consecutive nucleotides would add one codon and add one amino acid to the protein. One substitution would change only one codon and possibly (but not necessarily) change a single amino acid in the protein. Two consecutive substitutions would change either one or possibly two codons.

117. B. See the explanation for question 116. Deletion would change all of the remaining codons in a manner similar to a single insertion and have fairly drastic consequences for the coded protein. A duplication mutation would result in part of the protein being repeated and presumably would alter the function of the protein fairly dramatically.

118. C. A missense mutation changes a single nucleotide and results in a codon that codes for a different amino

acid. Choice A is a nonsense mutation. See also the explanation for question 116.

119. D. There are often more than one three letter codon that codes for the same amino acid in a polypeptide and therefore a mutation between two such codons has no effect on the functioning of the resulting protein.

120. B. This is a way to remember the start and three stop codons. What month does school start? Answer: August (AUG). Then take this abbreviation and switch the first two letters to give the first stop codon UAG. Then switch the second two letters of this codon to give the second stop codon UGA. Then replace the G of this codon with an A, to give UAA.

SECTION 2 CONTENT REVIEW PROBLEMS

1) D. The shell coating of a virus is called the capsid, which is made of protein and encloses the genetic material.

2) B. A bacteriophage is a virus that acts on bacteria, which are prokaryotes.

3) A. Unlike a lysogenic infection, in lytic infections the viral genetic information is not incorporated into the DNA of the host cell.

4) D. Prokaryotes do not have organelles.

5) C. The negatively charged head of a phospholipid consists of a phosphate group that forms a phosphate ester with glycerol, which is also attached to two fatty acids, forming a diglyceride. In addition, the phosphate can be bonded to other groups such as serine, choline, ethanolamine, inositol or an additional glycerol. None of these groups have aromatic rings in their structures.

6) A. A micelle is a spherical structure in which lipids come together to form a hydrophobic interior and a hydrophilic exterior.

7) B. Bacilli are a pathogenic form of bacteria that typically are rod shaped; spirilli are helically shaped bacteria; and gram positive bacteria give a positive response to the Gram staining test (crystal violet).

8) C. Peripheral proteins adhere to the surface of a membrane; G-proteins are attached to the inner surface of a membrane and bind GDP and GTP; glycoproteins have oligosaccharides and are attached to membrane surfaces, facilitating interactions of cells.

9) C. Osmosis occurs when a membrane is permeable to water but not permeable to other solutes. If the concentration of a solute is higher (hypertonic) in the cytosol than in the surrounding extracellular fluid, water will pass through the membrane in an attempt to equalize the concentrations of solute.

10) C. Gram-positive bacteria only have a single cell membrane surrounded by a thick cell wall. Some, but not all, such bacteria have a polysaccharide capsule.

11) A. In this case the name of the protein is pretty much a dead giveaway. Peptidoglycans are polymers of amino acids and saccharides that form a encapsulating layer on the outside of the cell membrane of bacteria; tubulin is a protein polymer that helps form the cytoskeleton of eukaryotic cells; chitin is a structural polymer of N-acetylglucosamine, an important component of the exoskeletons of insects and crustaceans, as well as the cell walls of fungi.

12) D. Binary fission is an asexual reproductive process observed in prokaryotic cells.

13) A. A plasmid is a small circular double stranded DNA found in bacteria and can be transmitted from one bacterium to another by transformation, transduction and conjugation. Meiosis is a sexual reproduction process that occurs in eukaryotes such as mammals in which DNA reproduction is followed by two rounds of cell division and gene shuffling.

14) D. Bacterial conjugation is a transfer of genetic material between cells that occurs by direct contact by way of a bridge-like structure. Transduction is the process in which genetic material is transferred from one bacterium to another by a virus. Transformation is a process in which external genetic material is brought into the cell and incorporated into the cell's own genetic material.

15) A. See the explanation for question 14. The virus is the vector.

16) B. Septa are the cell walls of fungi, which are typically comprised of chitin. See the explanations for questions 7 and 11. Hyphae are fibrous structures associated with molds and fungi.

17) A. See the explanation for question 11.

18) A. Unlike the diploid life cycle observed for most multicellular organisms (including humans), where the multicellular form is diploid and gametes are haploid, fungi (and algae) have a haploid life cycle, where the multicellular form is haploid and the diploid stage (spores) is unicellular.

19) C. Budding is an asexual reproductive process used by yeast in which a new cell develops as a small outgrowth of the original cells and remains attached until maturity.

20) A. Cholesterol is a component of eukaryotic cell membranes. Bacterial cell membranes have compounds called hopanoids, which are pentacyclic, and serve a similar function as cholesterol, which is a tetracyclic.

21) C. Autotrophs (plants) are organisms that convert simple molecules such as carbon dioxide and water into higher energy compounds, such as sugars, by using light, i.e. photosynthesis.

22) A. The prefix chemo- clearly refers to chemicals and the suffix -taxis refers to movement resulting from a stimulus.

23) B. See the explanation for question 14. Bacterial cells that undergo conjugation are asexual and therefore are neither male nor female. "Franco" means "French" and

these cells "ne parle pas Francais." Fungi do not undergo conjugation.

24) D. See the explanation for question 4. The suffix -oid means that it has a similar function.

25) C. Antibiotics are substances that kill microorganisms, such as bacteria. While viruses have genetic material, they are not living organisms and antibiotics usually have no effect on viruses.

26) C. A prion is an infectious agent comprise entirely of protein that acts somewhat like a virus, and have been implicated in spongiform diseases such as "Mad cow disease." An active virus is one that has entered a cell and is using it to replicate the viral genetic material. Viroids are the smallest pathogens and consist of very short strands of circular RNA without a coating.

27) D. Endocytosis is when a cell membrane engulfs a foreign material and brings it into the cell cytoplasm. Exocytosis is essentially the opposite process, in which a cell transports a material, like a protein, out of the cell. Both endocytosis and exocytosis are active transport mechanisms that require energy. G-protein cascade is a method of cell signaling as a response to stimuli outside of the cell, where a protein interacts with GTP. See also the explanation for question 8.

28) B. Large molecules generally can't pass through a cell membrane and therefore the virus must provide a path through the membrane.

29) A. The word "temperate" does not specifically refer to temperature in this case, but means "mild." A temperate virus is a phage that does not immediately lyse the host cell. The lysogenic cycle involves either incorporation of the viral genetic material into the genome of the host cell or replication in the cytoplasm. The lytic cycle involves lysis, or destruction of the host cell's membrane. Hydrophobic means water hating and it is not clear how this might be related to a temperate virus.

30) A. A vaccine often contains agents that resemble a disease-causing microorganism, and is often made from a weakened or killed form of a microbe, which induces an immune response when exposed to that microorganism.

31) A. Archaea are prokaryotes that were originally classified as archaebacteria, but are now placed in their own kingdom. Protists, fungi, and autotrophs are all eukaryotes. Fungi include unicellular microorganisms such as yeasts and molds, as well as multicellular mushrooms. Protists are unicellular animals and plants that do not form tissues. See also the explanation for question 21.

32) C. See the explanation for question 21. Chemotrophs are organisms that obtain energy by the oxidation of

chemicals in their environment. Phototrophs use light to carry out various cellular metabolic processes. Heterotrophs are organisms such as animals that can not fix carbon, and use high energy carbon compounds (sugars) produced by autotrophs as a source of energy.

33) D. See the explanation for question 32.

34) B. See the explanation for question 32.

35) B. Oxidation generally produces energy, whereas reduction, phosphorylation and polymerization generally require energy.

36) C. A helical structure is synonymous with a spiral or twisting structure. See also the explanation for question 7.

37) D. Bacilli are rod-shaped bacteria.

38) B. Hydrophilic means water loving and water is a polar molecule.

39) B. The prefix "amphi-" means "both." Amphipathic molecules are both hydrophilic and hydrophobic, i.e. soaps (fatty acid salts) and phospholipids. Amphoteric molecules are capable of being an acid or a base.

40) D. Phospholipids are the major component of cell membranes. Bacteria are prokaryotes and do not have organelles such as a nucleus or mitochondria. Cell walls for plants are generally made of polysaccharides (cellulose). See also the explanation for question 11.

41) B. The hydrophobic intermolecular interactions (London dispersion forces) of the fatty acid tails are primarily responsible for holding the cell membrane together.

42) C. The fluid mosaic model compares the complex structure of a cell membrane that contains many different molecules such as phospholipids, cholesterol, and proteins, to the art form in which small shapes come together to form a larger picture.

43) B. See the explanation for question 14.

44) C. Binary fission is an asexual reproduction process, and is the most common method for prokaryotes to reproduce. Fungi such as mushrooms reproduce by producing spores, which is essentially a sexual reproductive process and yeast undergo asexual budding.

45) D. Bacteria are prokaryotes and do not undergo the same stages of the cell life cycle as eukaryotes in which there are distinct phases such as G_1, G_2 and S.

46) C. See the explanation for question 25.

47) C. The term "obligate," means that it is "required." An anaerobe is a living organism that does not require oxygen for metabolism. Viruses are not living organisms and do not undergo metabolism by themselves, but require a host and its metabolic processes to provide energy, hence it is a parasite. See also the explanations for questions 21 and 32.

48) D. The host is required to do all of the normal processes that a living organism would perform, since a virus is simply genetic material enclosed in a package and is not a living entity.

49) D. Viruses are much smaller than prokaryotic or eukaryotic cells and can't be seen by a typical light microscope.

50) A. Shown below is a schematic drawing of a bacteriophage (virus). The genetic material is enclosed in the head. The tail fibers are used to make the initial attachment to the host cell membrane and the tail is used to inject the genetic material into the host cell.

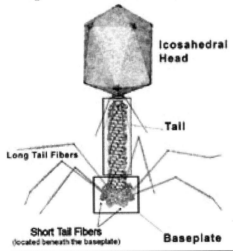

51) B. The lysogenic cycle involves integration of the viral nucleic acid into the host bacterium's genome. Reverse transcriptase is an enzyme used to generate complementary DNA from an RNA template.

52) B. In the lytic cycle, the host cell does not survive and the viral DNA is not incorporated into the host genome. See also the explanations for questions 29 and 51.

53) A. His+ bacteria can make their own histidine from other simpler molecular components.

54) C. HIV is a retrovirus that contains a single stranded RNA and must undergo reverse transcription to replicate. See also the explanation for question 51.

55) A. Histones are associated with nuclear DNA. Prokaryotes do not have nuclei. See also the explanation for question 4.

56) B. Lysozyme is an enzyme that helps dissolve the cell walls of bacteria.

57) C. The generalized structure of bacteria consists of nucleic acids and ribosomes suspended in the cytoplasm, which is surrounded by a cell membrane, which is subsequently encapsulated by a cell wall (see the explanation for question 11) and finally protected by the capsule. A capsid is the protein shell of a virus (See the explanation for question 1).

58) A. Motile means that the cell can move. A flagellum is a whip like structure that helps a cell to move and examples can be found in both prokaryotes (bacteria) and eukaryotes (sperm cells). Cilia are short hair like structures used by some eukaryotes for locomotion.

59) B. ATP supplies the energy required for proton pumping associated with the molecular motors driving the rotary motion of a flagellum. Action potentials are associated with nerve cells of multicellular organisms.

60) B. A pilus is a hair like structure that is used to attach the cell to other structures and or cells (conjugation).

61) C. The suffix "-trophs" (autotrophs and heterotrophs) means "the use of nutrients."

62) A. A photoautotroph uses light, carbon dioxide and water to produce sugars. See also the explanation for question 32.

63) B. An auxotroph is unable to synthesize a particular compound required for its growth. Chemoheterotrophs utilize inorganic energy sources such as elemental sulfur. See also the explanation for question 21, and 32.

64) C. The prefix thermo- refers to "temperature (high)" and the suffix -phile means "loving."

65) C. An aerobe uses oxygen and an anaerobe does not use oxygen. The term "obligate" means that it is "required", eliminating choices A and D. A facultative anaerobe is an organism that makes ATP by aerobic respiration if oxygen is present, but is capable of switching to fermentation or anaerobic respiration if oxygen is absent.

66) A. Since these organisms can't be exposed to oxygen, they are obligated to be anaerobes. See also the explanation for question 65.

67) D. Since these organisms must have oxygen, they are obligated to be aerobes. See also the explanation for question 65.

68) B. Since the question indicates that these organisms can survive exposure to oxygen but presumably produce

energy anaerobically by fermentation, they are classified as tolerant anaerobes, i.e. lactobacillus that is used to make yogurt.

69) B. Human beings must have oxygen to survive. While under certain conditions humans can temporarily use glycolysis as a source of energy, but in the long term our cells will die without breathing in fresh air containing oxygen. A virus is not alive and does not use oxygen, but its host might need oxygen. Yeasts can use undergo both aerobic respiration and anaerobic fermentation (facultative anaerobes).

70) C. See the explanation for question 65.

71) C. Since each cell divides and produces two new cells the process increases the number of cells exponentially, 1 $\rightarrow$ 2 $\rightarrow$ 4 $\rightarrow$ 8, etc., where the number of cells is equal to 2^n, where n represents the number of cell divisions.

72) B. Most fungi, i.e. mushrooms are multicellular. All fungi, including yeasts, are eukaryotes.

73) A. Mushrooms break down plant material such as wood (cellulose and lignin) into simpler molecules by excreting enzymes through their cell walls. Yeasts can metabolize simple sugars, glucose and sucrose, but are not capable to using starch as a nutrient.

74) A. Yeast can reproduce asexually by budding and many mushrooms reproduce by producing seed like spores. Mammals and birds can only reproduce sexually. Archaea reproduce asexually by fission, fragmentation, or budding

75) A. Most fungi are mushrooms and reproduce by the production of spores, a type of sexual reproduction requiring meiosis. Fungi are facultative anaerobes. Lactic acid fermentation occurs primarily in bacteria and animals. See also the explanations for questions 13, 44, 68 and 74.

76) B. Strictly speaking, viruses are not cells, because they can not reproduce by themselves. Prokaryotes do not have membrane bound organelles, but eukaryotes do have organelles. Bacteria generally reproduce asexually and hence do not undergo meiosis.

SECTION 3 CONTENT REVIEW PROBLEMS

1) D. The "t" in tRNA stands for "transfer" that functions along with the ribosomes located in the rough endoplasmic reticulum outside of the nucleus. The tRNA brings amino acids to the ribosomes to be assembled into proteins and translated from the mRNA, which was transcribed from the DNA in the nucleus.

2) A. See the explanation for question 1.

3) B. The rough endoplasmic reticulum is located in the cytoplasm and is attached to the nuclear membrane as seen below.

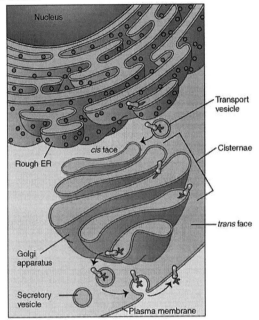

See also the explanation for question 1.

4) C. See the explanation for question 1.

5) B. The smooth ER participates in several metabolic processes, including the synthesis of lipids, the metabolism of carbohydrates and detoxification. See also the explanation for question 1.

6) B. Skin oils are typically triglycerides, which are lipids. See also the explanation for question 5.

7) D. Cytokinesis is the process in which a cell, and its associated cytoplasm, is divided into two new cells. The suffix "-kinesis" means "movement or motion", making choice A very tempting as a distractor.

8) D. Proteins from the endoplasmic reticulum are packaged by the Golgi apparatus, and transported as vesicles to their ultimate destinations. See also the explanations for questions 1, 3 and 5.

9) D. See the explanation for question 3.

10) B. See the explanation for question 3.

11) A. Mitochondria have their own nucleic acids, separate from the nuclear DNA.

12) D. Mitochondria and the vesicles that make up peroxisomes and lysosomes can all undergo fission to reproduce.

13) B. Lysosomes are spherical structures that contain enzymes that function best under slightly acidic conditions and can break down most types of molecules, thereby acting as the waste disposal system of the cell by digesting unwanted materials.

14) B. See the explanation for question 13.

15) D. A monocyte is a single celled organism and must contain all of the organelles necessary to survive. Multi-celled organisms have specific cell types and organs with specific functions, such as the liver, one function of which is waste detoxification. Choices A-C are not organs that would be involved in waste detoxification in multi-cellular organisms.

16) B. The enzymes in lysosomes are proteins, which are synthesized by the ribosomes in the rough ER and packaged by the Golgi bodies. See the explanations for questions 1 and 3.

17) A. Apoptosis is programmed cell death, and lysosomes are required to release the degradative enzymes that cause this cell death.

18) B. Mitochondria play a critical role in energy production by way of aerobic cellular respiration.

19) A. Spermatogenesis is a continuous process whereas oogenesis is arrested prior to ovulation and again prior to fertilization.

20) B. The cytoskeleton is a structure that helps cells maintain their shape. Muscle cells have a linear fibrous structure. Neurons or nerve cells have various portions of the cell that have fibrous or linear characteristics, i.e. the axon or dendrites, but overall the structure is much more complex, with the dendrite forming complex branching systems. Hepatocytes or liver cells essentially have cubic shapes. There are a number of types of leukocytes or white blood cells, all of which are roughly spherical and important for fighting disease and infections.

21) A. A neutrophil is a phagocytic leukocyte capable of engulfing solid particles by phagocytosis. See also the explanation for question 20. Erythrocytes are red blood cells.

22) B. The liver plays a key role in lipid metabolism. See also the explanations for questions 20 and 21.

23) A. Peroxisomes are organelles that break down a variety of compounds such as fatty acids and amino acids, as well as the detoxification of reactive oxygen species such as hydrogen peroxide. See the explanations for questions 12, 13 and 16.

24) C. Spermatogenesis is the production of sperm, which occurs in the male reproductive organs known as the testes. The prostrate is a male gland associated with reproduction. Somatic cells are all cells of a multicellular organism that are not associated with sexual reproduction. The pancreas is associated with the production of digestive enzymes.

25) A. The nucleolus is a structure within the nucleus of eukaryotic cells that is primarily responsible for the synthesis and assembly of ribosomes, which are macromolecular complexes of RNA and proteins used for the synthesis of other proteins required by the cell. See also question 1 and 3.

26) C. Flagella are used by sperm cells for movement. Spermatogonia are undifferentiated male germ cells. Gametes are mature reproductive cells and therefore could be either a female ovum or a male sperm cell. Therefore choice B is not specific enough to represent an appropriate choice. Neurons do not move but do have dendrites (see also the explanation for question 20).

27) D. The cytoskeleton is comprised of fibrous structures that help cells maintain their shape and internal organization, and provides mechanical support so that cells can carry out functions like division and movement. See also the explanation for question 20.

28) C. See the explanation for question 27.

29) A. The Fluid Mosaic Model describes the cell membrane as a complex assembly of phospholipids (the primary component), cholesterol, carbohydrates and proteins. Microtubules are a structural component of the cell located in the cytoplasm.

30) D. Peptidoglycan is a polymer of sugars and amino acids forming a mesh-like layer on the outside of the plasma membrane of most bacteria. See the explanation for question 29.

31) C. Transport proteins are transmembrane proteins that help various molecules and ions move across the cell membrane. Immunoglobulins (antibodies) are glycoproteins produced by white blood cells. Albumin is a blood serum protein. See also the explanation for question 1.

32) C. Cholesterol stabilizes and maintains the cell membrane while reducing membrane permeability.

33) A. The plasma membrane has an interior nonpolar region comprised of the hydrocarbon chains of phospholipids. Small non-polar molecular species, such as carbon dioxide and oxygen will most likely be able to diffuse through the nonpolar region.

34) D. See the explanation for question 33.

35) D. See the explanation for question 33.

36) C. The side chain on the alpha carbon of valine is an isopropyl group, which is nonpolar. Lysine and arginine are basic amino acids and positively charged at physiological pHs. Aspartic acid will be negatively charged (-ate suffix) at physiological pHs. See the explanation for question 33.

37) B. Isoleucine, leucine and alanine are all nonpolar amino acids. See the explanations for questions 33 and 36.

38) A. Potassium channels provide a path for potassium ions (K^+) to pass through the cell membrane. See also the explanation for question 1. Myosin is a protein component of muscles and histones help package DNA. See also the explanation for question 31.

39) C. The main function of centrioles is to produce spindle fibers (microtubules) during cell division. The centromere is the part (center) of a chromosome that links sister chromatids. Chromatin is a complex package of macromolecules consisting of DNA, protein and RNA. In metaphase, the DNA centromeres assemble themselves on the equatorial plate that is equidistant from the centrosome poles due to the pulling forces generated by the opposing spindle fibers. During mitosis, spindle fibers attach to the centromere via the kinetochore (See Figure 11.2).

40) B. See the explanation for question 39.

41) B. Histones are proteins found in nucleus of eukaryotic cells, whose purpose is to package and order DNA. See also the explanations for questions 38 and 39.

42) C. A solution that is isotonic has the same concentration of solutes as the cytosol of the cell and will not undergo osmosis, such that the cell will not change size.

43) A. Osmosis results when water (the solvent) can diffuse through a membrane but other solutes such as salt can not. Water will diffuse towards the higher solute concentration side of a membrane in order to equalize the concentrations of solute. This process is eventually balanced by the osmotic pressure at equilibrium.

44) B. The prefix "hypo-" means "beneath or below," therefore hypotonic means that the concentration of

solute is lower than the solution on the other side of the membrane.

45) A. The prefix "hyper-" means "above or higher," therefore hypertonic means that the concentration of solute is higher than the solution on the other side of the membrane.

46) C. The prefix "iso-" means "the same." See the explanation for question 42.

47) D. Pure water would not have solutes, and would be hypotonic compared with the cytosol of the cell. See the explanations for questions 43 and 44.

48) A. See the explanation for question 47. At some point the cell membrane will expand to the point where it will rupture, unless it can exert enough osmotic pressure to come to equilibrium, which is unlikely with pure water.

49) A. This is the opposite situation to question 47, and the concentration of NaCl in the cell will be lower than the surrounding solution.

50) B. Osmosis will result in water leaving the cell. See the explanation for question 43 and 48.

51) A. Seawater is a hypertonic salt solution compared to cytosol. See the explanation for question 50.

52) C. See the explanation for question 33. Water molecules travel through cell membranes by way of small trans-membrane proteins similar to those responsible for facilitated diffusion in ion channels. The term "pumping" indicates an active transport process requiring energy, which is typically against a concentration or electrical potential gradient.

53) B. See the explanation for question 52.

54) D. See the explanations for questions 33 and 52.

55) D. See the explanation for question 52.

56) B. Facilitated diffusion requires membrane pores and passively moves solutes from high to low concentration.

57) A. See the explanation for question 43.

58) C. Each checkpoint is a potential stopping point in the middle of the appropriate phase of the cell cycle to allow for proper functioning and progression to the next stage. There are three checkpoints in G_1, G_2 and M. The only stage without a checkpoint is the synthesis (S) phase, which occurs between G_1 and G_2.

59) D. Cell division occurs in the Mitotic (M) phase and the cell must grow enough in the gap phase (G_2) right

before M, in order to undergo mitosis. See also the explanation for question 58.

60) D. Prophase, anaphase and telophase are all stages of mitosis (M). G_0 occurs when a cells stops dividing and is an alternative stage that occurs before G_1 begins. Interphase represents all of the cell cycle stages except M.

61) D. The S phase does not have a checkpoint so the next checkpoint after replication is G_2. See the explanation for question 58.

62) D. After mitosis, each daughter cell begins the cycle again, $G_1 \rightarrow S \rightarrow G_2 \rightarrow M$, and repeat.

63) B. See the explanation for question 60.

64) C. See the explanation for question 62.

65) D. See the explanation for question 60.

66) C. DNA is made during the synthesis (S) phase.

67) B. The stages of mitosis are: (1) during prophase chromosomes condense and spindle fibers begin to form, the nuclear membrane breaks down and spindle fibers attach to the centromere; (2) during metaphase the spindle fibers that are attached to the chromosomes pull in opposite directions and align the chromosomes along the equatorial plane (metaphase plate); (3) during anaphase sister chromatids separate and are pulled towards opposite ends of the cell; and (4) during telophase two new nuclear membranes form and cytokinesis results in the formation of two new daughter cells.

68) D. See the explanation for question 67.

69) D. See the explanation for question 67.

70) A. See the explanation for question 67.

71) D. See the explanation for question 67.

72) C. See the explanation for question 67.

73) C. See the explanations for questions 62 and 67. An acronym for the stages of mitosis is PMAT.

74) A. Meiosis is associated with sexual reproduction, where the organism produces haploid gamete cells. See also the explanation for question 26. Both meiosis I and II produce haploid cells with half the original number of chromosomes.

75) A. See the explanation for question 74.

76) B. Mitosis is associated with asexual reproduction or cell replication in multicellular organisms and produces

two daughter cells that are identical to the original parent cell.

77) D. Anaphase in mitosis is where sister chromatids are separated. See the explanation for question 67. In meiosis there are two rounds of cell division. In Meiosis I, after the S phase and during the prophase, cross over of genes can occur, such that during metaphase homologous pairs of chromosomes line up and the intact chromosomes are separated in anaphase, with subsequent production of two haploid daughter cells. Then these daughter cells undergo Meiosis II, which functions like mitosis in that the replicated chromatids of the chromosomes are separated in anaphase II and result in a total of four haploid daughter cells.

78) A. See the explanation of question 77.

79) A. See the explanations for questions 62 and 67.

80) C. Meiosis is required for sexual reproduction. Somatic cells are any cells in a multicellular organism that are not involved in sexual reproduction. Skin cells are a type of soma cell. A germ cell is any biological cell that gives rise to the gametes that are produced by meiosis.

81) D. See the explanation for question 80.

82) B. See the explanation for question 76.

83) D. See the explanation for question 77.

84) C. Neurons are in G_0 of the cell cycle and generally do not replicate after the birth of an animal.

85) A. The most rapidly replicating cells would most likely be undergoing mitosis. Skin cells have a life span of a couple of weeks. Neurons and heart muscle cells essentially do not undergo mitosis during the life span of the animal. See the explanation for question 84. Liver cells have an intermediate life span and the liver is one of the few organs that if a portion is removed or transplanted, it can regenerate itself in a few months.

86) B. Menstruation is part of the reproductive cycle of a mammal in which the uterine lining is sloughed off if an embryo is not implanted and choice D should be fairly easily eliminated. The term "genesis" means "to create." Gametogenesis is the process that creates sperm (spermatogenesis) or egg (oogenesis) cells and is therefore too general to be the answer in this case.

87) C. Spermatogonia are cells produced at a very early stage of sperm formation that produce spermatocytes by way of mitosis. Spermatids are immature male sex cells lacking flagella, are in the process of becoming sperm and have already undergone meiosis. Primary spermatocytes are diploid cells that will undergo meiosis I, and

secondary spermatocytes are haploid cells that will undergo meiosis II. See the explanation for question 77.

88) D. See the explanation for question 87.

89) A. See the explanations for question 87 and 77.

90) A. Unlike spermatogenesis, meiosis I in oogenesis produces a haploid secondary oocyte and a polar body (that rarely undergoes meiosis II). The former does undergo meiosis II to produce an ovum (egg) and a second infertile polar body.

91) A. See the explanation for question 90.

92) A. See the explanations for questions 87 and 90.

93) A. See the explanation for question 90.

94) B. See the explanations for questions 77, 87 and 90.

95) B. See the explanation for question 67.

96) A. Prokaryotes do not have membrane bound organelles. Ribosomes are not organelles. See the explanation for question 19.

97) B. Eukaryotic DNA is linear and in the nucleus. Prokaryotic DNA is circular and located in the cytoplasm, since there are no organelles such as nuclei and lysosomes. Both eukaryotic and prokaryotic organisms can use oxidative phosphorylation.

98) D. Bulk transport is the movement of solutions containing macromolecular compounds, such as proteins or polysaccharides, into or out of a cell, i.e. exocytosis and endocytosis.

99) A. See the explanation for question 21.

100) C. Endocytosis is a form of active transport in which a cell engulfs extracellular material(s) and exocytosis is the opposite process in which materials are transported out of the cell. Phagocytosis and pinocytosis are both endocytotic processes, involving solid particles and liquid solutions, respectively. See also the explanation for question 21.

101) C. Phagocytosis (cell eating) and pinocytosis (cell drinking) are forms of endocytosis. Apoptosis is cell death.

102) C. See the explanation for question 13.

103) D. See the explanations for questions 21 and 100.

104) B. See the explanation for question 100. Neurons excrete neurotransmitters at synapses.

105) A. Endocytosis involves the cell taking in new material and thus getting larger.

106) B. Exocytosis involves a membrane-bound vesicle fusing with the plasma membrane. This addition of membrane material means the cell membrane gets slightly larger.

107) A. See the explanation for question 23.

108) C. See the explanations for questions 22 and 23.

109) A. See the explanation for question 23.

110) C. See the explanation for question 23.

111) D. See the explanation for question 19.

112) B. The membrane associated with the mitochondria has both an inner lipid bilayer membrane and an outer lipid bilayer membrane.

113) C. See also the explanation for question 29.

114) B. Muscles require a lot of energy to function. See also the explanation for question 18.

115) C. Unlike prokaryotes, eukaryotes have membrane-based organelles. Eukaryotes can be unicellular or multicellular organisms. Plants are eukaryotes that have chloroplasts, but not all eukaryotes are plants.

116) A. One theory is that mitochondria evolved from a symbiotic relationship between two different prokaryotic cells, in which a bacterium that was capable of generating ATP by way of the Krebs cycle underwent endocytosis by another cell.

117) D. See the explanation for question 116.

118) C. Adenosine triphosphate (ATP) is often called the "molecular currency" of intracellular energy and adenosine diphosphate (ADP) is the lower energy form of ATP. Nicotinamide adenine dinucleotide (NADH) is also an important energy molecule involved in respiration. Cyclic adenosine monophosphate (cAMP) is a messenger molecule.

119) D. T-cell receptors are molecules found on the surface of T-lymphocytes that are responsible for recognizing antigens. Coenzyme Q is a component of the electron transport chain and is primarily found in mitochondria. DNA polymerase creates DNA by assembling nucleotides in the nucleus. Helicase is an enzyme that functions during DNA replication and separates double-stranded DNA, allowing each strand to be copied.

120) A. Bacteria only have a single lipid bilayer, whereas mitochondria have a double lipid bilayer. See the explanation for question 116.

SECTION 4 CONTENT REVIEW PROBLEMS

1) C. See the diagram of a neuron shown below.

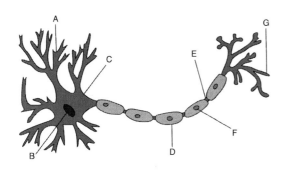

The signal begins at the dendrites (A) and travels to the cell body (B), the axon hillock (C), axon (D) which is insulated by the myelin sheath (F) between which are the nodes of Ranvier (E), and finally the signal reaches the branched axon terminals (G).

2) C. See the explanation for question 1.

3) C. Sodium ions are actively transported out of the neurons to maintain the resting potential. The sodium pumps require energy provided by ATP.

4) D. As sodium ions flow through channels into the neuron the potential increases from the rest potential of approximately -70 mV, to a maximum value of around +30 mV. This process is known as depolarization. Repolarization subsequently occurs after the ion channels close and ion pumps return the cell potential back to the normal resting potential. Hyperpolarization means that the neuron is more polarized (a more negative voltage) than the normal resting potential.

5) B. The ion channels are proteins that provide a path through the cell membrane and therefore must be transmembrane proteins. Peripheral proteins are only on the surface of the membrane. G-proteins are peripheral proteins, which bind either GTP or GDP. Free-floating proteins are part of the cytosol or extracellular fluids.

6) C. Gap junctions allow electrical impulses to travel through several cells without the use of neurotransmitters. Conduction along muscle cells is an example.

7) A. The action potential triggers an influx of calcium ions through ion selective gates, which quickly stimulates the exocytosis of the neurotransmitters.

8) B. When the neurotransmitter binds to the receptor it stimulates, or excites, an action potential. The term "temporal" means "time" and "spatial " means regions of "space."

9) A. Efferent nerves carry impulses away from the CNS and afferent neurons carry impulses towards the CNS.

Interneurons create circuits and connect sensory or motor neurons with the CNS.

10) B. See the explanation for question 9.

11) C. A reflex involves a direct connection between a sensory neuron and a motor neuron, with only one synapse. Reflexes do not require thought or the brain, eliminating choices A and D. Choice B is in the wrong order, and should state that a reflex is a motor response to a sensory input.

12) A. The somatic nervous system is part of the peripheral nervous system associated with voluntary muscle control. The autonomic nervous system is associated with involuntary muscle movement, such as breathing, heartbeat, and digestion. The central nervous system is the brain and spinal cord. The parasympathetic nervous system is part of the autonomic nervous system and is associated with "rest and digest (and reproduce)" processes.

13) C. See the explanation for question 12. The sympathetic nervous system is associated with the "fight or flight" response.

14) B. See the explanation for question 13. Dilation of the pupil would allow additional light to enter the eye and help prepare the person to respond to a threat.

15) A. Stimulation of the urge to urinate is an unconscious process. See the explanation for question 12.

16) B. The medulla oblongata is responsible for multiple autonomic functions. See the explanation for question 12. The cerebellum is mainly responsible for coordinating and regulating muscular activity. The posterior pituitary gland is part of the endocrine system, and is associated with hormones. The frontal cortex is associated with reward, attention, memory, and planning.

17) B. Nociceptors are sensory neurons that respond to damaging stimuli (chemical, temperature, etc.) and stimulation of nociceptors is typically interpreted as pain.

18) D. See the explanation for question 17. Electromagnetic receptors are the same as photoreceptors.

19) A. Rod and cone cells are photoreceptors. See the explanations for question 17 and 18.

20) B. The tympanic membrane is the eardrum; the auricle is the external portion of the ear; the stapes is one of the small bones in the middle ear; the cochlea is a spiral-shaped cavity that senses sound and transforms pressure waves into nerve impulses to be sent to the brain.

21) D. The amplitude of a pressure wave is associated with the loudness of a sound; the wavelength of a pressure

wave is inversely related to both frequency and pitch; the speed of sound in air is not related to pitch.

22) C. The position of liquid in the semicircular canals of the ear is associated with the sense of balance.

23) A. See the following figure.

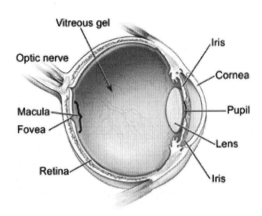

24) D. The optic disc is the point in the back of the eye where axons leave the eye into the optic nerve and there are no rods or cones overlying the optic disc, therefore there is a small blind spot.

25) A. Emmetropia is when the eye is completely relaxed and focused on an object more than 6 meters away, resulting in essentially parallel light rays that are focused on the retina without effort; hyperopia is also known as farsightedness; presbyopia is a type of farsightedness caused by loss of elasticity of the lens of the eye.

26) C. See the explanation for question 25.

27) B. See the explanation for question 25.

28) C. See the explanation for question 17.

29) B. T3 and T4 are thyroid hormones that help control how the body uses energy.

30) D. Catecholamines contain a 1,2-dihydroxyl benzene group, as well as an amine, and are water soluble. Important catecholamines are epinephrine (adrenaline), norepinephrine and dopamine. The first two are hormones released by the adrenal medulla and act in conjunction with the sympathetic nervous system (see the explanation for question 13). Dopamine is a neurotransmitter.

31) C. TSH stands for thyroid stimulating hormone.

32) A. The sex hormones are steroid based hormones derived from cholesterol, a lipid that is hydrophobic.

33) A. Aldosterone, cortisol and progesterone are all steroid hormones. See also the explanation for question 32.

34) C. Peptides are short polymers of amino acids, many of which have hydrophilic and polar side-chains. Peptide hormones are very often hydrophilic because they must dissolve directly in the water of the plasma for transport throughout the body.

35) D. FSH stands for follicle-stimulating hormone, which is secreted by the pituitary gland and in males stimulates primary spermatocytes to undergo meiosis. LH stands for luteinizing hormone, and is produced by the pituitary gland and in males stimulates the production of testosterone by Leydig cells in the testes.

36) B. Steroid hormones are generally lipophilic and can pass through cell membranes, therefore the receptors are found on the plasma membrane, in the cytosol and also in the nucleus of target cells.

37) A. The smooth ER is responsible for lipid metabolism and steroid production. See also the explanation for question 32.

38) B. ACTH stands for adrenocorticotropic hormone and is secreted by the pituitary gland as part of the "fight or flight" response to stress. Its primary effects are increased production and release of cortisol to help increase blood glucose levels.

39) D. Glucagon is a peptide hormone, produced by alpha cells of the pancreas, which raises the concentration of glucose in the blood and acts on the liver; the gall bladder stores bile; and the kidney processes and excretes waste.

40) D. Capillaries are the smallest and most numerous blood vessels, and are primarily where exchange of nutrients, oxygen and carbon dioxide with cells occurs.

41) B. The inferior vena cava brings deoxygenated blood back to the heart from the body and enters the right atrium.

42) D. Arteries transport blood away from the heart. The pulmonary artery transports deoxygenated blood from the heart to the lungs.

43) B. The ventricles are larger and more muscular than the atria and therefore can create more pressure.

44) A. During the diastolic phase the atria contract, but the ventricles remain relaxed, allowing for blood to flow into the ventricles from the atria.

45) C. When the ventricles contract, the pressure increases above that in the atria and the mitral and tricuspid valves

close, while the semilunar valves open, allowing blood to flow into the arteries.

46) A. Increasing the total volume of the blood in the body would increase the pressure in the veins and thereby increase the flow rate. Decreasing heart rate and decreasing stroke volume will decrease the rate of blood returning to the heart. Increasing the number of platelets in the blood will not have a significant effect on the rate of blood flow, unless a clot forms, which would reduce blood flow.

47) C. The plateau phase (see stage 2 in the figure below) is due to a balance between the inward movement of calcium and the outward movement of potassium through ion selective channels.

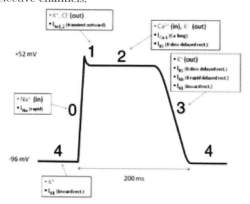

48) B. Pacemaker cells are located in the sinoatrial node (SN). The atrioventricular (AV) node makes an electrical connection between atrial and ventricular chambers. The bundle of His transmits electrical impulses from the AV node to the branches that distribute the impulse throughout the ventricles by way of the Purkinje fibers.

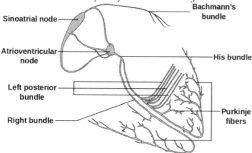

49) B. See the explanation for question 48.

50) B. The vagus nerve is part of the autonomic nervous system and allows parasympathetic (see the explanation for question 12) control of the heart and digestive system.

51) C. A person with type B blood can not receive blood from a person with A type antigens. O- type blood is considered a universal donor, since it does not have A or B type antigens and does not have the RhD antigen.

52) D. A buffer .s a combination of a weak acid and its conjugate base. Generally the pK_a of the weak acid should be within one pH unit of the desired pH. The pK_{a1} of carbonic acid is 6.4 and normal physiological pH is slightly above 7. Iron and elemental oxygen are not weak acids. The pK_a of lactic acid is 3.9.

53) C. See the explanation for question 52.

54) C. Plasma is the aqueous component of blood; erythrocytes are red blood cells; and electrolytes are ionic solutes dissolved in the plasma.

55) A. Urea is a nitrogen containing metabolite of proteins. Catabolism is a metabolic process that breaks down compounds.

56) C. Actin is a protein that forms microfilaments found in all eukaryotic cells; myosin is critical in muscle contraction; collagen is probably the most abundant protein in the human body and is a structural substance found in bones, muscles, skin and tendons.

57) A. Hemoglobin in red blood cells is made up of four protein subunits, each containing an iron/heme group that can bind oxygen. Once one iron/heme binds an oxygen molecule, the shape of the remaining subgroups is changed, cooperating to facilitate the further binding of oxygen to the remaining three subgroups.

58) B. Pressure is typically on the x-axis of an oxygen-dissociation curve. Fetal hemoglobin has a greater affinity for oxygen than adult hemoglobin and therefore it takes less pressure for oxygen to bind, causing a shift to the left.

59) A. A decrease in the affinity means that it would require more oxygen pressure to bind. See also the explanation for question 58.

60) C. An arteriole is a smaller blood vessel than an artery (see the explanation for question 42), connecting and branching out from an artery and ultimately leading to the capillaries. Venules connect the capillaries to the veins. Arteries and arterioles are highly elastic and surrounded by smooth muscle to withstand the high pressures generated by the heart. The pressure in the veins and venules is generally much lower than in the arteries and arterioles, eliminating choices B and D. Capillaries have very thin walls to allow exchange of gases and nutrients, and have the lowest blood pressure.

61) A. Lymph nodes are important for the proper functioning of the immune system, acting as filters for foreign particles and cells. Most blood cells, and platelets are produced by bone marrow. Antidiuretic hormone (ADH) is released by the pituitary gland. Lymph nodes do not play a role in digestion, but the lymph system does distribute digested fatty acids absorbed by lacteals in the small intestines.

62) C. Innate immunity refers to nonspecific defense mechanisms and the skin provides a barrier that prevents bacteria and pathogens from entering the body. Antibodies and immunoglobulins target specific types of pathogens. Platelets are a component of blood that helps stop bleeding and helps heal a wound. Once a scab is formed it could be argued that the platelets have become part of the skin.

63) D. An antibody or immunoglobulin is produced by plasma cells or mature B lymphocytes, which are a type of white blood cell. The antibody is a Y-shape protein that selectively attaches to antigens and is used by the immune system to fight pathogens such as bacteria and viruses.

64) C. One of the major functions of B cells is to produce antibodies.

65) B. The primary (1°) immune response occurs when the body is exposed to an antigen for the first time, and there is a delay in the production of antibodies but differentiated B-lymphocytes are produced. The secondary (2°) response occurs after a second exposure to an antigen, in which the body quickly recognizes the antigen due to the presence of memory cells produce from the first exposure.

66) C. T helper cells play an important role in the adaptive immune system. They help the activity of other immune cells by releasing cytokines, which are relatively small proteins that are important in cell signaling. See also the explanation for question 65. Epithelial cells line the surface of major cavities of the body, such as the lungs and digestive tract.

67) A. The immune system does not normally attack healthy cells. This happens in autoimmune diseases.

68) C. See the explanation for question 67.

69) C. Stem cells are the undifferentiated cells of a multicellular organism. See the explanation for question 61. The thymus is a specialized primary lymphoid organ of the immune system whose cells are differentiated.

70) C. Peristalsis is a series of wave-like involuntary muscle contractions that moves food through the digestive tract. Smooth muscles are not under voluntary control. Skeletal muscles are generally involved in motion of the body and are under voluntary control.

71) A. Exocrine secretion is when a substance leaves the body in some way and generally requires a duct. Endocrine secretions, i.e. hormones, stay within the body and often travel within the blood.

72) B. Amylase is an enzyme, produced by both the salivary glands and pancreas, which catalyzes the hydrolysis of starch into sugars.

73) B. The epiglottis is cartilage at the root of the tongue and the tube that connects it to the stomach is the esophagus. The trachea leads to the lungs. The jejunum is the largest portion of the small intestine.

74) D. Mastication or chewing, crushes and grinds food that is shaped into a bolus that is suitable for swallowing.

75) B. Saliva contains amylase, which helps enzymatically breaks down starch into carbohydrates, which are absorbed in the small intestine, not the mouth. See also the explanation for question 72. The salivary glands produce saliva that is released by way of ducts into the mouth.

76) A. Lysozyme is an enzyme in saliva that degrades the peptidoglycan portion of bacterial cell walls and therefore acts as part of the innate immune system. Lipase is an enzyme that breaks down fat and is produced primarily by the pancreas and released into the duodenum of the small intestine. Trypsin is an enzyme produced by the pancreas that helps digest proteins. Proteolysis enzymes generally aid in the hydrolysis of proteins.

77) B. The stomach secretes hydrochloric acid, producing low pHs that are optimal for enzymatic hydrolysis of proteins. See the explanation for question 76. Choices C and D are not pHs that are acidic.

78) B. Chief cells release pepsinogen that is activated into pepsin when it comes in contact with acid. Gastrin is a hormone that stimulates secretion of acid in the stomach. See also the explanations for questions 76 and 77.

79) C. See the explanation for question 70.

80) C. Bile is produced by the liver and stored in the gall bladder. See also the explanations for questions 39 and 76. The spleen is an organ involved in forming and removal of blood cells, and is part of the immune system.

81) D. Enteropeptidase is an enzyme produced by the duodenum and converts trypsinogen into the active form of trypsin. See also the explanations for questions 72, 76 and 78.

82) B. Proteins can not be absorbed by the digestive system and must be broken down into amino acids to be absorbed. Chyme is partially digested food produced by the stomach. See also the explanation for question 80.

83) A. See the explanation for question 71.

84) A. See the explanation for question 39. Glucagon is a hormone produced by the pancreas that raises the concentration of glucose in the bloodstream.

85) B. The liver catabolizes proteins and kidneys remove the waste from the blood stream, which is excreted in the urine.

86) A. The nephron is the basic functional unit of the kidney; a neuron is a nerve cell; and a cardiac cell is a heart cell.

87) C. The glomerulus is a series of capillaries that are surrounded by the cup shaped Bowman's capsule, which begins the filtration process of the kidney, by allowing small molecular waste products and ions to pass into the proximal portion of the loop of Henle and then the distal tube of the nephron. The collecting ducts connect the nephrons to the ureter that transfers urine to the bladder.

88) A. Glucose is primarily reabsorbed in the proximal tube, whereas the distal tubes primarily reabsorb ions and water. See also the explanation for question 87.

89) B. ADH (see the explanation for question 61) or vasopressin, is a hormone whose primary function is to retain water and to constrict blood vessels. Aldosterone is a hormone produced by the adrenal gland and helps regulate blood pressure, mainly by increasing reabsorption of ions and water in the kidney, thereby increasing blood volume and pressure.

90) A. Tendon is made of fibers that attach muscles to bone, whereas ligaments connect bones to one another. Cartilage is a firm material that can act as connective or structural tissue and is found in many areas of the body including the cushioning of joints between bones.

91) D. Skeletal muscle cells are striated and voluntary but do not contract on their own. That is a property of cardiac and some smooth muscle.

92) D. Once a muscle cell receives an action potential, calcium gates open and release calcium ions into the cytoplasm where the actin and myosin filaments are located. Proteins bound to the actin filaments normally prevent binding to myosin, but calcium ions can bind to these proteins and allow the coupling of the myosin and actin.

93) B. The sarcoplasmic reticulum is a specialized type of smooth ER that regulates calcium ion concentrations in the cytoplasm of striated muscle cells. Ribosomes are located in the rough ER.

94) C. See the explanations for questions 6 and 91.

95) C. Striated muscles are multinucleated and fibrous, not smooth. T-tubules are found in striated muscle cells

and allows for the quick depolarization of the membrane, facilitating rapid contraction. Smooth muscle cells have one nucleus. See also the explanation for question 70.

96) C. The prefix epi-, means: above, on, over, nearby, upon; outer; besides, in addition to; among; attached to; or toward. Physis is a Greek term meaning "nature".

97) A. The two types of bone marrow are red and yellow. The red marrow is actively producing red blood cells, platelets and white blood cells. See also the explanation for question 61.

98) B. Erythropoiesis is the synthesis of red blood cells. See also the explanation for question 97.

99) B. Hydroxyapatite, $Ca_5(PO_4)_3(OH)$, is the mineral component of bone.

100) C. Chondrocytes are the cells responsible for creating and maintaining cartilage.

101) D. Bone is constantly being remodeled through creation by osteoblasts and degradation by osteoclasts.

102) A. Synovial fluid is a viscous lubricating fluid found in joints. Mucus is a secretion produced by, and covering, membranes such as the digestive tract. Both synovial fluids and mucus are aqueous solutions of proteins.

103) B. Surfactants are organic compounds that lower surface tension of liquids and are typically amphiphilic (both hydrophilic and hydrophobic). Alveoli are the small sac-like structures in lungs that help exchange gases with the blood and are coated by surfactants to help them to inflate easily.

104) D. The diaphragm is the muscular membrane at the base of the lungs, contraction of which allows air to flow into the lungs, by increasing lung volume and decreasing the pressure of air in the lungs relative to the external atmosphere.

105) B. Intercostal muscles are between (inter-) the ribs, which surround the lungs.

106) D. Functional Residual Capacity (FRC) is the volume of air present in the lungs at the end of passive expiration of air due to the elasticity of the lungs. Tidal volume is the volume difference between normal inhalation and exhalation. Total lung capacity is the inspiratory capacity plus the functional residual capacity.

107) A. An increase in carbon dioxide concentration in the blood would create carbonic acid, which could then be removed from the blood by increasing the respiration rate, exchanging the CO_2 with the air.

108) C. An organ is a collection of tissues joined in a structural unit to serve a particular function. Skin covers the surface of the exterior of the body and is considered an organ.

109) B. Keratin is a protein that is present in the skin, is hydrophobic and does not dissolve in water.

110) B. The dermis is located between the epidermis, the dead layer of skin on the outside of the body, and the hypodermis, the inside layer of skin. Bone and muscles are located beneath the skin.

111) D. Humans use sweating and shivering, along with changes in vasoconstriction or dilation to regulate temperature. Increasing respiratory rate to shed heat is typical of an animal like a dog (panting) that cannot sweat.

112) B. An androgen is a chemical that increases and maintains male sex characteristics.

113) A. Leydig cells are found adjacent to the seminiferous tubules in the testicles and produce testosterone in the presence of luteinizing hormone (LH). See also the explanation for question 35. Sertoli cells in the seminiferous tubules help in spermatogenesis.

114) C. The male and female gonads are known as the testes and ovaries, respectively.

115) A. Gametogenesis is the synthesis of gametes, which are the unfertilized haploid sex cells, i.e. sperm and egg.

116) D. Human males do not produce sperm until puberty.

117) C. A primary spermatocyte is a precursor to meiosis I, during which a diploid cell produces two haploid cells, which is a division that reduces the number of chromosomes. Spermatids are produced after meiosis II.

118) B. The acrosome is at the head of the sperm cell and allows the cell to penetrate the ovum.

119) C. The endometrium is the inner lining of the uterus. Ovaries are the female reproductive organs that produce eggs. Fallopian tubes are passages that deliver eggs from the ovaries to the uterus. LH is the hormone that stimulates ovulation. See also the explanation for question 35.

120) D. Meiosis I in a female produces a secondary oocyte and a polar body from a primary oocyte.

121) B. When a female hits puberty, every menstrual cycle one or more primary oocytes undergo meiosis I and create secondary oocytes; menopause is when a female stops producing eggs; and fertilization is when an egg and sperm combine to form a zygote.

122) D. After ovulation, each oocyte continues to metaphase of meiosis II, which is completed only if fertilization occurs. See also the explanation for question 121.

123) C. The corpus luteum is a temporary endocrine structure produced in the ovaries of females after ovulation and is involved in the production of relatively high levels of progesterone and moderate levels of estrogen. This prevents menstruation.

124) C. Ovulation is when the ovary discharges the egg.

125) C. Human chorionic gonadotropin (hCG) is a hormone produced by the embryo after implantation and promotes the maintenance of the corpus luteum (see the explanation for question 123).

126) A. The morula is produced by a series of cleavage divisions of the early embryo, starting with the single-celled zygote. Further development produces a blastula, which is a hollow sphere of cells, which after some cell differentiation produces a blastocyst. See also the explanation for question 121.

127) C. An embryo in an early stage of development has a spherical shape and three layers of cells, the endoderm (inside), mesoderm (middle) and ectoderm (outside) layers, which roughly corresponds to various portion of the body. The ectoderm generally produces organs on the outside of the body, such as the skin. One exception to this rule is the nervous system, which is derived from the ectoderm layer, but is folded into the body during the process of neurulation.

SECTION 5 CONTENT REVIEW PROBLEMS

1) B. Humans have 23 pairs of chromosomes in their diploid cells.

2) C. One chromosome of a homologous pair comes from the mother and one comes from the father. Homologous chromosomes are similar, but not identical, with each carrying the same genes, but potentially having different alleles for each gene.

3) A. The prefix "hetero-" means different and in this case it is referring to the nature of the alleles, i.e. dominant and recessive. If both alleles are recessive, or both are dominant, then it would be homozygous. If there is only one allele then it is hemizygous.

4) C. A genotype represents the specific combination of alleles for an individual, but the phenotype is the specific physical traits that result from the genotype, i.e. brown eyes versus blue eyes. See also the explanation for question 3.

5) B. An allele is a variant form of a gene. See also the explanations for questions 2, 3 and 4.

6) A. Both the A and B blood type alleles are dominant over O, therefore, a child of an AB blood type parent and an O blood type parent (OO genotype) could either have A type blood (AO genotype) or B type blood (BO genotype). Incomplete dominance is when the heterozygous genotype produces a phenotype has traits intermediate between the two homozygous phenotypes. Complete dominance is when a heterozygous individual produces the phenotype of the dominant allele.

7) B. See the explanation for question 6.

8) C. Human males have XY chromosomes, whereas females have XX chromosomes. The Punnett square for this combination produces two XX and two XY offspring, which is a 50% probability for the offspring to be a son.

9) C. The Punnett square is

	X*	X
X	XX*	XX
Y	X*Y	XY

50% of the male offspring should have the disease.

10) C. The Punnett square is

	X*	X
X*	X*X*	X*X
Y	X*Y	XY

50% of the male and 50% of the female offspring should have the disease.

11) D.

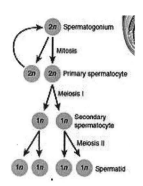

12) A

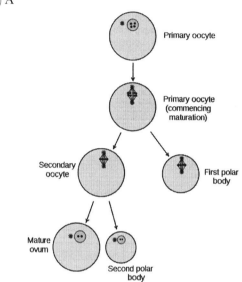

13) B. During meiosis chromosomes duplicate during interphase and homologous chromosomes exchange genetic information, which is known as chromosomal crossover. Conjugation is the transfer of genetic material between bacterial cells by direct contact via a bridge-like connection; transformation is an alteration of the genetic material of a cell from incorporation of exogenous DNA through the cell membrane; and transduction is the process by which DNA is transferred from one bacterium to another by a virus.

14) D. If the woman shows the symptoms of hemophilia, then she must be homozygous. The Punnett square is

	X*	X*
X*	X*X*	X*X
Y	X*Y	X*Y

100% of the offspring, both male and female, will be hemophiliacs.

15) B. A test cross involves breeding of a dominant phenotype of unknown genotype (PP or Pp) with a phenotypically recessive (pp) individual. There are two possible outcomes for this experiment, depending upon the unknown genotype. One of the Punnett squares is

	p	p

P	Pp	Pp
P	Pp	Pp

and 100% of the offspring will display the dominant phenotype and have the Pp genotype. The other possible Punnett square is

	p	p
P	Pp	Pp
p	pp	pp

And 50% of the offspring will display the dominant phenotype.

16) A. The term "disjunction" means to "disjoin" or to separate, therefore "nondisjunction" means to "not disjoin". Ectopic is a type of pregnancy in which the fertilized egg doesn't implant in the uterus; a mutation is when there is an alteration in a DNA sequence; a genetic linkage is the tendency of certain genes to be inherited together.

17) A. The law of independent assortment states that when two or more characteristics are inherited, alleles assort independently, giving different traits an equal opportunity of occurring together. The principle of segregation states that two alleles separate from each other in the formation of gametes; inbreeding is when closely related individuals, like siblings or cousins are involved in sexual reproduction, thereby reducing genetic diversity. Non-Mendelian genetics violate the principle of segregation and law of independent assortment.

18) D. This technique is often used for the production of livestock or pets, in order to preserve a specific trait or body type, i.e. Beagles or Labrador Retrievers.

19) C. A dihybrid cross is a cross between two individuals that differ in two observed traits and there are completely dominant and recessive traits. For example a cross between AABB and aabb parents results in offspring that are all heterozygous for both traits (AaBb). Crossing two AaBb individuals produces a 9:3:3:1 ration of phenotypic possibilities.

20) C. See the explanation for question 16.

21) B. A chromosome in a diploid organism is hemizygous when only one copy is present, as would be the case when a gene is located on a particular sex chromosome (X), but not the other (Y). The term degenerative suggests deterioration. See also the explanations for questions 3 and 6.

22) B. A pedigree is a diagram of family relationships that uses symbols to represent people and lines to represent genetic relationships. In a pedigree, squares represent males and circles represent females.

23) A. A species is a group of organisms that interbreed and produce fertile or viable offspring. Accordingly, one species is distinguished from another when it is not

possible for mating between individuals from different species to produce fertile offspring, i.e. the offspring of a female horse and a male donkey is an infertile mule.

24) B. A gene pool is the set of genetic information for a particular breeding population of a particular species.

25) C. The Hardy-Weinberg population equilibrium theorem states that allele and genotype frequencies in a population will remain constant from generation to generation, assuming: (1) organisms are diploid; (2) only sexual reproduction occurs; (3) generations are non-overlapping; (4) mating is random; (5) population size is infinitely large; (6) allele frequencies are equal in the sexes; (7) there is no migration, mutation or natural selection.

26) B. See the explanation for question 25.

27) C. $p + q = 1$, where p is the frequency of the dominant allele and q is the frequency of the recessive allele. Since p = 0.60, then q = 0.4, or 40%.

28) B. See the explanation for question 27, where q = 0.46, then p = 0.54.

29) B. See the explanation for question 27. In this case p = 0.50 and q = 0.50, and $p^2 + 2pq + q^2 = 1$, where p^2 is the frequency of the homozygous dominant genotype, q^2 is the frequency of the homozygous recessive genotype and 2pq is the frequency of the heterozygous combination, or 2(0.50)(0.50) = 0.50, or 50%.

30) C. See the explanations for questions 27 and 29. In this case q = 0.40 and p = 0.60, therefore $p^2 = 0.6^2 = 0.36$, or 36%.

31) D. See the explanations for questions 27 and 29. In this case 2pq = 0.4, which is an equation that can not be solved without another equation also containing p and q.

32) B. See the explanation for question 25.

33) C. Migration is when individuals in a population move from one geographic location to another and can cause a bifurcation of the gene pool.

34) C. In the context of genetics, "fitness" is related to the production of viable, healthy offspring. See also the explanation for question 23.

35) A. Speciation is the evolutionary process by which new biological species arise.

36) A. Homologous structures are portions of the anatomy that are similar in different species that evolved from a common ancestor. Vestigial structures are the remains of anatomical structures that were present in earlier ancestral species, i.e. the human tailbone and appendix; analogous structures are anatomical structures in different

species that have similar evolutionary functions, but the species are not closely related, i.e. the wing of a bird and the wing of a bat.

37) C. See the explanation for question 36.

38) C. See the explanation for question 36.

39) B. Convergent evolution is the process whereby two organisms not closely related independently evolve similar traits as a result of having to adapt to similar environments or ecological niches, but remain different species.

40) B. Parallel evolution is the production of similar traits in response to similar environmental conditions, starting from two species with a similar ancestral background and usually results from more closely related lineages than in convergent evolution.

41) A. Humans are animals, not plants, fungi, or single celled organisms.

42) C. Chordates are bilaterally symmetric animals that possess a neural chord, pharyngeal slits, and a tail for at least some period of their development. Humans are in the chordate phylum. Animalia is the kingdom of animals, primate is an order, and hominidae is a class.

43) B. A Barr body is the inactive X chromosome in a female's somatic cells.

44) C. The order of taxonomic ranks is: kingdom > phylum > class > order > family > genus > species, or "King Phillip Came Over From Great Spain."

45) D. The order of taxonomic ranks for humans is: Animalia; Chordate; Mammalia, Primate; Hominidae; Homo; and Homo Sapiens.

46) C. The "r-strategy" (r stands for reproductive) involves species that produce many energetically "cheap" offspring and live in unstable environments; "K-strategy" involves species that produce few energetically "expensive" offspring and live in stable environments. Most mammals are considered K-strategists.

47) A. A population bottleneck is a sharp reduction in the size of a population due to environmental events and produces a much smaller and less diverse gene pool. See also the explanation for question 25.

48) B. In evolutionary biology, adaptive radiation occurs when organisms diversify rapidly into new forms, particularly when a change in the environment makes new resources available, creates new challenges, or opens new niches. See also the explanation for question 35. Symbiosis is a mutually beneficial relationship between two species; parasitism is when one species benefits

exclusive from another; and mutualism is the way two organisms of different species exist in a relationship in which both species benefit from the activity of the other.

49) B. See the explanation for question 48. Commensalism is an association between two organisms in which one benefits and the other neither benefits nor is harmed by the relationship.

50) C. See the explanations for question 48 and 49.

51) B. See the explanation for question 42.

52) C. The Punnett square is

	X*	X
X*	X*X*	X*X
Y	X*Y	XY

And there is 50% chance that a daughter will be a hemophiliac.

53) B. And there is 50% chance that a son will be a hemophiliac. See the explanation for question 52.

54) B. The Punnett square is

	X	X*
X	XX	XX*
Y	XY	X*Y

If the mother is a carrier, then half of the male children will be hemophiliacs and half of the female children will be carriers.

55) D. If the disease is dominant then the mother could be either homozygous or heterozygous and have the disease. Either way, 100 % of the children will have the disease. If the disease is recessive, then the mother must be homozygous and again 100 % of the offspring with have the disease.

56) A. See the explanation for question 44.

57) D. Evolution is a change in the genetic traits of biological populations over successive generations; genetic drift is a change in frequency of a gene variant in a population; apoptosis is programmed cell death.

58) D. A diploid dihybrid would have two alleles (A and B) to consider (see the explanation for question 19), with possible combinations of 2^{2n}, where n represents the number of alleles. For example, a dihybrid cross between two AaBb individuals would have sixteen possible combinations (n = 2).

	AB	Ab	aB	ab
AB	AABB	AABb	AaBB	AaBb
Ab	AABb	AAbb	AaBb	Aabb
aB	AaBB	AaBb	aaBB	aaBb
ab	AaBb	Aabb	aaBb	aabb

59) A. See the Punnett square in the explanation for question 58.

60) A. See the explanation for question 4 and the Punnett square in the explanation for question 58.

61) C. See the explanation for question 17. Inbreeding results in an increase in homozygosity, which can increase the chances of offspring being affected by potentially deleterious traits.

62) C. Mendel found in his monohybrid pea crosses, an idealized 3:1 ratio between dominant and recessive phenotypes.

63) C. Outbreeding is when individuals not closely related to a population contribute to genetic diversity of the population. See also the explanations for questions 17 and 61.

64) B. If the mother is a carrier for both diseases, and they are unlinked then one of her X chromosomes will have the recessive genes and one will not ($X^{hd}X$ or X^hX^d). The male father does not have the recessive gene (XY).

	X	X^h	X^d	X^{dh}
X	XX	X^hX	X^dX	$X^{dh}X$
Y	XY	X^hY	X^dY	$X^{dh}Y$

65) A. A niche is an unusual or specific type of environmental condition that is exploited by a particular species in order to proliferate. Darwin was particularly interested in Galápagos Finches (a type of bird) and their adaptations to specific environmental niches as an example of speciation. However, niches are not specific to birds.

66) A. See the explanations for questions 35 and 65. Geographic separation is one common way that two populations can diverge into different species.

67) C. See the Punnett square for the cross of PP and pp shown in the explanation for question 15. See also the explanation for question 3.

68) B. See the explanation for question 4.

69) C. See the explanation for question 15.

70) B. The suffix -metry in nouns refers to procedures and systems corresponding to quantitative measurements, and statistics is the analysis of data.

71) B. A locus, in genetics, is the specific location or position of a specific DNA sequence on a chromosome. See also the explanations for question 2, 3, and 4. A wild type gene is one that is prevalent under natural conditions.

72) C. See the explanation for question 71.

73) A. See the explanation for question 6. Penetrance is the extent to which a gene or set of genes is reflected in the phenotypes of individuals carrying that gene, whereas, expressivity quantifies (a percentage) variations in a phenotype among individuals carrying a particular genotype. For example, penetrance answers the question "If someone has the gene for red hair, what are they odds that they actually have red hair?" whereas expressivity answers the question "If someone has the gene for red hair, will their hair be slightly red or bright red?"

74) D. See the explanation for question 73. Penetrance cannot be determined from a single individual.

75) A. See the explanation for question 73.

76) B. Some of the genes that can be present on the X chromosome are not present in the Y chromosome, which can lead to sex linked traits.

77) D. See the explanation for question 73.

SECTION 6 CONTENT REVIEW PROBLEMS

1) A. Enzymes lower the activation energy and speed up chemical reactions.

2) A. A peptide bond is a C-N bond formed between two amino acids when the carboxyl group of one molecule reacts with the amino group of the other molecule, releasing water (H_2O). Peptides are a type of amide, whose general formula is

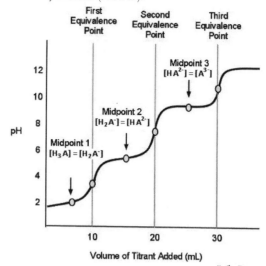

where R' is another amino acid residue and R" is hydrogen.

3) B. Prosthetic groups (cofactors or coenzymes) are non-protein groups, such as vitamins, sugars, lipids or metal ions, required for effective enzymatic action. Holoenzymes are the active forms of enzymes, including any prosthetic groups. Apoenzymes are enzymes that require a cofactor but do not yet have the cofactor. Zwitterions are molecules that have both positively and negatively charged groups, resulting in no net charge.

4) D. The **R** and **S** refer to the absolute configuration around the alpha carbon of an amino acid and are determined by the relative priority of the groups. D and L are determined by the rotation of plane polarized light and do not necessarily correspond to the **R** and **S** configurations. All naturally occurring proteins and polypeptides contain **L** amino acids.

5) C. The lower the pK_a, the more acidic the group and the α-carboxylic acid group is generally the most acidic group in an amino acid.

6) D. The degree to which a weak acid (or base) is protonated depends upon the acid (or base) equilibrium. The strength of the acid (or base), is measured by the pK_a (or pK_b) and the concentration of hydrogen ions (pH) determines the extent of protonation.

7) A. When the pH equals the pI, the net charge of the amino acid is zero. If the pH < pI, then both the amino group and the carboxylate group will be protonated, with the former group being positively charged and the latter being neutral, producing a net positive charge.

8) C. Since there is neither an acidic or basic group on the side chain, the pI will be the average of the two pK_as, $(2.35 + 9.78)/2 = 12.13/2 = 6.05$.

9) B. In this case, since the side chain is acidic, we must average the side chain pK_a and the pK_a of the acid group, giving $(2.05 + 3.86)/2 = 2.97$.

10) C. Shown below is a titration curve for a triprotic acid, such as phosphoric acid (H_2PO_4) with a strong base such as sodium hydroxide (NaOH).

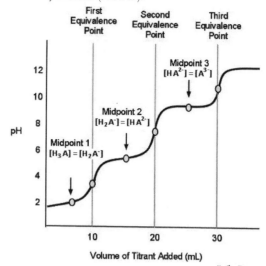

11) B. For any weak acid and its conjugate base the maximum buffer capacity occurs when the pH equal the pK_a.

12) D. In order to form hydrogen bonds the side chain must contain either oxygen or nitrogen atoms bonded to hydrogen or having a lone pair, in order to be either a hydrogen bond donor or acceptor, respectively. Asparagine and glutamine have amide groups as part of their side chains and aspartic acid has a carboxylic acid group as part of its side chain.

13) A. The isoelectric point is the pH where the amino group is protonated and the carboxylic acid group is deprotonated, forming a zwitterion, where there is a positively charged group and a negatively charged group, with a net charge of zero. To experience mobility in an electrophoresis experiment the molecule must have a nonzero net charge.

14) C. Transamination is a chemical reaction that replaces an amine functional group with another amine, or when an amine is replaced by a ketone (C=O). In the transamination of an amino acid, the NH_2 group on one molecule is replaced by a =O group, such that the original amino acid is converted to a keto acid. The structures of aspartic acid and oxaloacetate, both have four carbon atoms. α-ketoglutaric acid has five carbons atoms. Fumaric acid has a carbon-carbon double bond. Succinic acid does not have the appropriate keto group.

Aspartic acid   Oxaloacetate

α-ketoglutaric acid   Fumaric acid

Succinic acid

15) A. The phase "membrane-anchoring domain" in the stem of the question suggests that the group should be hydrophobic. Isoleucine, valine and phenylalanine are all hydrophobic (lipophilic) amino acids.

16) C. An essential amino acid must be supplied in the diet and can not be synthesized by the body from other compounds.

17) B. Enantiomers are optically active molecules that are mirror images, which can rotate plane-polarized light in opposite directions. Epimers are optically active molecules with more than one chiral center, but have opposite configurations at one of the chiral centers. Anomers are epimers of cyclic saccharides that differ in configuration at the hemiacetal/acetal carbon. Diastereomers are stereoisomers that are not mirror images.

18) D. Aspartic acid and glutamic acid would be in their deprotonated (negatively charge) forms at a pH of 8. Neutral amino acids like asparagine, glutamine, leucine, and glycine will not be charged. Basic amino acids, like histidine and lysine may not be completely deprotonated at a pH of 8, since their pK_as are >8.

19) B. Tryptophan, tyrosine and phenylalanine have aromatic p-bonding system in their side chains that could strongly absorb UV light at 280 nm.

20) C. Hydroxyproline is not one of the twenty one proteinogenic amino acids for eukaryotic organisms, while proline and choice A, B and D are.

21) A. A disulfide bond can form between two sulfur atoms that are present in the side chains of cysteines.

22) D. The imidazole group is a five atom aromatic structure containing two nitrogen atoms.

23) A. Coomassie Brilliant Blue is negatively charged and arginine is a basic amino acid that will be positively charged at physiological pHs.

24) D. Specific activity presumably refers to the activity of an enzyme, typically a protein, some of which could be lost or chemically decomposed during a purification process.

25) A. Ion exchange chromatography retains molecules on the stationary phase based on ionic interactions. The stationary phase surface displays ionic functional groups that interact with proteins of opposite charge, with the strength of the interactions being related to the net charge of the protein.

26) A. Gel filtration chromatography (also known as size exclusion chromatography) is a separation based primarily on molecular size, with molecular shape being a secondary consideration for separation when two molecules have similar size, i.e. globular versus fibrous proteins. The stationary phase consists of porous beads with a defined range of pore sizes, where species that are smaller than the pore size are retained on the column longer than molecules that are larger than the pore.

27) A. Affinity chromatography is used to separate biochemical mixtures based on specific interactions such as between antigen and antibody, or enzyme and substrate.

28) A. 1 unit x (1 mmol/s) x (1 / 1.0 µg) x (10^3 µg/mg) = 10^3 units/mg

29) A. Hemoglobin has four tertiary subunits and experiences a cooperative effect, in which the binding of an oxygen molecule to one of the subunits causes a conformational change that makes it easier for more oxygen molecules to bind to the other subunits. The T and R states stand for "tense" and "relaxed", respectively.

30) D. See the explanation for question 29.

31) C. Carbon dioxide also binds to hemoglobin and when dissolved in water, carbon dioxide produces carbonic acid. Reducing the concentration of carbon dioxide in the blood raises the pH and makes more free hemoglobin available to bind oxygen.

32) B. Typically the shape and types of intermolecular interactions of the binding site must match those of the substrate and these properties are determined by the properties of the amino acids that create the active site.

33) B. The primary structure is determined by the sequence of amino acids; the secondary structure is determined by the nature of the non-covalent bonding interactions that typically produce alpha helices and beta sheets; the tertiary structure is determined by how the

secondary structure combines to form various shapes and/or globular structures or subunits; quaternary structures result when the subunits combine to form the overall shape and structure of the protein.

34) C. A signal peptide is a short peptide added at the end of many proteins that leave the cell through the cell membrane by various mechanisms.

35) B. Collagen is a fibrous protein often used in connective tissues such as in bones, muscles, skin and tendons, where it provides strength and structure.

36) B. Cyclins are proteins that help control progression of the cell life cycle by activating kinase (phosphorylation) enzymes.

37) B. p53 is a protein that suppresses tumor growth, such that damage to this protein can lead to cancer development.

38) B. Chaperones proteins assist the folding or unfolding and the assembly or disassembly of other macromolecular structures.

39) D. See the explanations for questions 29 and 33.

40) D. Increasing the concentration of an enzyme speeds up the chemical reaction. Choice A, B and C each essentially increase the concentration of an enzyme in a specific portion of the cell.

41) C. Enzymes do not change the ΔG for a reaction, but do lower the activation energy. The shape of an enzyme is critical for it proper functioning. Catalysts participate in a chemical reaction, but after the reaction is completed, the catalyst is regenerated and available to repeat the process.

42) A. An enzyme can lower the activation energy of a reaction by interacting with a substrate and holding it in the proper orientation so that the activation energy is lowered, resulting in a faster chemical reaction than would otherwise be expected under the given set of conditions.

43) B. If the hydrogen bonding interactions did not occur at regular intervals, then the relatively uniform shape of the alpha helix would not be produced; the hydrogen bonding interactions must be perpendicular to the principle axis of the alpha helix; most of the amino residues in a protein are involved in peptide bond formation; and hydrogen bonding is a type of non-covalent bonding interaction, i.e. Van de Waals bonding.

44) C. Peptide bonds have restricted rotation and are planar due to partial multiple bond character. The trans configuration is energetically more favorable than the cis configuration due to steric interactions. Proline is an amino acid that is often present in naturally occurring

proteins and polypeptides, and hence forms peptide bonds.

45) B. Peptide bond formation is a type of dehydration reaction, such that for each peptide bond formed, the formula for the polymer loses one oxygen atom and two hydrogen atoms. The polypeptide described in the question has nine peptide bonds.

46) D. See the explanation for question 33.

47) A. The preferred coordination number for Fe^{2+} is six. The heme group has four nitrogen atoms that coordinate in a square-planar geometry. One of the axial positions is occupied by the coordination of a nitrogen lone-pair from a histidine and the other position is occupied by the coordination of the lone-pair of electrons from a water molecule.

48) A. Disulfide bonds are usually formed from the oxidation of thiol groups of cysteine residues in proteins, which would be facilitated under aerobic aqueous conditions, external to the cell.

49) D. Immunoglobulin G (IgG) is a type of antibody, being a protein complex composed of four peptide chains, two of which are heavy and two are light, arranged in a Y-shape. Each IgG has two antigen binding sites. Antibody fragmentation can be accomplished using reducing agents to cleave disulfide bonds and proteases that cleave certain portions of the protein and produce active fragments, such as F_{ab} and F_c. These fragments can be used in immunoassays.

50) D. Antibodies produced by the immune system respond to various types of infections. See also the explanation for question 49.

SECTION 7 CONTENT REVIEW PROBLEMS

1) C. During replication, two new DNA molecules are produced from the original DNA molecule by reading base pair combinations. Transcription is the process in which mRNA is produced from nuclear DNA; translation is the process in which proteins are produced from RNA; and gene expression is associated with a particular genetic trait.

2) B. See the explanation for question 1.

3) A. Prokaryotes do not have membrane-bound organelles and hence do not have a nucleus. The only membrane in a prokaryote is the cell membrane, whereas eukaryotes have both a cell membrane and a nuclear membrane.

4) D. Nucleic acids are polymers of nucleotides, which are comprised of nucleosides (a nitrogenous base such as A, C, G, T or U and a five-carbon sugar) and a single phosphate group. A nucleoside triphosphate (ATP or GTP) is a high-energy molecule associated with energy transfer.

5) A. The numbering of the carbon atoms in the five-carbon sugar starts with the glycosidic carbon next to the oxygen in the five atom ring, which is bonded to the base (adenine) as shown in the nucleotide below. The phosphate which is bonded to the 5' carbon then forms an additional ester linkage with the 3-hydroxyl of the next nucleotide.

6) B. DNA is synthesized from the 5' end to the 3' end which must have a free hydroxyl group. See also the explanation for question 5.

7) D. There are $4^3 = 64$ possibilities. Note that $3^4 = 81$ and is not one of the answer choices.

8) C. Base-pairs interact by way of hydrogen bonding, not the phosphate groups.

9) A. The planar aromatic bases interact due to temporary dipoles created by the movement of electron density in the p-ring systems.

10) A. There are two hydrogen bonding interactions for the A-T base pair combination, whereas there are three hydrogen bonding interactions in the C-G combination, therefore it takes more energy to break the hydrogen bonding interactions of the C-G combination.

11) A. Naturally occurring DNA is right handed. Imagine that DNA is a screw, and the strands are the grooves in the screw. Imagine using a screwdriver to screw the DNA into a piece wood, the direction you twist the screwdriver determines the handedness.

12) D. There are a fewer number of hydrogen bonding interactions per molecule with more A/T content.

13) A. DNA replication. The double helix of the parent molecule is unwound and each of these original strands acts as a template for a daughter strand. Bases of the nucleotides are matched appropriately to synthesize the new strands.

14) D. See the explanations for question 4 and 13.

15) C. The hydrogen bonding interactions in the double helix structure of DNA are thermodynamically more stable than the uncoiled single stranded form and therefore require energy to break the hydrogen bonds. Topoisomerases are enzymes that regulate the degree of winding of DNA by cutting the phosphate backbone allowing the DNA to be untangled. At the end of the replication processes, the DNA backbone must be resealed to form two daughter DNA strands. Helicases are enzymes whose function is to move along the DNA phosphate backbone and separate the two annealed strands using energy from ATP.

16) B. New DNA is synthesized in the 5' to 3' direction, but the original strand is read in the 3' to 5' direction. See also the explanation for question 6.

17) C. Endonucleases are a class of enzymes that cleave the phosphodiester bond at various spots within a polynucleotide. Exonucleases are enzymes that specifically cleave nucleotides, one at a time, from the end of a polynucleotide. DNA primase is an enzyme that synthesizes a short RNA primer that allows the initiation of DNA polymerization. DNA ligases are a type of enzyme that joins DNA strands by catalyzing the formation of phosphodiester bonds. See also the explanation for question 15.

18) A. See the explanations for questions 5, 6, 16 and 17.

19) C. DNA Polymerase I, II and III are all found in prokaryotes, but DNA polymerase III is the primary enzyme complex involved in prokaryotic DNA replication. The stem of the question specifically asks about "DNA replication", not RNA synthesis.

20) D. This question requires a highly specific knowledge of background information and would most likely be part

of a passage. DNA gyrase is most often used in prokaryotes, whose circular DNA is cut by DNA gyrase to relieve strain.

21) B. Primase is an enzyme that synthesizes short RNA sequences called primers that serve as a starting point for DNA synthesis.

22) B. See the explanations for questions 15 and 17.

23) A. See the explanations to question 16.

24) C. See the explanations for questions 5 and 6.

25) B. Both strands of DNA must be replicated.

26) A. The sugar in RNA is ribose, whereas the in DNA it is deoxyribose. The hydroxyl groups on the 3' and 5' carbons are essential for the phosphodiester bonds in both polymers. It is the hydroxyl group on the second carbon that is removed in DNA. See also the explanations for questions 5 and 6.

27) D. RNA is typically single stranded in both prokaryotes and eukaryotes, however, some viruses have double stranded RNA. RNA is produced by transcription of DNA. Messenger RNA (mRNA) is degraded relatively quickly after translation, compared with transfer RNA (tRNA) degradation.

28) B. See the explanations for questions 13, 15 and 27. The double stranded DNA must be unwound and the hydrogen bonding interactions broken over the section containing the needed gene, such that during transcription the base-pair combinations between the DNA and the mRNA that is being synthesized can be formed.

29) D. Transcriptional regulation is important for the functioning of a cell and controls the conversion of DNA to RNA, thereby orchestrating gene activity. A single gene can be regulated in many ways, from altering the number of copies of RNA that are transcribed, to the moment in time, in response to a stimulus, when the gene is transcribed. See also the explanation for question 28.

30) A. Promoters are DNA sequences located in the 5' region adjacent to the transcriptional start site. RNA polymerase and accessory proteins must recognize and bind to the promoter to initiate production of an mRNA transcript.

31) C. The thymine that is present in DNA, is replaced by uracil in RNA. See also the explanation for question 4.

32) C. The coding strand sequence is not the same as the sequence in the RNA because of the required base-pair combinations A-U and C-G.

33) B. A palindromic sequence reads the same backward or forward, and often results in hairpin loops that are important for transcriptional termination. The hairpin loops are formed due to hydrogen bonding interactions, not covalent bonds. Consensus sequences are important for the binding of RNA polymerase to the proper positions in the DNA so that the appropriate mRNAs can be formed.

34) B. Use of the drug would kill the bacteria that were not resistant to the drug, but would not affect the mutated form that is resistant. Bacteria are prokaryotes, therefore it is unclear how this drug would affect eukaryotic cells.

35) D. 7-Methylguanosine is a modified purine nucleoside that plays a role in RNA as a blocking group at the 5′ end for most eukaryotic cells in which the mRNA must be protected while it is transported from the nucleus to the rough endoplasmic reticulum.

36) A. Polyadenylation is the addition of a poly(A) tail to the 3' end of an mRNA and helps prevent degradation of the RNA while being transferred from the nucleus to the ribosomes in eukaryotic cells.

37) C. It is possible to splice together a given RNA sequence in several different ways. This is known as alternative splicing.

38) C. The transcription units are transcribed by RNA polymerase I into giant RNA molecules, primary transcripts, which are processed into the mature rRNAs. Prokaryotes don't the same rRNA as eukaryotes.

39) A. A single strand of a nucleic acid has a phosphoryl end, attached to the 5' end, and a hydroxyl on the 3' end. These define the 5' → 3' direction. See also the explanations for question 5 and 6. There are three reading frames that can be read in this 5'→3' direction, each beginning from a different nucleotide in a triplet or codon.

40) C. Codons are a group of three nucleotides.

41) C. The start codon is AUG and the stop codons are UAG, UGA are UAA.

42) A. Aminoacyl-tRNA synthetase is an enzyme that attaches the appropriate amino acid onto the 3' end of tRNA. Peptidyl transferase forms peptide bonds between adjacent amino acids using tRNAs during the translation process of protein biosynthesis.

43) D. The net reaction is:

amino acid + ATP + tRNA ↔
    aminoacyl-tRNA + AMP + PP_i (diphosphate)

44) A. Regulation at the level of transcription is the most common method of regulation.

45) A. A start codon always codes for methionine in eukaryotes and a modified Met in prokaryotes. By far the most common start codon in eukaryotes is AUG. AAA and AAG code for lysine. N-formylmethionine and trimethyllysine are derivatives of methionine and lysine, respectively, and do not have codons.

46) B. The 30S (large) subunit binds to the mRNA template at a purine-rich region, the Shine-Dalgarno sequence, upstream of the AUG initiation codon.

47) D. The initiator tRNA is a distinct species ($tRNA_i^{Met}$) from the tRNA that delivers methionine during translation. Initiation of translation begins when $tRNA^{met}$ binds to a peptidyl binding site, or P site and the various subunits of the ribosome are assembled. At this point, the aminoacyl site (A site) and the E sites are empty. Subsequently, an appropriate aminoacyl-tRNA molecule binds to the A site, the peptide bond is formed, and the RNAs shift positions, P to E and A to P, freeing up the A site so that a new charged tRNA can occupy the A site and continue the process.

48) D. Two GTPs are used in the direct formation of a peptide bond. One ATP is converted to AMP and P_iP_i when the tRNA is charged. This is equivalent to two more high-energy bonds. See also the explanation for question 43.

49) D. The suffix "-ase" in peptidyl transferase implies that it is acting as an enzyme. The pepti- prefix suggests that this enzyme has something to do with peptide bond formation, which is the key to forming proteins in ribosomes.

SECTION 8 CONTENT REVIEW PROBLEMS

1) B. If the enthalpy of unfolding is positive then the enthalpy of folding must be negative, with the later favoring the process. At low temperatures most proteins spontaneously adopt a structure that results from folding, whereas at high temperatures the protein spontaneously can be denatured or unfolded.

2) B. London dispersion forces result from temporary dipoles created by the uneven distribution of electron density around an atom or molecule. LD forces are the weakest of all intermolecular forces and are present in all atoms and molecules.

3) C. Protein folding produces alpha helices and beta sheets in the secondary structure and further interactions in the tertiary and quaternary structures that generally produce the hydrophobic interior regions of globular proteins.

4) D. Addition of a catalyst would lower the activation energy and speed up the process. For the reaction

$$P_f <==> P_u$$

Where P_f and P_u are the folded and unfolded species, the mid-point of the temperature transition curve does represent equal amounts of the reactants and products, which means $[P_f] = [P_u]$ and $K_{eq} = [P_f]/[P_u] = 1$. Since $\Delta G° = -RT \ln K_{eq}$, and since the natural logarithm of one is zero, then $\Delta G = 0$.

5) B. The positively and negatively charged amino acids would most likely be on the exterior of the protein's globular structure so that they would be in a hydrophilic environment, but this does not mean they could not sometimes be on the inside, which is usually hydrophobic. Likewise hydrophobic amino acids would most likely be on the inside, but could also occasionally be on the outside. Tyrosine is a polar amino acid, with a phenol functional group, which would favor a hydrophilic environment.

6) C. The natural logarithm of 10 is 2.3. Since the equation has a negative sign (-RT), the free energy change becomes more negative (goes down) as the equilibrium constant increases.

7) A. Denaturing does not change the order in which the amino acids are attached to each other by peptide bonds and just affects the relatively weak interactions that are responsible to secondary, tertiary and quaternary structures.

8) D. Hydrogen bonding is a type of electrostatic interaction that is typically stronger than dipole-dipole interactions.

9) B. if $\Delta G = \Delta H - T\Delta S$ and $\Delta H = 0$, then $\Delta G = 0 - T\Delta S$.

10) D. Coupling a nonspontaneous reaction with other spontaneous reactions that have free energies that are more negative than the nonspontaneous reaction will make the overall process spontaneous. Note that $\Delta G°$ is under standard conditions with the concentration of reactants and products being 1 M, whereas ΔG is not under standard conditions and the relative concentrations of reactants and products could produce a spontaneous reaction.

11) D. The $\Delta G°$ means a Gibbs free energy change, or the free energy difference between the final (products) and initial (reactants) states of the reaction under standard conditions (indicated by the ° symbol), which are 1 M solutions, 1 atm of pressure and 273 K.

12) A. $\Delta G° = G_f° - G_i°$
If the free energy of the products is greater than the reactants, then the difference will be positive, and the reactants are more thermodynamically stable than the products, making the reaction nonspontaneous and the equilibrium constant will be a value smaller than one. When K < 1, generally the concentration of products are smaller than reactants at equilibrium and we say the reactants are favored. See also the explanation for question 4.

13) D. The folded structure is more ordered than the unfolded structure, with the later having more entropy.

14) D. Since glycolysis produces energy that is stored in the form of the high-energy molecule ATP, by combining the lower energy molecule ADP and phosphate. Effective regulation would result from feedback when ATP concentrations are high which mechanistically occurs by way of allosteric inhibition of the enzyme by ATP and allosteric stimulation when ADP concentrations are high.

15) A. Catabolism is a form of metabolism in which molecules are broken down to produce energy. If the energy is not stored in other molecules, then it is released from the system, in the form of heat. Glycolysis is the metabolic pathway that converts glucose into pyruvate, with the production of the high-energy molecules ATP and NADH, not $NADP^+$.

16) A. There are ten separate steps (chemical reactions) in the glycolysis pathway, three of which have large negative Gibbs free energy changes and are thus irreversible reactions that drive the overall process towards the ultimate products.

17) C. See the explanation for question 15.

18) B. A kinase is an enzyme that catalyzes the transfer of phosphate groups from high-energy phosphate-donating molecules, like ATP, to specific substrates.

19) B. The formula for glucose ($C_6H_{12}O_6$) has six carbon atoms, whereas the formula for pyruvate ($C_3H_4O_3$) has three carbons atoms. Hence two pyruvate molecules are produced per glucose molecule.

20) C. Glycogen synthase, also known as glycosyltransferase, catalyzes the reaction of uridine diphosphate glucose (UDP-glucose) and short polymers of glucose and converts them into long polymers of glycogen.

21) A. See the explanation of question 20.

22) C. Glycolysis or anaerobic respiration occurs in the cytosol, whereas aerobic respiration occurs in the mitochondria.

23) C. The glycolysis pathway reduces NAD^+ to NADH.

24) B. Diffusion tends to be a relatively slow and is a nonspecific process that does not provide a mechanism for regulation.

25) C. Phosphofructokinase is a kinase enzyme that phosphorylates fructose 6-phosphate, so that it can participate in glycolysis. See the explanations for questions 14, 15 and 18.

26) D. See the explanation for question 25. Fructose-1,6-bisphosphatase is an enzyme that converts fructose-1,6-bisphosphate back to fructose 6-phosphate, which can then not participate in glycolysis.

27) D. Glycogen can be stored in both the liver and in muscles. Reversal of the glycogen synthesis process will produce glucose 6-phosphate by way of phosphorylation.

28) A. See the explanation for question 27. It is not necessary to transfer the glucose 6-phosphate from the muscles into the blood, since it will be used directly to produce energy.

29) C. Unlike starch, which is a linear polymer of glucose, with only α-1,4 linkages, glycogen is a branched polymer of glucose with both α-1,4 and α-1,6 linkages. β-1,4 linkages are found in cellulose, which can not be easily metabolized by eukaryotic cells.

30) A. Oxidative phosphorylation is the metabolic pathway in which mitochondria use the energy released by the Krebs cycle and electron transport chain to form ATP. The energy released by electrons flowing through the electron transport chain is used to transport protons across the inner mitochondrial membrane, which simultaneously generates a pH gradient and an electrical potential due to differences in charges on either side of the membrane.

31) D. Commitment steps are thermodynamically irreversible, and furthermore, the hydrolysis reaction removes the product, such that it can not undergo the reverse reaction. The initial thiokinase reactions could form acyl-CoA compounds regardless of the number of carbon atoms in the fatty acid. Acyl-CoA is a group of coenzymes involved in the metabolism of fatty acids and is a temporary compound formed when coenzyme A attaches to the end of a long-chain fatty acid.

32) A. The first step in the oxidation of an alcohol is the formation of an aldehyde. In the case of methanol (CH_3OH), the product is formaldehyde (CH_2O).

33) C. Both NAD^+ and FAD are reduced to NADH and $FADH_2$ in the Krebs cycle and feed into the electron transport chain. Lactate fermentation and glycolysis both involve reduction of NAD^+ to NADH, but do not involve FAD.

34) B. See the explanation for question 15.

35) D. Coenzyme Q is a hydrophobic, vitamin-like substance containing a benzoquinone-like functional group that readily accepts and donates electrons. Coenzyme Q is a component of the electron transport chain of aerobic respiration.

36) A. The Krebs cycle is an aerobic process that requires the presence of elemental oxygen. Glycolysis, substrate-level phosphorylation and fermentation are anaerobic processes.

37) A. The balanced reaction is $C + O_2 \rightarrow CO_2$.

38) A. Lactic acid is produced pyruvate under anaerobic respiration conditions. See also the explanation for question 15.

39) B. See the diagram below.

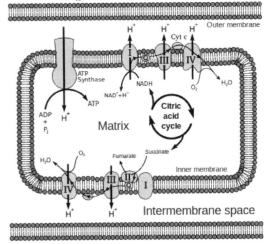

40) B. Pyruvate is the product of glycolysis and is the feedstock for the Krebs cycle. See also the explanations for questions 15 and 22.

41) C. See the explanation for question 31. Carnitine transports long-chain acyl groups from fatty acids into the mitochondrial matrix.

42) B. Each cycle of beta-oxidation of a fatty acid produces one acetyl-CoA, removing two carbon atoms from the fatty acid, as well as producing the reduced forms of $FADH_2$ and NADH.

43) B. The acetyl portion of acetyl-CoA has two carbon atoms that are derived from the catabolic process. Each round of beta-oxidation removes two carbon atoms from the fatty acid to form new acetyl-CoA that enters the Krebs cycle.

44) A. In the Krebs cycle, ascorbic acid gets oxidized to carbon dioxide, donating its electrons to the production of NADH, and therefore ascorbic acid is a reducing agent.

45) A. Biotin is a B vitamin that is involved in the synthesis of fatty acids.

46) D. The key word here is hormone. Lipase, pepsin, and amylase are enzymes used in the digestion of fats, proteins and sugars, respectively.

47) D. Folic acid is a synthetically produced food supplement and must be reduced to its active form of tetrahydrofolate, which is a B vitamin involved in numerous biological functions.

48) C. Vitamin A is a group of unsaturated lipophilic nutritional compounds including retinol and beta-carotene, which are thought to help maintain good vision.

49) B. Vitamins A, D, E, and K are all lipophilic compounds, whereas vitamin C (ascorbic acid) is hydrophilic.

50) B. FAD stands for flavin adenine dinucleotide.

SECTION 9 CONTENT REVIEW PROBLEMS

1) A. The structure of cholesterol is shown below.

2) B. Molecules or ions can be actively transported across a cell membrane by transmembrane proteins. An integral membrane protein is a type of protein that is permanently attached to the biological membrane, including transmembrane proteins.

3) A. The fluid mosaic model describes a cell membrane as a fluid comprised mainly of a phospholipid bilayer, with additional complexity provided by various other molecules such as cholesterol, proteins and carbohydrates that contribute to the overall structure and function of the membrane, similar to a mosaic painting.

4) C. Phospholipids contain two long hydrocarbon tails and ionic heads, making them both hydrophilic and hydrophobic (amphi- means "both"). Amphoteric molecules can act as both acids and bases.

5) A. Pinocytosis is a form of endocytosis, in which the cell brings fluids and small particles into the cell by invagination. Prokaryotes do not absorb materials by way of endocytosis.

6) A. The prefix exo- indicates that material is exiting the cell.

7) D. Active transport, i.e. proton pumping moves ions or molecules in a specific direction across a cell membrane against a concentration gradient and requires the expenditure of energy, usually in the form of ATP.

8) A. Passive transport involves the movement of ions or molecules in the direction of a gradient and does not require additional metabolic energy. Passive diffusion can involve protein channels, but can also occur directly through the cell membrane, as in the case of oxygen and carbon dioxide.

9) A. Peptidoglycan is a polymer consisting of amino acids (pepti-) and short polymers of sugars (-gly-) that form a mesh-like layer outside the plasma membrane of most bacteria, forming the cell wall. Oligosaccharides are relatively small carbohydrate polymers, whereas polysaccharides are large carbohydrate polymers.

10) A. The smooth endoplasmic reticulum lacks ribosomes and functions in lipid manufacture and metabolism. The rough endoplasmic reticulum is involved in protein synthesis.

11) D. Membranes define the boundaries of both prokaryotic and eukaryotic cells, as well as organelles such as the nucleus and mitochondria. The cell membrane and transmembrane proteins allow certain molecules to selectively pass through the membrane, while excluding others. See also the explanation for question 3.

12) D. Glycerophospholipids are sometimes simply referred to as phospholipids. Sphingolipids are a class of lipids often found in the cell membranes of the nervous system and play important roles in signal transmission and cell recognition. Sterols are the precursors to steroid hormones, and cholesterol is a sterol.

13) A. Arachidonic acid is an important polyunsaturated omega-6 fatty acid found in peanut oil.

14) C. Acetyl-CoA formed from either pyruvate (glycolysis) or from fatty acids (b-oxidation), enters the Krebs Cycle when it is joined to oxaloacetate to produce citrate. The decarboxylation of pyruvate to acetyl-CoA is a thermodynamically irreversible reaction.

15) A. See the explanation for question 4.

16) D. The solvent is water. The carboxylic acid groups (heads) are hydrophilic and the hydrocarbon chains (tails) are hydrophobic.

17) C. Chylomicrons are small milk like materials consisting of lipoprotein particles that contain primarily triglycerides, with lesser amounts of phospholipids, cholesterol and proteins. They transport lipids from the intestines to other locations in the body, by way of the lymph and circulatory systems.

18) B. Vitamin A is a group of unsaturated lipophilic nutritional compounds including retinol (structure shown below) and beta-carotene, which are thought to help maintain good vision.

Retinol

See also the explanations for questions 1 and 12. Cholesterol is a lipid and one of the components of bile.

19) C. A catecholamine is an organic compound that has a catechol and a side-chain amine. Catechol is a common name for the 1,2-dihydroxybenzene group. Biologically important catecholamines include the neurotransmitter

dopamine and the hormones epinephrine (adrenaline), and norepinephrine (noradrenaline).

20) B. The stem of the question specifically refers to "tyrosine kinase receptors", therefore choice A can be eliminated. Tyrosine is an amino acid and kinases phosphorylate various molecules. GDP stands for guanosine-diphosphate and is a nucleoside. To eliminate choice D as a possible allosteric cofactor, you would need to have very specific background knowledge concerning the function of the SH2 domain of this protein or information from a passage.

21) A. Paracrine signaling is a form of cellular communication in which a signal induces changes in nearby cells.

22) D. Adenylate cyclase is a class of enzymes, as indicated by the -ase suffix, that catalyzes the conversion of ATP into cAMP. Testosterone, insulin and thyroxin are all hormones.

23) A. Phosphorylation is a chemical process in which a phosphate group is added to another molecule, such as nucleosides or proteins, often forming a phosphate ester, which changes the shape, energetics and function of an enzyme.

24) C. G proteins, also known as guanine nucleotide-binding proteins, are a family of proteins that act as molecular switches inside cells, and are involved in transmitting signals from a variety of stimuli outside a cell to its interior. They are switched on when bound to GTP, and they are switched off when they are bound to GDP.

25) C. Primary signaling molecules are species such as hormones that travel through the circulatory system to a specific organ and bind to a receptor on cells of that organ in order to induce the G-proteins to transfer information across the cell membrane and into the cell.

26) C. Nitric oxide (NO) is a highly reactive molecule, being a radical. If it could not pass through membranes, it couldn't get into lung cells and affect them, either.

27) D. The "surface" of a cell is defined by the cell membrane, not the nuclear membrane.

28) B. If the signaling molecule is hydrophilic, it would not be able to cross the cell membrane by itself. Therefore, it would have to bind to a receptor on the outside surface of the cell membrane, triggering a protein to produce a signal cascade across the cell membrane to produce a response.

29) A. See the explanation for question 22.

30) D. Nitric oxide (NO) is a soluble gas continuously synthesized from the amino acid L-arginine in endothelial cells and is responsible for vascular dilation. Smooth muscle cells surround blood vessels and receive stimulus from the endothelial cells in order to maintain homeostasis.

31) A. Insulin stimulates the conversion of excess blood glucose into glycogen, to be temporarily stored in muscles, or the liver. Insulin is produced in the pancreas.

32) D. Oxygen is reduced at the end of oxidative phosphorylation. NADH and $FADH_2$ are oxidized to NAD and FAD, respectively. Fatty acids are oxidized in the mitochondria during normal metabolism.

33) D. See the explanations for questions 20, 24 and 28. Kinases can phosphorylate proteins and like GTP, in this mechanism the phosphorylated proteins induce the transmembrane protein to transduce the signal.

34) B. A phospholipase is an enzyme that hydrolyzes phospholipids. The products described in the stem of the question, inositol triphosphate (IP_3) and diacylglycerol (in other words a diglyceride) would be components of a phospholipid. See also the explanation for question 20 concerning kinases.

35) A. Signal transduction occurs when an extracellular signaling molecule, such as a hormone or first messenger binds to and activates a specific receptor located on the cell surface, causing a signal to be transmitted into the cell by a transmembrane protein, such as a G-protein, resulting in the production of intracellular second messenger molecules.

36) C. "Signal integration" can provide either enhanced or inhibitory combinations. See the explanation for question 35 for an explanation of "signal transduction." "Signal reception" is the receiving of a signal. "Signal amplification" would only produce an enhanced effect.

37) D. Leucine is non-polar and thus leucine residues are more likely to be found in a non-polar environment such as the inside of the lipid bilayer.

38) D. The prostaglandins (PG) are a group of lipids having diverse hormone-like effects and are derived from fatty acids such as arachidonic acid. See also the explanation for question 21.

39) C. Adrenaline is a hydrophilic molecule that binds to G-protein coupled receptors. See the explanations for questions 19, 26 and 28. Nitric oxide is not a hormone. Progesterone and estrogen are steroidal hormones derived from cholesterol that readily diffuse across the cell membrane.

40) A. A hormone is any member of a class of signaling molecules produced by glands that are transported by the circulatory system to target distant organs and regulates

processes. A first messenger is an extracellular substance, such as a hormone or neurotransmitter that binds to a cell-surface receptor and initiates intracellular activity, whereas second messengers are molecules that relay signals to target molecules in the cytosol and/or nucleus.

41) B. The function of ATPase is to transport a variety of different compounds, like sodium ions, across a membrane using ATP hydrolysis for energy. In nerve cells this creates a resting potential due to the sodium gradient created by pumping sodium ions out of the cell.

42) A. Second messengers are either produced enzymatically, as in the case of cAMP (see the explanation for question 22) or released from intracellular components, as in the case of calcium ions.

43) A. Desmosomes link two cells together, while hemidesmosomes attach one cell to the extracellular matrix of the skin. Gap junctions are intercellular connections between cells that connect the cytoplasm of two cells, allowing various molecules, ions and electrical impulses to directly pass through a regulated gate between the cells. Tight junctions seal adjacent epithelial cells together and prevent the passage of molecules and ions through the space between cells.

44) C. See the explanation for question 5.

45) C. The resting membrane potential of a neuron is slightly negative, which means that the inside of the neuron has less electrical potential energy to move current (positive charges) than the outside. At rest, relatively speaking, there are more sodium ions outside the neuron and more potassium ions inside that neuron.

46) C. See the explanation for question 12. Gangliosides, cerebrosides, and sphingomyelin all are associated with the nervous system. Phosphatidylserine is an important phospholipid that plays a key role in cell cycle signaling.

47) A. Osmosis is a spontaneous process in which water moves across a semipermeable membrane due to a concentration gradient of a solute that is not permeable. Active transport requires energy and moves species against a concentration or electrical gradient. Symport is when two solutes are pumped in the same direction across a membrane and antiport is when two solutes are pumped in opposite directions across a membrane.

48) D. Note the prefix "glycol-" which has to do with "sugar." The glycocalyx is a glycoprotein-polysaccharide covering that surrounds the cell membranes of some bacteria, whereas phospholipids would be part of the cell membrane.

49) A. A neuromuscular junction is a chemical synapse formed by the contact between a motor neuron and a muscle fiber. Acetylcholine is released for the neuron and binds to receptors on the muscle cell which then stimulates a twitch in the fiber. Acetylcholine serves as the ligand for the ligand-gated receptor on the postsynaptic membrane.

50) D. See the explanation for question 42. Phospholipase C is a class of enzymes that cleave phospholipids and plays an important role in signal transduction pathways.

FINAL EXAM CONTENT REVIEW PROBLEMS

1) A. The side chains (R) attached to the alpha carbon of amino acids create a chiral center. Glycine does not have a side chain (R = H) and hence is not chiral.

2) B. Tyrosine has a phenol as the functional group in its side chain, which is polar and hydrophilic.

3) C. Cysteine has a thiol (R-SH) functional group and upon oxidation can form disulfide bonds.

4) D. All amino acids contain an amino group (R-NH$_2$) and an organic acid group (R-CO$_2$H). An imide is a functional group consisting of two acyl groups bound to nitrogen; an alkene is an organic compound with a carbon-carbon double bond; and ether is a functional group in which two alkyl groups are bonded to an oxygen atom.

5) C. Proline's side chain forms a cyclic structure that includes the amino group, which restricts the degrees of freedom of movement for this amino acid.

6) A. Leucine is a hydrophobic amino acid with an aliphatic isobutyl group as the side chain.

7) D. Each of these amino acids has an aromatic ring structure in its side chain. None of these amino acids are acidic; tryptophan does have a nitrogen atom in its side chain; and none of these amino acids have imide functional groups.

8) C. Glutamate is the deprotonated form of glutamic acid, i.e. the food additive monosodium glutamate (MSG).

9) C. The adrenal cortex produces aldosterone, which plays a central role in the regulation of blood pressure. Epinephrine, or adrenaline, is produced by the adrenal medulla. Oxytocin and antidiuretic hormone (ADH, also known as ADH or Vasopressin) are produced in the hypothalamus of the brain.

10) A. Calcitonin acts to reduce blood calcium ion concentrations, opposing the effects of parathyroid hormone.

11) A. See the explanation for question 9. Vasopressin regulates the body's retention of water by acting to increase reabsorption in the kidney's collecting ducts. Luteinizing hormone (LH) is a sex glycoprotein hormone produced by the pituitary gland that triggers ovulation in females. Erythropoietin is a hormone secreted by the kidneys that increases the production of red blood cells (erythrocytes). Aldosterone increases reabsorption of both ions and water.

12) D. Thyroid-stimulating hormone (TSH) is a glycoprotein hormone produced by the pituitary gland that stimulates the production of hormones by the thyroid gland. Triiodothyronine (T3) is a thyroid hormone derived from tyrosine; Norepinephrine, or noradrenaline is a catecholamine derived from tyrosine; Cortisol is a steroid hormone produced by the adrenal cortex.

13) C. Estrogen is a female steroid hormone derived from cholesterol. See the explanation for question 11; human growth hormone (hGH) is a peptide hormone produced by the anterior pituitary gland; prolactin is a protein hormone produced by the pituitary gland that, and as the name implies, is associated with the production of milk.

14) C. Glucagon is the hormone that signals the production of glucose from glycogen and other sources (gluconeogenesis), when blood sugar levels are too low. Insulin signals the conversion of glucose to glycogen, when blood glucose levels are too high. See also the explanations for questions 9 and 13.

15) C. Insulin is produced in the pancreas. See the explanation for question 13. T4 is similar to T3 (see the explanation for question 12), except that it has four iodine atoms, rather than three.

16) B. See the explanations for questions 9 and 12. Epinephrine is also a catechol amine. Follicle-stimulating hormone (FSH) is a glycoprotein hormone produced by the pituitary gland. Adrenocorticotropic hormone (ACTH) is a polypeptide hormone produced by the pituitary gland. Parathyroid hormone (PTH) is a polypeptide hormone.

17) B. See the explanations for questions 9, 12, and 13.

18) C. Mitosis is a process in which chromosomes in a cell nucleus are separated into two identical sets of chromosomes, and each set ends up in its own nucleus. An acronym for the steps of mitosis is PMAT.

19) A. Interphase includes two growth phases and a synthesis phase, G1, S and G2.

20) D. Transcription is the process in which RNA is produced from DNA in the nucleus of eukaryotic cells.

21) C. Translation is the process in which mRNA is read and produces appropriately coded proteins in the ribosomes of the rough endoplasmic reticulum.

22) B. rRNA is ribosomal RNA, which like all RNA is produced from DNA in the nucleus of eukaryotic cells. This occurs in the nucleolus, the largest substructure in the nucleus; it assembles ribosomal subunits.

23) D. The electron transport system involves the pumping of hydrogen ions across the inner membrane of the mitochondria in order to establish both a potential

and concentration gradient that helps drive ATP synthesis.

24) A. Hydrolytic enzymes break down molecules by way of hydrolysis reactions. Apoptosis is programmed cell death and involves autolysis, which is self-digestion through the action of a cell's own enzymes. Mitosis is a process in which asexual reproduction of a cell results and involves the synthesis on new nucleic acids.

25) B. Microfilaments or actin filaments are the thinnest filaments of the cytoskeleton, a structure found in the cytoplasm of eukaryotic cells. Myosin is a protein found in muscles and is responsible for movement. Tubulin is protein that forms microtubules, which are also a major component of the eukaryotic cytoskeleton. Collagen is a protein found in the bones, muscles, skin and tendons, where it forms a scaffold to provide strength and structure.

26) B. A centriole is a small set of microtubules arranged in a specific way within the centrosome, which is the organelle in which the microtubules get organized. The mitotic spindle is comprised of microtubules that help segregate the chromosome during mitosis.

27) D. Connective tissue connects, supports, binds, or separates other tissues or organs and includes bone, ligament, tendon, cartilage, fat, and blood.

28) D. An organelle is located within a cell and typically has its own plasma membrane, as does mitochondria. Ribosomes in eukaryotic cells are part of the organelle known as the endoplasmic reticulum. Both eukaryotes and prokaryotes have plasma membranes, which are not organelles.

29) D. The smooth ER is responsible for the synthesis of lipids; the nucleus is where nucleic acids such as DNA and RNA are synthesized; lysosomes are organelles containing enzymes capable of breaking down most biological molecules; the rough ER is where proteins are synthesized.

30) A. Peptidoglycan is a polymer consisting of sugars and amino acids that forms a mesh-like layer outside the plasma membrane of most bacteria; chitin is a polymer of an N-acetylglucosamine and is a component of the cell walls of fungi and the exoskeletons of arthropods; actin is a globular multi-functional protein that forms microfilaments; tubulin is a protein that forms microtubules which are a component of the cytoskeleton.

31) B. See the explanation for question 30.

32) C. Bacteria are prokaryotes and do not have organelles. Besides producing some ATP by glycolysis, bacteria can also produce ATP by pumping protons across their cell membrane into the space between the cell

membrane and the cell wall, producing a gradient that is used by enzymes to make ATP, analogous to what happens in mitochondria.

33) B. Transection is a term that refers to a cut. Conjugation is the transfer of genetic material between bacterial cells by direct cell-to-cell contact; Transduction is the process by which DNA is transferred from one bacterium to another by a virus; Transformation is the genetic alteration of a cell resulting from the direct uptake and incorporation of exogenous genetic through the cell membrane.

34) C. See the explanation for question 33.

35) A. See the explanation for question 33.

36) C. Viruses are not living organisms capable of producing energy and reproducing on their own, therefore they do not have organelles such as mitochondria.

37) C. Normally, DNA is used to transcribe RNA, but reverse transcriptase does the opposite and makes DNA from RNA.

38) B. A retro virus that replicates in a host cell through the process of reverse transcription of its single stranded RNA. See also the explanation for question 37.

39) B. The lysogenic cycle is a viral reproduction process characterized by integration of the viral nucleic acid into the host's genome or formations of a circular replicon in the cytoplasm, allowing the host to continue to live and function normally. In the lytic cycle the infected cell is destroyed and the viral DNA exists as a separate molecule and replicates separately from the host DNA. Mitosis is not a life cycle for viruses and dormancy is a stage in the life cycle of a virus in which it is not reproducing and is not incorporated into or part of a living cell.

40) C. A facultative anaerobe is an organism that can undergo aerobic respiration if oxygen is present, but is capable of switching to anaerobic respiration if oxygen is absent.

41) B. The S stands for synthesis in which DNA replication occurs. after which humans still have 46 chromosomes, but now have 92 chromatids, which will separate to produce two new cells, each with 46 chromosomes.

42) C. See the explanation for question 41.

43) A. Most human cells are diploid, having 46 chromosomes, but after Meiosis II the resulting spermatids are haploid, with half the number of normal chromosomes.

44) A. Prior to release from the ovary oocytes (eggs and ova) are arrested at an early stage of the first meiotic division as a primary oocyte.

45) B. Sperm are produce by the testes and stored in the epididymis, which is a collection of tubes located on the top of the testes. The vas deferens is a tube that connects the testes to the urethra and the seminal vesicle produces the fluid components of semen and connects with the urethra near its junction with the vas deferens.

46) C. Leydig cells are found adjacent to the seminiferous tubules in the testicle and produce testosterone in the presence of luteinizing hormone. Sertoli cells are the somatic cells (diploid cells) of the testis that are essential for spermatogenesis and facilitate the progression of germ cells to spermatozoa (sperm).

47) C. See the explanations for questions 43 and 46. Spermatids are the immature product.

48) A. In vertebrates, the oviduct is the passageway from the ovaries to the outside of the body, but for mammals this is more commonly known as the Fallopian tube, which connects the ovary to the uterus, which is then connected to the vagina by way of the cervix.

49) C. An oogonia an immature female reproductive cell that produces primary oocytes, which undergo meiosis I to produce a secondary oocyte and a first polar body. The secondary oocyte then undergoes meiosis II, producing an ovum and a second polar body.

50) C. The corpus luteum is a structure that develops in an ovary after an ovum has been discharged but degenerates unless pregnancy occurs. The hormone that is secreted is progesterone, which helps maintain the endometrial lining of the uterus for implantation and maturation of the fetus during pregnancy. See the explanation for question 11. Testosterone is a hormone primarily produced by males. Gonadotropin-releasing hormone (GnRH), is responsible for the release of follicle-stimulating hormone (FSH) and luteinizing hormone (LH) from the anterior pituitary gland.

51) C. See the explanation for question 50.

52) B. See also the explanation for question 48. Sperm are more mobile than the ovum, and are able to travel through the reproductive tract to reach the ovum in the oviduct, after which the fertilized egg travels to the uterus, where it is implanted and matures.

53) B. After fertilization, the cell begins to divide.

54) C. Fraternal twins result from the fertilization of two separate eggs, resulting in similar but not identical genetic makeups, as seen in identical twins, which results from the fertilization of a single egg, that after cleavage, the cells

separate and produce two fetuses. Conjoined twins are two separate fetuses that are attached (joined) to each other in some way. An ectopic pregnancy is when the fertilized egg is implanted somewhere other than the uterus (most commonly the fallopian tube).

55) D. After fertilization, a zygote cleaves and forms a spherical group of cells known as the morula, which by way of blastulation, becomes a hollow spherical layer of cells, known as the blastula.

56) C. Gastrulation is an early phase of embryonic development in which the single-layered blastula is transformed into a three-layered structure known as the gastrula. The inner, middle and outer layers are known as the endoderm, mesoderm and ectoderm, respectively. Generally after differentiation, the endoderm produces cells and organs associated with the gut, the mesoderm produces muscles, sex organs, bones and tendons, and the ectoderm produces the outer layer of skin and the nervous system.

57) C. See the explanation for question 56.

58) C. Cell differentiation results from selective transcription of proteins in which genes produce different kinds of proteins depending upon how and when the gene is activated. Neurulation is the folding process in which vertebrate embryos, produce the neural tube. See the explanations for questions 18 and 56.

59) A. Totipotent stem cells can give rise to all the differentiated cell types in the body. The prefix toti-means total, whole or complete and the root "potent" in this case means "potential to become."

60) C. See the explanation for question 59. Pluripotent stem cells can differentiate into several different cell types and multipotent stem cells can only develop into relatively few cell types.

61) B. Autocrine signaling is a form of cell signaling in which a cell secretes a hormone that binds to receptors on that same cell, leading to changes in the cell. The endocrine system involves glands that secrete hormones that travel through the body and act on other cells in the body. Paracrine signaling is a form of communication in which a cell produces a signal to induce changes in nearby cells. Juxtacrine signaling requires physical contact between cells.

62) B. Apoptosis is when a cell destroys itself.

63) C. Necrosis is a form of traumatic cell death that results from an acute injury. See also the explanation for question 62.

64) A. The terms "incomplete" and "detached" suggest that the tissue is not "identical." The term "functional"

suggests that the tissue operates in the same way, but may not be "identical."

65) C. Arteries carry blood away from the heart. Since the umbilical cord is part of the fetus, umbilical arteries are arteries that are in the umbilical cord carrying blood away from the fetus' heart.

66) B. A developing human is an embryo until approximately the ninth week following fertilization, after which it is considered a fetus.

67) C. Sodium must be continuously pumped out of the nerve cell, to counteract leakage through sodium channels back into the cell. Active transport requires energy from ATP.

68) B. The dendrites connect to the cell body, or soma, which pass the signal through the axon hillock to the axon and then finally to the nerve terminals.

69) A. The myelin sheath surrounds the axon and acts as an electrical insulator. The myelin is comprised of Schwann cells for the peripheral nervous system, whereas oligodendrocytes form the myelin of the central nervous system (CNS).

70) C. The Nodes of Ranvier are gaps in the myelin sheath surrounding the axon, which function as points of signal amplification.

71) A. See the explanation for question 67.

72) D. The action potential causes the sodium-gated channels to open, after which sodium rushes into of the nerve cell, followed by the opening of potassium channels, allowing potassium ions to exit the cell. The inward flow of sodium ions increases the concentration of cations in the cell and causes depolarization, where the potential of the cell is higher than the slightly negative resting potential.

73) C. The relative refractory period is shortly after the firing of a nerve fiber when hyperpolarization has occurred and a greater than normal stimulus is required to stimulate a second response; the absolute refractory period is the period immediately following the firing of a nerve fiber when it cannot be stimulated no matter the magnitude of the stimulus.

74) D. Saltatory conduction is the propagation of action potentials along axons from one node of Ranvier to the next node, which are the only un-insulated places along the axon where ions are exchanged across the axon membrane, regenerating the action potential between regions of the axon that are insulated by myelin. See also the explanation for question 70. This is unlike conduction of electrical signals in an insulated copper wire, where gaps in the insulation would dissipate or weaken the

electrical impulse. Brownian motion describes the diffusion of fluids. Peristalsis is the rhythmic contraction of muscles that moves food through the digestive tract.

75) C. Serotonin is an amine neurotransmitter derived from tryptophan. Dopamine is a catecholamine neurotransmitter derived from tyrosine. See also the explanations for question 12.

76) C. Acetylcholinesterase catalyzes the hydrolysis of acetylcholine, an ester that functions as a neurotransmitter.

77) C. Grey matter typically consists of cell bodies and unmyelinated axons whereas white matter consists of fewer cell bodies and many myelinated axons.

78) C. The sympathetic nervous system produces the "fight or flight" response, whereas the parasympathetic nervous system is responsible for the "rest and digest" response.

79) A. A reflex response does not involve the brain and therefore, is a result of a direct connection between a sensory neuron and a motor neuron, with only one synaptic junction.

80) A. See the explanation for question 12.

81) C. One of the most important functions of the hypothalamus is to link the nervous system to the endocrine system by way of the pituitary gland.

82) D. A follicle is a portion of the ovary from which an egg is released. The hormone controlling the follicular phase of the female reproductive cycle is estradiol.

83) C. See the explanation for question 16.

84) D. The anterior pituitary secretes FSH, LH, ACTH, TSH, prolactin, endorphins, GH, and leptin.

85) B. See the explanation for question 13.

86) C. See the explanations for questions 12 and 15.

87) D. Renin is secreted by the juxtaglomerular cells and helps regulate blood pressure as part of the renin-angiotensin-aldosterone system.

88) C. Angiotensinogen is activated by renin. It is converted to ATI which is then converted to ATII by ACE.

89) A. Glucagon is a peptide hormone, produced by alpha cells of the pancreas, and it raises the concentration of glucose in the bloodstream. Its effect is opposite to that of insulin, which is produced by the beta cells of the

pancreas, and lowers glucose concentrations in the blood. See also the explanation for question 14.

90) C. Somatostatin is a peptide hormone that regulates the endocrine system and affects neurotransmission and inhibits the release of insulin and glucagon.

91) C. Atrial natriuretic peptide (ANP) is a powerful vasodilator, a polypeptide hormone secreted by heart muscle cells in response to high blood pressure.

92) B. Type I diabetes results from the autoimmune destruction of the insulin-producing cells. Resistance to insulin is type II diabetes. See also the explanation for question 89.

93) A. Circadian rhythms are cycles associated with physical processes such as night and day and melatonin helps regulate sleep cycles. See also the explanation for question 9 and 12.

94) D. The epiglottis is a flap of cartilage at the root of the tongue, which covers the opening of the windpipe (larynx) when food is swallowed. The pharynx is the back of the mouth that connects to the esophagus (and larynx).

95) D. Contraction of the diaphragm causes the expansion of the lungs, reducing the pressure of air in the lungs and causing air to flow into the lungs. Expiration of air occurs when the diaphragm relaxes and the elasticity of the lungs cause the lung volume to be reduced, pushing air out of the lungs.

96) B. The diaphragm is a sheet of internal skeletal muscles that is important for respiration. Skeletal muscles are under voluntary control.

97) D. The definition of residue is a small amount of something that remains after the main portion has been removed.

98) B. The prefix "hypo-" indicates a low level, with the root of the word, "-oxia", indicating something having to do with oxygen. Note that when a prefix and a root end and begin with the same vowel, the word is not written with two sequential vowels. Hypoglycemia is low glucose levels in the blood. Hypokalemia is low potassium.

99) A. Veins carry blood to the heart.

100) A. Alkalosis or alkalemia, is the opposite of acidosis, and refers to a process of reducing hydrogen ion concentrations and raising pH in the blood. Since carbon dioxide forms carbonic acid, a slower respiration rate would build up carbonic acid in the blood and lower the pH.

101) B. See the explanation for question 100.

102) C. A macrophage is a large white blood cell (leukocytes). T-cells are also white blood cells that are involved in an immune response because of the presence of specialized specific receptors on the cell surface. B cells are a type of white blood cell that is part of the adaptive immune system and secretes antibodies. Red blood cells, or erythrocytes, primary function is to carry gases such as oxygen and carbon dioxide throughout the body and are not part of the immune system.

103) B. The human heart has two atria and two ventricles, left and right.

104) B. The left ventricle is the largest chamber, since it must force oxygenated blood throughout the body, at high pressure.

105) C. See the explanation for question 104. The aorta is the largest artery, which carries blood away from the heart.

106) A. The atrioventricular valves separate the ventricles from atria for both the right and left chambers of the heart. Therefore there are two atrioventricular valves, the mitral (bicuspid) valve and the tricuspid valve, which are on the left and right respectively. See the diagram below.

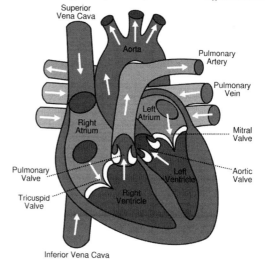

107) C. See the explanation for question 106.

108) D. See the explanation for question 106.

109) B. The oxygenated and deoxygenated blood does not mix, because there is no opening between the right and left chambers of the heart. See the explanation for question 106.

110) B. See the explanations for questions 104, 105 and 106.

111) C. See the explanation for question 106.

112) D. Pacemaker cells in the sinoatrial (SA) node initiate and regulate the rhythmic contractions of the heart. See the diagram below.

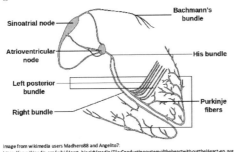

Image from wikimedia users Madhero88 and Angelito7:
https://en.wikipedia.org/wiki/Heart_block#/media/File:ConductionsystemoftheheartwithouttheHeart-en.svg

113) C. Cardiac muscle consists of individual cells connected by intercalated discs to work as a single functional organ. Note that the prefix "inter-" means "between". Note that Purkinje fibers are nerves (see the explanation for question 112) and do not act to physically connect one heart cell to another. Valves connect the chambers, not the cells.

114) B. The vagus nerve is part of the parasympathetic autonomic nervous system.

115) A. Heart rate is defined as the strokes per unit time (stroke/s) and the stroke volume is the average volume of blood pumped per stroke (L/stroke), therefore the cardiac output is the volume of blood pumped for a given amount of time, which is heart rate times the stroke volume.

116) B. Systole is the ventricular contraction phase of the cardiac cycle that results in the ejection of blood into an adjacent chamber or blood vessel, whereas diastole is the relaxation phase of the cardiac cycle.

117) D. The blood vessels that have the thinnest walls, the lowest pressure and the slowest flow rate are the capillaries.

118) A. Veins have much lower blood pressure than arteries and therefore need valves to keep the blood moving towards the heart.

119) A. Varicose veins occur when blood flow is reduced and the blood expands the veins so that the valves can not close. Blood clots can result. See also the explanation for question 118. Compression socks can help relieve this situation.

120) C. There are two vena cavae, which are the largest veins in the body and returns blood to the right ventricle of the heart. The superior vena cava returns blood from the upper body and the inferior vena cava returns blood from the lower body.

121) B. A portal system occurs when a capillary bed (associated with arteries) pools into another capillary bed (associated with veins). There are hepatic, hypophyseal, and renal portal systems in the body.

122) C. Pathogens are foreign substances and are not normally part of the blood. See also the explanations for questions 11 and 102. Platelets are the component of blood that is responsible for clotting.

123) D. Red blood cells are unusual in that they lack most of the organelles found in eukaryotes and since they do not reproduce themselves (they are produced from stem cells in the bone marrow), there is no need for these cells to have a nucleus and they produce energy by way of anaerobic respiration.

124) A. The Krebs cycle and electron transport chain for aerobic respiration occurs in the mitochondria of most eukaryotic cells. See also the explanation for question 123.

125) C. The prefix heme- refers to the prosthetic group in the oxygen carrying protein hemoglobin, which is found in red blood cells.

126) B. A granulocyte is a white blood cell with secretory granules in its cytoplasm, e.g., an eosinophil, basophil, or neutrophil (note the suffix). A monocyte is a large phagocytic white blood cell.

127) C. The prefix "a-" means "not". See the explanation for question 126.

128) C. See the explanation for question 125. The number of oxygen molecules depends upon if the red blood cells are oxygenated or deoxygenated. Myoglobin is an oxygen-carrying molecule found in muscles, not red blood cells.

129) B. The T stands for thymus. See also the explanations for questions 102 and 122.

130) A. See the explanation for question 102.

131) C. Thrombosis is local coagulation or clotting of the blood in a part of the circulatory system. Platelets are derived from megakaryocytes. See the explanation for question 122.

132) C. See the explanation for question 122.

133) A. See the explanation for question 11.

134) B. See the explanation for question 11 and 131.

135) A. An antigen is any substance that causes an immune response and the production of antibodies against the antigen. If a person with A type blood donates blood to a person with B type blood, the donor's blood would be rejected.

136) C. An allele is a variant form of a gene, which can be either dominant or recessive. Co-dominance occurs when the contributions of both alleles are visible in the phenotype. In this case AB type blood would be rejected by both A type and B type recipients (as well as O type).

137) D. O type blood lacks both the A and B type alleles, and therefore would not produce an immune response in a recipient having A, B or AB type blood. See also the explanations for questions 135 and 136.

138) C. Since people with AB type blood already have the A and B alleles, they would not reject other blood types (including O). See the explanation for question 137.

139) C. The Rh factor is a type of protein on the surface of red blood cells.

140) B. Interpreting the Latin, erythroblastosis fetalis refers to a process (-sis) that affects the red blood cells (erythro-) of the fetus (fetalis). See also the explanations for questions 24, 62 and 63. Sudden infant death syndrome (SIDS) occurs after birth.

141) A. Oxygen from the air is absorbed by hemoglobin in the lungs. See the explanations for questions 117 and 128.

142) C. Competitive inhibitors establish a dynamic equilibrium in which they bind to the same enzymatically active site as the substrate and high concentrations of the substrate can displace the inhibitor.

143) D. Hydride is the highly reactive H⁻ ion.

144) B. Fetal hemoglobin binds oxygen more tightly than the hemoglobin in the mother's blood.

145) B. A hypertonic environment means that the concentration of solutes in the solution surrounding the cell is higher than the concentrations within the cell, such that osmosis would cause water to diffuse out of the cell, creating a higher osmotic pressure for the external solution. Isotonic means that the concentration of solute within the cell is the same as the external solution.

146) C. Edema is swelling due to extracellular fluid accumulation, possibly due to an injury or poor blood circulation.

147) A. Clotting factors are proteins in the blood that control bleeding, one disorder of which is known as hemophilia.

148) C. Thrombosis is a local coagulation or clotting of the blood in a part of the circulatory system. Trypsin is a digestive enzyme. Thromboplastin converts prothrombin to thrombin.

149) C. Innate immunity refers to nonspecific defense mechanisms associated with an antigen. These include physical barriers such as skin, chemicals and cells in the blood, that attack foreign cells and materials introduced into the body.

150) D. The spleen acts as a filter, removing old red blood cells and holds a reserve of blood, which can be valuable in case of hemorrhaging. The liver also is involved in processing dead red blood cells (among many other things), but does not act as a storage vessel as does the spleen. The heart pumps blood, but does not store it. The pancreas is an endocrine gland.

151) A. Bone marrow produces blood cells (red and white) from stem cells. T-cells mature in the thymus. See also the explanation for question 150. The thyroid is an endocrine gland.

152) C. A B-cell is a white blood cell that can be processed into a plasma cell, which produces antibodies.

153) A. See the explanation for question 152.

154) B. See the explanation for question 102.

155) B. Monocytes are a type of white blood cell that can differentiate into macrophages, osteoclasts, dendritic cells, and other types of cells.

156) C. Humoral immunity results from the action of white blood cells that produce antibodies. See the explanation for question 152.

157) A. Interferons are a group of signaling proteins made and released by host cells in response to the presence of several pathogens, such as viruses, bacteria, parasites, and also tumor cells.

158) D. See the explanation for question 152 concerning "plasma cells." There is no such thing as a "plasma T cell."

159) C. Lacteals are the lymph system's equivalent to capillaries and absorb nutrients (fatty acids) in the villi of the small intestine.

160) B. The salivary glands in the mouth produce amylase, which helps hydrolyze starch into sugars.

161) A. Peristalsis is a series of wave-like muscle contractions that moves food to different processing stations in the digestive tract.

162) B. Mastication is chewing and a bolus is a ball of food. The pharynx connects the mouth to the esophagus, which connects the pharynx to the stomach, whereas the larynx connects the pharynx to the trachea, which connects to the lungs.

163) A. Gastric chief cells release the precursor to the protein digestive enzyme pepsin, which is activated when it comes in contact with hydrochloric acid produced by gastric parietal cells in the stomach.

164) C. See the explanation for question 163.

165) D. The ileocecal sphincter or valve separates the small intestine from the large intestine; the pupillary sphincter is in the eye; and the cardiac sphincter (near the heart, not in the heart) separates the esophagus from the stomach.

166) C. Mucus is a protective fluid produced by mucous cells, located on the mucous membrane that lines virtually the entire digestive tract.

167) C. A zymogen is an inactive enzyme precursor and enterokinase is an enzyme produced by the small intestine that activates trypsinogen by phosphorylation, forming trypsin, which digests proteins. Pepsinogen is produced in the stomach and produces pepsin, which also digests proteins. Secretin and cholecystokinin (CCK) are both hormones.

168) B. Bile is a digestive fluid produced by the liver and stored in the gall bladder, whose function is to interact with and break up clumps of hydrophobic lipids. Bile has properties similar to soaps and detergents.

169) A. Glucose can be stored in the human body as the branched polymer glycogen. Glucagon is a hormone that signals the body to convert glycogen into glucose, whereas insulin is a hormone that signals the body to convert glucose into glycogen. Galactose is a monosaccharide sugar.

170) B. See the explanation for question 168.

171) A. Vitamin C is ascorbic acid, which is highly water-soluble. Vitamins A, D, E, and K are fat-soluble.

172) B. Chylomicrons are lipophilic blood proteins that adsorb and transport lipids.

173) C. The glomerulus is a cluster of capillaries associated with the cup-shaped structure (Bowman's capsule) in the nephron of the kidney that filters the blood plasma, which flows to the proximal convoluted tubule.

174) C. Amino acids are deaminated in the liver, which produces the waste product urea, which is excreted in urine.

175) D. The proximal tube, prior to the loop of Henle is where glucose is reabsorbed back into the blood stream.

176) D. The descending limb of the loop of Henle has low permeability to ions and urea, while being highly permeable to water. The ascending limb of the loop of Henle is where ions such as K$^+$ and Na$^+$ are reabsorbed, and is impermeable to water.

177) A. The renal medulla is the inner portion of the kidney. The renal cortex is the outer portion of the kidney. The terms anterior means near the front, and superior means on top. The loop of Henle goes from the cortex to the medulla and then back to the cortex.

178) B. The carbonic acid/bicarbonate pK$_a$ is close to physiological pH and the amount of carbonic acid in the blood can be regulated by the rate of respiration.

179) B. Hair is primarily composed of the structural protein keratin.

180) C. Melanin is the substance that causes skin pigmentation, and it absorbs light.

181) B. Sweating causes the evaporation of water and cools the body; piloerection is the standing upright of hairs, which helps hold warm air near the surface of the skin; vasodilation increases blood flow and can help dissipate heat.

182) C. A sarcomere is the basic unit of striated muscles in which the proteins myosin and actin combine to produce a contraction.

183) C. Smooth muscles and cardiac muscles are not under voluntary control.

184) A. Myosin can only bind to actin and cause a contraction when the binding sites on actin are exposed by calcium ions released by the sarcoplasmic reticulum, which is a specialized type of smooth ER that regulates the calcium ion concentration in the cytoplasm of striated muscle cells.

185) C. See the explanation for question 184.

186) C. Osteo**c**lasts dissolve (**c**hew up) bone, whereas osteo**b**lasts **b**uild up bone.

187) D. Bone is comprised of collagen, calcium, and hydroxyapatite.

188) C. Incomplete dominance occurs when the observed phenotype has properties intermediate between the homozygous phenotypes.

189) B. A silent mutation is one with no effect on the gene product. A nonsense mutation would result in a nonfunctional protein. A missense mutation is a type of point mutation where a single nucleotide is changed and

results in a codon that codes for a different amino acid. A lethal mutation will kill the organism.

190) D. A translocation involves the movement of chunks of DNA between positions in the genome.

191) B. Homozygosity is when an individual has the same alleles in their genotype as opposed to heterozygosity, which is when the alleles are different. Factors that reduce genetic diversity would favor the reproduction of the homozygotes.

192) B. A test cross would be between an individual of unknown genotype and a homozygous recessive individual, where the resulting phenotype ratio identifies the unknown genotype.

193) C. The Hardy–Weinberg principle states that allele and genotype frequencies in a population will remain constant from generation to generation in the absence of evolutionary influences, such as choices A, B and D.

194) C. Natural selection is the differential survival and reproduction of individuals due to differences in multiple phenotypes. Is the evolution of multiple different forms from a single ancestor.

195) B. Amphoteric compounds can act as either an acid or a base.

196) D. The isoelectric point is the pH at which the net charge of an amino acid is zero.

197) B. Peptide bonds are formed by the loss of water when combining a carboxylic acid and an amine, to form an amide [R-CO-NHR'].

198) B. Alpha helices and beta sheets are due to intermolecular interactions that form the secondary structure. The primary structure comes from how the amino acids are connected by peptide bonds. Tertiary structures come from how the secondary structures form larger units, which can further combine to form the overall gross quaternary structure.

199) A. Disulfide bonds are formed when the sulfhydryl side groups of cysteine combine to form sulfur-sulfur bonds by way of oxidation. See the explanations for questions 197 and 198.

200) C. Catalysts lower the activation energy of a reaction but do not affect the relative free energies of the reactants and products (DG).

201) D. The stem of the question essentially describes the transfer of a functional group.

202) D. You must put energy into (energy is a reactant) an endergonic reaction.

203) C. Reactions that have positive free energy changes indicate that the products have more energy than the reactants and the reaction is said to be nonspontaneous.

204) A. If the concentration of the enzyme is increased then more substrate will bind and undergo reaction.

205) C. An allosteric binding site is some other position on the enzyme beside the substrate-binding site, which can change the shape and nature of the substrate binding to the enzyme.

206) D. An uncompetitive inhibitor only binds to the enzyme-substrate complex after it has been formed. A competitive inhibitor will bind to the substrate-binding site and establish a dynamic equilibrium, whereas an irreversible inhibitor will bind and not be released. Mixed inhibition occurs when the inhibitor can bind to the enzyme, whether or not the enzyme has already bound the substrate.

207) C. Cell adhesion molecules help cells stick to each other and to their surroundings. See the explanation for question 179.

208) A. A ligand is a compound that binds to a receptor.

209) A. Sodium dodecyl sulfate polyacrylamide gel electrophoresis (SDS-PAGE) involves the addition and binding of a negatively charged surfactant to a mixture of proteins, which produces analytes with roughly the same amount of charge, but whose size and mass vary, which dictates the rate of movement through the stationary phase.

210) B. In any electrochemical cell, the cathode attracts cations and the anode attracts anions.

211) A. The mobile phase is the moving solvent and if the analyte is attached to the stationary phase it will take a longer time to pass through the column compared with an analyte that spends more time dissolved in the mobile phase.

212) D. Edman degradation is a method of sequencing amino acids in polypeptides.

213) D. Mannose in its linear form is an aldehyde with six carbons atoms in the formula.

214) C. Epimers are stereoisomers that differ in configuration at only one chiral center. Anomers are stereoisomers of carbohydrate ring structures that differ in how the ring structure has closed. Enantiomers are stereoisomers that are mirror images of one another.

215) C. Diastereomers are stereoisomers of a compound having different configurations at one or more (but not all)

of the chiral centers and are not mirror images of each other. Diastereomers can have different physical properties, such as density, since the molecules have the same mass, but may occupy different molecular volumes.

216) A. A furan is a five membered ring, in which one of the atoms is an oxygen atom.

217) A. Reducing sugars have aldehydes in their linear forms, that when they close the ring they form hemiacetal functional groups. Hemiketals are formed when a carbohydrate ring structure is formed from a ketone functional group in a carbohydrate.

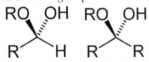
Hemiacetal   Hemiketal

218) C. The Tollen's test is the reduction of aqueous ammonium hydroxide solutions of silver ion to silver metal by a reducing sugar. See also the explanation for question 217.

219) D. The structure of an acetal is related to the corresponding hemiacetal by replacing the -OH with an -OR group of an alcohol. See the explanation for question 217.

220) C. Ribose is the monosaccharide found in the nucleic acid RNA.

221) C. The prefix homo- indicates that the polymer is comprised of all the same monomers, which in this case is a monosaccharide.

222) C. Saturated hydrocarbons contain the maximum amount of hydrogen and only have carbon-carbon single bonds, whereas unsaturated compounds have at least one carbon-carbon multiple bond, i.e. either a double or a triple bond.

223) C. Ceramide is the simplest sphingolipid with only a hydrogen atom on the head of the molecule.

224) A. Waxes are lipids that are malleable solids at room temperature, but have relatively low melting points, forming viscous liquids.

225) D. Steroids are lipids containing multiple carbon rings and are often metabolically made from cholesterol. Terpenes are organic compounds, produced by a variety of plants, particularly conifers, and also have multiple carbon ring structures, similar to cholesterol.

226) A. Cholesterol is a component of cell membranes.

227) D. Rickets results from a deficiency of lipid soluble vitamin D in children; in adults this is called osteomalacia.

228) B. Adipocytes are cells whose function is to store fat.

229) B. Triacylglycerols, also known as triglycerides, are commonly known as fat. Base hydrolysis of fat is a common way to make soap, which is known as saponification.

230) A. While a nucleoside is a nucleobase (A, C, G, T or U) linked to a sugar, a nucleotide is composed of a nucleoside and one or more phosphate groups.

231) C. The base A binds to T or U in DNA or RNA, respectively, and the base C always binds to G.

232) A. A, T and U are capable of forming two hydrogen bonds. See also the explanation for question 231.

233) C. Nucleobases come in pairs due to the number of hydrogen bonds they can form with each other, A and T (or U) form two hydrogen bonding interactions, whereas C and G form three hydrogen bonding interactions. The purines (A and G) have two rings, whereas the pyrimidines (C, T and U) have only one ring, in their structures.

234) A. Histones are proteins containing a large proportion of basic (positively charged) amino acids and are found in the nucleus, functioning to organize DNA into structural units called nucleosomes, by interaction with the negatively charge phosphate backbone. They are the chief protein components of chromatin, acting as spools around which DNA winds.

235) D. A telomere is a region of repetitive nucleotide sequences at the end of a chromosome that protects the chromosome from deterioration. Polyadenylation is the addition of a poly-A tail to protect an mRNA molecule while it is being transported from the nucleus to the rough ER, where it will participate in translation of proteins.

236) C. The prefix "hetero-" means "different". Heterochromatin is a tightly wound form of inactive DNA that is difficult to unwind and hence energetically more costly to reproduce than normal chromatin.

237) B. DNA forms a double helical structure that must be unwound in order to be replicated.

238) B. Okazaki fragments are short fragments of DNA synthesized from the lagging strand of DNA. The leading strand is replicated as a single, unfragmented molecule.

239) A. The polymerase chain reaction (PCR) is a technology in molecular biology used to amplify a single copy or a few copies of DNA, generating thousands to millions of copies of the DNA sequence. A Southern blot is an analytical technique used in molecular biology for detection of a specific DNA sequence in samples. The

northern blot is a technique used in molecular biology research to study gene expression by detection of RNA. Electrophoresis is an electrochemical method of separating charged species based on size, including proteins and nucleic acids.

240) C. A single strand of mRNA can code for several different proteins (polycistronic) in prokaryotes.

241) D. The start codon AUG, codes for methionine.

242) D. See the explanation for question 241.

243) C. Degenerate means more than one equivalent possibility.

244) A. See the explanation for question 189.

245) A. A specific DNA sequence in a promoter region involves the repeated nucleobases A and T, which indicates where a genetic sequence should begin to be read in order to transcribe the appropriate RNA.

246) B. Introns are noncoding sections of an RNA transcript, or the DNA encoding it, that are spliced out before the RNA molecule is translated into a protein. The sections of DNA (or RNA) that code for proteins are called exons.

247) C. mRNA is made in the nucleus by transcription and must pass through the nuclear membrane to get to the ribosomes. Exocytosis only occurs for the cell membrane, not the nuclear membrane.

248) C. Phosphorylation would change the shape of the protein, which could significantly alter the functional properties of a protein.

249) B. A chaperone assists in the folding and formation of the secondary protein structure. See also the explanation for question 198.

250) A. Prenylation is the addition of hydrophobic groups to a protein or other compounds and usually facilitates their attachment to lipid bilayers.

251) B. An operon is a functioning unit of DNA that contains genes that are translated. They are found in both prokaryotes and eukaryotes.

252) B. See the explanation for question 234. Acylation of the histones weakens the interactions of the histones with the DNA and allows the DNA to unwind so that it can be transcribed.

253) B. Triglycerides are the fatty acid esters of glycerol, in which all three alcohol groups of glycerol are turned into esters. Triglycerides are essentially acylated alcohols. See also the explanation for question 229.

254) D. Phospholipids are amphipathic, being both hydrophilic and hydrophobic as the same time, and capable of forming micelles, a spherical arrangement of lipid molecules in aqueous solution.

255) B. Transmembrane proteins form structures that extend completely from the inside to the outside of a cell membrane.

256) C. Gap junctions allow for electrical signals to be transmitted between cells.

257) C. Passive transport does not require an energy input like active transport does. Osmosis occurs when a semipermeable membrane allows water to diffuse, but doesn't allow other solutes to pass. See also the explanation for question 145.

258) B. Colligative properties only depend upon the number of particles present in solution, not on the chemical properties of those properties.

259) C. See the explanation for question 67. Most active transport mechanisms only involve one substance, whereas secondary active transport involves two substances. Exocytosis would involve transport out of the cell only, not in both directions.

260) B. It "pumps" 3 Na^+ ions **out** of the cell and 2 K^+ **into** the cell.

261) D. The net reaction is

$$C_6H_{12}O_6 + 2\ NAD^+ + 2\ ADP + 2\ P_i \rightarrow$$
$$2\ C_3H_4O_3 + 2\ NADH + 2\ ATP + 2\ H_2O$$

Where $C_6H_{12}O_6$ is the formula of glucose, P_i is phosphate and $C_3H_4O_3$ is the formula of pyruvic acid.

262) C. See the explanation for question 123.

263) C. Gluconeogenesis is a process that produces glucose from non-carbohydrate sources, such as amino acids. See also the explanation for question 14.

264) C. The electron transport chain is a series of compounds that transfer electrons from electron donors (NADH and $FADH_2$) to electron acceptors (O_2) via redox reactions, and couples this electron transfer with the transfer of protons (H^+ ions) across a membrane.

265) C. Ketone bodies are the water-soluble molecules acetoacetate, beta-hydroxybutyrate and acetone that are produced by metabolism of fatty acids in the liver.

266) A. See the explanation for question 263.

267) C. Fats have the greatest number of carbon-hydrogen bonds per molecule and therefore have the highest energy density of the answer choices.

268) C. See the explanation for question 14.

269) B. Ghrelin is known as the "hunger hormone" and is a peptide hormone produced by cells in the gastrointestinal tract, which functions on the central nervous system. Leptin is the "fullness hormone".